CHILTON'S Repair and Tune-Up Guide

Datsun

ILLUSTRATED

Second Edition

Prepared by the

Automotive Editorial Department

Chilton Book Company
Chilton Way
Radnor, Pa. 19089
215—687-8200

managing editor **JOHN D. KELLY**; assistant managing editor **PETER J. MEYER**; editor **STEPHEN J. DAVIS**; technical editors **Jon C. Jay, Howard Kenig, Zane C. Binder, N. Banks Spence Jr, George S. Rizzo, Alan E. Holt III, Ronald L. Sessions**

CHILTON BOOK COMPANY RADNOR, PENNSYLVANIA

Published in Radnor, Pa., by Chilton Book Company
and simultaneously in Ontario, Canada,
by Thomas Nelson & Sons, Ltd.
Second Edition
ISBN: 0-8019-5660-9 Library of Congress Catalog Card No. 72-188664
Manufactured in the United States of America *Fifth Printing, April 1974*

Acknowledgments

Devon Datsun, West Lancaster Avenue, Devon, Pa., 19333
Nissan Motor Corporation in USA, Secaucus, N.J. 07094

Although information in this guide is based on industry sources and is as complete as possible at the time of publication, the possibility exists that the manufacturer made later changes which could not be included here. While striving for total accuracy, Chilton Book Company can not assume responsibility for any errors, changes, or omissions that may occur in the compilation of this data.

Contents

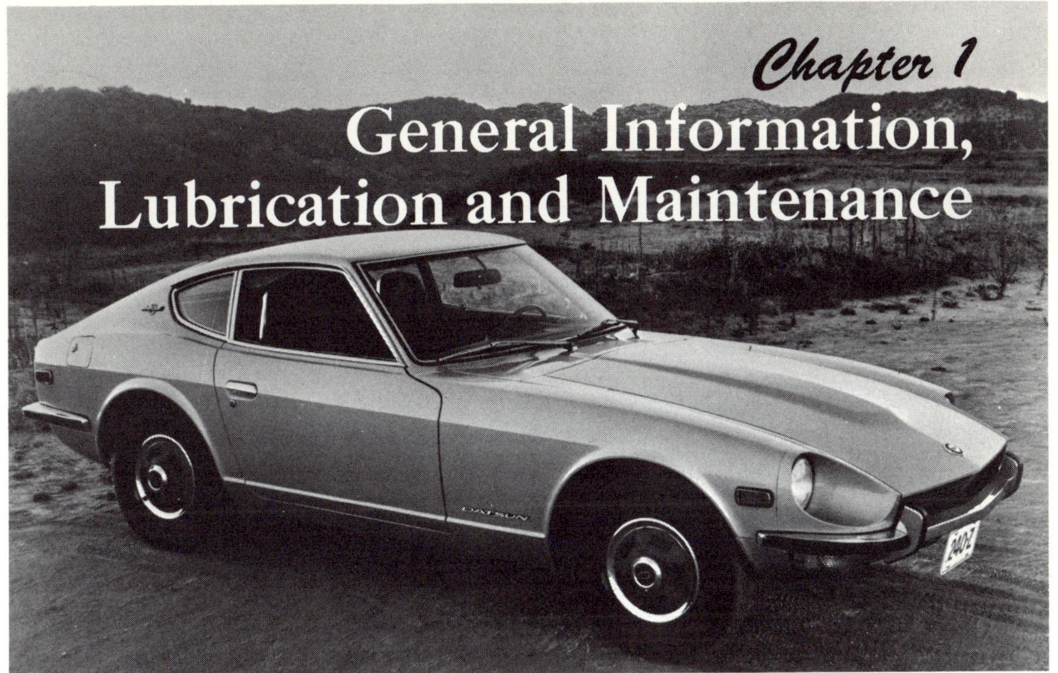

Introduction

Datsun, then known as D.A.T., began producing cars in 1913. The name D.A.T. was derived from the beginning letters of the three founder's last names. The name Datson, for son of D.A.T., was used later and finally evolved into Datsun. The first Datsun was a two seater with motorcycle fenders and a four-speed transmission. In 1933, a reorganization led to the formation of Nissan Motor Company, Ltd., which is now the parent company of Datsun. Datsun cars made their first United States appearance at the 1958 Los Angeles Imported Car Show. Cars were first imported in 1960, and since then sales have risen to a yearly total of over 150,000.

Datsun has had much success in several types of automotive competition. A Datsun 1600 roadster took the F-Production class trophy in 1967 and 1970. Datsun 240Z's swept the first three places in the C-Production class at the 1970 American Road Race of Champions. The 510 two door sedan has been declared the overall winner in the 2.5 Liter Challenge of SCCA Trans-Am racing. A Datsun 510 four door sedan won the 1970 East African Safari and in 1971, the same grueling cross-country rally was won by a 240Z sports car.

The intention of *Chilton's Repair and Tune-up Guide for the Datsun* is to cover maintenance and repair procedures that the owner or the average repair shop will be able to perform without special tools or equipment. Jobs that absolutely require special factory tools, such as automatic transmission overhaul, are best left to an authorized Datsun dealer. Datsun models that were imported since 1961 are covered. The tune-up and troubleshooting section is especially designed to enable the owner to diagnose and correct any minor problems before they become major repair jobs. A chapter is devoted to each operating system and includes repair and overhaul procedures.

Model Identification

Nissan Patrol, four-wheel drive (L60)

RL411 sedan. PL410 and PL411 are similar with slightly different grilles.

SPL310 1,500 cc. sportscar, SPL311 1,600 cc. sportscar, SRL311 2,000 cc. sportscar

L320 1,200 cc. pickup

L520 1,300 cc. pickup

PL521 1,600 cc. pickup

PL510 sedan, 1970 model

LB110 1,200 cc. sedan

KLB110 1,200 cc. coupe

HLS30 (240 Z) coupe

Serial Number Identification

ENGINE

The engine number, on the Nissan Patrol engine, is stamped on the lower right front corner of the cylinder block. On all other models, the engine number is stamped on the right side top edge of the cylinder block. The engine serial number is preceded by the engine model code.

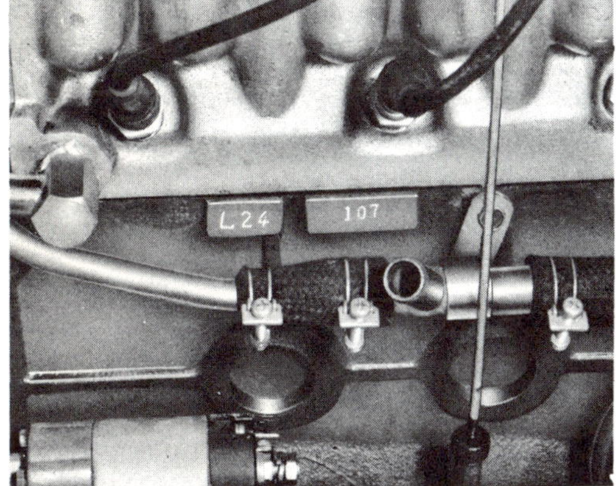

Engine model and serial number, L24 OHC six

Engine Identification Chart

Number of Cylinders	*Cu. In. Displacement (cc. Displacement)*	*Type*	*Engine Model Code*
6	241.3 (3,956)	OHV	P
4	72.5 (1,189)	OHV	E1
4	90.6 (1,488)	OHV	G
4	79.0 (1,299)	OHV	J
4	97.3 (1,595)	OHV	R
4	120.9 (1,982)	OHC	U20
4	97.3 (1,595)	OHC	L16
6	146.0 (2,393)	OHC	L24
4	71.5 (1,171)	OHV	A12

CHASSIS

The Nissan Patrol and L320 pickup chassis number is located on top of the right frame member, in the engine compartment. On all other models, the chassis number is on the firewall under the hood. Late model vehicles also have the chassis number on a plate attached to the top of the instrument panel on the driver's side. The chassis serial number is preceded by the model designation.

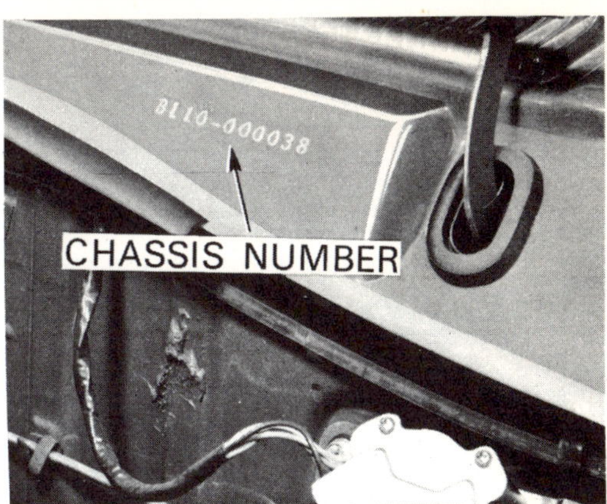

Chassis model and serial number, LB110 1,200 cc. sedan

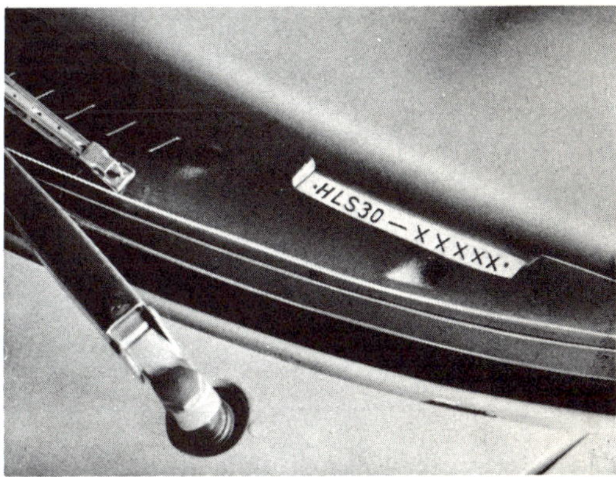

Chassis model and serial number, 240 Z coupe

VEHICLE

The vehicle identification plate is attached to the hood ledge or the firewall. This plate is mounted on the right front suspension strut housing on the HLS30 (240 Z). The identification plate gives the vehicle model, engine displacement in cc., SAE horsepower rating, wheelbase, engine number, and chassis number.

DATSUN TYPE HLS30

ENGINE CAPACITY	2,393 cc
MAX. HP at RPM	151 HP at 5,600 rpm
WHEEL BASE	2,305 mm
ENGINE NO.	L24- □□□□□□
CAR NO.	HLS30- □□□□□

NISSAN MOTOR CO., LTD.
YOKOHAMA JAPAN

Vehicle identification plate, 240 Z coupe (HLS30)

Vehicle Identification

Year	Model	Serial Numbers	
1961-1969	L60 Patrol (4 wheel drive)		
To 1966	L320 (1200 Pickup)		
1965	L520 (1300 Pickup)	L520-00001—L520-004603	April 1965—Sept. 1965
1966	L520 (1300 Pickup)	L520-004604—L520-019000	Oct. 1965—Sept. 1966
1967	L520 (1300 Pickup)	L520-019001—L520-160000	Oct. 1966—Sept. 1967
1968	L520 (1300 Pickup)	L520-160001—termination	Oct. 1967—termination
1968	L521 (1300 Pickup)	L521-000001—L521-038554	May 1968—Sept. 1968
1969	L521 (1300 Pickup)	L521-038555—L521-180000	Oct. 1968—June 1969
1970	PL521 (1600 Pickup)	PL521-180071—PL521-255904 PL521-255905—PL521-350000 PL521-350001—	July 1969—Sept. 1969 Oct. 1969—Jan. 1970 Feb. 1970—
1963-1965	PL410 Sedan		
1965-1967	PL411 Sedan	PL411-300000	
1966-1968	RL411 Sedan		
From 1971	LB110 (1200 Sedan)	LB110-00001	
From 1971	KLB110 (1200 Coupe)	LB110-70001	
1968	PL510 (1600 Sedan)	L510-00011—L510-009999 PL510-00011—PL510-040010	Oct. 1967—Sept. 1968
1969	PL510 (1600 Sedan)	L510-010000— PL510-040011—	Oct. 1968—Sept. 1969
1970	PL510 (1600 Sedan)	L510-040000— PL510-095000—	Oct. 1969— July 1969—
1971	PL510 (1600 Sedan)	PL510-200011—	Aug. 1970—
1968	WPL510 (1600 Wagon)	WPL510-800001—WPL510-805000	Oct. 1967—Sept. 1968
1969	WPL510 (1600 Wagon)	WPL510-805001—	Oct. 1968—
1970	WPL510 (1600 Wagon)	WPL510-842001— WPL510-11499—	Oct. 1969— July 1969—
1971	WPL510 (1600 Wagon)	WPL510-883501—	Aug. 1970—
1962-1965	SPL310 (1500 Roadster)		
1965, 1966, 1967	SPL311 (1600 Roadster)	SPL311-10001—SPL311-11000	To engine No. R-40000
Late 1967	SPL311 (1600 Roadster-Metric)	SPL311-11001—SPL311-17000	From engine No. R-40001—Sept. 1967
1968	SPL311 (1600 Roadster)	SPL311-17001—SPL311-24000	Oct. 1967—Sept. 1968
1969	SPL311 (1600 Roadster)	SPL311-24001—SPL311-27000	Oct. 1968—June 1969
Late 1967	SRL311 (2000 Roadster)	SRL311-00001—SRL311-01000	To Sept. 1967
1968	SRL311 (2000 Roadster)	SRL311-01001—SRL311-03000	Oct. 1967—Sept. 1968
1969	SRL311 (2000 Roadster)	SRL311-07001—SRL311-13000	Oct. 1968—June 1969
From 1971	HLS30 (240 Z Coupe)	HLS30-03013—	

Lubrication

Recommended Lubricants

Temperature (°F)	*Under 10*	*10-32*	*32-90*	*Over 90*
Engine Oil API Designation: MS, SD, SE	10W-30, 10W, or 5W-20	10W-30, 10W-40, or 10W	10W-30, 10W-40, or 20W	10W-30, 10W-40, 20W-40, or 30W *
Gear Oil API Designation: MP, EP, or MPS	80	90	90	140

* 40W may be used for high speeds in temperatures over 90.

Recommended Fuels

Regular	*Premium*
Patrol, L320 Pickup, PL410 Sedan, L520 Pickup, L521 Pickup, PL411 Sedan, RL411 Sedan, 510 Sedan and Wagon, PL521 Pickup, LB110 Sedan and Coupe	SPL310, SPL311, and SRL311 Roadsters, 240Z Coupe.

OIL CHANGES

All Datsun engines use a wet sump type oil supply in their lubrication systems. Draining the oil is accomplished by removing the drain plug at the bottom of the oil pan. Always drain the oil when the engine is hot, as contaminants will remain in the system when oil is drained cold. Do not overtighten the drain plug when installing.

OIL FILTER

The oil filter should be replaced every 6,000 miles on all models. Some early engines use a replaceable inner element within a permanent housing. All others use a throw-away cartridge type filter.

Components of replaceable element oil filter

Lubrication Intervals

Service	*Every 500 miles*	*Every 1,000 miles*	*Every 2,000 miles*	*Every 3,000 miles*	*Every 6,000 miles*	*Every 12,000 miles*	*Every 24,000 miles*	*Every 30,000 miles*
Grease suspension	L320	SPL310	L60 L520 L521 PL521 PL410		PL411 SPL311 SRL311	Early PL510 WPL510 RL411		Late PL510 WPL510 LB110 KLB110 HLS30
Change engine oil①	L320		L60 L520 L521 PL521 SPL310 PL410	RL411 PL411 SPL311 SRL311 PL510 WPL510 LB110 KLB110 HLS30				
Change oil filter①					All models			
Change transmission oil①					L320 PL410 SPL310		L60 L520 L521 PL521 RL411 PL411 SPL311 SRL311 Early PL510 WPL510	Late PL510 WPL510 LB110 KLB110 HLS30
Change differential oil①					L320 PL410 SPL310		L60 L520 L521 PL521 RL411 PL411 SPL311 SRL311	PL510 WPL510 LB110 KLB110 HLS30
Pack wheel bearings					L320 PL410 SPL310	L60 L520 L521 PL521	RL411 PL411 SPL311 SRL311	PL510 WPL510 LB110 KLB110 HLS30

① These services should be performed after the first 600-1000 miles on a new car or rebuilt units.

Oil Filter Applications

Year	*Model*	*AC*	*Fram*	*Purolator*
1962-65	Patrol, SPL310, SPL311, PL410, L520 Pickup, L320 Pickup	AC-32A	CH-820PL	MF-52A
1966-On	PL411, LB110, KLB110, L520 Pickup, RL411, SPL311, SRL311, L521 Pickup	PF-34	PH-2825	PER-42
1968-On	PL521 Pickup, 24OZ, PL510, WPL510	—	PH-2850	PER-17

Engine	*Filter type*	*Location on engine*
P	Replaceable element	Left side, on bracket
E1, G	Replaceable element	Right side, on bracket
R	Replaceable element or cartridge	Right side, on bracket
J, U20	Cartridge	Right side, on bracket
L16, L24	Cartridge	Right side, screwed into block
A12	Cartridge	Right side, on oil pump

R&R, Replaceable Element Filter

1. Unscrew mounting bolt which passes through housing.
2. Remove housing, element seat, and element. Discard element.
3. Wash out housing in a safe solvent. Dry thoroughly. If bolt is removed from housing, note location of spring, felt washer, and rubber washer.
4. Install new rubber sealing ring into bracket. A tiny bit of grease may help keep the ring in position.
5. Install new element into housing. Replace element seat. Torque bolt to 14-18 ft. lbs.

R&R, Throw-Away Cartridge Filter

1. Unscrew cartridge and discard. A strap wrench is a great help in removing these filters. If the cartridge has been overtightened and cannot be unscrewed, drive a long punch through it. Then use the punch as a handle to unscrew the cartridge.

Removing spin-off oil filter

2. Screw on the new cartridge with a new gasket. Tighten it by hand until it just contacts the block or bracket.
3. Tighten the cartridge 1/2 turn farther by hand. Overtightening these cartridges will cause leaking or extreme difficulty in removing.

Routine Maintenance

AIR CLEANER

All Datsuns, except the Patrol, use a replaceable paper element air cleaner. The Patrol element is permanent, and should be washed with solvent and refilled with oil. Air filters should be cleaned or replaced every 20,000 miles or sooner under severe conditions.

FLUID LEVEL CHECKS

Engine Oil

All Datsuns use the conventional dipstick oil level gauge. Maintain the oil level between the high and low marks.

Transmission

Datsun manual transmissions have two oil level checking methods. Depending on the transmission type, the oil level is checked either by a dipstick located under a rubber cover over the transmission or at the filler plug on the side of the transmission. The dipstick is marked for the correct oil level. On the other type, gear oil level should be maintained just below the filler plug. The Patrol transmission is checked at the top by a dipstick, and the transfer case at the side filler plug. The automatic transmission dipstick is at the right rear of the engine. It has a scale on each side, one for COLD and the other for HOT. The transmission is considered hot after 15 miles of highway driving.

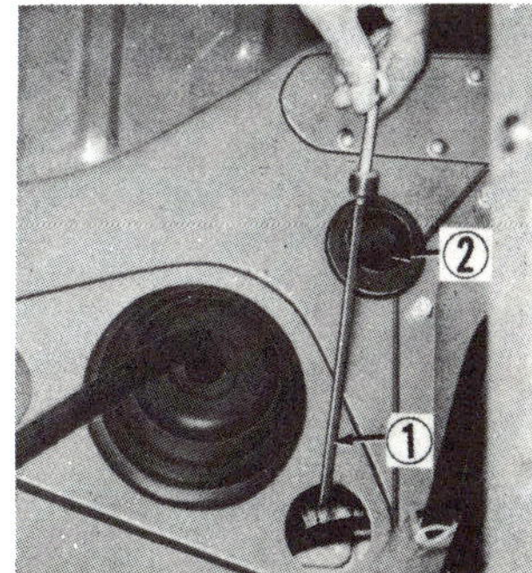

Checking Patrol transmission oil level

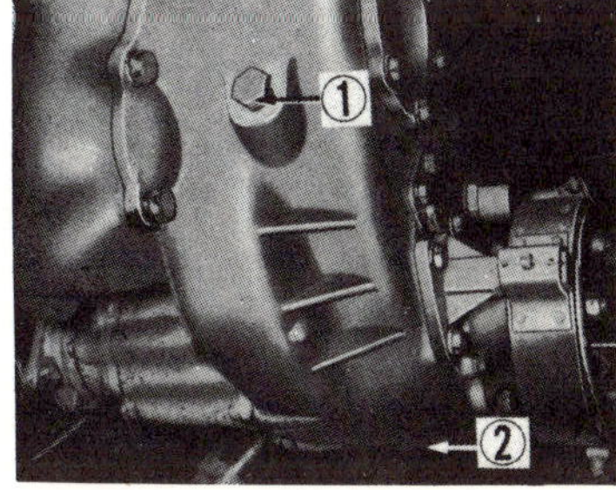

Transfer case plugs

1. Park on a level surface with the engine running. If transmission is not hot, shift into Drive, Low, then Neutral. Shift into Neutral (PL510, WPL510) or Park (HLS30). Block the wheels and set the handbrake.
2. Remove, wipe, and replace dipstick. Check fluid level on appropriate scale. The level should be at F.
3. If fluid level is below F, leave the engine running and add fluid through the dipstick tube until the F mark is reached.

CAUTION: *Do not overfill, as this may cause transmission malfunction and damage.*

Fluids recommended by the manufacturer are:

British BW Unit	*American BW Unit*	*Nissan Unit*
See owner's manual	Caltex (Texaco) Texamatic Fluid 6673	Caltex (Texaco) Texamatic Fluid 6991 or Texamatic 4571A
	Shell Automatic Transmission Fluid Dexron	Chevron RPM ATF Special
	BP Autran DX	Castrol TQF
	Mobil ATF 220	BP Autran B
	Castrol TQ Dexron	Esso (Enco) Glide
	Union ATF Dexron	Mobil ATF 210
	Humble 1956	Shell ATF Donax T7

Brake and Clutch Master Cylinders

Brake and clutch fluid level should be maintained at the normal mark located on the reservoir.

Brake and clutch master cylinders

Rear Axle

Rear axle oil level should be maintained just below the filler plug located on the rear cover of the third member. Front axle level on the Patrol should be checked at the same time as the rear axle.

TIRE ROTATION

Tires should be rotated according to the proper diagram every 3,000 miles on the L320 pickup and SPL310 Roadster, and every 6,000 miles on all other models.

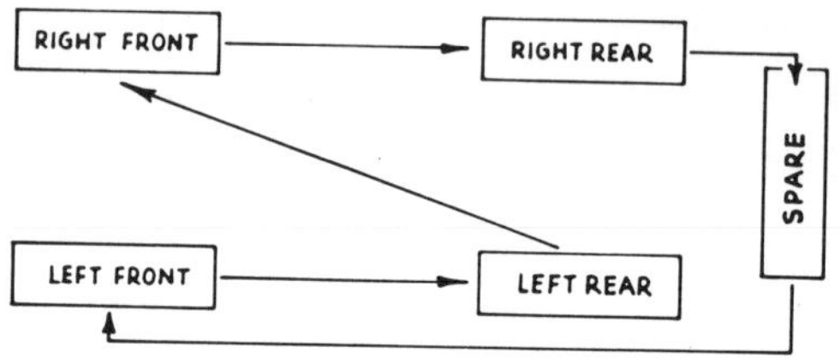

Tire rotation diagram No. 1

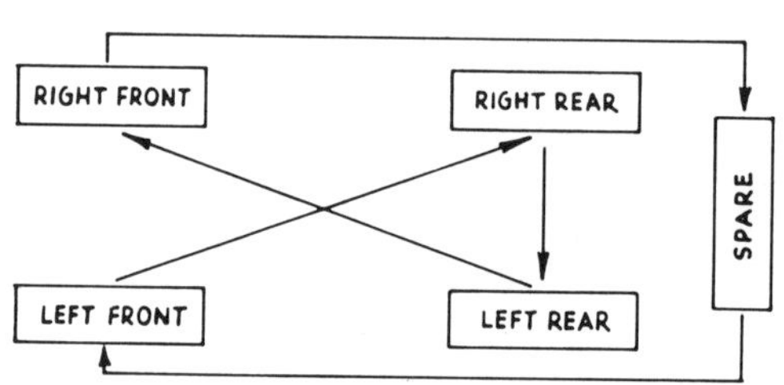

Tire rotation diagram No. 2

FUEL FILTER

All engines have a filter in the fuel line. The filter is mounted in the engine compartment. L16, L24, and A12 engines have a nonserviceable cartridge filter. This unit is simply replaced every 24,000 miles. All other models have a glass bowl type filter, with a removeable element. Both types of filter can be visually checked for the presence of excessive sediment or water.

510 cartridge fuel filter

Capacities and Pressures

Model	*Engine Crankcase Refill after Draining (qts.)*		*Transmission Refill after Draining (pts.)*				*Differential (pts.)*	*Fuel Tank (gals.)*	*Cooling System (qts.)*	*Normal Fuel Pressure (psi)*	*Maximum coolant pressure (psi)*
	With Filter	*Without Filter*	*Manual*			*Auto. (total capacity)*					
			3-Speed	*4-Speed*	*5-Speed*						
L60	3.6	N.A.	4.2①				2.6 front and rear	19.0	5.2	N.A.	N.A.
PL410	3.3	3.0	3.8				2.0	10.8	5.4	N.A.	6
SPL310	N.A.	4.2		4.6			1.8	11.3	6.9	N.A.	4-6
PL411	N.A.	3.1	3.8	4.7			2.2	11.0	5.7	N.A.	6
RL411	N.A.	3.5		4.3			1.9	11.0	7.1	N.A.	4-6
SPL311	N.A.	4.3		4.6			2.0	11.4	8.4	3.4-4.3	4-6
SRL311	N.A.	4.3			5.4		2.0	11.4	9.0	3.4-4.3	13
SRL311 with two twin-choke carburetors	N.A.	7.5			5.4		2.0	11.4	9.0	3.4-4.3	13
L320	3.8	3.2		4.3			1.8	9.3	5.7	N.A.	N.A.
L520, L521	3.8	3.2		4.2			1.7	10.8	5.9	2.1-2.5	6
PL510	5.2	4.4		6.4		11.4②	1.7	11.9	6.8, 7.2 with heater	2.6-3.4	13
WPL510	5.2	4.4		6.4		11.4②	2.1	11.9	6.8, 7.2 with heater	2.6-3.4	13
PL521	4.4	3.6		4.2			1.7	10.8	6.8, 7.4 with heater	2.6-3.4	13
HLS30	4.7	4.3		3.2	3.2	12.8	2.1	15.9	8.5	3.4-4.3	13
LB110	N.A.	2.9		4.3			1.8	9.3	5.7	N.A.	13

①—4.8 pts.—without power takeoff, 7.8 pts.—transfer case
②—1.5 pts.—oil cooler

Tire Rotation Patterns

No. 1	*No. 2*
L60	SPL311
PL410	SRL311
SPL310	L521
PL411	PL, WPL510
RL411	PL521
L320	HLS30
L520	LB, KLB110

Tire Pressures

Model	*Lightly Loaded (psi) front/rear*	*Heavily loaded or high speed (psi) front/rear*
SPL310 SPL311 SRL311	22/22	25.5/25.5
PL410 PL411 RL411	22/22	24/24
PL510 WPL510	24/28	28/32
HLS30	28/28①	32/32
LB110 KLB110	17/17②	22/22②
L320③	22/60	22/60
L520③	22/60	22/60
L521④ PL521	21/25	21/42
L60	22/30-35⑤	24/50-60⑥

① 24/24 with non-radial tires
② 24/24 with radial tires
③ 6.00x14, 6 ply/6.00x14, 8 ply
④ 6.00x14, 6 ply/6.00x14, 6 ply
⑤ 6 ply
⑥ 8 ply

BATTERY

All Datsun models are equipped with a 12-volt battery. Vehicles with the El and G engines are unusual in having a positive ground electrical system, rather than the more usual negative ground. The battery is located under the hood in all models except the L60. On the L60, the battery is under the front seat. To gain access to the battery in the HLS30 (240 Z coupe), first open the hood, then the inspection flap in the fender. The inspection flap must be closed before the hood.

Pushing, Towing and Jump Starting

Cars equipped with a manual transmission may be push started. Cars with automatic transmissions must never be push started, or towed with the driveshaft connected. To push start a manually shifted car: turn the ignition on, depress the clutch and place the shift lever in high gear. Before pushing, make sure that the bumpers of the cars do not override or body damage could result. Push the disabled car to about 10 or 15 mph and slowly release the clutch pedal. Before pushing or towing with the driveshaft connected, check for engine seizure. Check the oil level. If no oil shows on the dipstick, or if the oil is contaminated by water, further checking may require engine disassembly. CAUTION: *If the car is towed or push started in this condition, a broken crankshaft or bent connecting rod(s) could result. Water leakage into the cylinders causes a hydrostatic lock. Water will not compress, and if the engine is forced to turn over against this trapped water, damage will result.*

240Z towing bracket

Unit bodied cars are equipped with towing brackets similar to the one shown for the 240Z. Vehicles with separate frame and body may be towed with the line attached to the bumper brackets or front crossmember. Under no circumstances should a towing connection be made at the steering linkage or suspension members. It is not recommended that a car be flat towed, i.e., with all four wheels on the ground, farther than 50 miles or faster than 35 mph unless the driveshaft is disconnected. On cars equipped with a steering wheel lock, turn the ignition to the on position if steering control is necessary. If there is known or suspected engine-driveline damage or if it is necessary to tow longer distances and/or at higher speeds, tow the car with either the rear wheels raised or on a dolly, or disconnect the driveshaft.

Maintenance Intervals

Service	*Every 2,000 miles*	*Every 3,000 miles*	*Every 6,000 miles*	*Every 12,000 miles*
Torque cylinder head bolts①	L320	SPL310 PL410	L60 L520 L521 PL521 PL411 RL411 SPL311 SRL311	PL510 WPL510 HLS30 LB110 KLB110
Adjust valves			All models	
Clean and regap spark plugs	L60, L320 L520 L521 PL521	All other models		
Replace spark plugs				All models
Regap breaker points, check timing	L320 L520 L521 PL521	PL410 PL411 RL411 SPL310 SPL311 SRL311 PL510 WPL510 LB110 KLB110 HLS30	L60	
Replace breaker points, check timing				All models
Rotate tires②		L320 SPL310	All other models	
Check front end alignment		L320 PL410 SPL310		All other models
Adjust brakes, check lining③	L520 L521 PL521			All other models
Check emission control systems				All models

① Perform this operation after the first 600-1000 miles on a new car or a rebuilt engine.

② Do not rotate tires on trucks with 6/8 ply tires, front/rear.

③ Every 1,000 miles on L320, PL410, SPL310

Chapter 2
Tune-up and Troubleshooting

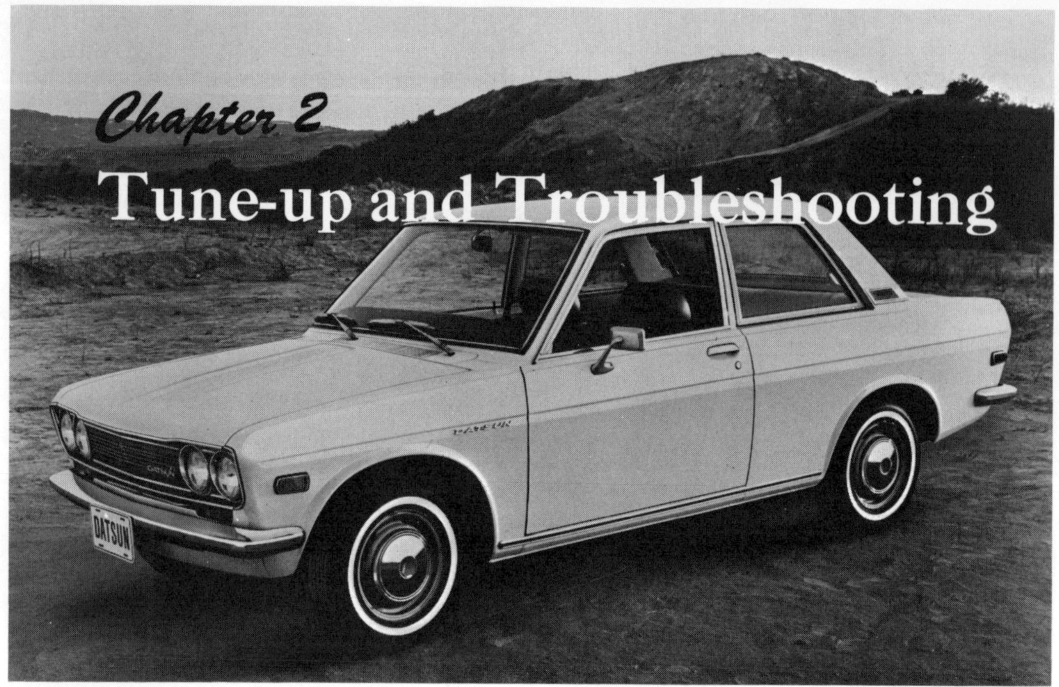

Tune-up Procedures

SPARK PLUGS

Clean any foreign material from around the spark plugs prior to removing them. Use a spark plug socket with a rubber insert to remove the plugs. This will prevent cracking the porcelain insulator. Each spark plug should be individually inspected and, if necessary, replaced. Refer to the spark plug diagnosis section for an analysis of plug tip conditions. Clean reusable spark plugs and file the center electrode flat. Adjust the spark plug gap according to the Tune-Up Specifications chart with a wire type feeler gauge. Inspect the spark plug hole threads for rust and cleanliness and, if necessary, use a 14 mm plug tap to clean the threads. Lightly oil the threads and torque the spark plugs to 11–15 ft. lbs.

BREAKER POINT R&R

Release the distributor cap latches and remove the cap and rotor. Check the points for pitting or burning. Use a point file to clean the points. Turn the engine by hand until the distributor cam opens the breaker points. Loosen the setscrew. Adjust the points to the specified gap using a feeler gauge. Tighten the setscrew and recheck the gap. Apply a trace of bearing lubricant to the breaker cam. Replace the cap and rotor. Point dwell may be checked at this point if a dwell meter is available. Point dwell figures are given in the Tune-Up Specifications Chart. The ignition timing should be checked each time the breaker points are adjusted.

NOTE: Some distributors are equipped with dual points. Adjust both point sets to the specified gap.

IGNITION TIMING

Ignition timing should be adjusted with the distributor vacuum line disconnected and the engine running at idle speed. A stroboscopic timing light must be used to obtain an accurate setting. The setting is indicated by the pointer on the engine front cover and the markings on the crankshaft pulley. The top dead center, or 0°, mark is located at the extreme left. The next mark may be either 5° or 10° before top dead center, depending on the engine model. The succeeding marks are 5° apart. To set the timing, disconnect the vacuum line and loosen the distributor clamp. Connect the

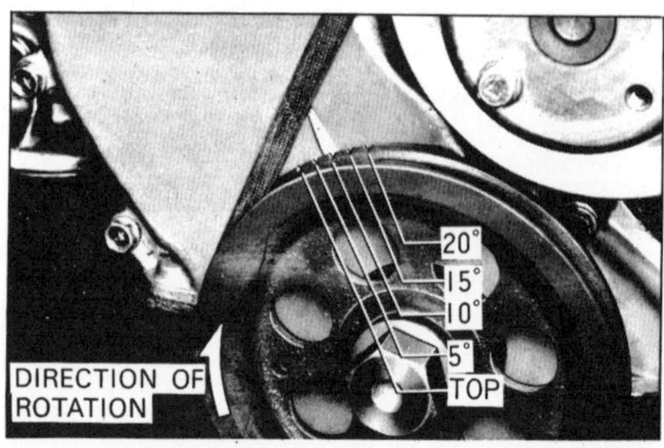

Timing marks, A12 engine

Tune-up Specifications

Year	Model	Spark Plugs Make, Type ①②	Spark Plugs Gap (in.)	Distributor Point Dwell (deg.)	Distributor Point Gap (in.)	Basic Ignition Timing (deg.)	Compression Pressure (psi) @ 350 rpm	Valves Clearance (in.) In.	Valves Clearance (in.) Ex.	Intake Opens (deg.) BTDC	Idle Speed (rpm)	Air:Fuel Ratio (:1) at idle	Percentage of CO at idle
1961-1969	L60	NGK BP-6E	.028-.032	35-45	.018-.022	10 BTDC @ 450	145	.016 Hot	.016 Hot	N.A.	450	N.A.	N.A.
1969	L60 with emission control	NGK BP-6E	.028-.032	35-45	.020	0 TDC @ 700	145	.016 Hot	.016 Hot	N.A.	750	N.A.	N.A.
1963-1965	PL410	NGK BP-6E, Hitachi L45	.028-.032	49-55	.018-.022	15 BTDC @ 600	165	.014 Hot	.014 Hot	14	600	N.A.	N.A.
1962-1965	SPL310	N.A.	.028-.032	49-55	.018-.022	16 BTDC @ 600	182	.017 Hot	.017 Hot	20	600	N.A.	N.A.
1965-1967	PL411	NGK BP-6E	.028-.032	49-55	.018-.022	15 BTDC @ 600	165	.014 Hot	.014 Hot	14	700	N.A.	N.A.
1966-1968	RL411	N.A.	.028-.032	49-55	.018-.022	18 BTDC @ 700	182	.017 Hot	.017 Hot	20	700	N.A.	N.A.
1965-1969	SPL311	NGK BP-6E	.028-.032	49-55	.018-.022	16 BTDC @ 600	181	.017	.017	20	600	N.A.	N.A.
1969	SPL311 with emission control	NGK BP-6E	.032-.036	49-55	.018-.022	0 TDC @ 700	181	.017	.017	20	700	12.0-12.5③	5-7③ 1.8-2.2⑥

Tune-up Specifications, continued

1967-1969	SRL311	NGK BP-6E	.028-.032	49-55	.018-.022	16 BTDC @ 600	166	.008 Hot	.012 Hot	18	600	N.A.	N.A.
1969	SRL311 with emission control	NGK BP-6E	.032-.036	49-55	.018-.022	0 TDC @ 700	166	.008 Hot	.012 Hot	18	700	12.0-12.5③	5-7③ 1.8-2.2⑥
1967-1969	SRL311 with two twin-choke side-draft carburetors	N.A.	.028-.032	51-58	.016-.022	20 BTDC @ 700④	166	.008 Hot	.012 Hot	30	700	N.A.	N.A.
To 1966	L320	NGK BP-6E	.028-.032	49-55	.018-.022	15 BTDC @ 600	163	.014	.014	14	600	N.A.	N.A.
1965-1968	L520	NGK BP-6E	.028-.032	50-55	.018-.022	8 BTDC @ 600⑤	163	.014	.014	14	600	N.A.	N.A.
1969	L520 with emission control, L521	NGK BP-6E	.032-.036	50-55	.018-.022	0 TDC @ 700	163	.014	.014	14	700	13.3-14.5	1-3
1968-1971	PL510, WPL510	NGK BP-6E	.028-.032	49-55	.018-.022	10 BTDC @ idle speed	171	.008 Cold, .010 Hot	.010 Cold, .012 Hot	16 PL510, 12 WPL510	600-700 manual, 575-650 automatic	N.A.	N.A.
1969-1971	PL510, WPL510 with emission control	NGK BP-6E	.032-.036	49-55	.018-.022	5 ATDC @ idle speed	171	.008 Cold, .010 Hot	.010 Cold, .012 Hot	16 PL510, 12 WPL510	700 manual, 600 automatic	12.0-12.5③	1969 2.0-2.4 1970 2-4③
1970-1971	PL521 with emission control	NGK BP-6E	.032-.036	49-55	.018-.022	10 BTDC @ 700	163	.008 Cold, .010 Hot	.010 Cold, .012 Hot	12	700	N.A.	2-4 ③

Tune-up Specifications, continued

1971	HLS30 with emission control	NGK BP-6E	N.A.	35-41	.016-.020	5 BTDC @ 750 ⑦	171-185	.008 Cold, .010 Hot	.010 Cold, .012 Hot	16	750 manual, 600 automatic	N.A.	5-7 ③
1971	HLS30	NGK BP-6E	.031-.035	35-41	.018-.022	17 BTDC @ 550	171-185	.008 Cold, .010 Hot	.010 Cold, .012 Hot	16	550	N.A.	N.A.
1971-1972	LB110, KLB110 with emission control	NGK BP-6E, Hitachi L46P	.031-.035	49-55	.018-.022	5 BTDC @ 700	193	.010 Cold, .014 Hot	.010 Cold, .014 Hot	14	700	N.A.	2-3
1972	PL510, WPL510 with emission control	NGK BP-6E	.032-.036-	49-55	.018-.022	7 BTDC@ idle speed	171	.008 Cold, .010 Hot	.010 Cold, .012 Hot	16 PL510, 12 WPL510	700 manual, 600 automatic	12.0-12.5③	2
1972	All other ⑧ models												

①—Torque to 11-15 ft. lbs.
②—NGK BP-6E corresponds to: Autolite AG22
Bosch W175T30.
③—Air pump disconnected
④—Vacuum line disconnected
⑤—Some early models are set at 15 BTDC @ 600.
⑥—Air pump connected
⑦—Automatic with dual point distributor OTDC @ 600 above 40°F, 10BTDC @ 600 below 40°F
⑧—See engine compartment sticker for tune-up specifications.

NOTE: Emission control requires a very precise approach to tune-up. Timing and idle speed are peculiar to the engine and its application, rather than to the engine alone. Data for the particular application will be found on a sticker in the engine compartment on all late models. The results of any adjustments or modifications should be checked with an air-fuel or CO meter.

timing light, start the engine, and allow it to idle. Direct the timing light at the pulley markings. Turn the distributor head until the timing pointer and the correct pulley mark are aligned. Some early distributors have a knurled knob for fine adjustments. Tighten the clamp and replace the vacuum line. Timing settings for each model are given in the Tune-Up Specifications Chart. The best setting for an individual engine may vary somewhat from the manufacturer's recommendations and can be found only by a trial and error method. However, the recommended setting is a good general figure. Engines with emission controls must be set exactly to the manufacturer's recommendations.

NOTE: There are two different timing settings for the HLS30 with automatic transmission: an advanced setting for temperatures below 40°F, and a retarded setting for temperatures above 40°F.

VALVE ADJUSTMENT

Remove the rocker arm or camshaft cover. Both valves for each cylinder may be adjusted while they are fully closed, on the compression stroke. After the valves have closed, turn the engine another quarter turn to insure that the cam lobes are not exerting pressure on the valves. This can readily be seen on overhead camshaft engines. Loosen the locknuts. Insert the proper size feeler gauge between the valve stem and rocker arm on overhead valve engines, or between the cam lobe and cam follower on overhead cam engines. Valve clearance figures are given in the Tune-Up Specifications Chart. Tighten the adjusting screw until there is a slight drag on the feeler gauge. Tighten the locknut and recheck the clearance. After adjusting the valves for the first cylinder, turn the engine in the normal direction of rotation until the valves for the next cylinder in the firing order close. Repeat the adjusting procedure until all valves have been adjusted. Install a new gasket and replace the rocker arm or camshaft cover.

NOTE: Do not run engine with rocker arm or camshaft cover removed. Do not adjust valves with engine running.

Adjusting valve clearances on L24 overhead cam engine

CARBURETOR

(See fuel system for further adjustments.) Two Hitachi sidedraft carburetors are used on G, R, U20, and L24 engines. A few high performance U20 engines are equipped with two twin-choke sidedraft carburetors. All other engines use one down-draft carburetor of various makes and types.

Synchronization and Idle Mixture

HITACHI/SU TYPE

Two types of dual carburetor linkage have been used. The early type utilizes a flexible cable from the accelerator pedal. The cable turns a cable drum attached to a throttle shaft, which is mounted on the intake manifold. The throttle shaft is connected to each carburetor throttle by a threaded turnbuckle. Each carburetor has an individual throttle adjusting (idle speed) screw. Some models have another idle adjusting screw on the throttle shaft.

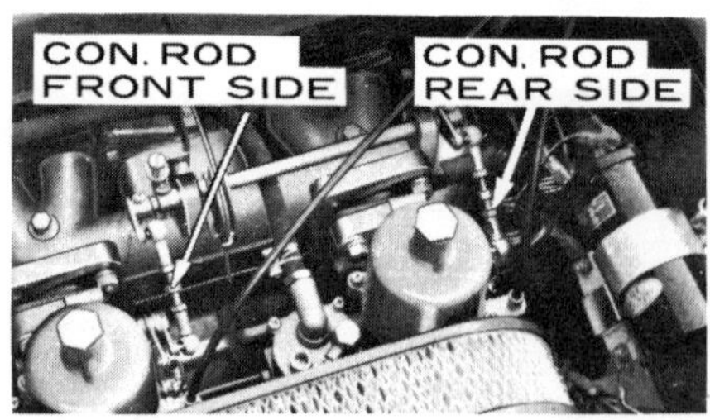

Early Hitachi/SU throttle linkage

Synchronization adjustments are made at the turnbuckles. The late type uses a rod linkage from the accelerator pedal to turn an auxiliary throttle shaft. This shaft is connected by a nonadjustable link rod to a throttle shaft linking the carburetor throttles. Each carburetor has an individual throttle adjusting (idle speed) screw. There is also an idle speed adjusting screw

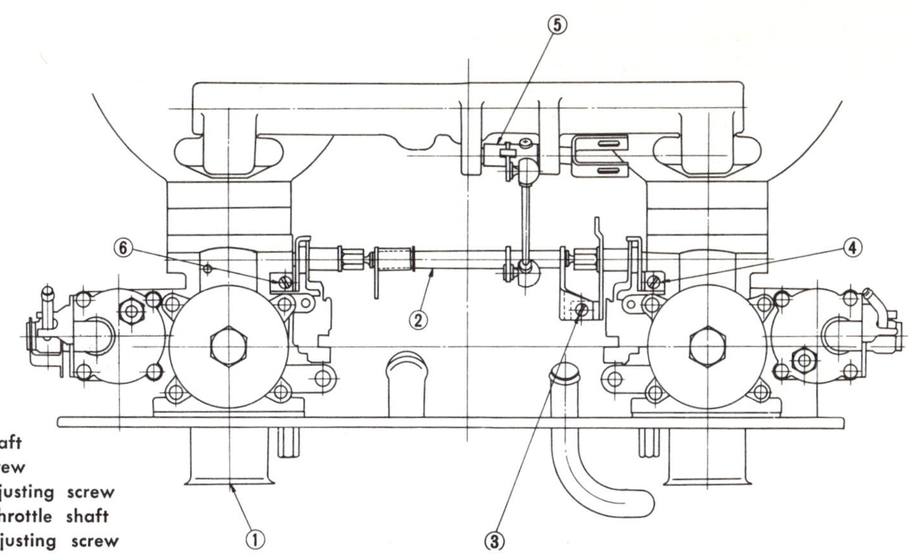

Late Hitachi/SU throttle linkage

on the auxiliary throttle shaft. Synchronizing adjustments are made at a balance screw on the throttle shaft.

The engine must be at normal operating temperature to perform carburetor adjustments. Check that the piston damper oil level is correct. If the plunger has one mark, the oil level should be within .2″ of the mark. If the rod has two marks, the oil level should be between the marks. SAE 20 oil should be used in the dampers, except in extremely cold areas where a lighter viscosity may be necessary. To adjust the carburetors:

1. Remove air cleaner.
2. Back out individual carburetor throttle adjusting screws.
3. On early linkage, disconnect front turnbuckle. On late linkage, back out balance screw.
4. On early linkage, adjust rear turnbuckle to standard measurement.

Engine	*Vehicle*	*Std. measurement*
G	SPL310	3.4-3.6″
R	SPL311	2.8″
R	RL411	3.1″
U20	SRL311	2.8″

5. Tighten both carburetor mixture adjusting nuts fully. Back them off an equal number of turns (2-3) until they reach their stops. Tighten both nuts about 1/2 turn.
6. Turn in individual carburetor throttle adjusting screws a few turns and start engine. Adjust both screws equally to obtain a reasonable idle speed.

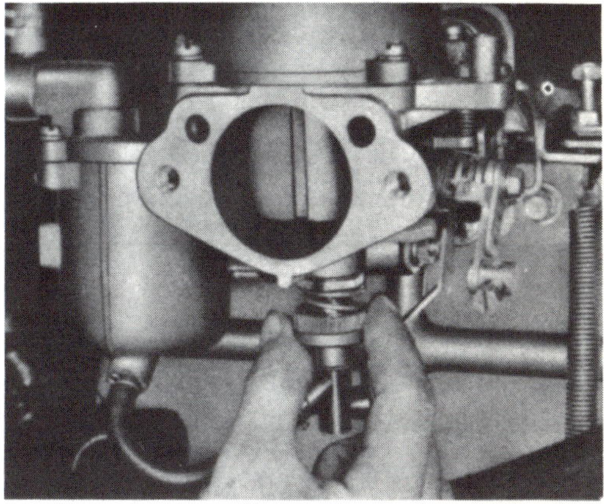

Hitachi/SU carburetor mixture adjusting nut

7. Using an air flow meter (Unisyn), measure air flow through each carburetor. Equalize the readings at each carburetor by adjusting the individual throttle adjusting screws. An alternate, and more difficult, method is to equalize air flow by listening to the hiss of each carburetor air intake through a length of rubber hose. The carburetors are now synchronized. This can be checked visually by stopping the engine, raising both carburetor pistons, and observing whether the throttle plates are parallel.
8. Tighten both mixture adjusting nuts simultaneously in increments of 1/8 turn. Tightening the nut leans the mixture. Stop at the point which gives the

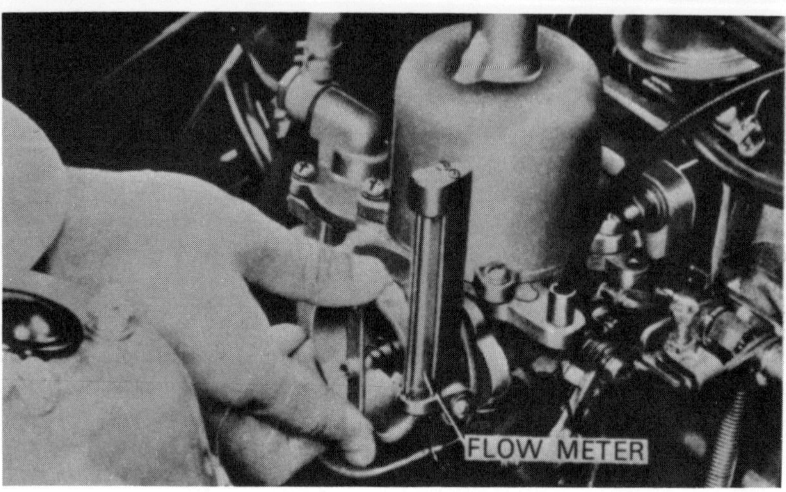

Measuring air flow through Hitachi/SU carburetor

fastest smooth idle. If the nuts are tightened all the way and idle is still unsatisfactory, return the nuts to their initial positions as in Step 5. Loosen the nuts simultaneously in increments of 1/8 turn. Loosening the nuts richens the mixture. Stop at the point which gives the fastest smooth idle.

9. Lift the piston of the rear carburetor 1/2″. This makes the carburetor inoperative. If the engine stalls, richen the front carburetor until it will keep the engine running. Now lift the piston of the front carburetor, and adjust the mixture of the back carburetor. The mixture adjustment is now completed.
10. On early linkage, adjust and connect front turnbuckle. On late linkage, turn in the balance screw to interlock the front and rear throttle shafts.
11. Open throttle suddenly. Engine should accelerate immediately with no hesitation. Both pistons should rise an equal amount. If this is not the case, recheck the synchronization and mixture adjustments.
12. Adjust the idle speed to that specified in the Tune-Up Specifications Chart. If there is a manufacturer's sticker in the engine compartment, it takes precedence.
13. Stop engine and replace air cleaner.

NOTE: On engines with emission control, the mixture adjusting nuts are held by locknuts and are not to be adjusted, except after carburetor overhaul. Adjust the mixture to obtain the air:fuel ratio or percentage of CO at idle speed specified in the Tune-Up Specifications Chart.

MIKUNI/SOLEX TWIN CHOKE

The engine must be at normal operating temperature before making any carburetor adjustments. There is a separate idle mixture adjusting screw for each of the four choke tubes. The relationship between the throttle shafts for the two carburetors is adjusted by a balance screw. A throttle (idle speed) adjusting screw is provided on the linkage between the carburetors. Some installations may also have an individual idle speed adjusting screw for each carburetor.

1. Remove air cleaner, if any. Disconnect turnbuckles from throttle linkage. Back out idle speed adjusting screw(s).
2. Gently screw idle mixture screws in all the way, then back them out about 1-1 1/2 turns.
3. Turn in idle speed screw(s) until it just contacts lever, then tighten one turn.
4. Start engine. Adjust idle speed screw(s) to obtain a reasonable idle speed.
5. Measure air flow at each choke tube with an air flow meter (Unisyn). Equalize air flow in all four choke tubes by use of idle speed screw(s) and balance screw. Carburetors are now balanced.
6. Adjust and reconnect linkage turnbuckles.
7. Adjust each idle mixture screw, one at

a time, to obtain the fastest possible smooth idle. Screw in to lean mixture, and out to richen it. Idle mixture is now set.

8. Adjust idle speed to that given in the Tune-Up Specifications Chart. If there is a manufacturer's sticker in the engine compartment, it takes precedence.
9. Open throttle suddenly. Engine should accelerate immediately with no hesitation. If this is not the case, recheck first the idle mixture and then the synchronization adjustments.
10. Stop engine and replace air cleaner.

Downdraft Carburetors

Both single and dual throat carburetors have only one idle mixture adjusting screw. Tighten the screw to lean mixture and loosen to richen.

1. For a starting point, gently turn the idle mixture adjusting screw all the way in and back out 2-3 turns.
2. Start the engine and adjust the mixture screw for the fastest smooth idle.
3. Adjust the idle speed screw to obtain the idle speed given in the Tune-Up Specifications Chart.
4. Open the throttle suddenly. The engine should accelerate immediately, without hesitation. If it stumbles or stalls, richen the mixture slightly.
5. On engines with emission control, adjust idle mixture to obtain the air: fuel ratio or percentage CO at idle speed given in the Tune-Up Specifications Chart. Some carburetors have idle mixture limiter caps to prevent unauthorized idle mixture adjustments.

NOTE: If turning the idle mixture screw has no effect, the idling passages are probably clogged.

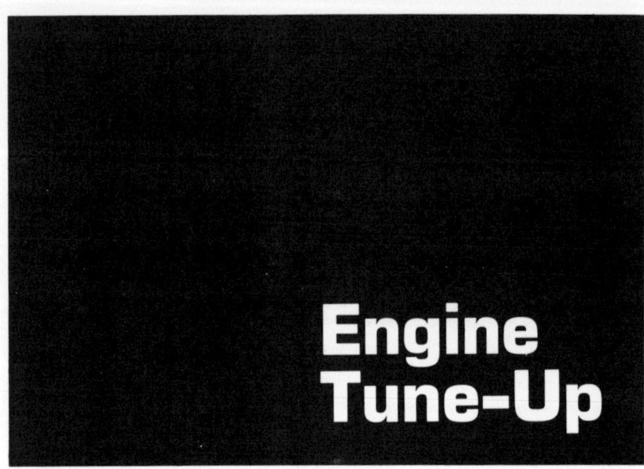

Engine Tune-Up

Engine tune-up is a procedure performed to restore engine performance, deteriorated due to normal wear and loss of adjustment. The three major areas considered in a routine tune-up are compression, ignition, and carburetion, although valve adjustment may be included.

A tune-up is performed in three steps: *analysis*, in which it is determined whether normal wear is responsible for performance loss, and which parts require replacement or service; *parts replacement or service*; and *adjustment*, in which engine adjustments are returned to original specifications. Since the advent of emission control equipment, precision adjustment has become increasingly critical, in order to maintain pollutant emission levels.

Analysis

The procedures below are used to indicate where adjustments, parts service or replacement are necessary within the realm of a normal tune-up. If, following these tests, all systems appear to be functioning properly, proceed to the Troubleshooting Section for further diagnosis.

—Remove all spark plugs, noting the cylinder in which they were installed. Remove the air cleaner, and position the throttle and choke in the full open position. Disconnect the coil high tension lead from the coil and the distributor cap. Insert a compression gauge into the spark plug port of each cylinder, in succession, and crank the engine with the starter to obtain the highest possible reading. Record the readings, and compare the highest to the lowest on the compression pressure limit chart. If the difference exceeds the limits on the chart, or if all readings are excessively low, proceed to a wet compression check (see Troubleshooting Section).

Maxi. Press. Lbs. Sq. In.	*Min. Press. Lbs. Sq. In.*	*Max. Press. Lbs. Sq. In.*	*Min. Press. Lbs. Sq. In.*
134	101	188	141
136	102	190	142
138	104	192	144
140	105	194	145
142	107	196	147
146	110	198	148
148	111	200	150
150	113	202	151
152	114	204	153
154	115	206	154
156	117	208	156
158	118	210	157
160	120	212	158
162	121	214	160
164	123	216	162
166	124	218	163
168	126	220	165
170	127	222	166
172	129	224	168
174	131	226	169
176	132	228	171
178	133	230	172
180	135	232	174
182	136	234	175
184	138	236	177
186	140	238	178

Compression pressure limits
(© Buick Div. G.M. Corp.)

—Evaluate the spark plugs according to the spark plug chart in the Troubleshooting Section, and proceed as indicated in the chart.

—Remove the distributor cap, and inspect it inside and out for cracks and/or carbon tracks, and inside for excessive wear or burning of the rotor contacts. If any of these faults are evident, the cap must be replaced.

—Check the breaker points for burning, pitting or wear, and the contact heel resting on the distributor cam for excessive wear. If defects are noted, replace the entire breaker point set.

—Remove and inspect the rotor. If the contacts are burned or worn, or if the rotor is excessively loose on the distributor shaft (where applicable), the rotor must be replaced.

—Inspect the spark plug leads and the coil high tension lead for cracks or brittleness. If any of the wires appear defective, the entire set should be replaced.

—Check the air filter to ensure that it is functioning properly.

Parts Replacement and Service

The determination of whether to replace or service parts is at the mechanic's discretion; however, it is suggested that any parts in questionable condition be replaced rather than reused.

—Clean and regap, or replace, the spark plugs as needed. Lightly coat the threads with engine oil and install the plugs. CAUTION: *Do not over-torque taper-seat spark plugs, or plugs being installed in aluminum cylinder heads.*

SPARK PLUG TORQUE

Thread size	*Cast-Iron Heads*	*Aluminum Heads*
10 mm.	14	11
14 mm.	30	27
18 mm.	34*	32
7/8 in.—18	37	35

* 17 ft. lbs. for tapered plugs using no gaskets.

—If the distributor cap is to be reused, clean the inside with a dry rag, and remove corrosion from the rotor contact points with fine emery cloth. Remove the spark plug wires one by one, and clean the wire ends and the inside of the towers. If the boots are loose, they should be replaced.

If the cap is to be replaced, transfer the wires one by one, cleaning the wire ends and replacing the boots if necessary.

—If the original points are to remain in service, clean them lightly with emery cloth, lubricate the contact heel with grease specifically designed for this purpose. Rotate the crankshaft until the heel rests on a high point of the distributor cam, and adjust the point gap to specifications.

When replacing the points, remove the original points and condenser, and wipe out the inside of the distributor housing with a clean, dry rag. Lightly lubricate the contact heel and pivot point, and install the points and condenser. Rotate the crankshaft until the heel rests on a high point of the distributor cam, and adjust the point gap to specifications. NOTE: *Always replace the condenser when changing the points.*

—If the rotor is to be reused, clean the contacts with solvent. Do not alter the spring tension of the rotor center contact. Install the rotor and the distributor cap.

—Replace the coil high tension lead and/or the spark plug leads as necessary.

—Clean the carburetor using a spray solvent (e.g., Gumout Spray). Remove the varnish from the throttle bores, and clean the linkage. Disconnect and plug the fuel line, and run the engine until it runs out of fuel. Partially fill the float chamber with solvent, and reconnect the fuel line. In extreme cases, the jets can be pressure flushed by inserting a rubber plug into the float vent, running the spray nozzle through it, and spraying the solvent until it squirts out of the venturi fuel dump.

—Clean and tighten all wiring connections in the primary electrical circuit.

Additional Services

The following services *should* be performed in conjunction with a routine tune-up to ensure efficient performance.

—Inspect the battery and fill to the proper level with distilled water. Remove the cable clamps, clean clamps and posts thoroughly, coat the posts lightly with petroleum jelly, reinstall and tighten.

—Inspect all belts, replace and/or adjust as necessary.

—Test the PCV valve (if so equipped), and clean or replace as indicated. Clean all crankcase ventilation hoses, or replace if cracked or hardened.

—Adjust the valves (if necessary) to manufacturer's specifications.

Adjustments

—Connect a dwell-tachometer between the distributor primary lead and ground. Remove the distributor cap and rotor (unless equipped with Delco externally adjustable distributor). With the ignition off, crank the engine with a remote starter switch and measure the point dwell angle. Adjust the dwell angle to specifications. NOTE: *Increasing the gap decreases the dwell angle and vice-versa.* Install the rotor and distributor cap.

—Connect a timing light according to the manufacturer's specifications. Identify the proper timing marks with chalk or paint. NOTE: *Luminescent (day-glo) paint is excellent for this purpose.* Start the engine, and run it until it reaches operating temperature. Disconnect and plug any distributor vacuum lines, and adjust idle to the speed required to adjust timing, according to specifications. Loosen the distributor clamp and adjust timing to specifications by rotating the distributor in the engine. NOTE: *To advance timing, rotate distributor opposite normal direction of rotor rotation, and vice-versa.*

—Synchronize the throttles and mixture of multiple carburetors (if so equipped) according to procedures given in the individual car sections.

—Adjust the idle speed, mixture, and idle quality, as specified in the car sections. Final idle adjustments should be made with the air cleaner installed. CAUTION: *Due to strict emission control requirements on 1969 and later models, special test equipment (CO meter, SUN Tester) may be necessary to properly adjust idle mixture to specifications.*

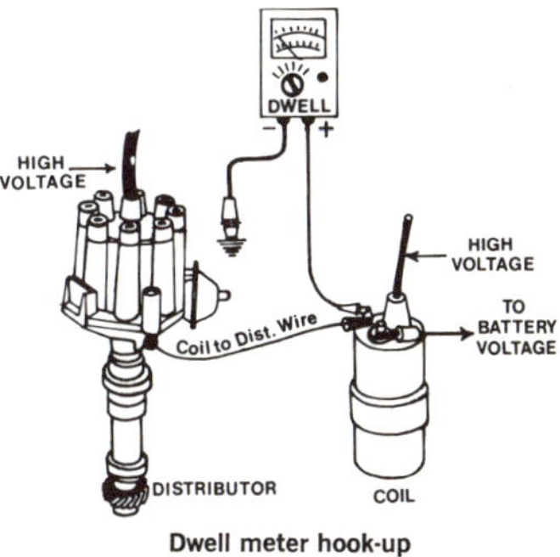

Dwell meter hook-up

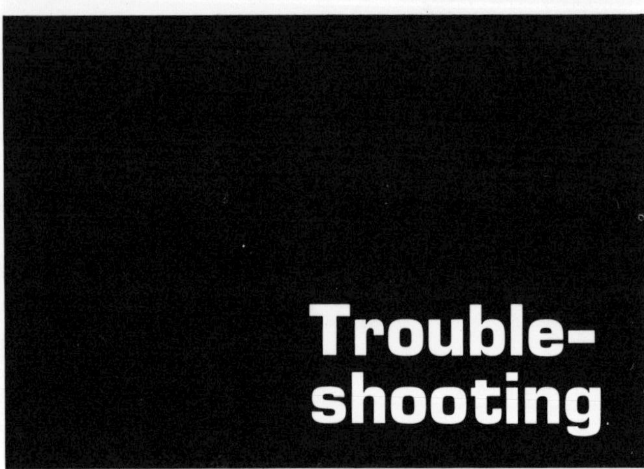

The following section is designed to aid in the rapid diagnosis of engine problems. The systematic format is used to diagnose problems ranging from engine starting difficulties to the need for engine overhaul. It is assumed that the user is equipped with basic hand tools and test equipment (tach-dwell meter, timing light, voltmeter, and ohmmeter).

Troubleshooting is divided into two sections. The first, *General Diagnosis*, is used to locate the problem area. In the second, *Specific Diagnosis*, the problem is systematically evaluated.

General Diagnosis

PROBLEM: *Symptom*	*Begin diagnosis at Section Two, Number* ———
Engine won't start:	
Starter doesn't turn	1.1, 2.1
Starter turns, engine doesn't	2.1
Starter turns engine very slowly	1.1, 2.4
Starter turns engine normally	3.1, 4.1
Starter turns engine very quickly	6.1
Engine fires intermittently	4.1
Engine fires consistently	5.1, 6.1
Engine runs poorly:	
Hard starting	3.1, 4.1, 5.1, 8.1
Rough idle	4.1, 5.1, 8.1
Stalling	3.1, 4.1, 5.1, 8.1
Engine dies at high speeds	4.1, 5.1
Hesitation (on acceleration from standing stop)	5.1, 8.1
Poor pickup	4.1, 5.1, 8.1
Lack of power	3.1, 4.1, 5.1, 8.1
Backfire through the carburetor	4.1, 8.1, 9.1
Backfire through the exhaust	4.1, 8.1, 9.1
Blue exhaust gases	6.1, 7.1
Black exhaust gases	5.1
Running on (after the ignition is shut off)	3.1, 8.1
Susceptible to moisture	4.1
Engine misfires under load	4.1, 7.1, 8.4, 9.1
Engine misfires at speed	4.1, 8.4
Engine misfires at idle	3.1, 4.1, 5.1, 7.1, 8.4

PROBLEM: *Symptom*	*Probable Cause*
Engine noises: ①	
Metallic grind while starting	Starter drive not engaging completely
Constant grind or rumble	*Starter drive not releasing, worn main bearings
Constant knock	Worn connecting rod bearings
Knock under load	Fuel octane too low, worn connecting rod bearings
Double knock	Loose piston pin
Metallic tap	*Collapsed or sticky valve lifter, excessive valve clearance, excessive end play in a rotating shaft
Scrape	*Fan belt contacting a stationary surface
Tick while starting	S.U. electric fuel pump (normal), starter brushes
Constant tick	*Generator brushes, shreaded fan belt
Squeal	*Improperly tensioned fan belt
Hiss or roar	*Steam escaping through a leak in the cooling system or the radiator overflow vent
Whistle	*Vacuum leak
Wheeze	Loose or cracked spark plug

①—It is extremely difficult to evaluate vehicle noises. While the above are general definitions of engine noises, those starred (*) should be considered as possibly originating elsewhere in the car. To aid diagnosis, the following list considers other potential sources of these sounds.

Metallic grind:
Throwout bearing; transmission gears, bearings, or synchronizers; differential bearings, gears; something metallic in contact with brake drum or disc.

Metallic tap:
U-joints; fan-to-radiator (or shroud) contact.

Scrape:
Brake shoe or pad dragging; tire to body contact; suspension contacting undercarriage or exhaust; something non-metallic contacting brake shoe or drum.

Tick:
Transmission gears; differential gears; lack of radio suppression; resonant vibration of body panels; windshield wiper motor or transmission; heater motor and blower.

Squeal:
Brake shoe or pad not fully releasing; tires (excessive wear, uneven wear, improper inflation); front or rear wheel alignment (most commonly due to improper toe-in).

Hiss or whistle:
Wind leaks (body or window); heater motor and blower fan.

Roar:
Wheel bearings; wind leaks (body and window).

Specific Diagnosis

This section is arranged so that following each test, instructions are given to proceed to another, until a problem is diagnosed.

INDEX

Group		*Topic*
1	*	Battery
2	*	Cranking system
3	*	Primary electrical system
4	*	Secondary electrical system
5	*	Fuel system
6	*	Engine compression
7	**	Engine vacuum
8	**	Secondary electrical system
9	**	Valve train
10	**	Exhaust system
11	**	Cooling system
12	**	Engine lubrication

*—The engine need not be running.
**—The engine must be running.

SAMPLE SECTION

Test and Procedure	*Results and Indications*	*Proceed to*
4.1—Check for spark: Hold each spark plug wire approximately ¼″ from ground with gloves or a heavy, dry rag. Crank the engine and observe the spark.	→ If no spark is evident: →	4.2
	→ If spark is good in some cases: →	4.3
	→ If spark is good in all cases: →	4.6

DIAGNOSIS

Test and Procedure	*Results and Indications*	*Proceed to*
1.1—Inspect the battery visually for case condition (corrosion, cracks) and water level.	If case is cracked, replace battery:	1.4
	If the case is intact, remove corrosion with a solution of baking soda and water (CAUTION: *do not get the solution into the battery*), and fill with water:	1.2
1.2—Check the battery cable connections: Insert a screwdriver between the battery post and the cable clamp. Turn the headlights on high beam, and observe them as the screwdriver is gently twisted to ensure good metal to metal contact.	If the lights brighten, remove and clean the clamp and post; coat the post with petroleum jelly, install and tighten the clamp:	1.4
	If no improvement is noted:	1.3

Testing battery cable connections using a screwdriver

1.3—Test the state of charge of the battery using an individual cell tester or hydrometer.

Spec. Grav. Reading	*Charged Condition*
1.260-1.280	Fully Charged
1.230-1.250	Three Quarter Charged
1.200-1.220	One Half Charged
1.170-1.190	One Quarter Charged
1.140-1.160	Just About Flat
1.110-1.130	All The Way Down

State of battery charge

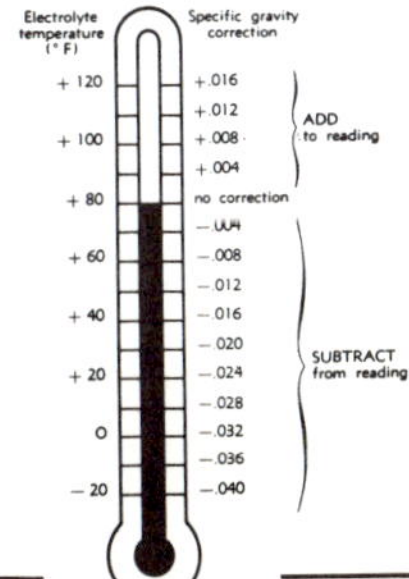

The effect of temperature on the specific gravity of battery electrolyte

If indicated, charge the battery. NOTE: *If no obvious reason exists for the low state of charge (i.e., battery age, prolonged storage), the charging system should be tested:* — 1.4

Test and Procedure	*Results and Indications*	*Proceed to*
1.4—Visually inspect battery cables for cracking, bad connection to ground, or bad connection to starter.	If necessary, tighten connections or replace the cables:	2.1

Tests in Group 2 are performed with coil high tension lead disconnected to prevent accidental starting.

Test and Procedure	*Results and Indications*	*Proceed to*
2.1—Test the starter motor and solenoid: Connect a jumper from the battery post of the solenoid (or relay) to the ignition post of the solenoid (or relay).	If starter turns the engine normally:	2.2
	If the starter buzzes, or turns the engine very slowly:	2.4
	If no response, replace the solenoid (or relay).	3.1
	If the starter turns, but the engine doesn't, ensure that the flywheel ring gear is intact. If the gear is undamaged, replace the starter drive.	3.1
2.2—Determine whether ignition override switches are functioning properly (clutch start switch, neutral safety switch), by connecting a jumper across the switch(es), and turning the ignition switch to "start".	If starter operates, adjust or replace switch:	3.1
	If the starter doesn't operate:	2.3
2.3—Check the ignition switch "start" position: Connect a 12V test lamp between the starter post of the solenoid (or relay) and ground. Turn the ignition switch to the "start" position, and jiggle the key.	If the lamp doesn't light when the switch is turned, check the ignition switch for loose connections, cracked insulation, or broken wires. Repair or replace as necessary:	3.1
	If the lamp flickers when the key is jiggled, replace the ignition switch.	3.3

Checking the ignition switch "start" position

Test and Procedure	*Results and Indications*	*Proceed to*
2.4—Remove and bench test the starter, according to specifications in the car section.	If the starter does not meet specifications, repair or replace as needed:	3.1
	If the starter is operating properly:	2.5
2.5—Determine whether the engine can turn freely: Remove the spark plugs, and check for water in the cylinders. Check for water on the dipstick, or oil in the radiator. Attempt to turn the engine using an 18″ flex drive and socket on the crankshaft pulley nut or bolt.	If the engine will turn freely only with the spark plugs out, and hydrostatic lock (water in the cylinders) is ruled out, check valve timing:	9.2
	If engine will not turn freely, and it is known that the clutch and transmission are free, the engine must be disassembled for further evaluation:	Next Chapter

Tests and Procedures	*Results and Indications*	*Proceed to*
3.1—Check the ignition switch "on" position: Connect a jumper wire between the distributor side of the coil and ground, and a 12V test lamp between the switch side of the coil and ground. Remove the high tension lead from the coil. Turn the ignition switch on and jiggle the key.	If the lamp lights:	3.2
	If the lamp flickers when the key is jiggled, replace the ignition switch:	3.3
	If the lamp doesn't light, check for loose or open connections. If none are found, remove the ignition switch and check for continuity. If the switch is faulty, replace it:	3.3
Checking the ignition switch "on" position		
3.2—Check the ballast resistor or resistance wire for an open circuit, using an ohmmeter.	Replace the resistor or the resistance wire if the resistance is zero.	3.3
3.3—Visually inspect the breaker points for burning, pitting, or excessive wear. Gray coloring of the point contact surfaces is normal. Rotate the crankshaft until the contact heel rests on a high point of the distributor cam, and adjust the point gap to specifications.	If the breaker points are intact, clean the contact surfaces with fine emery cloth, and adjust the point gap to specifications. If pitted or worn, replace the points and condenser, and adjust the gap to specifications: NOTE: *Always lubricate the distributor cam according to manufacturer's recommendations when servicing the breaker points.*	3.4
3.4—Connect a dwell meter between the distributor primary lead and ground. Crank the engine and observe the point dwell angle.	If necessary, adjust the point dwell angle: NOTE: *Increasing the point gap decreases the dwell angle, and vice-versa.*	3.6
	If dwell meter shows little or no reading:	3.5
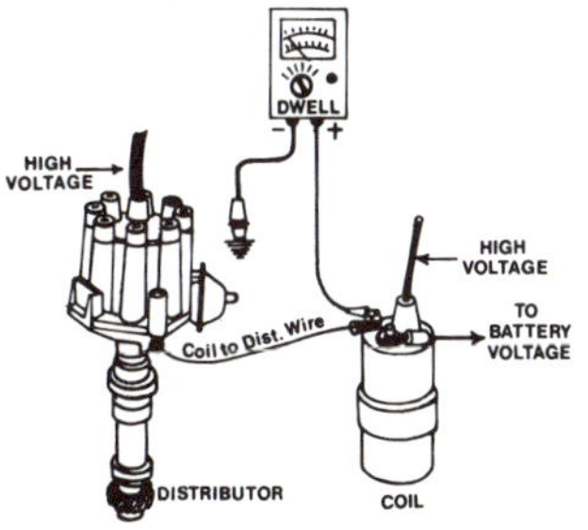 Dwell meter hook-up	Dwell angle	
3.5—Check the condenser for short: Connect an ohmmeter across the condenser body and the pigtail lead.	If any reading other than infinite resistance is noted, replace the condenser:	3.6
Checking the condenser for short		

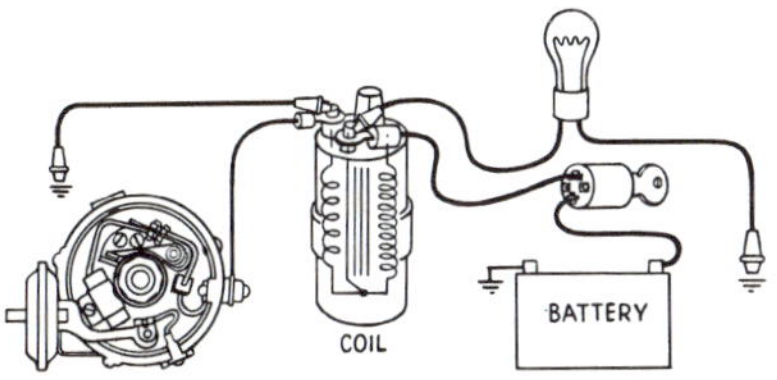

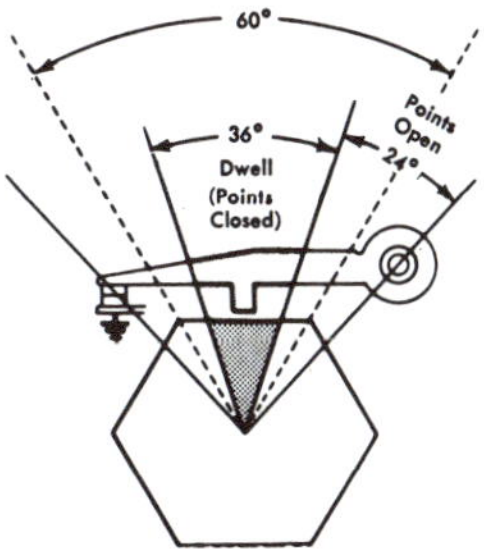

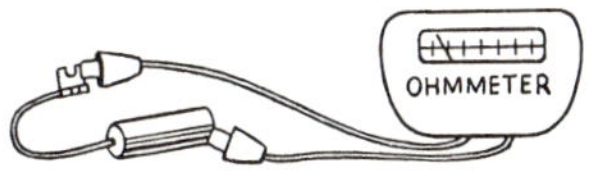

Test and Procedure	*Results and Indications*	*Proceed to*
3.6—Test the coil primary resistance: Connect an ohmmeter across the coil primary terminals, and read the resistance on the low scale. Note whether an external ballast resistor or resistance wire is utilized. 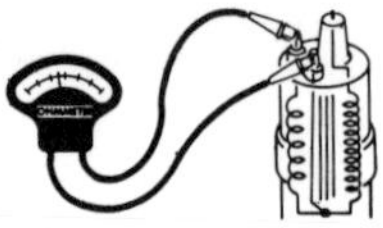 Testing the coil primary resistance	Coils utilizing ballast resistors or resistance wires should have approximately 1.0Ω resistance; coils with internal resistors should have approximately 4.0Ω resistance. If values far from the above are noted, replace the coil:	4.1
4.1—Check for spark: Hold each spark plug wire approximately ¼″ from ground with gloves or a heavy, dry rag. Crank the engine, and observe the spark.	If no spark is evident:	4.2
	If spark is good in some cylinders:	4.3
	If spark is good in all cylinders:	4.6
4.2—Check for spark at the coil high tension lead: Remove the coil high tension lead from the distributor and position it approximately ¼″ from ground. Crank the engine and observe spark. CAUTION: *This test should not be performed on cars equipped with transistorized ignition.*	If the spark is good and consistent:	4.3
	If the spark is good but intermittent, test the primary electrical system starting at 3.3:	3.3
	If the spark is weak or non-existent, replace the coil high tension lead, clean and tighten all connections and retest. If no improvement is noted:	4.4
4.3—Visually inspect the distributor cap and rotor for burned or corroded contacts, cracks, carbon tracks, or moisture. Also check the fit of the rotor on the distributor shaft (where applicable).	If moisture is present, dry thoroughly, and retest per 4.1:	4.1
	If burned or excessively corroded contacts, cracks, or carbon tracks are noted, replace the defective part(s) and retest per 4.1:	4.1
	If the rotor and cap appear intact, or are only slightly corroded, clean the contacts thoroughly (including the cap towers and spark plug wire ends) and retest per 4.1:	
	If the spark is good in all cases:	4.6
	If the spark is poor in all cases:	4.5
4.4—Check the coil secondary resistance: Connect an ohmmeter across the distributor side of the coil and the coil tower. Read the resistance on the high scale of the ohmmeter. 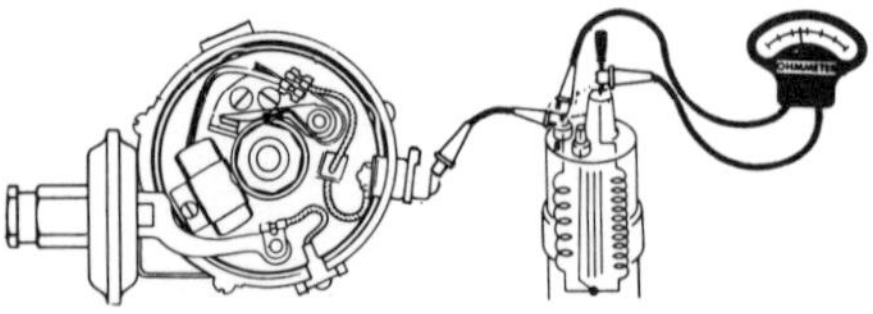 Testing the coil secondary resistance	The resistance of a satisfactory coil should be between 4KΩ and 10KΩ. If the resistance is considerably higher (i.e., 40KΩ) replace the coil, and retest per 4.1: NOTE: *This does not apply to high performance coils.*	4.1

Test and Procedure	*Results and Indications*	*Proceed to*
4.5—Visually inspect the spark plug wires for cracking or brittleness. Ensure that no two wires are positioned so as to cause induction firing (adjacent and parallel). Remove each wire, one by one, and check resistance with an ohmmeter.	Replace any cracked or brittle wires. If any of the wires are defective, replace the entire set. Replace any wires with excessive resistance (over 8000Ω per foot for suppression wire), and separate any wires that might cause induction firing.	4.6
4.6—Remove the spark plugs, noting the cylinders from which they were removed, and evaluate according to the chart below.	See below.	See below.

Condition	*Cause*	*Remedy*	*Proceed to*
Electrodes eroded, light brown deposits.	Normal wear. Normal wear is indicated by approximately .001″ wear per 1000 miles.	Clean and regap the spark plug if wear is not excessive: Replace the spark plug if excessively worn:	4.7
Carbon fouling (black, dry, fluffy deposits).	If present on one or two plugs:		
	Faulty high tension lead(s).	Test the high tension leads:	4.5
	Burnt or sticking valve(s).	Check the valve train: (Clean and regap the plugs in either case.)	9.1
	If present on most or all plugs: Overly rich fuel mixture, due to restricted air filter, improper carburetor adjustment, improper choke or heat riser adjustment or operation.	Check the fuel system:	5.1
Oil fouling (wet black deposits)	Worn engine components. NOTE: *Oil fouling may occur in new or recently rebuilt engines until broken in.*	Check engine vacuum and compression:	6.1
		Replace with new spark plug	
Lead fouling (gray, black, tan, or yellow deposits, which appear glazed or cinderlike).	Combustion by-products.	Clean and regap the plugs: (Use plugs of a different heat range if the problem recurs.)	4.7

Condition	Cause	Remedy	Proceed to
Gap bridging (deposits lodged between the electrodes).	Incomplete combustion, or transfer of deposits from the combustion chamber.	Replace the spark plugs:	4.7
Overheating (burnt electrodes, and extremely white insulator with small black spots).	Ignition timing advanced too far.	Adjust timing to specifications:	8.2
	Overly lean fuel mixture.	Check the fuel system:	5.1
	Spark plugs not seated properly.	Clean spark plug seat and install a new gasket washer: (Replace the spark plugs in all cases.)	4.7
Fused spot deposits on the insulator.	Combustion chamber blow-by.	Clean and regap the spark plugs:	4.7
Pre-ignition (melted or severely burned electrodes, blistered or cracked insulators, or metallic deposits on the insulator).	Incorrect spark plug heat range.	Replace with plugs of the proper heat range:	4.7
	Ignition timing advanced too far.	Adjust timing to specifications:	8.2
	Spark plugs not being cooled efficiently.	Clean the spark plug seat, and check the cooling system:	11.1
	Fuel mixture too lean.	Check the fuel system:	5.1
	Poor compression.	Check compression:	6.1
	Fuel grade too low.	Use higher octane fuel:	4.7

Test and Procedure	Results and Indications	Proceed to
4.7—Determine the static ignition timing: Using the flywheel or crankshaft pulley timing marks as a guide, locate top dead center on the *compression* stroke of the No. 1 cylinder. Remove the distributor cap.	Adjust the distributor so that the rotor points toward the No. 1 tower in the distributor cap, and the points are just opening:	4.8
4.8—Check coil polarity: Connect a voltmeter negative lead to the coil high tension lead, and the positive lead to ground (NOTE: *reverse the hook-up for positive ground cars*). Crank the engine momentarily. Checking coil polarity	If the voltmeter reads up-scale, the polarity is correct:	5.1
	If the voltmeter reads down-scale, reverse the coil polarity (switch the primary leads):	5.1

Test and Procedure	*Results and Indications*	*Proceed to*
5.1—Determine that the air filter is functioning efficiently: Hold paper elements up to a strong light, and attempt to see light through the filter.	Clean permanent air filters in gasoline (or manufacturer's recommendation), and allow to dry. Replace paper elements through which light cannot be seen:	5.2
5.2—Determine whether a flooding condition exists: Flooding is identified by a strong gasoline odor, and excessive gasoline present in the throttle bore(s) of the carburetor.	If flooding is not evident:	5.3
	If flooding is evident, permit the gasoline to dry for a few moments and restart.	
	If flooding doesn't recur:	5.6
	If flooding is persistant:	5.5
5.3—Check that fuel is reaching the carburetor: Detach the fuel line at the carburetor inlet. Hold the end of the line in a cup (not styrofoam), and crank the engine.	If fuel flows smoothly:	5.6
	If fuel doesn't flow (NOTE: *Make sure that there is fuel in the tank*), or flows erratically:	5.4
5.4—Test the fuel pump: Disconnect all fuel lines from the fuel pump. Hold a finger over the input fitting, crank the engine (with electric pump, turn the ignition or pump on), and feel for suction.	If suction is evident, blow out the fuel line to the tank with low pressure compressed air until bubbling is heard from the fuel filler neck. Also blow out the carburetor fuel line (both ends disconnected):	5.6
	If no suction is evident, replace or repair the fuel pump:	5.6
	NOTE: *Repeated oil fouling of the spark plugs, or a no-start condition, could be the result of a ruptured vacuum booster pump diaphragm, through which oil or gasoline is being drawn into the intake manifold (where applicable).*	
5.5—Check the needle and seat: Tap the carburetor in the area of the needle and seat.	If flooding stops, a gasoline additive (e.g., Gumout) will often cure the problem:	5.6
	If flooding continues, check the fuel pump for excessive pressure at the carburetor (according to specifications). If the pressure is normal, the needle and seat must be removed and checked, and/or the float level adjusted:	5.6
5.6—Test the accelerator pump by looking into the throttle bores while operating the throttle.	If the accelerator pump appears to be operating normally:	5.7
	If the accelerator pump is not operating, the pump must be reconditioned. Where possible, service the pump with the carburetor(s) installed on the engine. If necessary, remove the carburetor. Prior to removal:	5.7
5.7—Determine whether the carburetor main fuel system is functioning: Spray a commercial starting fluid into the carburetor while attempting to start the engine.	If the engine starts, runs for a few seconds, and dies:	5.8
	If the engine doesn't start:	6.1

Test and Procedures	Results and Indications	Proceed to
5.8—Uncommon fuel system malfunctions: See below:	If the problem is solved:	6.1
	If the problem remains, remove and recondition the carburetor.	

Condition	Indication	Test	Usual Weather Conditions	Remedy
Vapor lock	Car will not restart shortly after running.	Cool the components of the fuel system until the engine starts.	Hot to very hot	Ensure that the exhaust manifold heat control valve is operating. Check with the vehicle manufacturer for the recommended solution to vapor lock on the model in question.
Carburetor icing	Car will not idle, stalls at low speeds.	Visually inspect the throttle plate area of the throttle bores for frost.	High humidity, 32-40° F.	Ensure that the exhaust manifold heat control valve is operating, and that the intake manifold heat riser is not blocked.
Water in the fuel	Engine sputters and stalls; may not start.	Pump a small amount of fuel into a glass jar. Allow to stand, and inspect for droplets or a layer of water.	High humidity, extreme temperature changes.	For droplets, use one or two cans of commercial gas dryer (Dry Gas) For a layer of water, the tank must be drained, and the fuel lines blown out with compressed air.

Test and Procedure	Results and Indications	Proceed to
6.1—Test engine compression: Remove all spark plugs. Insert a compression gauge into a spark plug port, crank the engine to obtain the maximum reading, and record.	If compression is within limits on all cylinders:	7.1
	If gauge reading is extremely low on all cylinders:	6.2
	If gauge reading is low on one or two cylinders: (If gauge readings are identical and low on two or more adjacent cylinders, the head gasket must be replaced.)	6.2

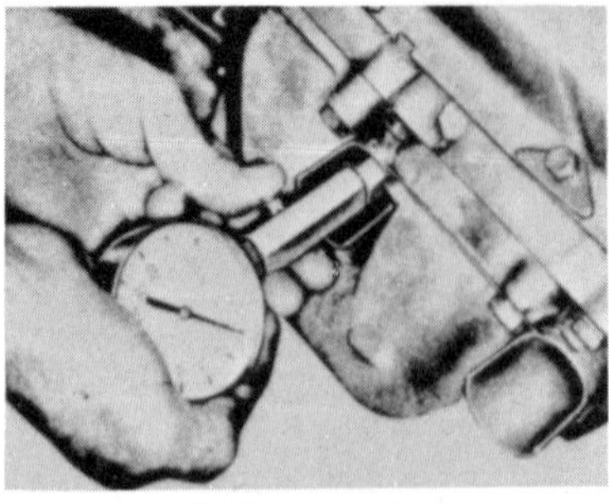

Testing compression
(© Chevrolet Div. G.M. Corp.)

Maxi. Press. Lbs. Sq. In.	*Min. Press. Lbs. Sq. In.*	*Maxi. Press. Lbs. Sq. In.*	*Min. Press. Lbs. Sq. In.*	*Max. Press. Lbs. Sq. In.*	*Min. Press. Lbs. Sq. In.*	*Max. Press. Lbs. Sq. In.*	*Min. Press. Lbs. Sq. In.*
134	101	162	121	188	141	214	160
136	102	164	123	190	142	216	162
138	104	166	124	192	144	218	163
140	105	168	126	194	145	220	165
142	107	170	127	196	147	222	166
146	110	172	129	198	148	224	168
148	111	174	131	200	150	226	169
150	113	176	132	202	151	228	171
152	114	178	133	204	153	230	172
154	115	180	135	206	154	232	174
156	117	182	136	208	156	234	175
158	118	184	138	210	157	236	177
160	120	186	140	212	158	238	178

Compression pressure limits
(© Buick Div. G.M. Corp.)

Test and Procedure	Results and Indications	Proceed to
6.2—Test engine compression (wet): Squirt approximately 30 cc. of engine oil into each cylinder, and retest per 6.1.	If the readings improve, worn or cracked rings or broken pistons are indicated: If the readings do not improve, burned or excessively carboned valves or a jumped timing chain are indicated: NOTE: *A jumped timing chain is often indicated by difficult cranking.*	Next Chapter 7.1
7.1—Perform a vacuum check of the engine: Attach a vacuum gauge to the intake manifold beyond the throttle plate. Start the engine, and observe the action of the needle over the range of engine speeds.	See below.	See below

Reading	Indications	Proceed to
 Steady, from 17-22 in. Hg.	Normal.	8.1
 Low and steady.	Late ignition or valve timing, or low compression:	6.1
 Very low	Vacuum leak:	7.2
 Needle fluctuates as engine speed increases.	Ignition miss, blown cylinder head gasket, leaking valve or weak valve spring:	6.1, 8.3
 Gradual drop in reading at idle.	Excessive back pressure in the exhaust system:	10.1
 Intermittent fluctuation at idle.	Ignition miss, sticking valve:	8.3, 9.1
 Drifting needle.	Improper idle mixture adjustment, carburetors not synchronized (where applicable), or minor intake leak. Synchronize the carburetors, adjust the idle, and retest. If the condition persists:	7.2
 High and steady.	Early ignition timing:	8.2

Test and Procedure	*Results and Indications*	*Proceed to*
7.2—Attach a vacuum gauge per 7.1, and test for an intake manifold leak. Squirt a small amount of oil around the intake manifold gaskets, carburetor gaskets, plugs and fittings. Observe the action of the vacuum gauge.	If the reading improves, replace the indicated gasket, or seal the indicated fitting or plug: If the reading remains low:	8.1 7.3
7.3—Test all vacuum hoses and accessories for leaks as described in 7.2. Also check the carburetor body (dashpots, automatic choke mechanism, throttle shafts) for leaks in the same manner.	If the reading improves, service or replace the offending part(s): If the reading remains low:	8.1 6.1
8.1—Check the point dwell angle: Connect a dwell meter between the distributor primary wire and ground. Start the engine, and observe the dwell angle from idle to 3000 rpm.	If necessary, adjust the dwell angle. NOTE: *Increasing the point gap reduces the dwell angle and vice-versa.* If the dwell angle moves outside specifications as engine speed increases, the distributor should be removed and checked for cam accuracy, shaft endplay and concentricity, bushing wear, and adequate point arm tension (NOTE: *Most of these items may be checked with the distributor installed in the engine, using an oscilloscope*):	8.2
8.2—Connect a timing light (per manufacturer's recommendation) and check the dynamic ignition timing. Disconnect and plug the vacuum hose(s) to the distributor if specified, start the engine, and observe the timing marks at the specified engine speed.	If the timing is not correct, adjust to specifications by rotating the distributor in the engine: (Advance timing by rotating distributor opposite normal direction of rotor rotation, retard timing by rotating distributor in same direction as rotor rotation.)	8.3
8.3—Check the operation of the distributor advance mechanism(s): To test the mechanical advance, disconnect all but the mechanical advance, and observe the timing marks with a timing light as the engine speed is increased from idle. If the mark moves smoothly, without hesitation, it may be assumed that the mechanical advance is functioning properly. To test vacuum advance and/or retard systems, alternately crimp and release the vacuum line, and observe the timing mark for movement. If movement is noted, the system is operating.	If the systems are functioning: If the systems are not functioning, remove the distributor, and test on a distributor tester:	8.4 8.4
8.4—Locate an ignition miss: With the engine running, remove each spark plug wire, one by one, until one is found that doesn't cause the engine to roughen and slow down.	When the missing cylinder is identified:	4.1

Test and Procedure	Results and Indications	Proceed to
9.1—Evaluate the valve train: Remove the valve cover, and ensure that the valves are adjusted to specifications. A mechanic's stethoscope may be used to aid in the diagnosis of the valve train. By pushing the probe on or near push rods or rockers, valve noise often can be isolated. A timing light also may be used to diagnose valve problems. Connect the light according to manufacturer's recommendations, and start the engine. Vary the firing moment of the light by increasing the engine speed (and therefore the ignition advance), and moving the trigger from cylinder to cylinder. Observe the movement of each valve.	See below	See below

Observation	Probable Cause	Remedy	Proceed to
Metallic tap heard through the stethoscope.	Sticking hydraulic lifter or excessive valve clearance.	Adjust valve. If tap persists, remove and replace the lifter:	10.1
Metallic tap through the stethoscope, able to push the rocker arm (lifter side) down by hand.	Collapsed valve lifter.	Remove and replace the lifter:	10.1
Erratic, irregular motion of the valve stem.*	Sticking valve, burned valve.	Recondition the valve and/or valve guide:	Next Chapter
Eccentric motion of the pushrod at the rocker arm.*	Bent pushrod.	Replace the pushrod:	10.1
Valve retainer bounces as the valve closes.*	Weak valve spring or damper.	Remove and test the spring and damper. Replace if necessary:	10.1

*—When observed with a timing light.

Test and Procedure	Results and Indications	Proceed to
9.2—Check the valve timing: Locate top dead center of the No. 1 piston, and install a degree wheel or tape on the crankshaft pulley or damper with zero corresponding to an index mark on the engine. Rotate the crankshaft in its direction of rotation, and observe the opening of the No. 1 cylinder intake valve. The opening should correspond with the correct mark on the degree wheel according to specifications.	If the timing is not correct, the timing cover must be removed for further investigation:	

Test and Procedure	*Results and Indications*	*Proceed to*
10.1—Determine whether the exhaust manifold heat control valve is operating: Operate the valve by hand to determine whether it is free to move. If the valve is free, run the engine to operating temperature and observe the action of the valve, to ensure that it is opening.	If the valve sticks, spray it with a suitable solvent, open and close the valve to free it, and retest.	
	If the valve functions properly:	10.2
	If the valve does not free, or does not operate, replace the valve:	10.2
10.2—Ensure that there are no exhaust restrictions: Visually inspect the exhaust system for kinks, dents, or crushing. Also note that gasses are flowing freely from the tailpipe at all engine speeds, indicating no restriction in the muffler or resonator.	Replace any damaged portion of the system:	11.1
11.1—Visually inspect the fan belt for glazing, cracks, and fraying, and replace if necessary. Tighten the belt so that the longest span has approximately ½″ play at its midpoint under thumb pressure.	Replace or tighten the fan belt as necessary:	11.2

Checking the fan belt tension
(© Nissan Motor Co. Ltd.)

Test and Procedure	*Results and Indications*	*Proceed to*
11.2—Check the fluid level of the cooling system.	If full or slightly low, fill as necessary:	11.5
	If extremely low:	11.3
11.3—Visually inspect the external portions of the cooling system (radiator, radiator hoses, thermostat elbow, water pump seals, heater hoses, etc.) for leaks. If none are found, pressurize the cooling system to 14-15 psi.	If cooling system holds the pressure:	11.5
	If cooling system loses pressure rapidly, reinspect external parts of the system for leaks under pressure. If none are found, check dipstick for coolant in crankcase. If no coolant is present, but pressure loss continues:	11.4
	If coolant is evident in crankcase, remove cylinder head(s), and check gasket(s). If gaskets are intact, block and cylinder head(s) should be checked for cracks or holes.	
	If the gasket(s) is blown, replace, and purge the crankcase of coolant:	12.6
	NOTE: *Occasionally, due to atmospheric and driving conditions, condensation of water can occur in the crankcase. This causes the oil to appear milky white. To remedy, run the engine until hot, and change the oil and oil filter.*	

Test and Procedure	*Results and Indication*	*Proceed to*
11.4—Check for combustion leaks into the cooling system: Pressurize the cooling system as above. Start the engine, and observe the pressure gauge. If the needle fluctuates, remove each spark plug wire, one by one, noting which cylinder(s) reduce or eliminate the fluctuation. Radiator pressure tester (© American Motors Corp.)	Cylinders which reduce or eliminate the fluctuation, when the spark plug wire is removed, are leaking into the cooling system. Replace the head gasket on the affected cylinder bank(s).	
11.5—Check the radiator pressure cap: Attach a radiator pressure tester to the radiator cap (wet the seal prior to installation). Quickly pump up the pressure, noting the point at which the cap releases. Testing the radiator pressure cap (© American Motors Corp.)	If the cap releases within ± 1 psi of the specified rating, it is operating properly:	11.6
	If the cap releases at more than ± 1 psi of the specified rating, it should be replaced:	11.6
11.6—Test the thermostat: Start the engine cold, remove the radiator cap, and insert a thermometer into the radiator. Allow the engine to idle. After a short while, there will be a sudden, rapid increase in coolant temperature. The temperature at which this sharp rise stops is the thermostat opening temperature.	If the thermostat opens at or about the specified temperature:	11.7
	If the temperature doesn't increase: (If the temperature increases slowly and gradually, replace the thermostat.)	11.7
11.7—Check the water pump: Remove the thermostat elbow and the thermostat, disconnect the coil high tension lead (to prevent starting), and crank the engine momentarily.	If coolant flows, replace the thermostat and retest per 11.6:	11.6
	If coolant doesn't flow, reverse flush the cooling system to alleviate any blockage that might exist. If system is not blocked, and coolant will not flow, recondition the water pump.	—
12.1—Check the oil pressure gauge or warning light: If the gauge shows low pressure, or the light is on, for no obvious reason, remove the oil pressure sender. Install an accurate oil pressure gauge and run the engine momentarily.	If oil pressure builds normally, run engine for a few moments to determine that it is functioning normally, and replace the sender.	—
	If the pressure remains low:	12.2
	If the pressure surges:	12.3
	If the oil pressure is zero:	12.3

Test and Procedure	*Results and Indications*	*Proceed to*
12.2—Visually inspect the oil: If the oil is watery or very thin, milky, or foamy, replace the oil and oil filter.	If the oil is normal:	12.3
	If after replacing oil the pressure remains low:	12.3
	If after replacing oil the pressure becomes normal:	—
12.3—Inspect the oil pressure relief valve and spring, to ensure that it is not sticking or stuck. Remove and thoroughly clean the valve, spring, and the valve body. Oil pressure relief valve (© British Leyland Motors)	If the oil pressure improves:	—
	If no improvement is noted:	12.4
12.4—Check to ensure that the oil pump is not cavitating (sucking air instead of oil): See that the crankcase is neither over nor underfull, and that the pickup in the sump is in the proper position and free from sludge.	Fill or drain the crankcase to the proper capacity, and clean the pickup screen in solvent if necessary. If no improvement is noted:	12.5
12.5—Inspect the oil pump drive and the oil pump:	If the pump drive or the oil pump appear to be defective, service as necessary and retest per 12.1:	12.1
	If the pump drive and pump appear to be operating normally, the engine should be disassembled to determine where blockage exists:	Next Chapter
12.6—Purge the engine of ethylene glycol coolant: Completely drain the crankcase and the oil filter. Obtain a commercial butyl cellosolve base solvent, designated for this purpose, and follow the instructions precisely. Following this, install a new oil filter and refill the crankcase with the proper weight oil. The next oil and filter change should follow shortly thereafter (1000 miles).		

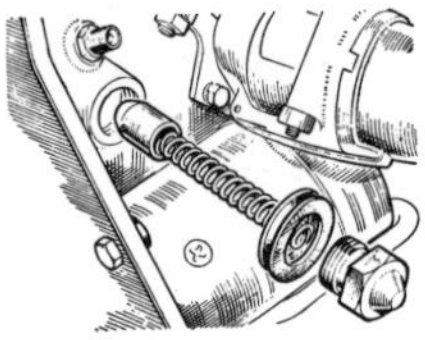

Chapter 3
Engine and Engine Rebuilding

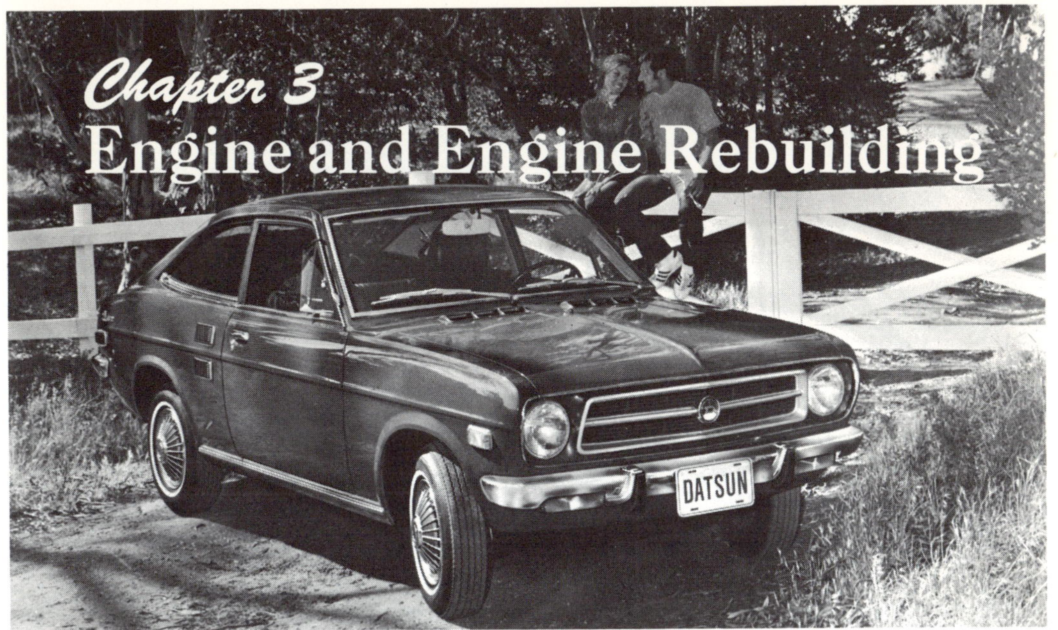

Engine Electrical

DISTRIBUTOR

Removal and Installation

When removing the distributor for any reason, note the location of the rotor and mark the relationship of the distributor body to the engine. The distributor can

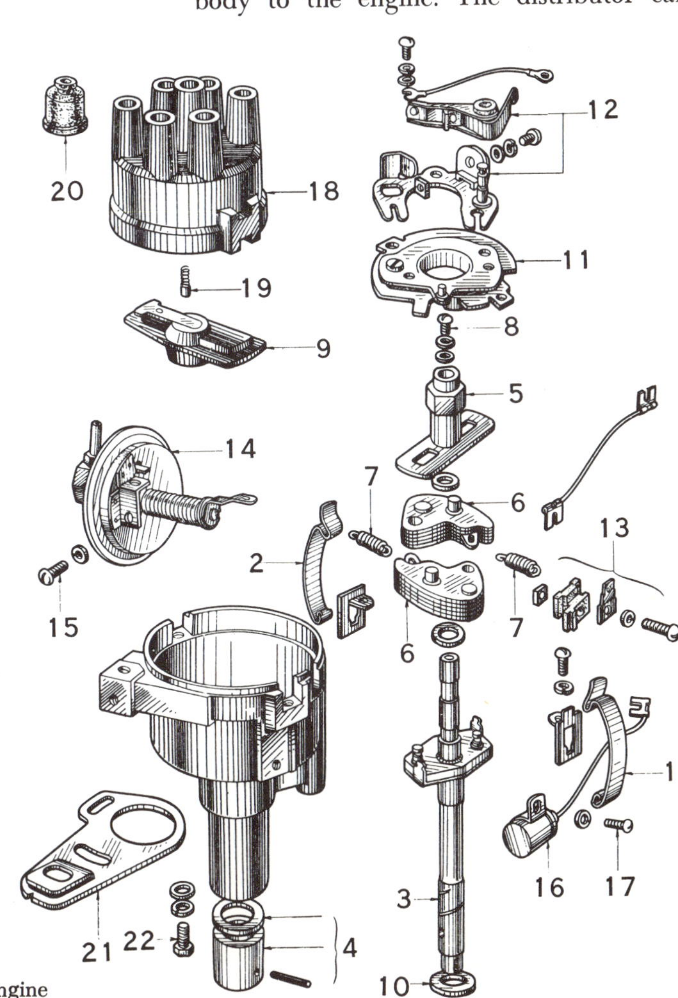

1. Cap holddown spring
2. Cap holddown spring
3. Shaft
4. Drive pinion
5. Cam
6. Centrifugal advance weights
7. Centrifugal advance springs
8. Screw
9. Rotor
10. Thrust washer
11. Breaker plate
12. Contact set
13. Terminal assembly
14. Vacuum control unit
15. Screw
16. Condenser
17. Screw
18. Cap
19. Carbon brush
20. Rubber boot
21. Holddown plate
22. Bolt

Exploded view of distributor, L16 engine

then be replaced precisely in its original location, if the engine has not been turned. If the engine has been turned while the distributor was removed, or the distributor location was not marked, proceed as follows: Find top dead center of the compression stroke of No. 1 cylinder by holding a finger in the spark plug hole and rotating the engine. Compression pressure will force the finger from the hole. The exact location of top dead center can then be found by use of the crankshaft pulley timing marks. Install the distributor so that the rotor is pointing at the No. 1 spark plug wire and the points are just opening. The ignition wires may now be installed in the distributor cap, following the firing order in the direction of rotation. Set the timing to specifications.

Firing Order

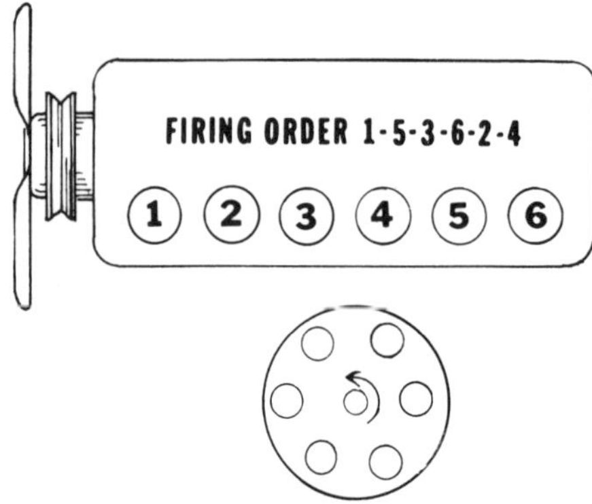

All six cylinder. L24 engine has spark plugs on right side and distributor at front. P engine is as shown.

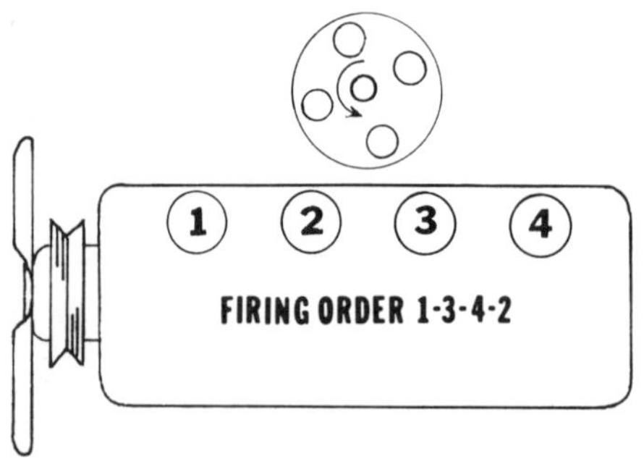

All four cylinder except L16

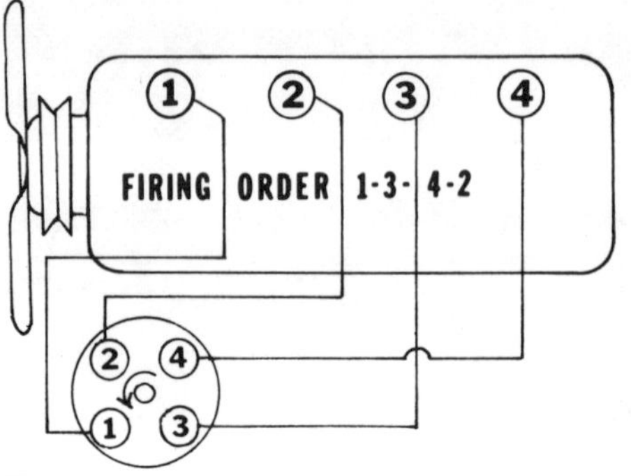

L16 engine

NOTE: Spark plug wiring arrangements are not shown, except for the L16 engine, as these vary with the placement of the distributor head in the different engine models.

Distributor Specifications

Engine Model	*Distributor*	*Centrifugal Advance*		*Vacuum Advance*	
		Start (rpm)	*End (deg. @ rpm)*	*Start (in. Hg.)*	*End (deg. @ in. Hg.)*
J	Hitachi D411-53	450	11-15 @ 2,400	3.9-4.7	6-9 @ 13.4
L16	Hitachi D410-58	450	10 @ 1,500	5.9	9 @ 12.4
L24	Hitachi D606-52	450	6 @ 1,000	3.9	5.5 @ 9.6
A12	Hitachi D412-63	550	12.5 @ 2,100	9.8	6.5 @ 13.8

GENERATOR AND REGULATOR

Only L320 and early L60 models are equipped with a DC generator. All other models have the more modern alternator. The generator used on the L320 is the Hitachi G115-53; that used on the L60 is the Hitachi G115-11. The voltage regulator is a Hitachi carbon pile unit.

Adjusting Carbon Pile Regulator

The adjustment most often required is that for output voltage. Proceed as follows:

1. Connect a voltmeter to the regulator terminal, A. Connect the other voltmeter lead to ground.
2. Make sure that all electrical loads are switched off. Disconnect the terminal, B.
3. With the engine running at about 1,900 rpm, read the voltage. It should be 15-16 volts.

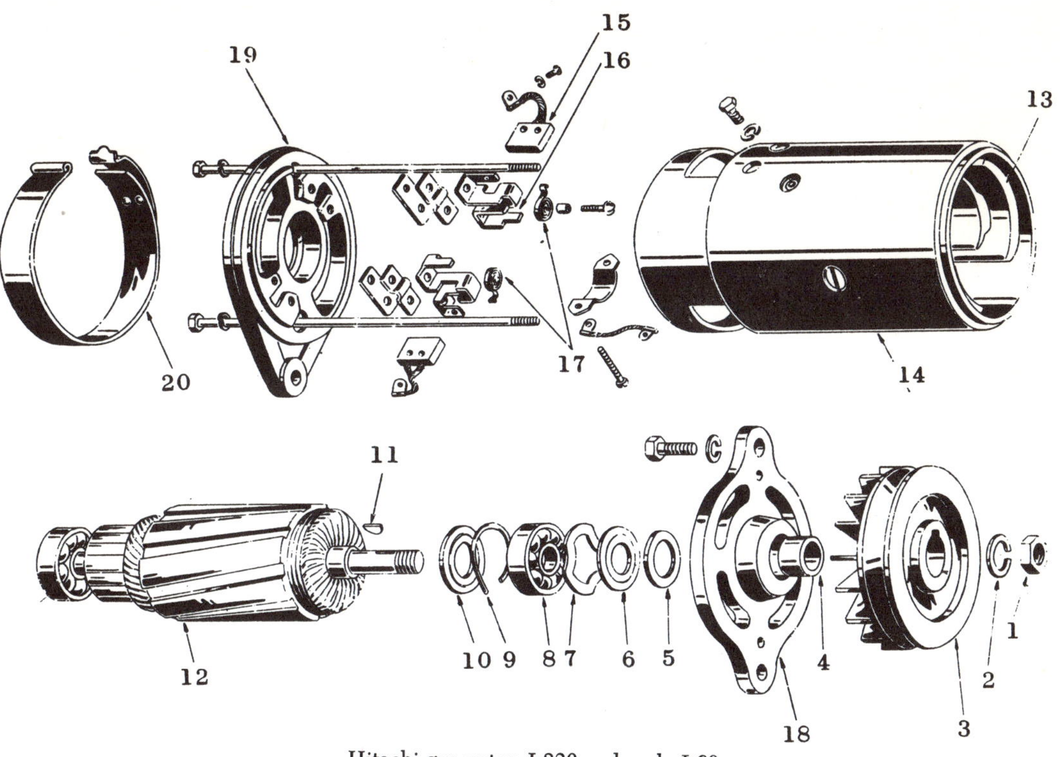

Hitachi generator, L320 and early L60

1. Nut
2. Washer
3. Pulley
4. Spacer
5. Packing
6. Retainer
7. Spring
8. Ball bearing
9. Clip
10. Oil cover
11. Key
12. Armature
13. Field coil
14. Housing
15. Brush
16. Brush holder
17. Brush spring
18. Front cover
19. Rear cover
20. Brush cover

Generating system diagram, models using Hitachi generator

1. Generator
2. Voltage regulator
3. Ammeter
4. Battery
5. Fuse
6. Lighting switch
7. Light (typical electrical load)

4. Loosen the pile compression screw lockscrew. To raise voltage, turn the pile compression screw in. To lower voltage, back it out. Tighten the lockscrew after adjustment.

The gaps in the cutout relay should be adjusted and the points dressed, periodically.

Gap	*Opening*
Relay point gap	.036″
Core to arm gap (open)	.028-.031″
Core to arm gap (closed)	.016-.020″

Hitachi carbon pile voltage regulator unit. P-screw is the pile compression screw, used to adjust output voltage. F-screw is flux adjusting screw, used for a preliminary setting when reassembling the unit.

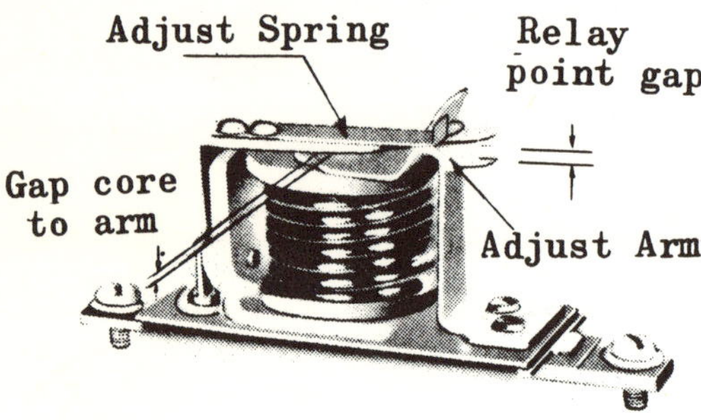

Cutout relay adjusting points for Hitachi carbon pile regulator

ALTERNATOR AND AC REGULATOR

An alternator (AC generator) is used on all current models. The following precautions must be observed to prevent alternator and regulator damage:

1. Be absolutely sure of correct polarity when installing a new battery, or connecting a battery charger.
2. Do not short across or ground any alternator or regulator terminals.
3. Disconnect the battery ground cable before replacing any electrical unit.
4. Never operate the alternator with any of the leads disconnected.
5. When steam cleaning the engine, be careful not to subject the alternator to excessive heat.
6. When charging the battery, remove it from the car or disconnect the alternator output terminal.

Regulated Voltage Check

All Regulators Except Hitachi TL1Z-37

1. Perform this test with the regulator cool. If voltage is not measured within one minute after starting the engine, stop the engine and allow the regulator to cool. It is imperative that the battery be fully charged.
2. Connect an ammeter and voltmeter as shown.
3. Run the engine at 2,500 rpm. Check that the charging current is less than 5 amps, and that the regulated voltage is as specified in the AC Regulator Electrical Specifications Table. If the charging current is too high, replace the battery with a fully charged one.
4. If voltage is incorrect, set regulator unit gaps to specified clearances.
5. Recheck voltage. If voltage is still incorrect, readjust air gap. Bend stopper up to raise the voltage and down to lower.

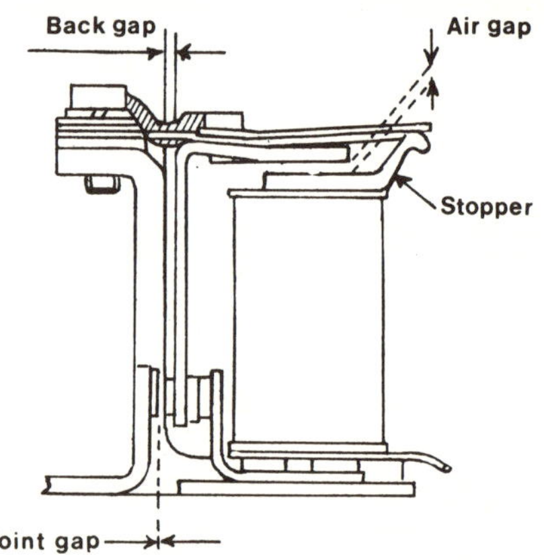

Regulator and charge indicator relay, all except Hitachi TL1Z-37

Hitachi TL1Z-37 Regulator

1. Connect an ammeter, voltmeter, fully charged battery, and resistor as shown.
2. Since this regulator is temperature compensated, the temperature of the regulator cover must be noted. Regulated voltage varies with ambient temperature.
3. Before starting check, bypass ammeter as shown to prevent ammeter damage.
4. Start engine, increase engine speed to 2,500 rpm gradually, and continue for several minutes.

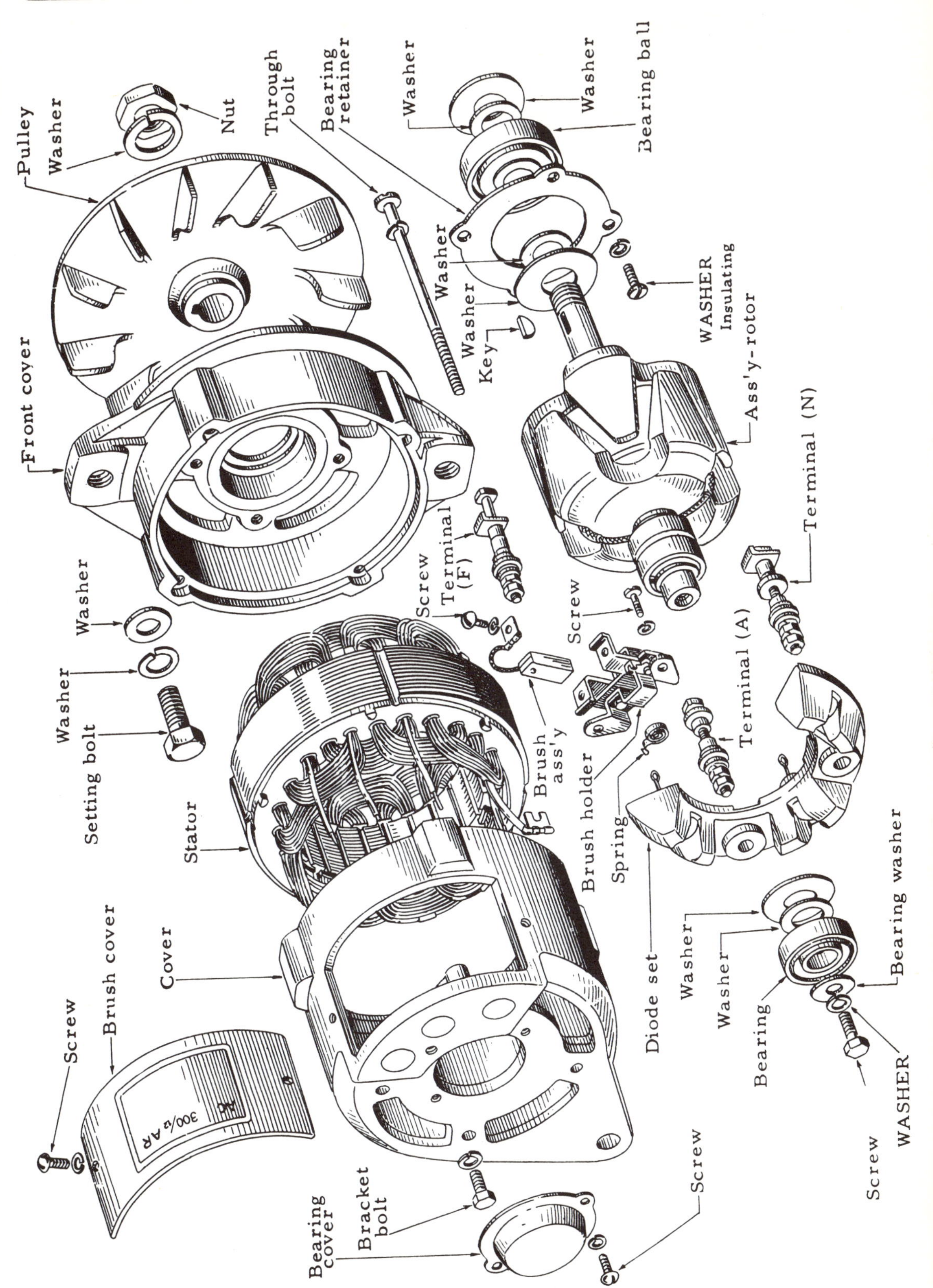

Mitsubishi alternator

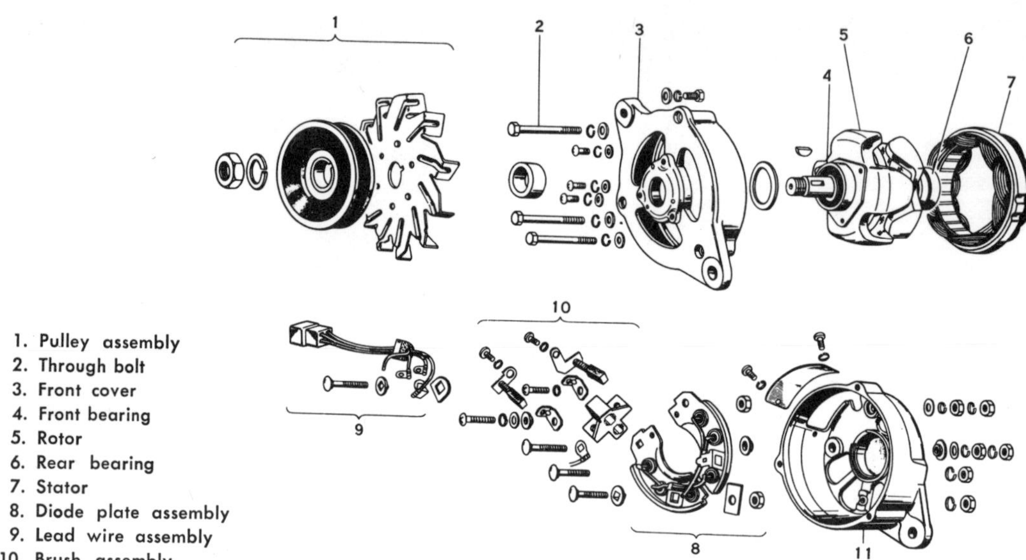

Hitachi alternator

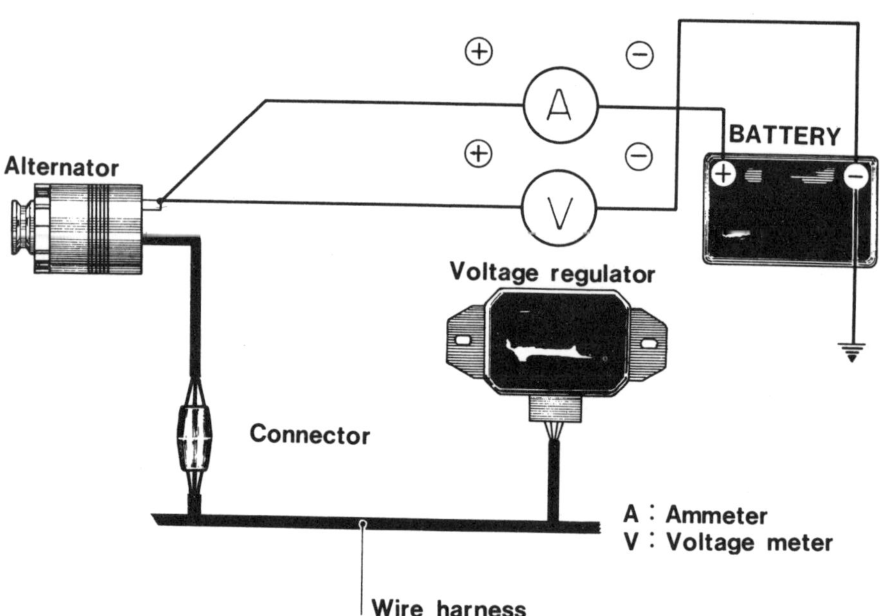

Test setup for AC regulators except Hitachi TL1Z-37

5. If ammeter reading is not below 5 amps, the battery is not fully charged. Replace it with a good one.
6. Return engine to idle speed.
7. Increase engine speed to 2,500 rpm and check voltage.

Ambient temperature (°F)	*Regulated voltage*
14	14.6-15.6
32	14.5-15.5
50	14.3-15.3
68	14.2-15.2
86	14.0-15.0
104	13.9-14.9

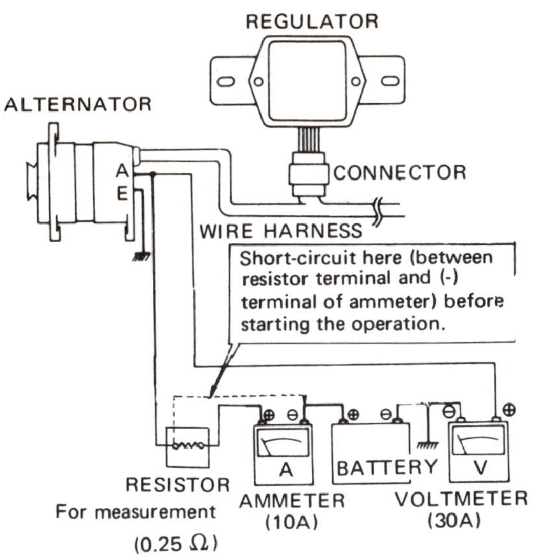

Test setup for Hitachi TL1Z-37 AC regulator

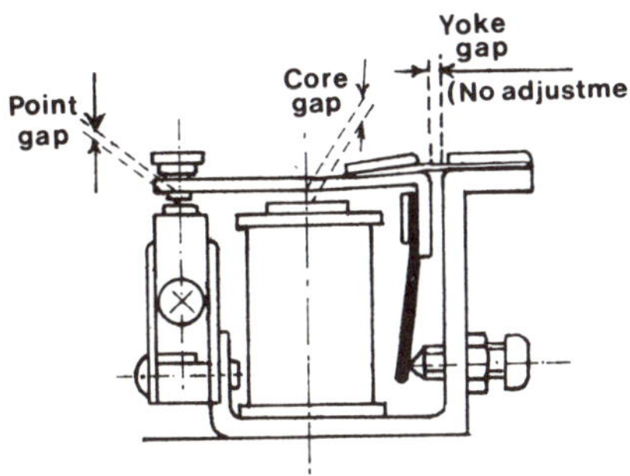

Regulator and charge indicator relay, Hitachi TL1Z-37

8. If voltage is incorrect, set regulator unit gaps to specified figures.
9. Recheck voltage. If voltage is still incorrect, turn in adjusting screw on voltage regulator unit to increase voltage, and turn out to decrease voltage.

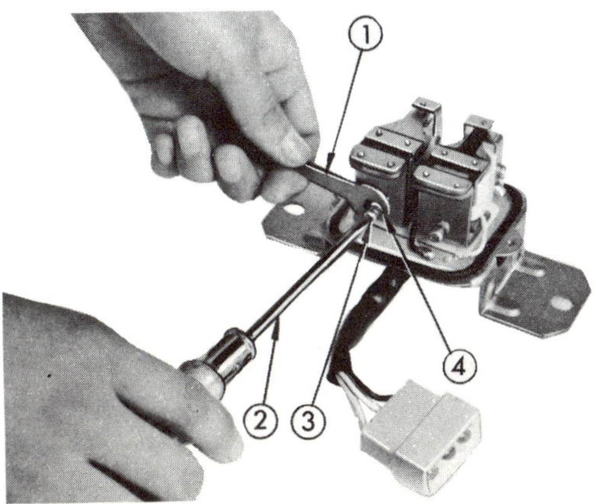

Adjustment of voltage on TL1Z-37 regulator. Wrench, 1, is used to loosen locknut, 4. Screwdriver, 2, is used to turn adjusting screw, 3.

Belt Tension

The correct belt tension for all alternators and generators gives .4-.6″ play on the longest span of the belt. The adjustment is usually made by pivoting the alternator (generator). Overtightening the belt will cause rapid wear to the alternator (generator) and water pump bearings.

Alternator Specifications

Engine Model	*Alternator*		
	Part Number	*Output @ Generator rpm*	
		rpm	*Amps (14v.)*
J	Mitsubishi AS203A1	2,500	24.5
R	Mitsubishi AC300/12X2R	2,500	24.5, 21.5 @ high temp.
U20	Mitsubishi AS2030A2	2,500	23
L16	Hitachi LT130-41	2,500	22
L24	Hitachi LT145-35	2,500 5,000	>34 >45
A12	Hitachi LT135-05	2,500 5,000	>24 >33

>More than

STARTER

The starter is mounted at the right rear of the engine. The solenoid is mounted on top of the starter and engages the drive pinion through a pivot yoke shift lever.

One model, the L320 pickup, does not have the solenoid mounted on the starter. This vehicle has a starter motor which uses an inertia drive for engagement.

Starter R&R, L320 Pickup

1. Disconnect battery ground cable.
2. Disconnect starter power cable. Disconnect starter ground cable, if any.
3. Remove both starter mounting bolts. Pull starter forward and out.
4. Reverse procedure to install.

AC Regulator Specifications

Engine Model	Part Number	Charge Indicator Relay① Core Gap (in.)	Back Gap (in.)	Air Gap (in.)	Point Gap (in.)	Voltage Regulator② Core Gap (in.)	Back Gap (in.)	Air Gap (in.)	Point Gap (in.)	Regulated Voltage
G	Mitsubishi RLA-1		.032-.044	.032-.048	.032-.044		.028-.036	.032-.040	.012-.016	N.A.
J	Mitsubishi RL2220B5		.032-.043	.032-.047	.032-.043		.028-.035	.032-.039	.012-.016	14-15
R	Mitsubishi RL-2B		.032-.043	.032-.047	.032-.043		.028-.035	.032-.035	.012-.016	14-15
U20	Mitsubishi RL2220B5		.035-.047	.030-.043	.030-.043		.032-.047	.032-.043	.012-.016	13.5-14.5
L16	Hitachi TL1Z-17		.007	.020-.024	.016-.020		.035-.039	.032-.047	.012-.016	14-15
L24	Hitachi TL1Z-37	.032-.039			.016-.024	.024-.039			.012-.016	14.3-15.3 @ 50F
A12	Hitachi TL1Z-37	.032-.039			.016-.024	.024-.039			.012-.016	14.3-15.3 @ 50F

①—Right unit in regulator case (left unit in TL1Z-17)
②—Left unit in regulator case (right unit in TL1Z-17)

NOTE: *Right and left are determined with the regulator terminals or harness plug downward.*

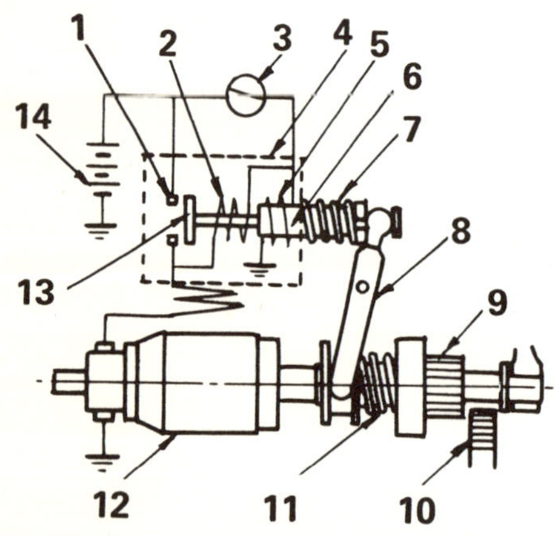

Starter circuit, all vehicles except L320

1. Stationary contact
2. Series coil
3. Ignition switch
4. Solenoid
5. Shunt coil
6. Plunger
7. Return spring
8. Shift lever
9. Drive pinion
10. Ring gear
11. Pinion sleeve spring
12. Armature
13. Moveable contact
14. Battery

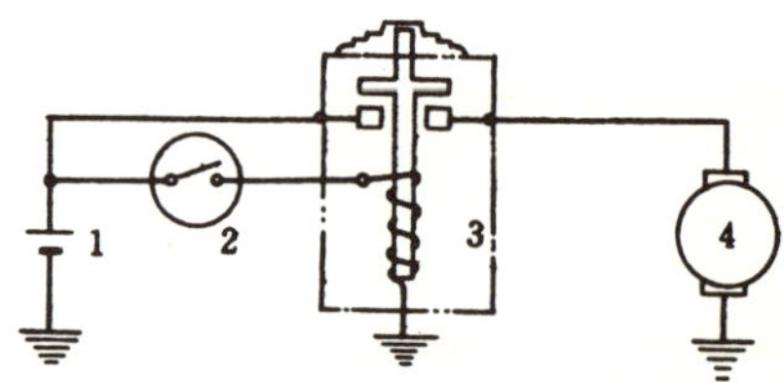

Starter circuit, L320. 1 is battery 2, is starter button, 3 is solenoid, and 4 is starter motor.

Starter R&R, All except L320 Pickup

1. Disconnect battery ground cable.
2. Disconnect switch lead from solenoid switch terminal. This terminal is usually labeled S.
3. Disconnect battery cable from solenoid battery terminal. This terminal is usually labeled B. There is a third solenoid terminal, labeled M, connected to the starter motor.
4. Remove both starter mounting bolts. Pull starter assembly forward and out.
5. Reverse procedure to install.

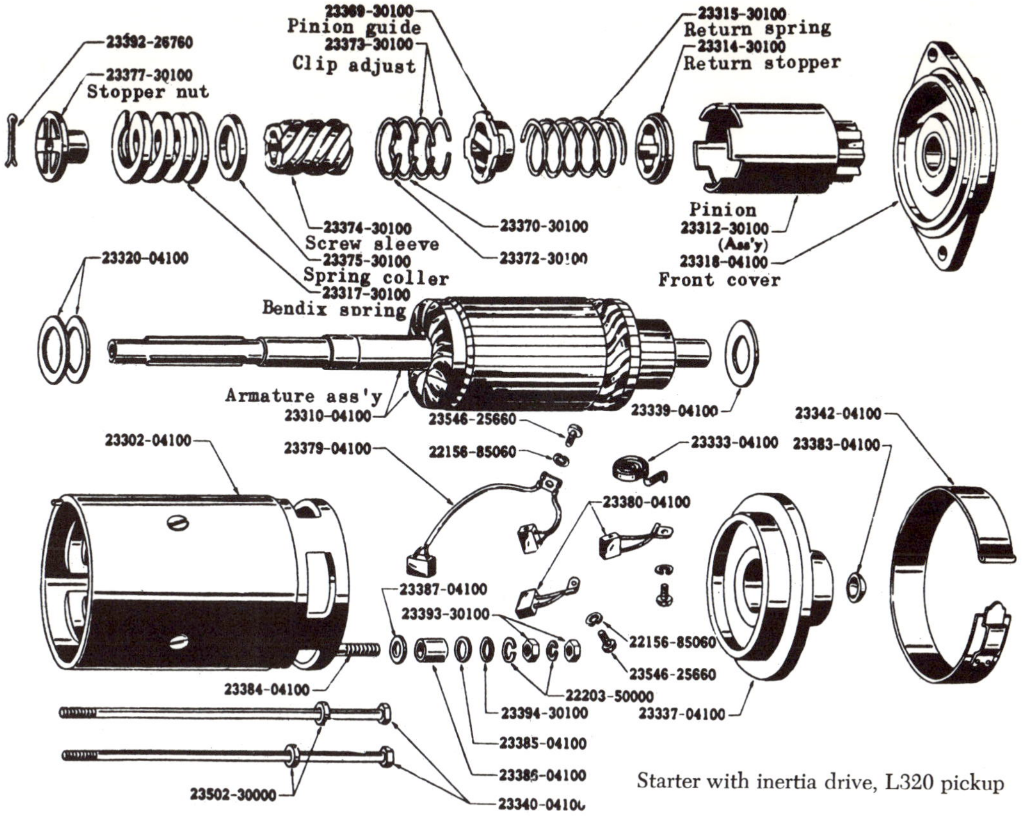

Starter with inertia drive, L320 pickup

Starter with top-mounted solenoid (magnetic switch), all vehicles but L320. L16 engine starter is shown.

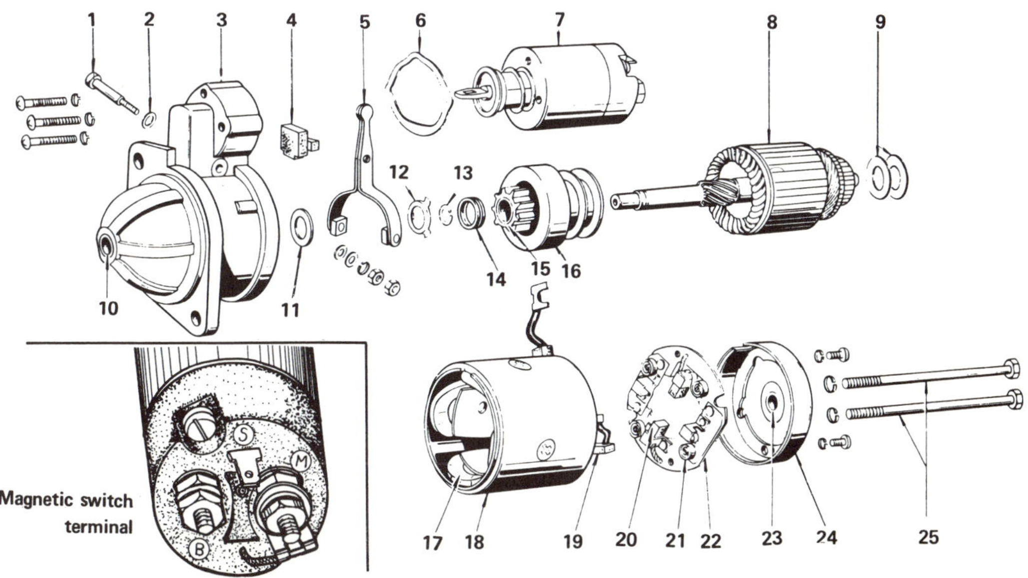

1. Shift lever pin
2. Packing
3. Gear case
4. Dust cover
5. Shift lever
6. Dust cover
7. Solenoid assembly
8. Armature
9. Thrust washer
10. Bushing
11. Thrust washer
12. Stopper washer
13. Stopper clip
14. Pinion stopper
15. Pinion
16. Overrunning clutch
17. Field coil
18. Housing
19. Positive brush
20. Negative brush
21. Brush spring
22. Brush holder assembly
23. Brushing
24. Rear cover
25. Through bolt

Battery and Starter Specifications

Engine Model	*Battery*			*Starter*						
				Lock Test			*No Load Test*			
	Capacity (Amp. Hrs.)	*Volts*	*Grounded Terminal*	*Amps*	*Volts*	*Torque (ft. lbs.)*	*Amps*	*Volts*	*rpm*	*Brush Minimum Length (in.)*
P	60	12	Neg.	N.A.	N.A.	N.A.	N.A.	N.A.	N.A.	N.A.
E1	50	12	Pos.	<500	8.0	>7.7	60	11	<7,000	N.A.
G	N.A.	12	Pos.	<500	9.5	>7.0	60	11	<7,000	N.A.
J	40,50	12	Neg.	N.A.	N.A.	N.A	60	12	>7,000	.37
R	40,50	12	Neg.	<500	9.5	>6.5	N.A.	N.A.	N.A.	N.A.
U20	50	12	Neg.	<500	6.0	>7.2	60	11	<6,000	.30
L16	50,60 PL510, WPL510; 40,50 L520; 40,50,60 PL521, L521	12	Neg.	<480	6.0	>7.9	60	12	>7,000	.28
L24	N.A.	12	Neg.	<460	6.0	10.1	60	12	>5,000	.49
A12	N.A.	12	Neg.	<420	6.3	>6.5	60	12	>7,000	.37

<—Less than
>—More than

Engine Mechanical

DESIGN

Datsun cars imported to the United States have been equipped with nine different engines. The P type engine used in the Patrol is an in-line six cylinder powerplant of 241 cu. in. This displacement is achieved with an undersquare bore-stroke relationship i.e., the stroke is larger than the cylinder bore. An engine of this design has the characteristic of high torque at low engine rpm, which is desired in a four wheel drive, off-the-road vehicle such as the Patrol. The P engine utilizes typical OHV valve gear: in-block camshaft, mechanical lifters, pushrods, and rocker arms pivoting on a common shaft.

The E1, G, J, and R model engines are basically similar four cylinder, overhead valve designs. All have three main bearing crankshafts and, except for the J, are slightly over-square with regard to bore and stroke. R engines from serial number R/40001 have been equipped with five main bearings. The U20 is a cam in cylinder block engine which was redesigned for overhead cam operation. A jackshaft replaces the camshaft in the cylinder block. The overhead camshaft is then chain driven by the jackshaft. This design has the drawback of two timing chains and the additional friction of the jackshaft, but still offers an improvement over the cam in-block.

The L16 and L24 are pure overhead camshaft engines, using only single timing chains. Both engines are very similar and have aluminum cylinder heads and cast iron blocks. The overhead cam operates the valves through short rocker arms. The A12 is a four cylinder overhead valve engine used to power the LB110 series coupe and sedan. The A12 has an aluminum cylinder head and a cast iron block. The camshaft is placed high in the cylinder block allowing short pushrods. Therefore, valve train reciprocating weight is reduced and higher engine speeds are possible. The forged steel crankshaft rides in five main bearings.

Engines are referred to by model designation codes throughout this section. Use the Engine Identification Chart for identification of engines by model, number of cylinders, displacement, and camshaft location.

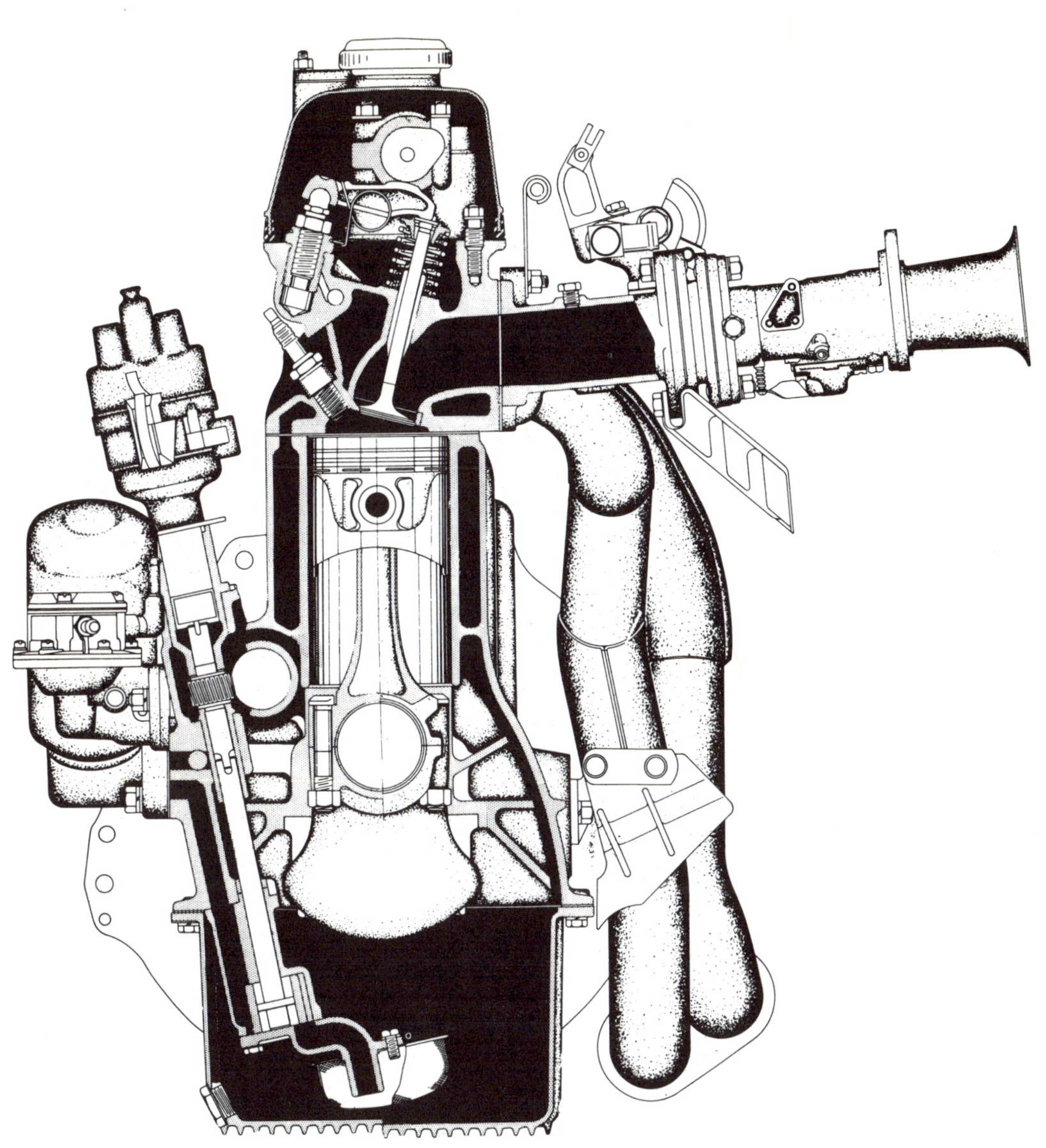

Cutaway end view of U20 engine equipped with optional Mikuni/Solex carburetors.

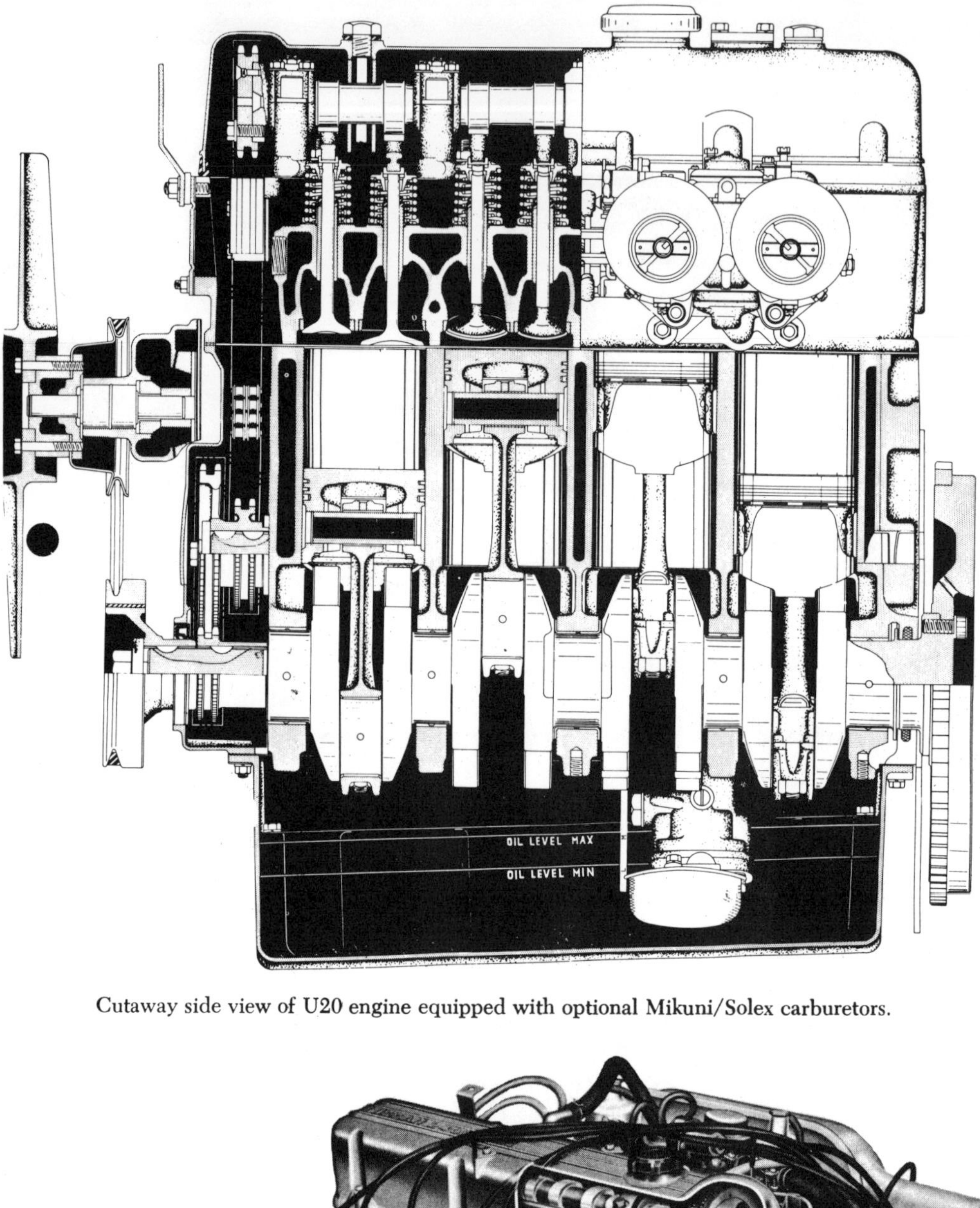

Cutaway side view of U20 engine equipped with optional Mikuni/Solex carburetors.

Cutaway view of L24 engine

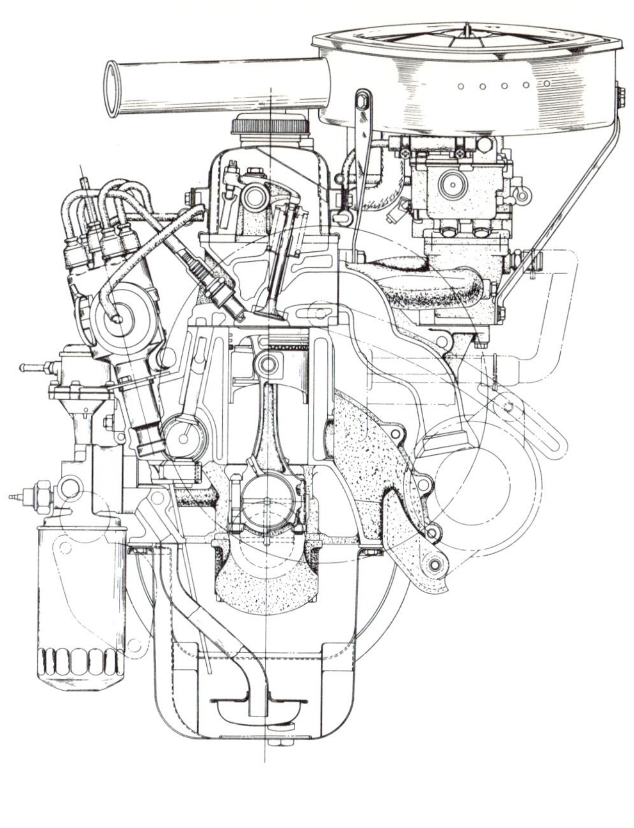

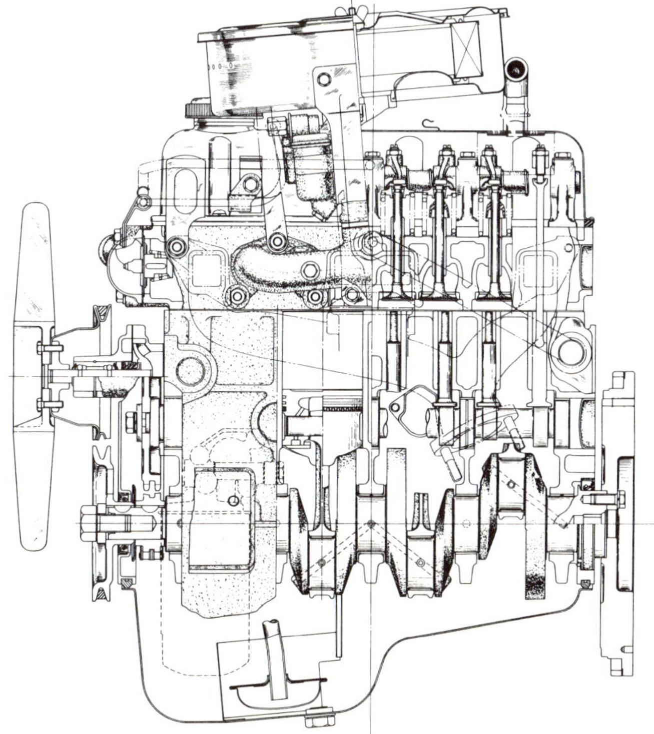

Cutaway end and side views of A12 engine

General Engine Specifications

Year	Type (code)	Cu. In. Displacement (cc. Displacement)	Carburetor	Developed Horsepower (SAE) @ rpm	Developed Torque (ft. lbs.) @ rpm	Bore X Stroke inches (mm.)	Compression Ratio	Normal Oil Pressure (psi)
1961-1969 L60 Patrol	OHV 6 (P)	241.3 (3,956)	Single throat downdraft	145 @ 3,600	235 @ 2,000	3.314 X 4.5 (85.7 X 114.3)	7.6:1	50-57
To 1966 L320 1200 Pickup, 1963-1965 PL410 Sedan	OHV 4 (E1)	72.5 (1,189)	Dual throat downdraft	60 @ 5,000	63.7 @ 5,000	2.89 X 2.80 (73 X 71)	8.2:1	54-57
1962-1965 SPL310 1500 Roadster	OHV 4 (G)	90.6 (1,488)	Two SU type side-draft	85 @ 5,600	92 @ 4,400	3.15 X 2.93 (80 X 74)	9.0:1	54-57
1965-1968 L520 1300 Pickup, 1968-1969 L521 1300 Pickup, 1965-1967 PL411 Sedan	OHV 4 (J)	79.0 (1,299)	Dual throat downdraft	67 @ 5,200	77 @ 2,800	2.89 X 3.06 (73 X 77.6)	8.2:1	54-57
1966-1968 RL411 Sedan, 1965-1969 SPL311 1600 Roadster	OHV 4 (R)	97.3 (1,595)	Two SU type side-draft	96 @ 6,000	103 @ 4,000	3.43 X 2.63 (87.2 X 66.8)	9.0:1	54-57
1967-1969 SRL311 2000 Roadster	OHC 4 (U20)	120.9 (1,982)	Two SU type side-draft	135 @ 6,000	132 @ 4,400	3.43 X 3.27 (87.2 X 83)	9.5:1	54-57
1967-1969 SRL311 2000 Roadster	OHC 4 (U20)	120.9 (1,982)	Two Solex type twin-choke sidedraft	150 @ 6,000	138 @ 4,800	3.43 X 3.27 (87.2 X 83)	9.5:1	54-57
From 1968 PL510 1600 Sedan, From 1968 WPL510 1600 Wagon, From 1970 PL521 1600 Pickup	OHC 4 (L16)	97.3 (1,595)	Dual throat downdraft	96 @ 5,600	100 @ 3,600	3.27 X 2.90 (83 X 73.7)	8.5:1	54-57
From 1971 HLS30 240 Z Coupe	OHC 6 (L24)	146.0 (2,393)	Two SU type side-draft	151 @ 5,600	145.7 @ 4,400	3.27 X 2.90 (83 X 73.7)	9.0:1	54-60
From 1971 LB110 1200 Sedan	OHV 4 (A12)	71.5 (1,171)	Dual throat downdraft	69 @ 6,000	70 @ 4,000	2.87 X 2.76 (73 X 70)	9.0:1	54-60

Engine Rebuilding Specifications
Crankshaft

Engine Model	Main Bearing Journals (in.)					Connecting Rod Bearing Journals (in.)			
	Journal Diameter		Oil Clearance	Shaft End-Play	Thruslon No.	Journal Diameter		Oil Clearance	Side-Play
	New	Minimum				New	Minimum		
P	2.727, 2.685 for No. 1 journal	N.A.	.001-.003 ①	.003-.008 ②	N.A.	2.225	N.A.	N.A.	N.A.
E1	2.000	N.A.	.001-.002 ①	.002-.003 ②	N.A.	1.875	N.A.	N.A.	N.A.
G	2.360	N.A.	.001-.002 ①	.001-.006 ②	N.A.	2.047	N.A.	N.A.	N.A.
J	2.0021-2.0025	N.A.	.001-.002	.002-.003	Center	1.860-1.878	N.A.	N.A.	.008-.012
R	2.3598-2.3602	N.A.	.001-.003	.002-.006	Center	2.0457-2.0463	N.A.	.001-.002	.008-.012
U20	2.4780-2.4785	N.A.	.001-.003 ①	.002-.007 ③	Center	2.0449-2.0454	N.A.	.001-.003	.008-.012
L16	2.1631-2.1636	2.1237-2.1242	.001-.003 ①	.002-.006 ③	3	1.9670-1.9675	1.9276-1.9281	.001-.003	.008-.012
L24	2.1631-2.1636	2.1237-2.1242	.001-.003 ①	.002-.007 ③	Center	1.9670-1.9675	1.9276-1.9281	.001-.002	.008-.012
A12	1.9671-1.9668	1.9272-1.9277	.001-.002 ④	.002-.006 ③	3	1.7701-1.7706	1.7307-1.7313	.001-.002	.008-.012

①—Wear limit—.005
②—Wear limit—.010
③—Wear limit—.012
④—Wear limit—.006

Torque Specifications

Engine Model	Cylinder Head Bolts (ft. lbs.)	Main Bearing Bolts (ft. lbs.)	Rod Bearing Bolts (ft. lbs.)	Crankshaft Pulley Bolt (ft. lbs.)	Flywheel to Crankshaft Bolts (ft. lbs.)
P	63-65	65	65	N.A.	57
E1	35-45	72-87	20-25	N.A.	35-44
G	50-60	72-87	32-43	N.A.	35-44
J	45	75-80	22-25	N.A.	35-44
R	45-50	71-81	35-45	N.A.	35-44
U20	65	65	65	145	58
L16	40	33-40	20-24	116-130	69-76
L24	47	33-40	20-24	116-130	101
A12	33-35	36-38	25-26	108-116	47-54

Engine Rebuilding Specifications
Block, Pistons, Rings

Engine Model	Block: Bore (in.) New	Block: Bore (in.) Maximum Oversize	Pistons: Piston Diameter (in.) New	Pistons: Piston Diameter (in.) Maximum Oversize	Pistons: Wrist Pin Fit	Rings: Side Clearance (in.)	Rings: End-Gap (in.)	Piston to Bore Clearance (in.)
P	N.A.	N.A.	N.A.	N.A.	push fit	.001-.003 top, .001-.003 2nd, N.A. oil	.010-.016 top, .006-.012 2nd, N.A. oil	N.A.
E1	N.A.	N.A.	N.A.	N.A.	push fit	.001-.003 top, .001-.003 2nd, .002-.003 oil	.008-.013 top, .008-.013 2nd, .008-.013 oil	N.A.
G	N.A.	N.A.	N.A.	N.A.	push fit	.002-.003 top, .001-.003 2nd, .001-.003 oil	.010-.016 top, .006-.012 2nd, .006-.012 oil	N.A.
J	N.A.	N.A.	N.A.	N.A.	push fit	.002-.004 top, .002-.004 2nd, .002-.004 oil	.008-.013 top, .008-.013 2nd, .008-.013 oil	.001-.002
R	3.4281-3.4357	N.A.	N.A.	N.A.	push fit	N.A. top, .001 2nd, .001 oil	.010-.016 top, N.A. 2nd, N.A. oil	.001-.002
U20	3.4331-3.4351	N.A.	3.4323-3.4342	3.4905-3.4925	push fit	.002-.003 top, .001-.003 2nd, .001-.003 oil	.010-.016 top, .006-.012 2nd, .006-.012 oil	.001-.002
L16	3.2677-3.2697	N.A.	3.267-3.269	3.326-3.328	push fit	.002-.003 top, .001-.003 2nd, .001-.003 top,	.009-.015 top, .006-.012 2nd, .006-.012 oil	.001-.002
L24	3.2677-3.2697	N.A.	3.267-3.269	3.326-3.328	push fit	.002-.003 top, .001-.003 2nd, .001-.003 oil	.009-.015 top, .006-.012 2nd, .006-.012 oil	.001-.002
A12	2.8760-2.8740	N.A.	2.8727-2.8747	2.9318-2.9239	push fit	.002-.003 top, .002-.003 2nd, .002-.003 oil	.008-014 top, .008-.014 2nd, .001-.014 oil	.001-.002

Engine Rebuilding Specifications
Valves

Engine Model	Seat Angle (deg.)	Valve Seat Width (in.)	Valve Lift (in.)	Valve Spring Pressure (lbs. @ in.)		Valve Spring Free Length (in.)		Stem to Guide Clearance (in.)		Valve Guide Removable
				Outer	Inner	Outer	Inner	Intake	Exhaust	
P	45	N.A.	.374	132 @ 1.57	None	2.26	None	.002-.003	.002-.003	N.A.
E1	45	N.A.	.323	47 @ 1.13	105 @ 1.21	1.97	2.05	.002-.003	.002-.003	N.A.
G	45	N.A.	.335	47 @ 1.13	134 @ 1.19	1.97	1.93	.001-.002	.002-.003	N.A.
J	45	.064-.065 intake, .064-.065 exhaust	N.A.	N.A.	N.A.	1.97	2.05	.002-.003	.002-.003	Yes
R	45	N.A.	.335	N.A.	N.A.	1.97	1.93	.001-.002	.002-.003	N.A.
U20	45	.055 intake, .069 exhaust	.44②	168 @ 1.17 71 @ 1.62	29 @ 1.54	1.96	1.91	.001-.002	.002-.003	Yes
L16	45	.055-.071 intake, .063-.079 exhaust	.394	105 @ 1.21 64 @ 1.53	56 @ .96 27 @ 1.38	2.05	1.77	.001-.002	.002-.003	Yes
L24	45	.055-.063 intake, .071-.087 exhaust	.413	47 @ 1.57 108 @ 1.16	56 @ .96	1.97	1.76	.001-.002	.002-.003	Yes
A12	45	.051 intake, .071 exhaust	.295	66 @ 1.52 135 @ 1.23	None	1.80	None	.001-.002	.002-.003	Yes

①—Valve angle is 45.5.
②—With two twin-choke sidedraft carburetors—.46

ENGINE REMOVAL AND INSTALLATION

Nissan Patrol (L60)

The engine, transmission, and transfer case should be removed as a unit.

1. Drain coolant. Open hood fully and rest on windshield.
2. Disconnect front lights at junction block.
3. Disconnect main wiring harness from voltage regulator and junction block on left hood ledge.
4. Disconnect radiator hoses. Unbolt radiator panel and radiator from fenders. Remove radiator and panel as an assembly.
5. Disconnect:
   A. distributor primary wire,
   B. coil high tension wire,
   C. fuel line from fuel pump,
   D. throttle and choke controls from carburetor, and
   E. exhaust pipe from exhaust manifold.
6. Remove transmission cover from floorboards. Remove transmission control lever, hand brake linkage, and the two transfer case levers.
7. Disconnect clutch linkage at cross shaft.
8. Unbolt universal joints of both driveshafts from transfer case.
9. Support the engine and remove the rear mounts. Remove the front mounts.
10. Attach a lifting device and raise the engine up and forward over the front crossmember. The chassis may be rolled back to free the engine.
11. Reverse procedure to install the engine and transmission.

SPL310, SPL311, SRL311, PL410, PL411, L320, L520, L521

It is best to remove the engine and transmission as a unit. On the sportscars, this must be done.

1. Mark location of hinges on hood. Unbolt and remove hood.
2. Drain coolant. Drain automatic transmission.
3. Remove air cleaner, battery, and tray.
4. Remove radiator hoses. Remove radiator. On automatic transmission, disconnect oil cooler lines from bottom of radiator, remove oil filler tube and cooler lines from transmission case, and disconnect shift linkage.
5. Disconnect heater hoses.
6. Disconnect fuel line(s) at pump.
7. Disconnect throttle and choke linkage.
8. Remove all electrical connections from ignition coil, distributor, starter, alternator (generator), and oil pressure and water temperature sending units.
9. Remove clutch linkage or slave cylinder. Do not disconnect hydraulic line.
10. Disconnect speedometer cable and reverse switch from transmission. Disconnect neutral start switch on automatic transmission.
11. Remove shift lever from floorshift units. Disconnect column shift linkage.
12. Remove exhaust pipe from manifold. On sportscars, remove manifold from engine first, detach bottom of left rear shock absorber so exhaust system can be pulled to one side, then separate manifold and exhaust pipe.
13. Mark relationship of driveshaft flanges at rear end. Unbolt flanges and remove driveshaft.
14. Jack up rear of transmission. Unbolt crossmember from frame, then from transmission. Detach handbrake cable clamp from transmission.
15. Unbolt front motor mounts. Remove if necessary.
16. Attach hoist to lifting hooks on engine. As the engine is hoisted, lower the jack under the transmission. It will be necessary to tilt the engine rather steeply to remove it.
17. Reverse procedure to install.

PL510, WPL510, PL521, HLS30, LB110, KLB110

It is best to remove the engine and transmission as a unit.

1. Mark location of hinges on hood. Unbolt and remove hood.
2. Disconnect battery cables. Remove battery from models with L16 engine.
3. Drain coolant and automatic transmission fluid.
4. Remove grille on models with L16 engine. Remove radiator after disconnecting automatic transmission coolant tubes.
5. Remove air cleaner.
6. Remove fan and pulley from L16 engine.

7. Disconnect:
   a. water temperature gauge wire,
   b. oil pressure sending unit wire,
   c. ignition distributor primary wire,
   d. starter motor connections,
   e. fuel hose,
   f. alternator leads,
   g. heater hoses, and
   h. throttle and choke connections.
8. Disconnect power brake booster hose from engine.
9. Remove clutch operating cylinder and return spring.
10. Disconnect speedometer cable from transmission. Disconnect backup light switch and any other wiring or attachments to transmission.
11. Disconnect column shift linkage. Remove floorshift lever. On LB110 and KLB110, remove boot, withdraw lock pin, and remove lever from inside car.
12. Detach exhaust pipe from exhaust manifold. Remove front section of exhaust system.
13. Mark relationship of driveshaft flanges and remove driveshaft.
14. Place a jack under the transmission. Remove rear crossmember. On LB110 and KLB110, remove the rear engine mounting nuts.
15. Attach a hoist to the lifting hooks on the engine (at either end of the cylinder head). Support engine.
16. Unbolt front engine mounts. Tilt the engine by lowering the jack under the transmission and raising the hoist.
17. Reverse procedure to install.

CYLINDER HEAD

Removal and Installation

NOTE: To prevent distortion or warping of the cylinder head, allow the engine to cool completely before removing the head bolts.

P, E1, G, J, R, A12 Overhead Valve Engines

To remove the cylinder head on OHV engines:

1. Drain coolant.
2. Disconnect battery ground cable.
3. Remove upper radiator hose. Remove water outlet elbow and thermostat.
4. Remove air cleaner, carburetor, rocker arm cover, and both manifolds.
5. Remove spark plugs.
6. Disconnect temperature gauge connection.
7. On A12, remove head bolts and remove head and rocker arm assembly together. On all other OHV engines, the rocker arm assembly is held down by four of the head bolts and must be removed before the cylinder head. There is a special locking plate under the right rear rocker stud nut. Rap the head with a mallet to loosen it from the block. Remove the head and discard the gasket.
8. Remove the pushrods, keeping them in order.

To replace the cylinder head on OHV engines:

1. Check that head and block surfaces are clean. Check the cylinder head surface with a straightedge and a feeler gauge for flatness. If the head is warped more than .003″, it must be trued. If this is not done, there will probably be a leak. The block surface should also be checked in the same way. If the block is warped more than .003″, it must be trued.
2. Install a new head gasket. Most gaskets have a TOP marking. Make sure that the proper head gasket is used on the A12 so that no water passages are blocked off.
3. Install the head. Install the pushrods in their original locations. Install the rocker arm assembly. Loosen the rocker arm adjusting screws to prevent bending pushrods when tightening the head bolts. Tighten the head bolts finger tight. On A12, the single bolt marked T must go in the No. 1 position on the center right side of the engine.
4. Refer to the Torque Specifications Chart for the correct head bolt torque. Tighten the bolts to one third of the specified torque in the order shown in the head bolt tightening sequence illustration. On A12, torque the rocker arm mounting bolts to 15-18 ft. lbs.
5. Tighten the bolts to two thirds of the specified torque in sequence.
6. Tighten the bolts to the full specified torque in sequence.
7. Adjust the valves as described under Valve Train. If no cold setting is given, adjust the valves to the normal hot setting.
8. Reassemble the engine. On A12, intake

	I	II
Cylinder block side (Steel sheet)	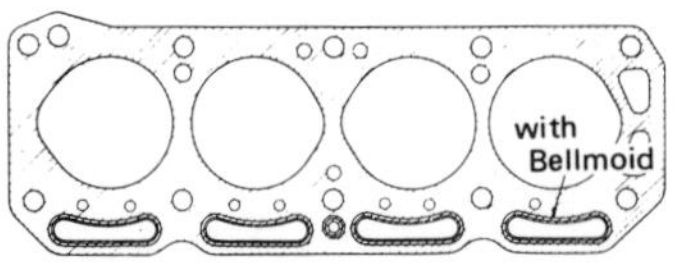 with Bellmoid Apply sealing agent on overall surface	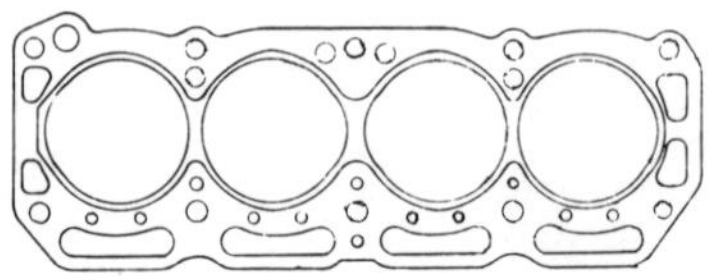 Sealing agent; not required
Cylinder head side (Joint sheet)	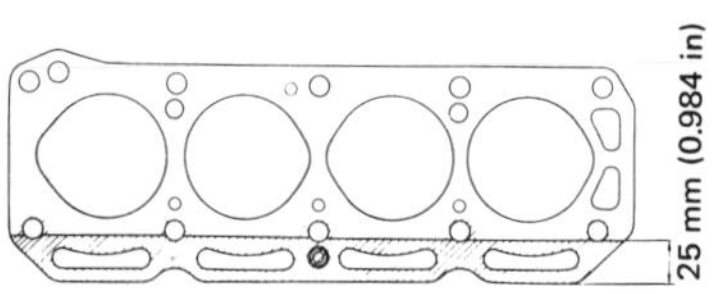 25 mm (0.984 in) Apply sealing agent to oblique lined portion	 Sealing agent; not required
Remarks	. Install immediately after applying sealing agent. . Be sure to apply sealing agent to the push rod side sufficiently.	. Install without applying sealing agent. . Be careful not to damage the push rod side because this side has previously been provided with sealing agent.

Two types of head gasket which will both fit A12 engine. Note that gasket I requires sealant. Note that gasket II requires no sealant and has two additional triangular cooling passages. Be sure to match the gasket to both the head and the block before installation. If the proper gasket is not installed, leakage or immediate overheating will result.

and exhaust manifold bolt torque is 7-10 ft. lbs. Fill the cooling system. Start the engine and run until normal temperature is reached. Remove the rocker arm cover. Torque the bolts in sequence once more. Check the valve clearances.

9. Retorque the head bolts after 600 miles of driving. Check the valve clearances after torquing, as this may disturb the settings.

U20, L16, L24 Overhead Cam Engines

To remove the cylinder head on OHC engines:

1. Drain coolant.
2. Disconnect battery ground cable.
3. Remove upper radiator hose. Remove water outlet elbow and thermostat.
4. Remove air cleaner, carburetor, camshaft cover, and both manifolds.
5. Disconnect temperature gauge at head.
6. Remove spark plugs.
7. Mark the relationship between the camshaft, camshaft sprocket, and timing chain. Remove camshaft sprocket. On L16 and L24, a wooden wedge may be used to prevent the timing chain from slipping off the crankshaft sprocket. If this tool is not available, support the timing chain in some way so that the relationship of the crankshaft sprocket and the timing chain will be unchanged. On U20, unbolt camshaft sprocket, remove cylinder head front cover plate and upper chain tensioner. Support camshaft sprocket to chain guide with a screw. The camshaft sprocket and chain will be left in place when the head is removed.
8. Remove cylinder head front plate and chain tensioner on L16 and L24.
9. Unbolt the cylinder head from the block and the front timing cover. The L16 and L24 use three different size head bolts. Note the original locations of these bolts.

To replace the cylinder head on OHC engines:

1. Check that the head and block surfaces are clean. Check the cylinder head surface for flatness. If the head is warped more than .003″, it must be trued. If this is not done, there will probably be a leak. The block surface should also be checked. If the block is warped more than .003″, it must be trued.

2. Install the new gasket. On L16, apply sealant to both sides of the gasket.
3. Install head. Install bolts in proper locations. Tighten bolts finger tight.
4. Refer to the Torque Specifications Chart for the correct bolt torque. Tighten the bolts to one third of the specified torque in the order shown in the head bolt tightening sequence illustration.
5. Tighten the bolts to two thirds of the specified torque in sequence.
6. Tighten the bolts to the full specified torque in sequence.
7. If the engine has not been disturbed, and the timing chain has not slipped off the crankshaft sprocket (jackshaft sprocket on U20), reinstall the camshaft sprocket, aligning the marks made on disassembly. On L16 and L24, replace fuel pump drive cam. Camshaft sprocket torque is 13 ft. lbs. on the U20 and 36-43 ft. lbs. on the L16 and L24. If the relationship of the crankshaft, camshaft, and timing chain has been disturbed, correct this relationship as described later under Camshaft and Timing Chain.
8. Adjust the valves as described under Valve Train. If no cold setting is given, adjust the valves to the normal hot setting.
9. Reassemble the engine. On U20, intake and exhaust manifold bolt torque is 10-20 ft. lbs. Fill the cooling system. Start the engine and run until normal temperature is reached. Remove the camshaft cover. Torque the bolts in sequence once more. Check the valve clearances.
10. Retorque the head bolts after 600 miles of driving.

VALVE GUIDE REPLACEMENT

See Engine Rebuilding Section for specific procedures.

Cylinder Head Torque Sequences

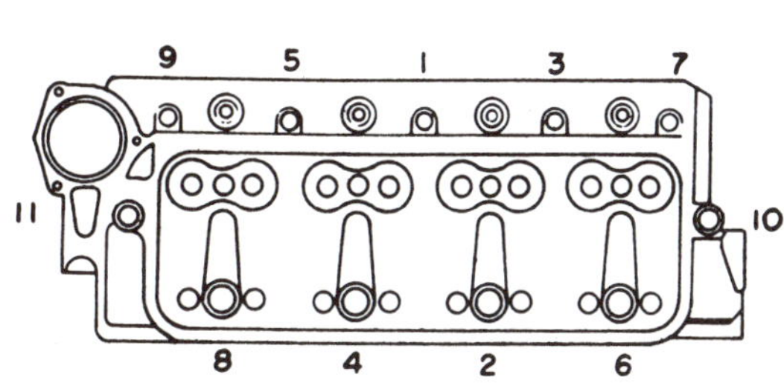

Cylinder head, E1 and J engines

12 8 4 2 6 10 14
11 7 3 1 5 9 13

Cylinder head, L24 engine

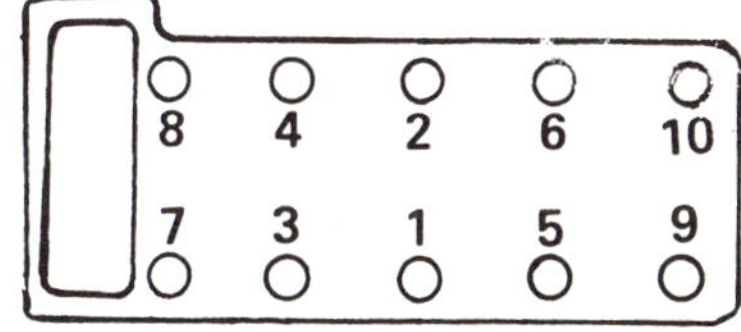

Cylinder head, L16 and U20 engines

Cylinder head, A12, G, and R engines

EXHAUST SYSTEM

Exhaust systems for current models are shown in the accompanying illustrations. Removal and replacement of the various components should be made obvious by studying the illustrations.

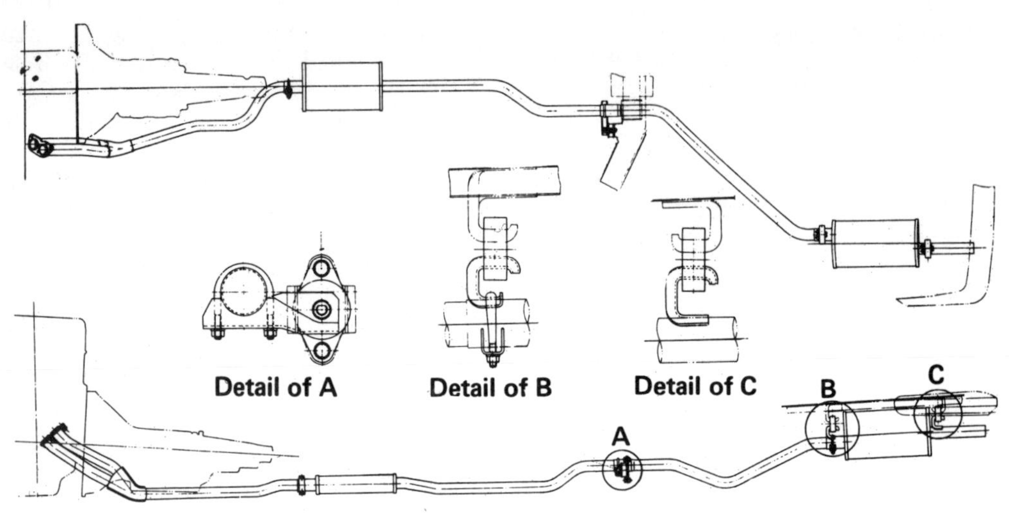

Exhaust system, PL510 and WPL510

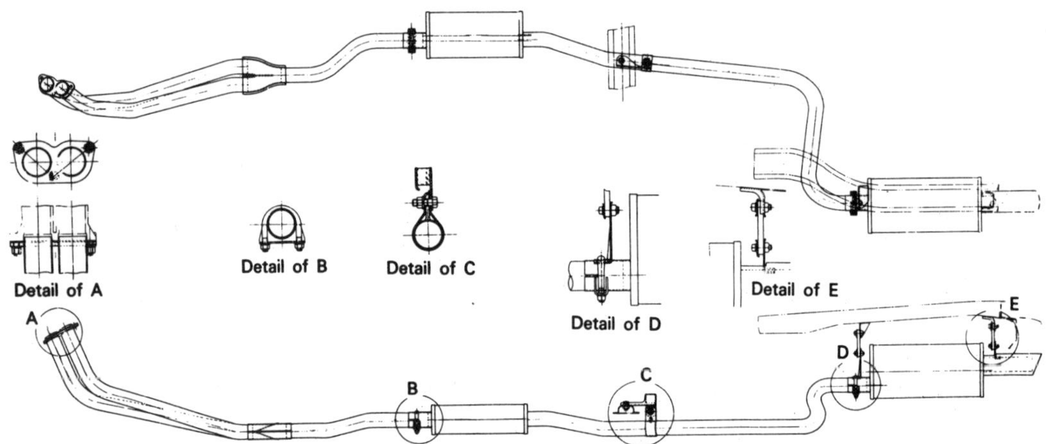

Exhaust system, HLS30 (240 Z coupe)

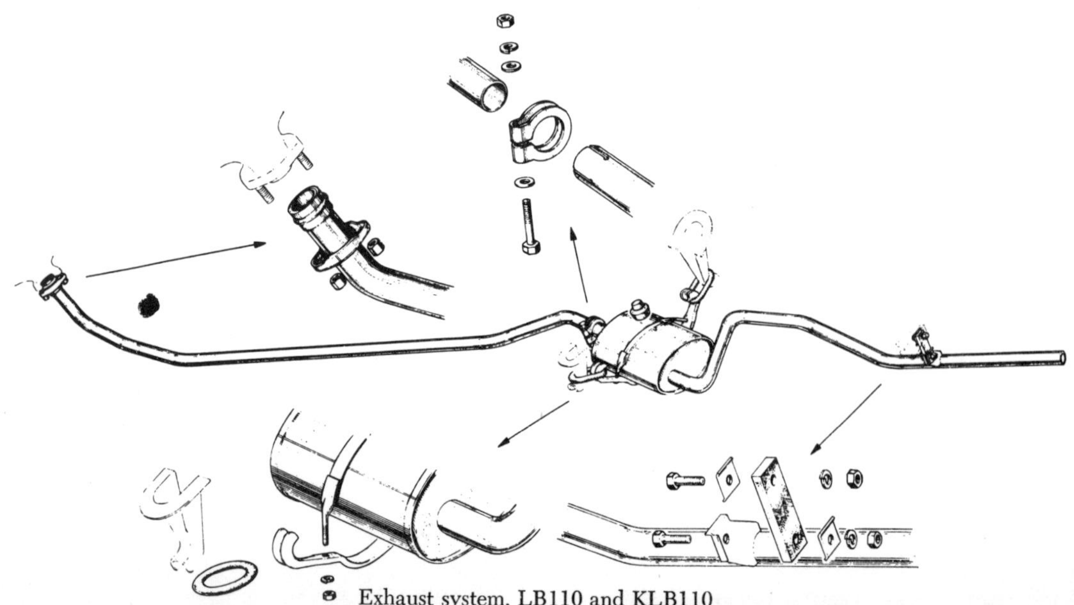

Exhaust system, LB110 and KLB110

Valve Guide Replacement

When replacing cylinder head valve guides, be sure that the guide height above the top of the cylinder head surface is as follows.

Engine	*Guide height*
E1, J	.610-626″
U20	.508-.516″
L16, L24	.409-.417″
A12	.709″
P, G, R	not specified

TIMING CHAIN COVER AND OIL SEAL

Removal and Installation

E1, G, J, R, A12 Overhead Valve Engines

1. Remove radiator. Loosen alternator (generator) adjustment and remove belt. Loosen air pump adjustment and remove belt on engines with air pump system.
2. Remove fan and/or water pump. Water pump should be removed from A12 engine.
3. Bend back lock tab from crankshaft pulley nut. Remove nut by affixing a heavy wrench and rapping the wrench with a hammer. The nut must be unscrewed in the opposite direction of normal engine rotation. Pull off pulley.
4. On A12, it is recommended that the oil pan be removed or loosened before the front cover is removed.
5. Unbolt and remove timing chain cover.
6. Replace the crankshaft oil seal in the cover. Most models use a felt seal.
7. Reverse procedure to install, using new gaskets. Apply sealant to both sides of timing cover gasket. On A12 engine, front cover bolt torque is 4 ft. lbs., water pump bolt torque is 7-10 ft. lbs., and oil pan bolt torque is 4 ft. lbs.

U20, L16, L24 Overhead Cam Engines

While it may be possible to perform this operation with the engine in place, Datsun recommends that the engine be removed from the vehicle.

1. Loosen and remove alternator and air pump belts. Remove alternator and air pump.
2. Remove distributor on L16 and L24. Remove cylinder head. This may not be necessary on some engines.
3. Remove fan and pulley.
4. Bend back lock tab from crankshaft pulley nut. Remove nut by affixing a heavy wrench and rapping the wrench with a hammer. The nut must be unscrewed in the opposite direction of normal engine rotation.
5. Remove water pump.
6. Remove oil pan.
7. Remove timing chain cover.
8. Remove old crankshaft oil seal from cover. Press in new seal.
9. Reverse procedure to install, applying sealant to both sides of cover gasket. On L16, check that height difference between cylinder block upper surface and front cover upper surface is less than .006″. Oil pan bolt torque is 4-5 ft. lbs. for all three engines.

TIMING CHAIN AND CAMSHAFT

Removal and Replacement

E1, G, J, R, A12 Overhead Valve Engines

It is recommended that this operation be done with the engine removed from the vehicle.

1. Remove timing chain cover.
2. Unbolt and remove chain tensioner.
3. Remove camshaft sprocket retaining bolt.
4. Pull off the camshaft sprocket, easing off the crankshaft sprocket at the same time. Remove both sprockets and chain as an assembly. Be careful not to lose the shims and oil slinger from behind the crankshaft sprocket.
5. Remove distributor, distributor drive spindle, pushrods, and valve lifters.

NOTE: On G, R, and A12, the lifters cannot be removed until the camshaft has been removed.

Remove oil pump and pump drive-shaft.

6. Remove engine front mounting plate on El and J.
7. Unbolt and remove camshaft locating plate.
8. Remove camshaft carefully. On G, R, and A12, this will be easier if the block is inverted to prevent the lifters from falling down.
9. Camshaft bearings can be pressed out and replaced. They are available in

undersizes, should it be necessary to regrind the camshaft journals.

10. Reinstall camshaft. If locating plate has an oil hole, it should be to the right of the engine. On A12, locating plate is marked with the word LOWER and an arrow. A12 locating plate bolt torque is 3-4 ft. lbs. Be careful to engage drive pin in rear end of camshaft with slot in oil pump driveshaft.
11. Camshaft end-play can be measured after temporarily replacing the camshaft sprocket and securing bolt.

Engine	*Camshaft end-play*
P, E1, J	.003-.007″
G, R	.002-.011″
A12	.001-.003″

If end-play is excessive, replace locating plate. They are available in several sizes.

12. On El and J, replace engine front mounting plate.
13. If crankshaft or camshaft has been replaced, install sprockets temporarily and check that they are parallel. Adjust by shimming under crankshaft sprocket.
14. Assemble sprockets and chain, aligning as illustrated.

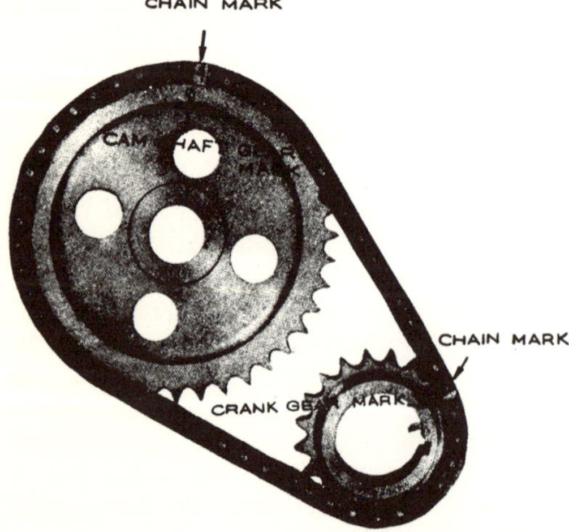

Assembly of sprockets and timing chain, G, J, and R engines

15. Turn crankshaft until keyway and No. 1 piston is at top dead center. Install sprockets and chain. Oil slinger behind crankshaft sprocket must be replaced with concave surface to the front. If chain and sprocket installation is correct, sprocket marks must be aligned between the shaft centers when No. 1 piston is at top dead center. A12 camshaft sprocket retaining bolt torque is 33-36 ft. lbs.

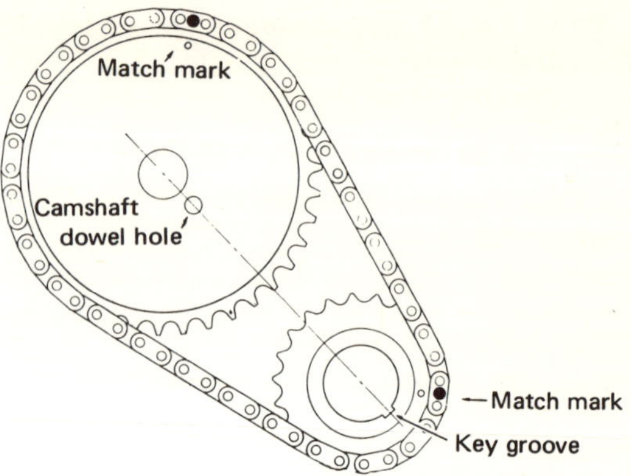

Assembly of sprockets and timing chain, A12 engine

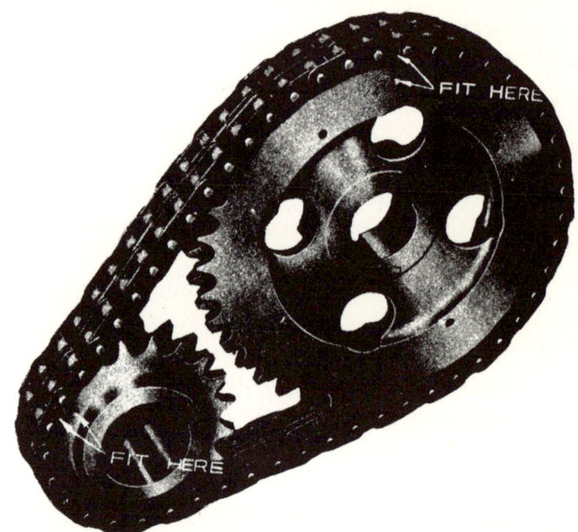

Assembly of sprockets and timing chain, E1 engine

Alignment of timing sprockets with No. 1 cylinder at top dead center, overhead valve (pushrod) engines

16. The rest of the reassembly procedure is the reverse of disassembly. A12 chain tensioner bolt torque is 4-6 ft. lbs.

U20 Overhead Cam Engine

This engine is basically an overhead valve type redesigned to use an overhead camshaft cylinder head. A jackshaft replaces the camshaft in the cylinder block. The overhead camshaft is chain driven from the jackshaft. Thus there are two timing chains. To remove the timing chains:

1. Remove the timing chain cover.
2. Remove the lower chain tensioner.
3. Remove jackshaft outer sprocket retaining bolt.
4. Pull off jackshaft outer sprocket, easing off crankshaft sprocket at same time. Remove both sprockets and chain as an assembly.
5. Remove screw which was installed during cylinder head removal holding camshaft sprocket to chain guide. If head was not removed, unbolt camshaft sprocket.
6. Remove camshaft chain. Remove jackshaft inner sprocket.
7. Jackshaft may now be removed if necessary.

To replace timing chains:

U20 engine. Note that camshaft sprocket is temporarily supported on the chain guide by a screw.

8. Place camshaft sprocket and jackshaft inner sprocket in camshaft chain, aligning timing marks on sprockets with marks on chain.

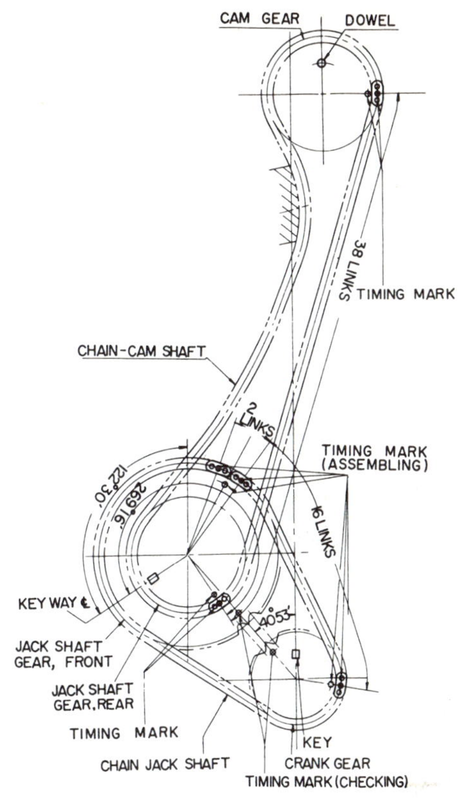

Timing marks for camshaft sprockets and chain, assembling and timing marks for jackshaft sprockets and chain, U20 engine

9. Holding sprockets in position, engage jackshaft inner sprocket keyway with key on jackshaft.
10. Replace screw removed in Step 5.
11. Assemble jackshaft outer sprocket and crankshaft sprocket to chain. Install sprockets and chain on shafts. Jackshaft bolt torque is 33-36 ft. lbs. If assembly is correct, lower chain sprocket marks will be aligned between the shaft centers when No. 1 piston and the crankshaft key are at top dead center.
12. Replace lower chain tensioner and timing chain cover.

The camshaft can be removed from the cylinder head with the head either in place on the engine or removed. To remove the camshaft:

1. Remove cylinder head or remove camshaft cover, unbolt camshaft sprocket.

and support sprocket with a screw to chain guide.

2. Unbolt all camshaft bearing caps. Do not remove lower camshaft bearings. If these bearings are removed, an alignment boring procedure will be required to properly realign them.
3. Remove camshaft.

To replace camshaft:

4. Replace camshaft. Torque large bearing cap nuts to 13 ft. lbs. and small nuts to 5 ft. lbs.
5. Check camshaft end-play. It should be .004-.012″.
6. Replace camshaft sprocket, torquing bolts to 13 ft. lbs.
7. Press down valve springs and reinstall rocker arms.
8. Adjust valves.

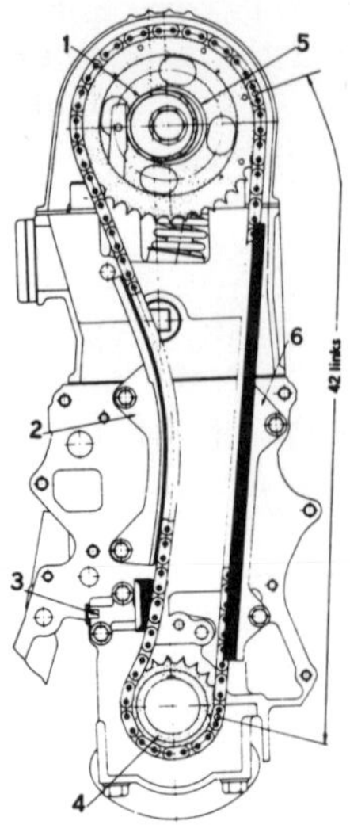

1. Fuel pump drive cam
2. Chain guide
3. Chain tensioner
4. Crankshaft sprocket
5. Camshaft sprocket
6. Chain guide

Camshaft chain installation, L16 and L24 engines

L16, L24 Overhead Cam Engines

These engines are of true overhead camshaft design, using only a single timing chain. The L16 and L24 are very similar in appearance and construction. To remove the timing chain:

1. Remove timing chain cover. Remove camshaft sprocket if head has not been removed.
2. Remove chain and tensioner.
3. Remove oil slinger and distributor drive gear from crankshaft. Pull off sprocket.

To replace the chain:

4. Install cylinder head (removed during timing chain cover removal).
5. Install crankshaft sprocket, distributor drive gear, and oil slinger with concave side out.
6. Set crankshaft and camshaft keys upward. When turning the shafts, be careful not to force the valves against the pistons.
7. Install sprockets to chain, aligning marks on chain with marks on sprockets at left side of engine. There are 42 links between the two chain marks.
8. Install chain and sprockets to engine. Install fuel pump drive cam. Torque camshaft sprocket bolt to 36-43 ft. lbs.
9. Install chain tensioner.
10. Replace timing chain cover.

The camshaft can be removed from the cylinder head with the head either in place on the engine or removed. To remove the camshaft:

1. Remove camshaft cover or cylinder head. Remove fuel pump drive cam and camshaft sprocket. Remove rocker arm springs.
2. Loosen rocker pivot lock nuts and remove rocker arms by pressing down valve springs.
3. Remove camshaft locating plate.
4. Withdraw camshaft carefully. Do not remove camshaft bearings. If these bearings are removed, an alignment boring procedure will be required to properly realign them.

To replace camshaft:

5. Replace camshaft. Install locating plate.
6. Check camshaft end-play. It should be .003-.015″. Adjust by replacing locating plate.
7. Replace sprocket, torquing bolt to 36-43 ft. lbs.
8. Install rocker arms, pressing down valve springs with a screwdriver. Install rocker arm springs.
9. Adjust valves.

PISTONS AND CONNECTING RODS

On all engines, it is advisable to mark the connecting rods on removal so that they will be reinstalled in the same cylinder, facing in the same direction. On early engines with a clamp bolt at the top of the connecting rod, the clamp bolt must face toward the camshaft side of the engine. On P, L16, L24, and A12 engines, the oil hole at the bottom of the connecting rod must face to the right side. On E1, J, G, and R engines, the split in the piston skirt must face toward the camshaft side of the engine. If the piston has a mark on its top, the mark must be to the front. P, U20, L16, L24, and A12 engines have F marks on the tops of their pistons.

Engine Lubrication

TYPE

All Datsun engines use a wet sump oil supply. Oil is delivered under pressure by a gear type oil pump. Every engine model is equipped with a filter in the lubrication system.

Oil Pump Removal and Installation

E1, J, G, R, U20

On these engines, the oil pump is mounted inside the oil pan.

1. Drain oil.
2. Remove oil pan and pickup strainer.
3. Unscrew three long bolts holding pump to crankcase.
4. Reverse procedure to install. Torque pump mounting bolts to 6-7 ft. lbs. and oil pan bolts to 4-5 ft. lbs.

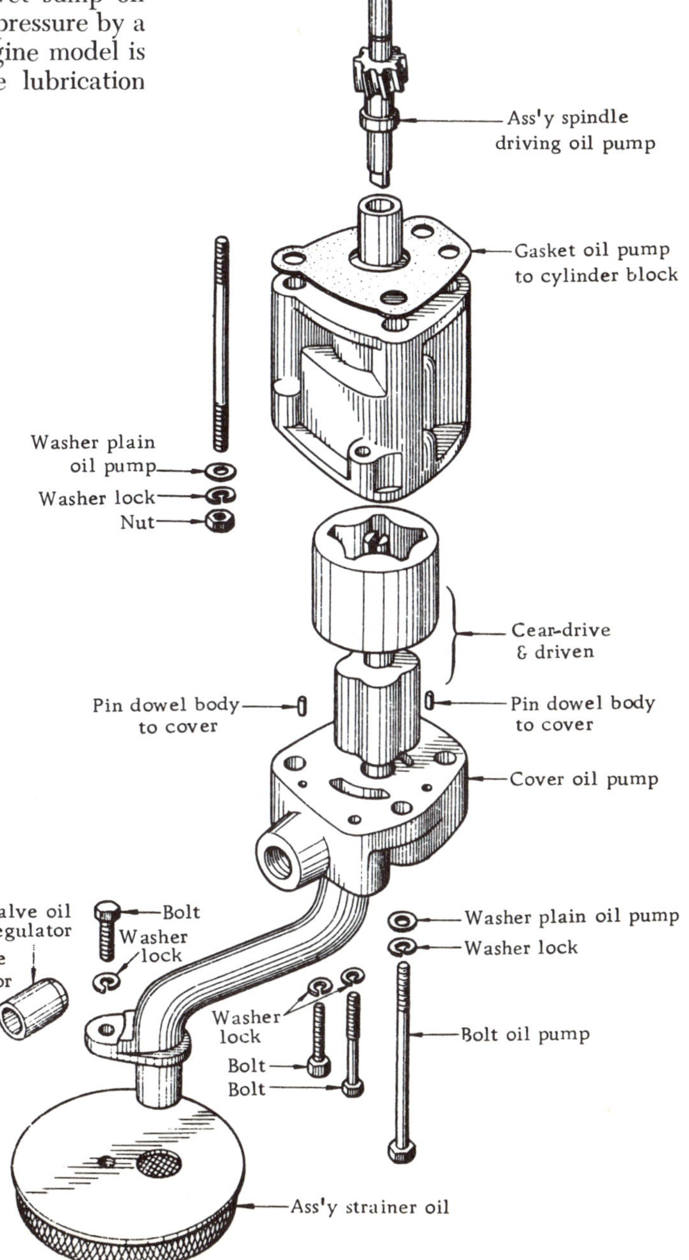

Rotor oil pump, J engine

A12

The A12 oil pump is mounted on the right side of the engine.

1. Drain oil.
2. Remove front stabilizer.
3. Remove splash shield.
4. Unbolt and withdraw pump from side of engine.
5. Reverse procedure to install. Torque pump mounting bolts to 9-11 ft. lbs.

L16, L24

These oil pumps are mounted at the bottom of the engine front cover.

1. Remove distributor.
2. Drain oil.
3. Remove front stabilizer on L16 models.
4. Remove splash shield.
5. Unbolt and remove oil pump.
6. Before replacing pump, position No. 1 cylinder at top dead center. Install oil pump with spindle punch mark to the front. Torque mounting bolts to 11-15 ft. lbs.
7. Install distributor with rotor pointing to No. 1 spark plug lead in cap.
8. Reverse rest of removal procedure.

Oil Pump Inspection

The pump can readily be disassembled and checked for wear. Refer to the Oil Pump Specifications Chart for clearances. The rotor pump used on E1 and J engines has a chamfered edge on the outer rotor. On reassembly, the chamfer must be toward the base of the pump body.

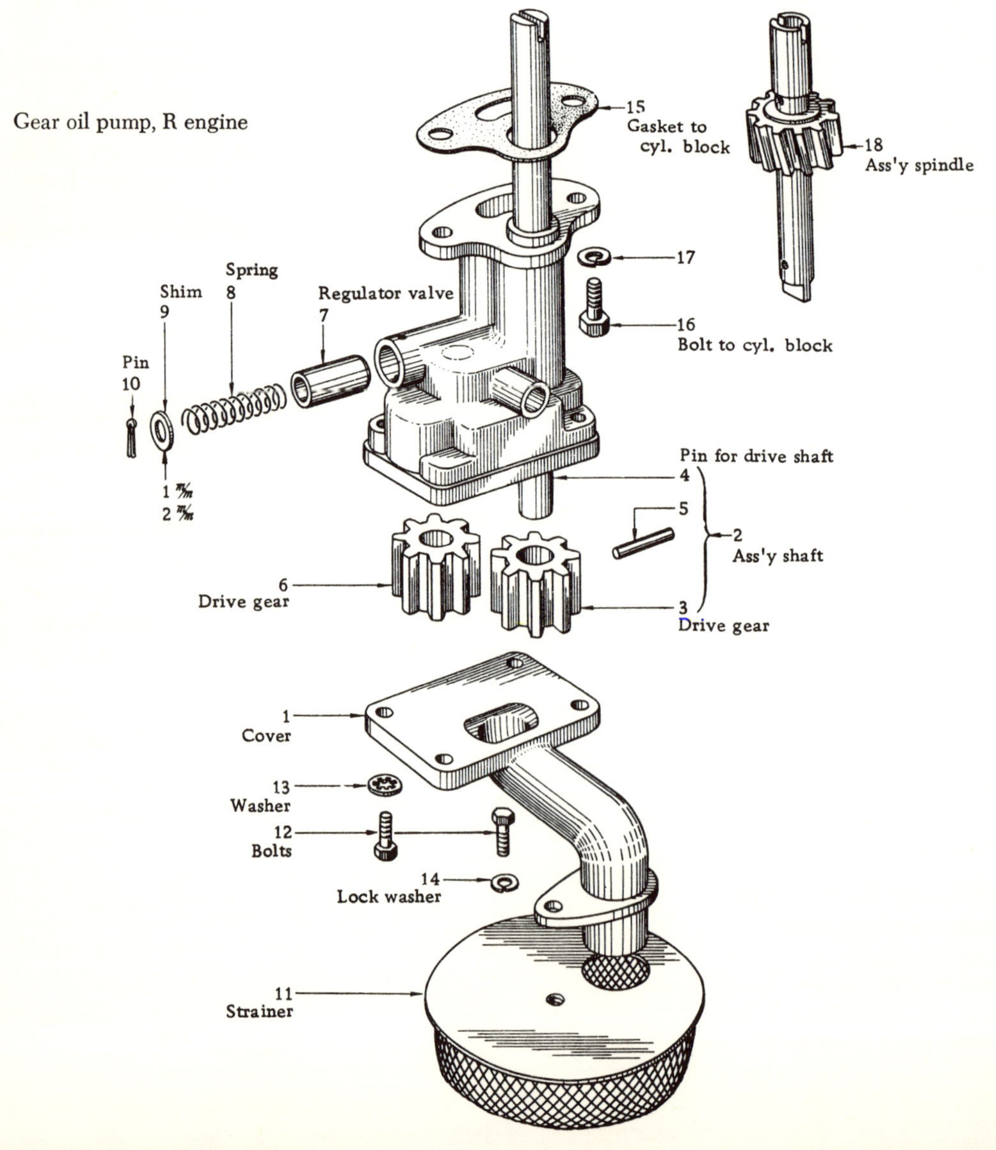

Gear oil pump, R engine

Oil Pump Specifications

Engine	*Pump type*	*Clearance between inner and outer rotor (in.)*	*Tip clearance—gear or rotor to cover (in.)*	*Clearance between outer rotor and body (in.)*	*Gear backlash (in.)*	*Side clearance—gear to body (in.)*	*Maximum oil pressure (psi)*	*Minimum oil pressure (psi) at idle*	*Relief valve spring free length (in.)*	*Relief valve opening pressure (psi)*
P	Gear	—	.006-.009	—	.001-.003	.006-.010	50-57	7-10	1.634	N.A.
E1, J	Rotor	.002-.005	.005-.008	N.A.	—	—	54-57	14-17	N.A.	N.A.
G, R	Gear	—	.002-.004	—	.010-.012	N.A.	54-57	7-10	N.A.	N.A.
U20	Gear	—	.006-.009	—	.012-.016	.002-.004	54-57	7-10	2.453	63.9
L16, L24	Rotor	.002-.005	.005	.006-.008	—	—	54-60	14-17	2.24	54.0-59.7
A12	Rotor	.002-.005	.005	.006-.008	—	—	54-60	13-17	1.71	54.0-59.7

Engine Cooling System

The coolant level should be checked regularly, at least every two weeks. Loosen the cap a quarter turn to allow the system pressure to escape. On models with an expansion tank, hold the pressure release button on the tank cap. Never remove the cap when the engine is hot or overheated. Scalding from steam may result. When all the pressure has escaped, remove the cap cautiously. The coolant level should be 1/2-1 in. below the filler neck.

Only permanent type antifreeze should be used. Follow the directions on the antifreeze container to determine the quantity necessary for the particular vehicle and the temperature expected. Refer to the Capacities and Pressures Chart for cooling system capacity. The cooling system should be drained and flushed out with clean water once a year. Open both the block and radiator drains. The rust inhibitor in antifreeze gradually loses effectiveness, so it is unwise to reuse antifreeze after flushing the system. In summer weather, a solution of rust inhibitor and water may be used.

RADIATOR

Removal and Installation

To remove the radiator:

1. Drain coolant.
2. Disconnect upper hose, lower hose, and expansion tank hose.
3. Disconnect automatic transmission oil cooler lines after draining the transmission. Cap the lines to exclude dirt.
4. Remove radiator mounting bolts and radiator. On Nissan Patrol (L60), the grille shell/headlight mounting panel and radiator can be removed as an assembly.
5. Reverse procedure to replace. Fill automatic transmission to proper level.

EXPANSION TANK

Some sports models have an expansion tank arrangement in the cooling system. The function of the expansion tank is to collect coolant forced out of the radiator by heat expansion. The coolant is returned to the radiator by vacuum created in the radiator upon cooling. With this system, proper coolant level is always maintained and the antifreeze is not diluted. Expansion tank systems are available on the accessory market, or may easily be constructed. Details are shown in the illustration.

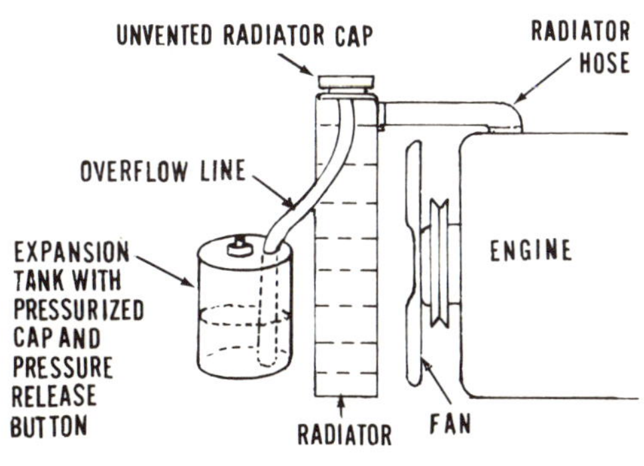

Coolant expansion tank details

WATER PUMP

Removal

To remove the water pump, first drain the coolant. Loosen the adjusting bolt at the alternator (generator) and remove the fan belt. Remove the fan and pulley and unbolt the pump. This job will be made easier by removing the radiator beforehand.

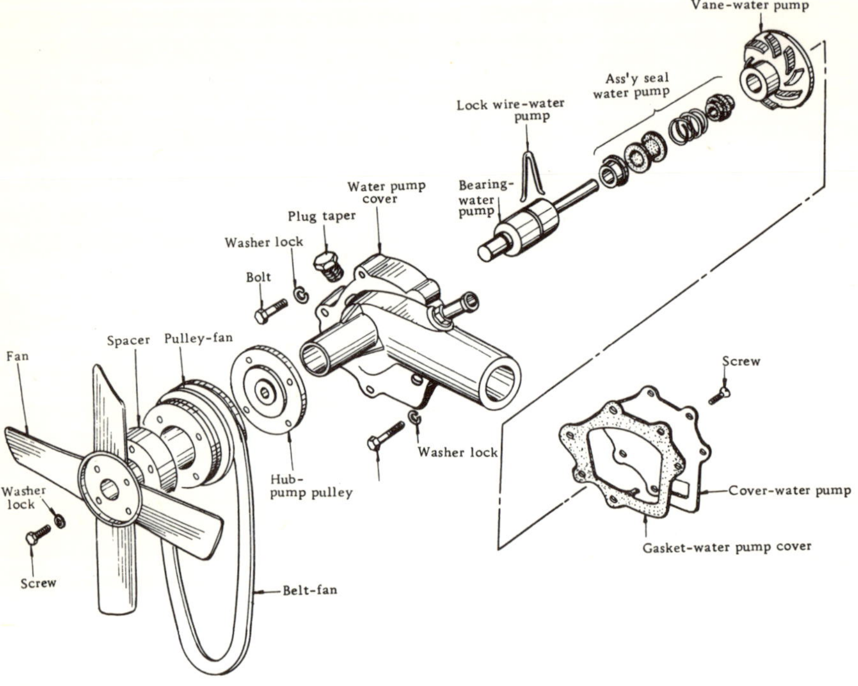

U20 engine water pump. E1, G, J, and R engine water pumps are similar.

Disassembly and Repair

The water pump on the L16 and L24 engine is made of aluminum and may not be disassembled for repairs. To disassemble and repair the pump on all other engines, proceed as follows:

1. Pull off the pulley hub. Remove the pump rear cover.
2. Remove the lock wire through the opening in the pump body.
3. Press out the shaft from the vanes. The shaft cannot be withdrawn from the hub side.
4. Remove the shaft from the body.
5. Press out the seal. Clean the seal seating surfaces.
6. Apply adhesive to the seal seating edge. Install the new seal.
7. Reassemble the pump. The clearance between the vanes and the pump body should be .016-.020 in. On the A12 engine, the vanes face away from the pump body. On all other models, the vanes face into the pump body.
8. Replace the lock wire. Install the pump with new gaskets.

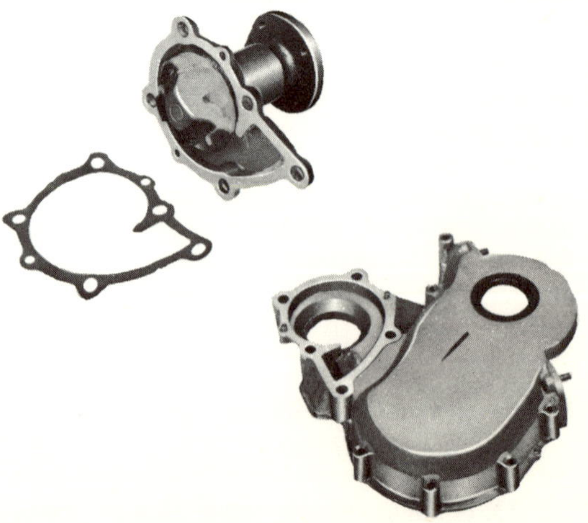

A12 engine water pump and front cover. Note that this pump has no rear cover. The nonrepairable aluminum water pump on the L16 and L24 engines is similar.

THERMOSTAT

The engine thermostat is housed in the water outlet casting on the cylinder head. The thermostat controls the flow of coolant, providing quick engine warmup and regulating coolant temperature. To remove the thermostat, first drain the coolant. Remove the upper radiator hose and unbolt the water outlet elbow. The thermostat may now be removed. To check the thermostat for proper operation, submerge it in a pan of water with a thermometer. The unit should open when the water temperature is the same as that marked on the body of the thermostat. Check that the unit opens fully. Refer to the accompanying chart for data on original equipment thermostats.

Engine	*Opening Temperature of Thermostat (°F)*	*Full Opening of Thermostat (in.)*
P	180	—
E1	164	—
J	170 or 180	—
G,R	176	.374
U20, L16, L24, A12	180	.315 @ 203°F

When heater output is insufficient, the original equipment thermostat may be replaced with one having a higher temperature rating. An engine should never be run without a thermostat, except in an emergency. Reverse the removal procedure to replace a thermostat. When installing a thermostat, be sure that the side with the spring faces into the engine. Always use a new gasket.

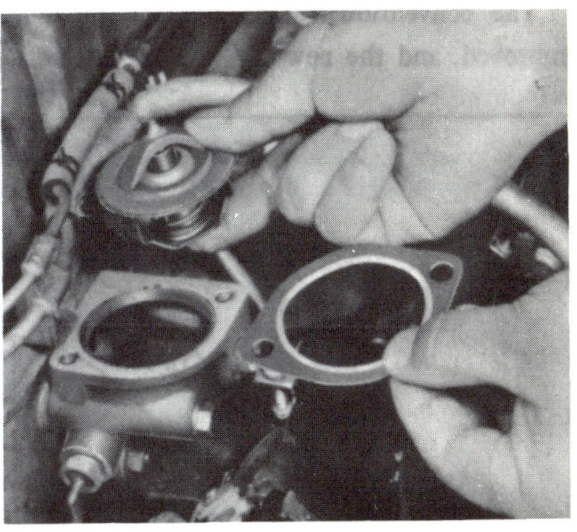

Correct thermostat installation

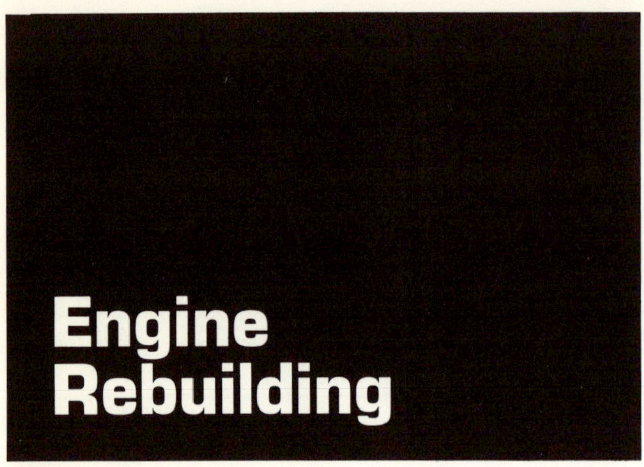

Engine Rebuilding

This section describes, in detail, the procedures involved in rebuilding a typical engine. The procedures specifically refer to an inline engine, however, they are basically identical to those used in rebuilding engines of nearly all design and configurations. Procedures for servicing atypical engines (i.e., horizontally opposed) are described in the appropriate section, although in most cases, cylinder head reconditioning procedures described in this chapter will apply.

The section is divided into two sections. The first, Cylinder Head Reconditioning, assumes that the cylinder head is removed from the engine, all manifolds are removed, and the cylinder head is on a workbench. The camshaft should be removed from overhead cam cylinder heads. The second section, Cylinder Block Reconditioning, covers the block, pistons, connecting rods and crankshaft. It is assumed that the engine is mounted on a work stand, and the cylinder head and all accessories are removed.

Procedures are identified as follows:

Unmarked—Basic procedures that must be performed in order to successfully complete the rebuilding process.

Starred (*)—Procedures that should be performed to ensure maximum performance and engine life.

Double starred (**)—Procedures that may be performed to increase engine performance and reliability. These procedures are usually reserved for extremely heavy-duty or competition usage.

In many cases, a choice of methods is also provided. Methods are identified in the same manner as procedures. The choice of method for a procedure is at the discretion of the user.

The tools required for the basic rebuilding procedure should, with minor exceptions, be those

TORQUE (ft. lbs.)*

U.S.

Bolt Diameter (inches)	Bolt Grade (SAE) 1 and 2	5	6	8	Wrench Size (inches) Bolt	Nut
1/4	5	7	10	10.5	3/8	7/16
5/16	9	14	19	22	1/2	9/16
3/8	15	25	34	37	9/16	5/8
7/16	24	40	55	60	5/8	3/4
1/2	37	60	85	92	3/4	13/16
9/16	53	88	120	132	7/8	7/8
5/8	74	120	167	180	15/16	1
3/4	120	200	280	296	1-1/8	1-1/8
7/8	190	302	440	473	1-5/16	1-5/16
1	282	466	660	714	1-1/2	1-1/2

Metric

Bolt Diameter (mm)	Bolt Grade 5D	8G	10K	12K	Wrench Size (mm) Bolt and Nut
6	5	6	8	10	10
8	10	16	22	27	14
10	19	31	40	49	17
12	34	54	70	86	19
14	55	89	117	137	22
16	83	132	175	208	24
18	111	182	236	283	27
22	182	284	394	464	32
24	261	419	570	689	36

*—Torque values are for lightly oiled bolts. CAUTION: Bolts threaded into aluminum require much less torque.

General Torque Specifications

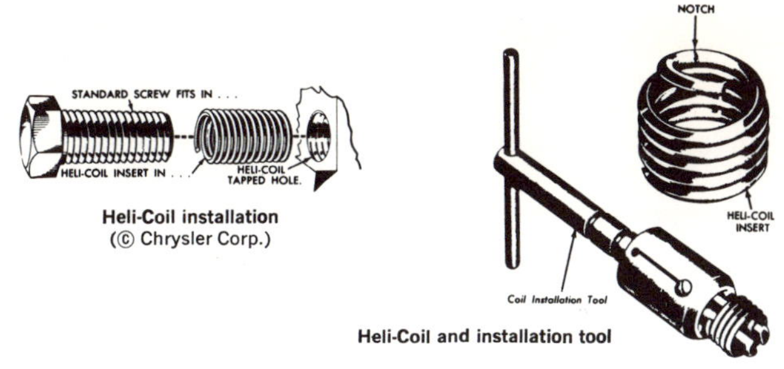

Heli-Coil installation
(© Chrysler Corp.)

Heli-Coil and installation tool

Heli-Coil Insert			*Drill*	*Tap*	*Insert. Tool*	*Extracting Tool*
Thread Size	*Part No.*	*Insert Length (In.)*	*Size*	*Part No.*	*Part No.*	*Part No.*
1/2 -20	1185-4	3/8	17/64(.266)	4 CPB	528-4N	1227-6
5/16-18	1185-5	15/32	Q(.332)	5 CPB	528-5N	1227-6
3/8 -16	1185-6	9/16	X(.397)	6 CPB	528-6N	1227-6
7/16-14	1185-7	21/32	29/64(.453)	7 CPB	528-7N	1227-16
1/2 -13	1185-8	3/4	33/64(.516)	8 CPB	528-8N	1227-16

Heli-Coil Specifications

included in a mechanic's tool kit. An accurate torque wrench, and a dial indicator (reading in thousandths) mounted on a universal base should be available. Bolts and nuts with no torque specification should be tightened according to size (see chart). Special tools, where required, all are readily available from the major tool suppliers (i.e., Craftsman, Snap-On, K-D). The services of a competent automotive machine shop must also be readily available.

When assembling the engine, any parts that will be in frictional contact must be pre-lubricated, to provide protection on initial start-up. Vortex Pre-Lube, STP, or any product specifically formulated for this purpose may be used. NOTE: *Do not use engine oil.* Where semi-permanent (locked but removable) installation of bolts or nuts is desired, threads should be cleaned and coated with Loctite. Studs may be permanently installed using Loctite Stud and Bearing Mount.

Aluminum has become increasingly popular for use in engines, due to its low weight and excellent heat transfer characteristics. The following precautions must be observed when handling aluminum engine parts:

—Never hot-tank aluminum parts.

—Remove all aluminum parts (identification tags, etc.) from engine parts before hot-tanking (otherwise they will be removed during the process).

—Always coat threads lightly with engine oil or anti-seize compounds before installation, to prevent seizure.

—Never over-torque bolts or spark plugs in aluminum threads. Should stripping occur, threads can be restored according to the following procedure, using Heli-Coil thread inserts:

Tap drill the hole with the stripped threads to the specified size (see chart). Using the specified tap (NOTE: *Heli-Coil tap sizes refer to the size thread being replaced, rather than the actual tap size*), tap the hole for the Heli-Coil. Place the insert on the proper installation tool (see chart). Apply pressure on the insert while winding it clockwise into the hole, until the top of the insert is one turn below the surface. Remove the installation tool, and break the installation tang from the bottom of the insert by moving it up and down. If the Heli-Coil must be removed, tap the removal tool firmly into the hole, so that it engages the top thread, and turn the tool counter-clockwise to extract the insert.

Snapped bolts or studs may be removed, using a stud extractor (unthreaded) or Vise-Grip pliers (threaded). Penetrating oil (e.g., Liquid Wrench) will often aid in breaking frozen threads. In cases where the stud or bolt is flush with, or below the surface, proceed as follows:

Drill a hole in the broken stud or bolt, approximately ½ its diameter. Select a screw extractor (e.g., Easy-Out) of the proper size, and tap it into the stud or bolt. Turn the extractor counterclockwise to remove the stud or bolt.

Magnaflux and Zyglo are inspection techniques used to locate material flaws, such as stress cracks. Magnafluxing coats the part with fine magnetic particles, and subjects the part to a magnetic field. Cracks cause breaks in the magnetic field, which are outlined by the particles. Since Magnaflux is a magnetic process, it is applicable only to ferrous materials. The Zyglo process coats the material with a fluorescent dye penetrant, and then subjects it to blacklight inspection, under which cracks glow bright-

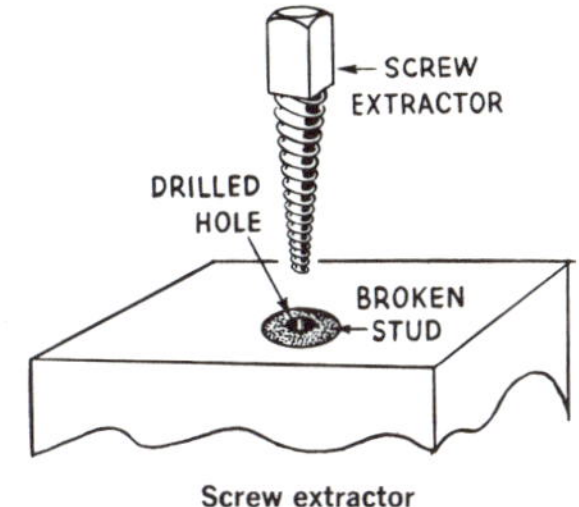

Screw extractor

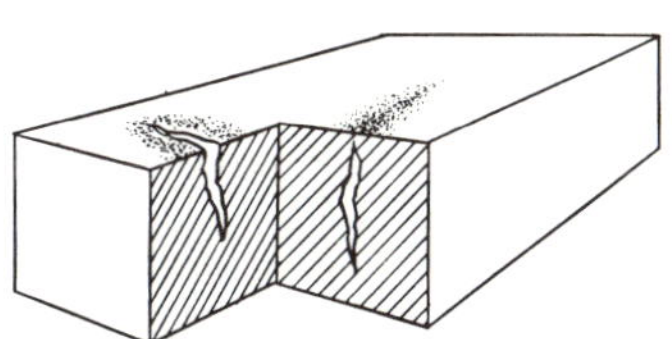

Magnaflux indication of cracks

ly. Parts made of any material may be tested using Zyglo. While Magnaflux and Zyglo are excellent for general inspection, and locating hidden defects, specific checks of suspected cracks may be made at lower cost and more readily using spot check dye. The dye is sprayed onto the suspected area, wiped off, and the area is then sprayed with a developer. Cracks then will show up brightly. Spot check dyes will only indicate surface cracks; therefore, structural cracks below the surface may escape detection. When questionable, the part should be tested using Magnaflux or Zyglo.

CYLINDER HEAD RECONDITIONING

Procedure	*Method*
Identify the valves: Valve identification (© SAAB)	Invert the cylinder head, and number the valve faces front to rear, using a permanent felt-tip marker.
Remove the rocker arms:	Remove the rocker arms with shaft(s) or balls and nuts. Wire the sets of rockers, balls and nuts together, and identify according to the corresponding valve.
Remove the valves and springs:	Using an appropriate valve spring compressor (depending on the configuration of the cylinder head), compress the valve springs. Lift out the keepers with needlenose pliers, release the compressor, and remove the valve, spring, and spring retainer.
Check the valve stem-to-guide clearance:  Checking the valve stem-to-guide clearance (© American Motors Corp.)	Clean the valve stem with lacquer thinner or a similar solvent to remove all gum and varnish. Clean the valve guides using solvent and an expanding wire-type valve guide cleaner. Mount a dial indicator so that the stem is at 90° to the valve stem, as close to the valve guide as possible. Move the valve off its seat, and measure the valve guide-to-stem clearance by moving the stem back and forth to actuate the dial indicator. Measure the valve stems using a micrometer, and compare to specifications, to determine whether stem or guide wear is responsible for excessive clearance.
De-carbon the cylinder head and valves: 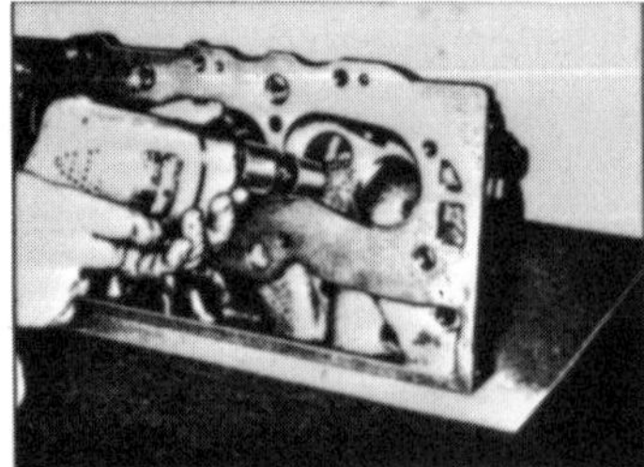 Removing carbon from the cylinder head (© Chevrolet Div. G.M. Corp.)	Chip carbon away from the valve heads, combustion chambers, and ports, using a chisel made of hardwood. Remove the remaining deposits with a stiff wire brush. NOTE: *Ensure that the deposits are actually removed, rather than burnished.*

Procedure	*Method*
Hot-tank the cylinder head:	Have the cylinder head hot-tanked to remove grease, corrosion, and scale from the water passages. NOTE: *In the case of overhead cam cylinder heads, consult the operator to determine whether the camshaft bearings will be damaged by the caustic solution.*
Degrease the remaining cylinder head parts:	Using solvent (i.e., Gunk), clean the rockers, rocker shaft(s) (where applicable), rocker balls and nuts, springs, spring retainers, and keepers. Do not remove the protective coating from the springs.
Check the cylinder head for warpage: **Checking the cylinder head for warpage** (© Ford Motor Co.)	Place a straight-edge across the gasket surface of the cylinder head. Using feeler gauges, determine the clearance at the center of the straight-edge. Measure across both diagonals, along the longitudinal centerline, and across the cylinder head at several points. If warpage exceeds .003″ in a 6″ span, or .006″ over the total length, the cylinder head must be resurfaced. NOTE: *If warpage exceeds the manufacturers maximum tolerance for material removal, the cylinder head must be replaced.* When milling the cylinder heads of V-type engines, the intake manifold mounting position is altered, and must be corrected by milling the manifold flange a proportionate amount.
** Porting and gasket matching: 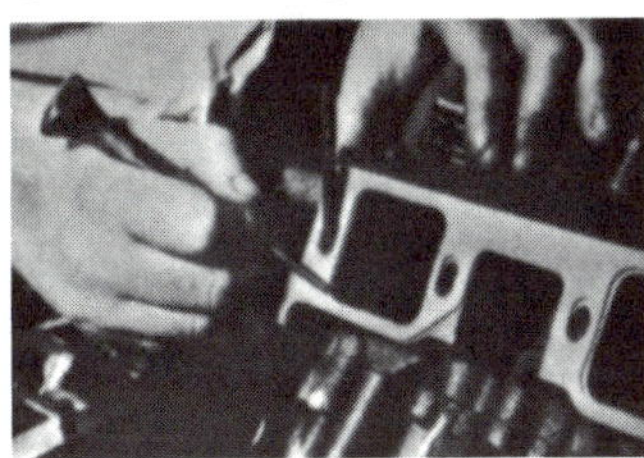 **Marking the cylinder head for gasket matching** (© Petersen Publishing Co.)  **Port configuration before and after gasket matching** (© Petersen Publishing Co.)	** Coat the manifold flanges of the cylinder head with Prussian blue dye. Glue intake and exhaust gaskets to the cylinder head in their installed position using rubber cement and scribe the outline of the ports on the manifold flanges. Remove the gaskets. Using a small cutter in a hand-held power tool (i.e., Dremel Moto-Tool), gradually taper the walls of the port out to the scribed outline of the gasket. Further enlargement of the ports should include the removal of sharp edges and radiusing of sharp corners. Do not alter the valve guides. NOTE: *The most efficient port configuration is determined only by extensive testing. Therefore, it is best to consult someone experienced with the head in question to determine the optimum alterations.*

Procedure	*Method*
** Polish the ports: 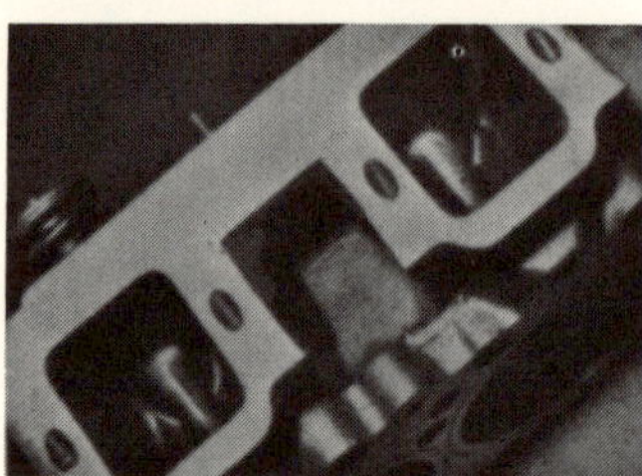 Relieved and polished ports (© Petersen Publishing Co.) 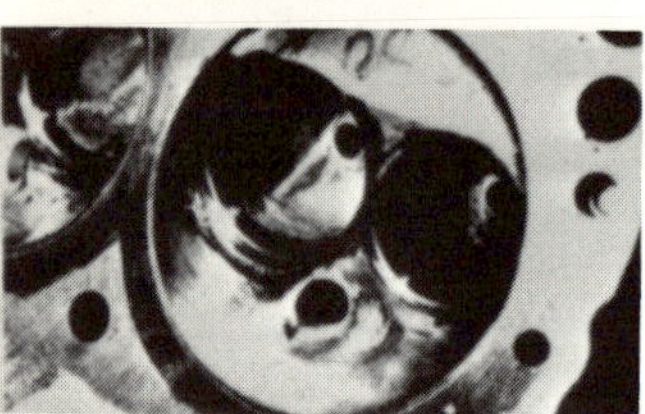 Polished combustion chamber (© Petersen Publishing Co.)	** Using a grinding stone with the above mentioned tool, polish the walls of the intake and exhaust ports, and combustion chamber. Use progressively finer stones until all surface imperfections are removed. NOTE: *Through testing, it has been determined that a smooth surface is more effective than a mirror polished surface in intake ports, and vice-versa in exhaust ports.*
* Knurling the valve guides: 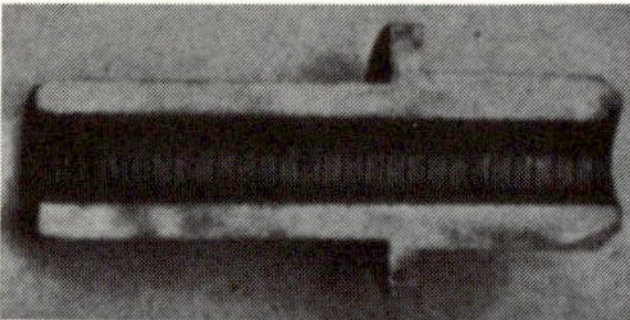 Cut-away view of a knurled valve guide (© Petersen Publishing Co.)	* Valve guides which are not excessively worn or distorted may, in some cases, be knurled rather than replaced. Knurling is a process in which metal is displaced and raised, thereby reducing clearance. Knurling also provides excellent oil control. The possibility of knurling rather than replacing valve guides should be discussed with a machinist.
Replacing the valve guides: NOTE: *Valve guides should only be replaced if damaged or if an oversize valve stem is not available.* A-VALVE GUIDE I.D. B-SLIGHTLY SMALLER THAN VALVE GUIDE O.D. Valve guide removal tool WASHERS A-VALVE GUIDE I.D. B-LARGER THAN THE VALVE GUIDE O.D. Valve guide installation tool (with washers used during installation)	Depending on the type of cylinder head, valve guides may be pressed, hammered, or shrunk in. In cases where the guides are shrunk into the head, replacement should be left to an equipped machine shop. In other cases, the guides are replaced as follows: Press or tap the valve guides out of the head using a stepped drift (see illustration). Determine the height above the boss that the guide must extend, and obtain a stack of washers, their I.D. similar to the guide's O.D., of that height. Place the stack of washers on the guide, and insert the guide into the boss. NOTE: *Valve guides are often tapered or beveled for installation.* Using the stepped installation tool (see illustration), press or tap the guides into position. Ream the guides according to the size of the valve stem.

Procedure	*Method*
Replacing valve seat inserts:	Replacement of valve seat inserts which are worn beyond resurfacing or broken, if feasible, must be done by a machine shop.
Resurfacing (grinding) the valve face: 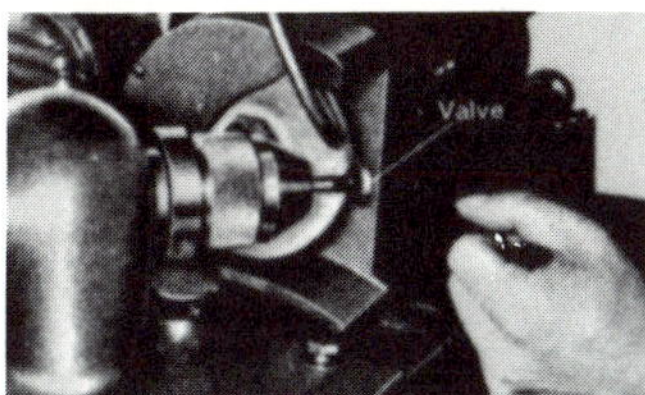 Grinding a valve (© Subaru) 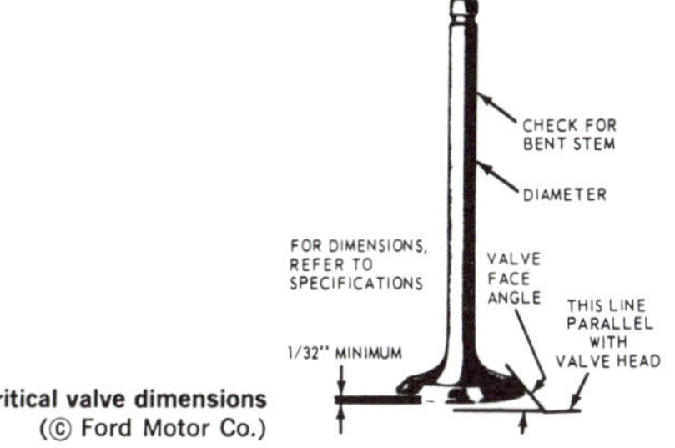 Critical valve dimensions (© Ford Motor Co.)	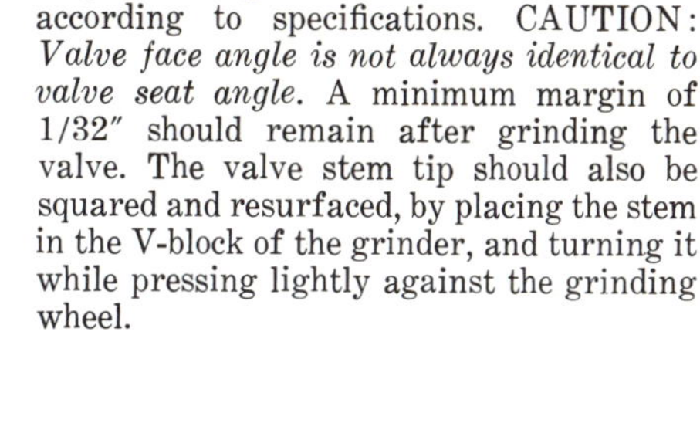 Using a valve grinder, resurface the valves according to specifications. CAUTION: *Valve face angle is not always identical to valve seat angle.* A minimum margin of 1/32" should remain after grinding the valve. The valve stem tip should also be squared and resurfaced, by placing the stem in the V-block of the grinder, and turning it while pressing lightly against the grinding wheel.
Resurfacing the valve seats using reamers: 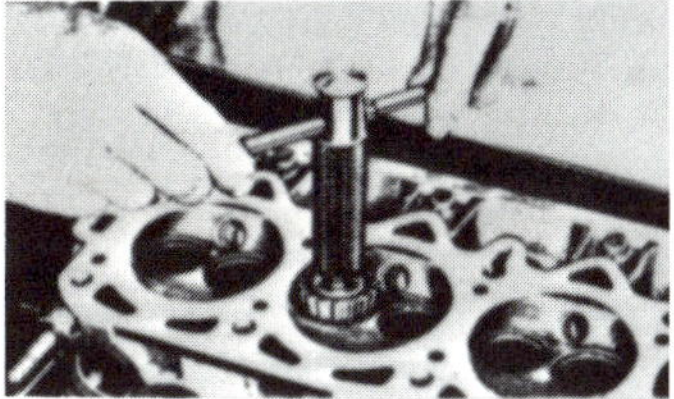 Reaming the valve seat (© S.p.A. Fiat) 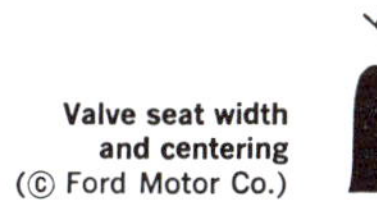 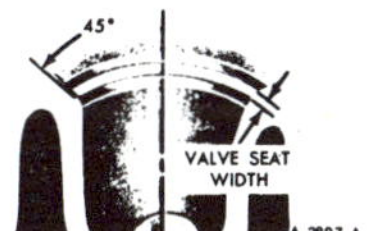 Valve seat width and centering (© Ford Motor Co.)	Select a reamer of the correct seat angle, slightly larger than the diameter of the valve seat, and assemble it with a pilot of the correct size. Install the pilot into the valve guide, and using steady pressure, turn the reamer clockwise. CAUTION: *Do not turn the reamer counter-clockwise.* Remove only as much material as necessary to clean the seat. Check the concentricity of the seat (see below). If the dye method is not used, coat the valve face with Prussian blue dye, install and rotate it on the valve seat. Using the dye marked area as a centering guide, center and narrow the valve seat to specifications with correction cutters. NOTE: *When no specifications are available, minimum seat width for exhaust valves should be 5/64", intake valves 1/16".* After making correction cuts, check the position of the valve seat on the valve face using Prussian blue dye.
* Resurfacing the valve seats using a grinder: 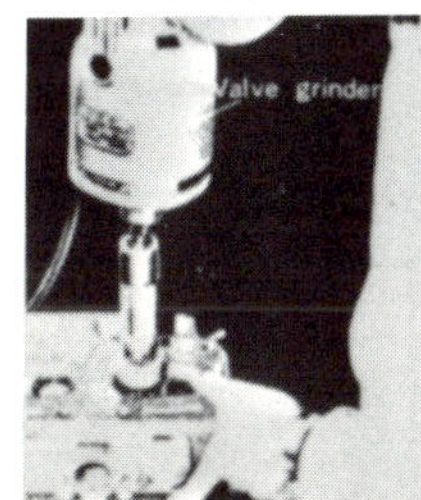 Grinding a valve seat (© Subaru)	Select a pilot of the correct size, and a coarse stone of the correct seat angle. Lubricate the pilot if necessary, and install the tool in the valve guide. Move the stone on and off the seat at approximately two cycles per second, until all flaws are removed from the seat. Install a fine stone, and finish the seat. Center and narrow the seat using correction stones, as described above.

Procedure	*Method*
Checking the valve seat concentricity: 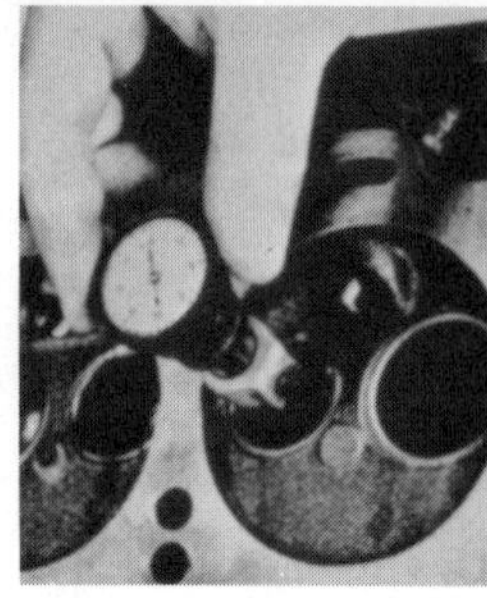 Checking the valve seat concentricity using a dial gauge (© American Motors Corp.)	Coat the valve face with Prussian blue dye, install the valve, and rotate it on the valve seat. If the entire seat becomes coated, and the valve is known to be concentric, the seat is concentric.
	* Install the dial gauge pilot into the guide, and rest the arm on the valve seat. Zero the gauge, and rotate the arm around the seat. Run-out should not exceed .002″.
* Lapping the valves: NOTE: *Valve lapping is done to ensure efficient sealing of resurfaced valves and seats. Valve lapping alone is not recommended for use as a resurfacing procedure.*  Hand lapping the valves	* Invert the cylinder head, lightly lubricate the valve stems, and install the valves in the head as numbered. Coat valve seats with fine grinding compound, and attach the lapping tool suction cup to a valve head (NOTE: *Moisten the suction cup*). Rotate the tool between the palms, changing position and lifting the tool often to prevent grooving. Lap the valve until a smooth, polished seat is evident. Remove the valve and tool, and rinse away all traces of grinding compound.
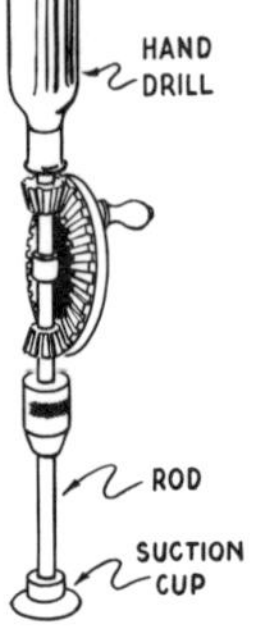 Home made mechanical valve lapping tool	** Fasten a suction cup to a piece of drill rod, and mount the rod in a hand drill. Proceed as above, using the hand drill as a lapping tool. CAUTION: *Due to the higher speeds involved when using the hand drill, care must be exercised to avoid grooving the seat.* Lift the tool and change direction of rotation often.
Check the valve springs: 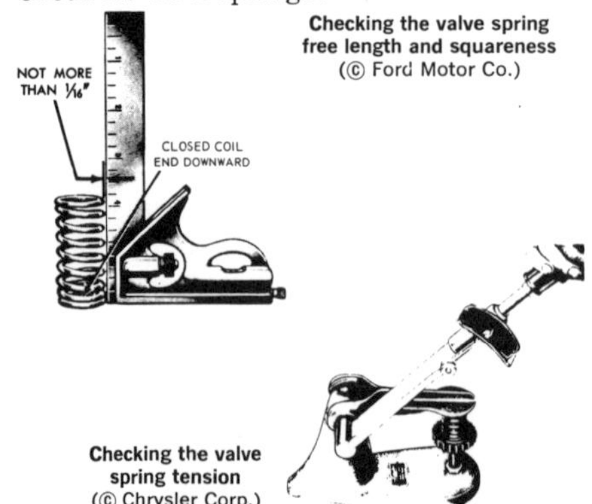 Checking the valve spring free length and squareness (© Ford Motor Co.) Checking the valve spring tension (© Chrysler Corp.)	Place the spring on a flat surface next to a square. Measure the height of the spring, and rotate it against the edge of the square to measure distortion. If spring height varies (by comparison) by more than 1/16″ or if distortion exceeds 1/16″, replace the spring.
	** In addition to evaluating the spring as above, test the spring pressure at the installed and compressed (installed height minus valve lift) height using a valve spring tester. Springs used on small displacement engines (up to 3 liters) should be ± 1 lb. of all other springs in either position. A tolerance of ± 5 lbs. is permissible on larger engines.

Procedure	*Method*
* Install valve stem seals: 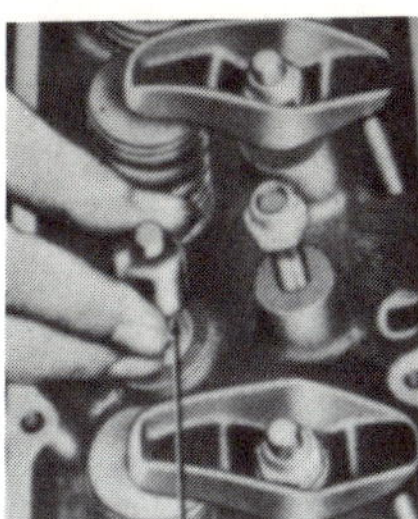 **Valve stem seal installation** (© Ford Motor Co.)	* Due to the pressure differential that exists at the ends of the intake valve guides (atmospheric pressure above, manifold vacuum below), oil is drawn through the valve guides into the intake port. This has been alleviated somewhat since the addition of positive crankcase ventilation, which lowers the pressure above the guides. Several types of valve stem seals are available to reduce blow-by. Certain seals simply slip over the stem and guide boss, while others require that the boss be machined. Recently, Teflon guide seals have become popular. Consult a parts supplier or machinist concerning availability and suggested usages. NOTE: *When installing seals, ensure that a small amount of oil is able to pass the seal to lubricate the valve guides; otherwise, excessive wear may result.*
Install the valves:	Lubricate the valve stems, and install the valves in the cylinder head as numbered. Lubricate and position the seals (if used, see above) and the valve springs. Install the spring retainers, compress the springs, and insert the keys using needlenose pliers or a tool designed for this purpose. NOTE: *Retain the keys with wheel bearing grease during installation.*
Checking valve spring installed height: 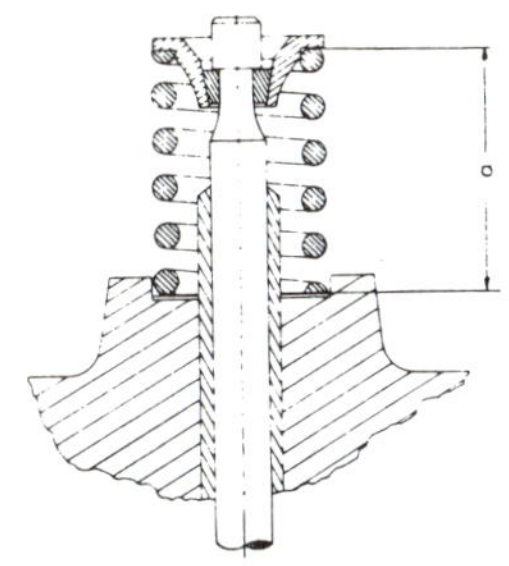 **Valve spring installed height dimension** (© Porsche) 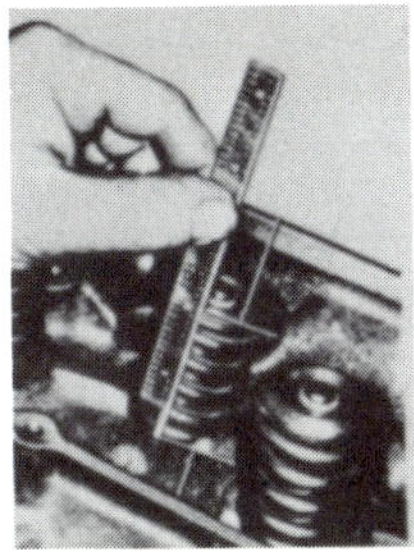 **Measuring valve spring installed height** (© Petersen Publishing Co.)	Measure the distance between the spring pad and the lower edge of the spring retainer, and compare to specifications. If the installed height is incorrect, add shim washers between the spring pad and the spring. CAUTION: *Use only washers designed for this purpose.*
** CC'ing the combustion chambers:	** Invert the cylinder head and place a bead of sealer around a combustion chamber. Install an apparatus designed for this purpose (burette mounted on a clear plate; see illustration) over the combustion chamber, and fill with the specified fluid to an even mark on the burette. Record the burette reading, and fill the combustion chamber with fluid. (NOTE: *A hole drilled in the plate will permit air to escape*). Subtract the burette reading, with the combustion chamber filled, from the previous reading, to determine combustion chamber volume in cc's. Duplicate this procedure in all combustion

Procedure	*Method*
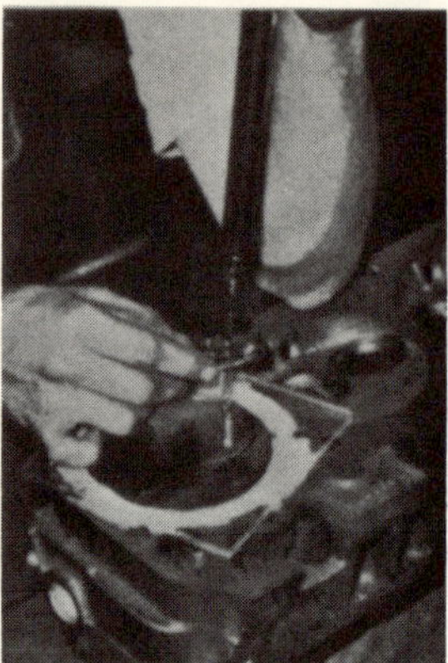 CC'ing the combustion chamber (© Petersen Publishing Co.)	chambers on the cylinder head, and compare the readings. The volume of all combustion chambers should be made equal to that of the largest. Combustion chamber volume may be increased in two ways. When only a small change is required (usually), a small cutter or coarse stone may be used to remove material from the combustion chamber. NOTE: *Check volume frequently.* Remove material over a wide area, so as not to change the configuration of the combustion chamber. When a larger change is required, the valve seat may be sunk (lowered into the head). NOTE: *When altering valve seat, remember to compensate for the change in spring installed height.*
Inspect the rocker arms, balls, studs, and nuts (where applicable): 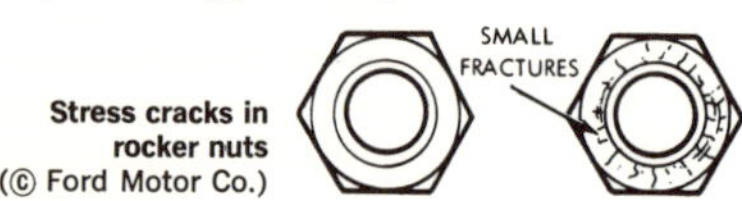 Stress cracks in rocker nuts (© Ford Motor Co.)	Visually inspect the rocker arms, balls, studs, and nuts for cracks, galling, burning, scoring, or wear. If all parts are intact, liberally lubricate the rocker arms and balls, and install them on the cylinder head. If wear is noted on a rocker arm at the point of valve contact, grind it smooth and square, removing as little material as possible. Replace the rocker arm if excessively worn. If a rocker stud shows signs of wear, it must be replaced (see below). If a rocker nut shows stress cracks, replace it. If an exhaust ball is galled or burned, substitute the intake ball from the same cylinder (if it is intact), and install a new intake ball. NOTE: *Avoid using new rocker balls on exhaust valves.*
Replacing rocker studs: 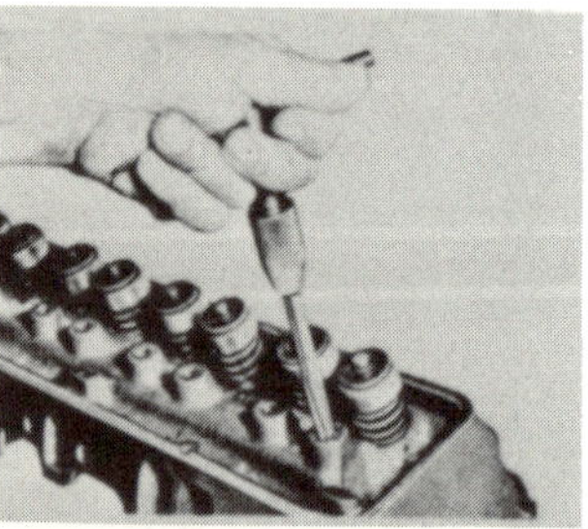 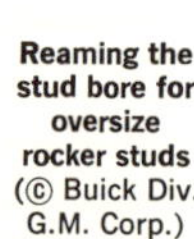 Reaming the stud bore for oversize rocker studs (© Buick Div. G.M. Corp.) 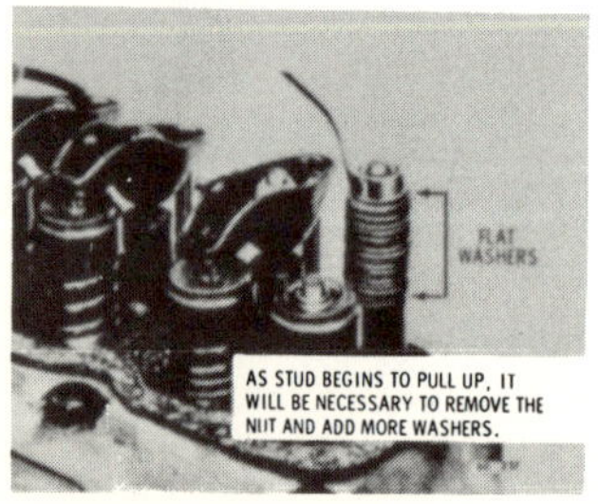 Extracting a pressed in rocker stud (© Buick Div. G.M. Corp.)	In order to remove a threaded stud, lock two nuts on the stud, and unscrew the stud using the lower nut. Coat the lower threads of the new stud with Loctite, and install. Two alternative methods are available for replacing pressed in studs. Remove the damaged stud using a stack of washers and a nut (see illustration). In the first, the boss is reamed .005-.006″ oversize, and an oversize stud pressed in. Control the stud extension over the boss using washers, in the same manner as valve guides. Before installing the stud, coat it with white lead and grease. To retain the stud more positively, drill a hole through the stud and boss, and install a roll pin. In the second method, the boss is tapped, and a threaded stud installed. Retain the stud using Loctite Stud and Bearing Mount.

Procedure	*Method*
Inspect the rocker shaft(s) and rocker arms (where applicable):  Disassembled rocker shaft parts arranged for inspection (© American Motors Corp.) 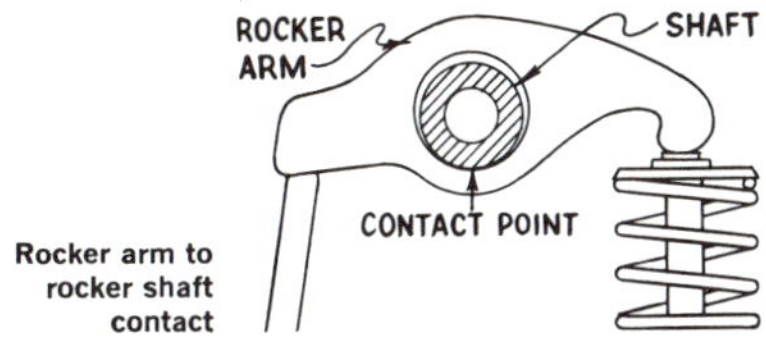 Rocker arm to rocker shaft contact	Remove rocker arms, springs and washers from rocker shaft. NOTE: *Lay out parts in the order they are removed.* Inspect rocker arms for pitting or wear on the valve contact point, or excessive bushing wear. Bushings need only be replaced if wear is excessive, because the rocker arm normally contacts the shaft at one point only. Grind the valve contact point of rocker arm smooth if necessary, removing as little material as possible. If excessive material must be removed to smooth and square the arm, it should be replaced. Clean out all oil holes and passages in rocker shaft. If shaft is grooved or worn, replace it. Lubricate and assemble the rocker shaft.
Inspect the camshaft bushings and the camshaft (overhead cam engines):	See next section.
Inspect the pushrods:	Remove the pushrods, and, if hollow, clean out the oil passages using fine wire. Roll each pushrod over a piece of clean glass. If a distinct clicking sound is heard as the pushrod rolls, the rod is bent, and must be replaced. * The length of all pushrods must be equal. Measure the length of the pushrods, compare to specifications, and replace as necessary.
Inspect the valve lifters: 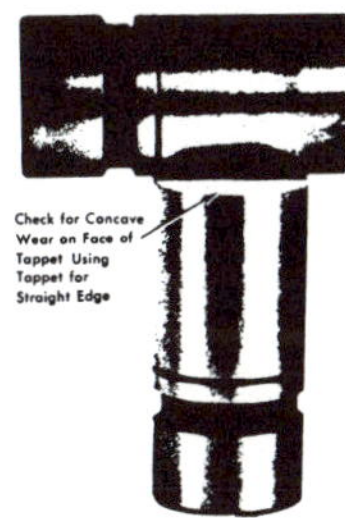 Checking the lifter face (© American Motors Corp.)	Remove lifters from their bores, and remove gum and varnish, using solvent. Clean walls of lifter bores. Check lifters for concave wear as illustrated. If face is worn concave, replace lifter, and carefully inspect the camshaft. Lightly lubricate lifter and insert it into its bore. If play is excessive, an oversize lifter must be installed (where possible). Consult a machinist concerning feasibility. If play is satisfactory, remove, lubricate, and reinstall the lifter.
* Testing hydraulic lifter leak down: 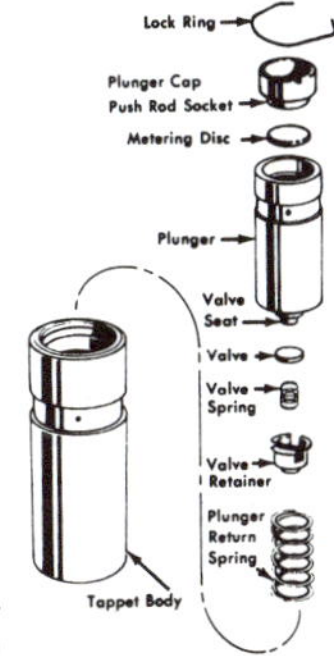 Exploded view of a typical hydraulic lifter (© American Motors Corp.)	Submerge lifter in a container of kerosene. Chuck a used pushrod or its equivalent into a drill press. Position container of kerosene so pushrod acts on the lifter plunger. Pump lifter with the drill press, until resistance increases. Pump several more times to bleed any air out of lifter. Apply very firm, constant pressure to the lifter, and observe rate at which fluid bleeds out of lifter. If the fluid bleeds very quickly (less than 15 seconds), lifter is defective. If the time exceeds 60 seconds, lifter is sticking. In either case, recondition or replace lifter. If lifter is operating properly (leak down time 15-60 seconds), lubricate and install it.

CYLINDER BLOCK RECONDITIONING

Procedure	*Method*
Checking the main bearing clearance:  Plastigage installed on main bearing journal (© Chevrolet Div. G.M. Corp.)  Measuring Plastigage to determine main bearing clearance (© Chevrolet Div. G.M. Corp.) 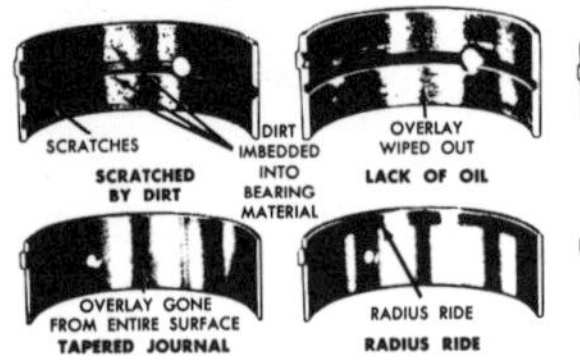 Causes of bearing failure (© Ford Motor Co.)	Invert engine, and remove cap from the bearing to be checked. Using a clean, dry rag, thoroughly clean all oil from crankshaft journal and bearing insert. NOTE: *Plastigage is soluble in oil; therefore, oil on the journal or bearing could result in erroneous readings.* Place a piece of Plastigage along the full length of journal, reinstall cap, and torque to specifications. Remove bearing cap, and determine bearing clearance by comparing width of Plastigage to the scale on Plastigage envelope. Journal taper is determined by comparing width of the Plastigage strip near its ends. Rotate crankshaft 90° and retest, to determine journal eccentricity. NOTE: *Do not rotate crankshaft with Plastigage installed.* If bearing insert and journal appear intact, and are within tolerances, no further main bearing service is required. If bearing or journal appear defective, cause of failure should be determined before replacement.
	* Remove crankshaft from block (see below). Measure the main bearing journals at each end twice (90° apart) using a micrometer, to determine diameter, journal taper and eccentricity. If journals are within tolerances, reinstall bearing caps at their specified torque. Using a telescope gauge and micrometer, measure bearing I.D. parallel to piston axis and at 30° on each side of piston axis. Subtract journal O.D. from bearing I.D. to determine oil clearance. If crankshaft journals appear defective, or do not meet tolerances, there is no need to measure bearings; for the crankshaft will require grinding and/or undersize bearings will be required. If bearing appears defective, cause for failure should be determined prior to replacement.
Checking the connecting rod bearing clearance:  Plastigage installed on connecting rod bearing journal (© Chevrolet Div. G.M. Corp.)	Connecting rod bearing clearance is checked in the same manner as main bearing clearance, using Plastigage. Before removing the crankshaft, connecting rod side clearance also should be measured and recorded.
	* Checking connecting rod bearing clearance, using a micrometer, is identical to checking main bearing clearance. If no other service

Procedure	Method
 **Measuring Plastigage to determine connecting rod bearing clearance** (© Chevrolet Div. G.M. Corp.)	is required, the piston and rod assemblies need not be removed.
Removing the crankshaft: 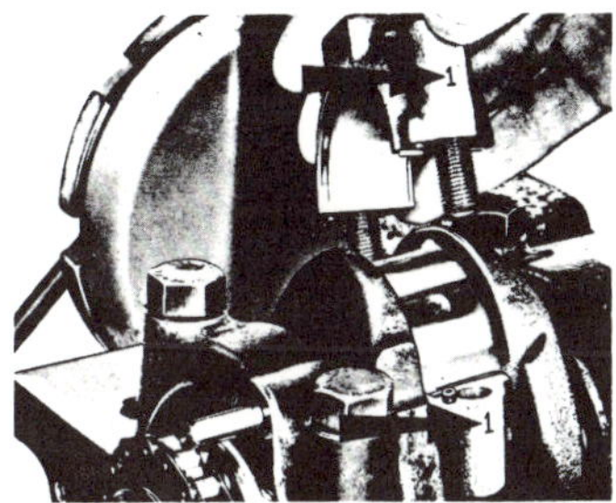 **Connecting rod matching marks** (© Ford Motor Co.)	Using a punch, mark the corresponding main bearing caps and saddles according to position (i.e., one punch on the front main cap and saddle, two on the second, three on the third, etc.). Using number stamps, identify the corresponding connecting rods and caps, according to cylinder (if no numbers are present). Remove the main and connecting rod caps, and place sleeves of plastic tubing over the connecting rod bolts, to protect the journals as the crankshaft is removed. Lift the crankshaft out of the block.
Remove the ridge from the top of the cylinder: 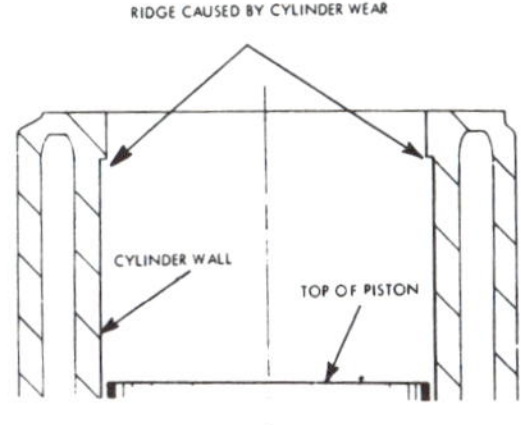 **Cylinder bore ridge** (© Pontiac Div. G.M. Corp.)	In order to facilitate removal of the piston and connecting rod, the ridge at the top of the cylinder (unworn area; see illustration) must be removed. Place the piston at the bottom of the bore, and cover it with a rag. Cut the ridge away using a ridge reamer, exercising extreme care to avoid cutting too deeply. Remove the rag, and remove cuttings that remain on the piston. CAUTION: *If the ridge is not removed, and new rings are installed, damage to rings will result.*
Removing the piston and connecting rod: 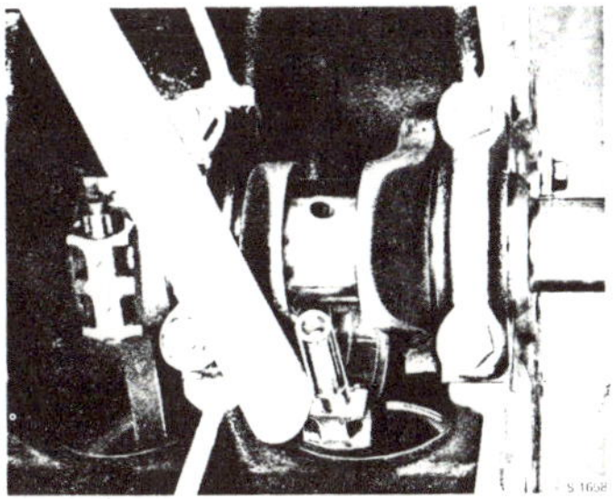 **Removing the piston** (© SAAB)	Invert the engine, and push the pistons and connecting rods out of the cylinders. If necessary, tap the connecting rod boss with a wooden hammer handle, to force the piston out. CAUTION: *Do not attempt to force the piston past the cylinder ridge* (see above).

Procedure	*Method*
Service the crankshaft:	Ensure that all oil holes and passages in the crankshaft are open and free of sludge. If necessary, have the crankshaft ground to the largest possible undersize.
	** Have the crankshaft Magnafluxed, to locate stress cracks. Consult a machinist concerning additional service procedures, such as surface hardening (e.g., nitriding, Tuftriding) to improve wear characteristics, cross drilling and chamfering the oil holes to improve lubrication, and balancing.
Removing freeze plugs:	Drill a hole in the center of the freeze plugs, and pry them out using a screwdriver or drift.
Remove the oil gallery plugs:	Threaded plugs should be removed using an appropriate (usually square) wrench. To remove soft, pressed in plugs, drill a hole in the plug, and thread in a sheet metal screw. Pull the plug out by the screw using pliers.
Hot-tank the block:	Have the block hot-tanked to remove grease, corrosion, and scale from the water jackets. NOTE: *Consult the operator to determine whether the camshaft bearings will be damaged during the hot-tank process.*
Check the block for cracks:	Visually inspect the block for cracks or chips. The most common locations are as follows: Adjacent to freeze plugs. Between the cylinders and water jackets. Adjacent to the main bearing saddles. At the extreme bottom of the cylinders. Check only suspected cracks using spot check dye (see introduction). If a crack is located, consult a machinist concerning possible repairs.
	** Magnaflux the block to locate hidden cracks. If cracks are located, consult a machinist about feasibility of repair.
Install the oil gallery plugs and freeze plugs:	Coat freeze plugs with sealer and tap into position using a piece of pipe, slightly smaller than the plug, as a driver. To ensure retention, stake the edges of the plugs. Coat threaded oil gallery plugs with sealer and install. Drive replacement soft plugs into block using a large drift as a driver.
	* Rather than reinstalling lead plugs, drill and tap the holes, and install threaded plugs.

Procedure	*Method*

Check the bore diameter and surface:

Visually inspect the cylinder bores for roughness, scoring, or scuffing. If evident, the cylinder bore must be bored or honed oversize to eliminate imperfections, and the smallest possible oversize piston used. The new pistons should be given to the machinist with the block, so that the cylinders can be bored or honed exactly to the piston size (plus clearance). If no flaws are evident, measure the bore diameter using a telescope gauge and micrometer, or dial gauge, parallel and perpendicular to the engine centerline, at the top (below the ridge) and bottom of the bore. Subtract the bottom measurements from the top to determine taper, and the parallel to the centerline measurements from the perpendicular measurements to determine eccentricity. If the measurements are not within specifications, the cylinder must be bored or honed, and an oversize piston installed. If the measurements are within specifications the cylinder may be used as is, with only finish honing (see below). NOTE: *Prior to submitting the block for boring, perform the following operation(s).*

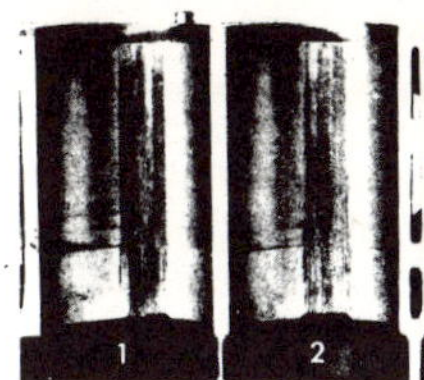
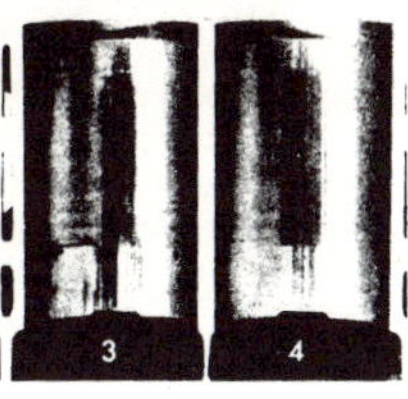

1, 2, 3 Piston skirt seizure resulted in this pattern. Engine must be rebored

4. Piston skirt and oil ring seizure caused this damage. Engine must be rebored

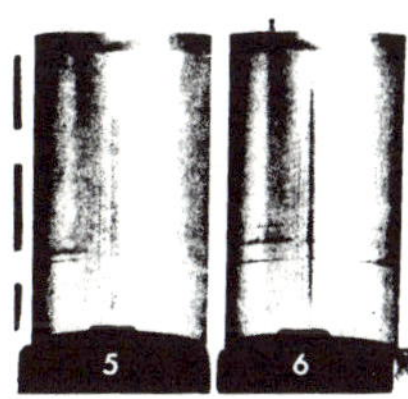

5, 6 Score marks caused by a split piston skirt. Damage is not serious enough to warrant reboring

7. Ring seized longitudinally, causing a score mark 1 3/16" wide, on the land side of the piston groove. The honing pattern is destroyed and the cylinder must be rebored

8. Result of oil ring seizure. Engine must be rebored

9. Oil ring seizure here was not serious enough to warrant reboring. The honing marks are still visible

Cylinder wall damage
(© Daimler-Benz A.G.)

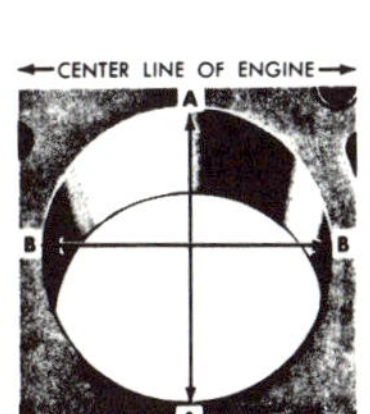

Cylinder bore measuring positions
(© Ford Motor Co.)

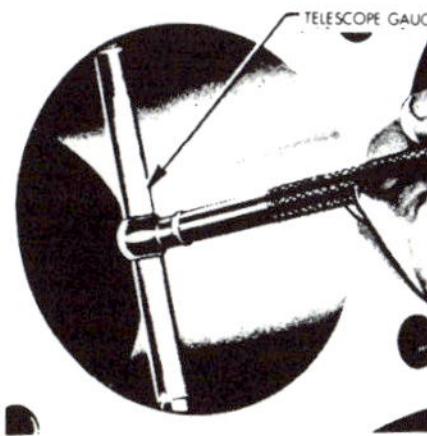

Measuring the cylinder bore with a telescope gauge
(© Buick Div. G.M. Corp.)

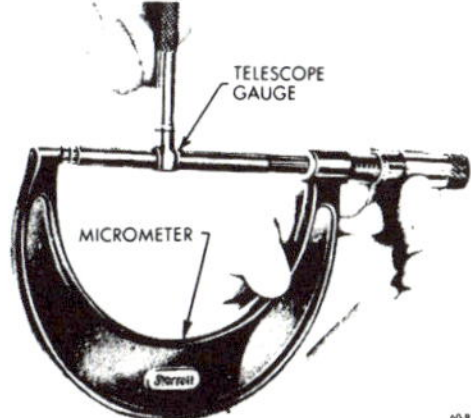

Determining the cylinder bore by measuring the telescope gauge with a micrometer
(© Buick Div. G.M. Corp.)

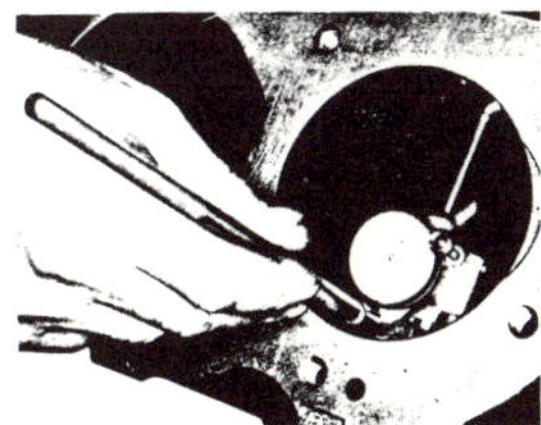

Measuring the cylinder bore with a dial gauge
(© Chevrolet Div. G.M. Corp.)

Procedure	*Method*
Check the block deck for warpage:	Using a straightedge and feeler gauges, check the block deck for warpage in the same manner that the cylinder head is checked (see Cylinder Head Reconditioning). If warpage exceeds specifications, have the deck resurfaced. NOTE: *In certain cases a specification for total material removal (Cylinder head and block deck) is provided. This specification must not be exceeded.*
* Check the deck height:	The deck height is the distance from the crankshaft centerline to the block deck. To measure, invert the engine, and install the crankshaft, retaining it with the center main cap. Measure the distance from the crankshaft journal to the block deck, parallel to the cylinder centerline. Measure the diameter of the end (front and rear) main journals, parallel to the centerline of the cylinders, divide the diameter in half, and subtract it from the previous measurement. The results of the front and rear measurements should be identical. If the difference exceeds .005″, the deck height should be corrected. NOTE: *Block deck height and warpage should be corrected concurrently.*
Check the cylinder block bearing alignment:  **Checking main bearing saddle alignment** (© Petersen Publishing Co.)	Remove the upper bearing inserts. Place a straightedge in the bearing saddles along the centerline of the crankshaft. If clearance exists between the straightedge and the center saddle, the block must be alignbored.
Clean and inspect the pistons and connecting rods: 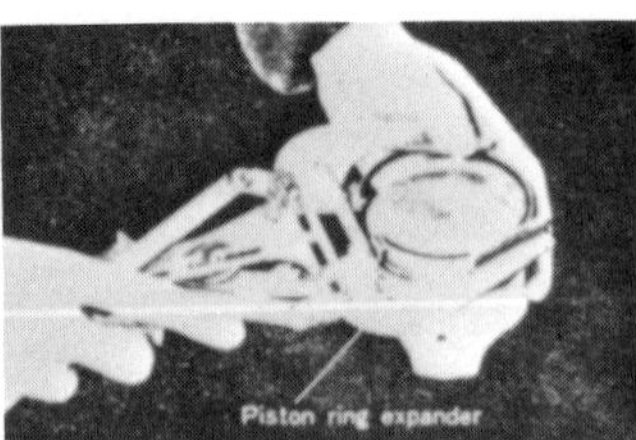 **Removing the piston rings** (© Subaru)	Using a ring expander, remove the rings from the piston. Remove the retaining rings (if so equipped) and remove piston pin. NOTE: *If the piston pin must be pressed out, determine the proper method and use the proper tools; otherwise the piston will distort.* Clean the ring grooves using an appropriate tool, exercising care to avoid cutting too deeply. Thoroughly clean all carbon and varnish from the piston with solvent. CAUTION: *Do not use a wire brush or caustic solvent on pistons.* Inspect the pistons for scuffing, scoring, cracks, pitting, or excessive ring groove wear. If wear is evident, the piston must be replaced. Check the connecting rod length by measuring the rod from the inside of the large end to the inside of the small end using calipers (see

Procedure	Method
 Cleaning the piston ring grooves (© Ford Motor Co.) 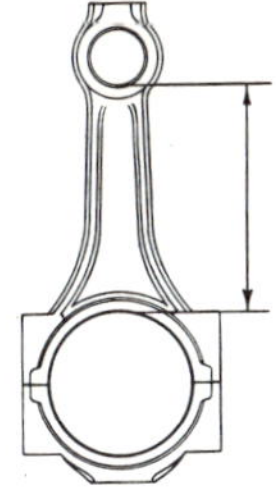 Connecting rod length checking dimension	illustration). All connecting rods should be equal length. Replace any rod that differs from the others in the engine. * Have the connecting rod alignment checked in an alignment fixture by a machinist. Replace any twisted or bent rods. * Magnaflux the connecting rods to locate stress cracks. If cracks are found, replace the connecting rod.
Fit the pistons to the cylinders: 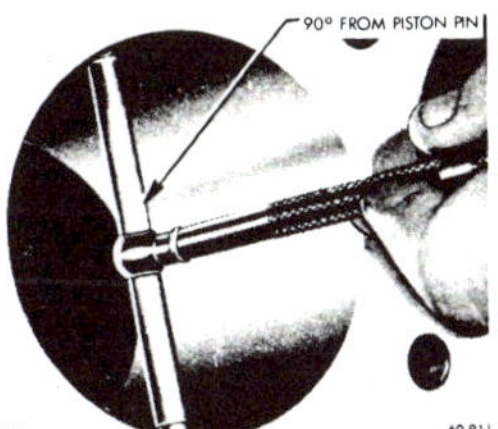 Measuring the cylinder with a telescope gauge for piston fitting (© Buick Div. G.M. Corp.) 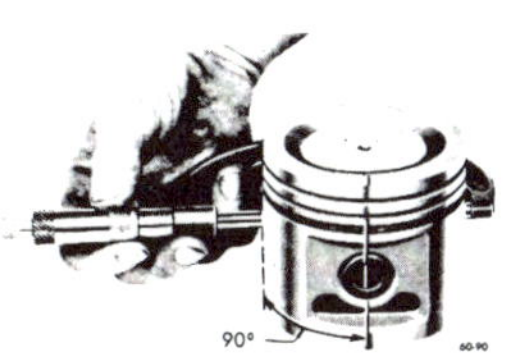 Measuring the piston for fitting (© Buick Div. G.M. Corp.)	Using a telescope gauge and micrometer, or a dial gauge, measure the cylinder bore diameter perpendicular to the piston pin, 2½″ below the deck. Measure the piston perpendicular to its pin on the skirt. The difference between the two measurements is the piston clearance. If the clearance is within specifications or slightly below (after boring or honing), finish honing is all that is required. If the clearance is excessive, try to obtain a slightly larger piston to bring clearance within specifications. Where this is not possible, obtain the first oversize piston, and hone (or if necessary, bore) the cylinder to size.
Assemble the pistons and connecting rods: 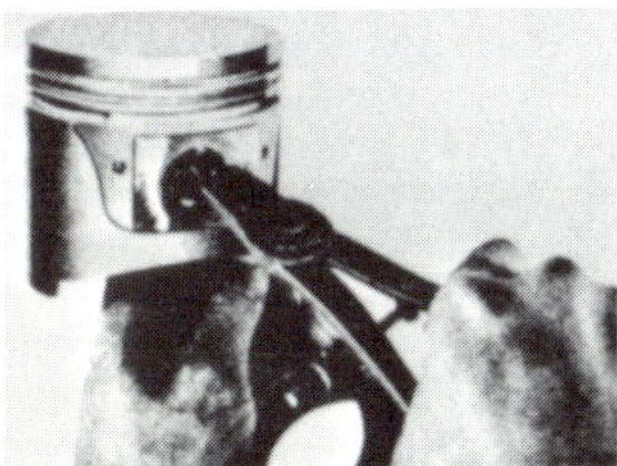 Installing piston pin lock rings (© Nissan Motor Co., Ltd.)	Inspect piston pin, connecting rod small end bushing, and piston bore for galling, scoring, or excessive wear. If evident, replace defective part(s). Measure the I.D. of the piston boss and connecting rod small end, and the O.D. of the piston pin. If within specifications, assemble piston pin and rod. CAUTION: *If piston pin must be pressed in, determine the proper method and use the proper tools; otherwise the piston will distort.* Install the lock rings; ensure that they seat properly. If the parts are not within specifications, determine the service method for the type of engine. In some cases, piston and pin are serviced as an assembly when either is defective. Others specify reaming the piston and connecting rods for an oversize pin. If the connecting rod bushing is worn, it may in many cases be replaced. Reaming the piston and replacing the rod bushing are machine shop operations.

Procedure	*Method*

Clean and inspect the camshaft:

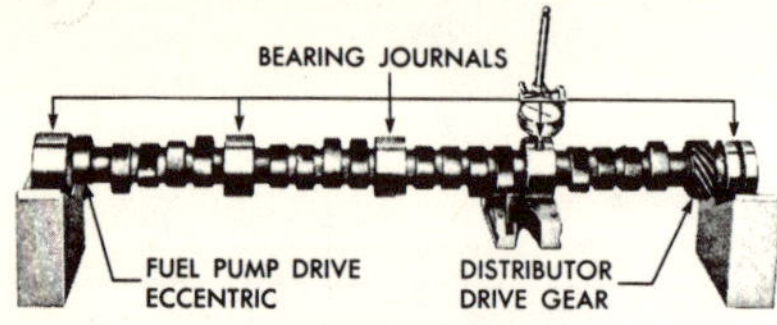

Checking the camshaft for straightness
(© Chevrolet Motor Div. G.M. Corp.)

Degrease the camshaft, using solvent, and clean out all oil holes. Visually inspect cam lobes and bearing journals for excessive wear. If a lobe is questionable, check all lobes as indicated below. If a journal or lobe is worn, the camshaft must be reground or replaced. NOTE: *If a journal is worn, there is a good chance that the bushings are worn.* If lobes and journals appear intact, place the front and rear journals in V-blocks, and rest a dial indicator on the center journal. Rotate the camshaft to check straightness. If deviation exceeds .001″, replace the camshaft.

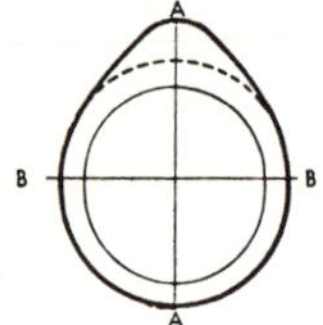

Camshaft lobe measurement
(© Ford Motor Co.)

* Check the camshaft lobes with a micrometer, by measuring the lobes from the nose to base and again at 90° (see illustration). The lift is determined by subtracting the second measurement from the first. If all exhaust lobes and all intake lobes are not identical, the camshaft must be reground or replaced.

Replace the camshaft bearings:

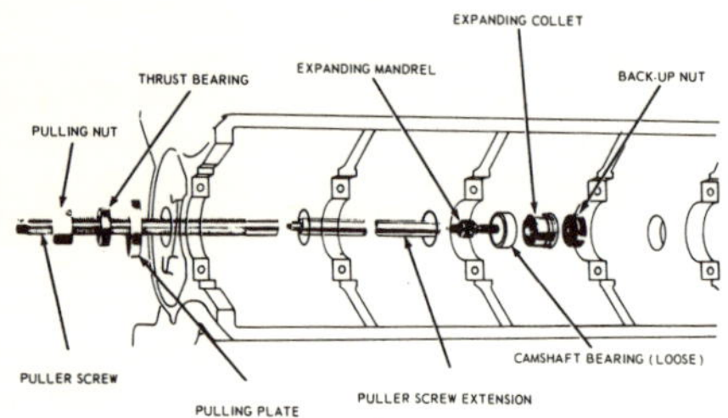

Camshaft removal and installation tool (typical)
(© Ford Motor Co.)

If excessive wear is indicated, or if the engine is being completely rebuilt, camshaft bearings should be replaced as follows: Drive the camshaft rear plug from the block. Assemble the removal puller with its shoulder on the bearing to be removed. Gradually tighten the puller nut until bearing is removed. Remove remaining bearings, leaving the front and rear for last. To remove front and rear bearings, reverse position of the tool, so as to pull the bearings in toward the center of the block. Leave the tool in this position, pilot the new front and rear bearings on the installer, and pull them into position. Return the tool to its original position and pull remaining bearings into position. NOTE: *Ensure that oil holes align when installing bearings.* Replace camshaft rear plug, and stake it into position to aid retention.

Finish hone the cylinders:

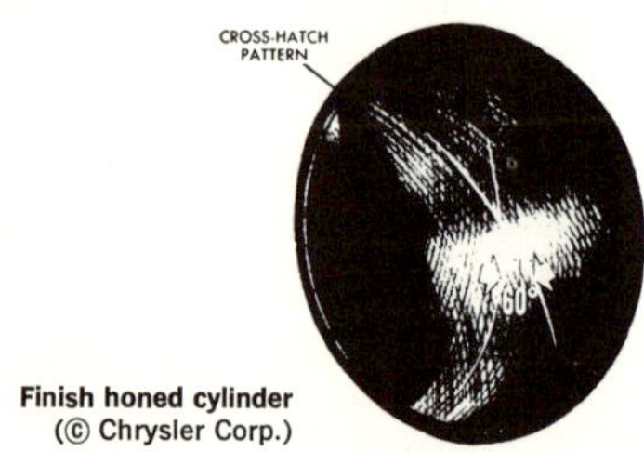

Finish honed cylinder
(© Chrysler Corp.)

Chuck a flexible drive hone into a power drill, and insert it into the cylinder. Start the hone, and move it up and down in the cylinder at a rate which will produce approximately a 60° cross-hatch pattern (see illustration). NOTE: *Do not extend the hone below the cylinder bore.* After developing the pattern, remove the hone and recheck piston fit. Wash the cylinders with a detergent and water solution to remove abrasive dust, dry, and wipe several times with a rag soaked in engine oil.

Procedure	*Method*
Check piston ring end-gap: 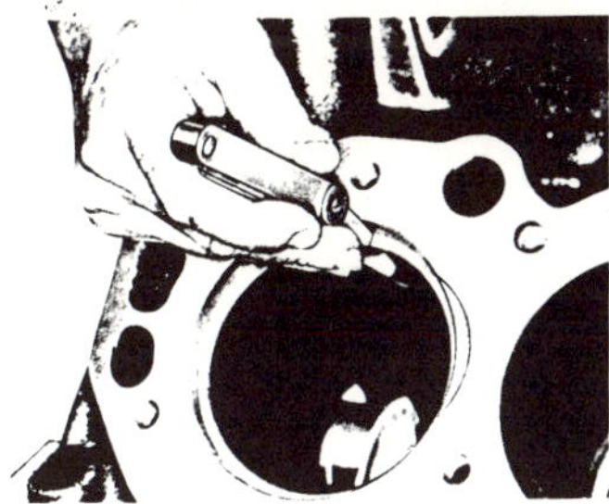 **Checking ring end-gap** (© Chevrolet Motor Div. G.M. Corp.)	Compress the piston rings to be used in a cylinder, one at a time, into that cylinder, and press them approximately 1″ below the deck with an inverted piston. Using feeler gauges, measure the ring end-gap, and compare to specifications. Pull the ring out of the cylinder and file the ends with a fine file to obtain proper clearance. CAUTION: *If inadequate ring end-gap is utilized, ring breakage will result.*
Install the piston rings: 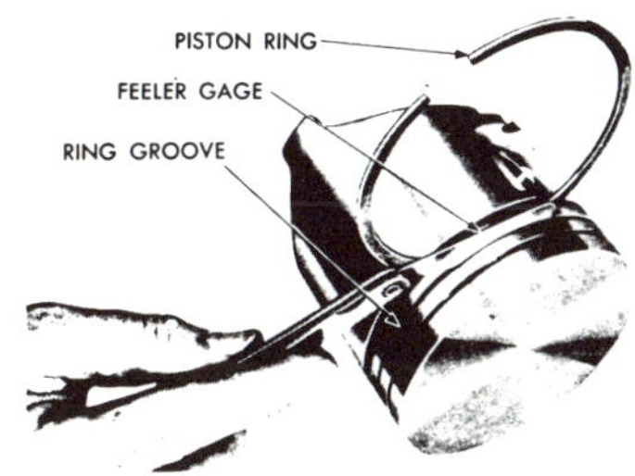 **Checking ring side clearance** (© Chrysler Corp.) 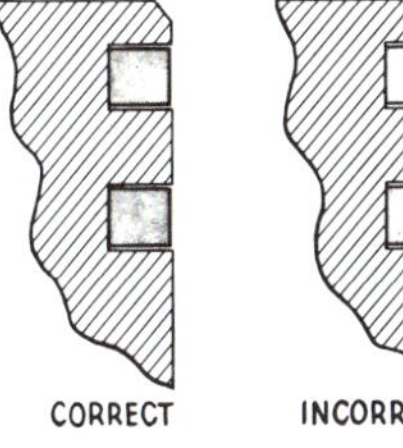 **Piston groove depth** **Correct ring spacer installation**	Inspect the ring grooves in the piston for excessive wear or taper. If necessary, recut the groove(s) for use with an overwidth ring or a standard ring and spacer. If the groove is worn uniformly, overwidth rings, or standard rings and spacers may be installed without recutting. Roll the outside of the ring around the groove to check for burrs or deposits. If any are found, remove with a fine file. Hold the ring in the groove, and measure side clearance. If necessary, correct as indicated above. NOTE: *Always install any additional spacers above the piston ring.* The ring groove must be deep enough to allow the ring to seat below the lands (see illustration). In many cases, a "go-no-go" depth gauge will be provided with the piston rings. Shallow grooves may be corrected by recutting, while deep grooves require some type of filler or expander behind the piston. Consult the piston ring supplier concerning the suggested method. Install the rings on the piston, lowest ring first, using a ring expander. NOTE: *Position the ring markings as specified by the manufacturer (see car section).*
Install the camshaft:	Liberally lubricate the camshaft lobes and journals, and slide the camshaft into the block. CAUTION: *Exercise extreme care to avoid damaging the bearings when inserting the camshaft.* Install and tighten the camshaft thrust plate retaining bolts.
Check camshaft end-play: 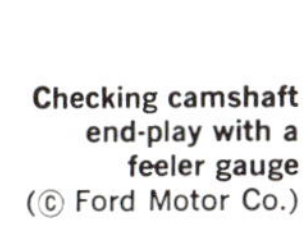  **Checking camshaft end-play with a feeler gauge** (© Ford Motor Co.)	Using feeler gauges, determine whether the clearance between the camshaft boss (or gear) and backing plate is within specifications. Install shims behind the thrust plate, or reposition the camshaft gear and retest end-play.

Procedure	*Method*
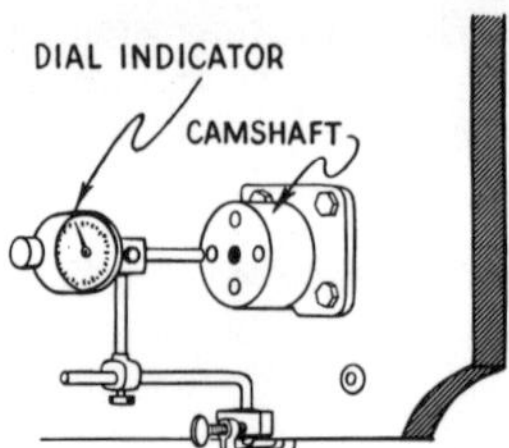 Checking camshaft end-play with a dial indicator	* Mount a dial indicator stand so that the stem of the dial indicator rests on the nose of the camshaft, parallel to the camshaft axis. Push the camshaft as far in as possible and zero the gauge. Move the camshaft outward to determine the amount of camshaft end-play. If the end-play is not within tolerance, install shims behind the thrust plate, or re-position the camshaft gear and retest.
Install the rear main seal (where applicable):  Seating the rear main seal (© Buick Div. G.M. Corp.)	Position the block with the bearing saddles facing upward. Lay the rear main seal in its groove and press it lightly into its seat. Place a piece of pipe the same diameter as the crankshaft journal into the saddle, and firmly seat the seal. Hold the pipe in position, and trim the ends of the seal flush if required.
Install the crankshaft: 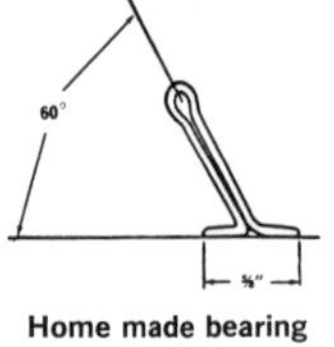 Home made bearing roll-out pin (© Pontiac Div. G.M. Corp.) 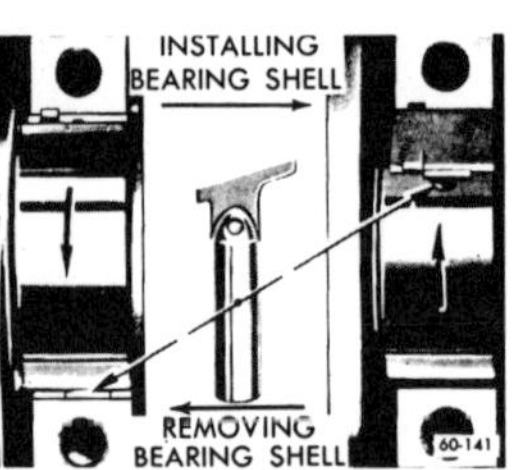 Removal and installation of upper bearing insert using a roll-out pin (© Buick Div. G.M. Corp.)	Thoroughly clean the main bearing saddles and caps. Place the upper halves of the bearing inserts on the saddles and press into position. NOTE: *Ensure that the oil holes align.* Press the corresponding bearing inserts into the main bearing caps. Lubricate the upper main bearings, and lay the crankshaft in position. Place a strip of Plastigage on each of the crankshaft journals, install the main caps, and torque to specifications. Remove the main caps, and compare the Plastigage to the scale on the Plastigage envelope. If clearances are within tolerances, remove the Plastigage, turn the crankshaft 90°, wipe off all oil and retest. If all clearances are correct, remove all Plastigage, thoroughly

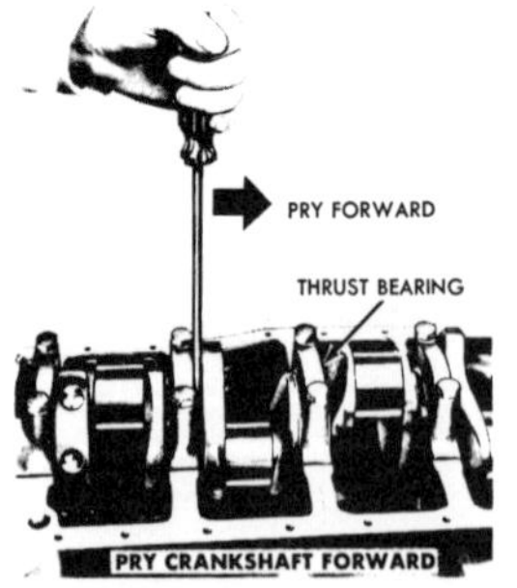

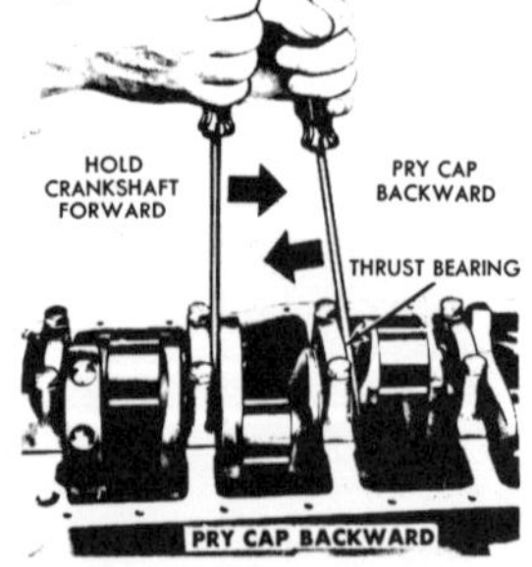

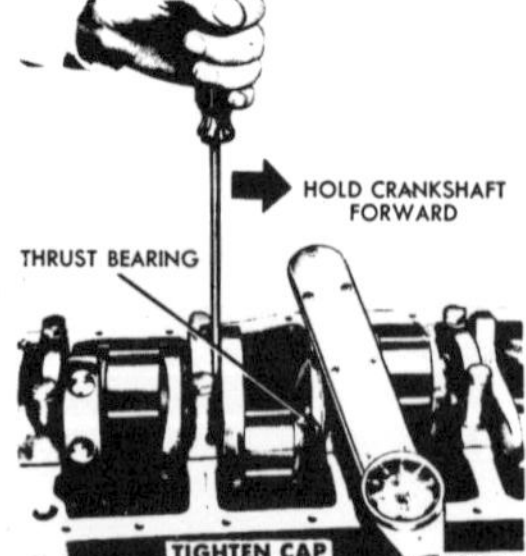

Aligning the thrust bearing
(© Ford Motor Co.)

Procedure	Method
	lubricate the main caps and bearing journals, and install the main caps. If clearances are not within tolerance, the upper bearing inserts may be removed, without removing the crankshaft, using a bearing roll out pin (see illustration). Roll in a bearing that will provide proper clearance, and retest. Torque all main caps, excluding the thrust bearing cap, to specifications. Tighten the thrust bearing cap finger tight. To properly align the thrust bearing, pry the crankshaft the extent of its axial travel several times, the last movement held toward the front of the engine, and torque the thrust bearing cap to specifications. Determine the crankshaft end-play (see below), and bring within tolerance with thrust washers.
Measure crankshaft end-play:  Checking crankshaft end-play with a dial indicator (© Ford Motor Co.) 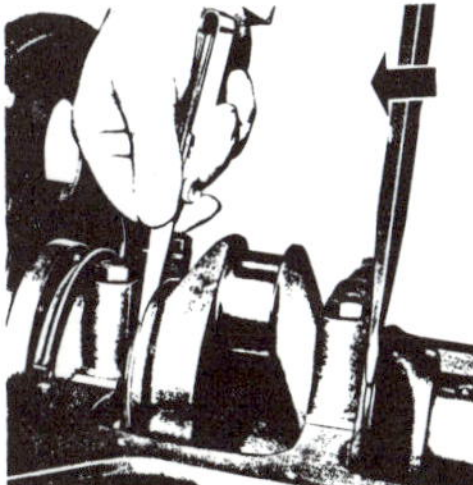 Checking crankshaft end-play with a feeler gauge (© Chevrolet Div. (G.M. Corp.)	Mount a dial indicator stand on the front of the block, with the dial indicator stem resting on the nose of the crankshaft, parallel to the crankshaft axis. Pry the crankshaft the extent of its travel rearward, and zero the indicator. Pry the crankshaft forward and record crankshaft end-play. NOTE: *Crankshaft end-play also may be measured at the thrust bearing, using feeler gauges* (see illustration).
Install the pistons:	Press the upper connecting rod bearing halves into the connecting rods, and the lower halves into the connecting rod caps. Position the piston ring gaps according to specifications (see car section), and lubricate the pistons. Install a ring compresser on a piston, and press two long (8″) pieces of plastic tubing over the rod bolts. Using the plastic tubes as a guide, press the pistons into the bores and onto the crankshaft with a wooden hammer handle. After seating the rod on the crankshaft journal, remove the tubes and install the cap finger tight. Install the remaining pistons in the same man-

Procedure	*Method*
 Tubing used as guide when installing a piston (© Oldsmobile Div. G.M. Corp.) 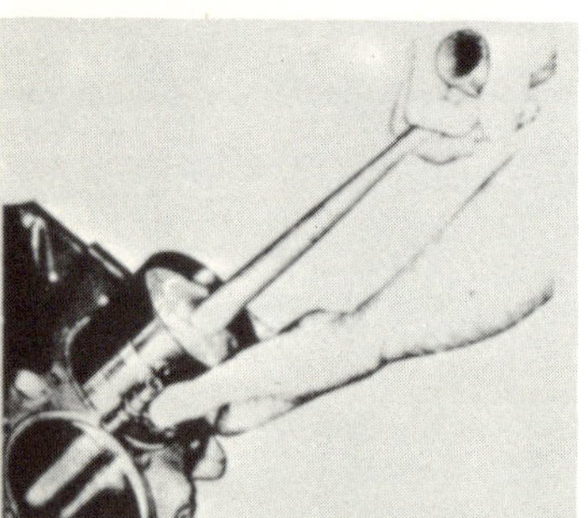 Installing a piston (© Chevrolet Div. G.M. Corp.)	ner. Invert the engine and check the bearing clearance at two points (90° apart) on each journal with Plastigage. NOTE: *Do not turn the crankshaft with Plastigage installed.* If clearance is within tolerances, remove *all* Plastigage, thoroughly lubricate the journals, and torque the rod caps to specifications. If clearance is not within specifications, install different thickness bearing inserts and recheck. CAUTION: *Never shim or file the connecting rods or caps.* Always install plastic tube sleeves over the rod bolts when the caps are not installed, to protect the crankshaft journals.
Check connecting rod side clearance: 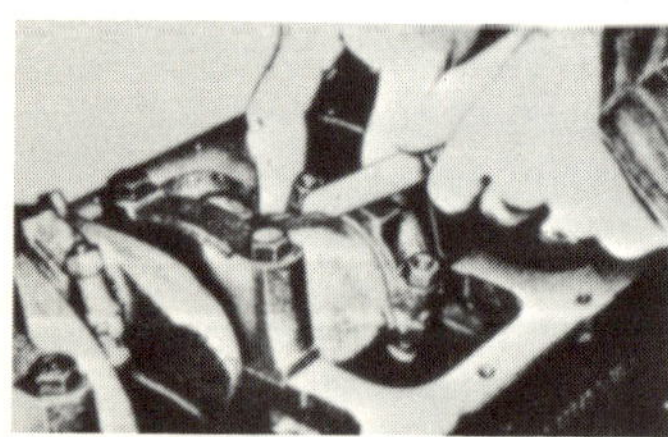 Checking connecting rod side clearance (© Chevrolet Div. G.M. Corp.)	Determine the clearance between the sides of the connecting rods and the crankshaft, using feeler gauges. If clearance is below the minimum tolerance, the rod may be machined to provide adequate clearance. If clearance is excessive, substitute an unworn rod, and recheck. If clearance is still outside specifications, the crankshaft must be welded and reground, or replaced.
Inspect the timing chain:	Visually inspect the timing chain for broken or loose links, and replace the chain if any are found. If the chain will flex sideways, it must be replaced. Install the timing chain as specified. NOTE: *If the original timing chain is to be reused, install it in its original position.*

Procedure	*Method*
Check timing gear backlash and runout:	Mount a dial indicator with its stem resting on a tooth of the camshaft gear (as illustrated). Rotate the gear until all slack is removed, and zero the indicator. Rotate the gear in the opposite direction until slack is removed, and record gear backlash. Mount the indicator with its stem resting on the edge of the camshaft gear, parallel to the axis of the camshaft. Zero the indicator, and turn the camshaft gear one full turn, recording the runout. If either backlash or runout exceed specifications, replace the worn gear(s).

Checking camshaft gear backlash
(© Chevrolet Div. G.M. Corp.)

Checking camshaft gear runout
(© Chevrolet Div. G.M. Corp.)

Completing the Rebuilding Process

Following the above procedures, complete the rebuilding process as follows:

Fill the oil pump with oil, to prevent cavitating (sucking air) on initial engine start up. Install the oil pump and the pickup tube on the engine. Coat the oil pan gasket as necessary, and install the gasket and the oil pan. Mount the flywheel and the crankshaft vibrational damper or pulley on the crankshaft. NOTE: *Always use new bolts when installing the flywheel.* Inspect the clutch shaft pilot bushing in the crankshaft. If the bushing is excessively worn, remove it with an expanding puller and a slide hammer, and tap a new bushing into place.

Position the engine, cylinder head side up. Lubricate the lifters, and install them into their bores. Install the cylinder head, and torque it as specified in the car section. Insert the pushrods (where applicable), and install the rocker shaft(s) (if so equipped) or position the rocker arms on the pushrods. If solid lifters are utilized, adjust the valves to the "cold" specifications.

Mount the intake and exhaust manifolds, the carburetor(s), the distributor and spark plugs. Adjust the point gap and the static ignition timing. Mount all accessories and install the engine in the car. Fill the radiator with coolant, and the crankcase with high quality engine oil.

Break-in Procedure

Start the engine, and allow it to run at low speed for a few minutes, while checking for leaks. Stop the engine, check the oil level, and fill as necessary. Restart the engine, and fill the cooling system to capacity. Check the point dwell angle and adjust the ignition timing and the valves. Run the engine at low to medium speed (800-2500 rpm) for approximately ½ hour, and retorque the cylinder head bolts. Road test the car, and check again for leaks.

Follow the manufacturer's recommended engine break-in procedure and maintenance schedule for new engines.

Chapter 4
Emission Controls and Fuel System

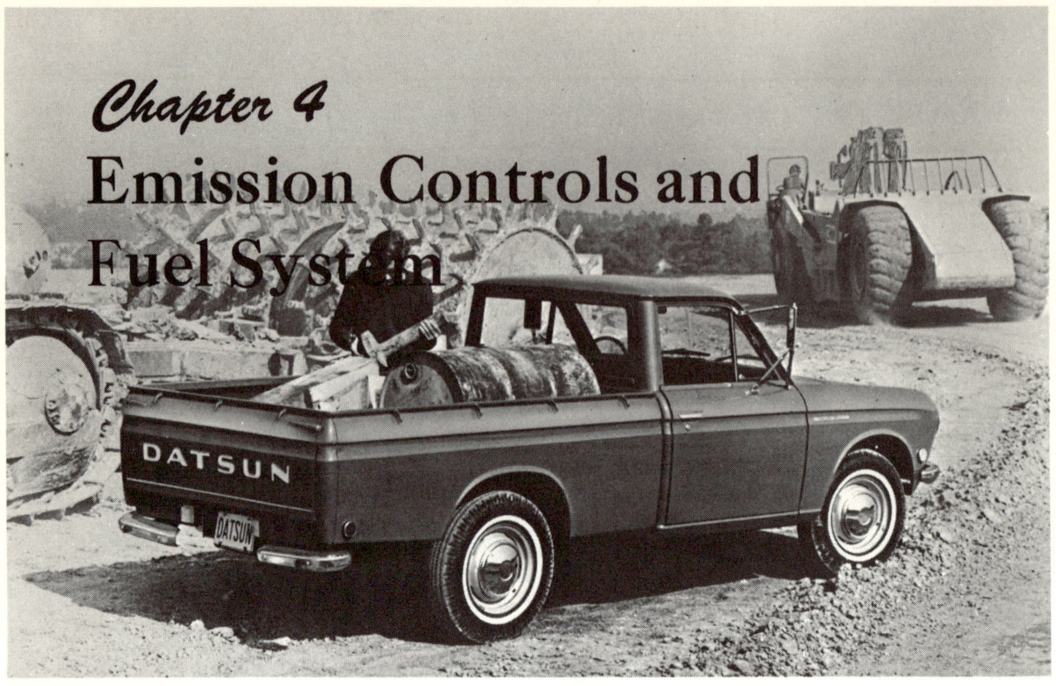

Emission Controls

Various systems are used to control crankcase vapors, exhaust emissions, and fuel vapors. The accompanying chart shows the systems used with various models and engines.

Year (approximate)	*Model*	*Engine*	*Emission Control Systems*
1969	PL510, WPL510	L16	1,3
1969	SPL311	R	2,3
1969	SRL311	U20	2,3
1969	L520, L521	J	2,4
1969	L60	P	2,4
Starting 1970	PL510, WPL510, PL521	L16	1,3,4,5
Starting 1970	SPL311	R	2,3,4,5
Starting 1970	SRL311	U20	2,3,5
Starting 1971	HLS30	L24	1,3,4,5
Starting 1971	LB110, KLB110	A12	1,4,5

1. Closed crankcase ventilation system
2. Sealed crankcase ventilation system
3. Air pump system
4. Engine modification system
5. Fuel vapor control system

CRANKCASE VENTILATION SYSTEM

The sealed system consists simply of a tube connecting the valve cover to the carburetor air cleaner. The oil filler cap and the dipstick are sealed. No provision is made for admitting ventilation air into the crankcase. Crankcase vapors are drawn through the carburetor and burned along with the air/fuel mixture.

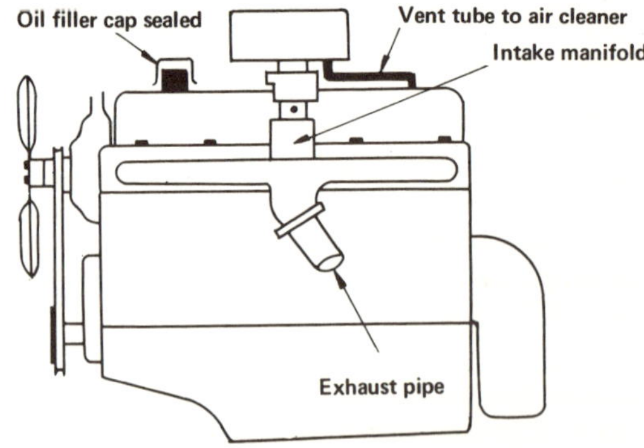

Sealed crankcase ventilation system

The closed system is identical to the sealed system, with the addition of a tube containing a variable orifice valve between the crankcase and the intake manifold. Under high vacuum conditions (idle), vapors are drawn into the intake manifold through the valve. The tube connected to the air cleaner admits ventilation air through the crankcase. Under low vacuum conditions (full-throttle), vapors are drawn through the carburetor as in the sealed system.

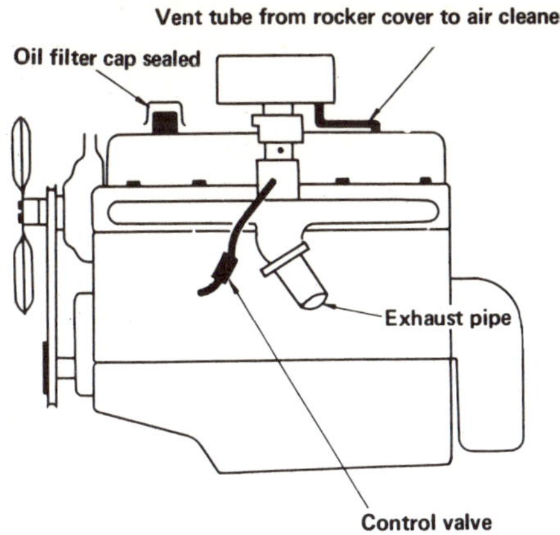

Closed crankcase ventilation system. The control valve is the variable orifice valve referred to in the text.

The crankcase ventilation system requires no periodic maintenance other than replacement of the variable orifice valve, should it become clogged.

Variable Orifice Valve Test

1. With engine idling, remove hose from valve on intake manifold.
2. A hissing sound should be heard and a vacuum felt at the valve inlet.
3. If valve is plugged, replace. Do not clean.

AIR PUMP SYSTEM

In this system, an air injection pump, driven by the engine, compresses, distributes, and injects filtered air into the exhaust port of each cylinder. The air combines with unburned hydrocarbons and carbon monoxide to produce harmless compounds. The system includes an air cleaner, the belt driven air pump, a check valve, and an anti-backfire valve.

The air pump draws air through a hose connected to the carburetor air cleaner or to a separate air cleaner. The pump is a rotary vane unit with an integral pressure regulating valve. The pump outlet pressure passes through a check valve which prevents exhaust gas from entering the pump in case of insufficient pump outlet pressure. An anti-backfire valve admits air from the air pump into the intake manifold on deceleration to prevent backfiring in the exhaust manifold.

All engines with the air pump system have a series of minor alterations to accommodate the system. These are:

1. Special close-tolerance carburetor.

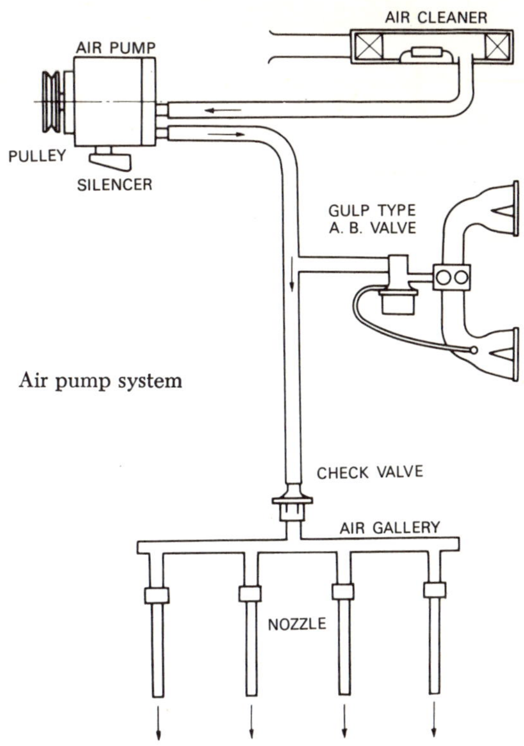

Air pump system

Most engines, except L16, require a slightly rich idle mixture adjustment.
2. Distributor with special advance curve. Ignition timing is retarded about 10° at idle in most cases.
3. Cooling system changes such as larger fan, higher fan speed, and thermostatic fan clutch. This is required to offset the increase in temperature caused by retarded timing at idle. The U20 engine has a thermal modulator valve which gives full distributor vacuum advance at idle if engine temperature becomes excessive.
4. Faster idle speed.
5. Heated air intake on some engines.

The only periodic maintenance required on the air pump system is replacement of the air filter element and adjustment of the drive belt.

Air Pump System Tests and Repairs

Air Pump Test, R&R

To test air pump output pressure:

1. Engine must be at normal operating temperature.
2. Stop engine. Disconnect air supply hose from check valve at exhaust manifold.

3. Start engine. Check pump pressure output at 1,500 rpm. With L16 engine, pressure should be .47″ (12 mm.) Hg or more. With R, U20, or L24 engine, pressure should be .63″ (16 mm.) Hg or more.

To remove and replace air pump:

1. Disconnect hoses from pump.
2. Remove bolt holding pump to belt adjustment arm or adjusting bracket.
3. Unbolt pump from mounting bracket. Remove belt.
4. Remove pump from car.
5. Reverse procedure to install, adjusting the belt to have about 1/2″ play under thumb pressure at the longest span between pulleys.

Check Valve Test, R&R

To test check valve action:

1. Engine must be at normal operating temperature.
2. Stop engine. Disconnect air supply hose from check valve at exhaust manifold.
3. Valve plate inside valve body should be lightly positioned against the valve seat away from the air distributor manifold.
4. Insert a small screwdriver into valve and depress valve plate. Plate should reset freely when released.
5. Start engine. Increase speed to 1,500 rpm and check for exhaust leakage. Valve pulsation or vibration at idle is a normal condition.

To remove and replace check valve:

1. Remove check valve from air gallery pipe, holding the air gallery flange with a wrench.
2. On reinstallation, the proper torque is 65-76 ft. lbs.

Anti-Backfire Valve Test, R&R

To test the anti-backfire valve:

1. Engine must be at normal operating temperature.
2. Disconnect air hose to intake manifold at anti-backfire valve. Plug the hose.
3. Open and close the throttle rapidly. Air flow should be felt at the valve for 1-2 seconds on decleration. If no air flow is felt or flow is felt continuously for more than 2 seconds, replace valve.

To remove anti-backfire valve, simply disconnect the hoses.

Thermal Modulator Test

The thermal modulator is used only on the U20 engine. It provides full vacuum advance at idle if coolant temperature exceeds about 220°F. To test the unit:

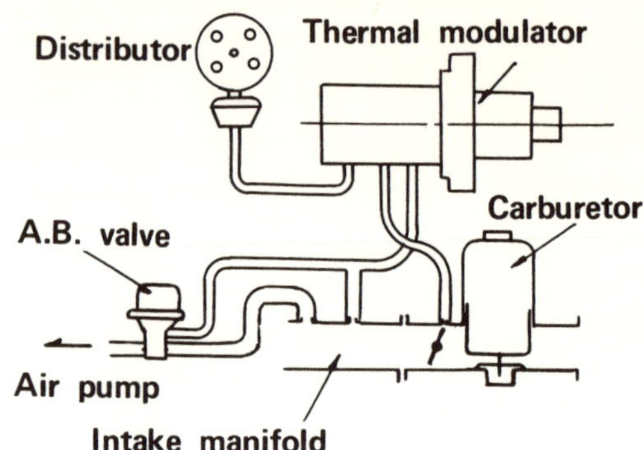

Thermal modulator, U20 engine

1. Remove vacuum tube at distributor.
2. Connect a vacuum gauge to the tube.
3. Run engine until it reaches normal operating temperature.
4. Vacuum should be no more than 4″ (102 mm.) Hg. If it is excessive, the modulator is leaking internally and must be replaced.

ENGINE MODIFICATION SYSTEM

Engine modifications used on the L520 or L521 pickup with the J engine are:

1. Special carburetor calibrated about three percent leaner than normal for cruise conditions. The idle speed is higher than normal and the extent of idle mixture adjustment is limited. A solenoid valve shuts off the idle fuel system on deceleration. The solenoid valve is regulated by four switches. The throttle valve switch attached to the carburetor is on when the throttle valve is open. The vacuum switch connected to the intake manifold is on when manifold vacuum is less than 22.8″ Hg. The clutch switch on the pedal bracket is on when the pedal is depressed. The neutral switch on the transmission rear extension is on when the transmission is in neutral. If any of these switches are on, the solenoid valve will not shut off the fuel.
2. Heated air intake to prevent icing with the leaner carburetor mixture.
3. Maximum ignition timing retard at low speed and small retard at middle speed

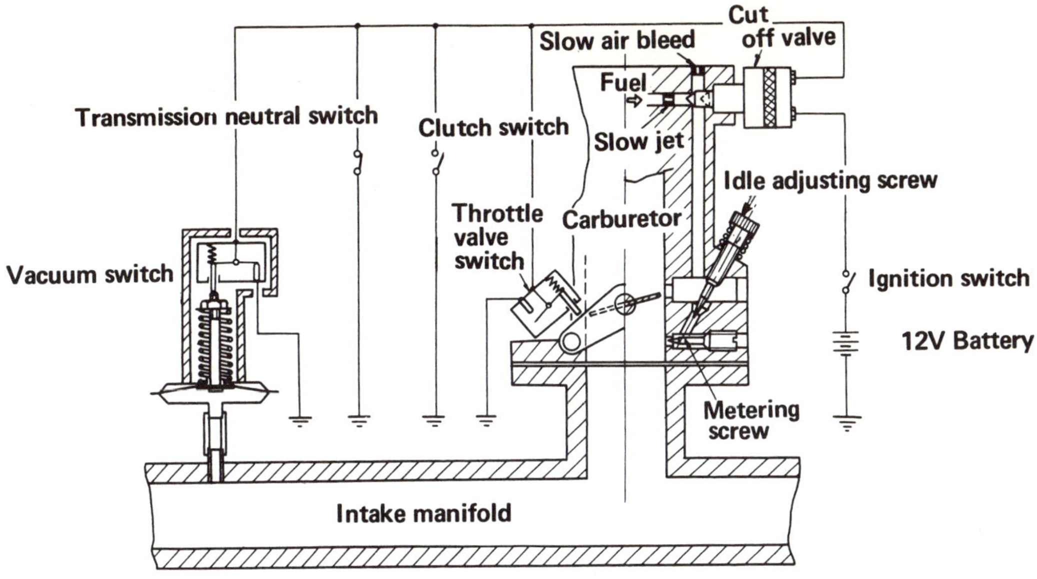

Engine modification system, pickup with J engine

ranges. Normal advance is provided at high speeds.

Engine modifications used on the L60 Nissan Patrol with the P engine are:

1. Rochester carburetor with leaner idle and low speed mixture. Faster idle speed.
2. Refined manifold heating for lessened cold starting emissions.
3. Retarded ignition timing at idle and low speed.
4. Vacuum control valve providing advanced ignition timing on deceleration.

Engine modifications used on vehicles with the L16 engine are:

1. Distributor with a secondary set of contact points which are retarded 5°. These secondary points are operational only when cruising or accelerating with a partially open throttle in third gear with manual transmission, or over 13 mph with automatic transmission. A speed sensor is located at the speedometer on automatic transmission models.
2. A solenoid valve in the carburetor opens to supply a lean fuel and air mixture, bypassing the throttle valve, in third gear or over 13 mph as above. The solenoid valve will not open if overridden by a closed throttle switch, a wide open throttle switch, a neutral switch, or a clutch disengaged switch. This arrangement is operational primarily during deceleration, when high intake manifold vacuum is present.

Engine modifications on the SPL311

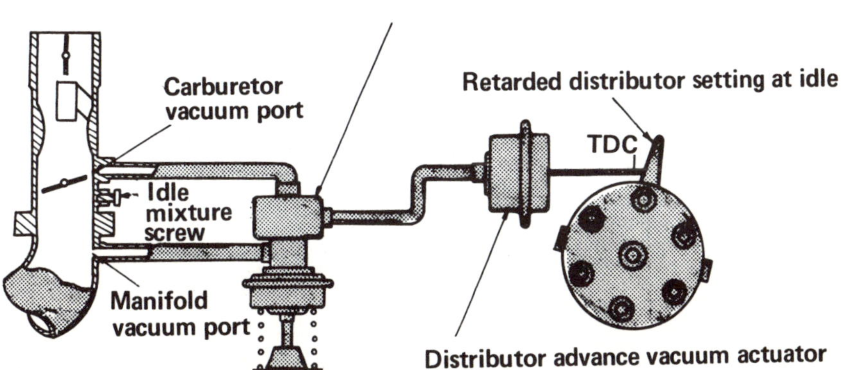

Vacuum control valve which regulates ignition timing, L60 Nissan Parol with P engine

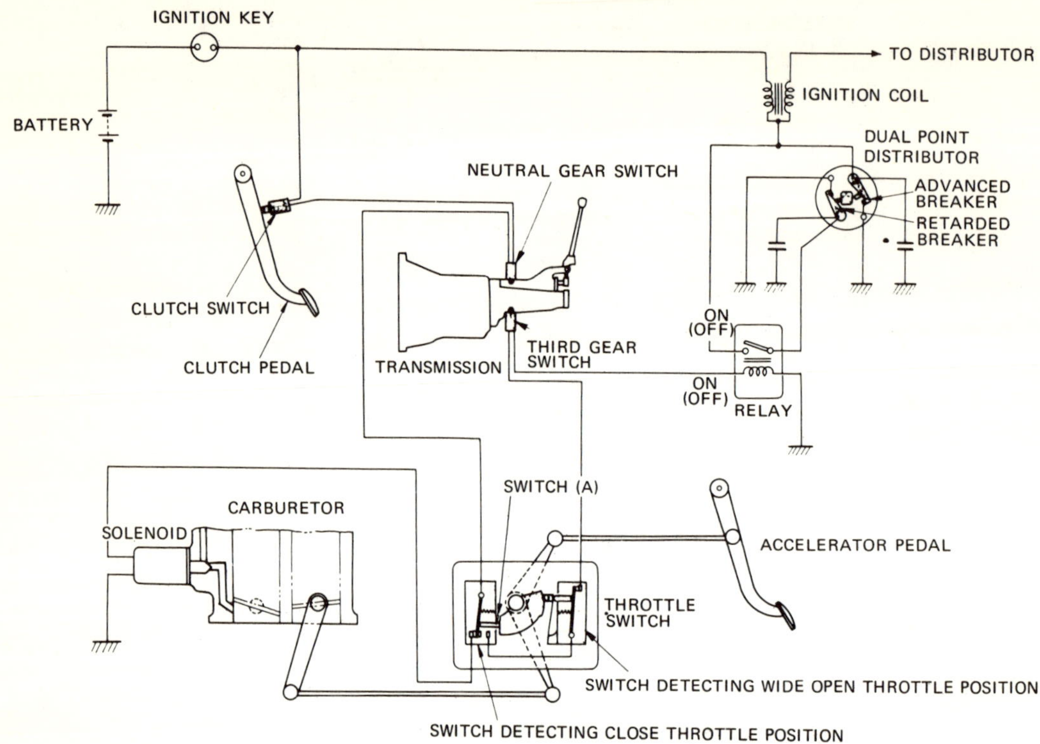

IGNITION KEY
TO DISTRIBUTOR
IGNITION COIL
BATTERY
DUAL POINT DISTRIBUTOR
NEUTRAL GEAR SWITCH
ADVANCED BREAKER
RETARDED BREAKER
CLUTCH SWITCH
ON (OFF)
THIRD GEAR SWITCH
CLUTCH PEDAL
TRANSMISSION
ON (OFF)
RELAY
SWITCH (A)
CARBURETOR
SOLENOID
ACCELERATOR PEDAL
THROTTLE SWITCH
SWITCH DETECTING WIDE OPEN THROTTLE POSITION
SWITCH DETECTING CLOSE THROTTLE POSITION

Engine modification system, PL510 and WPL510, manual transmission, L16 engine

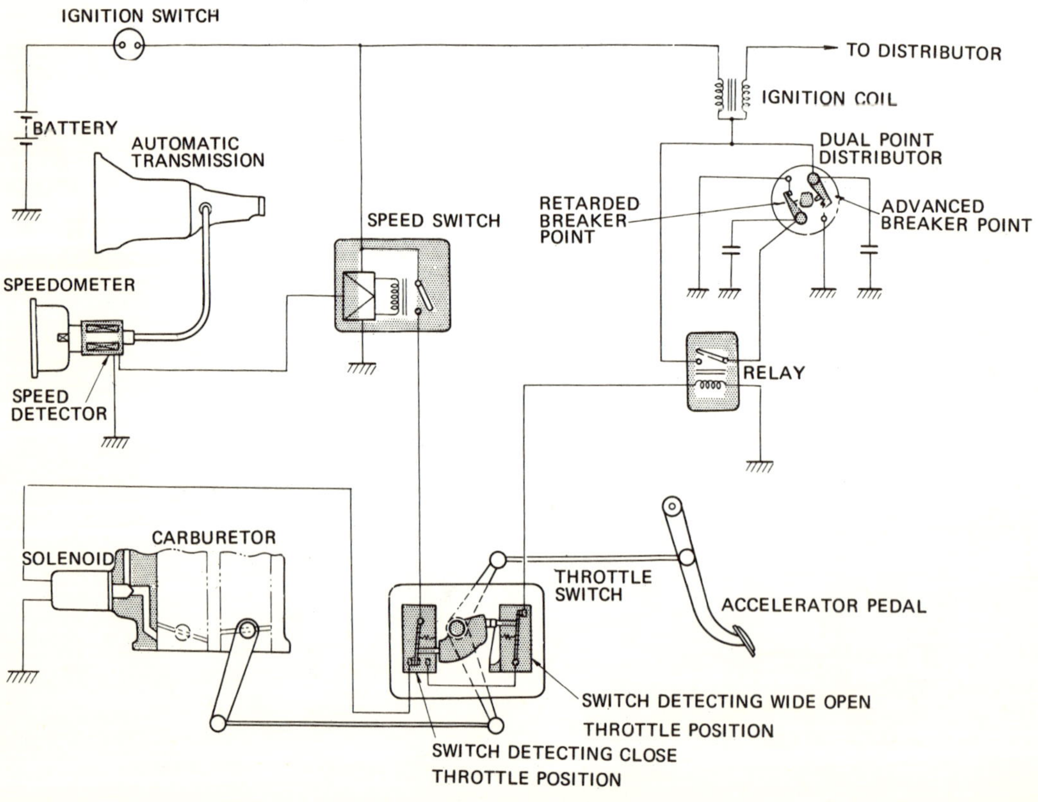
IGNITION SWITCH
TO DISTRIBUTOR
IGNITION COIL
BATTERY
AUTOMATIC TRANSMISSION
DUAL POINT DISTRIBUTOR
RETARDED BREAKER POINT
ADVANCED BREAKER POINT
SPEED SWITCH
SPEEDOMETER
SPEED DETECTOR
RELAY
CARBURETOR
SOLENOID
THROTTLE SWITCH
ACCELERATOR PEDAL
SWITCH DETECTING WIDE OPEN THROTTLE POSITION
SWITCH DETECTING CLOSE THROTTLE POSITION

Engine modification system, PL510 and WPL510, automatic transmission, L16 engine

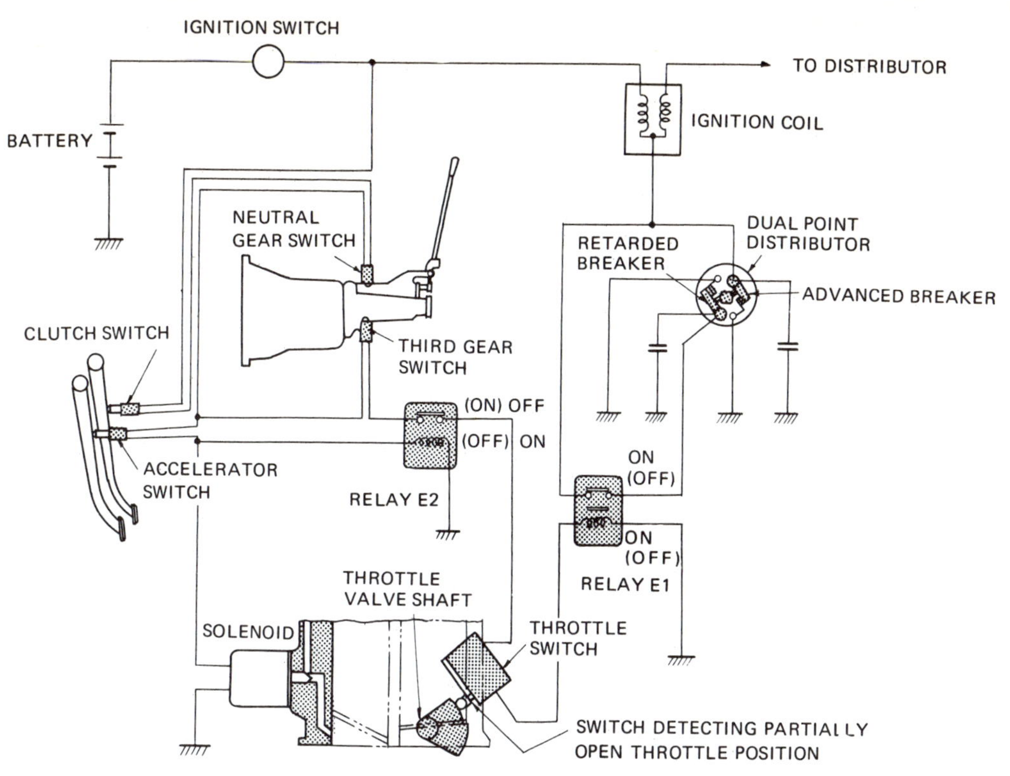

Engine modification system, PL521 pickup, L16 engine

By-pass valve operation

T/M \ Clutch	Engaged	Disengaged
3rd, 4th	Open	Close
1st, 2nd, neutral reverse	Close	Close

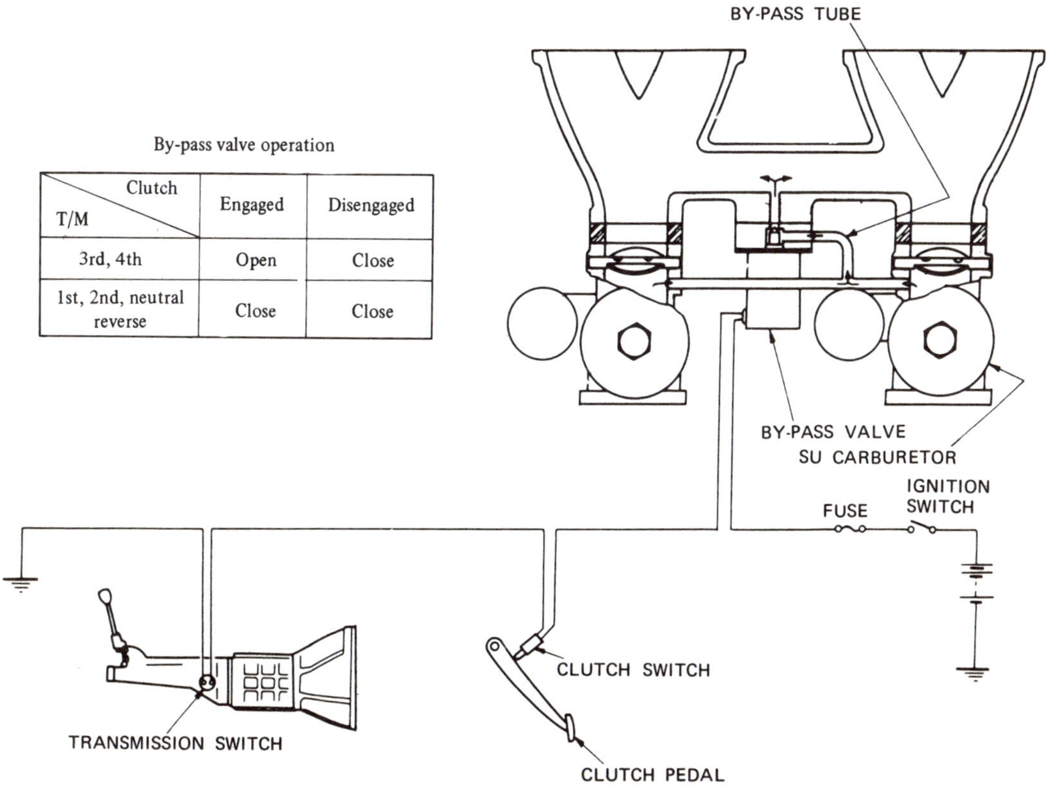

BY-PASS TUBE
BY-PASS VALVE
SU CARBURETOR
IGNITION
SWITCH
FUSE
CLUTCH SWITCH
TRANSMISSION SWITCH
CLUTCH PEDAL

Engine modification system, SPL311 sportscar, R engine

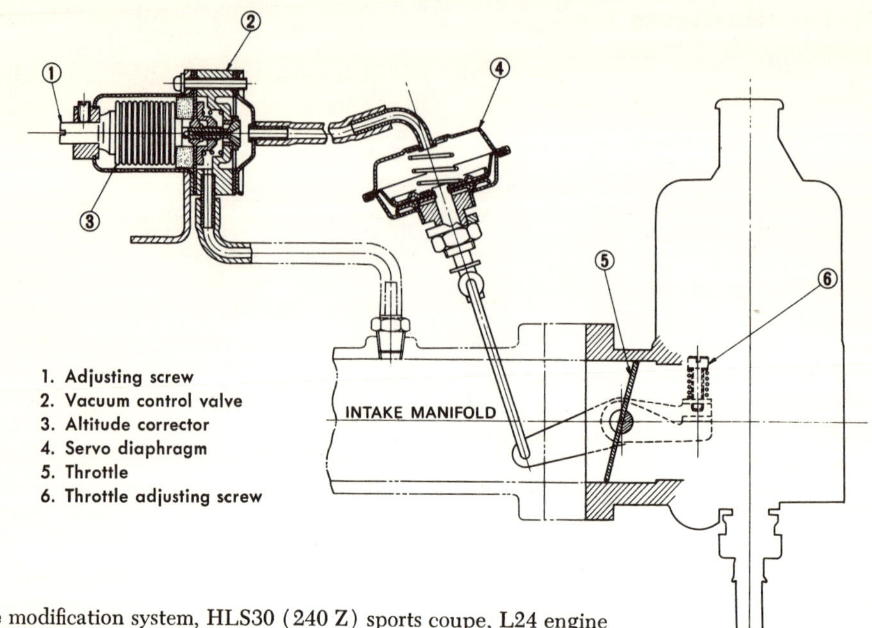

Engine modification system, HLS30 (240 Z) sports coupe, L24 engine

sports roadster with the R engine consist only of a solenoid valve which bypasses a lean fuel and air mixture into the intake manifold for improved combustion. The solenoid valve is overridden if the clutch is not depressed or the transmission is not in third or fourth gear. This arrangement is operational primarily during deceleration, when high intake manifold vacuum is present.

The engine modification system used on the LB110 and KLB110 1200 series with the A12 engine is relatively simple. It requires only a throttle positioner which holds the throttle slightly open on deceleration. A vacuum control valve connected to the intake manifold causes a vacuum servo to hold the throttle open slightly during the high vacuum condition of deceleration. The control valve is compensated for the effects of altitude and atmospheric pressure. The carburetor and distributor are specially calibrated for this engine.

The engine modification system for the HLS30 (240 Z) sports coupe with the L24 engine is quite similar to that for the A12 engine, using a vacuum control valve, vacuum servo, and throttle positioner. The HLS30 with automatic transmission has a dual point distributor. One set of points has a timing setting of 0°TDC and the other a setting of 10°BTDC. A thermo-switch under the instrument panel activates the advanced timing set of points for easier starting and warmup when the temperature inside the car is below 40°F.

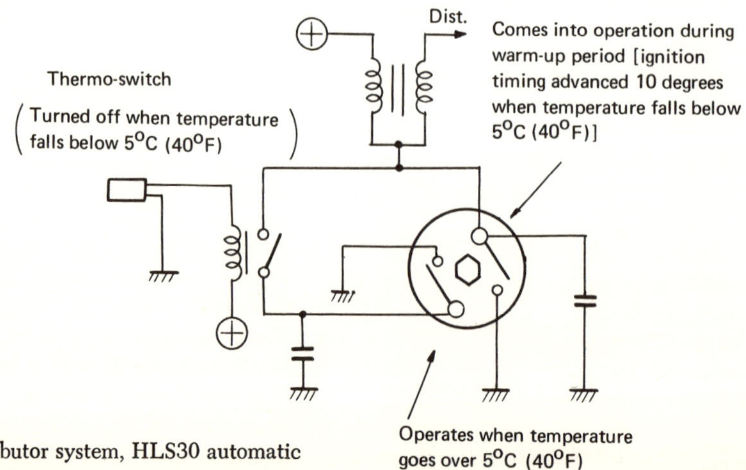

Dual point distributor system, HLS30 automatic

Engine Modification System Tests, Adjustments

Throttle Positioner Adjustment—L24, A12 Engines

Only the A12 and L24 engines use a throttle positioner. This device is regulated by a vacuum control valve with an adjusting screw.

1. Engine must be at normal operating temperature. A tachometer must be connected.
2. Increase engine speed to 3,000 rpm for A12 or 2,000 rpm for L24.
3. Release throttle. Time required to slow to 1,000 rpm should be:

Engine	*Transmission*	*Time in seconds*
A12	Manual	3.5-4.5
A12	Automatic	2.5-3.5
L24	Manual	3.0

4. To adjust time lag, first loosen lockscrew on vacuum control valve. Turn adjusting screw clockwise to increase time lag, and counterclockwise to decrease.
5. Tighten lockscrew.
6. Repeat Steps 2-5 to check adjustment. If adjustment is correct, engine will settle down to correct idle speed.

Idle Fuel Cutoff—J Engine

The solenoid valve used in this system is opened by electric current and spring-loaded to the closed position. If the solenoid valve circuit is shorted to ground by any one of the four circuit switches being in its on position, the idle fuel supply is cut off. Thus a short circuit or a sticking switch in the circuit will cause the engine to give the symptoms of a clogged idle fuel system. These are stalling, rough idle and low speed operation, but normal operation at higher speeds.

To test the solenoid valve:

1. With the engine running, disconnect the solenoid wires. Valve should cut off fuel and stall engine.
2. Ground one solenoid terminal. Connect battery voltage to the other. Valve should click open.

To test the function of all the system switches, disconnect the wires of the solenoid valve and connect them to a test light. Disconnect the wires of the clutch switch, vacuum switch, and neutral switch.

1. Turn ignition switch on. Do not start engine.
2. Reconnect transmission neutral switch. Check that test light is on with transmission in neutral and off in all other positions. Disconnect transmission neutral switch.
3. Reconnect throttle valve switch. Depress accelerator pedal. Test light should be on. Release accelerator. Light should be off. Disconnect throttle valve switch. Correct adjustment requires that the throttle arm depress the contact arm of the switch about .02″ at rest.
4. Reconnect clutch switch. Check that test light is on when pedal is down and off when pedal is released. Disconnect clutch switch.
5. Reconnect solenoid valve, installing the test lamp in series with the solenoid so that it will indicate when current is supplied. Reconnect transmission neutral switch, throttle valve switch, and vacuum switch but not clutch switch. T-connect a vacuum gauge into the vacuum line between the intake manifold and the vacuum switch. Start and warm up the engine. Depress clutch and shift transmission into gear. Race engine and close throttle rapidly. On deceleration, vacuum should rise and test light should go off. Light should go back on when gauge drops to 20.9-21.6″ Hg.
6. Reconnect all leads.

Distributor Vacuum Control Valve—P Engine

1. The engine must be at normal operating temperature.
2. T-connect a vacuum gauge into the distributor vacuum line.
3. Start engine. Hold speed of 2,000 rpm in neutral for about 5 seconds. Release throttle. When throttle is released, vacuum should increase to above 16″ Hg and remain steady for at least 1 second. The vacuum must fall below 4″ Hg within 3 seconds after the throttle is released.
4. Turn vacuum control valve adjusting screw counterclockwise to increase the time the vacuum remains above 4″ Hg. One turn of the adjusting screw will change the setting by about 1/2″ Hg. If

	IGNITION	ENGINE OR CAR OPERATIONS	Vacuum switch	Throttle valve switch	Clutch switch	Transmission neutral switch	Cut-off valve
PARKING	OFF	None	OFF	OFF	OFF	OFF	OFF
CAR STOPP-ING	ON	Engine starting & warming up with choke	ON (ON → OFF)	ON	OFF	ON	ON
		Idling	ON	OFF	OFF	ON	ON
		Engine racing	ON → OFF → CN	OFF → ON → OFF	OFF	ON	ON
CRUIS-ING	ON	Car starting & accelerating	ON	ON	OFF → ON → OFF	OFF	ON
		Gear shifting (neutral)	OFF	OFF	ON	ON	ON
		Cruising	ON	ON	OFF	OFF	ON
		Decelerating	OFF	OFF	OFF	OFF	OFF
		Just before car stopping	OFF → ON	OFF	OFF → ON → OFF	ON	ON
REMARK	Electric current ON		I. manifold V.P.; 20.9 ∿ 21.6 inHg	Throttle valve; opening	Pedal; operating	In neutral	
	Electric current OFF		I. manifold V.P.; less than 22.8 inHg	Throttle valve; closing	Pedal; not operating	1st, 2nd, 3rd, 4th rev. gear positions	

Switch position chart, pickup, J engine

adjustment is impossible, replace the valve.

Solenoid Bypass Valve—R Engine

This system uses a solenoid valve which is opened by electric current and spring loaded to the closed position. To test system operation:

1. Switch ignition on.
2. Shift into third or fourth gear.
3. Release clutch pedal slowly. When the clutch switch reaches its closed position, the bypass valve should make an audible click.
4. The operation of the two individual switches can be tested by use of a test light or an ohmmeter. The clutch switch should be closed when the pedal is released. The transmission switch should be closed only in third and fourth gears.

Solenoid Bypass Valve—L16 Engine With Manual Transmission

The solenoid valve is opened by electric current and spring-loaded to the closed position. To test system operation:

1. Disconnect solenoid valve ground lead (black wire). Connect an ammeter between the lead terminal and ground. A test light can also be used; but this only indicates whether current is present or not, while an ammeter measures the amount of current.
2. Switch ignition on.
3. With throttle closed, transmission in gear, and clutch pedal released, ammeter should read about .4 amps. In any other condition, ammeter should read 0 amps.
4. If ammeter reading is not as specified, check each switch and adjust or replace it as necessary. On throttle valve switch, clearance between cam and microswitch body should be .032″.

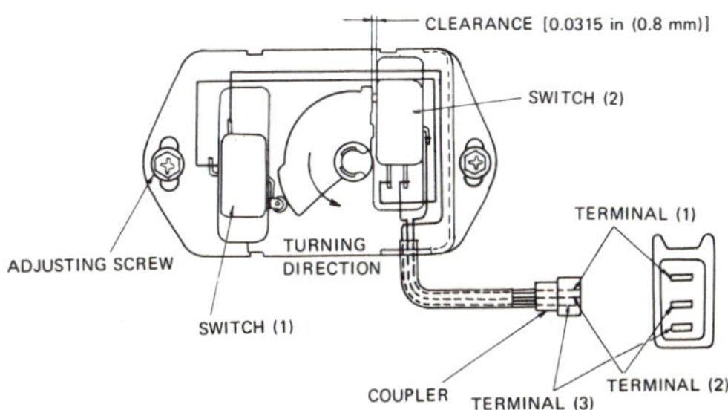

Throttle valve switch, L16 engine, manual transmission

Refer to the switch position charts for details.

5. Remove ammeter and replace solenoid valve ground lead. Start engine. Connect a jumper wire between the battery output terminal and the solenoid input terminal. The engine speed should rise to about 1,100 rpm.
6. If engine speed does not rise, check solenoid operation.
7. Reconnect leads in their normal locations.

Solenoid Bypass Valve—L16 Engine With Automatic Transmission

1. Disconnect solenoid valve ground lead (black wire). Connect an ammeter between the lead terminal and ground. A test light can also be used; but this only indicates whether current is present or not, while an ammeter measures the amount of current.
2. When speed is over 13 mph with closed throttle, ammeter should read about .4 amps. Below 13 mph or with throttle open, ammeter should read 0 amps.
3. If ammeter reading is not as specified, check each switch and adjust or replace it as necessary. Refer to the switch position charts for details.
4. Remove ammeter and replace solenoid valve ground lead. Start engine. Connect a jumper wire between the battery output terminal and the solenoid input terminal. The engine speed should rise to about 1,100 rpm.
5. If engine speed does not rise, check solenoid operation.
6. Reconnect leads in their normal locations.

Dual Point Distributor—L16 Engine With Manual Transmission

1. Disconnect lead wires from retarded and advanced terminals on distributor. Connect an ammeter between the lead wire for the retarded points and ground.
2. Switch ignition on.
3. With throttle partially open, shift lever in third gear, and clutch pedal released, ammeter should indicate about 3 amps.
4. With throttle valve wide open or nearly closed, or shift lever in some position other than third, or clutch

Engine or vehicle operations	Clutch switch	Neutral gear switch	Throttle switch		Third gear switch	Relay	Solenoid valve current	Spark timing	
			Switch detecting close throttle position	Switch detecting wide open throttle position				"Advanced"	"Retarded"
Engine starting & warming up with choke	ON	OFF	OFF	ON	OFF	OFF	OFF	O	——
Engine starting without choke (Hot restarting)	ON	OFF	ON	ON	OFF	OFF	OFF	O	——
Idling	ON	OFF	ON	ON	OFF	OFF	OFF	O	——
Engine racing	ON	OFF	ON → OFF → ON	ON or ON → OFF → ON	OFF	OFF	OFF	O	——
Cruising or accelerating in 3rd gear with partially open throttle	ON	ON	OFF	ON	ON	ON	OFF	——	O
Cruising or accelerating in 1st, 2nd and 4th gear with partially open throttle	ON	ON	OFF	ON	OFF	OFF	OFF	O	——
Cruising or accelerating with wide open throttle	ON	ON	OFF	OFF	ON (3rd) or OFF (1st, 2nd, 4th)	OFF	OFF	O	——
Coasting	ON	ON	ON	ON	ON (3rd) or OFF (1st, 2nd, 4th)	OFF	ON	O	——
Remarks	When the clutch pedal is depressed, this switch is "OFF". And when the pedal is released, the switch is "ON".	When the shift lever is in neutral gear position, this switch is "OFF". And when the lever is in another gear position, the switch is "ON".	When the throttle valve is nearly closed, this switch is "ON". And when the valve is even slightly opened the switch is "OFF".	When the throttle valve is partially opened, this switch is "ON". And when the valve is wide open, the switch is "OFF".	When the shift lever is in 3rd gear, this switch is "ON". And when the lever is in another gear position, the switch is "OFF".	When the relay is "ON", the primary ignition circuit from the ignition coil to "retarded" breaker point is closed, so the "retarded" spark timing is provided.	When the solenoid valve current is "ON", the fuel and air passage is opened and excessive mixture is supplied to reduce HC emission.	When the "retarded" spark timing is provided, HC emission is reduced.	

Switch position chart, PL510 and WPL510, manual transmission, L16 engine

Engine or vehicle operations	Neutral gear switch	Clutch switch	Accelerator switch (Detecting close throttle position)	Relay E_2	Third gear switch	Throttle switch (Detecting wide open throttle position)	Relay E_1	Solenoid valve current	Spark timing	
									"Advanced"	"Retarded"
Engine starting & warming up with choke	OFF	ON	OFF	ON	OFF	ON	OFF	OFF	O	——
Engine starting without choke (Hot restarting)	OFF	ON	ON	ON	OFF	ON	OFF	OFF	O	——
Idling	OFF	ON	ON	ON	OFF	ON	OFF	OFF	O	——
Engine racing	OFF	ON	ON → OFF → ON	ON	OFF	ON or ON → OFF → ON	OFF	OFF	O	——
Cruising or accelerating in 3rd gear with the partially open throttle	ON	ON	OFF	ON	ON	ON	ON	OFF	——	O
Cruising or accelerating in 1st, 2nd and 4th gear with partially open throttle	ON	ON	OFF	ON	OFF	ON	OFF	OFF	O	——
Cruising or accelerating with wide open throttle	ON	ON	OFF	ON	ON (3rd) or OFF (1st, 2nd, 4th)	OFF	OFF	OFF	O	——
Coasting	ON	ON	ON	OFF	ON (3rd) or OFF (1st, 2nd, 4th)	ON	OFF	ON	O	——
Remarks	When the shift lever is in neutral gear position, this switch if "OFF" And when the lever is in ano another gear position, the switch is "ON".	When the clutch pedal is depressed, this switch is "OFF". And when the pedal is released, the switch is "ON".	When the accelerator pedal is "OFF". And when the pedal is released, the switch is "ON".	This relay has the characteristic of "normal close"	When the shift lever is in 3rd gear, this switch is "ON". And when the lever is in another gear position, the switch is "OFF".	When the throttle valve is partially opened, this switch is "ON". And when the valve is wide open, the switch is "OFF".	When the relay E_1 is "ON", the primary ignition circuit from the ignition coil to "retarded" breaker point is closed. So the "retarded" spark timing is provided.	When the solenoid valve current is "ON", the fuel and air passage is opened and excessive mixture is supplied to reduce HC emission.	When the "retarded" spark timing is provided, HC emission is reduced.	

Switch position chart, PL521 pickup, L16 engine

Engine or vehicle operations	Speed switch	Throttle switch		Relay	Solenoid valve current	Spark timing	
		Switch detecting close throttle position	Switch detecting wide open throttle position			"Advanced"	"Retarded"
Engine starting & warming up with choke	OFF	OFF	ON	OFF	OFF	O	——
Engine starting without choke (Hot restarting)	OFF	ON	ON	OFF	OFF	O	——
Idling	OFF	ON	ON	OFF	OFF	O	——
Engine racing	OFF	ON → OFF → ON	ON or ON → OFF → ON	OFF	OFF	O	——
Cruising or accelerating over 13 mph with partially open throttle	ON	OFF	ON	ON	OFF	——	O
Cruising or accelerating under 13 mph with partially open throttle	OFF	OFF	ON	OFF	OFF	O	——
Cruising or accelerating with wide open throttle	ON (over 13 mph) or OFF (under 13 mph)	OFF	OFF	OFF	OFF	O	——
Coasting	ON (over 13 mph) or OFF (under 13 mph)	ON	ON	OFF	ON (over 13 mph) or OFF (under 13 mph)	O	——
Remarks	When the car speed is under 13 mph, this switch is "OFF" And when the speed is over 13 mph, the switch is "ON".	When the throttle valve is nearly closed, this switch is "ON". And when the valve is even slightly opened the switch is "OFF".	When the throttle valve is partially opened, this switch is "ON". And when the valve is widely opened, the switch is "OFF".	When the relay is "ON", the primary ignition circuit from ignition coil to "retarded" breaker point is closed, so the "retarded" spark timing is provided	When the solenoid valve current is "ON", the fuel and air passage is opened and excessive mixture is supplied to reduce HC emission.	When the "retarded" spark timing is provided, HC emission is reduced.	

Switch position chart, PL510 and WP510, automatic transmission, L16 engine

pedal depressed, ammeter should indicate 0 amps.

5. If ammeter reads 0 amps in Step 3, disconnect terminals of relay (relay E1 on PL521) and measure voltage between terminal with No. 1 punch mark and ground. If voltage is about 12 volts, replace relay. If voltage is 0 volts, check each switch and wiring.
6. If ammeter reads 3 amps in Step 4, check clutch switch, neutral switch, and third gear switch. On PL510 and WPL510, check throttle switch. On PL521, check throttle switch and accelrator switch. Refer to the switch position charts for details.

Dual Point Distributor—L16 Engine With Automatic Transmission

1. Disconnect lead wire of retarded side of distributor. Connect an ammeter between the lead wire and the retarded side terminal.
2. Start engine and drive vehicle.
3. Ammeter should not read 0 amps when speed is over 13 mph with a partially open throttle. Otherwise, ammeter should read 0 amps.
4. If ammeter reading is not as specified, check speed switch, throttle switch, speed detector, and relay. Refer to the switch position charts for details.

FUEL VAPOR CONTROL SYSTEM

The fuel vapor control system is used on all vehicles sold in the U.S., starting 1970. It has four major components:

1. A sealed gas tank filler cap to prevent vapors from escaping at this point.
2. A vapor separator which returns liquid fuel to the fuel tank, but allows vapors to pass into the system.
3. A vapor vent line connecting the vapor separator to a flow guide valve.
4. A flow guide valve which allows air into the fuel tank and prevents vapors from the crankcase ventilation system from passing into the vapor vent line and fuel tank.

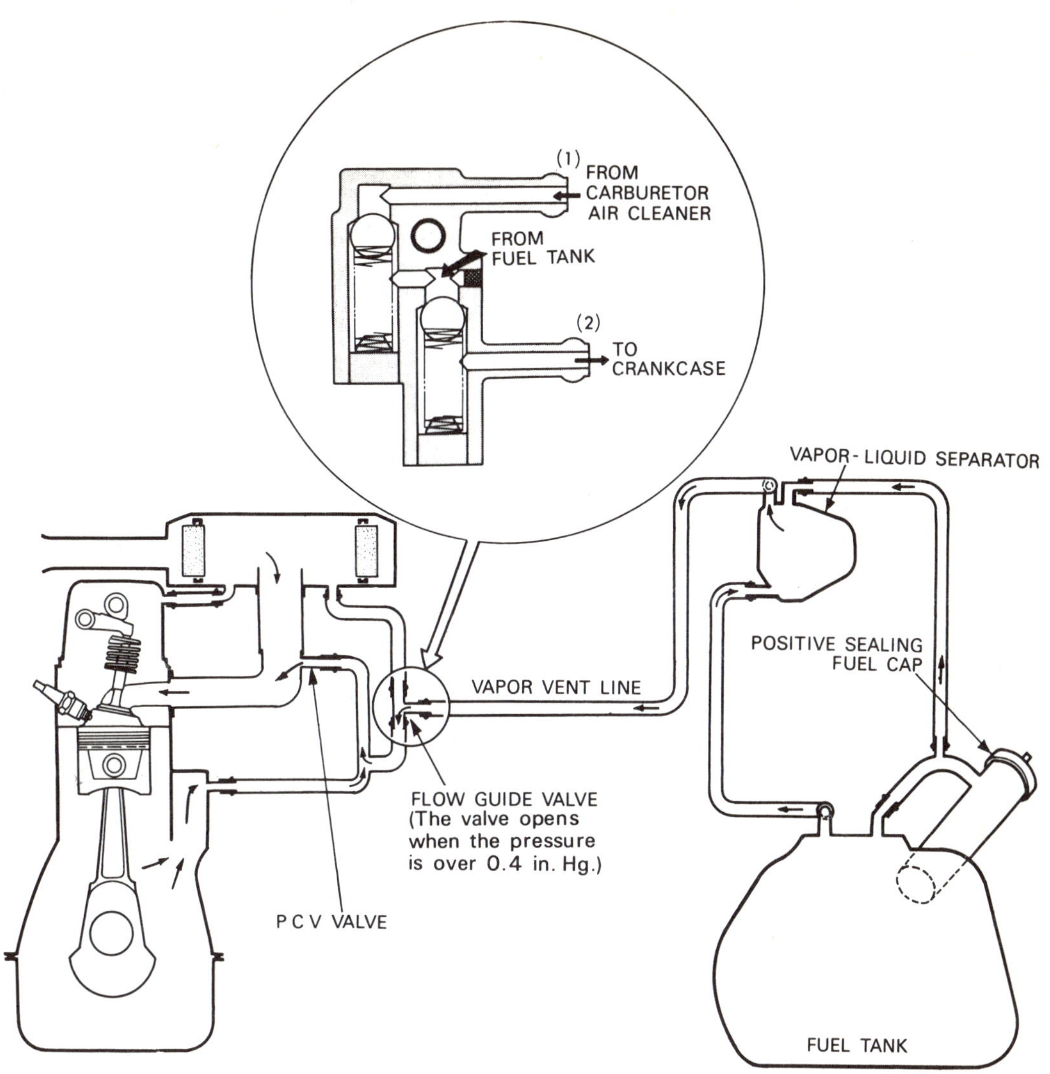

Fuel vapor control system, engines with downdraft carburetor

When the engine is not running, fuel vapors accumulate in the fuel tank, vapor separator, and vapor vent line. When the vapor pressure exceeds .4″ (10 mm.) Hg, the flow guide valve opens to allow the vapors to pass into the crankcase ventilation system. Fuel vapors are thus accumulated in the crankcase. When the engine starts, the vapors are disposed of by the crankcase ventilation system. When enough fuel has been used to create a slight vacuum in the fuel tank and fuel vapor control system, the flow guide valve opens to let fresh air from the carburetor air cleaner into the tank.

On engines with SU type carburetors, float bowl vapors are routed through the float bowl overflow tubes to the carburetor air cleaner.

Flow Guide Valve Test

The flow guide valve is mounted in the engine compartment. The valve fittings are marked A, from air cleaner; F, from fuel tank; and C, to crankcase.

1. Blow into the F fitting. Air should come out the C fitting.
2. Blow into the C fitting. Air should not escape.
3. Blow into the A fitting. Air should come out either the F or C fitting, or both.
4. Replace valve if defective.

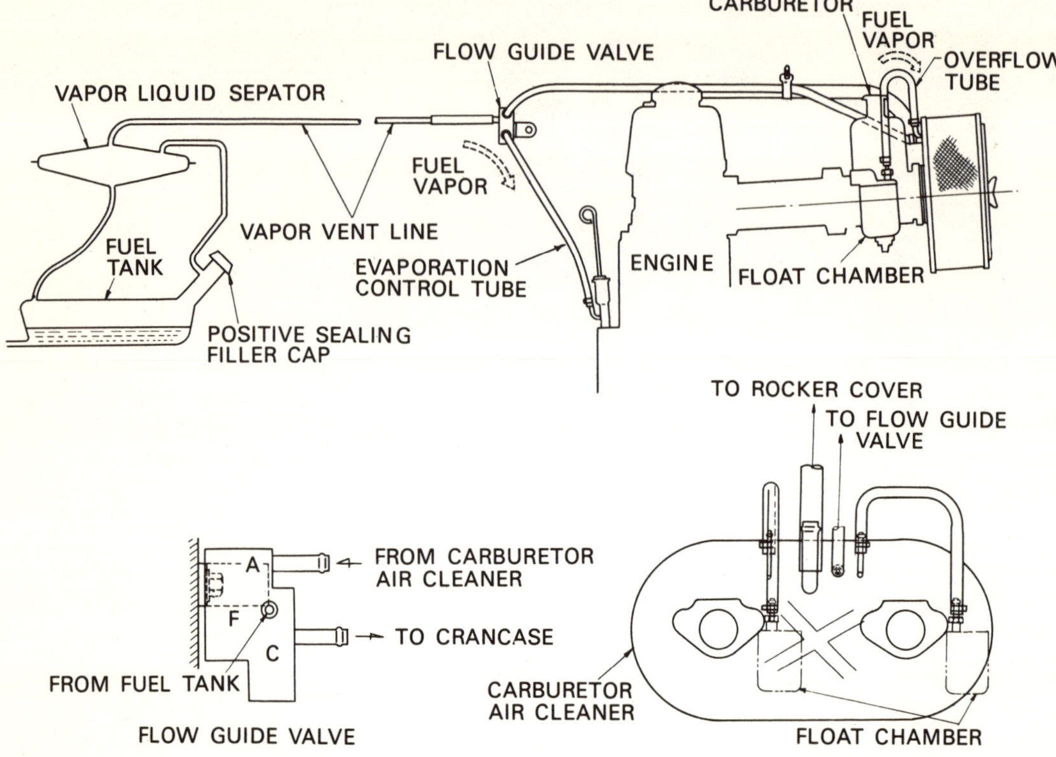

Fuel vapor control system, engines with SU type carburetors

Fuel System

FUEL PUMP

The diaphragm fuel pump is driven from the engine camshaft on all engines except the U20. On the U20 engine, the pump is driven off the engine jackshaft. It is mounted on the side of the engine block on overhead valve engines and the U20 and on the side of the cylinder head on all other overhead camshaft engines. The pump is on the left side of P, El, and J engines and on the right side of all others. The pump on P, El, and J engines has a primer lever which is useful in cold weather and in restarting after running out of fuel.

Fuel Pump R&R

1. Disconnect inlet and outlet lines from pump.
2. Remove mounting bolts.
3. Remove pump and discard gasket.
4. Lubricate the pump rocker arm, rocker arm pin, and lever pin before reinstallation.
5. Bolt the pump into position, using a new gasket.
6. Connect the fuel lines.

CARBURETOR

Two Hitachi sidedraft carburetors are used on G, R, U20, and L24 engines. These carburetors are virtually identical to the British SU carburetors. A few high performance U20 engines are equipped with two twin-choke sidedraft carburetors. These are identical to the German Solex carburetors and are built under license by Mikuni. All other engines use one downdraft carburetor of various makes and types. For complete details on carburetors see the Carburetor Specifications Chart.

Hitachi/SU Type

Fuel Level Adjustment

Float bowl fuel level should be .87-.95″ from the top edge of the bowl with the float in place.

To adjust the level:

1. Remove the float chamber covers.
2. Place the covers upside down.

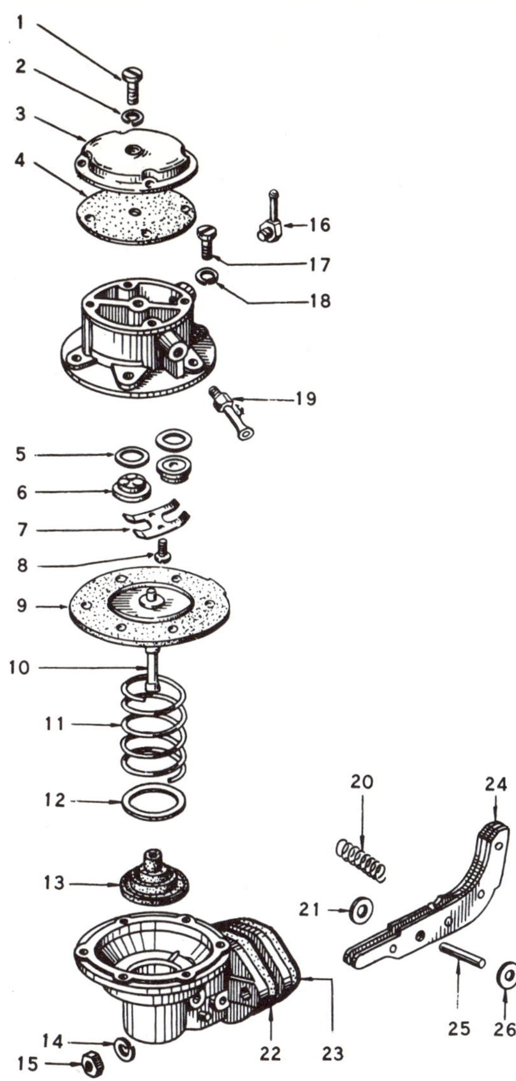

Details of fuel pump, L16 engine pump shown

1. Screw
2. Lockwasher
3. Cover
4. Cover gasket
5. Packing
6. Valve
7. Valve retainer
8. Valve retainer screw
9. Diaphragm
10. Pull rod
11. Spring
12. Seal washer
13. Seal
14. Lockwasher
15. Nut
16. Elbow
17. Screw
18. Lockwasher
19. Connector
20. Spring
21. Rocker arm slide spacer
22. Spacer
23. Gasket
24. Rocker arm
25. Pin
26. Rocker arm slide spacer

3. Lift the float lever and slowly lower it until the float lever seat just contacts the valve stem.
4. Check dimension H. It should be .55-.59″. Note that some carburetors have free floats and others have the float in unit with the float lever.
5. Reassemble carburetors. Fuel level should now be correct.

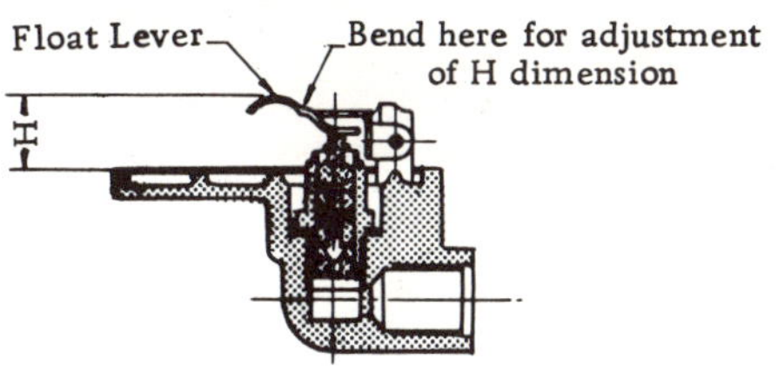

Float bowl fuel level adjustment for Hitachi/SU type carburetor with free float

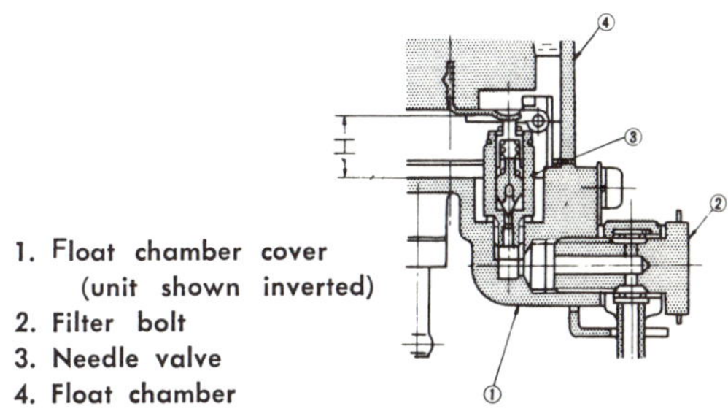

Float bowl fuel level adjustment for Hitachi/SU type carburetor with float in unit with float lever

Hitachi/SU Overhaul

These carburetors, being precision devices, are capable of being very finely adjusted. For the same reason, they require periodic attention. The factory recommends that they be disassembled and cleaned every six months. The suction piston and chamber often accumulate deposits of grit and varnish. To check for this condition, remove the air cleaner and raise the suction piston about 1/2″ with a finger. Release the piston. It should come down smoothly and evenly. If not, the carburetor must be disassembled and cleaned. If turning the mixture nuts seems to have no effect, the difficulty is probably an air leak at some point. The remedy for this is to replace all packings and gaskets. The same applies to fuel leaks. A common cause of air leaks is wear of the throttle shafts and the throttle shaft bore itself. The remedy for this condition is to install new throttle shafts and bushings. If the carburetor has no throttle shaft bushings, it may be necessary to drill out the throttle shaft bore to install bushings. The float chambers of these carburetors are very similar to those in conventional carburetors. However, the venturi and fuel system are precision made and require careful handling.

Hitachi/SU float bowl assembly

To disassemble the carburetors:

1. Remove screws and suction chamber.
2. Remove suction spring, nylon packing, and suction piston from chamber. Be extremely careful not to bend the jet needle.
3. Do not remove the jet needle from the suction pistion unless it must be replaced. To remove, loosen jet needle setscrew. Hold the needle with pliers at a point no more than .1″ from the piston. Remove needle by pulling and turning slowly. Replace the needle with the shoulder portion flush with the piston surface. Check this with a straightedge. Tighten the setscrew.

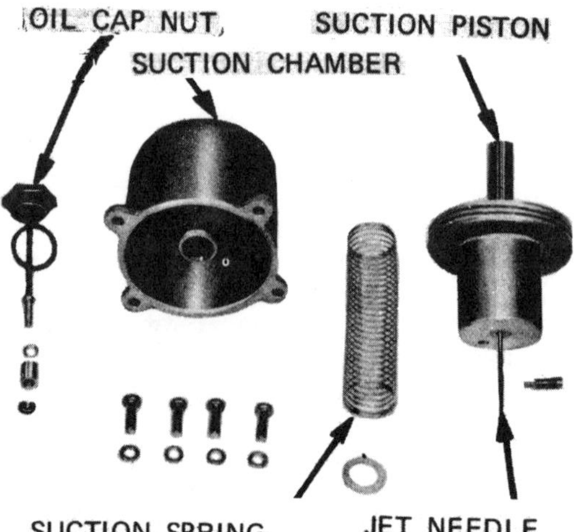

Hitachi/SU suction chamber assembly

4. Clean all parts of suction chamber assembly with a safe solvent. Reassemble, using all new parts supplied in overhaul kit. Do not lubricate piston.
5. To dismantle nozzle assembly, remove 4 mm. screw and remove connecting plate from nozzle head by pulling lightly on starter (choke) lever. Remove fuel line and nozzle. Be careful not to bend jet needle if suction chamber assembly is mounted on carburetor. Remove idle (mixture) adjusting nut and spring. Do not remove nozzle sleeve unless absolutely necessary. Special care is required to replace this part. Remove nozzle sleeve setscrew and nozzle sleeve.
6. Clean all parts of nozzle assembly with a safe solvent. Be very careful of nozzle. Do not pass anything through nozzle for cleaning purposes.
7. The jet needle must now be carefully centered in the nozzle, unless the nozzle sleeve and setscrew were not disturbed. Even so, it is a good idea to check this. To center the jet needle, insert nozzle sleeve into carburetor body with setscrew loose. Carefully install the suction piston assembly without the plunger rod. Insert the nozzle without spring and mixture adjusting nut until the nozzle contacts the nozzle sleeve. Position the nozzle sleeve so that the jet needle is centered inside the sleeve and does not contact the sleeve. Test centering by raising and releasing suction piston. It should drop smoothly, making a metallic sound when it hits the stop. Tighten the nozzle sleeve setscrew when the needle is centered.
8. Reassemble nozzle assembly. Replace fuel line. Replace damper plunger rod.
9. Pull starter lever slightly, replace connecting plate and 4 mm. screw.
10. Carburetor synchronization and mixture adjustments must be performed after reinstalling carburetors.

Mikuni/Solex Twin-Choke

Fuel Level Adjustment

Float bowl fuel level is controlled by the thickness of the washer under the float needle valve. The standard washer thickness is .04″ (1 mm.). A .02″ (.5 mm.) thick washer is available to raise the fuel level

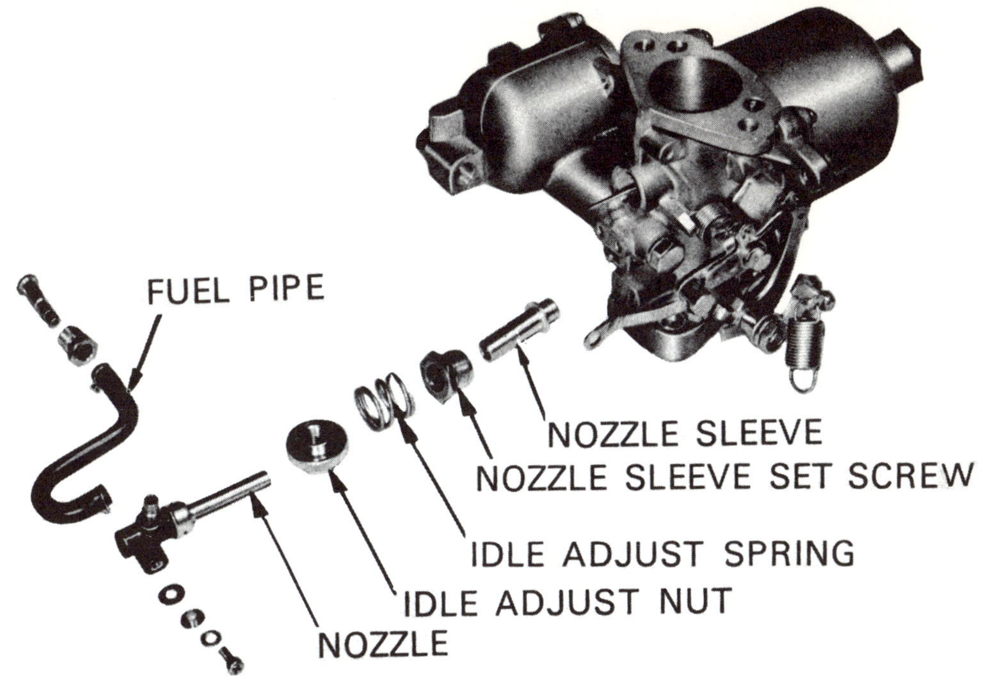

Hitachi/SU nozzle assembly

.08″ (2 mm.), and a .06″ (1.5 mm.) washer is available to lower it .08″ (2 mm.). Normal fuel level is .79″ above the center of the main bore. A special fuel level meter is available to measure this. When using the meter, fuel level on the scale should be .67-.75″. The float lever should never be bent to change the fuel level.

Jet Replacement

These carburetors are unique in that jet changes can be made simply be removing a jet chamber cover and replacing the main air, main fuel, or idling (pilot) jets. To maintain balance, the jets for each of the choke tubes in both carburetors must all be the same size. This means that four main air or fuel, or pilot jets must be changed together. Jet numbers relate directly to jet drilling diameter, except in the case of main fuel jets which are rated by flow. The larger the main air or pilot jet number, the leaner the mixture. The larger the main fuel jet number, the richer the mixture.

The carburetor venturi tubes can also be replaced readily and are available in a number of sizes.

Mikuni/Solex Overhaul

To remove from engine:

1. Remove air cleaner or velocity stacks. Disconnect fuel lines. Disconnect throttle cable or turnbuckles. Disconnect starter (choke) cable. Remove carburetors from intake manifold.

To disassemble float chamber:

2. Unbolt fuel inlet pipe from float chamber cover. Blow wire mesh fuel filter clean. Unbolt chamber cover. Remove cover and float. Remove and blow out float needle valve. Be careful not to bend the float arm. Remove jet chamber cover. Remove main air jets and jet blocks. Remove main fuel jets from jet blocks. Remove idling (pilot) jets. Clean all parts in a safe solvent. Blow out jets.

To dismantle the accelerator pump:

3. Invert carburetor body. Remove cotter pin, washer, and spring from pump rod. Remove screws and pump bottom cover, diaphragm, spring, top cover, and gasket. Check diaphragm for holes. Shake upper cover; listen for internal check ball. From top of carburetor remove plugs, pump weights, and balls.

NOTE: Installing the cotter pin in the endmost pump rod hole will result in the smallest possible pump discharge.

To dismantle the starting pump:

4. Remove snap-ring, washer, starter cover, spring, and starter disk from fuel bowl cover. Check that disk rub-

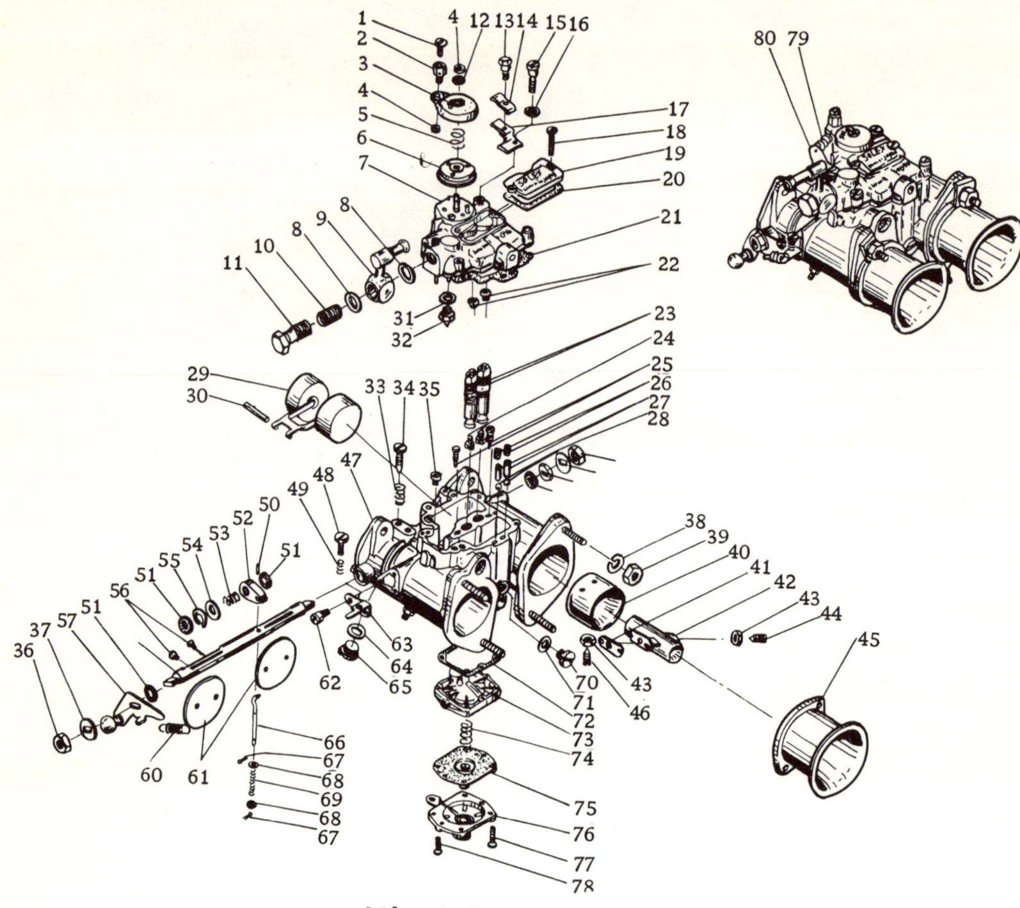

Mikuni/Solex 44PHH carburetor

1. Cable fixing bolt
2. Cable fixing collar
3. Starter cover
4. Snap ring
5. Starter spring
6. Starter disk
7. Float chamber cover
8. Washer
9. Fuel pipe
10. Filter
11. Banjo bolt
12. Washer
13. Spring washer bolt
14. Clip; cable bracket
15. Spring washer screw
16. Washer
17. Starter bracket
18. Fixing screw: jet chamber cover
19. Jet chamber cover
20. Gasket; jet chamber cover
21. Gasket; float chamber cover
22. Main air jet
23. Jet block
24. Main jet
25. Pilot jet
26. Plug
27. Pump weight
28. Ball
29. Float
30. Spindle; float
31. Washer
32. Needle valve
33. Volume control screw spring
34. Volume control screw
35. Starter jet
36. Nut
37. Washer
38. Spring washer
39. Nut
40. Outer venturi
41. Gasket-inner venturi
42. Inner venturi
43. Nut
44. Fixing screw
45. Air funnel
46. Fixing screw
47. Main body assembly
48. Slow running adjustment screw
49. Volume control screw spring
50. Stopper pin
51. Dustproof ring
52. Pump intermediate lever
53. Throttle spring
54. Thrust washer
55. Snap ring
56. Fixing screw; throttle
57. Throttle lever
58. Throttle spindle
59. Nut fixing collar
60. Throttle spring
61. Throttle butterfly
62. Spring washer screw
63. Bracket; slow running screw
64. Washer
65. Plug screw
66. Pump control rod
67. Split pin
68. Washer; pump control
69. Spring; pump control
70. Plug screw
71. Washer
72. Gasket; pump cover
73. Pump cover
74. Pump spring
75. Diaphragm assembly
76. Pump cover assembly
77. Fixing screw
78. Fixing screw
79. Starter spring
80. Starter spring bracket

bing surfaces are not scratched. Remove the starting jet, centered behind and between the main jet blocks.

NOTE: The starting jet is not effective after the engine has started.

The throttle shaft normally need not be removed, unless it is worn or bent. To remove:

5. Remove nut from end of shaft. File staked end of throttle valve retaining screws so screws can be removed. Remove throttle valves. Be sure to wash filings out of carburetor body. Remove shaft C-clip and stopper pin. Pull out shaft. When replacing shaft, be careful to replace dust seals and to avoid bending shaft. Stake the new throttle valve retaining screws to prevent their loosening.

Remove the idle mixture adjusting screws. Blow out all passages in carburetor body, particularly the idle bypass passages. Reassemble the carburetor, using new gaskets.

Downdraft Carburetors

Fuel Level Adjustment

All Nihonkikaki (Nikki) carburetors have a glass float chamber side cover marked with a fuel level line. Fuel level is adjusted by varying the thickness of the washer under the float valve.

The Hitachi VC42-4A single throat carburetor used on the P engine in the Nissan Patrol (L60) has a glass fuel level sight tube. The fuel level should be between the two red lines on the tube.

On the Hitachi DAF328 and DCG306, fuel level is adjusted by bending the float seat tab to obtain a gap of .051-.067″ between the needle valve and float seat tab with the float cover removed and inverted, and the float fully raised.

NOTE: All fuel level measurements are given with the float in place.

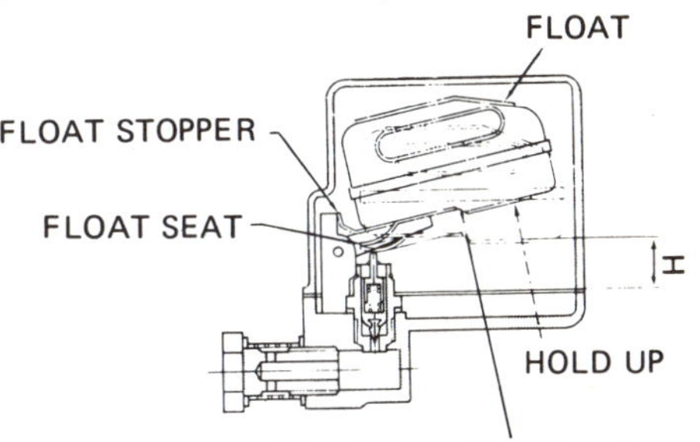

Float adjustment for Hitachi DAF328 and DCG306 carburetors

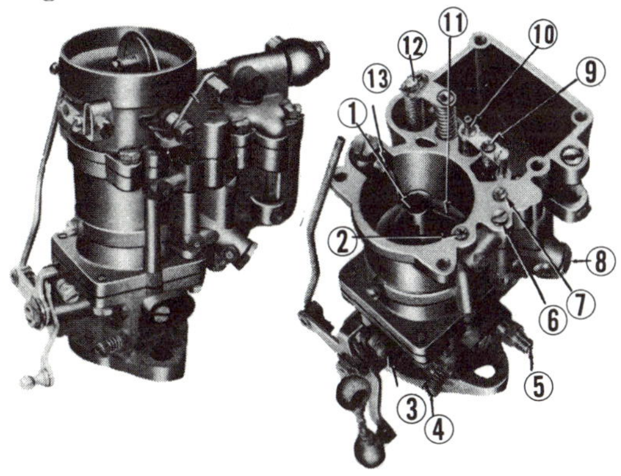

Hitachi VC42-4A single throat carburetor

1. Venturi
2. Idle air bleed
3. Idle speed (throttle) adjusting screw
4. Idle mixture adjusting screw
5. Vacuum fitting
6. Idle jet
7. Main air bleed
8. Main jet
9. Power valve
10. Vacuum piston
11. Main nozzle
12. Accelerating pump
13. Accelerating pump nozzle

Throttle Linkage Adjustment

On the PL410 and PL411 sedans, the accelerator linkage must be adjusted to obtain a measurement, D, of 3.4″. On all models, check that the throttle is wide open when the accelerator pedal is floored. Some models have an adjustable accelerator pedal stop to prevent strain on the linkage.

Starting Interlock Adjustment

With the choke valve fully closed, the primary throttle valve should be open the angle specified under Fast Idle in the Carburetor Specifications Chart. On the Hitachi DAF328, a throttle valve opening of 16° corresponds to a measurement of .051″ between the lower edge of the throttle valve and the inside edge of the primary bore.

Dashpot Adjustment

A dashpot is used on Hitachi DAF328 carburetors with automatic transmission. The dashpot slows the closing of the throttle valve to prevent stalling. The dashpot

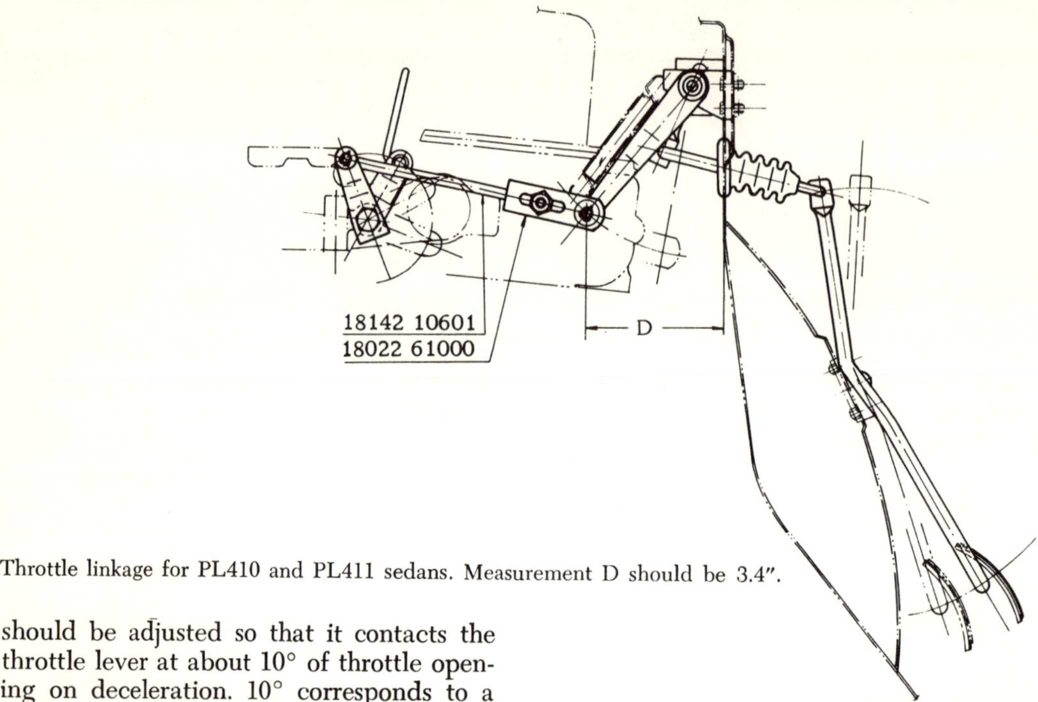

Throttle linkage for PL410 and PL411 sedans. Measurement D should be 3.4″.

should be adjusted so that it contacts the throttle lever at about 10° of throttle opening on deceleration. 10° corresponds to a measurement of .071″ between the throttle valve and the edge of the primary bore.

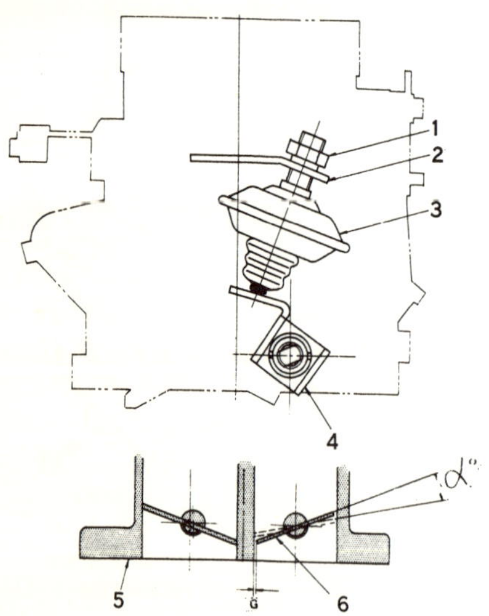

Dashpot installation on Hitachi DAF328 carburetor with automatic transmission

1. Locknut
2. Mounting arm
3. Dashpot
4. Throttle lever
5. Carburetor body
6. Primary throttle valve
α. Primary throttle opening in degrees
G. Primary throttle opening in inches

Secondary Throttle Adjustment

On all two throat carburetors except the Hitachi DAF328, the secondary throttle should begin to open when the primary throttle is open 48°. On the Hitachi DCG306, 48° corresponds to a measurement of .230″ between the lower edge of the primary throttle valve and the inside edge of the primary bore. On the Hitachi DAF328, the secondary throttle begins to open when the primary throttle is open 59° or .358″. Adjust the point of secondary throttle opening by bending the linkage between the two throttles.

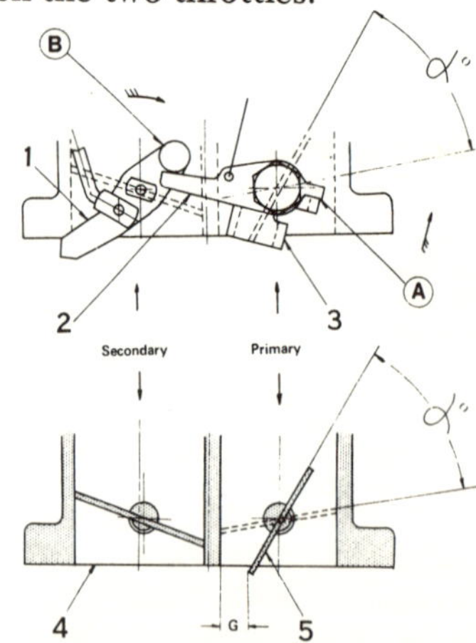

1. Connecting lever
2. Return plate
3. Adjusting plate
4. Secondary throttle chamber
5. Primary throttle valve

Measurement of point at which secondary throttle starts to open, Hitachi DAF328 carburetor. α is the primary throttle opening in degrees; G is the opening in inches.

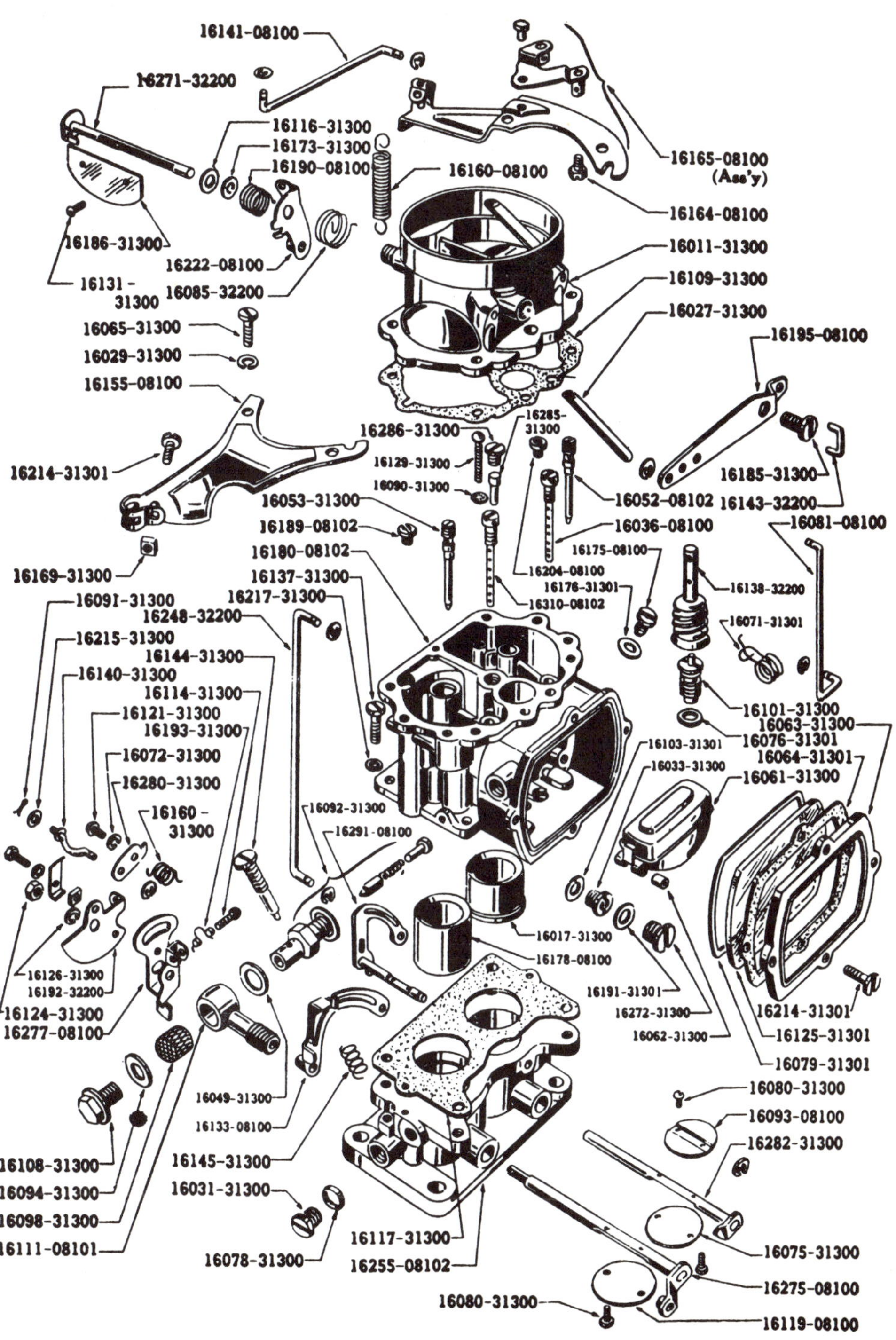

Nihonkikaki 2D30CE dual throat carburetor

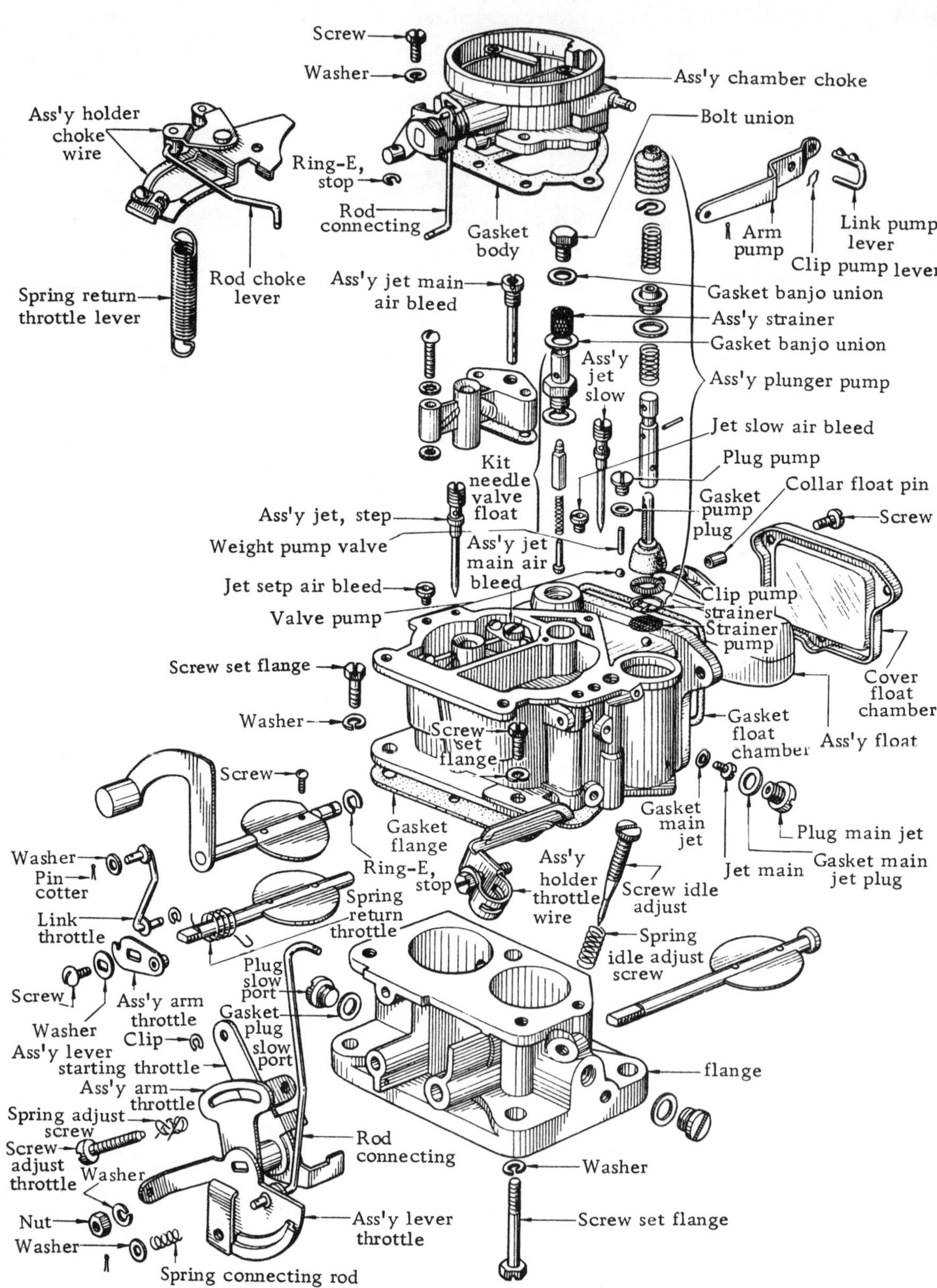

Nihonkikaki D2630A-5A dual throat carburetor

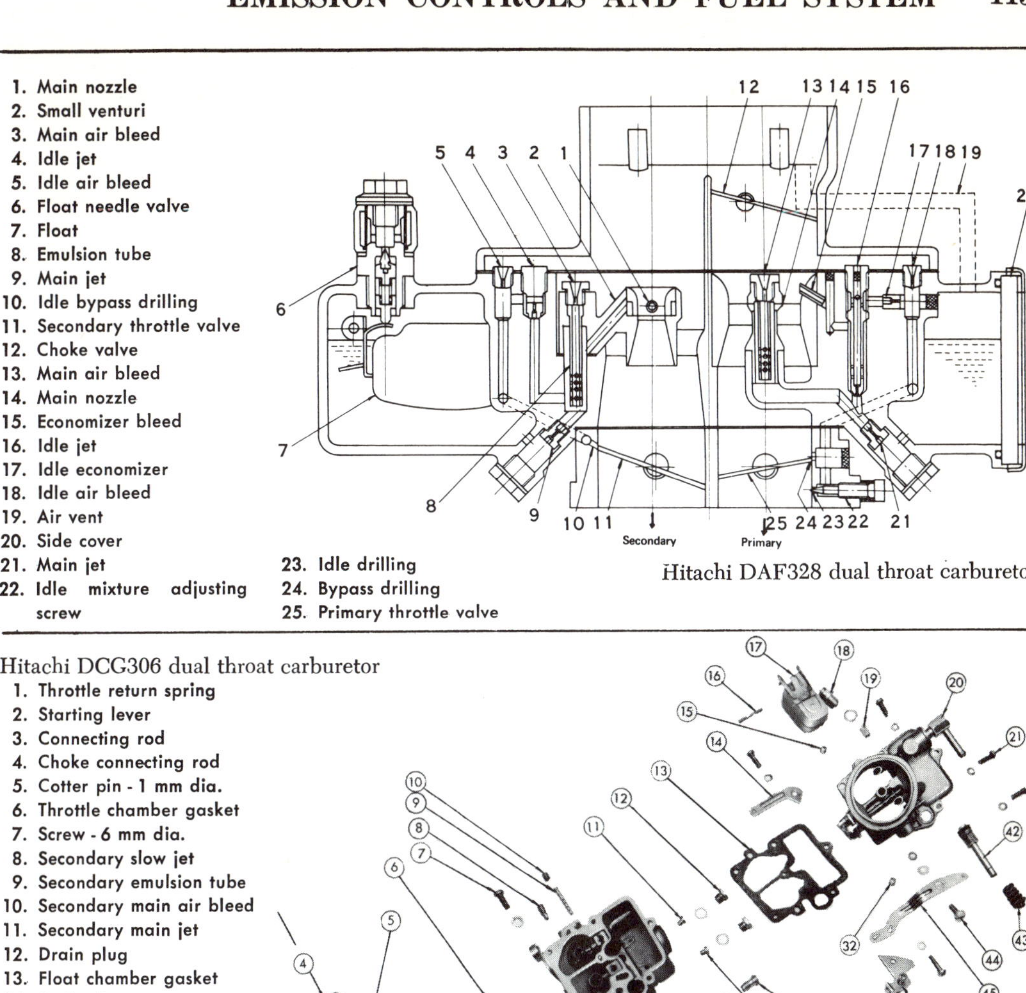

1. Main nozzle
2. Small venturi
3. Main air bleed
4. Idle jet
5. Idle air bleed
6. Float needle valve
7. Float
8. Emulsion tube
9. Main jet
10. Idle bypass drilling
11. Secondary throttle valve
12. Choke valve
13. Main air bleed
14. Main nozzle
15. Economizer bleed
16. Idle jet
17. Idle economizer
18. Idle air bleed
19. Air vent
20. Side cover
21. Main jet
22. Idle mixture adjusting screw
23. Idle drilling
24. Bypass drilling
25. Primary throttle valve

Hitachi DAF328 dual throat carburetor

Hitachi DCG306 dual throat carburetor

1. Throttle return spring
2. Starting lever
3. Connecting rod
4. Choke connecting rod
5. Cotter pin - 1 mm dia.
6. Throttle chamber gasket
7. Screw - 6 mm dia.
8. Secondary slow jet
9. Secondary emulsion tube
10. Secondary main air bleed
11. Secondary main jet
12. Drain plug
13. Float chamber gasket
14. Spring hanger
15. Secondary slow air bleed
16. Float shaft
17. Float
18. Needle valve
19. Filter
20. Choke chamber assembly
21. Screw - 5 mm dia.
22. Nut - 8 mm dia.
23. Throttle lever
24. Sleeve
25. Pump rod
26. Adjust plate
27. Screw - 6 mm dia.
28. Idle adjust screw spring
29. Idle adjust screw
30. Throttle adjust screw spring
31. Throttle adjust screw
32. Primary slow air bleed
33. Power valve
34. Primary main jet
35. Ball
36. Piston return spring
37. Injector weight
38. Primary emulsion tube
39. Primary main air bleed
40. Primary slow jet
41. Throttle wire arm
42. Piston
43. Pump cover
44. Pump lever shaft
45. Pump lever
46. Choke wire arm

DOWNDRAFT CARBURETOR OVERHAUL

Carburetor overhaul involves separating the major components, removing and blowing out all jets, blowing out all passages, washing all parts in a safe solvent, and reassembling with new gaskets. After overhaul, the idle mixture and speed must be adjusted. Carburetor overhaul kits are available, and generally contain complete instructions, a full set of gaskets, and a new float needle valve and accelerator pump parts.

Carbuertor Specifications

Engine Model —Vehicle	*Carburetor*	*Bore Size (in.)*	*Large Venturi (in.)*	*Small Venturi (in.)*	*Main Jet (Number)*	*Main Air Bleed (Number)*	*Main Nozzle (in.)*	*Idle (Slow) Jet (Number)*	*Idle (Slow) Air Bleed*	*Bypass Air Bleed (Number)*	*Power Jet*	*Accelerator Pump Injector*	*Fast Idle (deg. of throttle opening at full choke)*	*Suction Piston Lift (in.)*
P—L60	Hitachi VC42-4A	1.42			135	70		25	210					
P with emission control—L60	Rochester 7015013 single throat downdraft													
E1—PL410	Nihonki-kaki 2D30CE dual throat downdraft	1.102, 1.81 sec.	.827, 1.024 sec.		96, 115 sec.	80, 60 sec.		48, 48 sec.	100, 220 2nd, 120 sec.		#55		14	
E1—L320	Nihonki-kaki 2D30C dual throat downdraft	1.102, 1.81 sec.	.827, 1.024 sec.		96, 115 sec.	80, 60 sec.		48, 48 sec.	100, 220 2nd, 120 sec.		55		14	
J—L520	Nihonki-kaki D2630A-5A dual throat downdraft	1.022, 1.180 sec.	.788, 1.06 sec.		90, 145 sec.			48, 48 sec.			#40	#45	14	
J—PL411	Nihonki-kaki D2630A-5A dual throat downdraft	1.022, 1.180 sec.	.788, 1.06 sec.		92, 140 sec.	60, 60 sec.		48, 48 sec.	100, 240 2nd, 120 sec.		#40	.024″	14	

Carburetor Specifications, continued

Engine Model —Vehicle	Carburetor	Bore Size (in.)	Large Venturi (in.)	Small Venturi (in.)	Main Jet (Number)	Main Air Bleed (Number)	Main Nozzle (in.)	Idle (Slow) Jet (Number)	Idle (Slow) Air Bleed	Bypass Air Bleed (Number)	Power Jet	Accelerator Pump Injector	Fast Idle (deg. of throttle opening at full choke)	Suction Piston Lift (in.)
J with emission control—L520, L521	Hitachi DCA306-4 dual throat downdraft	1.022, 1.180 sec.	.827, 1.01 sec.	.315-.512 prim., .315-.433 sec., .551-.710 2nd	96, 130 sec.	100, 140 sec.	.106/.138 .118/.157 sec.	47, 100 sec.	200, 100 sec.	170	#60		13	
R	Hitachi HJB38W SU type sidedraft	1.495												
R with emission control	Hitachi HJB38W-5 or HJB38W-6 SU type sidedraft	1.495									.092″		6	1.400
U20	Hitachi HJ46W SU type sidedraft	1.81												
U20	Mikuni/ Solex 44PHH twin-choke sidedraft	1.74	.394, 1.456 sec.		180			60				.012″		1.337

U20 with emission control	Hitachi HJG46W-5 or HJG46W-7 SU type sidedraft	1.805								.100″		4.5
L16—PL510	Hitachi DAF328 dual throat downdraft	1.102, 1.260 sec.	.945, 1.102 sec.	.354	115, 155 sec.	240, 120 sec.		48, 180 sec.	180, 100 sec.			16
L16 with emission control	Hitachi DAF328-8 (auto.), DAF328-6 (std.) DAF328-10 (PL521)	1.101, 1.260 sec.	.906, 1.101 sec.	.355	117 (1969), 115 (1970)	240, 120 sec.	.255/.071 .118 sec.	48, 180 sec.	150, 100 sec.		.020″	16
L24 with emission control—HLS30	Hitachi HJG46W-3A SU type sidedraft	1.811			A							
A12 with emission control—LB110, KLB110	Hitachi DCG306 dual throat downdraft	1.024, 1.181 sec.	.787, 1.024 sec.	.315 prim., .276 sec., .512 2nd	98, 135 sec.	80, 80 sec.	.083, .110 sec.	43, 50 sec.	220, 100 sec.	#60	.020″	17.5

Carburetor Specifications, Continued

Engine Model —Vehicle	*Suction Spring (Number)*	*Metering Needle*	*Float Chamber Inclination (deg.)*	*Economizer (in.)*	*Fuel Level (in.)*	*Vacuum Jet (Number)*
P— L60					.80-.88①	
P with emission control —L60						
E1— PL410				.079	.75①	
E1— L320				#145	.75①	
J— L520					.85①	
J— PL411					.85①	
J with emission control —L520, L521					N.A.	
R					.87-.95①	
R with emission control	23	M-39 with 38W-5, M-70 with 38W-6	0		.87-.95①	
U20 (SU type)					.87-.95①	
U20 (Mikuni/ Solex)					See text	
U20 with emission control	32	N-17 with 46W-5, N-25 with 46W-7	8		.87-.95①	
L16— PL510				.071	.87-.95①	
L16 with emission control				.071	.87-.95①	150, 130 sec.
L24 with emission control —HLS30	23	N-27 .079″			.87-.95①	
A12 with emission control —LB110, KLB110					.71-.78①	

①—From float chamber top to fuel level

Chapter 5 Chassis Electrical

Heater Unit

Removal and Installation

PL510, WPL510

1. Drain coolant.
2. Disconnect water pipes to engine.
3. Disconnect blower motor electrical connector.
4. Remove three heater control wires at heater unit.
5. Remove two bolts and ventilator.
6. Remove four bolts and detach heater unit.

LB110, KLB110

1. Remove package tray and ashtray.
2. Disconnect two hoses between heater and engine.
3. Disconnect cables from heater unit and heater controls. Disconnect wiring.
4. Disconnect two control wires from water cock and interior valve, and control rod from shut valve. Set heater control upper lever to DEF and lower lever to OFF.
5. Pull off right and left defroster hoses.
6. Remove four screws holding heater unit to firewall. Remove control knob and remove screws holding control unit to instrument panel. Remove heater unit.

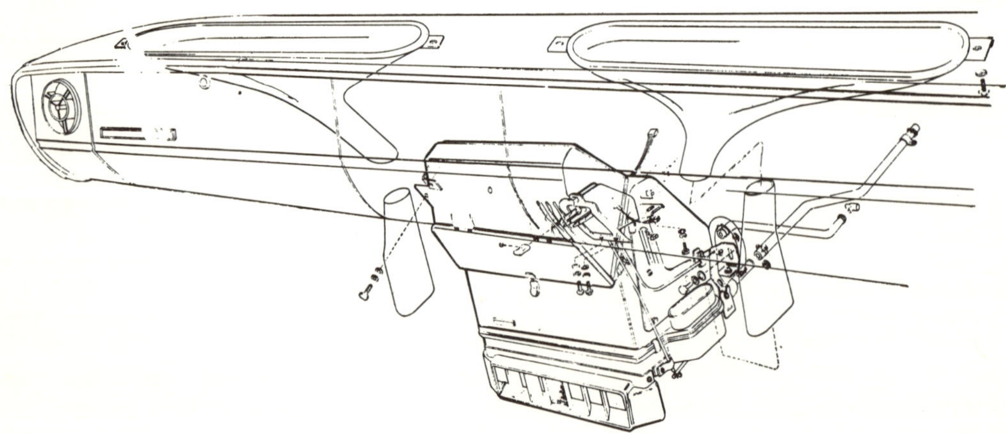

PL510, WPL510 heater unit

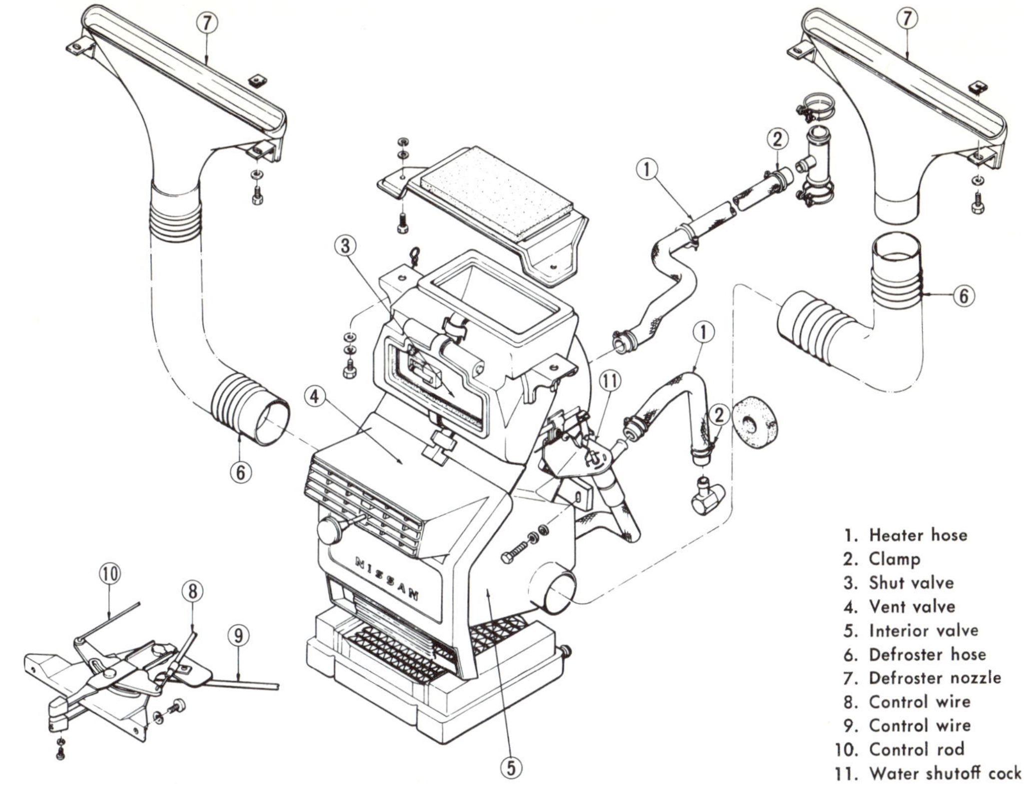

LB110 and KLB110 heater unit

Heater Core

Removal and Installation

PL510, WPL510

1. Remove four clips and separate lower cover.
2. Unbolt and remove heater core.

Radio

Removal and Installation

PL510, WPL510

1. Detach all electrical connections.
2. Remove radio knobs and retaining nuts.
3. Remove mounting screws, tip radio down at the rear, and remove.

LB110, KLB110

1. Remove the instrument cluster.
2. Detach all electrical connections.
3. Remove radio knobs and retaining nuts.
4. Remove rear support bracket.
5. Remove radio.

HLS30

The radio is mounted in the center console panel and the speaker in the left fender inner panel. The front face plate of the console must be removed to remove the radio.

Windshield Wiper Motor

Removal and Installation

PL510, WPL510

The wiper motor and operating linkage is on the firewall under the hood.

1. Lift wiper arms. Remove securing nuts and detach arms.
2. Remove nuts holding wiper pivots to body.
3. Open hood and unscrew motor from firewall.
4. Disconnect wiring connector and remove wiper motor with linkage.

NOTE: If wipers do not park correctly, adjust position of automatic stop cover on wiper motor.

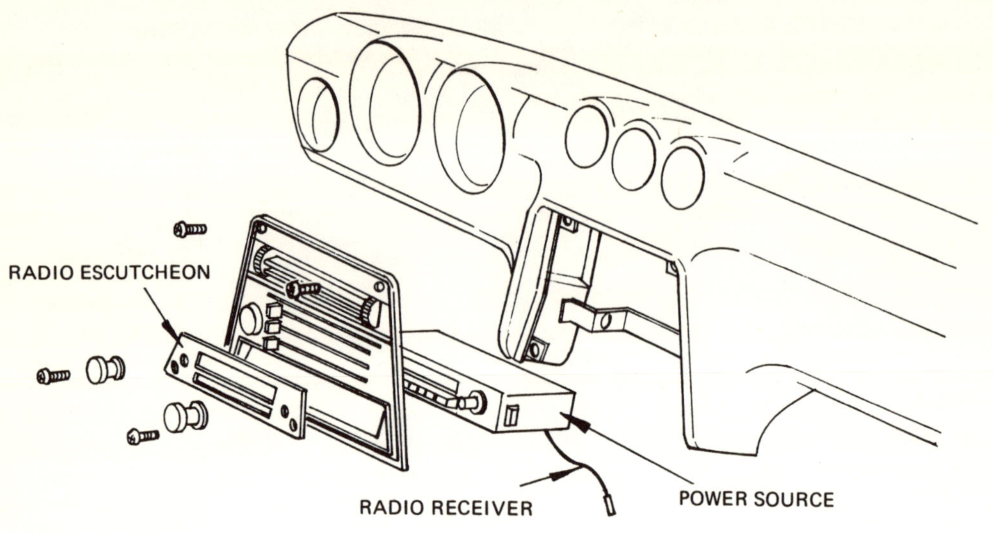

HLS30 radio installation

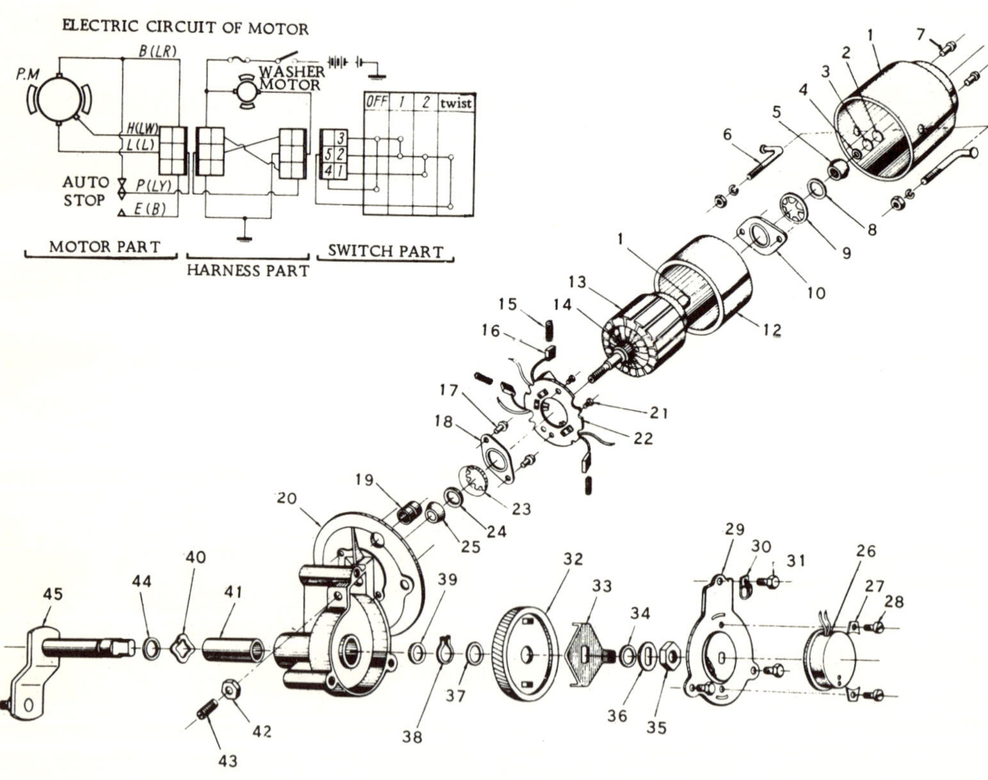

PL510, WPL510 wiper unit

1. Yoke
2. Damper
3. Armature stopper
4. Felt washer
5. Bearing
6. Hook bolt
7. Rivet
8. Felt washer
9. Plate spring
10. Spring retainer
11. Ball
12. Magnet ball
13. Armature
14. Commutator
15. Brush spring
16. Brush
17. Rivet
18. Spring retainer
19. Grommet
20. Gear case
21. Tapping screw
22. Brush holder
23. Plate spring
24. Felt washer
25. Bearing
26. Auto stop cover
27. Lock plate
28. Plain small screw
29. Gear cover
30. Clip
31. Tapping screw
32. Worm wheel
33. Wheel arm
34. Plain washer
35. Hexagon nut
36. Lock washer
37. Plain washer
38. C type stop ring
39. Thrust washer
40. Wave washer
41. Bearing
42. Hexagon nut
43. Thrust screw
44. Thrust washer
45. Gear shaft

LB110, KLB110

The wiper motor is on the firewall under the hood. The operating linkage is on the firewall inside the car.

1. Detach motor wiring plug.
2. Inside car, remove nut connecting linkage to wiper shaft.
3. Unbolt and remove wiper motor from firewall.

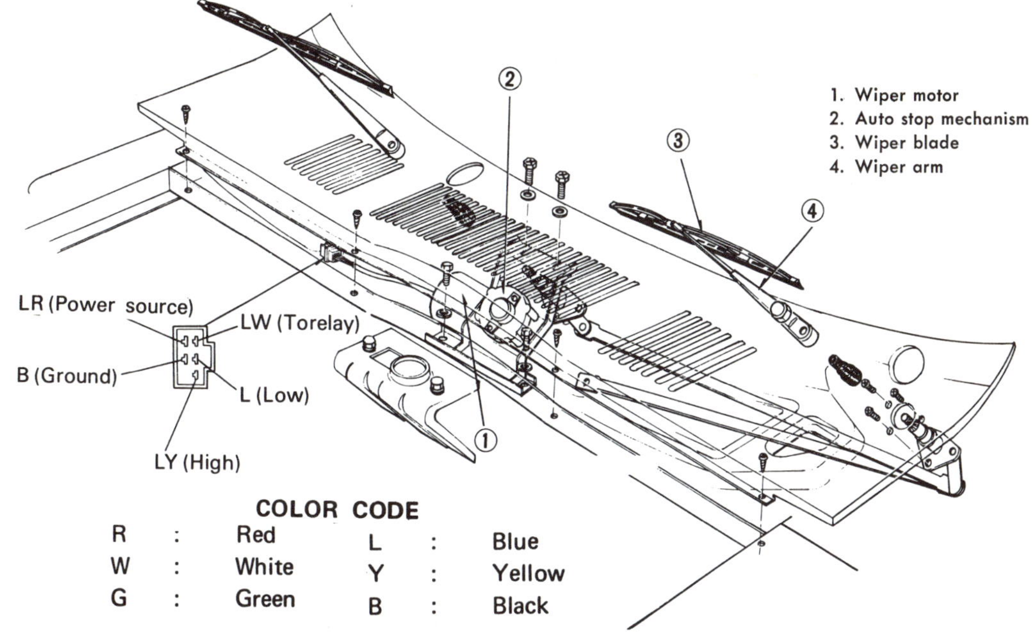

HLS30 wiper installation

Instrument Cluster

Removal and Installation

PL510, WPL510

1. Disconnect speedometer cable by unscrewing nut at back of speedometer.
2. Remove screws holding instrument cluster to instrument panel.
3. Pull out instrument cluster enough to detach wiring.
4. Remove cluster. Individual instrument units can be removed from the rear of the cluster.

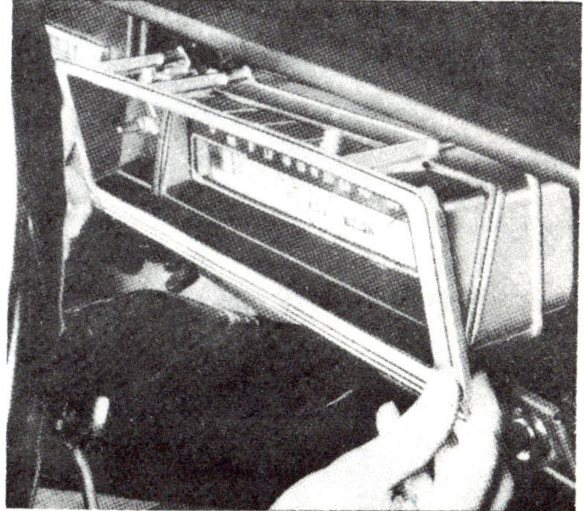
Instrument cluster removal from PL510, WPL510

LB110, KLB110

1. Disconnect battery negative lead.
2. Depress wiper, light switch, and choke knobs, turning counterclockwise to remove.
3. From the rear, disconnect the lighter wire. Turn and remove lighter outer case.
4. Remove radio and heater knobs.
5. Remove shell cover from steering column.
6. Remove screws holding instrument cluster to instrument panel. Pull out cluster.
7. Disconnect wiring connector. Disconnect speedometer cable by unscrewing nut at back of speedometer.
8. Individual instruments may be removed from the rear of the cluster.

Individual Instruments

Removal and Installation

HLS30

The speedometer and tachometer are both attached at the rear with two wingnuts. Access is from under the instrument panel. After the wingnuts are removed, the instrument can be pulled out through the instrument panel. The other three gauge units are held to brackets by slotted head hex bolts. To gain access, the center console panel must be removed.

LB110, KLB110

An optional clock or tachometer can be installed in the space provided to one side of the speedometer.

1. Remove instrument cluster.
2. Remove blank face and install tachometer or clock.
3. Connect wires as shown.
4. On clock, connect blue (or yellow/-red) wire to blue wire in harness along upper edge of instrument panel. On tachometer, connect black and white wires to black/white cable plug in harness.
5. Replace instrument cluster.

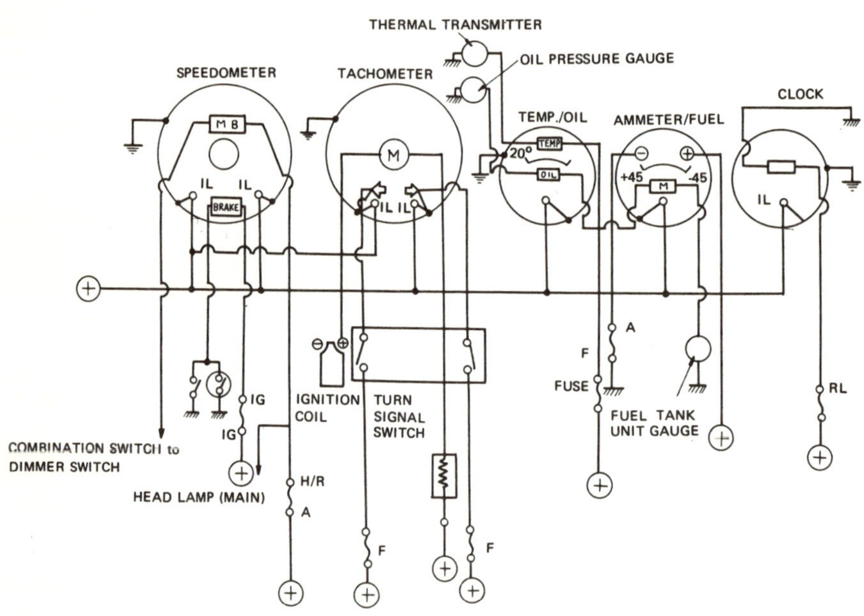

HLS30 instrument wiring diagram

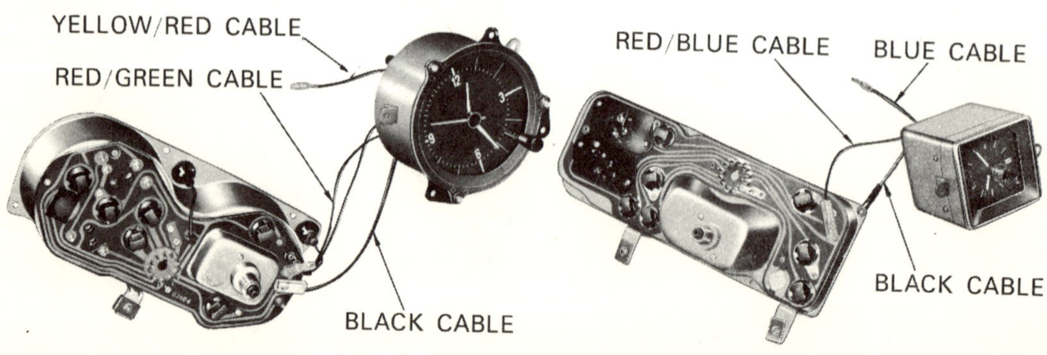

Wiring connections for two optional clocks, LB110 and KLB110

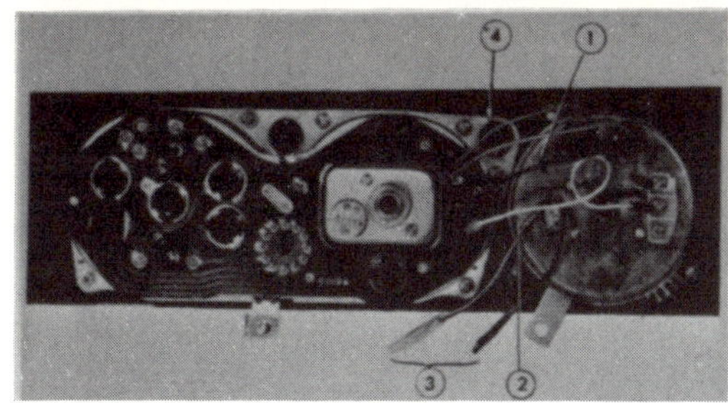
Wiring connections for optional tachometer, LB110 and KLB110

1. Black wire
2. Yellow/red wire
3. Black and white wires
4. Red/green wire

Headlights

Removal and Installation

PL510, WPL510

1. Remove headlight trim.
2. Remove screws and headlight retaining ring.
3. Pull out headlight carefully and pull off wiring plug from rear.

LB110, KLB110

1. On KLB110 coupe, remove screws holding grille to radiator support. On all other models, remove screws and headlight rim.
2. Remove screws and headlight retaining ring.
3. Pull out headlight carefully and pull off wiring plug.

HLS30

To remove the headlight, remove the four retaining screws from inside the wheel opening.

Light Bulb Specifications

Model	*Usage*	*Wattage*
L60	Headlights	50/42
	Front parking, turn	21/6
	Stop, tail, turn	21/6
	License plate	10
	Instrument panel	8
	Flasher warning light	1.5
PL410	Headlights	37.5/50
		37.5
	Parking	8
	Turn	25
	License plate	8
	Interior light	5
	Backup	25
	Warning lights	1.5
	Instrument	5
SPL310	Headlights	50/40
	Front parking, turn	25/5
	Tail, stop	21/6
	License plate	8
	Interior	6
	Instruments, warning	1.5
	Inspection lamp	8
	Radio	1.2
PL411, RL411	Headlights	37.5/50
		37.5
	Side markers	8
	Tail	8
	License plate	8
	Stop	25
	Backup	25
	Interior	5
	Fog	35
	Inspection	8
	Parking	8
	Turn	25
	Instrument	3
	Warning	1.5
SPL311, SRL311	Headlight	50/40
	Front turn, parking	25/8
	Stop, tail, turn	25/8
	Backup	15
	License plate	8
	Map	5
	Side marker	8

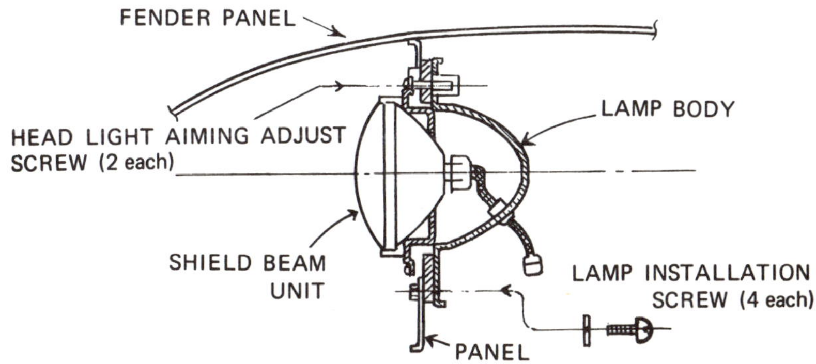

HLS30 headlight assembly details

L520	Headlights	37.5/50 50
	Front parking, turn	25/8
	Tail, stop	25/8
	Rear turn, backup	25
	License plate	8
	Interior	6
L521, PL521	Headlights	37.5/50 37.5
	Front turn, parking	25/8
	Tail, stop	25/8
	Rear turn	25
	Backup	25
	Interior	6
	License plate	8
PL510, WPL510	Headlights	37.5/50 37.5
	Front parking, turn	25/8
	Tail, turn	25/8
	Stop	25
	Backup	25
	License plate	8
	Interior	10
HLS30	Headlights	50/40
	Side marker, turn	23/7
	Side marker, license plate	7.5
	Tail	7
	Stop	23
	Rear turn	23
	Backup	23
	Instrument, warning, glove compartment, clock	3
	Four-way flasher	23
	Inspection	8

Fuses and Fusible Links

Model	*Fuse Box Location*	*Fusible Link Location*
L320, L520, L521 PL521, PL510, WPL510	Engine compartment, right rear	
L60	Engine compartment, right fender well	
SPL311, SRL311	Inside glove compartment	
LB110 KLB110	Under instrument panel, right of steering column	Between battery and alternator
HLS30	Under ash tray in console	At alternator, at starter

Wiring Diagrams

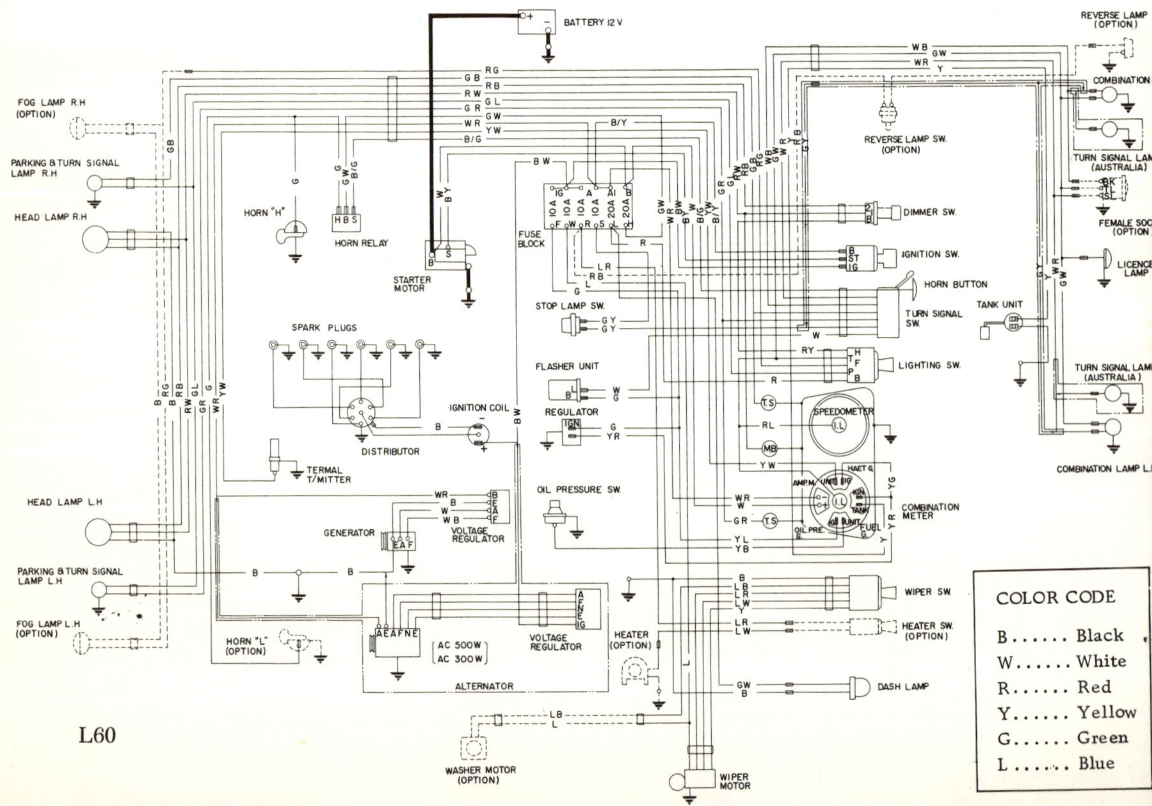

L60

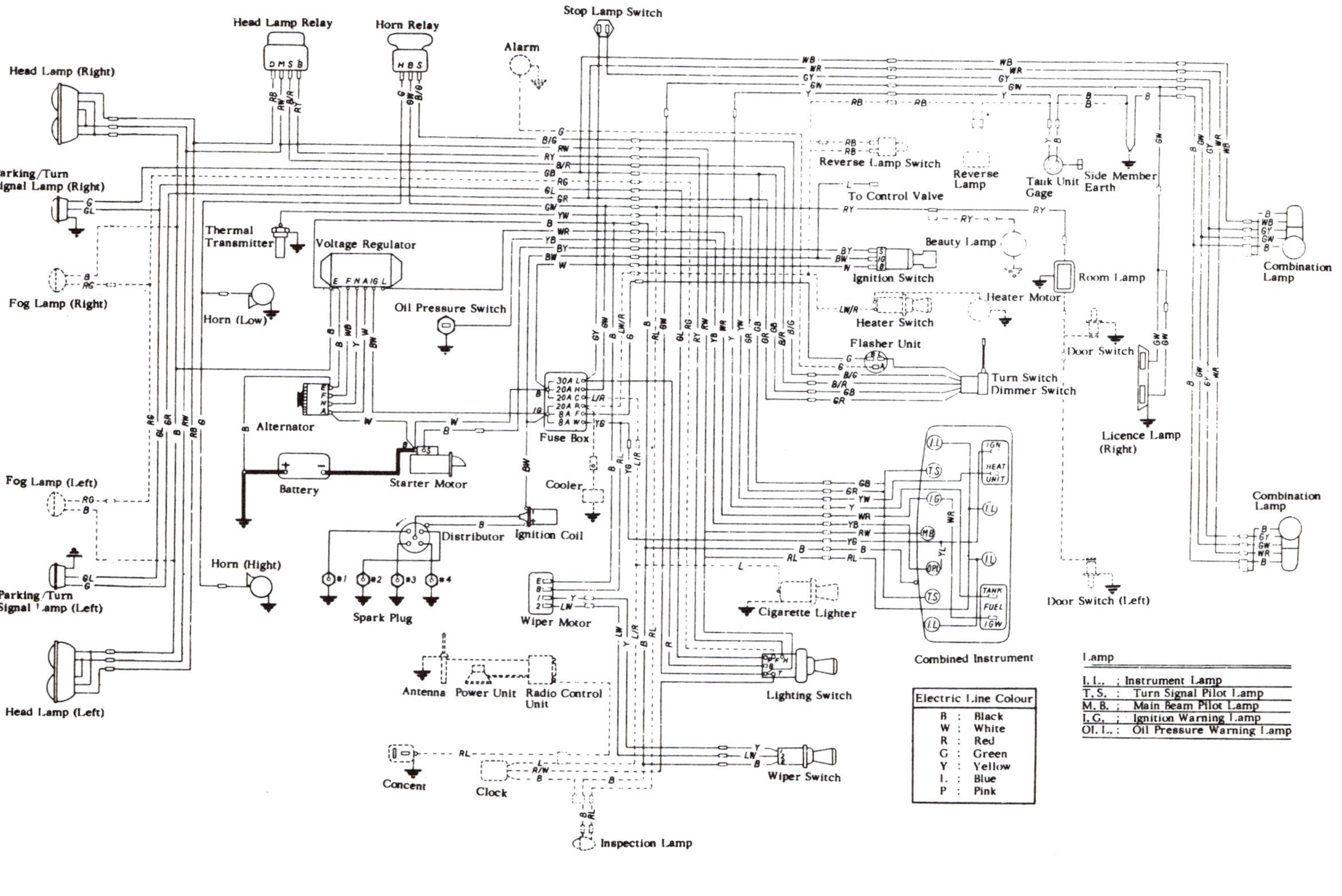

PL410

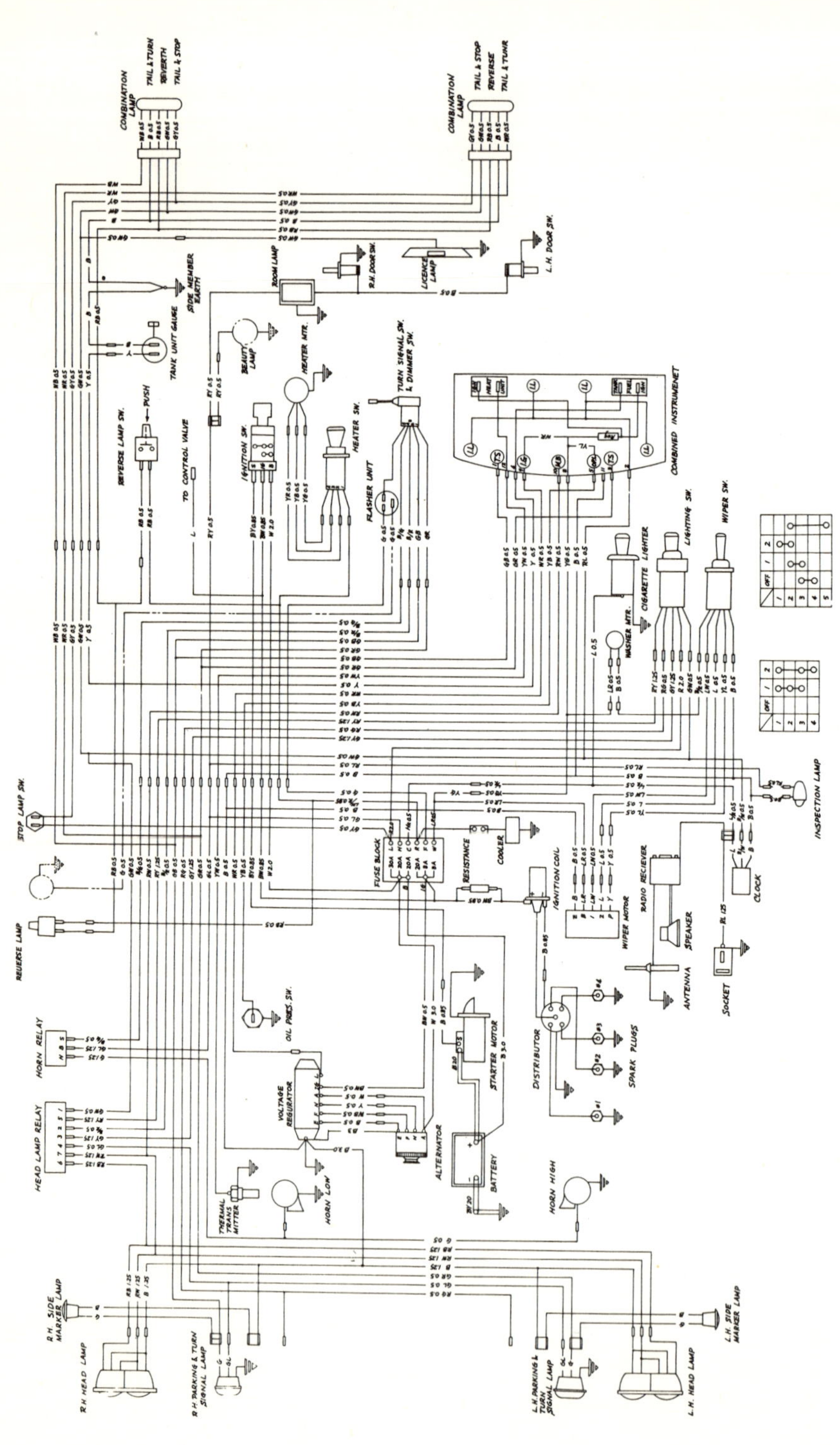
COMBINATION LAMP
TAIL & TURN
TAIL & STOP
REVERSE
ROOM LAMP
R.H. DOOR SW.
L.H. DOOR SW.
LICENCE LAMP
SIDE MEMBER EARTH
TANK UNIT GAUGE
REVERSE LAMP SW.
PUSH
TO CONTROL VALVE
IGNITION SW.
BEAUTY LAMP
HEATER MTR.
HEATER SW.
TURN SIGNAL SW. & DIMMER SW.
FLASHER UNIT
COMBINED INSTRUMENET
CIGARETTE LIGHTER
LIGHTING SW.
WIPER SW.
WASHER MTR.
INSPECTION LAMP
STOP LAMP SW.
REVERSE LAMP
FUSE BLOCK
RESISTANCE
COOLER
IGNITION COIL
WIPER MOTOR
RADIO RECIEVER
SPEAKER
ANTENNA
CLOCK
SOCKET
OIL PRES. SW.
HORN RELAY
HEAD LAMP RELAY
VOLTAGE REGURATOR
STARTER MOTOR
DISTRIBUTOR
SPARK PLUGS
ALTERNATOR
BATTERY
THERMAL TRANS MITTER
HORN LOW
HORN HIGH
R.H. SIDE MARKER LAMP
L.H. SIDE MARKER LAMP
R.H HEAD LAMP
L.H. HEAD LAMP
R.H PARKING & TURN SIGNAL LAMP
L.H PARKING & TURN SIGNAL LAMP
PL411

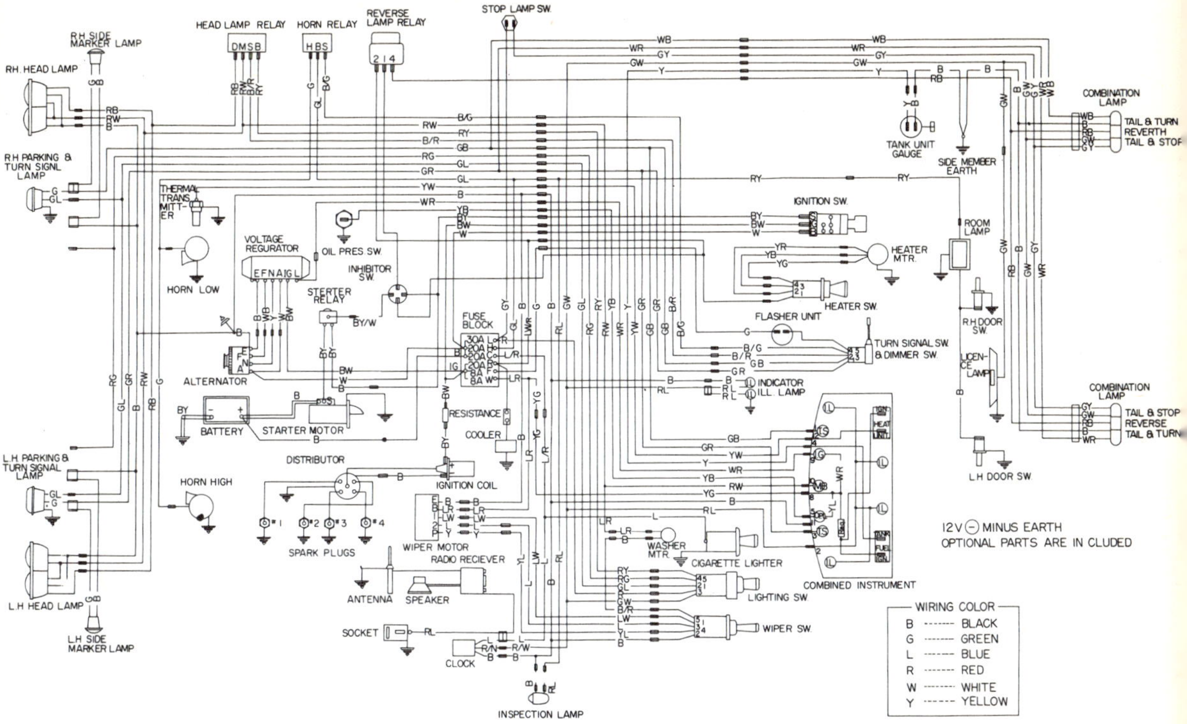

12V ⊖ MINUS EARTH
OPTIONAL PARTS ARE IN CLUDED

WIRING COLOR

B	BLACK
G	GREEN
L	BLUE
R	RED
W	WHITE
Y	YELLOW

RL411

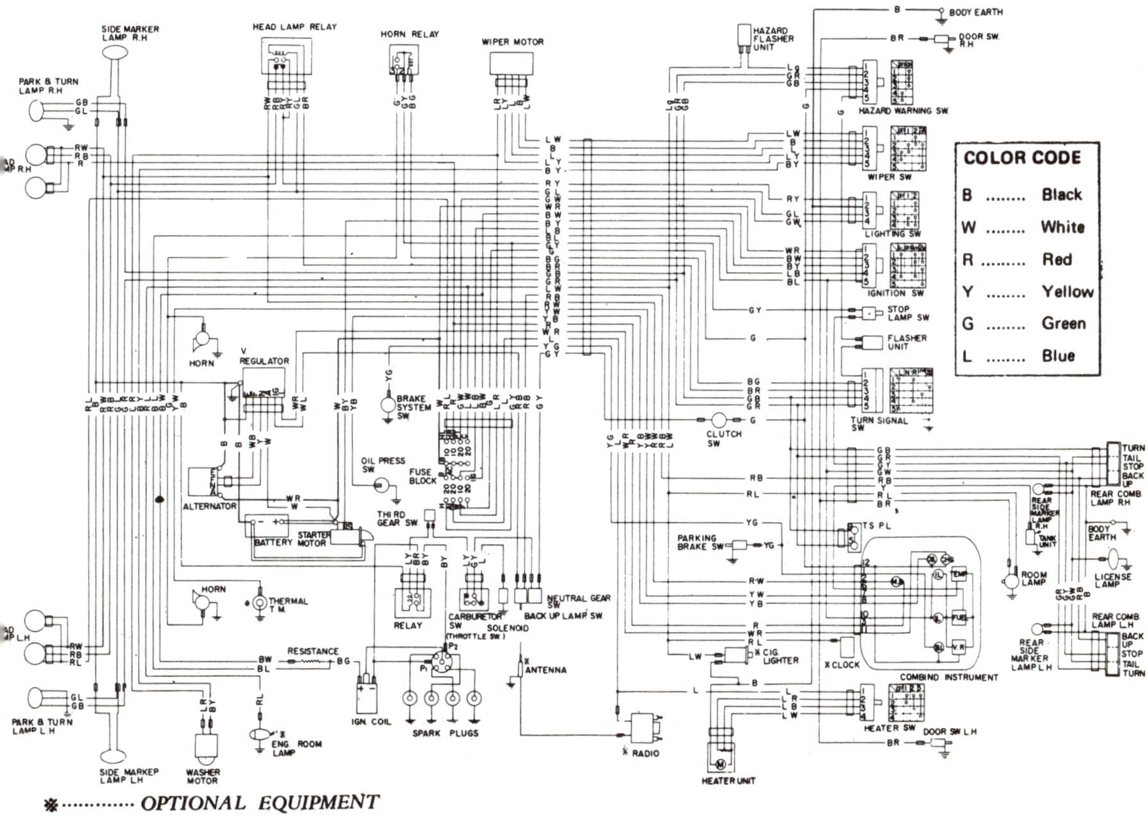

COLOR CODE

B	Black
W	White
R	Red
Y	Yellow
G	Green
L	Blue

✻ .... *OPTIONAL EQUIPMENT*

PL510, standard transmission

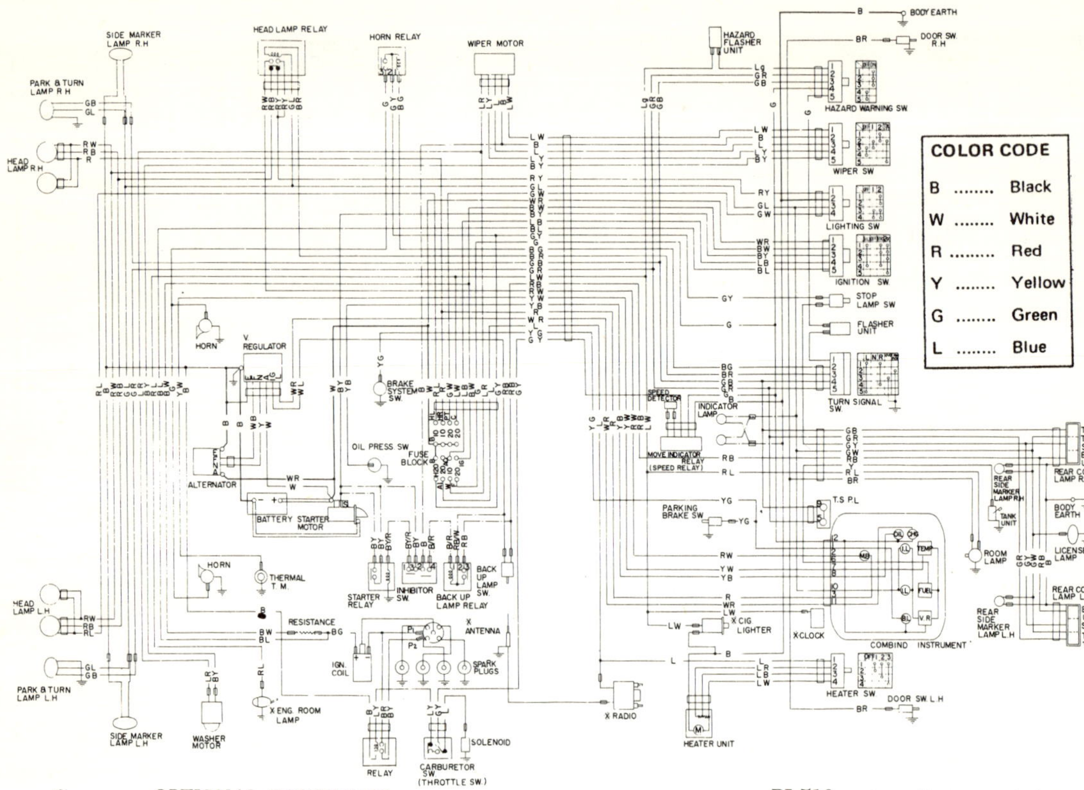

COLOR CODE

B	....	Black
W	....	White
R	....	Red
Y	....	Yellow
G	....	Green
L	....	Blue

※ .... *OPTIONAL EQUIPMENT*

PL510, automatic transmission

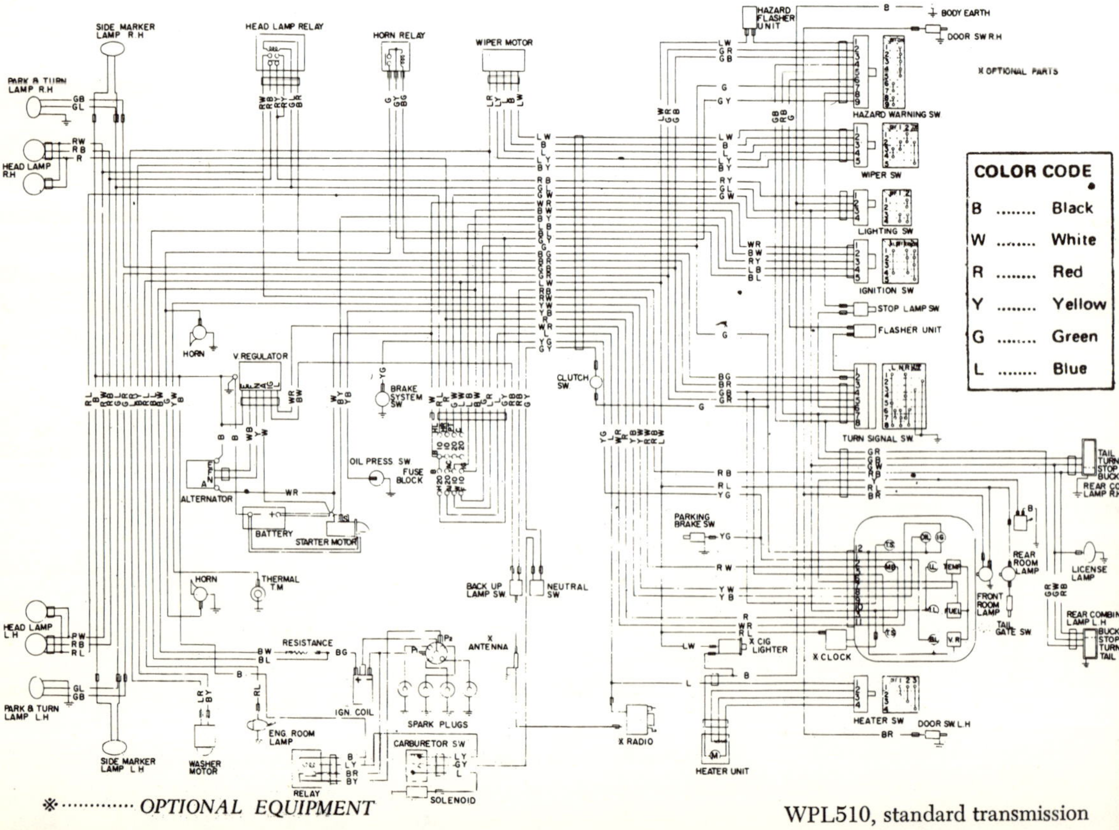

※ OPTIONAL PARTS

COLOR CODE

B	....	Black
W	....	White
R	....	Red
Y	....	Yellow
G	....	Green
L	....	Blue

※ .... *OPTIONAL EQUIPMENT*

WPL510, standard transmission

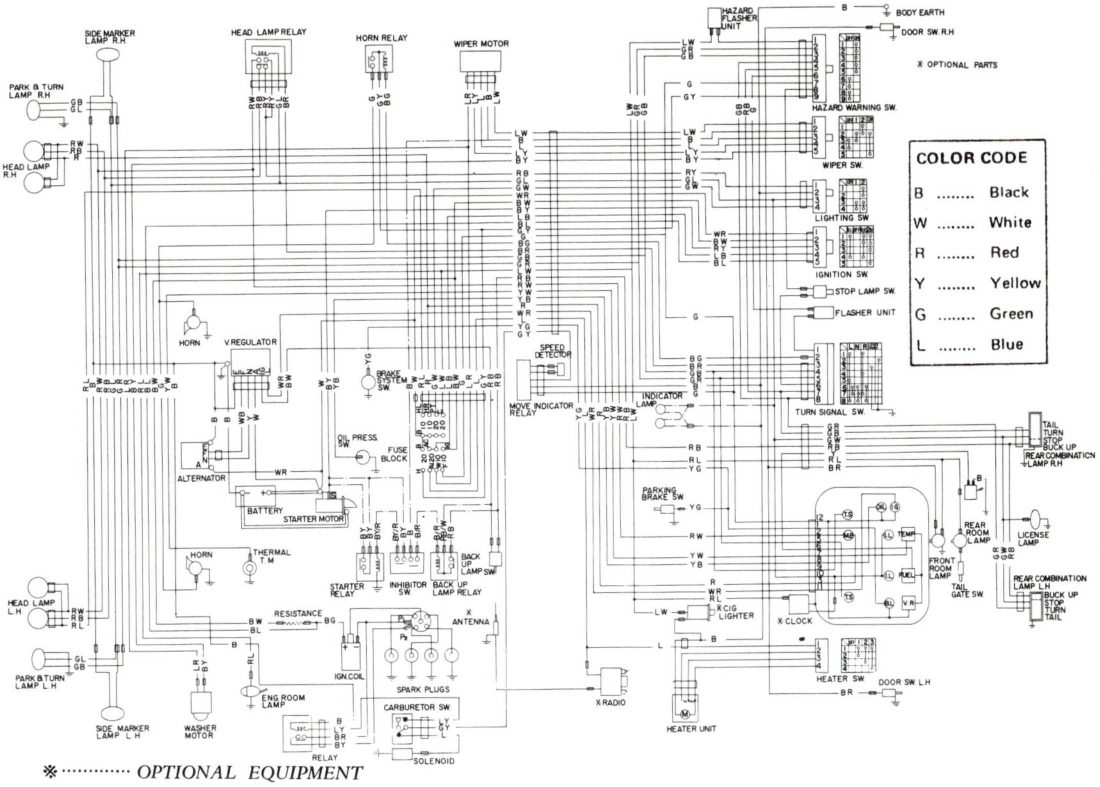

COLOR CODE

B	....	Black
W	....	White
R	....	Red
Y	....	Yellow
G	....	Green
L	....	Blue

※ ············ *OPTIONAL EQUIPMENT*

WPL510, automatic transmission

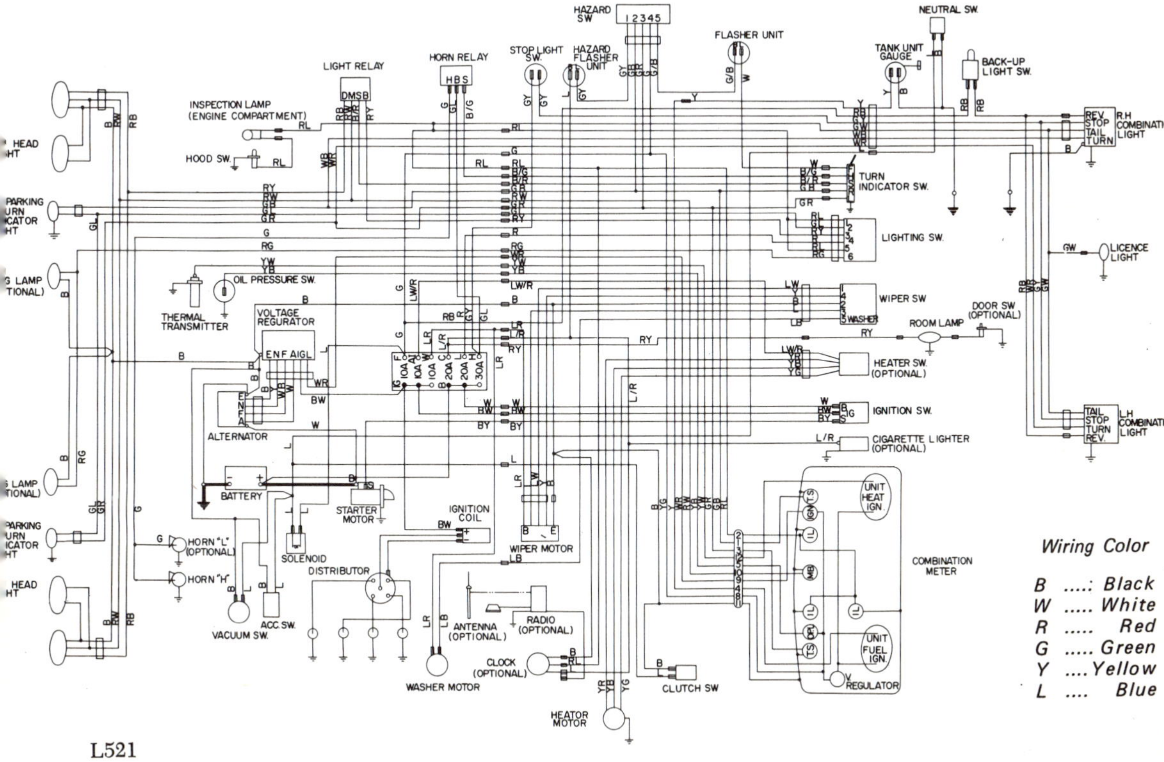

Wiring Color

B	*.....:*	*Black*
W	*.....*	*White*
R	*.....*	*Red*
G	*.....*	*Green*
Y	*....*	*Yellow*
L	*....*	*Blue*

L521

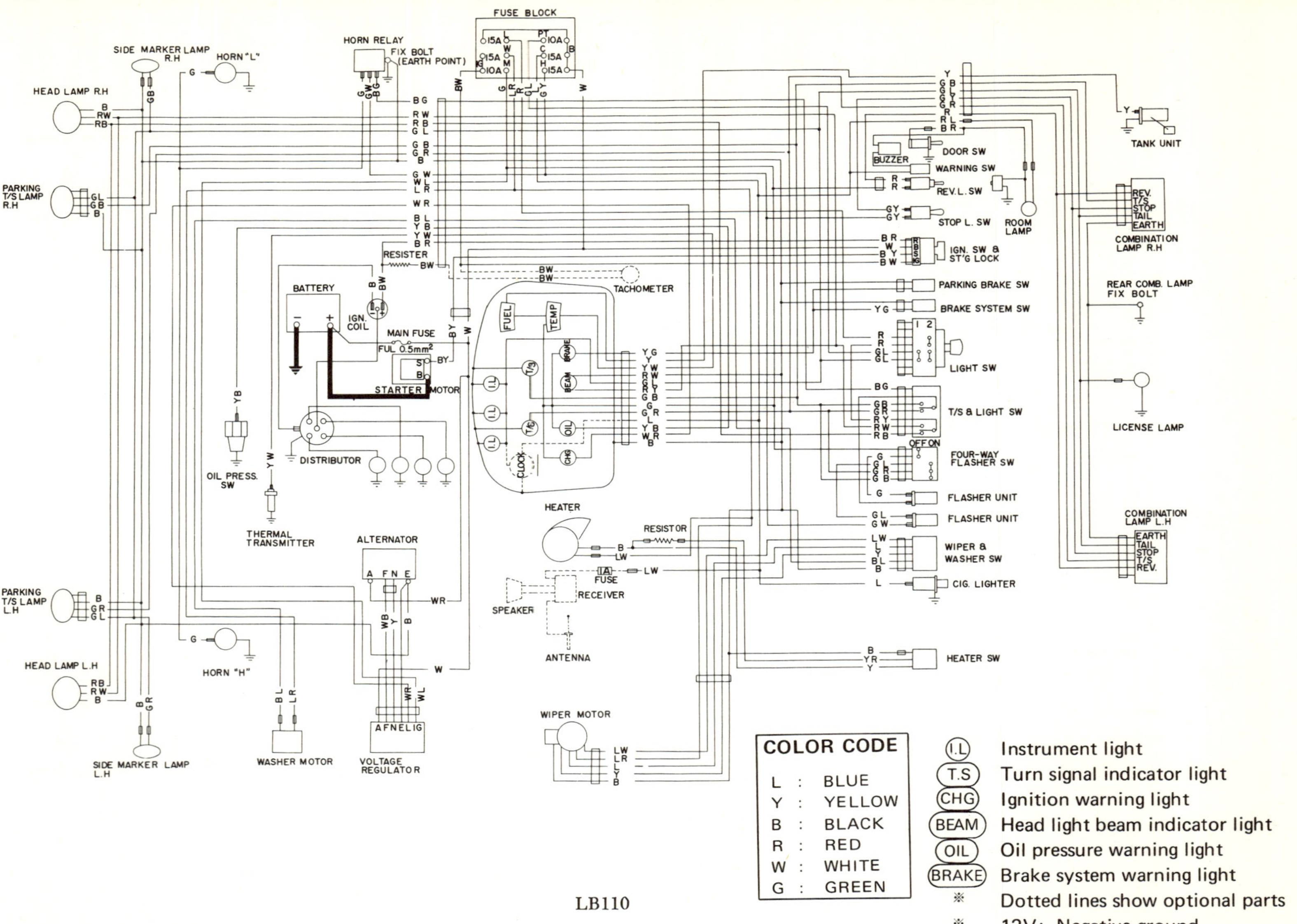

FUSE BLOCK
HORN RELAY
FIX BOLT (EARTH POINT)
SIDE MARKER LAMP R.H
HORN "L"
HEAD LAMP R.H
PARKING T/S LAMP R.H
PARKING T/S LAMP L.H
HEAD LAMP L.H
SIDE MARKER LAMP L.H
HORN "H"
WASHER MOTOR
VOLTAGE REGULATOR
ALTERNATOR
THERMAL TRANSMITTER
OIL PRESS. SW
DISTRIBUTOR
BATTERY
IGN. COIL
MAIN FUSE
FUL 0.5mm²
STARTER MOTOR
RESISTER
TACHOMETER
FUEL
TEMP
BRAKE
BEAM
OIL
CHG
CLOCK
HEATER
RESISTOR
FUSE
RECEIVER
SPEAKER
ANTENNA
WIPER MOTOR
TANK UNIT
DOOR SW
BUZZER
WARNING SW
REV.L. SW
STOP L. SW
ROOM LAMP
IGN. SW & ST'G LOCK
PARKING BRAKE SW
BRAKE SYSTEM SW
LIGHT SW
T/S & LIGHT SW
FOUR-WAY FLASHER SW
FLASHER UNIT
FLASHER UNIT
WIPER & WASHER SW
CIG. LIGHTER
HEATER SW
COMBINATION LAMP R.H
REV. T/S STOP TAIL EARTH
REAR COMB. LAMP FIX BOLT
LICENSE LAMP
COMBINATION LAMP L.H
EARTH TAIL STOP T/S REV.
COLOR CODE
L : BLUE
Y : YELLOW
B : BLACK
R : RED
W : WHITE
G : GREEN
I.L Instrument light
T.S Turn signal indicator light
CHG Ignition warning light
BEAM Head light beam indicator light
OIL Oil pressure warning light
BRAKE Brake system warning light
※ Dotted lines show optional parts
※ 12V: Negative ground
LB110

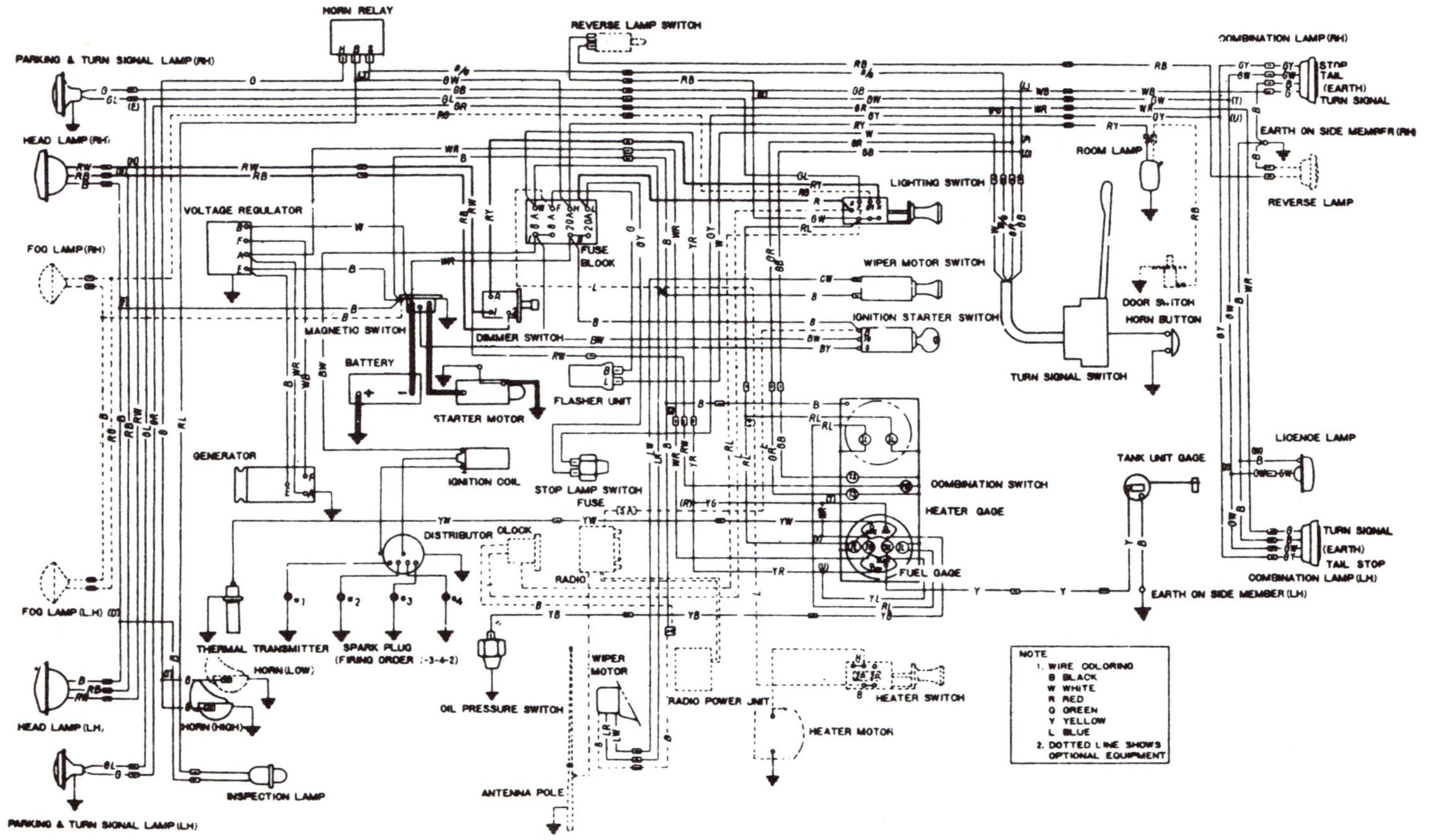

L320

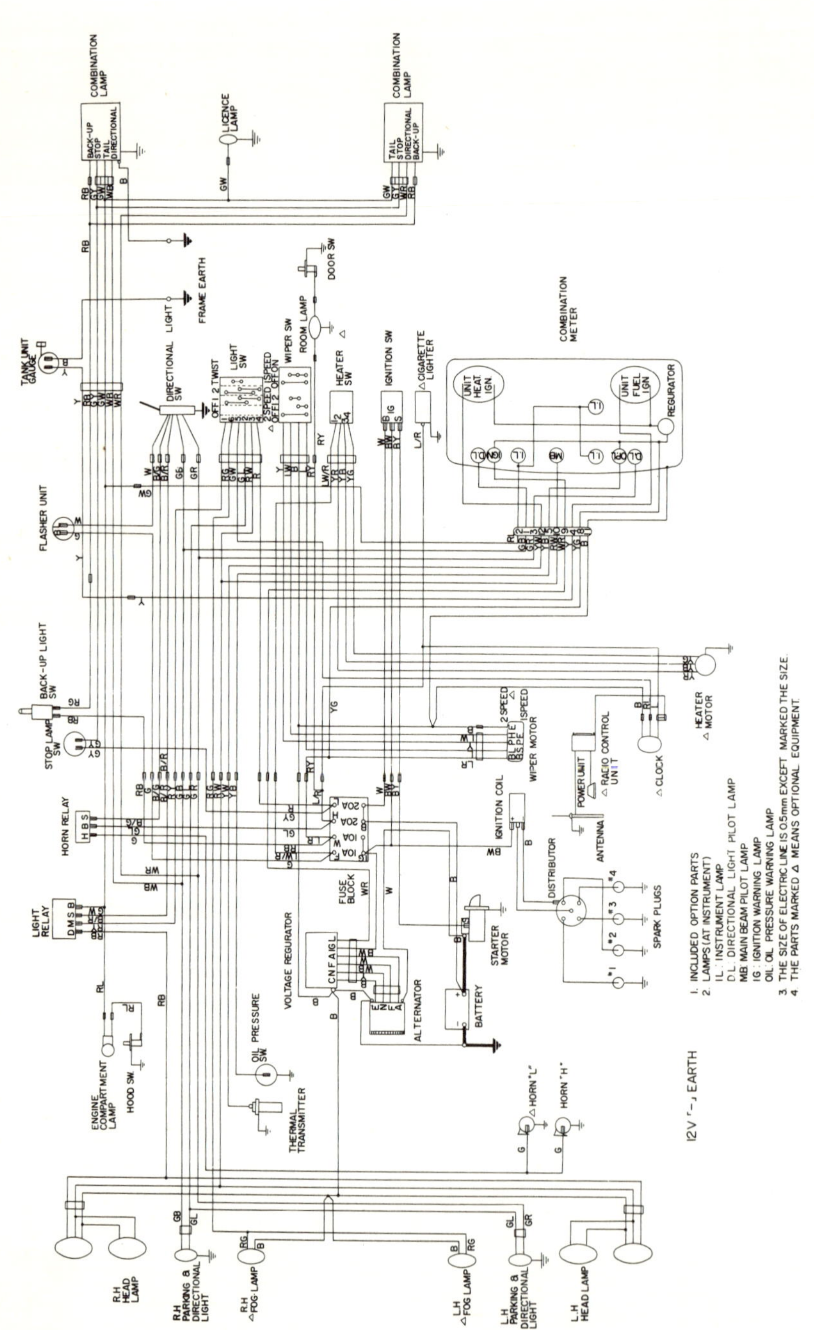
COMBINATION LAMP
BACK-UP
STOP
TAIL
DIRECTIONAL
LICENCE LAMP
TAIL
STOP
DIRECTIONAL
BACK-UP
COMBINATION LAMP
FRAME EARTH
DOOR SW
ROOM LAMP
TANK UNIT
GAUGE
DIRECTIONAL LIGHT
DIRECTIONAL SW
LIGHT SW
WIPER SW
HEATER SW
IGNITION SW
△ CIGARETTE LIGHTER
COMBINATION METER
UNIT HEAT IGN
UNIT FUEL IGN
REGURATOR
FLASHER UNIT
BACK-UP LIGHT SW
STOP LAMP SW
HORN RELAY
LIGHT RELAY
FUSE BLOCK
VOLTAGE REGURATOR
ALTERNATOR
BATTERY
STARTER MOTOR
IGNITION COIL
DISTRIBUTOR
SPARK PLUGS
WIPER MOTOR
ANTENNA
POWER UNIT
△ RADIO CONTROL UNIT
△ CLOCK
HEATER △ MOTOR
ENGINE COMPARTMENT LAMP
HOOD SW.
OIL PRESSURE SW
THERMAL TRANSMITTER
△ HORN "L"
HORN "H"
R.H HEAD LAMP
R.H PARKING & DIRECTIONAL LIGHT
R.H △ FOG LAMP
L.H △ FOG LAMP
L.H PARKING & DIRECTIONAL LIGHT
L.H HEAD LAMP
12V (-) EARTH
1. INCLUDED OPTION PARTS
2. LAMPS (AT INSTRUMENT)
IL : INSTRUMENT LAMP
D.L : DIRECTIONAL LIGHT PILOT LAMP
MB : MAIN BEAM PILOT LAMP
IG : IGNITION WARNING LAMP
OIL : OIL PRESSURE WARNING LAMP
3. THE SIZE OF ELECTRIC LINE IS 0.5mm EXCEPT MARKED THE SIZE.
4. THE PARTS MARKED △ MEANS OPTIONAL EQUIPMENT.
L520

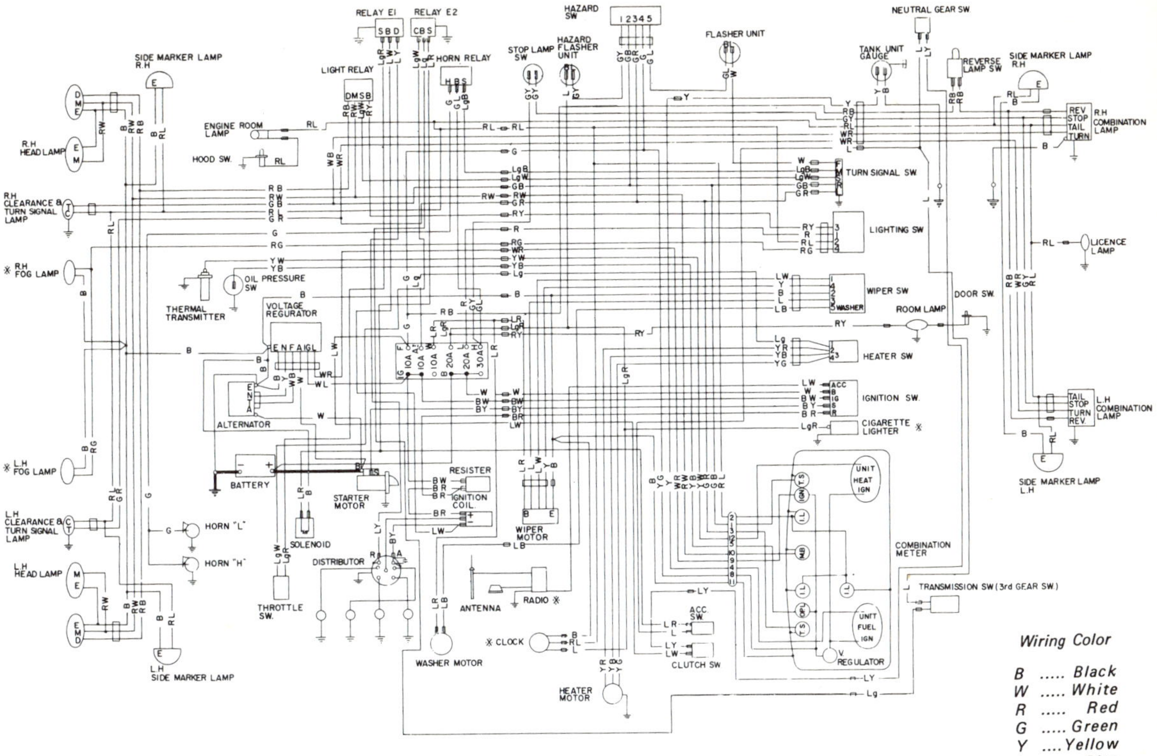

Wiring Color

B ..... Black
W ..... White
R ..... Red
G ..... Green
Y ..... Yellow
L ..... Blue

※········ OPTIONAL EQUIPMENT

PL521

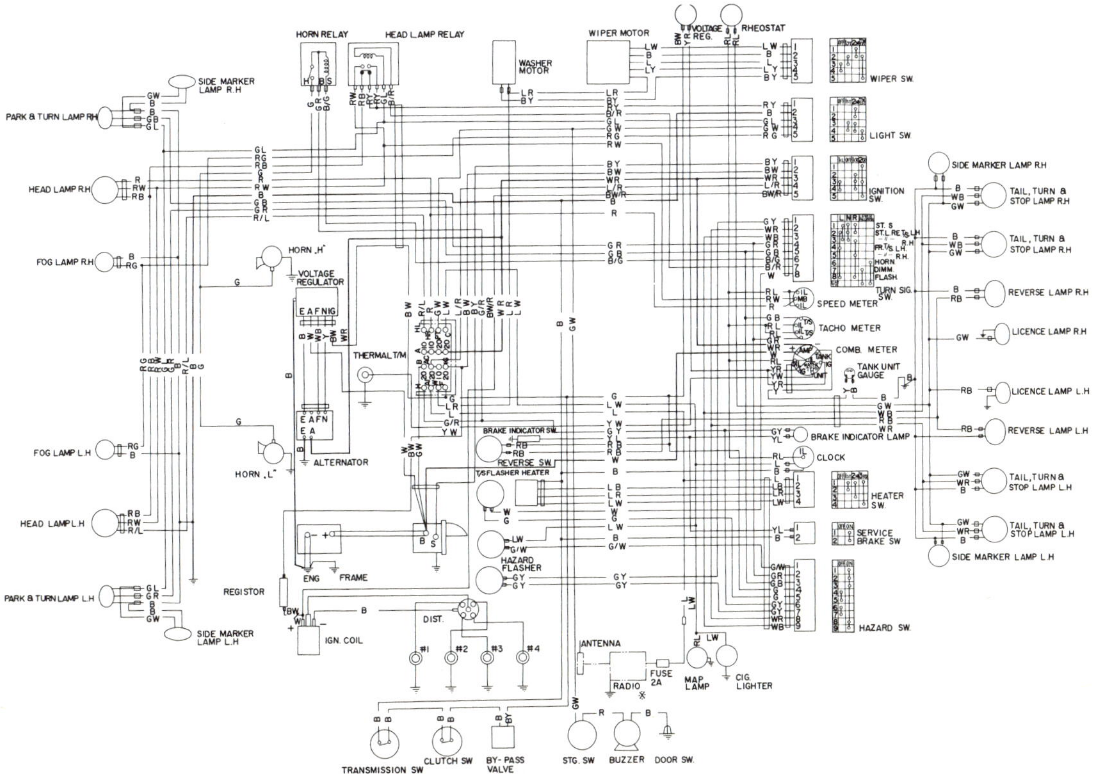

SPL311

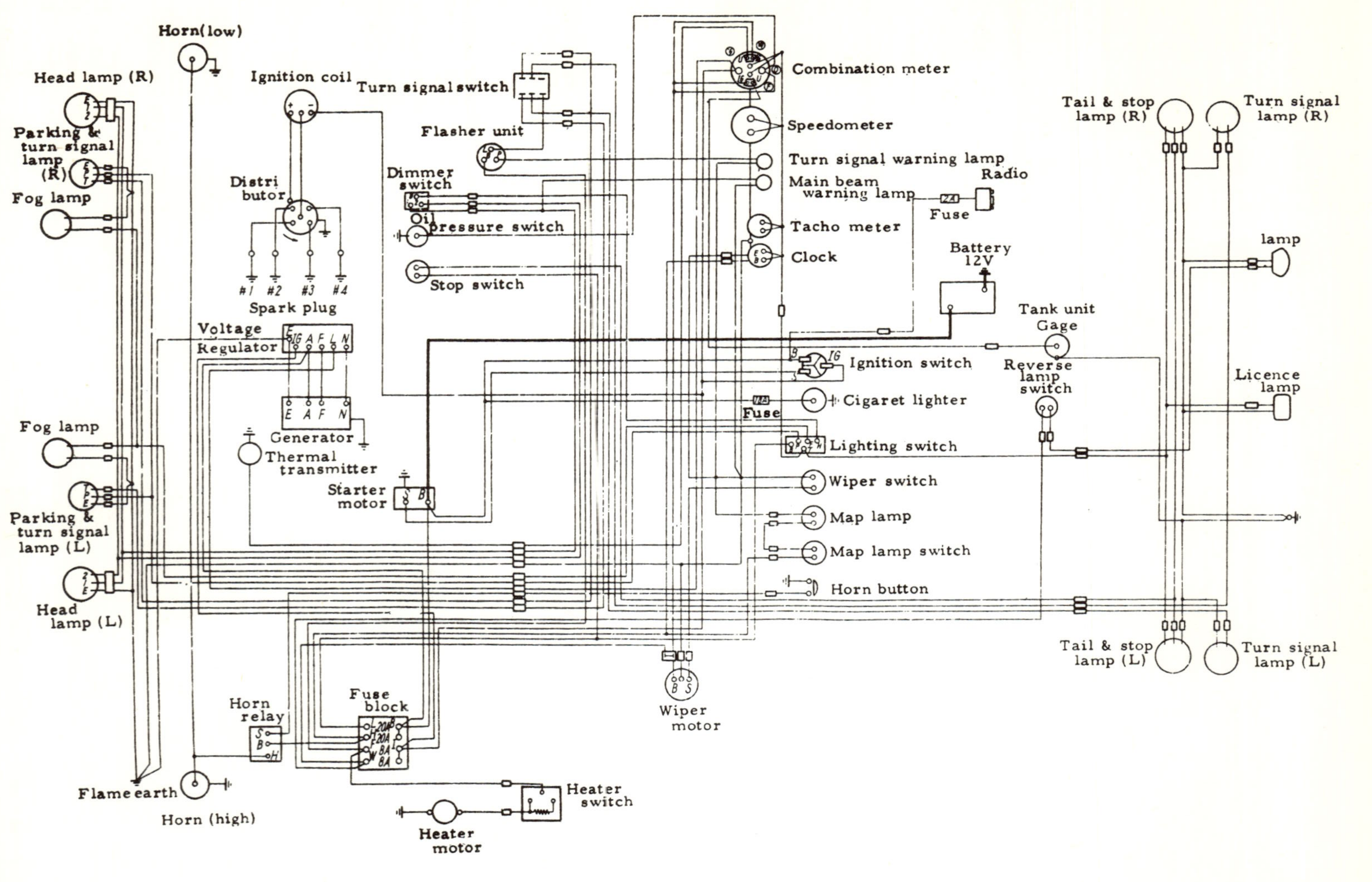
Horn(low)
Head lamp (R)
Parking & turn signal lamp (R)
Fog lamp
Ignition coil
Distri butor
Spark plug
Voltage Regulator
Generator
Thermal transmitter
Starter motor
Turn signal switch
Flasher unit
Dimmer switch
Oil pressure switch
Stop switch
Combination meter
Speedometer
Turn signal warning lamp
Main beam warning lamp
Radio
Fuse
Tacho meter
Clock
Battery 12V
Tank unit
Gage
Ignition switch
Reverse lamp switch
Cigaret lighter
Fuse
Lighting switch
Wiper switch
Map lamp
Map lamp switch
Horn button
Tail & stop lamp (R)
Turn signal lamp (R)
lamp
Licence lamp
Tail & stop lamp (L)
Turn signal lamp (L)
Fog lamp
Parking & turn signal lamp (L)
Head lamp (L)
Wiper motor
Horn relay
Fuse block
Flame earth
Horn (high)
Heater switch
Heater motor
SPL310

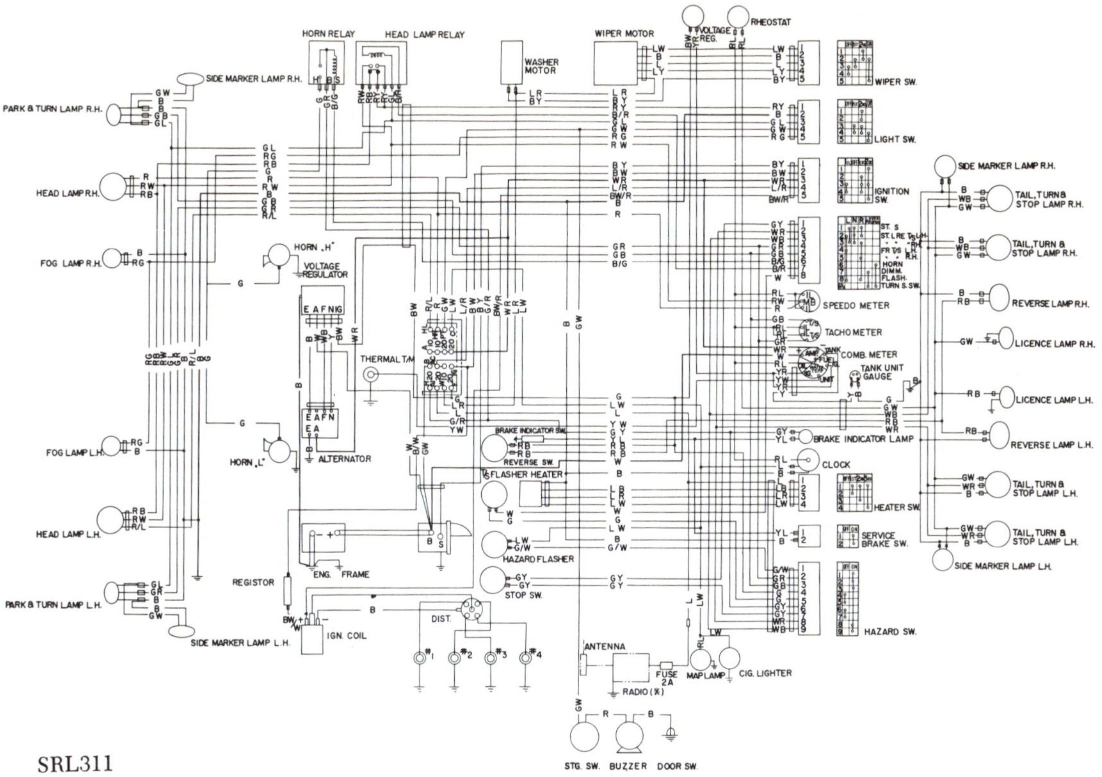

SRL311

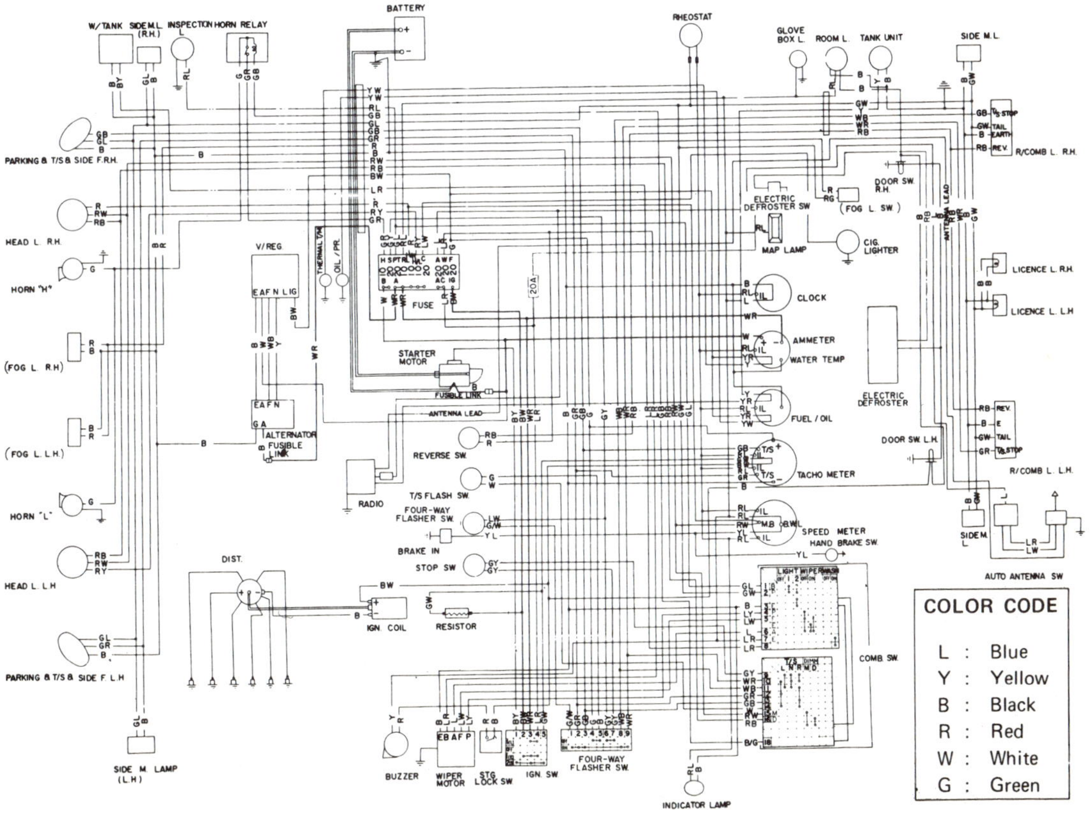

COLOR CODE

L	:	Blue
Y	:	Yellow
B	:	Black
R	:	Red
W	:	White
G	:	Green

HLS30, standard transmission

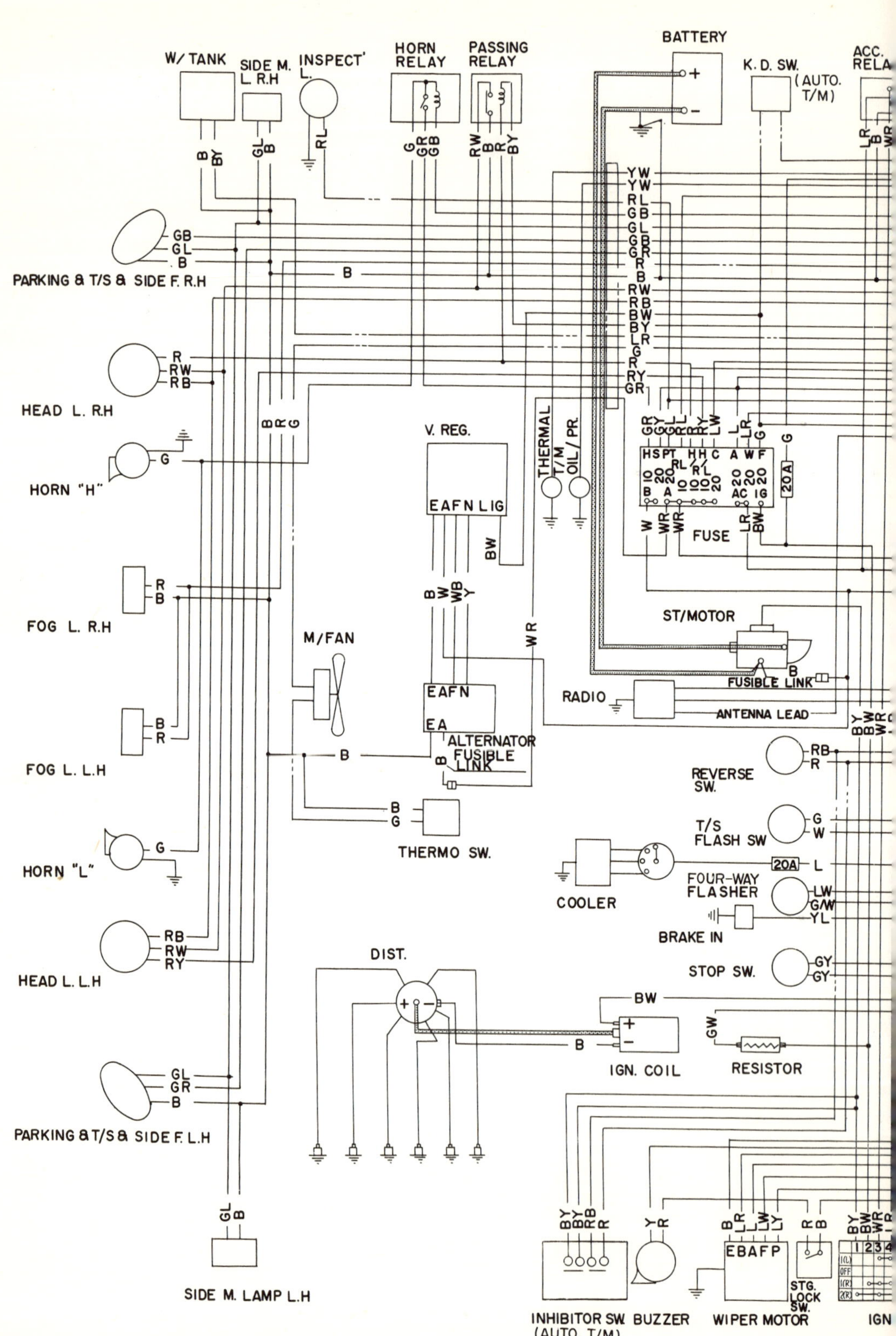

HLS30, automatic transmission

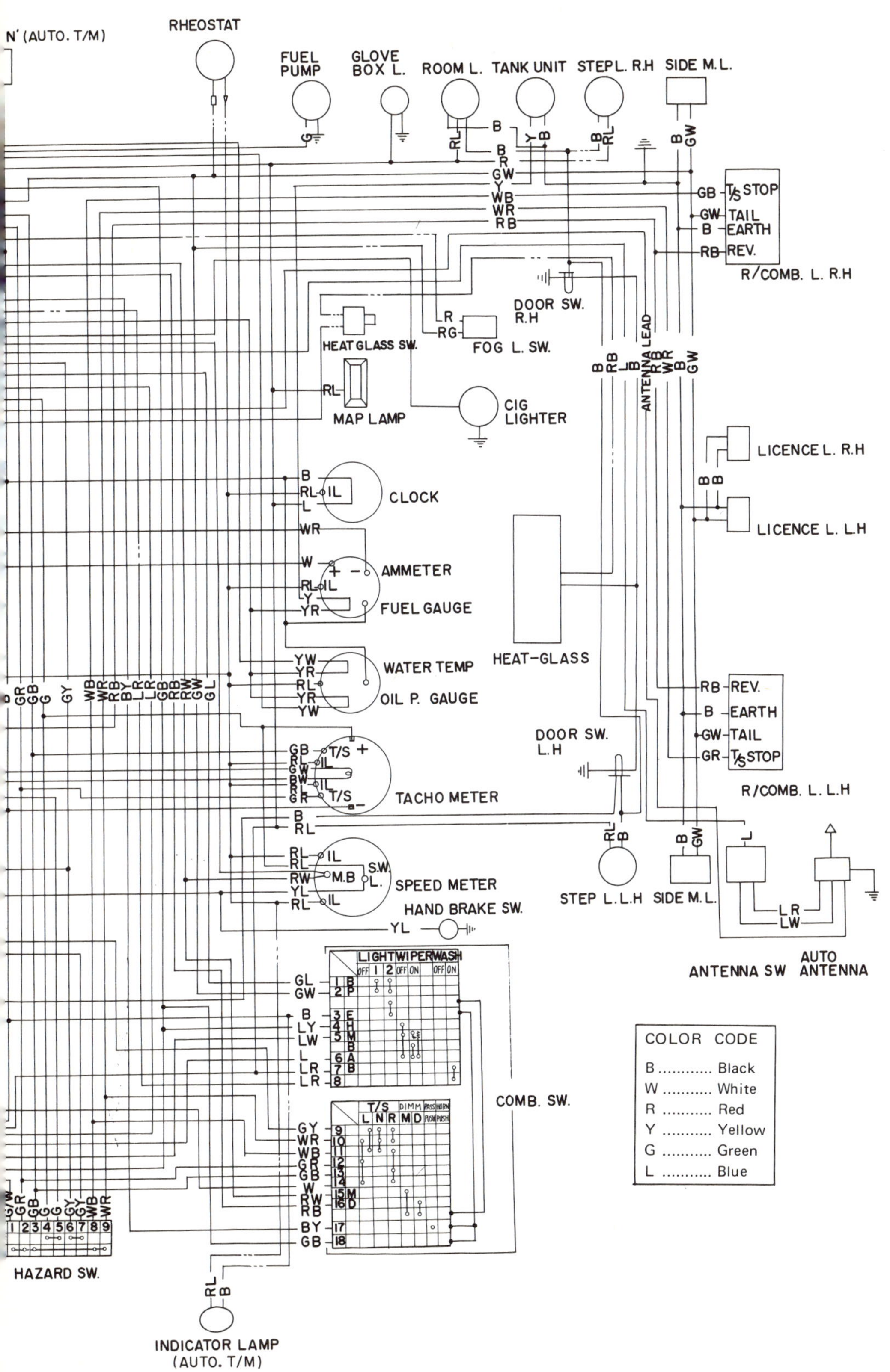

N' (AUTO. T/M)
RHEOSTAT
FUEL PUMP
GLOVE BOX L.
ROOM L.
TANK UNIT
STEP L. R.H
SIDE M.L.
T/S STOP
TAIL
EARTH
REV.
R/COMB. L. R.H
DOOR SW. R.H
HEAT GLASS SW.
FOG L. SW.
MAP LAMP
CIG LIGHTER
ANTENNA LEAD
LICENCE L. R.H
LICENCE L. L.H
CLOCK
AMMETER
FUEL GAUGE
HEAT-GLASS
WATER TEMP
OIL P. GAUGE
REV.
EARTH
TAIL
T/S STOP
R/COMB. L. L.H
DOOR SW. L.H
TACHO METER
STEP L. L.H
SIDE M.L.
SPEED METER
HAND BRAKE SW.
ANTENNA SW
AUTO ANTENNA
LIGHT WIPER WASH
T/S DIMM PASS HORN
COMB. SW.
HAZARD SW.
INDICATOR LAMP (AUTO. T/M)
COLOR CODE
B .... Black
W .... White
R .... Red
Y .... Yellow
G .... Green
L .... Blue

Manual Transmission

Removal and Installation

On SPL310, SPL311, and SRL311 sportscars, the transmission must be removed in unit with the engine; it cannot be removed separately. On all other models, the transmission may be removed separately from under the vehicle. Transmission removal and replacement procedure for early models is generally similar to that for PL510, WPL510, HLS30, LB110, KLB110 Manual Transmission.

NISSAN PATROL (L60), SEPARATION OF TRANSFER CASE AND TRANSMISSION

1. Drain transmission and transfer case. Disconnect front and rear driveshafts. Disconnect handbrake rod, shifter rods, and speedometer cable.
2. Remove transfer case rear cover.
3. Remove nut and washer securing drive gear to transmission mainshaft.
4. Pull off drive (mainshaft) gear.
5. Remove four capscrews and one nut securing transfer case to transmission.
6. Pull transfer case to rear on a jack.
7. Reverse procedure to reinstall. Adjust handbrake.

PL510, WPL510, HLS30, LB110, KLB110

1. Raise and support vehicle.
2. On PL510 and WPL510, disconnect handbrake cable at equalizer pivot. Disconnect backup light switch on all models.
3. On PL510 and WPL510, loosen muffler clamps and turn muffler to one side to allow room for driveshaft removal. On HLS30, remove exhaust system. On LB110 and KLB110, disconnect exhaust pipe from manifold.
4. Unbolt driveshaft at rear and remove. Seal the end of the transmission extension housing to prevent leakage.
5. Disconnect speedometer drive cable from transmission.
6. Remove shift lever.
7. Remove clutch operating cylinder from clutch housing.
8. Support the engine with a large wood block and a jack under the oil pan.

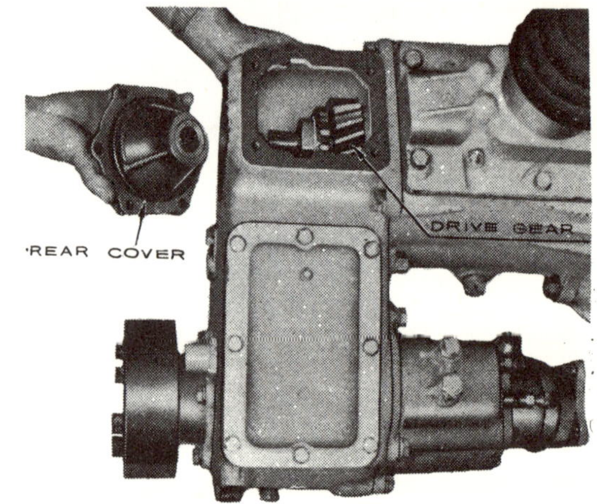

Removing transfer case rear cover

Main shaft (drive) gear and nut

9. Unbolt transmission from crossmember. Support the transmission with a jack. Remove crossmember.
10. Lower the rear of the engine to allow clearance.

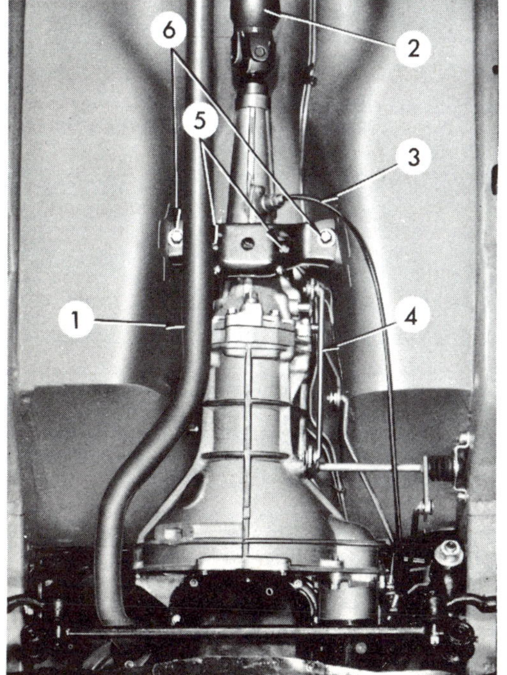

LB110 with manual transmission

1. Exhaust pipe
2. Driveshaft
3. Speedometer cable
4. Shift linkage
5. Transmission rear mounting bolts
6. Crossmember mounting bolts

11. Remove starter.
12. Unbolt transmission. Lower and remove to the rear.
13. Reverse procedure for reinstallation. Check clutch linkage adjustment.

Overhaul

Nissan Patrol (L60) Transmission

Disassembly

1. Separate transfer case from transmission.
2. Unbolt and remove gearshift cover.
3. Unbolt and remove bearing retainer and oil seal from front of transmission.
4. Bend back countershaft lockplate and unscrew nut. Drive countergear assembly back about ⅛". Hook a puller on the bearing snap-ring and pull out the bearing.
5. Drive mainshaft back enough to hook the rear bearing with a puller. Remove the bearing. Slide the rear mainshaft section rearward and upward, out of the top of the case.
6. Remove the front mainshaft bearing snap-ring. Drive the front mainshaft section in, then pull it out of the case. Drive the front bearing out from the inside.
7. Tap the countershaft in from the front and remove it through the top of the case. Remove countershaft front bear-

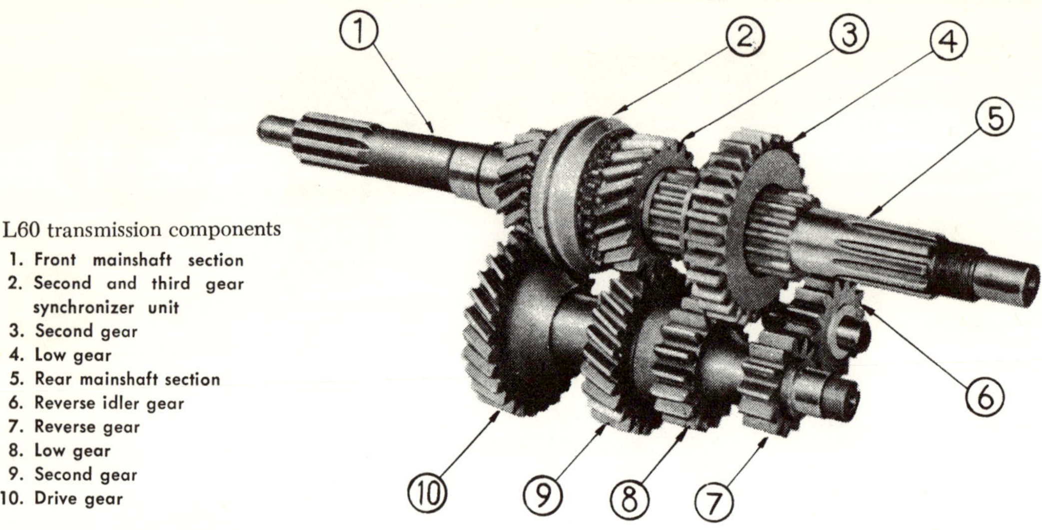

L60 transmission components
1. Front mainshaft section
2. Second and third gear synchronizer unit
3. Second gear
4. Low gear
5. Rear mainshaft section
6. Reverse idler gear
7. Reverse gear
8. Low gear
9. Second gear
10. Drive gear

ing by driving in the outer race.

8. Bend back reverse idler shaft lockplate and remove setscrew. Drive out shaft. Remove idler gear and thrust washer.

Inspection

1. Wash all parts in a safe solvent.
2. Oil the bearings immediately.
3. Slide first and reverse gear into the mainshaft. If play between gear and shaft exceeds .005″ (.125 mm.), replace gear, shaft, or both.
4. The inside diameter of second gear should not exceed 1.503″ (38.175 mm.). The outer diameter of the second gear bushing should not be less than 1.495″ (38 mm.). Replace the gear, bushing, or shaft, if worn. If the pin preventing the bushing from turning is loose, replace bushing and pin. To remove the bushing, remove the snap-ring and thrust washer. Slide off second gear and remove the pin. Drive or press off the bushing. Press on the new bushing.
5. The inside diameter of the idler gear bushing must be no more than .7509″ (19.073 mm.). If the bushing is replaced, ream the new one to fit. Clearance between bushing and shaft should be about .003-.004″.
6. If the idler gear shaft is less than .7432″ (18.879 mm.) in diameter, replace the shaft.
7. Needle bearing rollers must be at least .117″ (2.99 mm.) in diameter.
8. Gear backlash should be .03-.05″ (.075-.125 mm.).
9. Check all parts for excessive wear or damage, replacing as necessary.

Assembly

1. Dip each part in transmission lubricant before assembly.
2. Hold the reverse idler gear in place in the case with the cone end of the hub to the front and thrust washers at each side. Push the idler gear shaft into the case. Align the setscrew hole and insert the setscrew with its lockplate. Tighten the setscrew and bend up the lockplate.
3. Place the countergear in the case with the large gear to the front.

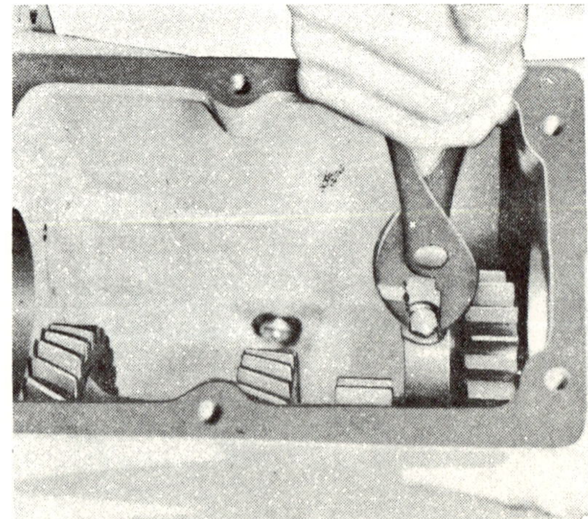

Bending setscrew lockplate, L60 transmission

4. Press second gear bushing onto front of rear mainshaft section. Insert bushing lockpin. Slide second gear onto shaft with tapered end to the front.

Install thrust washer and snap-ring. Gear end-play should be .0026-.0050″ (.067-.133 mm.). Thrust washers of different thicknesses are available to adjust the end-play. These are .1520-.1535″ (3.860-3.900 mm.), .1539-.1555″ (3.910-3.950 mm.), and .1559-.1575″ (3.960-4.000 mm.). The bushing should have no end-play. Slide the first and reverse gear onto the shaft, with the shift fork groove forward.

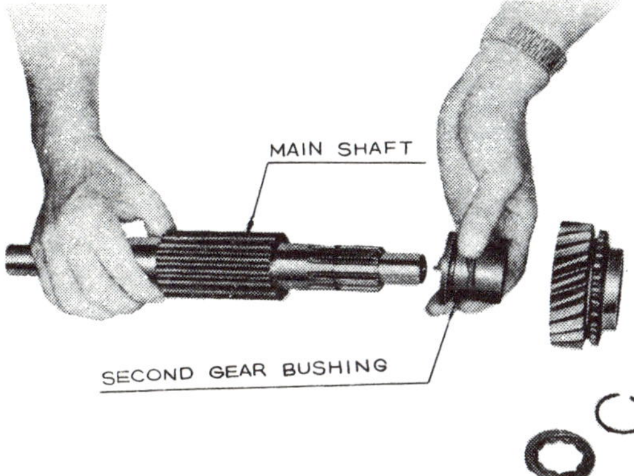

Replacing second gear bushing, L60 transmission

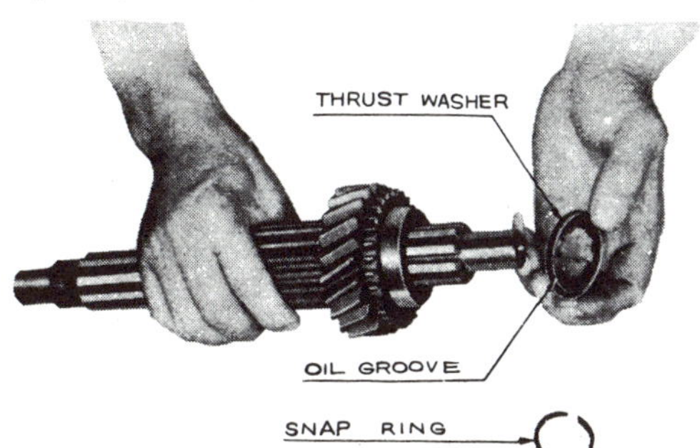

Thrust washer installation, L60 transmission

5. Assemble the synchronizer by installing the balls, springs, locking plates, and sleeve. Install the baulk rings in both sides of the hub. The pointed ends of the ring lugs must face in to the synchronizers. Slide the synchronizer assembly onto the mainshaft with the long side of the hub to the front and the deeper flange to the rear.
6. Insert rear mainshaft section into case through the top. Hold the front of the shaft in some way while driving in the rear bearing.
7. Drive front mainshaft section and bearing into place.
8. Insert counter gear assembly through power takeoff cover opening. Insert front washer and drive in roller bearing. Place rear bearing on countershaft and drive into case. Install lockplate and nut at rear. Bend lockplate.

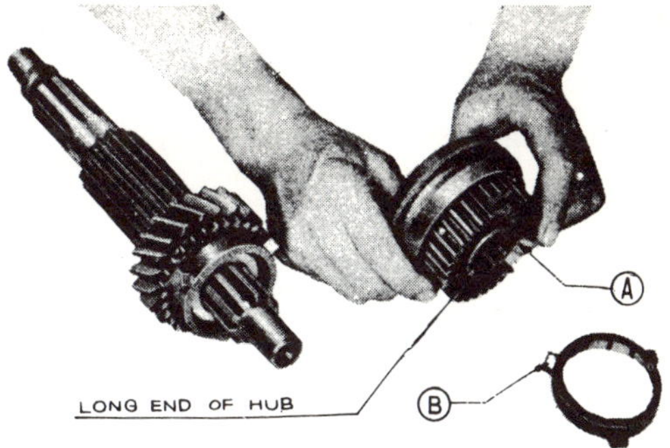

Align A with B when assembling synchronizer, L60 transmission

Mainshaft installation (rear section), L60 transmission

Installation of mainshaft front section, L60 transmission

9. Coat front mainshaft section with transmission lubricant where it contacts the front bearing. Install the front bearing retainer.
10. Install cover assembly and gasket, making sure that shifter forks enter their grooves.
11. Refill transmission with recommended gear oil. Note that units with power takeoff have a smaller fluid capacity. See Capacities and Pressures Chart.

Nissan Patrol (L60) Transfer Case

Disassembly

1. Separate transfer case from transmission.

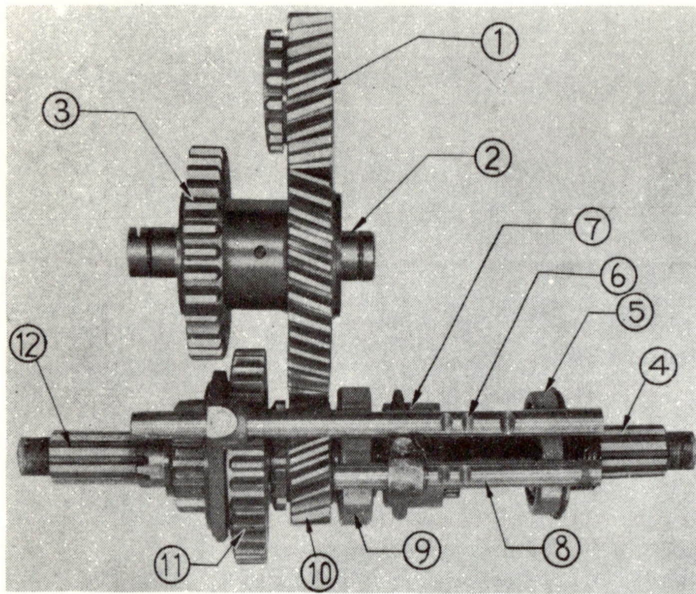

L60 transfer case components

1. Main drive gear
2. Countershaft
3. Countergear
4. Front driveshaft
5. Front bearing
6. High and low range shift rod
7. Front wheel drive sleeve
8. Front wheel drive shift rod
9. Front bearing of rear driveshaft
10. High range gear
11. Low range gear
12. Rear drive shaft

L60 transfer case components

1. Main drive gear
2. Countershaft
3. Countergear
4. Front driveshaft
5. Front bearing
6. High and low range shift rod
7. Front wheel drive sleeve
8. Front wheel drive shift rod
9. Front bearing of rear driveshaft
10. High range gear
11. Low range gear
12. Rear driveshaft

2. Remove the brake band assembly. Remove the brake drum. Unbolt and pull off the rear flange.
3. Remove both top covers.
4. Unbolt and pull off the front flange.
5. Unbolt and remove the front bearing retainer.
6. Remove two spring plugs from front cover. Remove two detent springs and balls.
7. Remove the two shift rod eyes from the rods.
8. Unbolt and carefully slide off the front cover, leaving long shift rod in place. Remove the front wheel drive shift rod with fork and sleeve from the front

Removing front cover, L60 transfer case

cover. Remove the bearing.

9. Remove the setscrew from the high and low range shift fork (long rod). Slide the shift rod out and remove the fork.
10. Remove the capscrew and countershaft lockplate. Drive the countershaft out with a drift. Remove the countergear and two thrust washers.
11. Remove rear bearing retainer. Remove driveshaft rear bearing with a puller or press driveshaft out to the front. Remove low range gear. If shaft was pressed out, drive rear bearing from case.
12. To disassemble driveshaft, remove snap-ring securing front bearing. Remove spacer washer and pull off bearing. Remove thrust washer and high range gear.

Inspection

1. Wash all parts in a safe solvent. Oil the bearings immediately.
2. Replace the shift rod oil seals.
3. The diameter of the pilot end (rear) of the front driveshaft should be at least .6693″ (17 mm.). If it is less, replace the shaft.
4. The countergear thrust washers must be at least .1311″ (3.33 mm.) thick. If not, replace them. The countershaft must be at least .1249″ (31.73 mm.) in diameter.
5. Drive out and replace the bearing retainer oil seals.
6. The rear driveshaft thrust washer must be at least .142″ (3.6 mm.) thick.
7. Gear backlash should be .004-.006″ (.102-.152 mm.).
8. Check all parts for excessive wear or damage, replacing as necessary.

Assembly

1. To install rear driveshaft, push rear bearing onto driveshaft. Place low range sliding gear into case, channel side to the rear. Insert driveshaft through the gear. Use a dummy bearing at the front to center the shaft. Drive in the rear bearing and driveshaft. Stick the rear bearing retainer gasket to the case with grease. Place the rear driveshaft bearing spacer on the shaft, chamfered side to the bearing. Install the rear bearing retainer and new oil seal. Tighten the bolts evenly. Coat the oil seal with grease and install the rear flange, using a new cotter pin. Remove the dummy bearing from the front. Slide the high range gear onto the driveshaft, small gear to the rear. Drive in the front bearing. Install the bearing spacer and snap-ring.
2. To install the countershaft, insert the two roller bearings, separated by the spacer, into the gear. Place rear thrust washer in case with the oil grooved side toward the countergear. Use grease to hold the washer in position. Insert a short dummy shaft into the countergear to hold the bearings. Place the rear O-ring onto the countershaft. Place the countergear with the large gear to the front. Insert the front thrust washer and drive the shaft in from the rear. Drive the shaft out to the front enough to install the front O-ring. Position the shaft and install the lockplate.
3. Place high and low range shift fork in case. Insert shaft and fork setscrew. Lockwire setscrew. Attach front wheel drive shift rod to fork. Lockwire setscrew. Place front wheel drive fork on sleeve gear. Insert shift rod into case and place sleeve on driveshaft. Insert needle bearings in driveshaft.
4. Install the front cover with a new gasket, tightening the bolts evenly. Drive in the front driveshaft and bearing assembly.
5. Install the shift rod detent balls, springs, and plugs. Slide the speedometer drive gear onto the shaft. Install the front bearing retainer with a new gasket. Grease the oil seal and install

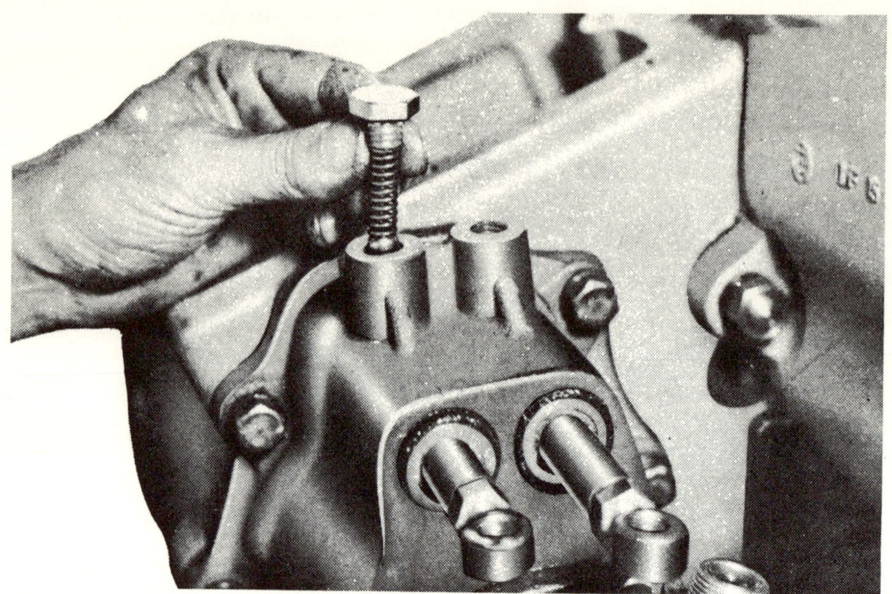

Replacing detent assembly, L60 transfer case

the flange, using a new cotter pin.

6. Replace the case top covers with new gaskets.
7. Replace the brake drum and band assembly. Adjust brake band.
8. Fill case with specified lubricant after reinstalling transfer case to transmission. See Capacities and Pressures Chart.

Flat, ribbed bottom cover of three speed transmission

Three Speed; Bottom Cover Transmission PL410, PL411

This transmission can readily be identified by the flat, ribbed bottom cover. The transmission and clutch housings are a single piece. It was used only with a column shift arrangement.

Disassembly

1. Drain transmission. Remove bottom cover.
2. Remove clutch withdrawal lever and front bearing retainer from clutch housing.
3. Remove speedometer pinion assembly from extension housing. Remove housing.
4. Remove shift shaft locking clips from inside the case. Unscrew the nuts holding the operating lever pins on the shift shafts. Drive out the pins and remove both shift shafts.
5. Remove countershaft and countergear with roller bearings and spacers.
6. Remove reverse idler shaft lockbolt. Remove shaft and gear.
7. Drive out shift fork pins. Unscrew detent plug, spring, and ball from base. Remove the second/third shift rod and fork. Remove the interlock plunger from the detent hole. Remove the first/reverse shift rod and fork. Remove the other detent ball and spring.
8. Pull the mainshaft assembly out through the rear of the case. Pull the clutch shaft out through the front of the case.
9. To disassemble the mainshaft, remove the snap-ring from the front of the shaft. Remove second/third synchronizer, hub, and second gear. Remove snap-ring, speedometer drive gear, and

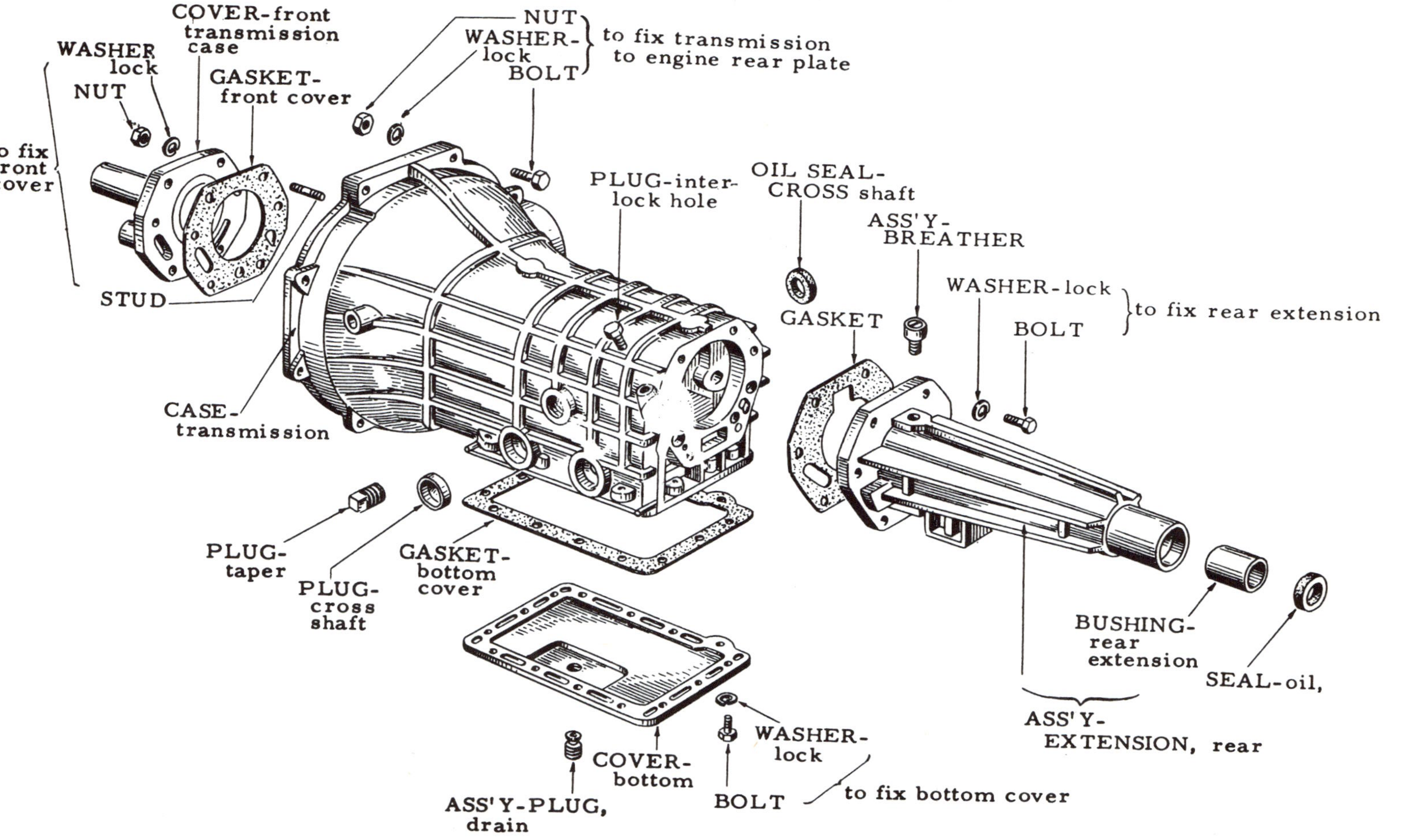

Three speed, bottom cover transmission external components

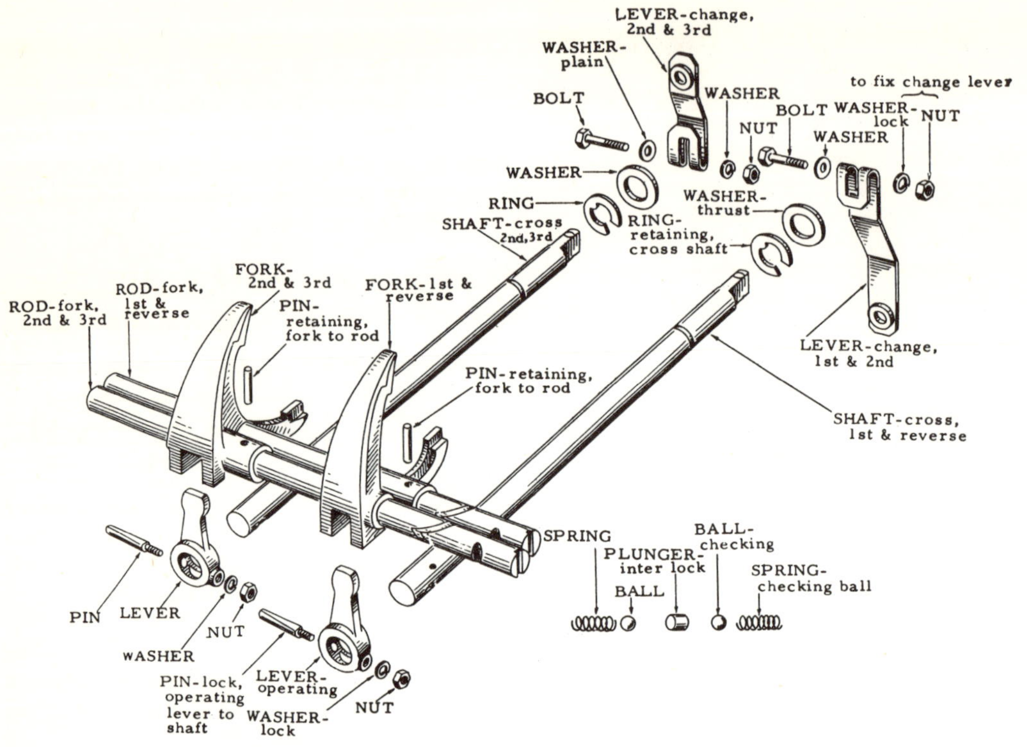

Shifting mechanism for three speed, bottom cover transmission

Countergear removal; three speed, bottom cover unit

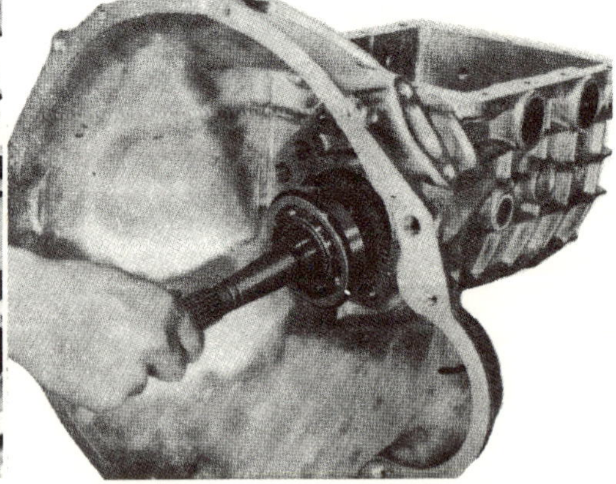
Clutch shaft removal; three speed, bottom cover unit

Mainshaft removal; three speed, bottom cover unit

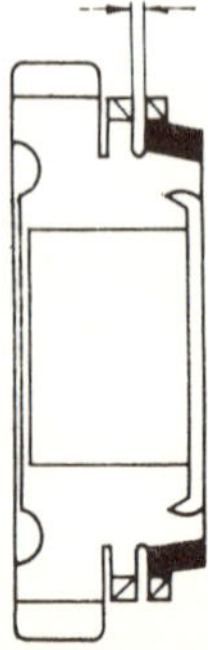
Checking synchronizer baulk ring gap

spacer with ball. Press off shaft bearing and retainer. Hold reverse gear and strike the end of the mainshaft on a block of wood. Remove reverse and first gears.

Inspection

1. Clean all parts with a safe solvent. Lubricate the bearings with gear oil.
2. Check the mainshaft for straightness. Runout at the rear of the shaft should not exceed .0059″ (.15 mm.). Check that synchronizer hubs slide freely without excessive clearance.
3. Place the synchronizer baulk ring in position on the cone of its gear. Check the gap between the baulk ring end face and the front face of the clutch teeth. The gap should be .0472-.0360″ (1.2-1.6 mm.). If it is less than .0315″ (.8 mm.), replace the ring.
4. The clearance between the shift forks and their grooves should be .0059-.0118″ (.15-.30 mm.).
5. Replace all O-rings and oil seals.

Assembly

1. Press the main drive gear onto the clutch shaft. Install the spacer and snap-ring. There must be no play between the bearing and snap-ring. Snap-rings are available in thicknesses from .0598″ (1.52 mm.) to 0747″ (1.89 mm.).

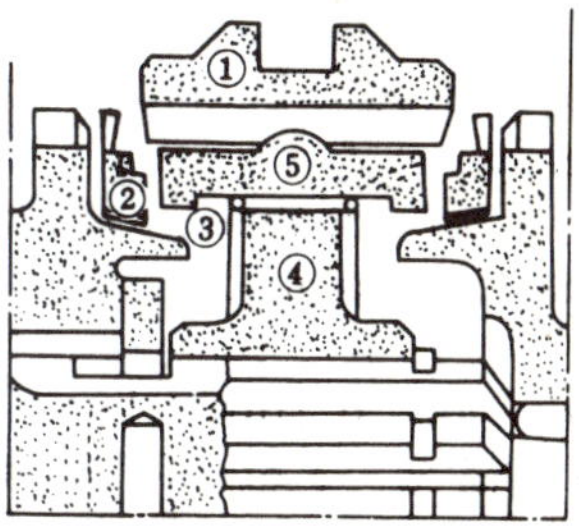

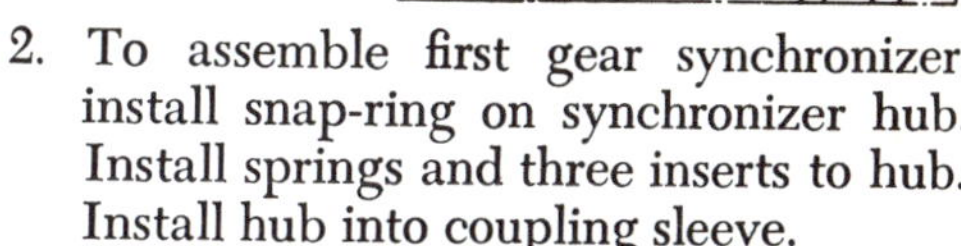

Synchronizer details

1. Synchronizer sleeve
2. Baulk ring
3. Spreader ring
4. Synchronizer hub
5. Insert

2. To assemble first gear synchronizer, install snap-ring on synchronizer hub. Install springs and three inserts to hub. Install hub into coupling sleeve.
3. To assemble second/third gear synchronizer, assemble hub and coupling sleeve. Install three inserts between hub and sleeve. Install a spring ring on each side of the hub.

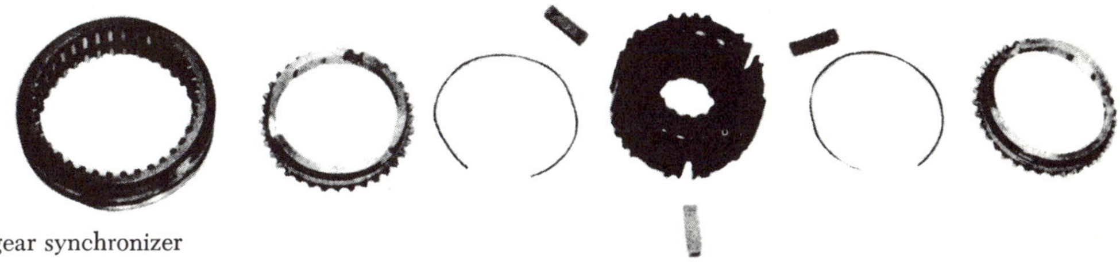

First gear synchronizer

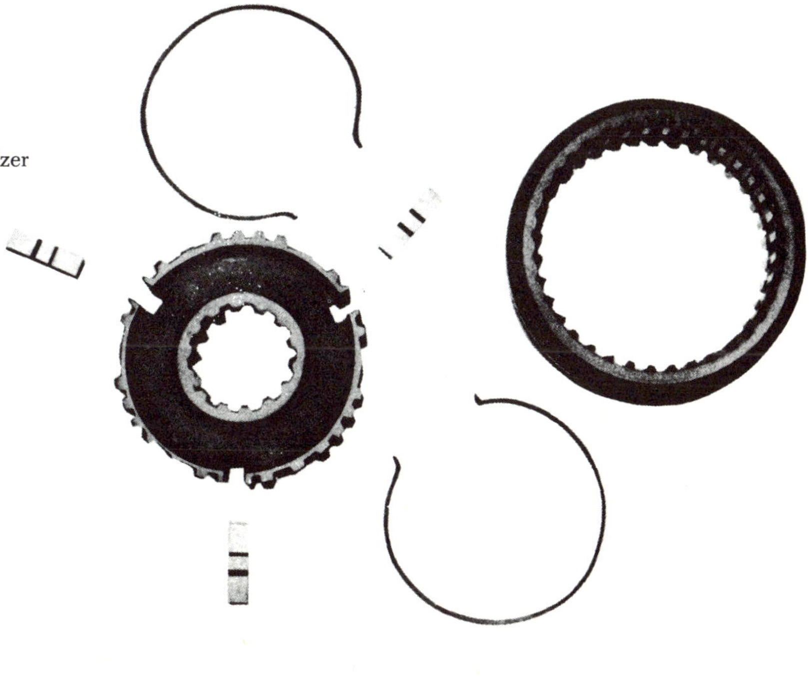

Second gear synchronizer

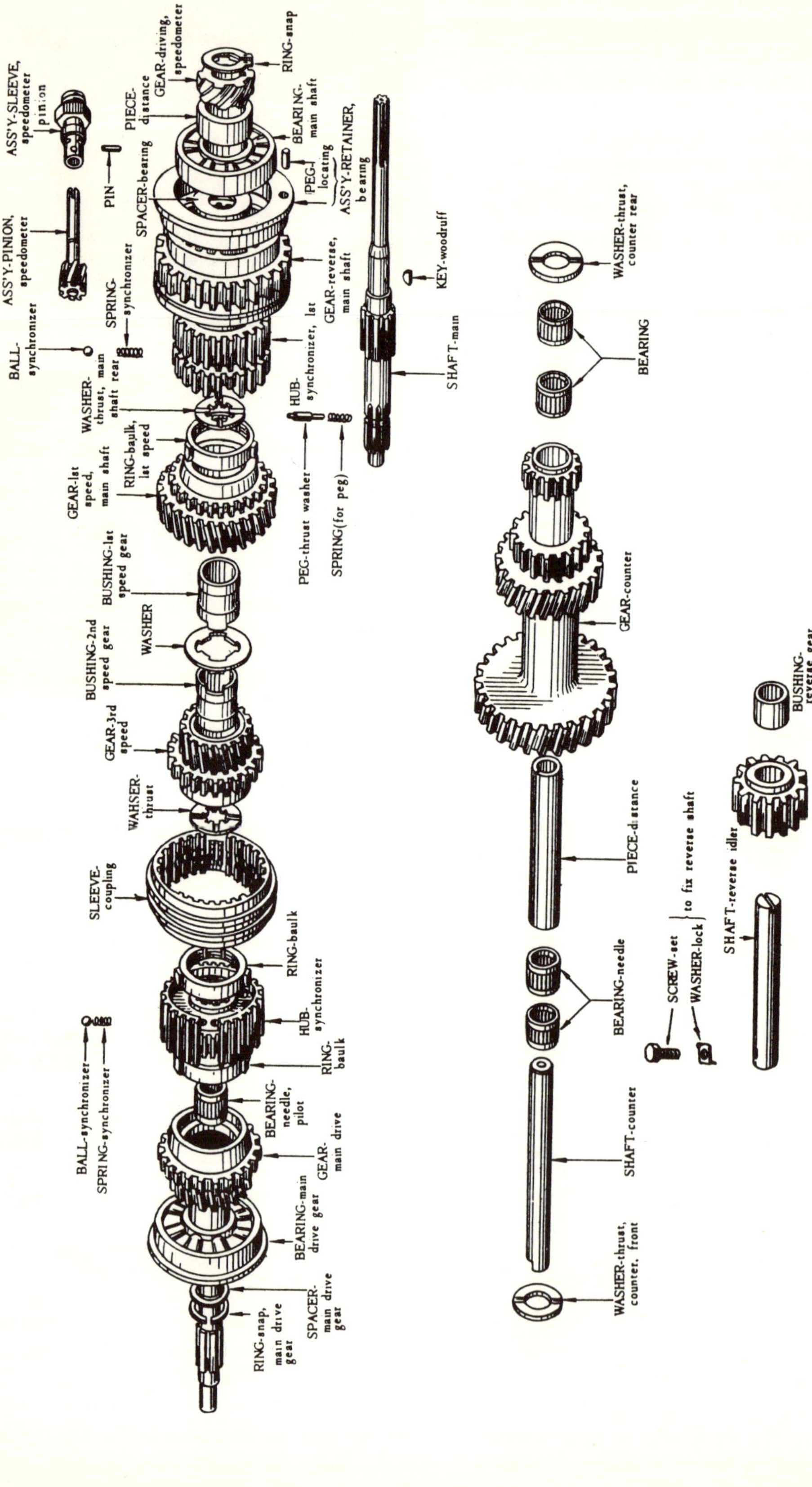

Internal components of three speed, bottom cover transmission

4. To assemble the mainshaft, slide on second gear with the tapered cone to the front. Install the second gear baulk ring. Install the second/third synchronizer assembly and snap-ring on the front of the shaft. Select a snap-ring which gives an end-play of .0020-.0087″ (.05-.25 mm.). Snap-rings are available in thicknesses from .0630″ (1.60 mm.) to .0709″ (1.80 mm.). Place first gear and its baulk ring on the rear of the shaft with the tapered cone to the rear. Install first gear synchronizer and reverse gear. Install the spacer and press on the mainshaft bearing and retainer. Replace the spacer, ball, speedometer drive gear, and snap-ring. Select a snap-ring to give a first gear end-play of .0020-.0087″ (.05-.22 mm.). Snap-rings are available in thicknesses from .0512″ (1.30 mm.) to .0669″ (1.70 mm.). Second gear end-play should be .0039-.0087″ (.10-.22 mm.).
5. Install clutch shaft and mainshaft into case.

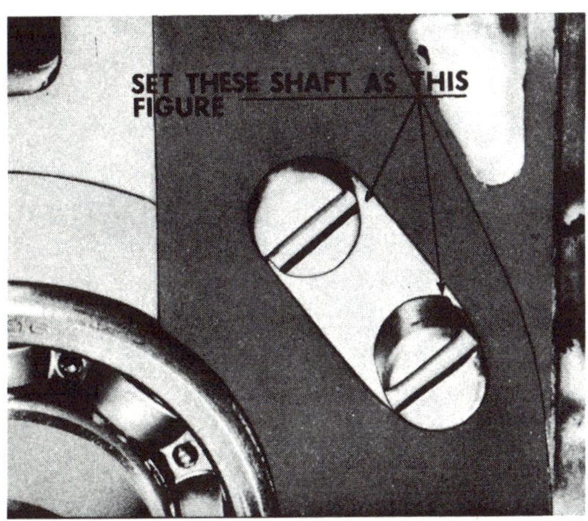

Shift rod alignment. Align rods as illustrated for three speed, bottom cover transmission.

6. Place case with detent hole upward. Place detent spring, then ball, into hole. Install first/reverse shift rod and fork. Insert interlock plunger into hole. Install second/third shift rod and fork. Place the other detent ball, spring, and plug into the detent hole. Use sealant on the plug threads. Fasten the forks to the shift rods with their retaining pins.
7. Install the reverse idler gear and shaft. Install the shaft lockbolt and plate.
8. Replace the countergear and countershaft. Select thrust washers to give a countergear end-play of .0016-.0047″ (.04-.12 mm.). Thrust washers are available in sizes from .151″ (3.83 mm.) to .159″ (4.03 mm.).

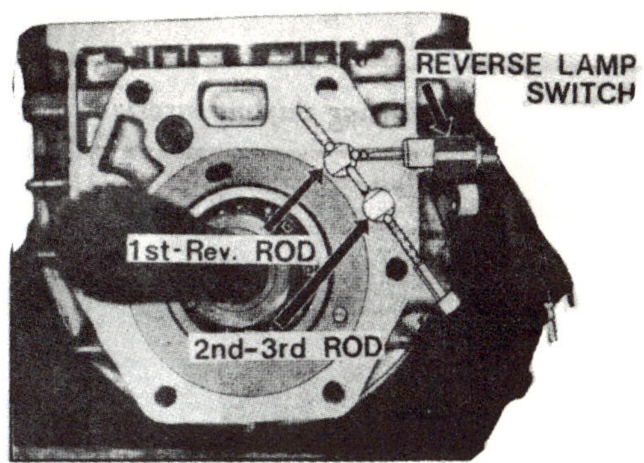

Shift rod interlock details; three speed, bottom cover unit

Shift rods and forks installed; three speed, bottom cover unit

9. Install shift shafts with thrust washers, locking clips, and operating levers.
10. Install extension housing to case. Torque bolts to 16-22 ft. lbs.
11. Insert speedometer pinion assembly.
12. Check gear backlash with a dial indicator. It should be .0031-.0051″ (.08-.13 mm.) for all gears.
13. Replace front bearing retainer. Torque bolts to 8-12 ft. lbs. Replace clutch withdrawal lever.
14. Replace bottom cover and torque bolts to 8-12 ft. lbs.
15. See Capacities and Pressures Chart for refill capacity.

Four Speed, Bottom Cover Transmission L520, PL411, RL411, SPL311, PL510, WPL510

This transmission is adapted from and quite similar in appearance to the three speed unit used in the PL410 and

Four speed, bottom cover transmission case details

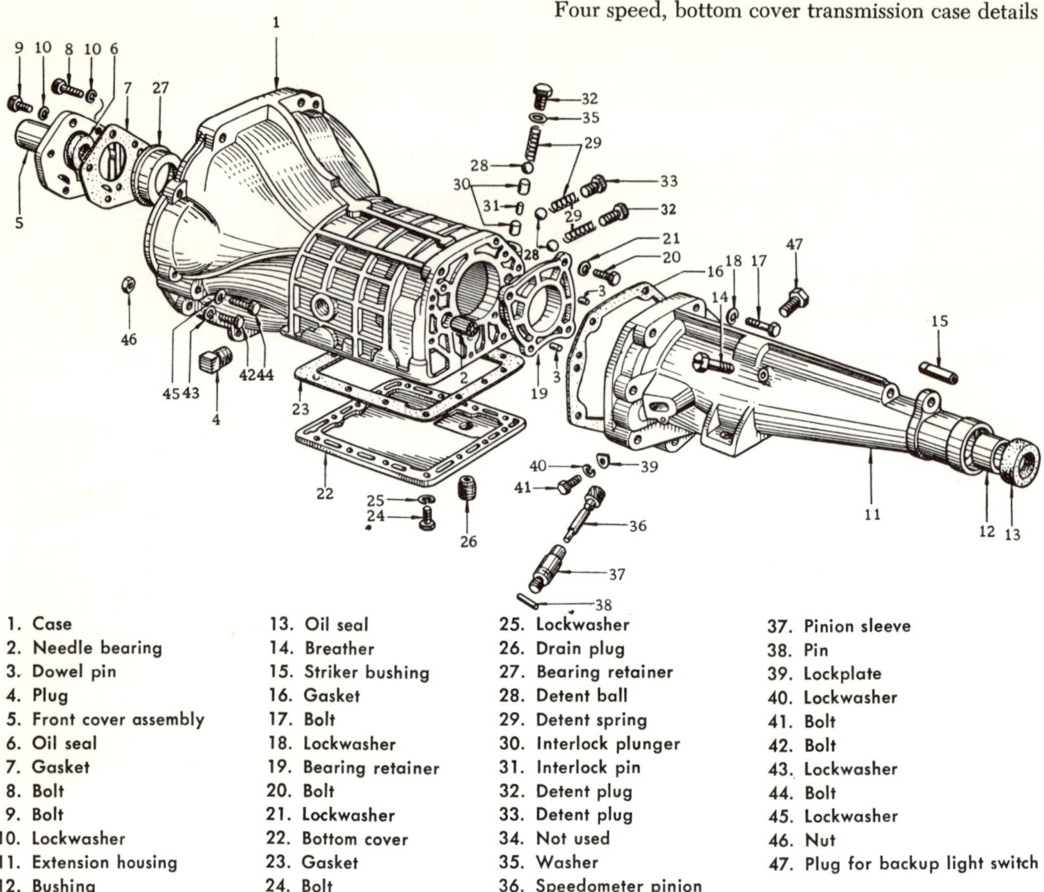

1. Case
2. Needle bearing
3. Dowel pin
4. Plug
5. Front cover assembly
6. Oil seal
7. Gasket
8. Bolt
9. Bolt
10. Lockwasher
11. Extension housing
12. Bushing
13. Oil seal
14. Breather
15. Striker bushing
16. Gasket
17. Bolt
18. Lockwasher
19. Bearing retainer
20. Bolt
21. Lockwasher
22. Bottom cover
23. Gasket
24. Bolt
25. Lockwasher
26. Drain plug
27. Bearing retainer
28. Detent ball
29. Detent spring
30. Interlock plunger
31. Interlock pin
32. Detent plug
33. Detent plug
34. Not used
35. Washer
36. Speedometer pinion
37. Pinion sleeve
38. Pin
39. Lockplate
40. Lockwasher
41. Bolt
42. Bolt
43. Lockwasher
44. Bolt
45. Lockwasher
46. Nut
47. Plug for backup light switch

PL411. The reverse and reverse idler drive gears are contained in the extension housing to make room for the additional internal gears. On some late units, the cast, ribbed bottom cover is replaced by a stamped steel cover. Virtually all of these transmissions imported to the US have a modified extension housing incorporating a floorshift mechanism. The transmission model number, on the PL510 and WPL510, is F4W(C)63L.

Disassembly

1. Drain transmission.
2. Remove clutch withdrawal lever and release bearing.
3. Remove clevis pin connecting striker rod to shift lever.
4. Remove speedometer drive pinion assembly.
5. Unbolt and remove extension housing, disengaging striker rod from shift rod gates.
6. Remove bottom and front covers.
7. Remove three detent plugs, springs, and balls.
8. Drive out shift fork retaining pins. Remove rods and forks.
9. Move first/second and third/fourth coupling sleeves into gear at the same time to lock the mainshaft.
10. Pull out the countershaft and countergear with the two needle roller bearings and spacers.
11. Remove snap-ring, reverse idler gears, and shaft.
12. Unbolt mainshaft rear bearing retainer.
13. Pull out mainshaft assembly to the rear. Pull out clutch shaft to the front.
14. To disassemble mainshaft, remove snap-ring, third/fourth synchronizer hub and coupling sleeve. Remove third gear, with roller bearing. Remove mainshaft nut, lockplate, speedometer drive gear, and steel ball. Take off reverse gear and hub. Press off bearing and retainer. Remove thrust washer and first gear with needle roller bear-

Four speed, bottom cover transmission gear train details

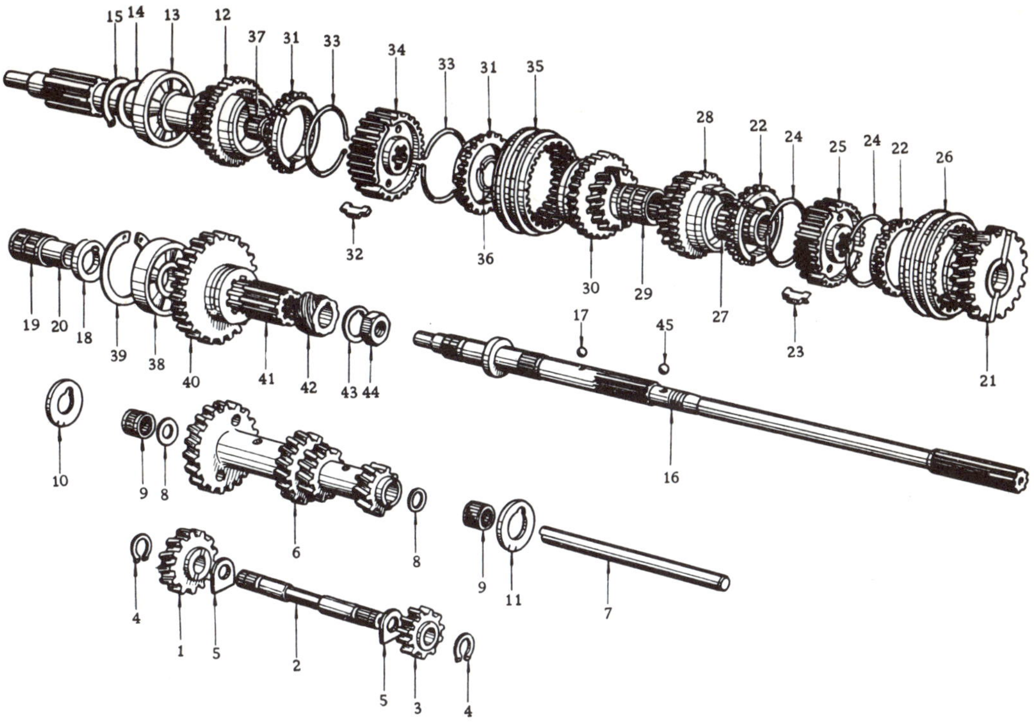

1. Reverse idler gear
2. Reverse idler shaft
3. Main reverse idler gear
4. Snap-ring
5. Thrust washer
6. Countergear
7. Countershaft
8. Spacer
9. Needle bearing
10. Front countershaft thrust washer
11. Rear countershaft thrust washer
12. Main drive gear
13. Main drive gear bearing
14. Washer
15. Snap-ring
16. Mainshaft
17. 5/32" steel ball
18. Thrust washer
19. Needle bearing
20. First gear bushing
21. First gear
22. Baulk ring
23. Shifting insert
24. Spreader ring
25. First/second synchro hub
26. Coupling sleeve
27. Needle bearing
28. Second gear
29. Needle bearing
30. Third gear
31. Baulk ring
32. Shifting insert
33. Spreader ring
34. Third/fourth synchro hub
35. Coupling sleeve
36. Snap-ring
37. Pilot bearing
38. Bearing
39. Snap-ring
40. Reverse gear
41. Reverse gear hub
42. Speedometer drive gear
43. Lockwasher
44. Nut
45. Steel ball

ing and bushing. Be careful not to lose the steel ball which locates the thrust washer. Take off the first/second synchronizer and hub. Remove second gear with needle roller bearing.

Inspection

Inspection procedures are the same as for the three speed transmission used in the PL410 and PL411.

Assembly

Assembly procedures are generally the reverse of disassembly, however the following special instructions are required.

1. On the clutch shaft, there should be no end-play between the bearing and the snap-ring. Snap-rings are available in sizes from .0598" (1.52 mm.) to .0697" (1.77 mm.).
2. Some of these transmissions use the same type of synchronizer (Borg Warner) as in the PL410 and PL411 three speed, bottom cover transmission. Others use a servo type synchronizer which utilizes brake bands. To assemble these synchronizers, place each gear on a flat surface. Install the synchronizer ring into the clutch gear. Place the thrust block and anchor block as shown and install the circlip into the groove.
3. Third gear should be adjusted to give an end-play of .0020-.0059" (.05-.15

mm.). Snap-rings for adjustment are available in sizes from .0551″ (1.40 mm.) to .0630″ (1.60 mm.).

4. Tighten the mainshaft nut to 65-80 ft. lbs.

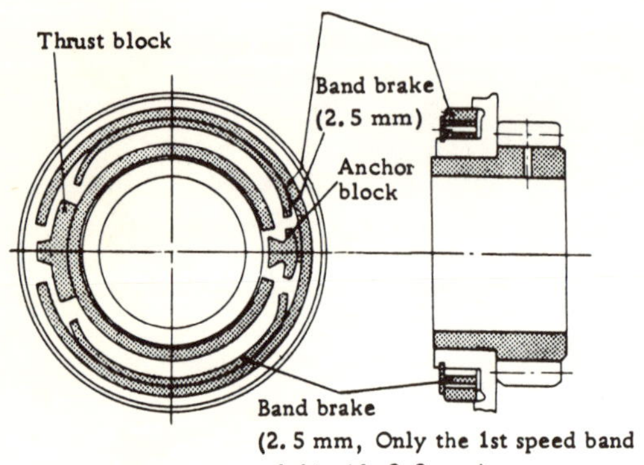

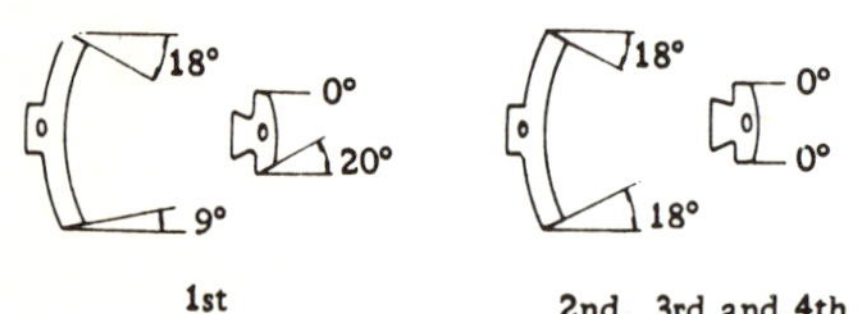

Servo type synchronizer assembly details

5. Install the reverse idler driving gear on the reverse shaft and fasten with a snap-ring. Install the shaft and gear into the case, placing a thrust washer between the gear and case. Place a thrust washer, idler gear, and snap-ring on the inside end of the shaft. Idler gear end-play should be .0039-.0118″ (.1-.3 mm.). Snap-rings are available in sizes from .0433″ (1.1 mm.) to .0591″ (1.5 mm.).
6. Countergear end-play should be .0020-.0059″ (.05-.15 mm.). Thrust washers for adjustment are available from .0945″ (2.40 mm.) to .1024″ (2.60 mm.).
7. To assemble shift mechanism, place first/second and third/fourth forks onto their sleeves. Insert first/second shift rod. Install an interlock plunger and then the third/fourth shift rod with interlock pin. Install the other interlock plunger and then the reverse shift fork and rod. Place a detent ball and spring into each detent hole. Use sealant on the plug threads and torque to 12-15 ft. lbs.
8. Install the extension housing, engaging the striker rod with the shift rod gates. Torque bolts to 16-22 ft. lbs. Torque front cover bolts to 8-12 ft. lbs. Torque bottom cover bolts to 8-12 ft. lbs. See Capacities and Pressures Chart for refill capacity.

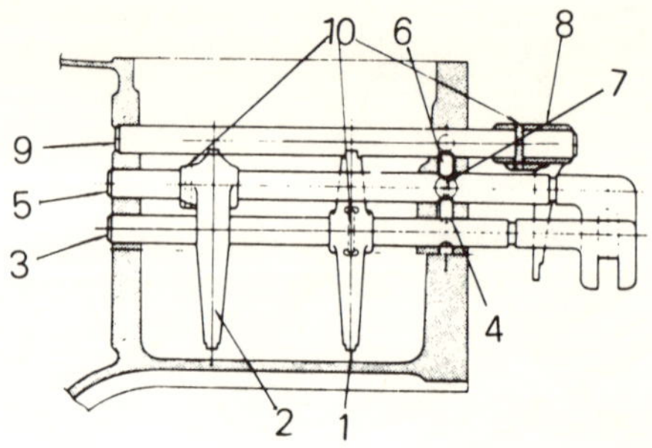

1. First/second shift fork
2. Third/fourth shift fork
3. First/second shift rod
4. Interlock plunger
5. Third/fourth shift rod
6. Interlock plunger
7. Interlock pin
8. Reverse shift fork
9. Reverse shift rod
10. Fork retaining pin

Shift rod and fork details; four speed, bottom cover transmission

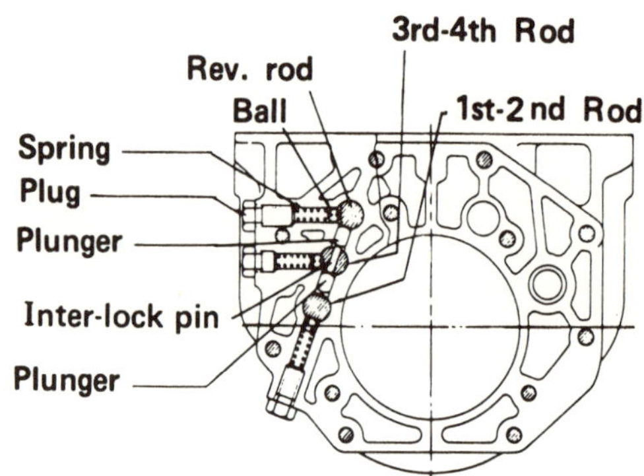

Shift rod interlock details for four speed, bottom cover transmission

FOUR SPEED TRANSMISSION—HLS30

This transmission is constructed in three sections: clutch housing, transmission housing, and extension housing. There are no case cover plates. There is a cast iron adapter plate between the transmission and extension housings. The transmission model number is F4W71A.

Disassembly

1. Remove clutch housing dust cover. Remove retaining spring, release bearing sleeve, and withdrawal lever.
2. Remove backup light/neutral safety switch.
3. Unbolt and remove clutch housing, rapping with a soft hammer if necessary. Remove gasket, mainshaft bear-

Shifting arrangement for four speed, bottom cover transmission

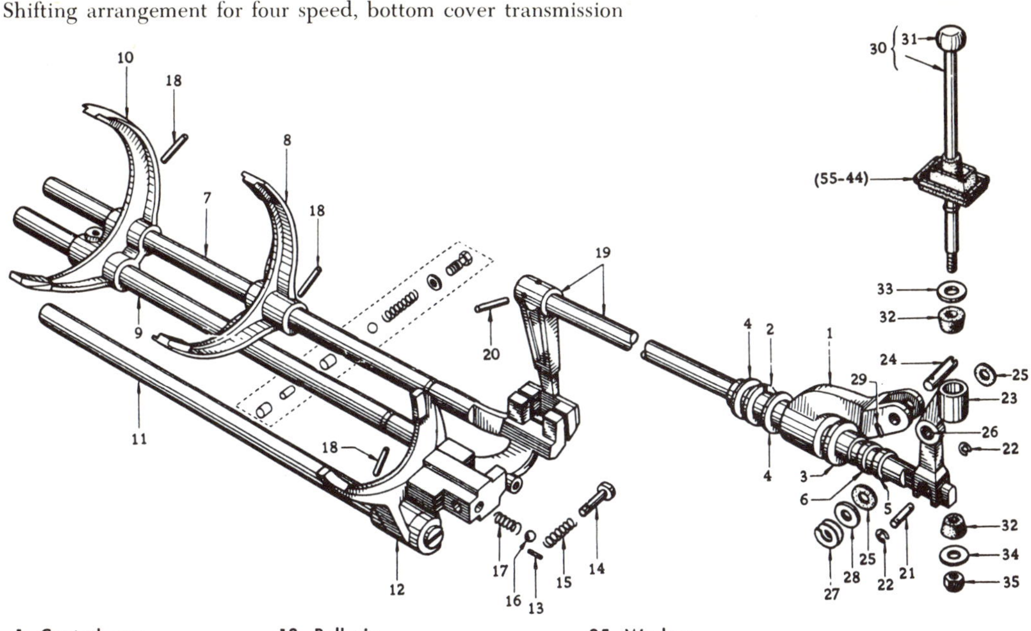

1. Control arm
2. Striker spring
3. Thrust washer
4. Thrust washer
5. O-ring cap
6. O-ring
7. First/second shift rod
8. First/second shift fork
9. Third/fourth shift rod
10. Third/fourth shift rod
11. Reverse shift rod
12. Reverse shift fork
13. Roll pin
14. Pin
15. Reverse pin return spring
16. Reverse fork check ball
17. Check spring
18. Pin
19. Striker rod
20. Pin
21. Pin
22. C-ring
23. Shift lever bracket
24. Pin
25. Washer
26. Bushing
27. Spring
28. Thrust washer
29. Pin
30. Shift lever assembly
31. Shift knob
32. Rubber bushing
33. Washer
34. Washer
35. Nut

55-44. Rubber boot

ing shim, and countershaft bearing shim.

4. Remove speedometer pinion sleeve.
5. Remove striker rod pin from rod. Separate striker rod from shift lever bracket.
6. Unbolt and remove rear extension. It may be necessary to rap the housing with a soft hammer.
7. Remove mainshaft bearing snap-ring.
8. Remove adapter plate and gear assembly from transmission case by rapping with a soft hammer. Hold adapter plate in a vise.
9. Punch out shift fork retaining pins. Remove shift rod snap-rings. Remove detent plugs, springs, and balls from adapter plate. Remove shift rods, being careful not to lose the interlock balls.
10. Remove snap-ring, speedometer drive gear, and locating ball.
11. Bend back mainshaft lock tab. Remove nut, lockwasher. thrust washer, reverse hub, and reverse gear.
12. Remove snap-ring and countershaft reverse gear. Remove snap-ring, reverse idler gear, thrust washer, and needle bearing.
13. Support gear assembly while rapping on the rear of the mainshaft with a soft hammer. An assistant would be helpful to avoid dropping any of the parts. The mainshaft will separate into the forward clutch shaft and the rear mainshaft.
14. Remove setscrew from adapter plate. Remove shaft nut, spring washer, plain washer, and reverse idler shaft.
15. Remove the machine screws holding the bearing retainer with an impact tool. Remove the bearing retainer and the mainshaft rear bushing.
16. To disassemble the mainshaft (rear section), remove the front snap-ring, third/fourth synchronizer assembly, third gear, and needle bearing. From the rear, remove the thrust washer, locating ball, first gear, needle bearing,

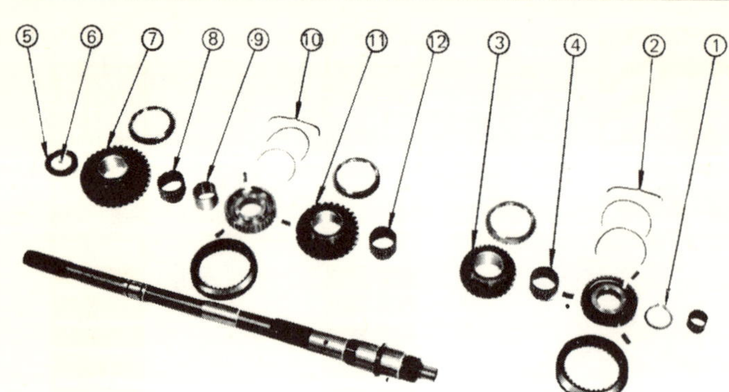

Mainshaft (rear section) assembly, HLS30 four speed

first gear bushing, first/second synchronizer assembly, second gear, and needle bearing.

17. To disassemble the clutch shaft, remove the snap-ring and bearing spacer. Press off the bearing.

Clutch shaft assembly, HLS30 four speed

18. To disassemble the countershaft, press off the front bearing. Press off the rear bearing. Press off the gears and remove the keys.
19. Remove the retaining pin, control arm pin, and shift control arm from the rear of the extension housing.

Inspection

1. Wash all parts in a safe solvent. Oil bearings immediately. Check all parts for wear or damage. Replace all seals, O-rings, and gaskets.
2. On reassembly, gear backlash between mating gears should be .0020-.0059″ (.05-.15 mm.). If it is excessive, replace both driving and driven gears.
3. Gear end-play should be .0047-.0075″ (.12-.19 mm.) for all gears except the reverse idler. Reverse idler gear end-play should be .0020-.0138″ (.05-.35 mm.). End-play is adjusted by installing snap-rings of different thicknesses.

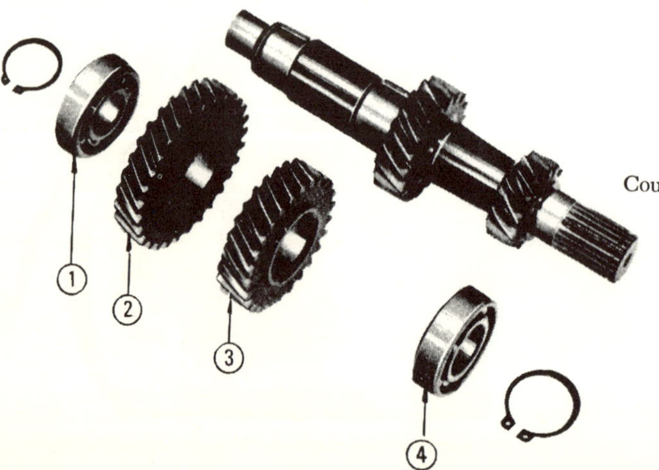

Countershaft assembly, HLS30 four speed

1. Countershaft front bearing
2. Countershaft drive gear
3. Third gear
4. Countershaft rear bearing

Checking end-play between second and third gears

4. Check the synchronizer baulk ring inside serration for wear. The slot should be .0472-.0550″ (1.2-1.4 mm.) wide.

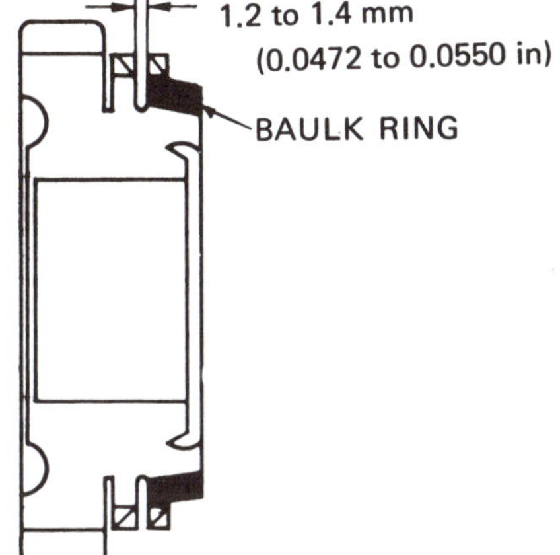

Checking synchronizer baulk ring wear

Assembly

1. Place the O-ring in the front cover. Install the front cover to the clutch housing with a press. Install the front cover oil seal.
2. Install the rear extension oil seal with a drift.
3. Assemble first/second and third/fourth synchronizer assembles. Make sure that the spreader ring gaps are not both on the same side of the unit.
4. On rear end of mainshaft, install needle bearing, second gear, baulk ring, first/second synchronizer assembly, baulk ring, first gear bushing, needle bearing, first gear, locating ball, and thrust washer.
5. Drive or press on mainshaft rear bearing.

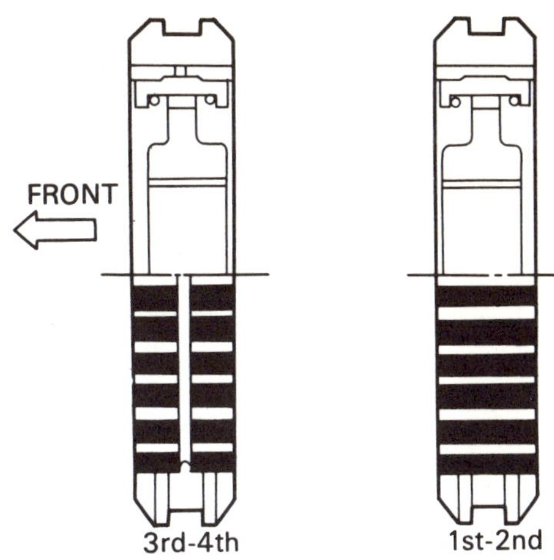

Synchronizer hubs must be installed as shown

6. Install countershaft rear bearing to adapter plate. Drive or press mainshaft rear bearing into adapter plate until bearing snap-ring groove comes through rear side of plate. Install the snap-ring. If it is not tight against the plate, press the bearing back in slightly.
7. Insert the countershaft bearing ring between the countershaft rear bearing and bearing retainer. Install the bearing retainer to the adapter plate, torquing the screws to 9-13 ft. lbs. Stake both ends of the screws with a punch.
8. Insert the reverse idler shaft from the rear of the adapter plate. Torque the setscrew to 9-13 ft. lbs. Install spring washer and plain washer to the idler shaft. Torque the shaft nut to 43-58 ft. lbs.

Reverse idler shaft, 1, is located by setscrew, 2.

9. Place the two keys on the countershaft and oil the shaft lightly. Press on third gear and install a snap-ring.
10. Install the countershaft into its rear bearing.
11. From the front of the mainshaft, install the needle bearing, third gear, baulk ring, third/fourth synchronizer assembly, and snap-ring. Snap-rings are available in thicknesses from .0561″ (1.425 mm.) to .0640″ (1.625 mm.) to adjust gear end-play to the figure specified under Inspection.
12. Press the main drive bearing onto the clutch shaft. Install the main drive gear spacer and a snap-ring. Snap-rings are available in thicknesses from .0710″ (1.80 mm.) to .0820″ (2.08 mm.) to adjust gear end-play to the figure specified under Inspection.
13. Insert a key into the countershaft. Insert the pilot bearing in the clutch shaft assembly. Engage the countershaft drive gear with fourth gear and drive on the countershaft fourth gear with a drift. The rear end of the countershaft should be held steady while driving on the gear, to prevent rear bearing damage.
14. Install the reverse hub, reverse gear, thrust washer, and lock tab on the rear of the mainshaft. Install the shaft nut temporarily.
15. Oil the reverse idler shaft lightly. Install the needle bearing, reverse idler gear, thrust washer, and snap-ring.
16. Place countershaft reverse gear and snap-ring on rear of countershaft. Snap-rings are available in thicknesses from .0433″ (1.1 mm.) to .0590″ (1.5 mm.) to adjust gear end-play to the figure specified under Inspection.
17. Engage both first and second gears to lock the shaft. Torque the mainshaft nut to 130-152 ft. lbs. and bend up the lock tab.
18. On the rear of the mainshaft, install the snap-ring, locating ball, speedometer drive gear, and snap-ring. Snap-rings are available in thicknesses from .0433″ (1.1 mm.) to .0590″ (1.5 mm.).
19. Recheck end-play and backlash of all gears. See Inspection.
20. Place reverse shift fork on reverse gear and install reverse shift rod. Install detent ball, spring, and plug. Install fork retaining pin. Place two interlock balls between reverse shift rod and third/fourth shift rod location. Install third/fourth shift fork and rod. Install detent ball, spring, and plug. This plug is shorter than the other two. Install fork retaining pin. Place two interlock balls between first/second shift rod location and third/fourth shift rod. Install first/second shift fork and rod. Install detent ball, spring, and plug. Apply locking agent to each detent plug and torque them to 16-22 ft. lbs. Install fork retaining pin.
21. Install shift rod snap-rings.

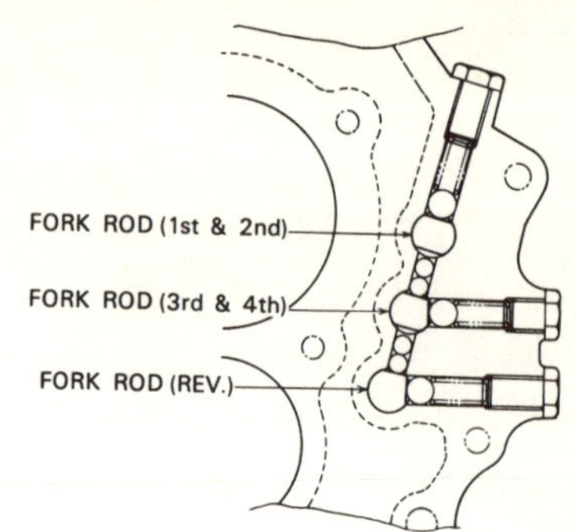

Interlock and detent arrangement, HLS30 four speed

Replacing shift rod snap-ring

22. Oil all moving parts and check that all gears can be shifted smoothly.
23. Apply sealant sparingly to the adapter plate and transmission housing. Install the transmission housing to the adapter plate and bolt it down temporarily.
24. Drive in countershaft front bearing with a drift. Place the snap-ring in the mainshaft front bearing.

25. Apply sealant sparingly to adapter plate and extension housing. Align shift rods in neutral positions. Position striker rod to shift rods and bolt down extension housing. Torque to 11-16 ft. lbs. Be careful not to damage the extension housing oil seal in installation.

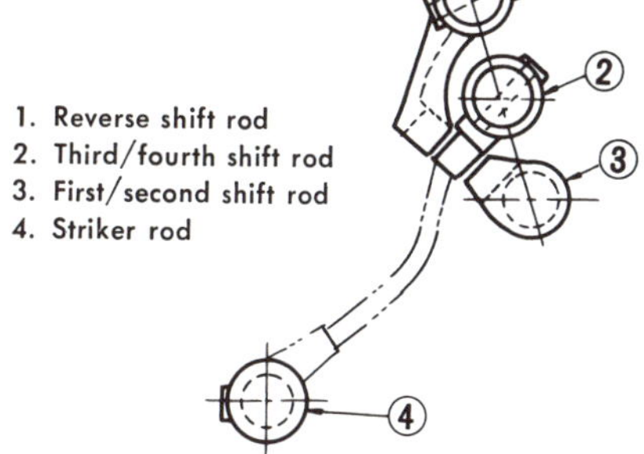

Striker rod and shift fork rod arrangement

26. Insert striker rod pin, connect rod to shift lever bracket, and install striker rod pin retaining ring. Replace shift control arm.
27. To select the proper mainshaft bearing shim, first measure the amount the bearing protrudes from the front of the transmission case. This is measurement B. Then measure the depth of the bearing recess in the rear of the clutch housing. This is measurement A.

Measurement A

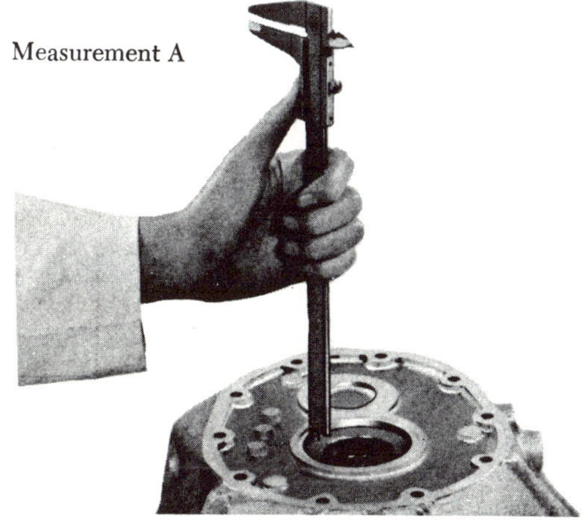

Required shim thickness is found by subtracting B from A. Shims are available in thicknesses of .0551″ (1.4 mm.) and .0630″ (1.6 mm.).
28. To select the proper countershaft front bearing shim, measure the amount that the bearing is recessed into the transmission case. Shim thickness should equal this measurement. Shims are available in thicknesses from .0157″ (.4 mm.) to .0394″ (1.0 mm.).
29. Apply sealant sparingly to clutch and transmission housing mating surfaces and torque bolts to 11-16 ft. lbs.
30. Replace clutch operating mechanism.
31. Install shift lever temporarily and check shifting action.
32. Refill transmission. See Capacities and Pressures Chart.

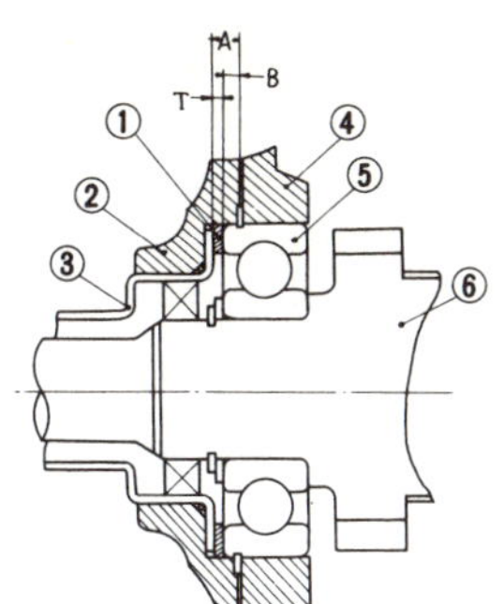

Mainshaft bearing and shim

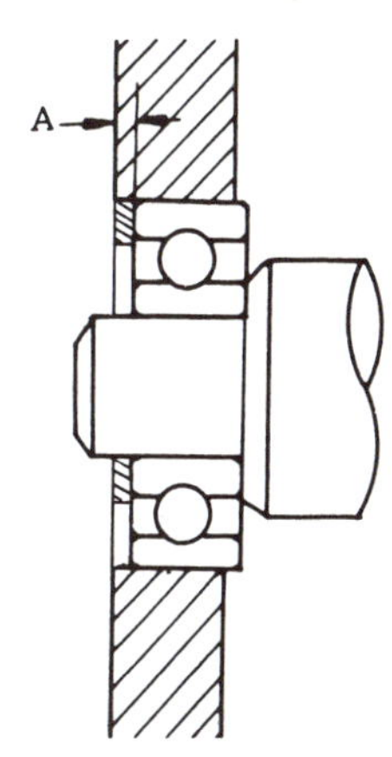

Countershaft bearing and shim, A

Five Speed Transmission—SRL311, HLS30

This transmission is quite similar to the four speed HLS30 unit. The model number is FS5C71A. Servo type synchromesh is used, instead of the Borg Warner type in the four speed. Shift linkage and interlock arrangements are the same, except that the reverse shift rod also operates fifth gear. Most service procedures are identical to those for the four speed unit. Those unique to the five speed follow.

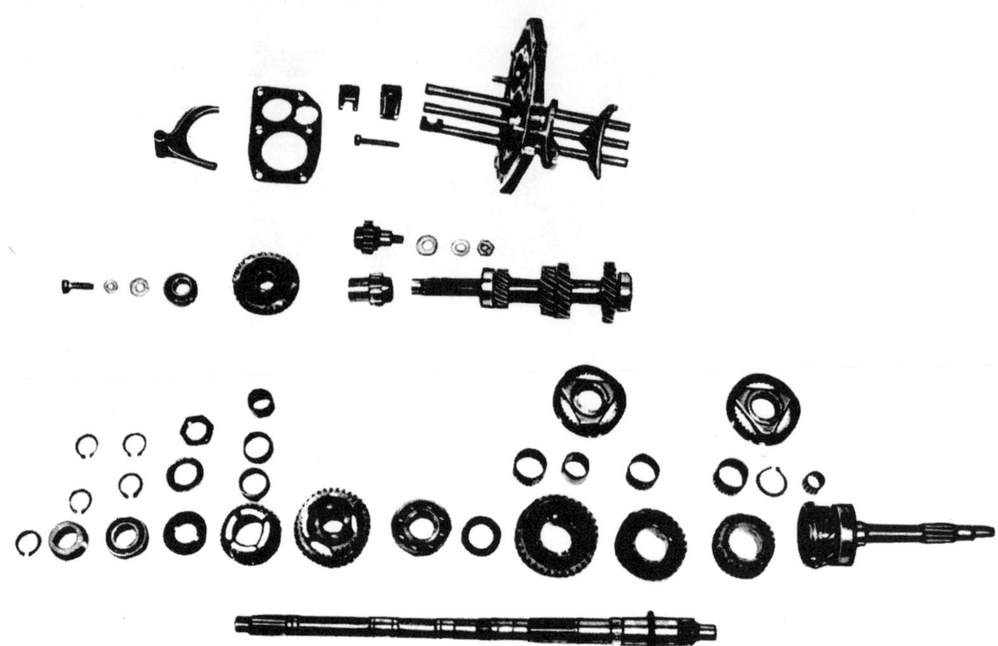

Components of five speed transmission gear train

Disassembly

1. To disassemble synchronizers, remove circlip, synchronizer ring, thrust block, brake band, and anchor block. Be careful not to mix parts of the different synchronizer assembles.

Inspection

1. Gear backlash should be .0016-.0059″ (.04-.15 mm.) for the main drive gear and reverse gear. For first, second, third, and fifth gears it should be .0016-.0079″ (.04-.20 mm.).
2. Gear end-play should be:

Gear	*End-Play*
First, Second, Fifth	.0039-.0075″ (.12-.19 mm.)
Third	.0039-.0094″ (.12-.24 mm.)
Reverse Idler	.0019-.0137″ (.05-.35 mm.)

Assembly

1. The synchronizer assemblies for second, third, and fourth are identical. Refer to the illustrations for identification of synchronizer components. When assembling the first gear synchronizer, be sure to install the .0866″ (2.2 mm.) thick brake band at the bottom.
2. When assembling the mainshaft, select a third gear synchronizer hub snapring to minimize hub end-play. Snaprings are available in thicknesses of

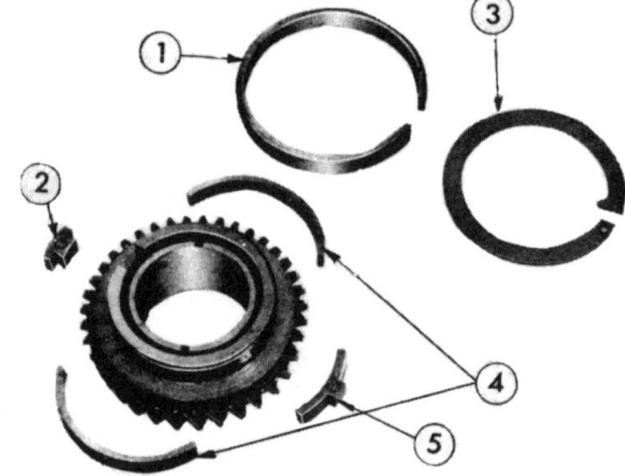

Servo type synchronizer unit disassembled

1. Synchronizer ring
2. Anchor block
3. Circlip
4. Brake band
5. Thrust block
6. Synchronizer sleeve
7. Synchronizer hub

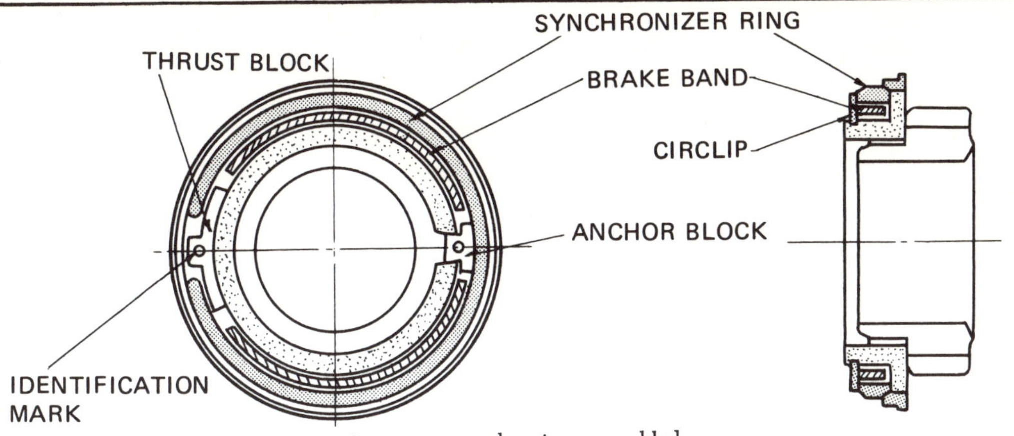

Servo type synchronizer assembled

.0610-.0630″ (1.55-1.60 mm.), .0591-.0610″ (1.50-1.55 mm.), and .0571-0591″ (1.45-1.50 mm.). The synchronizer hub must be installed with the longer boss to the rear.

3. When reassembling the gear train, install the mainshaft, countershaft, and gears to the adapter plate. To tighten the mainshaft locknuts, tighten the front nut to 15-22 ft. lbs. and the rear nut to 7-15 ft. lbs. Hold the rear nut and force the front nut against it to a torque of 217 ft. lbs. Select a snap-ring to minimize end-play of the fifth gear bearing at the rear of the mainshaft. Snap-rings are available in thicknesses from .0433″ (1.1 mm.) to .0551″ (1.4 mm.).

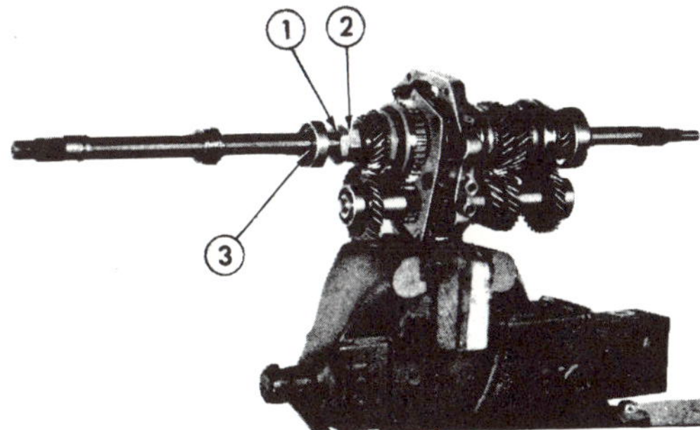

Mainshaft locknuts, 1 and 2, and snap-ring, 3

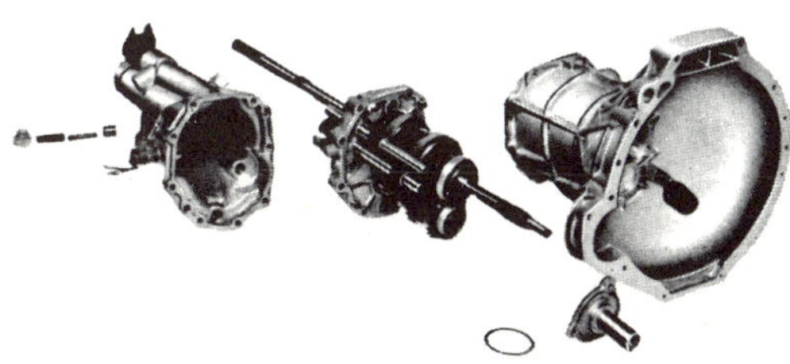

LB110 four speed transmission major assemblies

Four Speed Transmission—LB110, KLB110

This transmission is constructed in two sections: a combined clutch and transmission housing. and an extension housing. There is a cast iron adapter plate between the housings. There are no case cover plates. The transmission model number is F4W56.

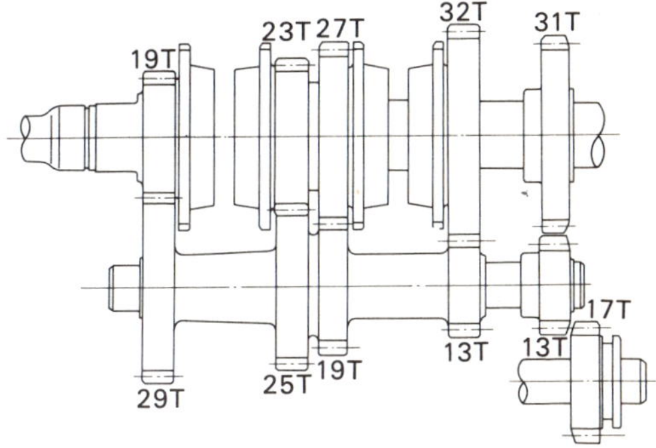

LB110 four speed transmission gear train

Disassembly

1. Drain oil.
2. Remove dust cover, spring, clutch withdrawal lever, and release bearing.
3. Remove front cover from inside clutch housing.
4. From extension housing, remove speedometer drive pinion. Remove striker rod return spring plug, spring, plunger, and bushing. Remove striker rod pin and separate striker rod from shift lever bracket.
5. Unbolt extension housing and remove. Tap it with a soft hammer, if necessary.
6. Separate the adapter plate from the transmission case, being careful not to lose the countershaft bearing washer.

Synchronizer assembly

The following table indicates three types of synchronizer. When assembling the individual components, be careful to combine appropriate components correctly.

Component parts of synchronizer assembly

mm (in)

	4th	3rd	2nd	1st	5th (OD)
Thrust block	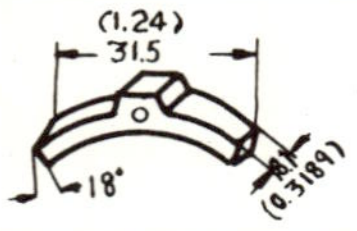 31.5 (1.24); 8.1 (0.3189); 18°	←	←	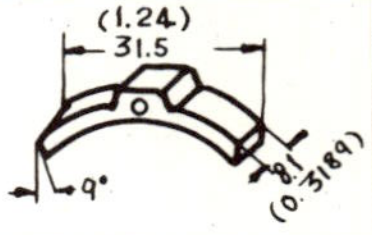 31.5 (1.24); 8.1 (0.3189); 9°	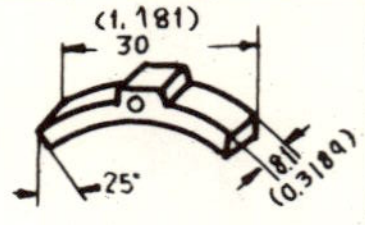 30 (1.181); 8.1 (0.3189); 25°
Anchor block	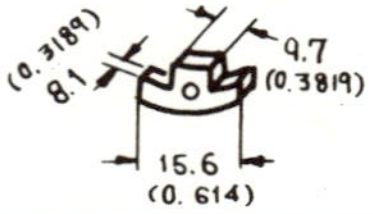 9.7 (0.3819); 8.1 (0.3189); 15.6 (0.614)	←	←	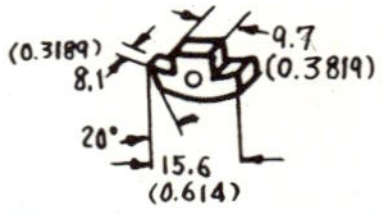 9.7 (0.3819); 8.1 (0.3189); 20°; 15.6 (0.614)	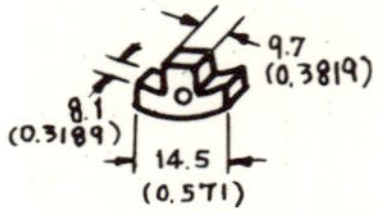 9.7 (0.3819); 8.1 (0.3189); 14.5 (0.571)
Brake band	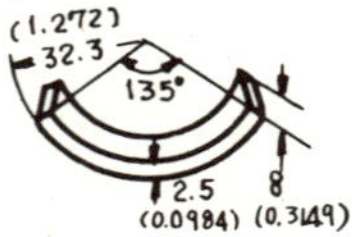 32.3 (1.272); 135°; 2.5 (0.0984); 8 (0.3149)	←	←	←	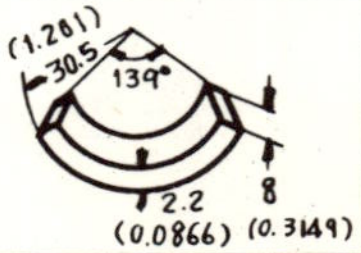 30.5 (1.201); 139°; 2.2 (0.0866); 8 (0.3149)
Brake band	Same as above	←	←	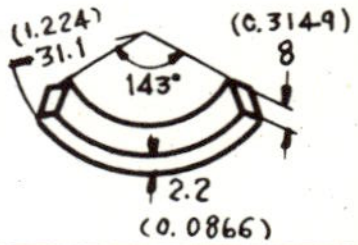 31.1 (1.224); 143°; 8 (0.3149); 2.2 (0.0866)	Same as above
Synchronizer ring	 67.7 (2.665); 3.9 (0.1535)	←	←	←	 63.5 (2500); 3.5 (0.1379)
Circlip	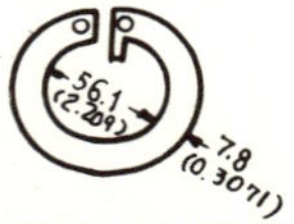 56.1 (2.209); 7.8 (0.3071)	←	←	←	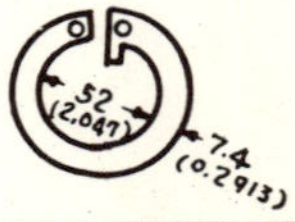 52 (2.047); 7.4 (0.2913)

Dimensions of components of servo type synchronizers for five speed transmission. Dimensions are in mm. and (ins.).

Striker rod return spring parts

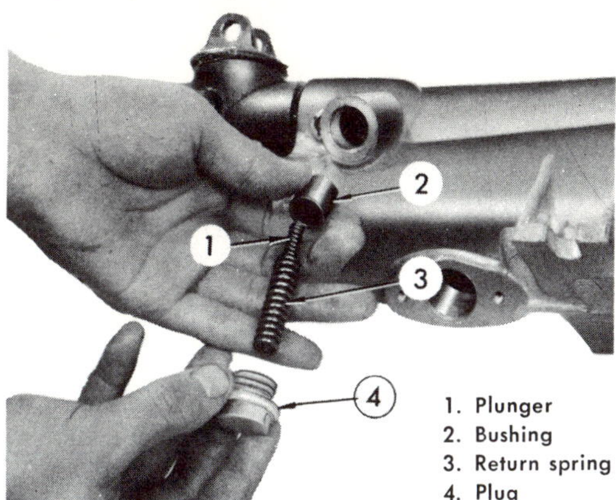

7. Clamp the adapter plate in a vise with the reverse idler gear up.
8. Drive out the retaining pin and remove the reverse shift fork and reverse idler gear.
9. Remove the mainshaft rear snap-ring, washer, and reverse gear.
10. Drive out remaining shift fork retaining pins. Remove all three detent plugs, springs, and balls. Remove forks and shift rods. Be careful not to lose the interlock plungers.
11. Tap the rear of the mainshaft with a soft hammer to separate the mainshaft and countershaft from the adapter plate. Be careful not to drop the shafts. Separate clutch shaft from mainshaft.
12. From the front of the mainshaft, remove the needle bearing, synchronizer hub thrust washer, steel locating ball, third/fourth synchronizer, baulk ring, third gear, and needle bearing.

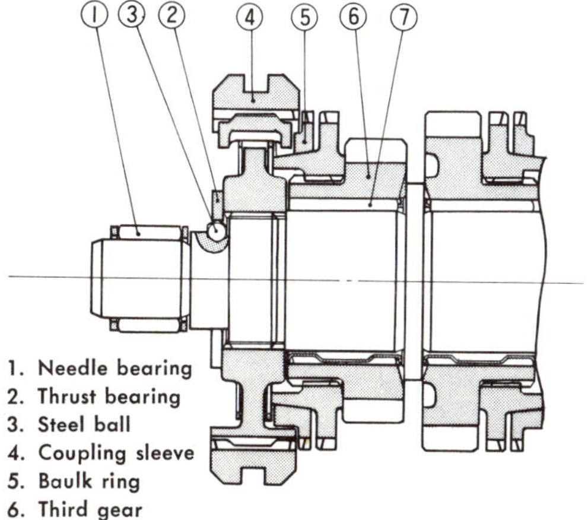

Front of LB110 and KLB110 transmission mainshaft

13. Press off the mainshaft bearing to the rear. Remove the thrust washer, first gear, needle bearing, baulk ring, first/second synchronizer, baulk ring, second gear, and needle bearing.

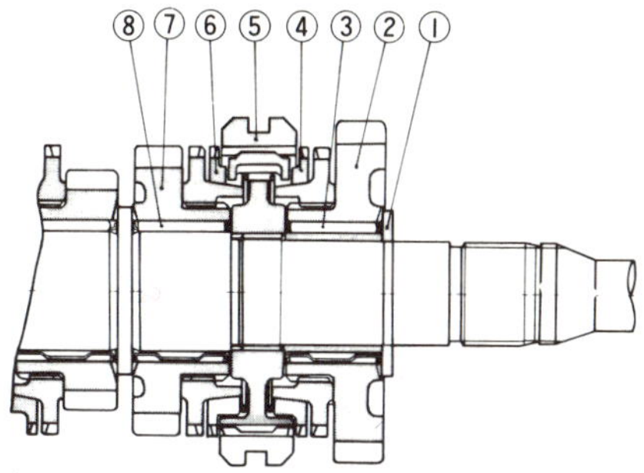

Rear of LB110 and KLB110 transmission mainshaft

1. Thrust washer
2. First gear
3. Needle bearing
4. Baulk ring
5. Coupling sleeve
6. Baulk ring
7. Second gear
8. Needle bearing

14. Remove countergear bearing.
15. Remove clutch shaft snap-ring and bearing.

Inspection

1. Clean all parts in a safe solvent. Oil the bearings immediately. Check all parts for wear or damage.
2. Backlash for each pair of gears should be .0031-.0059″ (.08-.15 mm.). If it is excessive, replace both drive and driven gears.
3. Gear end-play is adjusted by using snap-rings of different thicknesses.

Gear	*End-Play*
First, Second	.0059-.0098″ (.15-.25 mm.)
Third	.0059-.0138″ (.15-.35 mm.)

4. Place each baulk ring on the cone of its gear. Check the gap between the baulk ring end face and the clutch teeth front face. The gap should be .0413-.0551″ (1.05-1.40 mm.). If it is less than .0197″ (.5 mm.), replace the bulk ring.

Assembly

1. Press on the countershaft bearings. Install the countershaft assembly into the transmission case and replace the adapter plate temporarily. Countershaft end-play should be 0-.0079″ (0-.2 mm.). Front bearing shims are availa-

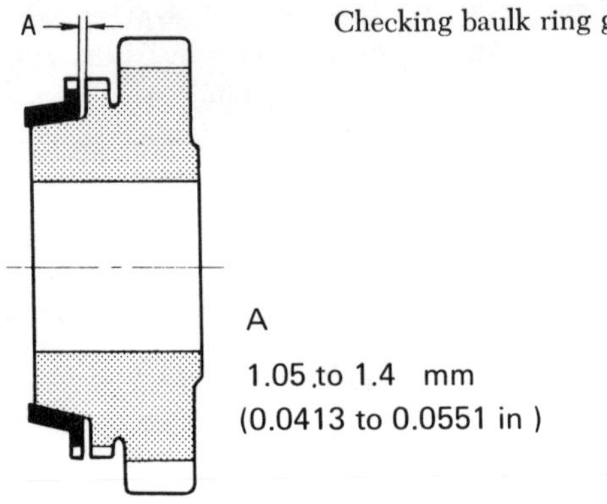

Checking baulk ring gap

ble for adjustment in thicknesses from .0315″ (.8 mm.) to .0512″ (1.3 mm.). Remove countershaft assembly from case.

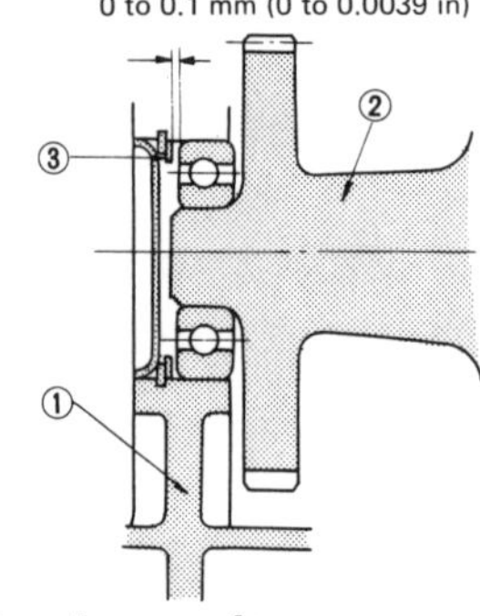

1. Transmission case
2. Countershaft
3. Shim

Selecting countershaft front bearing shim

2. Oil all moving parts on installation.
3. Install coupling sleeve, shifting inserts, and spring on synchronizer hub. Be careful not to hook front and rear ends of spring to same insert. Check that hub and sleeve operate smoothly.
4. Install needle bearing from rear of mainshaft. Install second gear, baulk ring, and synchronizer hub assembly. Align shifting insert to baulk ring groove. Install first gear side needle bearing, baulk ring, and first gear. Install mainshaft thrust washer and press on the rear bearing. On mainshaft front end, replace needle bearing, third gear, baulk ring, synchronizer hub assembly, steel locating ball, thrust washer, and pilot bearing. Be sure to grease the sliding surface of the steel ball and thrust washer. The dimpled side of the thrust washer must face to the front and the oil grooved side to the rear.
5. Replace main bearing, washer, and snap-ring on clutch shaft. The web side of the washer must face the bearing. Place the baulk ring on the clutch shaft and assemble clutch shaft to mainshaft.
6. Align mainshaft assembly with countershaft assembly and install them to the adapter plate by lightly tapping on the clutch shaft with a soft hammer.
7. Place first/second and third/fourth shift forks on shift rods, being careful that forks are not reversed. Install all three shift rods and detent and interlock parts. Apply locking agent to detent plug threads and screw plugs in flush. Make sure that shift forks are in their grooves and drive in the retaining pins.

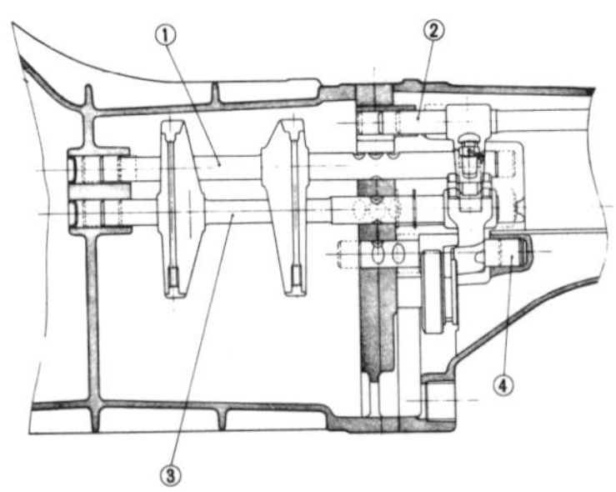

1. First/second shift rod
2. Striker rod
3. Third/fourth shift rod
4. Reverse shift rod

Shift rod and fork arrangement, LB110 and KLB110 four speed

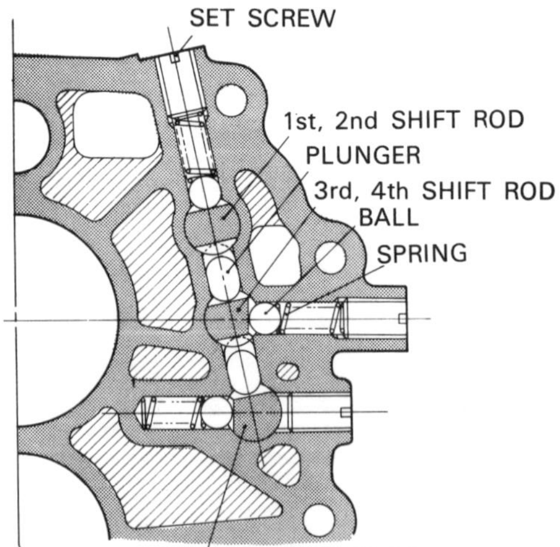

Detent ball and interlock details, LB110 and KLB110 four speed

8. Install mainshaft reverse gear, thrust washer, and snap-ring. Face web side of thrust washer to gear.
9. Replace reverse idler gear and pin on reverse shift fork. Check interlock

action by attempting to shift two shift rods at once.

10. Install adapter plate to transmission case. Make sure to install countergear front shim selected in Step 1. Use sealant on the joint and seat the plate by tapping with a soft hammer.
11. Align the striker lever and install the extension housing. Use sealant on the joint. Install bushing, plunger, return spring, and plug. Use sealant on the plug threads. Install striker rod pin and speedometer drive pinion.
12. Select clutch shaft bearing shim(s) by measuring amount bearing outer race is recessed below machined surface for front cover. The depth should be .1969-.2028″ (5.00-5.15 mm.). Shims are available for adjustment in thicknesses of .0039″ (.1 mm.), .0079″ (.2 mm.), and .0197″ (.5 mm.).

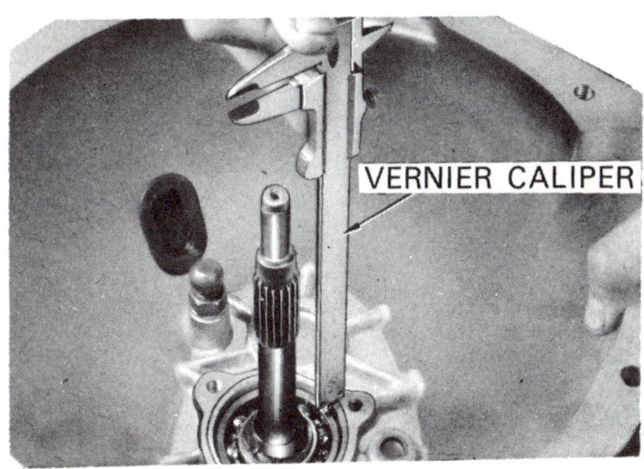

1. Clutch shaft
2. Front cover
3. Shim for adjusting front cover

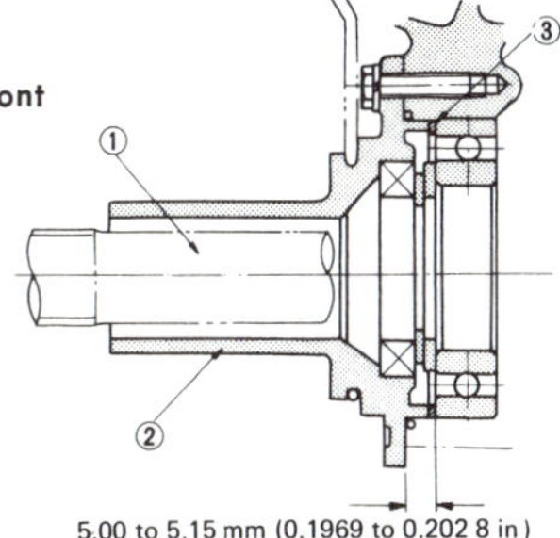

Selecting clutch shaft bearing shims

13. Place oil seal in front cover, grease the seal lip, and install the cover and O-ring with the shim(s) selected in Step 12.
14. Replace clutch release bearing, return spring, and withdrawal lever.
15. Check shifting action. Rotate clutch shaft slowly in neutral. The rear of the mainshaft should not turn.
16. Refer to the Capacities and Pressures Chart for refill capacity.

Four Speed, Top Cover Transmission—PL410, SPL310

This transmission may also be found in some early L520 and PL411 models. The transmission and clutch housings are combined in one piece. The floorshift mechanism is integrated with the top cover. On some models, the shift lever is located further back, above the extension housing.

Disassembly

1. Drain oil.
2. Remove the clutch withdrawal lever. Remove the transmission top cover.
3. Twist the cap at the base of the shift lever counterclockwise while pressing down.
4. Unbolt and remove top cover.
5. Straighten lock tab, remove setscrew, and tap reverse idler shaft forward. Remove shaft and gear.
6. Drive countershaft forward and out. Remove thrust washers. The countergear cannot be removed yet.
7. Pull the mainshaft out through the rear of the case.
8. Tilt the countergear to clear the clutch shaft gear. Insert a long drift through the mainshaft opening and drive the clutch shaft and bearing forward out of the case.
9. Remove the countergear from the case. To remove the needle roller bearing, break the retaining clips and drive out the bearing.
10. To disassemble the mainshaft, slide off the third/fourth synchronizer from the front. Insert a wire through the hole in the gear cone and depress the spring loaded plunger which locates the splined washer, aligning the washer with the splines. Pull third and second gears, with their bronze sleeves, over the plunger and off the shaft. It may be necessary to immerse the shaft in warm oil to expand the sleeve slightly. Remove the plunger and spring. Remove the splined washer and first gear. At the rear of the shaft, straighten the lock tab, remove the nut, speedometer drive gear, and key. Remove the distance piece (spacer) and bearing.
11. To dismantle the clutch shaft, first

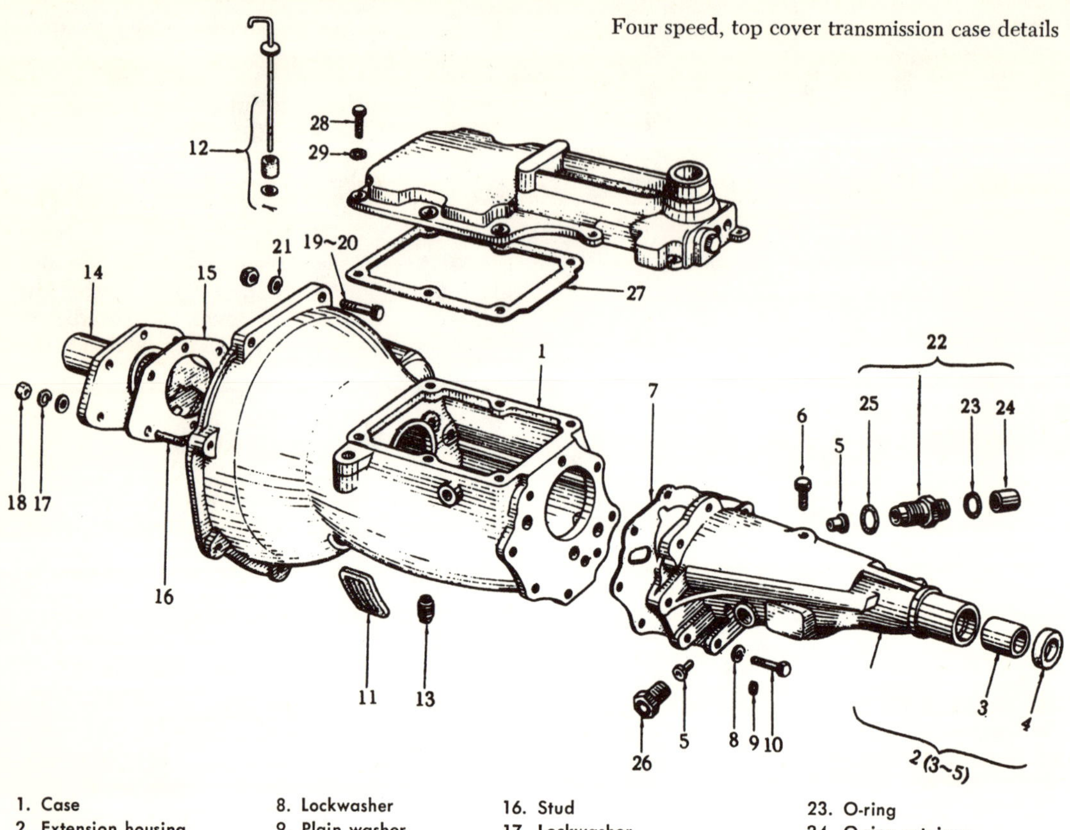

Four speed, top cover transmission case details

1. Case
2. Extension housing
3. Bushing
4. Oil seal
5. Speedometer pinion bushing
6. Breather
7. Gasket
8. Lockwasher
9. Plain washer
10. Bolt
11. Rubber boot
12. Dipstick assembly
13. Drain plug
14. Front cover
15. Gasket
16. Stud
17. Lockwasher
18. Nut
19. Bolt
20. Bolt
21. Lockwasher
22. Speedometer pinion sleeve assembly
23. O-ring
24. O-ring retainer
25. O-ring
26. Speedometer pinion plug
27. Cover gasket
28. Bolt
29. Lockwasher

remove the needle roller bearings from the rear. Bend back the lock tab, unscrew the left hand threaded nut, and press off the bearing.

Inspection

1. Wash all parts in a safe solvent. Oil bearings immediately.
2. Check all parts for wear or damage.
3. Pry out extension housing oil seal and install a new one.
4. Replace all gaskets.
5. Gear backlash should be .003-.005″ (.075-.125 mm.) between all pairs of gears.

Assembly

1. Install countergear in case with thrust washers. The larger washer must be at the front. Install countershaft. Countergear end-play should be .0015-.0023″ (.04-.06 mm.). End-play is adjusted by changing the rear thrust washer. Thrust washers are available in thicknesses from .0015-.0023″ (.04-.06 mm.) to .154-.156″ (3.91-3.96 mm.). Temporarily replace the countershaft with a smaller diameter rod so that the countergear will not mesh with the mainshaft and clutch shaft gears as they are installed.
2. Press the bearing onto the clutch shaft, replace the washer and nut. Some units may have a snap-ring instead of a nut. Place the 18 needle rollers into the rear of the shaft with a bit of grease. Turn transmission housing so that countergear is out of the way and drive in shaft and bearing from the front.
3. Press the mainshaft bearing on from the rear. Oil the shaft ahead of the bearing and install first gear with the synchronizer forward. Replace the thrust washer and baulk ring. Expand

Shaft assemblies, four speed, top cover transmission

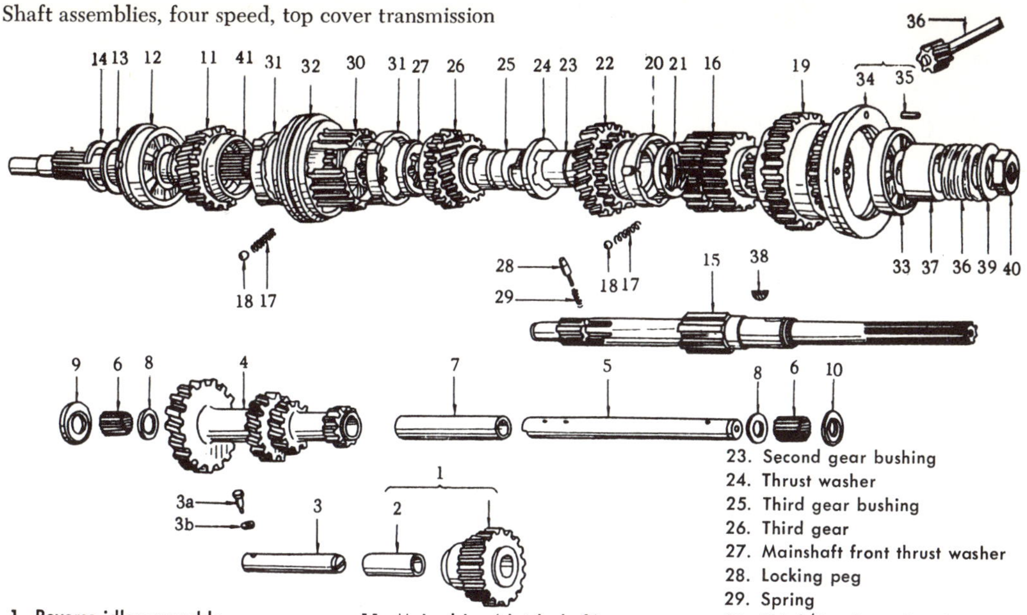

1. Reverse idler assembly
2. Bushing
3. Shaft
3a. Setscrew
3b. Lock tab
4. Countergear
5. Countershaft
6. Needle roller
7. Countershaft spacer
8. Needle roller retainer ring
9. Countergear front thrust washer
10. Countergear rear thust washer
11. Main drive (clutch shaft) gear
12. Bearing
13. Bearing spacer
14. Snap-ring
15. Mainshaft
16. Synchronizer hub
17. Synchronizer spring
18. Synchronizer ball
19. Mainshaft gear
20. Second gear baulk ring
21. Mainshaft rear thrust washer
22. Second gear
23. Second gear bushing
24. Thrust washer
25. Third gear bushing
26. Third gear
27. Mainshaft front thrust washer
28. Locking peg
29. Spring
30. Third/fourth synchronizer
31. Third/fourth baulk ring
32. Third/fourth synchronizer sleeve
33. Mainshaft bearing
34. Bearing retainer
35. Locking peg
36. Speedometer drive gears
37. Distance piece
38. Key
39. Lockwasher
40. Mainshaft nut
41. Mainshaft pilot bearing

Four speed, top cover transmission top cover and shifting arrangement

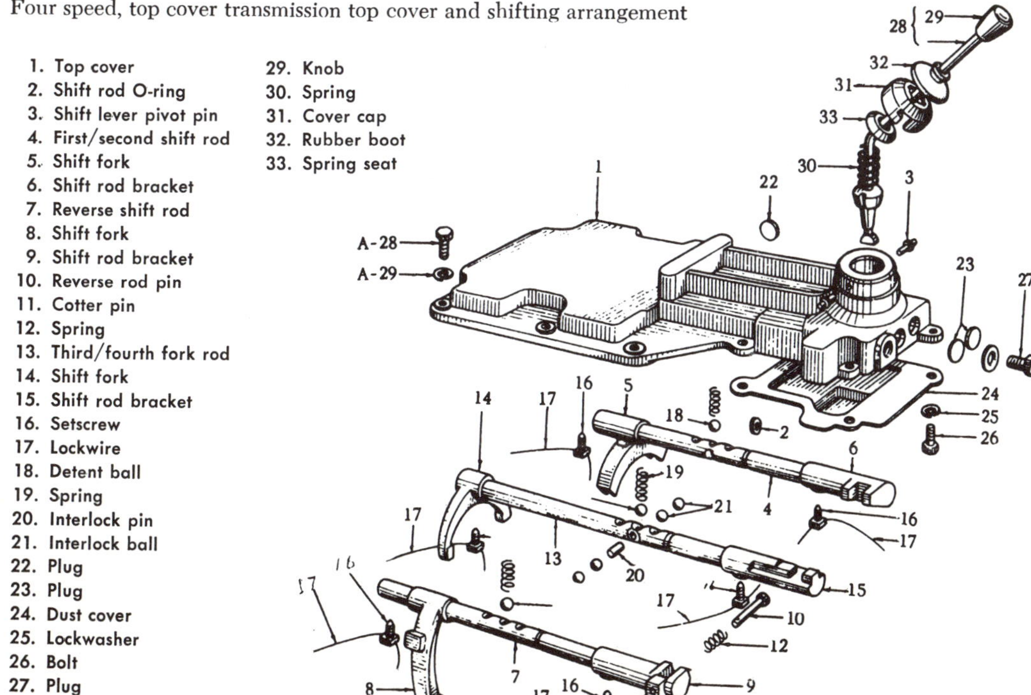

1. Top cover
2. Shift rod O-ring
3. Shift lever pivot pin
4. First/second shift rod
5. Shift fork
6. Shift rod bracket
7. Reverse shift rod
8. Shift fork
9. Shift rod bracket
10. Reverse rod pin
11. Cotter pin
12. Spring
13. Third/fourth fork rod
14. Shift fork
15. Shift rod bracket
16. Setscrew
17. Lockwire
18. Detent ball
19. Spring
20. Interlock pin
21. Interlock ball
22. Plug
23. Plug
24. Dust cover
25. Lockwasher
26. Bolt
27. Plug
28. Shift lever
29. Knob
30. Spring
31. Cover cap
32. Rubber boot
33. Spring seat

the second gear sleeve in warm oil and slide it over the shaft. Install second gear, the washer, and the third gear sleeve. The two sleeves are locked together by the washer. Replace third gear. Place spring and plunger into hole in shaft and slide on splined washer. Depress the plunger with a wire through the hole in third gear, and slide the splined washer over the plunger. Turn the washer so that the plunger engages with a groove in the washer. Assemble the two baulk rings to third/fourth synchronizer and coupling sleeve. The large boss of the synchronizer inner splines must face forward. The pointed ends of the baulk ring lugs must face into the synchronizer. Slide third/fourth synchronizer forward slightly to clear countergear and install mainshaft. Second and third gear end-play should be .0048-.0062″ (.12-.16 mm.).

4. Oil and install the countershaft.
5. Replace the reverse idler gear and shaft with setscrew and lock tab. Replace front cover.

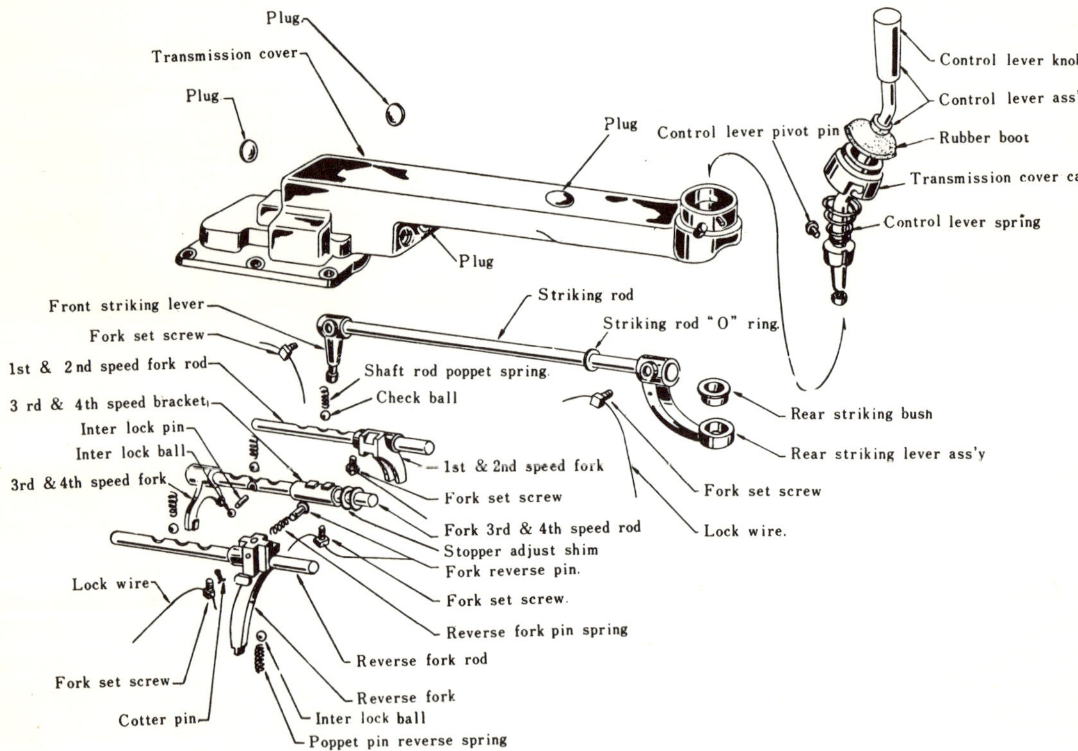

Rear mounted shift lever arrangement for four speed, top cover transmission

Four Speed, Side Cover Transmission—L320

This transmission has a two piece case with a side cover. The column shift linkage uses cross shafts with a coupling disc. Overhaul procedures are the same as that for the four speed top cover transmission used on the PL410 and SPL310, after the shift linkage and cross shafts are removed.

Four speed, side cover transmission case details

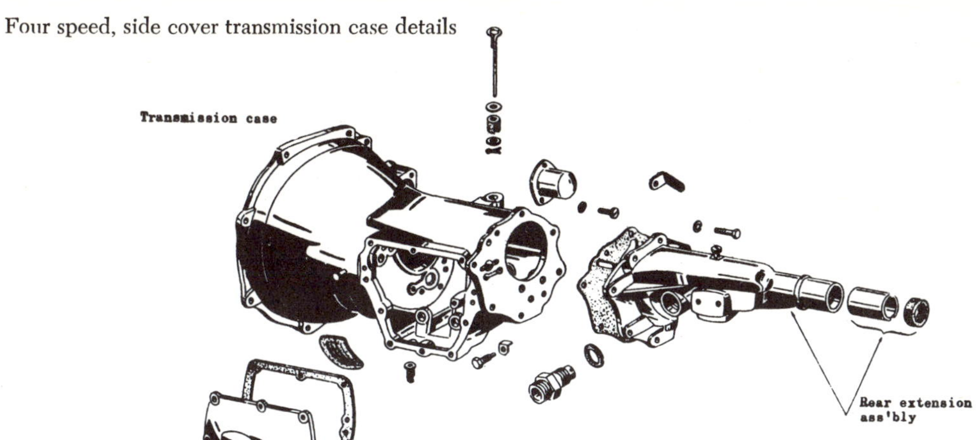

Details of shifting arrangement of four speed, side cover transmission

Shift linkage, four speed, side cover transmission

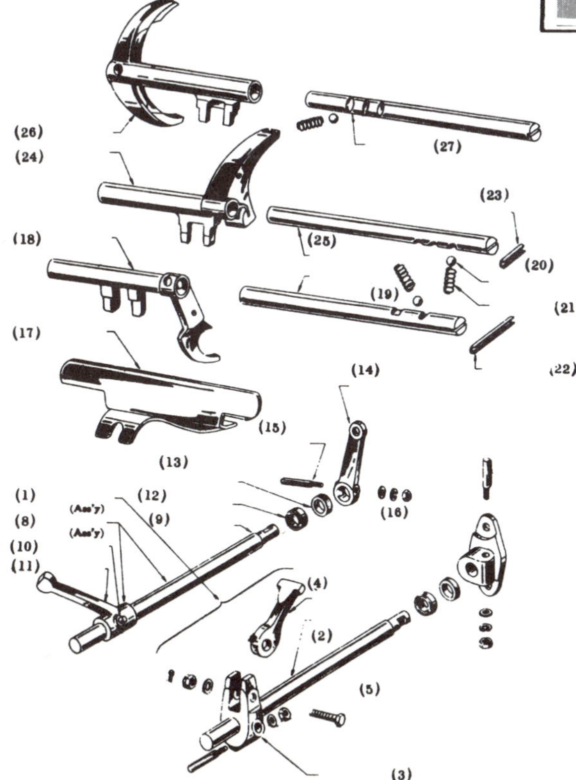

1. Fork assembly
2. Cross shaft
3. Shift fork
4. Operating fork
5. Fulcrum pin
6. Not used
7. Not used
8. Selector cross shaft assembly
9. Selector shaft
10. Taper pin
11. Selector shaft inner lever
12. Oil seal
13. Felt ring
14. Selector cross shaft lever
15. Lock pin
16. Plain washer, lockwasher, nut
17. Shift gate
18. Reverse fork
19. Reverse shift rod
20. Detent ball
21. Detent spring
22. Large shift rod locking strip
23. Small fork rod locking strip
24. First/second shift fork
25. First/second shift rod
26. Third/fourth shift fork
27. Third/fourth shift rod

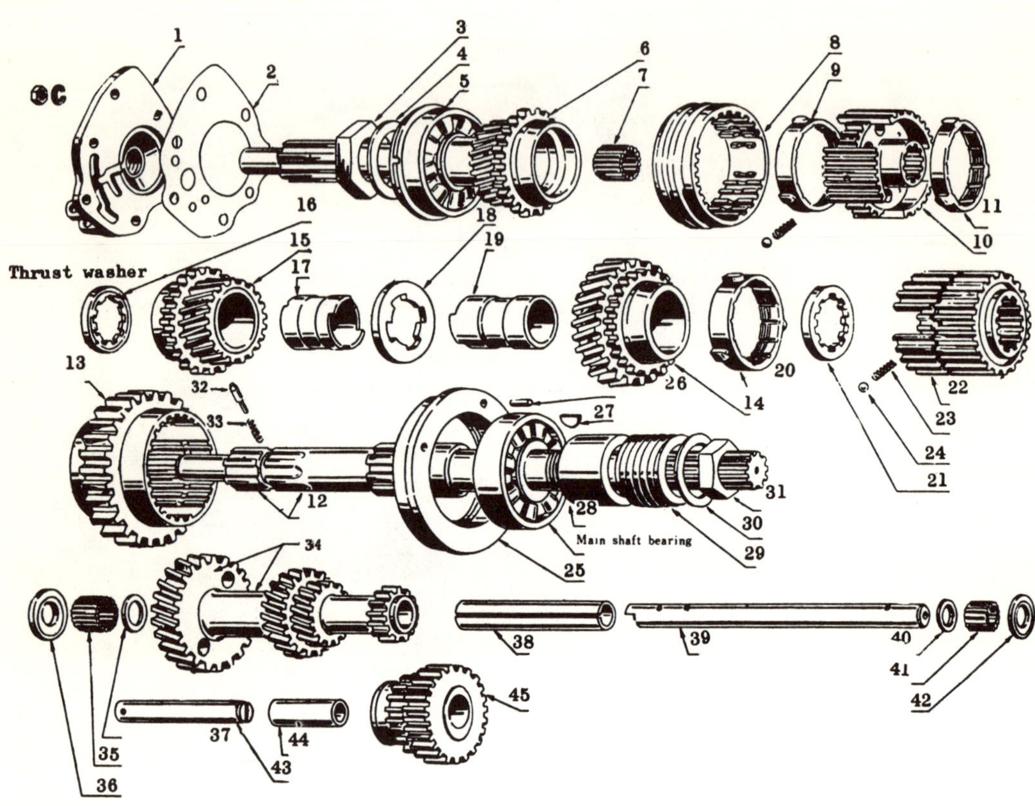

Shaft assemblies, four speed, side cover transmission

1. Front cover
2. Gasket
3. Clutch shaft bearing
4. Lockwasher
5. Clutch shaft gear
6. Clutch shaft gear
7. Mainshaft pilot bearing
8. Third/fourth synchronizer sleeve
9. Synchronizer ring
10. Synchronizer hub
11. Synchronizer ring
12. Mainshaft
13. First gear
14. Second gear
15. Third gear
16. Mainshaft front thrust washer
17. Third gear bushing
18. Thrust washer
19. Second gear bushing
20. Second gear synchronizer ring
21. Mainshaft rear thrust washer
22. Second gear synchronizer hub
23. Synchronizer spring
24. Ball
25. Bearing retainer
26. Bearing retainer locater
27. Key
28. Mainshaft spacer
29. Speedometer drive gear
30. Mainshaft lockwasher
31. Mainshaft nut
32. Locking peg
33. Spring
34. Countergear
35. Countershaft needle rollers
36. Countershaft front thrust washer
37. Snap-ring
38. Spacer
39. Countershaft
40. Snap-ring
41. Needle rollers
42. Thrust washer
43. Reverse idler shaft
44. Bushing
45. Reverse idler gear

Manual Transmission Ratios

Vehicle	First	Second	Third	Fourth	Fifth	Reverse
L60①	2.900	1.562	1.000	None	None	3.015
L320	4.94	3.01	1.73	1.00	None	6.46
L520	3.657	2.177	1.419	1.000	None	3.638
	4.941	3.009	1.726	1.000	None	6.462
PL521	3.657	2.177	1.419	1.000	None	3.638
PL410	3.518	1.725	1.00	None	None	4.125
	3.197	1.725	1.00	None	None	4.125
	3.945	2.94	1.490	1.000	None	5.159
	3.945	2.403	1.490	1.000	None	5.159
PL411	3.197	1.725	1.000	None	None	4.125
	3.94	2.40	1.49	1.00	None	5.159
	3.657	2.177	1.419	1.000	None	3.638
RL411, SPL311, PL510	3.382	2.013	1.312	1.000	None	3.365
SPL310	3.515	2.140	1.328	1.000	None	4.597
SRL311	2.957	1.858	1.311	1.000	.852	2.922
WPL510	3.657	2.177	1.419	1.000	None	3.638
	3.382	2.013	1.312	1.000	None	3.634
	3.382	2.013	1.312	1.000	None	3.634
HLS30	3.549	2.197	1.420	1.000	None	3.164
	2.957	1.857	1.311	1.000	.852	2.922
LB110, KLB110	3.757	2.169	1.404	1.000	None	3.640

① L60 transfer case ratios are 2.264:1 and 1:1.

Automatic Transmission

Only external transmission adjustments and repairs, and transmission removal and replacement, are covered in this book. Automatic transmission internal repairs and overhaul should be left to an authorized repair facility.

The RL411, PL510 up to serial number PL510-117464, and WPL510 up to serial number WPL510-853595 use a British built Borg Warner automatic transmission with a cable operated downshift. Later PL510 and WPL510 models use an American built Borg Warner transmission with vacuum pressure control and a solenoid operated downshift. The HLS30 uses a Nissan unit. There is a model and serial number tag on the left side of the Borg Warner units.

Model no.	Nissan Part no.	Transmission	Vehicle
AS14-35EC	31010-24500	British built BW	RL411, PL510, WPL510
AS2-41	31010A8500	American built BW	PL510, WPL510
3N71A		Nissan	HLS30

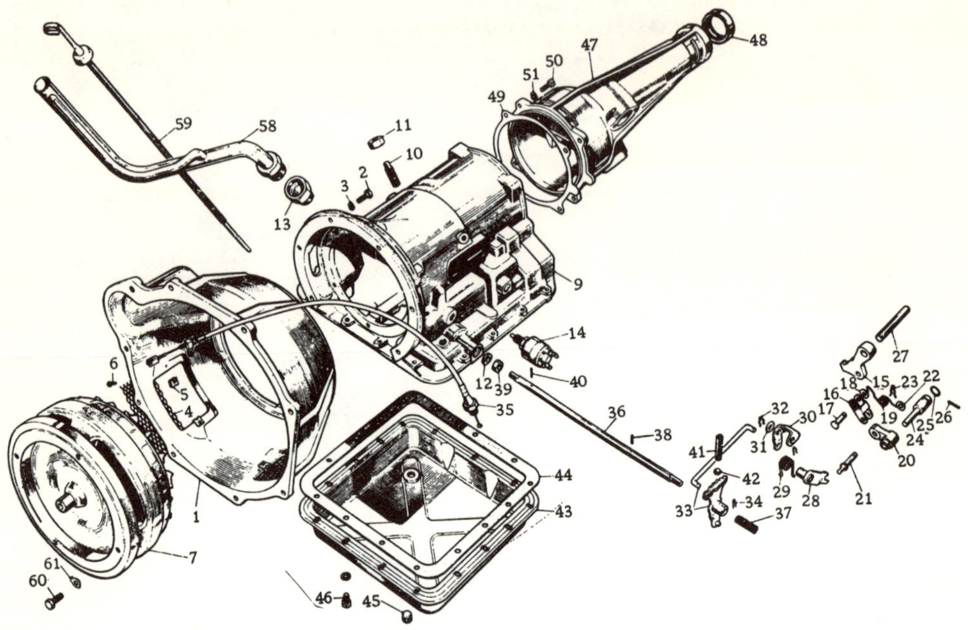

British built Borg Warner automatic transmission

1. Converter housing
2. Housing to case bolt
3. Lockwasher
4. Screen
5. Captive nut
6. Screw
7. Converter assembly
8. Not used
9. Case assembly
10. Rear band adjusting screw
11. Locknut
12. Seal
13. Adapter
14. Neutral safety switch
15. Park pawl
16. Toggle link
17. Toggle link pin
18. Washer
19. Spring
20. Toggle lever
21. Toggle pin
22. Washer
23. Retaining clip
24. Toggle pin
25. O-ring
26. Cotter pin
27. Pin
28. Toggle lift lever
29. Spring
30. Torsion lever
31. Washer
32. Retaining clip
33. Park linkage
34. Retaining clip
35. Downshift cable assembly
36. Manual valve shaft
37. Spring
38. Roll pin
39. Collar
40. Roll pin
41. Detent spring
42. Detent ball
43. Pan
44. Pan gasket
45. Drain plug
46. Bolt
47. Extension housing
48. Oil seal
49. Gasket
50. Bolt
51. Lockwasher
52-57. Not used
58. Filler, dipstick, and breather tube
59. Dipstick
60. Drive plate to converter bolt
61. Lockwasher

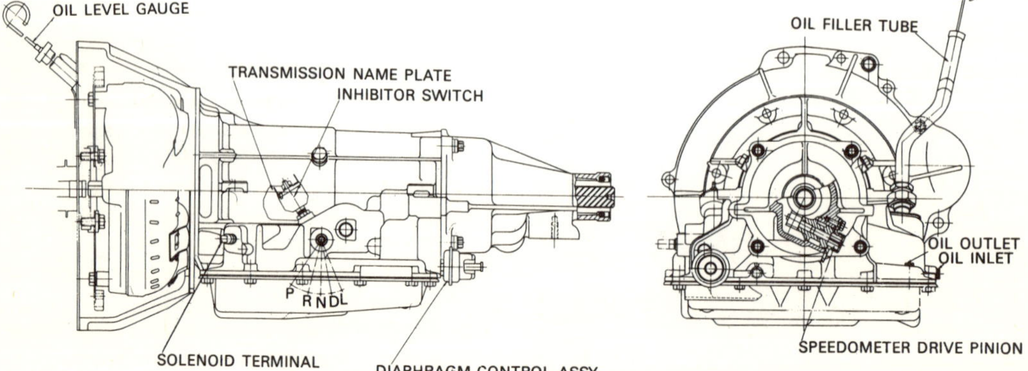

American built Borg Warner automatic transmission

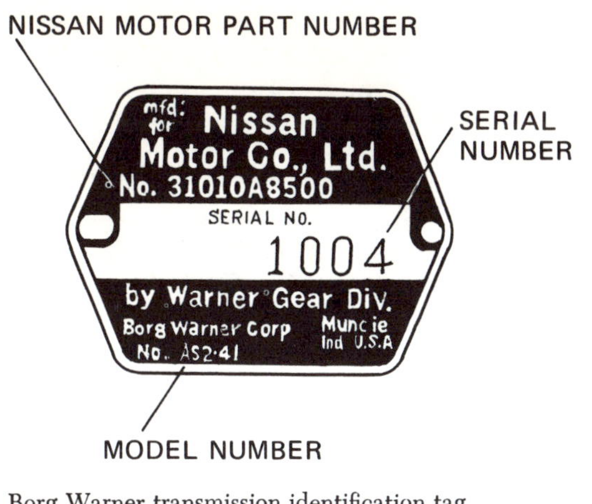

Borg Warner transmission identification tag

Nissan automatic transmission

1. Converter housing
2. Converter housing to transmission bolt
3. Transmission case
4. Case rear flange
5. Gasket
6. Rear extension housing
7. Not used
8. Bushing
9. O-ring
10. Washer
11. Manual plate
12. Park lever
13. Snap-ring
14. Park rod
15. Park actuator support
16. Breather baffle plate
17. Park lever pin

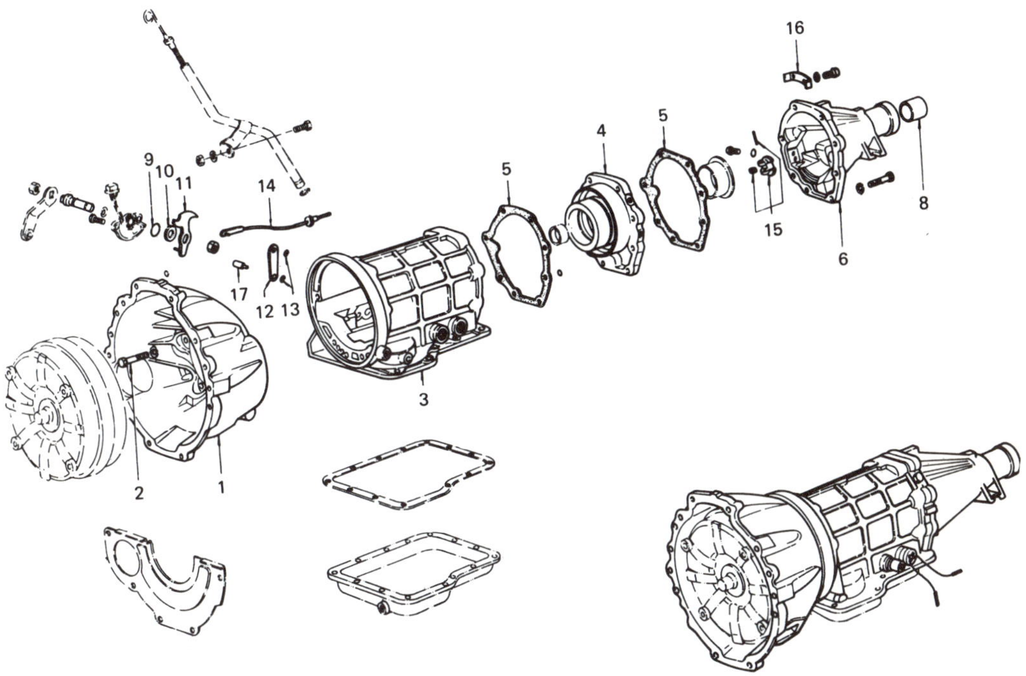

Removal and Installation

RL411, PL510, WPL510 With British BW Unit

1. Disconnect downshift cable from carburetor.
2. Drain transmission oil pan.
3. Remove driveshaft.
4. Disconnect handbrake mechanism if necessary.
5. Disconnect speedometer cable from transmission. Disconnect neutral safety switch.
6. Disconnect transmission shift linkage. Disconnect oil cooler tubes.
7. Remove filler tube.
8. Unbolt transmission from rear crossmember.
9. Support engine with a jack under the torque converter housing.
10. Remove crossmember. Lower rear of engine slightly.
11. Support transmission with a jack. Place a pan under the torque converter.
12. Remove starter.
13. Remove four bolts retaining torque

converter to drive plate. Access is from front through engine mounting plate.

14. Remove converter and transmission assembly to the rear. Be careful not to let converter fall when separating assembly from engine.
15. Reverse procedure to install. Check that drive plate is not warped more than .020″. Plate to crankshaft bolt torque is 40-50 ft. lbs. To ensure correct engagement of front oil pump drive, rotate converter so that drive fingers on hub will be in 9 and 3 o'clock positions. Rotate the slots of the front oil pump driving gear to the same positions. Torque drive plate to torque converter bolts to 25-30 ft. lbs. Torque ⅜″ converter housing to engine bolts to 30-34 ft. lbs. and 5/16″ bolts to 7-10 ft. lbs. There are two dowels for aligning the converter housing to the engine.
16. Refill transmission and check fluid level.

PL510, WPL510 with American BW Unit

1. Disconnect battery.
2. Remove carburetor torsion shaft and starter.
3. Remove two torque converter housing to engine capscrews at top.
4. Raise and support car.
5. Disconnect handbrake front cable from center lever.
6. Loosen oil pan bolts and drain transmission.
7. Loosen muffler clamps and turn muffler for clearance. Remove driveshaft after unbolting at rear.
8. Disconnect speedometer cable, vacuum hose, and inhibitor wiring. Disconnect solenoid wire at transmission.
9. Detach oil cooler tubes. Remove filler tube and plug opening.
10. Disconnect lower selector rod and remove cross shaft assembly.
11. Support the transmission with a suitable jack.
12. Remove rear crossmember. Lower transmission and rear of engine for access to converter to drive plate bolts. Place a pan under the converter.
13. Remove engine rear plate. Mark relationship of converter and drive plate. Remove torque converter to drive plate bolts, screwing bolts out completely one at a time. Remove remaining converter housing to engine capscrews. Pull transmission away from engine.

To replace American built Borg Warner transmission:

14. Check that drive plate is not warped more than .020″. Plate to crankshaft bolt torque is 50 ft. lbs. Place transmission and converter assembly on a jack. Pull transmission forward to start converter hub in crankshaft. Align engine block dowel pin with converter housing aligning hole. Install two lower converter housing attaching bolts and tighten to pull transmission assembly into place. Torque converter housing bolts to 32 ft. lbs. Tighten drive plate to converter bolts to 28 ft. lbs.
15. Install starter motor, shift linkage, speedometer cable, filler tube, and oil cooler tubes.
16. Connect vacuum hose and kickdown solenoid wire.
17. Raise transmission until it contacts floor pan, attach rear crossmember to side rails, lower transmission, and bolt transmission to crossmember.
18. Replace driveshaft, exhaust pipe, and handbrake cable.
19. Lower vehicle, replace battery cable, and carburetor torsion shaft.
20. Pour in 3 quarts of transmission fluid. Set handbrake and start engine. Add 3 more quarts. Move selector lever through all ranges. Add enough fluid to bring level up to F mark.

HLS30

1. Disconnect battery cable.
2. Remove carburetor torsion shaft.
3. Detach transmission control lever.
4. Disconnect inhibitor switch and downshift solenoid wiring.
5. Remove drain plug and drain torque converter.
6. Remove front exhaust pipe.
7. Remove vacuum tube and speedometer cable.
8. Disconnect oil cooler tubes.
9. Remove driveshaft and starter.
10. Support transmission with a jack under the oil pan. Support engine also.
11. Remove rear crossmember.
12. Mark relationship between torque converter and drive plate. Remove four bolts holding converter to drive plate through hole at front, under engine.

Unbolt transmission from engine.

13. Reverse procedure for installation. Check that drive plate is warped no more than .020″. Torque drive plate to torque converter and converter housing to engine bolts to 29-36 ft. lbs. Drive plate to crankshaft bolt torque is 8.5 ft. lbs.
14. Refill transmission and check fluid level.

Shift Linkage Adjustment

HLS30 Floorshift

1. Loosen trunnion locknuts at lower end of control lever. Remove selector lever knob and console.
2. Place selector lever in N.
3. Place transmission shift lever in neutral position by pushing it all the way back, then pulling it forward two stops.
4. Check vertical clearance between top of shift lever pin and transmission control bracket. The clearance, A in the illustration, should be .020-.059″. Adjust by turning the nut at the lower end of the selector lever compression rod.
5. Check horizontal clearance, B, of shift lever pin and transmission control bracket. This should be .020″. Adjust with trunnion locknuts.
6. Replace console, making sure that shift pointer is correctly aligned. Install knob.

RL411, PL510, WPL510 Column Shift

1. Loosen trunnion locknuts on upper selector rod. (On the steering column inside the engine compartment).
2. Place selector lever in N. Place transmission shift lever in neutral position, the central of its five positions.
3. Adjust locknuts so that the clearance between the stop pin on the lower selector lever and the position plate is .020-.039″.

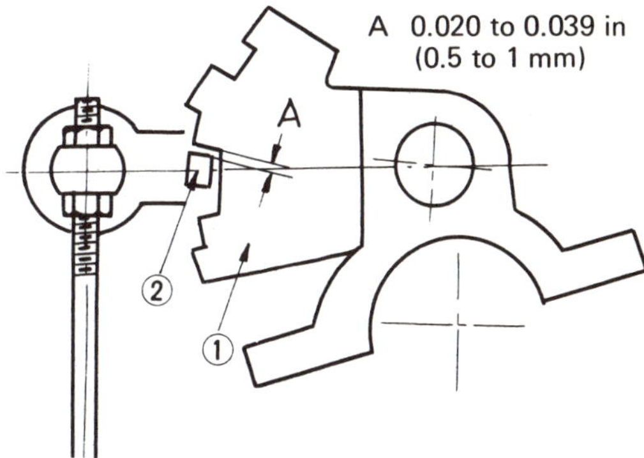

Column shift adjustment. 1 is selector position plate, 2 is stop pin.

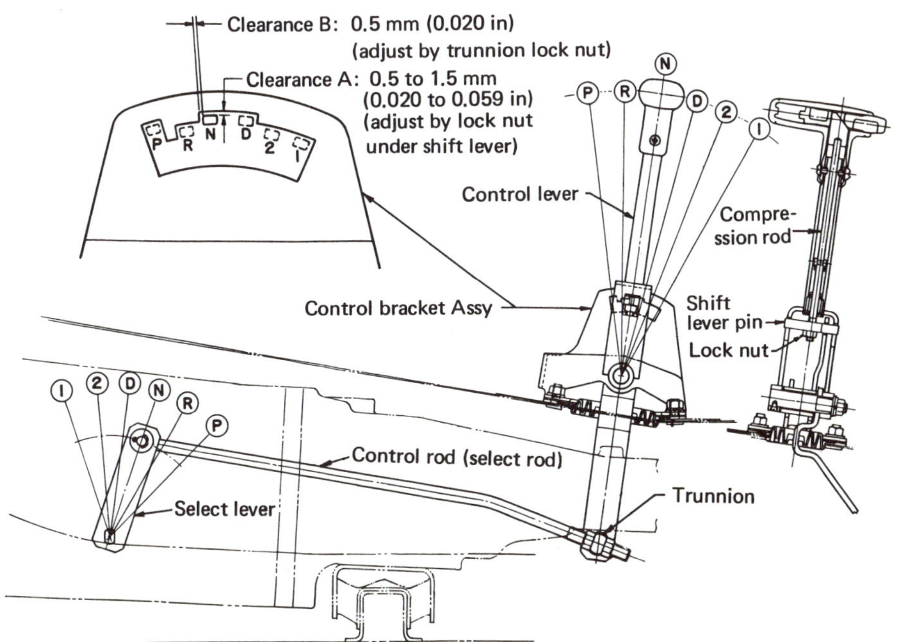

HLS30 floorshift linkage adjustment

Downshift Cable Adjustment

RL411, PL510, WPL510

This adjustment is necessary only on early models with the British built Borg Warner transmission. The adjustment is made at the carburetor end of the cable.

1. Check transmission fluid level. Connect a tachometer to the engine.
2. Connect a pressure gauge to the transmission line pressure outlet.

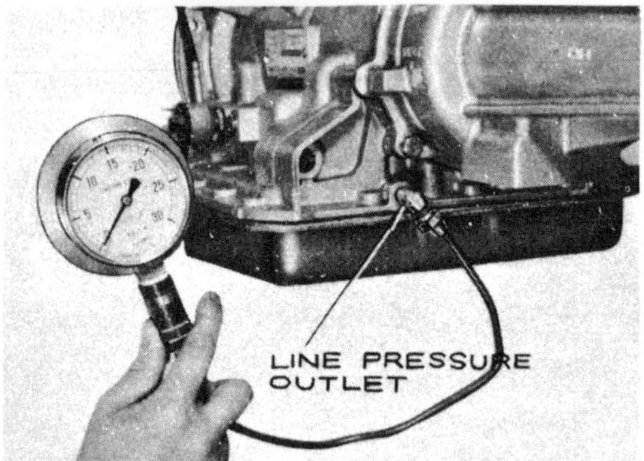

Pressure gauge connected to British BW transmission

3. Start engine and shift into D. The car should be safely blocked and the hand and footbrakes set.
4. Increase engine speed from 500 to 1,000 rpm. The line pressure should rise 15-20 psi.
5. If the pressure rise is less than 15-20 psi, shorten the inner cable with the adjuster.

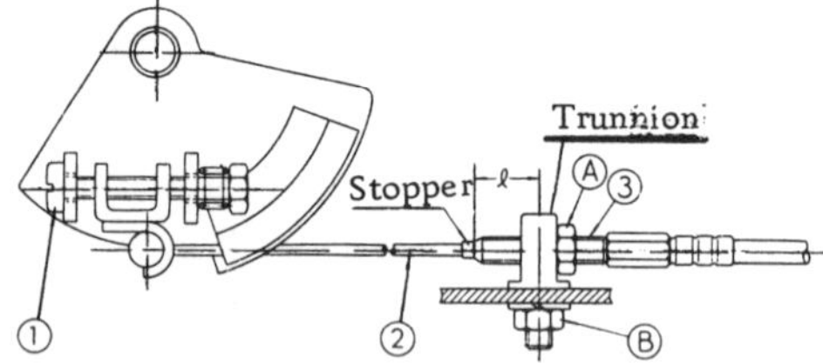

Downshift cable adjuster. 1 is adjuster, 2 is inner cable, 3 is outer cable.

6. If the pressure rise is excessive, lengthen the cable.

NOTE: Do not oil the cable.

Downshift Solenoid Check

PL510, WPL510, HLS30

This solenoid is used on the American Borg Warner and the Nissan transmissions. It is controlled by a downshift switch on the accelerator linkage inside the car. To test switch and solenoid operation:

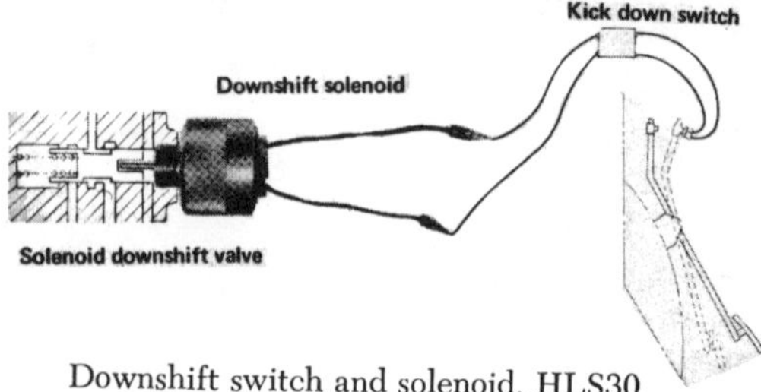

Downshift switch and solenoid, HLS30

1 Turn the ignition on.
2. Push the accelerator all the way down to actuate the switch.
3. The solenoid should click when actuated. Since the solenoid on the Borg Warner transmission is mounted inside the pan, it may be difficult to hear the click. The Nissan transmission solenoid is screwed into the outside of the case. If there is no click, check the switch, wiring, and solenoid.

Removal of Borg Warner downshift solenoid

To remove the solenoid from the Borg Warner transmission, drain and remove the pan. Then push in and turn the solenoid 1/2 turn clockwise to remove.

To remove the Nissan solenoid, first drain 2-3 pints of fluid, then unscrew the unit.

Front Band Adjustment

RL411, PL510, WPL510

This adjustment procedure is for the Borg Warner transmissions only.

1. Drain fluid and remove pan.
2. Clean fluid pickup screen.
3. Loosen locknut on front servo adjusting screw. Loosen adjusting screw.

4. Insert a .250″ thick gauge block between the adjusting screw and the servo piston rod.

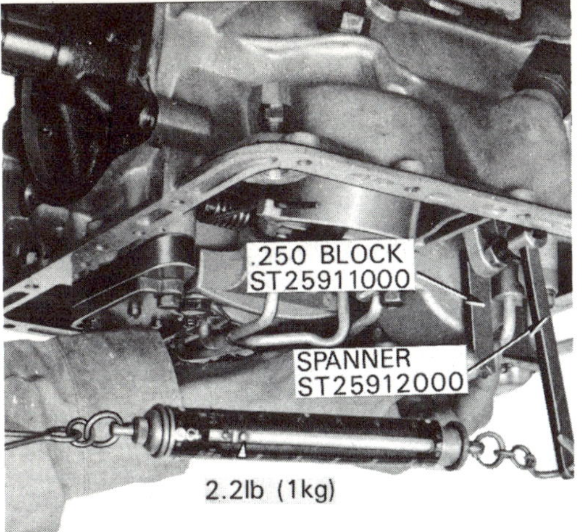

Front band adjustment on Borg Warner transmissions, using a special wrench and a spring scale

5. Tighten adjusting screw to 10 in. lbs. Tighten locknut to 18 ft. lbs.
6. Remove gauge block.
7. Clean and install pan with a new gasket.

Rear Band Adjustment

RL411, PL510, WPL510

This adjustment procedure is for the Borg Warner transmissions only. It may be necessary to unbolt the crossmember and lower the rear of the transmission to get at the adjusting screw on the right side of the case.

1. Loosen locknut. Tighten adjusting screw to 10 ft. lbs.
2. Back off adjusting screw ¾ turn on the American unit and one turn on the British unit.
3. Tighten locknut to 28 ft. lbs.

Neutral Safety and Backup Light Switch Adjustment

RL411, PL510, WPL510

The switch unit is screwed into the left side of the transmission case. The switch terminals marked 1 and 3 are for the neutral safety switch which prevents the engine from being started except in P or N. The terminals 2 and 4 are for the backup light switch.

1. Shift into D or L with the engine off. Disconnect switch leads.
2. Connect a test light in series with terminals 1 and 3 and battery current.
3. Loosen the switch locknut. Screw in the switch until the light goes out. The

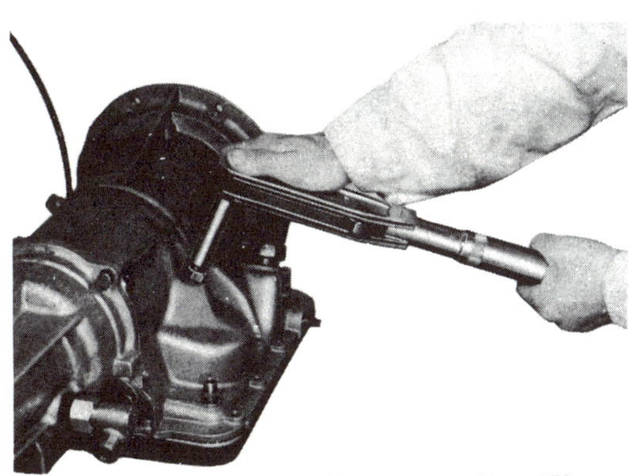

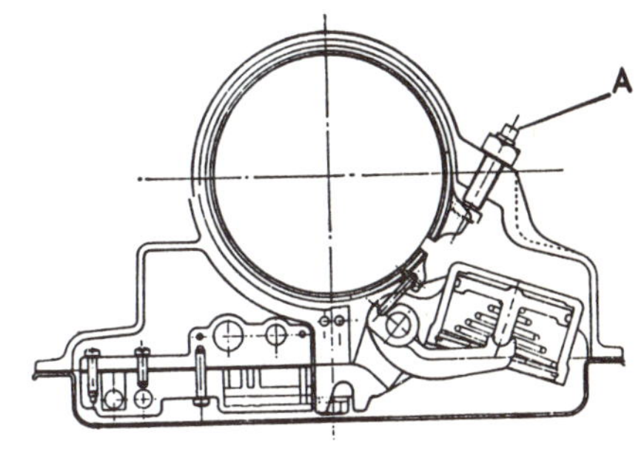

Rear band adjustment on Borg Warner transmissions. A is the adjusting screw.

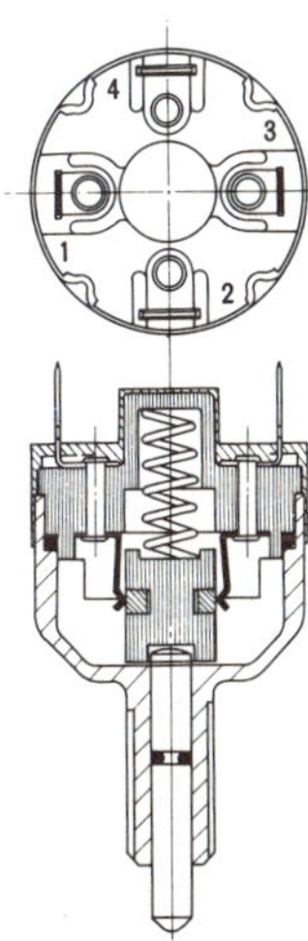

Neutral safety and backup light switch, Borg Warner transmissions

neutral safety switch is now open. Mark the switch position in the case.

4. Connect the test light to terminals 2 and 4. Screw the switch in until the test light goes on. The backup light switch is now closed. Mark the switch position in the case.
5. Screw the switch out to a position midway between the positions marked in Steps 3 and 4. Tighten the locknut to 5 ft. lbs.
6. Check, while holding the brakes on, that the engine will start only in P or N transmission positions. Check that the backup lights go on only in R.

HLS30

The switch unit is bolted to the left side of the transmission case, behind the transmission shift lever. The switch prevents the engine from being started in any transmission position except P or N. It also controls the backup lights.

1. Remove the transmission shift lever retaining nut and the lever.
2. Remove the switch.
3. Remove the machine screw in the case under the switch.
4. Align the switch to the case by inserting a .059″ (1.5 mm.) diameter pin through the hole in the switch into the screw hole. Mark switch location.
5. Remove pin, replace machine screw, install switch as marked, and replace transmission shift lever and retaining nut.
6. Check, while holding the brakes on, that the engine will start only in P or N. Check that the backup lights go on only in R.

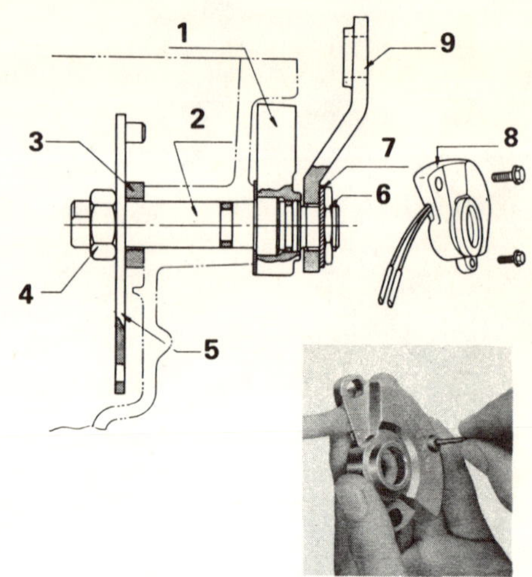

Neutral safety and backup light switch, Nissan transmission

1. Neutral safety switch
2. Manual shaft
3. Washer
4. Nut
5. Manual plate
6. Nut
7. Washer
8. Neutral safety switch
9. Transmission shift lever

Control Pressure Check and Adjustment

PL510, WPL510

This procedure applies only to the American built Borg Warner transmission. Before attempting to adjust transmission shifting control pressure, make sure that the engine vacuum is satisfactory.

1. T-connect a vacuum gauge to the hose at the transmission control unit. The unit is at the left rear of the transmission.
2. Connect a tachometer to the engine.
3. Apply the handbrake, chock the wheels, and set the footbrake.
4. Start the engine and shift into D.
5. Accelerate the engine to 1,200 rpm. Note engine vacuum.

CAUTION: Do not continue this test for more than 10 seconds or transmission overheating and damage will result.

6. The vacuum should be steady and no less than 12.0 in. Hg. (305 mm. Hg.). New engines usually have low and unsteady vacuum for the first 400-500 miles. If the vacuum is too low, correct this condition before any adjustment is made.

To adjust control pressure, proceed as follows:

1. Check transmission fluid level. Remove plug to the right of the transmission control unit at the left rear of the transmission. Connect a pressure gauge.
2. Connect a tachometer to the engine.
3. Apply the handbrake, chock the wheels, and lock the footbrake.
4. Start engine and shift into R. Accelerate engine to 1,200 rpm. See Caution above. Pressure should be 92-98 psi.
5. If pressure is low, remove hose from control unit and turn adjusting screw clockwise. To lower pressure, turn counterclockwise. Turning the screw one complete turn will change the pressure about 10 psi.

Adjusting transmission shifting control pressure on American BW unit

6. The test may be repeated in D and L. The pressure should also be 92-98 psi. The pressure must not be adjusted for D and L.
7. The pressure may also be checked with the engine idling. Idle vacuum must be at least 17.7 in. Hg. (305 mm. Hg.). Transmission pressure in R, D, or L should be 55-68 psi. Idle pressure must not be adjusted.
8. If pressure adjustment is unsuccessful, replacement of the control unit or transmission internal adjustments and repairs may be necessary.

Clutch

Removal and Installation

NISSAN PATROL (L60)

1. Remove transfer case and transmission from engine.
2. Remove clutch housing cover, clutch operating lever, shaft, and release bearing.
3. Loosen clutch retaining bolts gradually and in sequence to prevent distortion. Remove bolts.
4. Clutch assembly can be removed through the bottom of the clutch housing.
5. When replacing the clutch assembly, align the disc to the flywheel with a splined dummy shaft. If this is not done, it will be extremely difficult to assemble the transmission to the engine. Tighten bolts alternately and equally to prevent distortion.
6. Replace release bearing, shaft, operating lever, and housing cover.
7. Replace transmission.

MODELS WITH COIL SPRING CLUTCH (EXCEPT L60)

1. Remove transmission from engine.
2. On L16 engine, temporarily lock release lever.
3. Loosen retaining bolts in sequence, a turn at a time. Remove bolts.
4. Remove pressure plate and disc.
5. Replace the disc with the longer chamfered splined end of the hub toward the transmission.
6. Align the disc to the flywheel with a splined dummy shaft.
7. Install the pressure plate. Most models have two pressure plate locating dowels in the flywheel. Tighten the pressure plate bolts in sequence, a turn at a time. Torque to 35 ft. lbs., except on L16 engine. L16 torque is 17-19 ft. lbs.
8. Remove dummy shaft. Unlock release lever on L16.
9. Replace release bearing and transmission.

MODELS WITH DIAPHRAGM SPRING CLUTCH

1. Remove transmission from engine.
2. Loosen bolts in sequence, a turn at a time. Remove bolts.
3. Remove pressure plate and clutch disc.
4. On A12 and L24 engines, remove release mechanism. Apply multi-purpose grease to bearing sleeve inside groove, contact point of withdrawal lever and bearing sleeve, contact surface of lever ball pin and lever. Replace release mechanism.
5. Install disc, aligning with a splined dummy shaft.
6. Install pressure plate and torque to 17-18 ft. lbs. on L16 and L24, and 11-16 ft. lbs. on A12.
7. Remove dummy shaft.
8. Replace transmission.

CLUTCH LINKAGE

Adjustment

Refer to the Clutch Specifications Chart

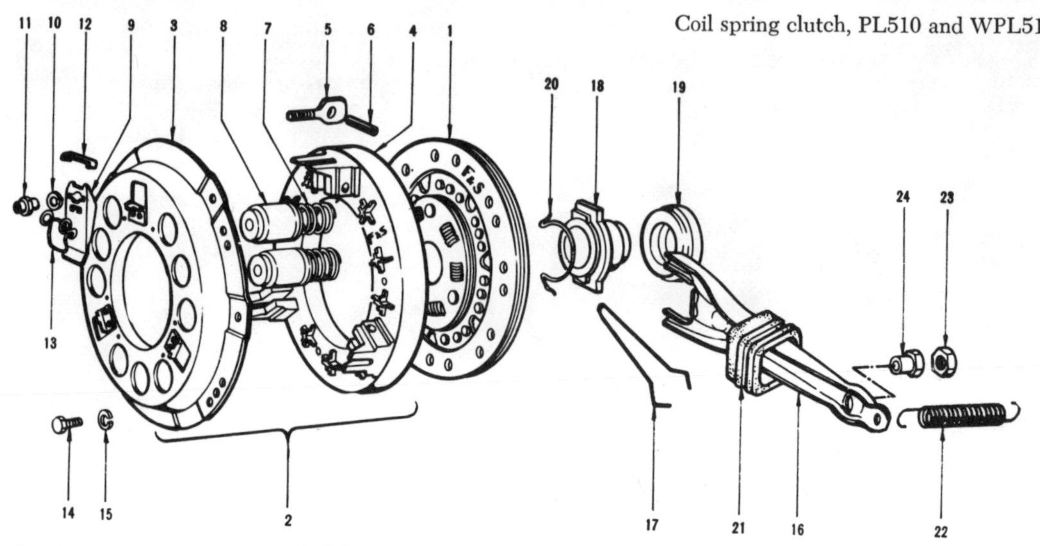

Coil spring clutch, PL510 and WPL510

1. Disc
2. Clutch assembly
3. Clutch cover
4. Pressure plate
5. Pressure plate bolt
6. Eye bolt pin
7. Spring
8. Spring retainer
9. Release lever
10. Release lever seat
11. Locknut
12. Release lever support
13. Retaining spring
14. Bolt
15. Lockwasher
16. Withdrawal lever
17. Retainer spring
18. Bearing sleeve
19. Release bearing
20. Bearing sleeve holder spring
21. Dust cover
22. Return spring
23. Locknut
24. Withdrawal lever push nut

Diaphragm spring clutch, PL510 and WPL510

1. Disc
2, 3. Clutch cover assembly with pressure plate
4. Bolt
5. Lockwasher
6. Withdrawal lever
7. Retainer spring 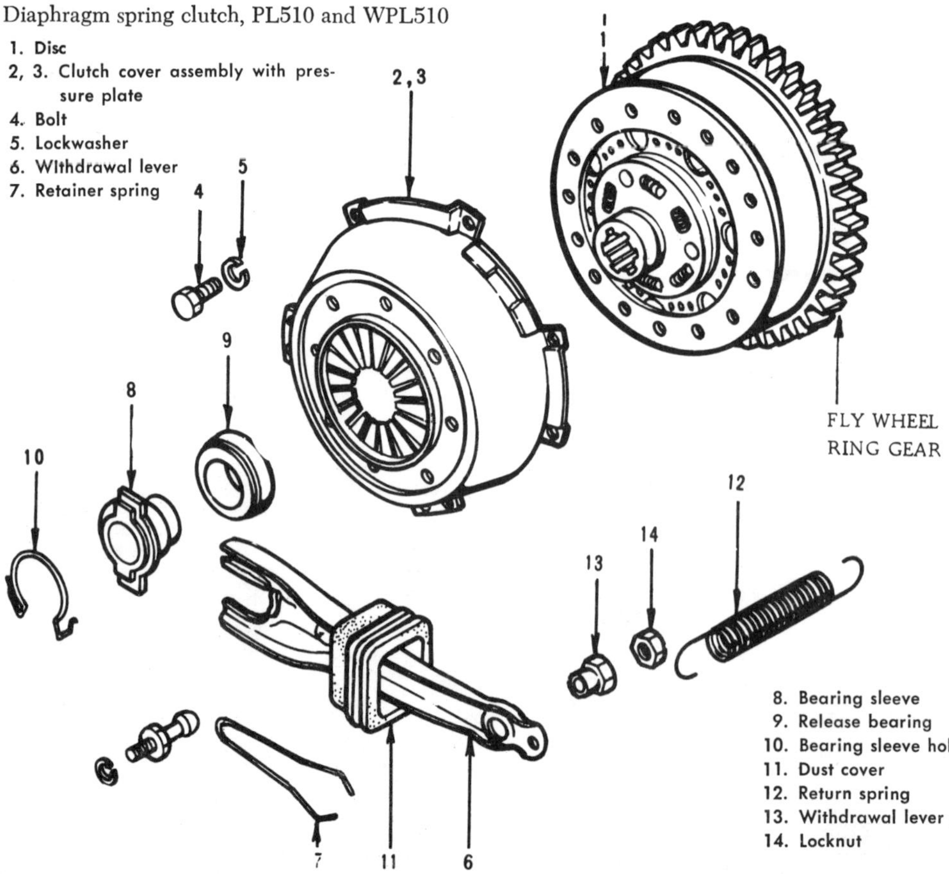
8. Bearing sleeve
9. Release bearing
10. Bearing sleeve holder spring
11. Dust cover
12. Return spring
13. Withdrawal lever push nut
14. Locknut

FLY WHEEL
RING GEAR

Clutch release mechanism, A12 and L24 engines. 1 is withdrawal lever, 2 is return spring, and 3 is release bearing.

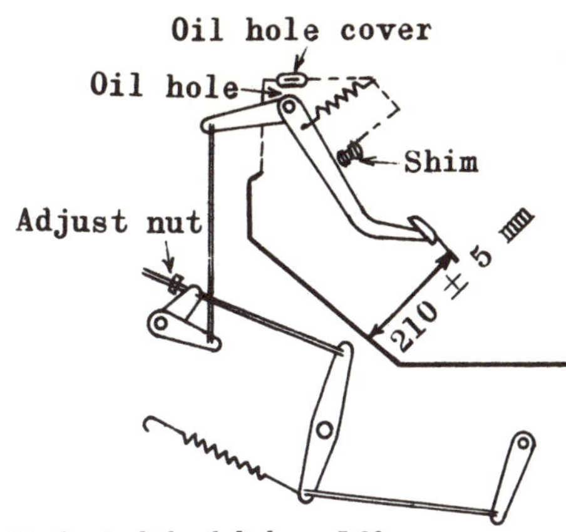

Mechanical clutch linkage, L60

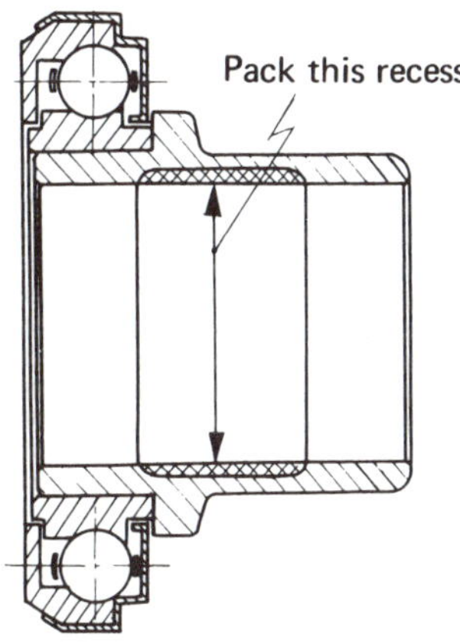

Apply multi-purpose grease where shown on throwout bearing for A12 and L24 engines.

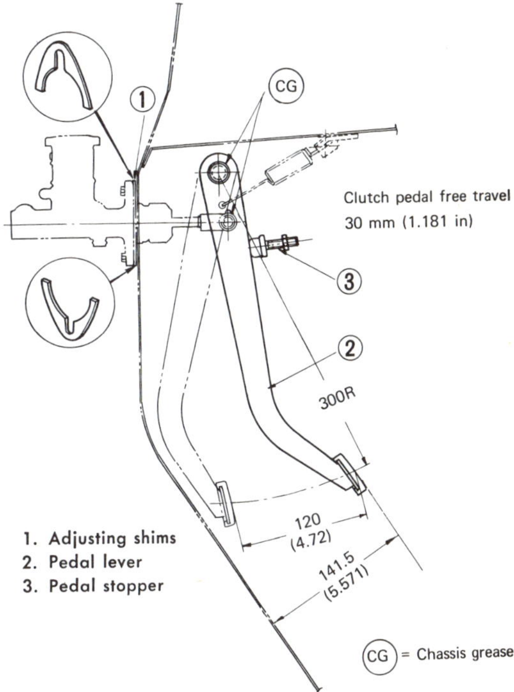

Clutch pedal height adjustment, LB110 and KLB110. A similar method of adjustment is used on all models without an adjustable master cylinder pushrod.

for clutch pedal height above floor and pedal free play.

Early L60

The early model has a mechanically actuated clutch. Adjust pedal height by changing shim thickness at the pedal stopper. Adjust free play by means of the adjusting nut on the intermediate clutch rod. Tighten the nut to decrease play and loosen to increase.

Models With Hydraulically Operated Clutch

All models except the early L60 have a hydraulically actuated clutch. On some early models, KLB110 and LB110, clutch pedal height is adjusted by placing shims between the master cylinder and the firewall. On some late models, as HLS30, PL-510, and WPL510, pedal height may be adjusted by varying the length of the master cylinder pushrod from the brake pedal. All models have an adjustable pedal stop which limits the upward travel of the pedal.

Clutch pedal free play is adjusted at the pushrod on the clutch operating cylinder. A few early models have no provision for this adjustment.

Clutch Hydraulic System Bleeding

Bleeding is required to remove air trapped in the hydraulic system. This oper-

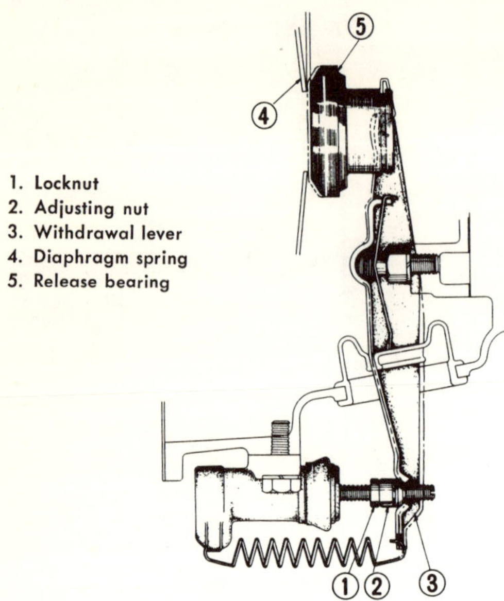

Detail of clutch operating cylinder and withdrawal lever, HLS30. Free play is adjusted at this point on most models with hydraulic clutch.

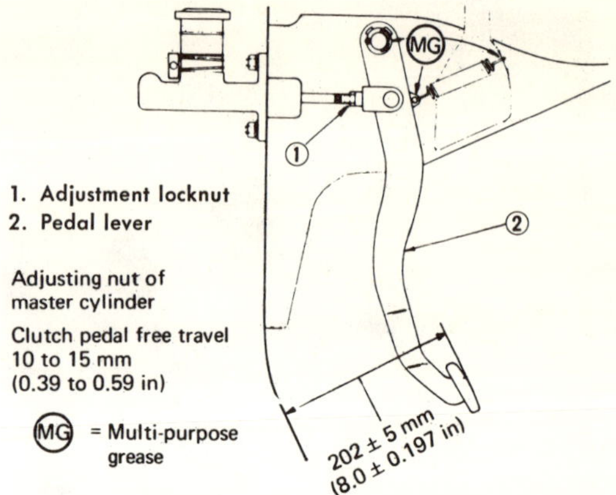

Clutch pedal height adjustment, HLS30. A similar method of adjustment is used on all models with an adjustable master cylinder pushrod.

ation is necessary whenever the system has been leaking or dismantled. The bleed screw is usually located on the clutch operating (slave) cylinder.

1. Remove bleed screw dust cap.
2. Open bleed screw about ¾ turn.
3. Attach a tube to the bleed screw, immersing the free end in a clean container of brake fluid.
4. Fill master cylinder with fluid.
5. Depress the clutch pedal quickly. Hold it down. Have an assistant tighten the bleed screw. Allow the pedal to return slowly.
6. Repeat steps 2 and 5 until no more air bubbles are seen in the fluid container.
7. Remove bleed tube. Replace dust cap. Refill master cylinder.

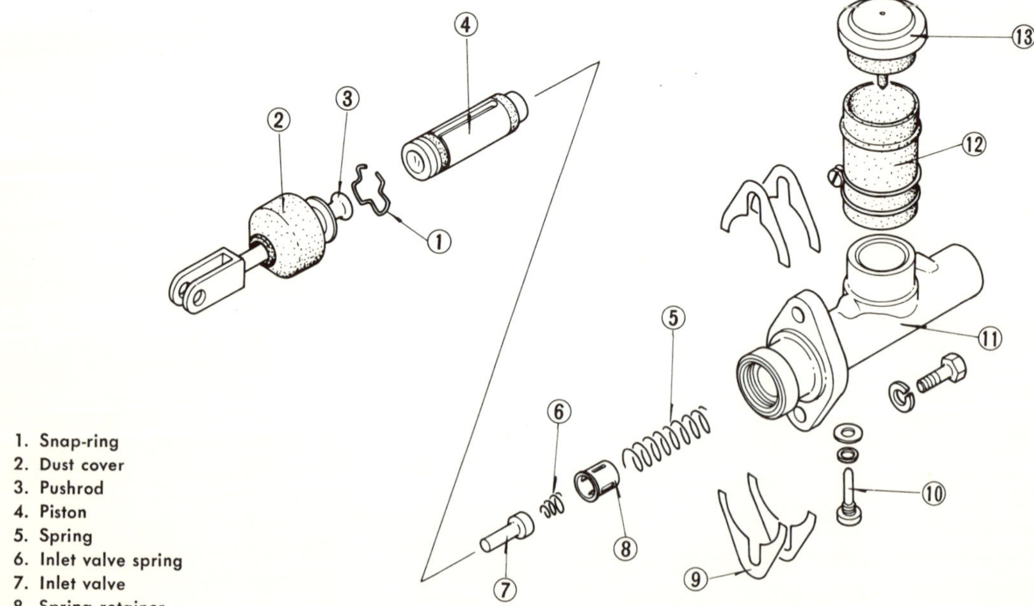

Clutch master cylinder, LB110 and KLB110

Clutch Hydraulic System Repairs

Clutch master and slave cylinders are repaired in much the same way as are brake master and wheel cylinders. Bleeding is required whenever the clutch hydraulic system has been dismantled.

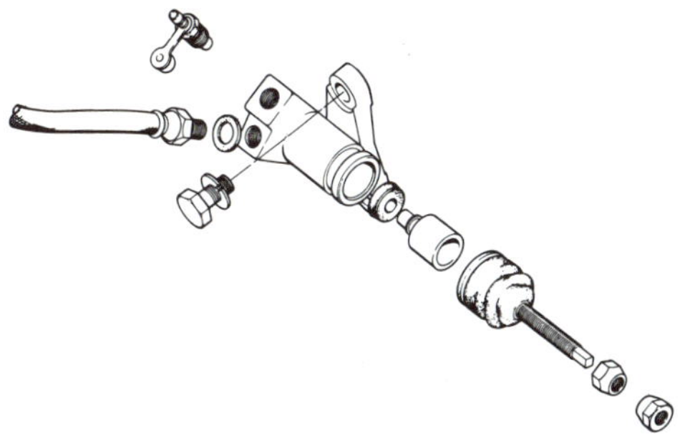

Clutch operating (slave) cylinder, LB110 and KLB110

Clutch Specifications

Vehicle model	*Clutch type*	*Spring tension, free length (lbs. @ in., in.)*	*Release lever or diaphragm distance from flywheel (in.)*	*Facing O.D. X I.D. X thickness (in.)*	*New disc thickness (in.)*	*No. disc springs*	*Minimum allowable depth of rivet head below facing (in.)*	*Maximum allowable disc runout (in.)*	*Pedal height above floor (in.)*	*Pedal free play (in.)*
L60	coil spring	180-190 @ 1.56, N.A.	2.5	10.8 X 6.9 X .14	.47	N.A.	.012	.020	8.1-8.5	1.0-1.5
Early L320	coil spring	132-176 @ 1.41, 1.95	2.26-2.32	7.25 X 5.00 X .14	.346	6	.012	.020	N.A.	.98-1.18
Late L320, PL410, PL411, RL411	coil spring	78-87 @ 1.15, 1.87-1.99	1.98-2.00	7.87 X 5.12 X .14	.338-.358	6	.012	.020	N.A.	1.0-1.5, 1.8-2.0 for PL411 & RL411

Clutch Specifications, continued

SPL310	coil spring	169-178 @ 1.56, 2.17	2.04-2.06	7.87 X 5.76 X .13	.333	6	.012	.020	6.10-6.60	.60-.80
SPL311, SRL311	diaphragm spring	—	N.A.	7.87 X 5.12 X .14	N.A.	N.A.	.012	.020	N.A.	1.9-2.1
PL510 WPL510	coil spring	92.6-101.4 @ 1.15, 2.06	1.97-2.01	7.87 X 5.12 X .14	.339-.354	6	.012	.020	8.15	.98
PL510, WPL510	diaphragm spring	—	1.69-1.77	7.87 X 5.12 X .14	.339-.354	6	.012	.020	8.15	.98
L520, L521, PL521	coil spring	161-179 @ 1.15, 1.87-1.99	1.98-2.01	7.87 X 5.12 X .14	.339-.354	9	.012	.020	5.34, 5.46 without pedal stop	.98
HLS30	diaphragm spring	—	1.69-1.77	8.86 X 5.90 X N.A.	.327-.350	6	.012	.020	8.00	.39-.59
LB110, KLB110	diaphragm spring	—	1.14-1.22	7.09 X 4.92 X N.A.	.299-.315	6	.012	.020	5.57	1.18

Driveshaft and U-Joints

Removal and Installation

L60

Both front and rear shafts are splined in the center and have a U-joint and flange at each end. There are grease fittings in both U-joints and in the splines. The U-joints also have a pressure relief to prevent over lubrication. To remove either driveshaft, simply unbolt the U-joint flanges at both ends and remove the shaft. The flange bolt torque is 43-51 ft. lbs.

L320, L520, L521, PL521, PL410, PL411, SPL310, SPL311, LB110, KLB110

These driveshafts are all one piece units with a U-joint and flange at the rear, and a U-joint and a splined sleeve yoke which fits into the rear of the transmission, at the front. Early models and trucks generally have U-joints with grease fittings. U-joints without grease fittings must be disassembled for lubrication, usually at 24,000 mile intervals. The splines are lubricated by transmission oil.

1. Be ready to catch oil coming from the rear of the transmission and to plug the extension housing.
2. Unbolt rear flange.
3. Pull driveshaft down and back.
4. Plug the transmission extension housing.
5. Reverse procedure to install, oiling the splines. Flange bolt torque is 15-20 ft. lbs.

PL510, WPL510

These driveshafts are the one piece type with a U-joint and flange at the rear, and a U-joint and a splined sleeve yoke which fits into the rear of the transmission, at the front. The U-joints must be disassembled for lubrication at 24,000 mile intervals. The splines are lubricated by transmission oil.

1. Release handbrake.
2. Loosen PL510 muffler and rotate out of the way.
3. On PL510, remove handbrake rear cable adjusting nut and disconnect left handbrake cable from adjuster.
4. Unbolt rear flange.
5. Pull driveshaft down and back.
6. Plug transmission extension housing.
7. Reverse procedure to install, oiling the splines. Flange bolt torque is 29-62 ft. lbs.

HLS30—Four Speed

This driveshaft is the same type used on the PL510 and WPL510. It is balanced as an assembly.

1. Check that there are spline/flange yoke match marks in two places. If not, mark with chalk.
2. Remove submuffler.
3. Unbolt rear flange.
4. Pull driveshaft down and back.
5. Plug the transmission extension housing.
6. Reverse procedure to install, aligning the match marks and oiling the splines. Flange bolt torque is 18 ft. lbs.

HLS30, SRL311—Five Speed

This driveshaft has a flange at either end and a splined coupling in the center.

1. Carry out Steps 1-3 for HLS30—Four Speed.
2. Unbolt front flange.
3. Remove driveshaft.
4. Reverse procedure to install, aligning match marks. Flange bolt torque is 18 ft. lbs.

U-Joint Overhaul

Disassembly

1. Mark relationship of all components for reassembly.
2. Remove snap-rings. On early units, the snap-rings are seated in the yokes. On later units, the snap-rings seat in the needle bearing races.
3. Tap the yoke with a soft hammer to

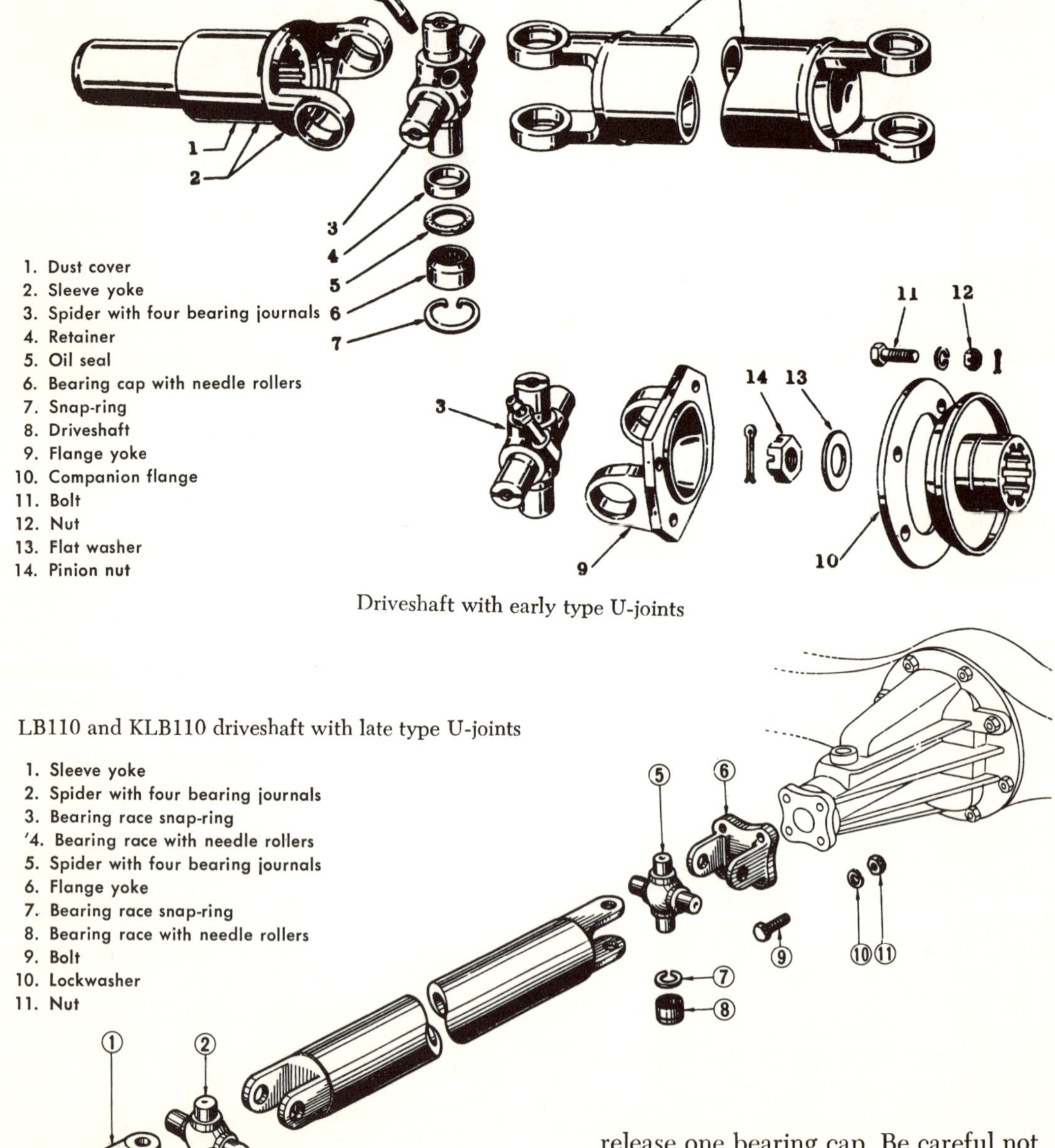

Driveshaft with early type U-joints

LB110 and KLB110 driveshaft with late type U-joints

release one bearing cap. Be careful not to lose the needle rollers.

4. Remove the other bearing caps. Remove the spiders from the yokes.

Inspection

1. Spline backlash should not exceed .0197″ (.5 mm.).
2. Driveshaft runout should not exceed .015″ (.4 mm.).
3. On late units with snap-rings seated in the needle bearing races, different thicknesses of snap-rings are available for U-joint adjustment. Play should not exceed .0008″ (.02 mm.).
4. U-joint spiders must be replaced if their bearing journals are worn more than .0059″ (.15 mm.) from their original diameter.

Assembly

1. Place the needle rollers in the races and hold them in place with grease.
2. Put the spider into place in its yokes.
3. Replace all seals.
4. Tap the races into position and secure with the snap-rings.

AXLE SHAFT

For axle shaft service, see Wheel Bearing, Seal, and Axle Shaft Service under Independent Rear Suspension—PL510, HLS30.

Final Drive Unit

Removal and Installation

All models have solid rear drive axles except the PL510 and HLS30, which have independent rear suspension with the differential carrier solidly mounted. The L60 has solid drive axles front and rear.

Nissan Patrol (L60) Front Axle

1. Drain gear oil. Raise vehicle to unload front springs.
2. Disconnect shock absorbers, drag link plug, drag link, stabilizer bar, center brake hose, vertical rebound stop rod, and steering damper.
3. Disconnect front driveshaft. Unbolt axle from springs.
4. Remove front spring shackles and roll axle assembly out.

To replace:

5. Roll axle assembly into place. Secure front spring shackles.
6. Bolt axle to springs with U-bolts and plates. Torque U-bolts to 50-60 ft. lbs.
7. Replace shock absorbers, stabilizer bar, and steering damper.
8. Replace vertical rebound stop rod. The end of the rod should protrude from the locknut .47″ (12 mm.). Operating stroke should be 3.34″ (85 mm.).
9. Replace driveshaft. Place drag link on steering arm ball and install plug and cotter pin. Connect brake hose.
10. Fill differential. Grease spindle housing and all fittings. Bleed brake system.

Nissan Patrol (L60) Rear Axle

1. Drain gear oil. Raise vehicle to unload rear springs.
2. Disconnect shock absorbers, stabilizer, and brake hose.
3. Disconnect driveshaft and spring U-bolts. Remove shackles from rear of springs.
4. Roll axle assembly out.

To replace:

5. Roll axle assembly into place. Secure spring shackles.
6. Bolt axle to springs with U-bolts and plates. Torque U-bolts to 50-60 ft. lbs.
7. Replace shock absorbers and stabilizer.
8. Replace driveshaft and brake hose. Fill differential.

Solid Rear Axle—L320, L520, L521, PL521, PL410, PL411, RL411, WPL510, LB110, KLB110, SPL310, SPL311, SRL311

1. Raise and support rear of vehicle. Remove wheels.
2. Remove screws and brake drums, backing off brake adjustment if necessary.
3. Disconnect and plug brake hose. Disconnect handbrake cable, driveshaft, and shock absorbers.
4. Support rear axle assembly with a floor jack.
5. Loosen spring U-bolts. Remove rear spring shackles.
6. Remove U-bolts. Lower and remove axle.
7. Reverse procedure to install.

HLS30, PL510

These vehicles have independent rear suspension with the final drive unit mounted solidly. Although the suspension arrangements differ, the final drive units are virtually identical.

HLS30

1. Chock the front wheels. Raise and support the rear of the vehicle.
2. Remove the main muffler.
3. Unbolt the driveshaft.
4. Loosen the transverse link spindle inner bolts (on the front of the front differential mounting crossmember) enough to free the crossmember.
5. Unbolt the axle shafts.
6. Support the differential unit with a jack.
7. Remove the two mounting nuts from the rear of the rear differential mounting crossmember.
8. Remove the four nuts from the bottom of the front crossmember.
9. Lower the front crossmember and final drive unit together.
10. Unbolt the front crossmember from the differential unit.
11. Reverse procedure to install. Tighten transverse link spindle inner bolts with vehicle lowered to the ground and with two 150 lb. passengers.

Fastener	*Torque*
Axle shaft bolts	36-43 ft. lbs.
Driveshaft bolts	18 ft. lbs.
Transverse link spindle inner bolts	101-116 ft. lbs.
Differential rear mounting nuts	54-69 ft. lbs.
Differential front mounting and crossmember bolts	23-31 ft. lbs.

PL510

1. Chock the front wheels. Raise and support the rear of the vehicle.
2. Disconnect handbrake rear cable, driveshaft, and axle shafts.
3. Support the differential unit with a jack.
4. Unbolt differential rear mounting crossmember from body.
5. Remove four bolts holding differential to rear suspension crossmember.
6. Remove differential to the rear.
7. Support rear suspension crossmember with stands to prevent damage to the insulators.
8. Unbolt differential rear mounting crossmember from differential.
9. Reverse procedure to install. Pry differential unit into position.

Fastener	*Torque*
Differential mounting crossmember to differential nuts	43-58 ft. lbs.
Differential mounting crossmember to body nuts	62 ft. lbs.
Differential to suspension crossmember nuts	43 ft. lbs.
Driveshaft bolts	29-62 ft. lbs.
Axle shaft bolts	51-58 ft. lbs.

Overhaul

Nissan Patrol (L60) Front Axle

Disassembly

1. Remove wheels.
2. Pry off hub cap. Remove snap-ring from axle shaft groove. Unbolt and pull off drive flange, being careful of shims.
3. Bend back lockwasher. Using a wheel bearing adjusting wrench, remove the locknut, lockwasher, and adjusting nut. Slide brake drum and hub with wheel bearings off the spindle.
4. Disconnect brake hose. Unbolt and remove backing plate. Slide spindle off axle shaft. Remove outer axle shaft and universal joint outer part from axle housing. Pull inner part of universal joint and inner axle shaft out.
5. Remove tie rod. Remove spindle housing upper cap, spring disc, and bearing cone. Remove lower cap. Remove eight capscrews from rear and remove spindle housing.
6. Remove differential cover and gasket. Remove bearing caps, marking their original locations for reassembly. Remove differential assembly, prying cautiously if necessary.
7. Mark differential case halves for reassembly. Remove four nuts and disassemble differential. Release lock plates and remove ring gear. Side bearings must be pulled off.
8. Unbolt and pull off pinion flange. Drive pinion shaft out with a brass drift. Remove pinion shaft shims and spacer, noting shim thickness.

Inspection and Repair

1. Clean all parts in a safe solvent. Oil the bearings immediately.
2. Check inside diameter of bushing

inside end of axle housing. If it is more than 1.350″ (35.3 mm.), the bushing must be replaced. A new bushing should be reamed to fit after being pressed in. Be sure that holes in bushing and case are aligned. Replace all axle housing oil seals.

3. When pulling out and replacing the inner and outer pinion bearing cups, be sure that the original shims behind the inner cup are replaced. If new parts are to be used, see Step 2 under Assembly. The new cups should be tapped in carefully with a brass drift.
4. The ring and pinion gears must be replaced only as a set.

Assembly

1. Press inner bearing onto pinion shaft. It must seat against the gear shoulder.
2. If original ring and pinion gears are to be replaced in the original carrier, use the original shims at each bearing. If new parts are used, place the pinion in the housing. Check the setting from the back face of the pinion to the differential case bearing centerline. The standard setting is 2.7706″ (70.36 mm.). There is a mark on the pinion head to indicate the shim thickness needed under the inner bearing cup (deviation from standard setting). The mark is read in thousandths of an inch. Add the indicated shim thickness to the standard setting to find the setting distance. Add .002″ for bearing preload.

	Example A	*Example B*
Standard setting	2.7706″	2.7706″
Pinion marking	(+) 2	(−) 2
Add for preload	.002″	.002″
Final setting	2.7746″	2.7706″

3. Replace spacer, original shims, and outer bearing on pinion shaft.
4. Install the pinion flange without the oil seal and torque the nut to 180-215 ft. lbs. The torque required to rotate the pinion shaft should be 9-12 in. lbs., provided that the bearing preload is correct.
5. Remove flange and install a new well-soaked oil seal. Replace flange, retorque nut, and install cotter pin. Recheck pinion setting distance as in Step 2.
6. Assemble side gear and thrust washer to ring gear half of differential case. Lubricate gears and thrust washers. Place spider with gears and thrust washers in case. Install the other thrust washer and side gear. Replace the other case half, aligning the marks made on disassembly. Replace the case bolts, torquing to 50-65 ft. lbs. Side gear backlash should be .003-.010″, and can be adjusted by replacing the thrust washers or gears. Lock the nuts with cotter pins. Position the ring gear on the case. Install the lock plates and torque the bolts to 32-42 ft. lbs. Bend up the lock plates.
7. Press the roller bearings on the differential case without shims. Place the bearing cups on the bearings. Tilt the cups to start the differential assembly into the housing, tapping lightly with a soft hammer until the bearings seat firmly. To determine the thickness of the bearing shims needed, slide the differential assembly from side to side.

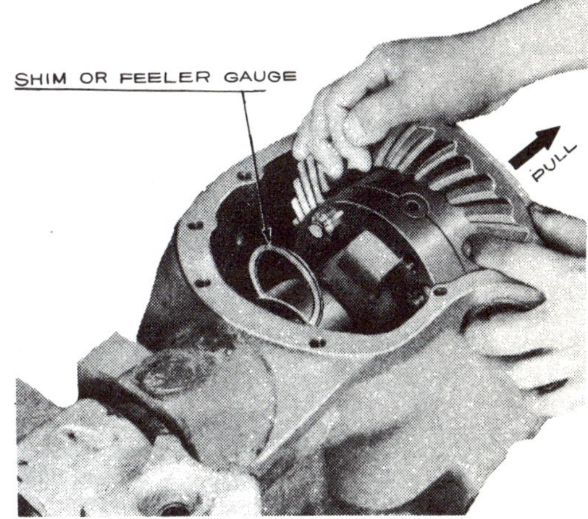

Checking differential side bearing shim thickness needed

Check the clearance between the bearing cup and differential housing with feeler gauges. Add .002″ to the left bearing measurement and .001″ to the right. This gives the proper shim thickness for each side. Now remove the differential assembly, pull off the side bearings, and install the shims. Press the bearings back on and install the differential assembly as above. Replace the bearing caps, aligning the marks made on disassembly. Torque the cap bolts to 62-72 ft. lbs. and lockwire.

8. Mount a dial indicator on the housing with the indicator against a ring gear tooth. Hold the pinion shaft stationary and move the ring gear back and forth to measure backlash. Correct backlash is .005-.007″. To correct backlash, remove differential assembly and move a thickness of shims equal to the backlash error from one side to the other. If backlash is too little, the ring gear must be moved away from the pinion. If it is excessive, the gears must be brought closer together.
9. Check ring gear runout with a dial indicator. If runout exceeds .0025″, remove differential assembly and check bearing seating surfaces for foreign matter. Check the bearings carefully.
10. Check tooth contact pattern with red lead.
11. Replace differential gasket and cover.
12. Grease spindle housing lower cap roller bearing. Install a new O-ring. The number of shims to be used with the lower cap depends upon the bearing width.

Bearing Width	*Number of .005″ (.127 mm.) Shims*	*Number of .003″ (.075 mm.) Shims*
.630-.634″ (16.0-16.1 mm.)	0	0
.634-.638″ (16.1-16.2 mm.)	0	1
.638-.643″ (16.2-16.3 mm.)	1	1
.643-.646″ (16.3-16.4 mm.)	1	2
.646-.650″ (16.4-16.5 mm.)	2	2

Install lower cap assembly, torquing nuts to 15 ft. lbs.

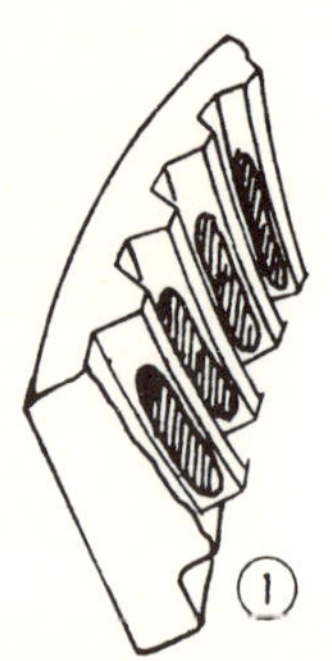

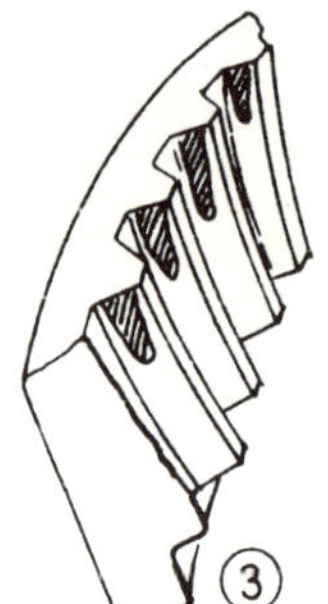

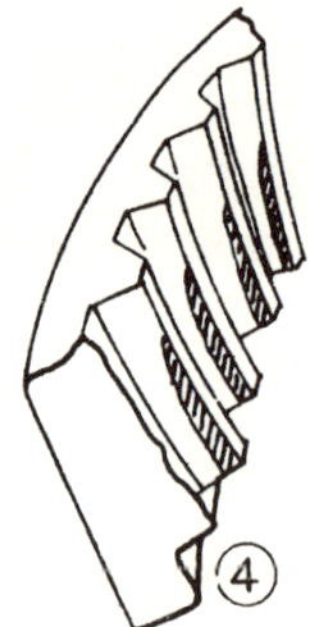

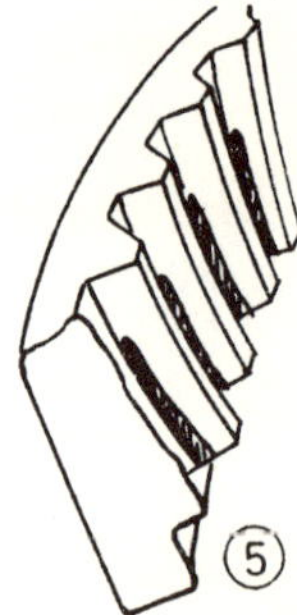

Ring gear tooth contact patterns obtained with red lead

1. Correct tooth contact
2. Short toe contact; move ring gear away from pinion.
3. Short heel contact; move ring gear toward pinion.
4. Contact too high and narrow; pinion should be moved toward center of axle.
5. Contact too low and narrow; pinion should be moved away from center of axle.

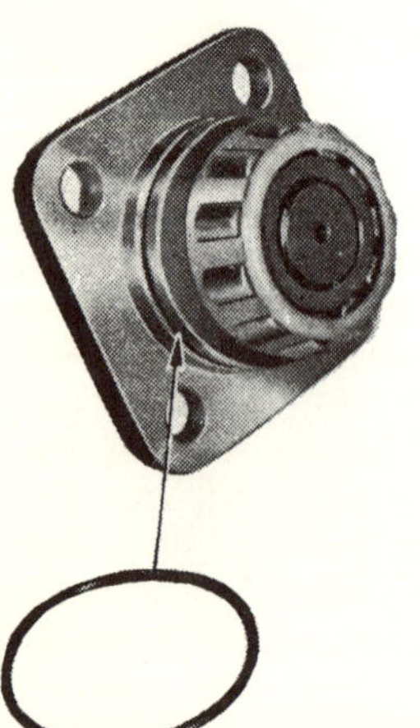

Front drive spindle housing lower cap assembly

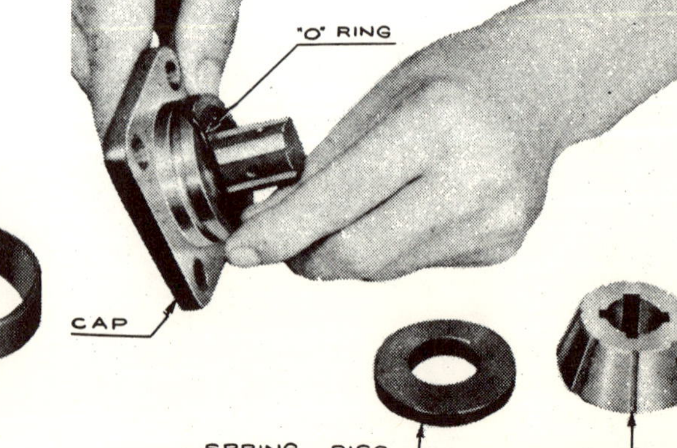

Front drive spindle housing upper cap assembly

13. Place new O-ring, spring disc, and bearing cone on upper cap, aligning grease holes. Insert upper cap assembly to spindle housing without shims. Tighten the four nuts equally until the bearing cone does not turn when the spindle housing is turned back and forth. Check the clearance between the upper cap and spindle housing with feeler gauges. Add .016″ to this measurement. This total is the thickness of shims required under the upper cap. Install the shims and torque the cap nuts to 15 ft. lbs. The force required to turn the spindle housing at the steering knuckle arm should be 20-22 lbs. Adjust by adding or removing shims.

Checking clearance between upper cap and spindle housing

14. Place oil seal on spindle housing flange. Start oil seal retainer bolts. Install oil seal and spring, connecting ends. Bolt down seal retainer.
15. Grease shaft and joint bearing surfaces. Slide in inner axle shaft and inner part of universal joint, aligning axle shaft and differential splines. Slide outer part of universal joint on outer axle shaft. Align universal joint slots and slide outer axle shaft into place.
16. Grease spindle bearing and secure in spindle with lockring. Place spindle on housing. Put backing plate and grease deflector plate on spindle with oil drain hole aligned toward bottom. Bolt in place.
17. Install spindle collar, greasing oil seal contact surface lightly. Pack wheel bearings. Place inner wheel bearing and oil seal in hub. Assemble hub and brake drum to spindle. Replace outer wheel bearing, thrust washer, and bearing adjusting nut. Tighten adjusting nut until the drum binds when turned, then back off ⅛ turn. Install lockwasher and locknut, bending up lockwasher. Hub turning torque should be 1-3 ft. lbs.
18. Place a straightedge across the spindle and measure between hub and straightedge with feeler gauges to determine the shim thickness required under the drive flange. Replace inner snap-ring, shims, drive flange, lock plates, and nuts. Torque nuts to 25-28 ft. lbs. and bend up lock plates. Replace outer snap-ring on axle shaft groove. Replace hub cap.
19. Reassemble other side in the same way.
20. Install tie rod.

Nissan Patrol (L60) Rear Axle

Disassembly

1. Unbolt and remove wheels.
2. Remove brake drum retaining screws. Remove brake drum.
3. Unbolt and remove brake backing plate with axle shaft from axle housing.
4. Remove lock plate and bearing locknut. Remove wheel bearing, spacer, backing plate, and bearing cage from axle shaft.
5. Press out four serrated bolts and remove bearing cage from backing plate. Pull outer bearing race and oil seal from bearing cage. Pull inner oil seal from axle housing.
6. The differential is the same as that used in the front axle. Service procedures are the same.
7. Replace all oil seals.

Assembly

1. Press the new oil seal and bearing cup into the bearing cage.
2. Place the bearing cage and brake disc in a press and press the four serrated bolts through both.
3. Put the axle shaft through the backing plate. Put the bearing spacer over the axle shaft into the bearing cage. Put the wheel bearing over the axle shaft and drive the bearing into the bearing cage. Install the lock plate and bearing locknut. Torque the nut to 157 ft. lbs. and bend the lock plate.

4. Place shims .059″ (1.405 mm.) thick between the bearing cage of one rear axle shaft assembly and the axle housing. Fasten the assembly to the housing, torquing the nuts to 21-28 ft. lbs.
5. Install the other axle shaft assembly without any shims and tighten the nuts temporarily. Measure the clearance between the axle housing and the bearing cage with feeler gauges. Subtract .00394″ (.1 mm.) from the measured clearance. The resulting figure is the thickness of shims required at that side. Remove the axle shaft assembly and replace with the shims. Torque the bolts to 21-28 ft. lbs.
6. Measure the end-play of the axle shaft with a dial indicator. It should be .002-.006″ (.05-.15 mm.) If not, install or remove shims to correct. The thickness of the shims on each side must not differ by more than .04″ (1 mm.) from the thickness on the other end of the axle housing. If it does, take some shims from the side with the greater thickness and add them to the other side.

Solid Rear Axle—L320, L520, L521, PL521, PL410, PL411, RL411, WPL510, LB110, KLB110, SPL310, SPL311, SRL311

Disassembly

1. Disconnect brake lines at wheel cylinders.
2. Remove handbrake linkage.
3. Drain oil.
4. Unbolt backing plate from axle housing. Pull axle shaft and backing plate out together with a slide hammer.
5. From the rear of the backing plate, press off the bearing collar or cut if off with a cold chisel. The collar should not be reused. Pull out the bearing. *NOTE: some units use a locknut instead of a bearing collar.*
6. Unbolt and pull out the differential carrier from the axle housing.

Differential Disassembly

1. Remove the side bearing caps, marking their locations for reassembly. Remove the differential assembly from the carrier.

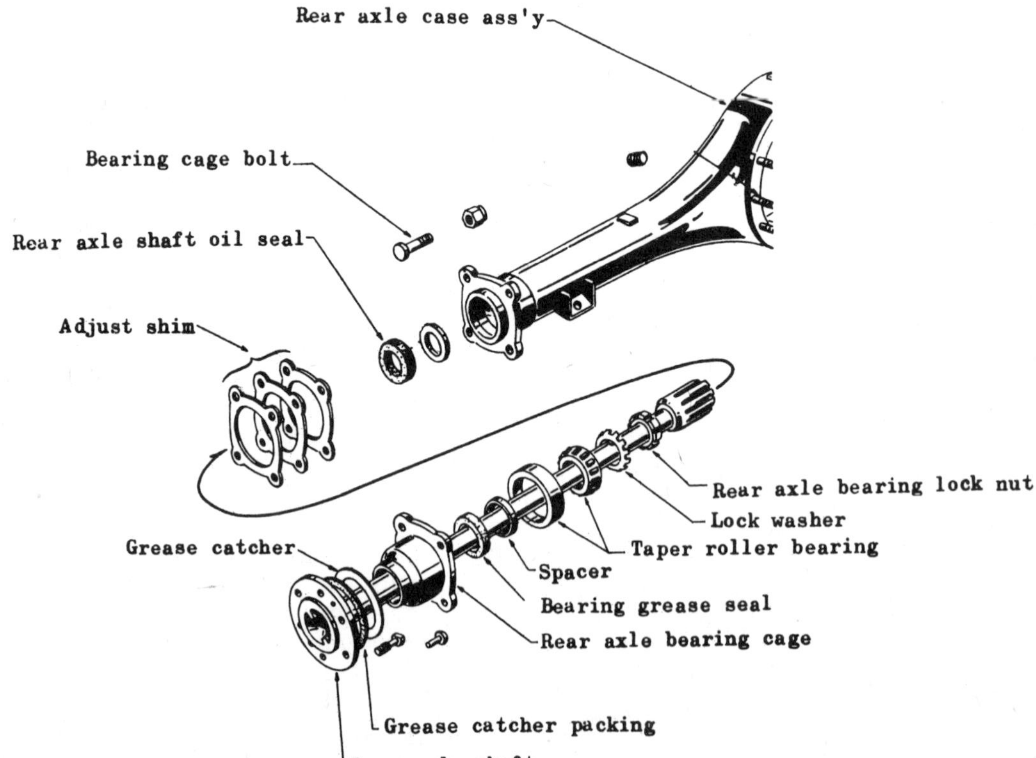

Detail of L320 axle shafts

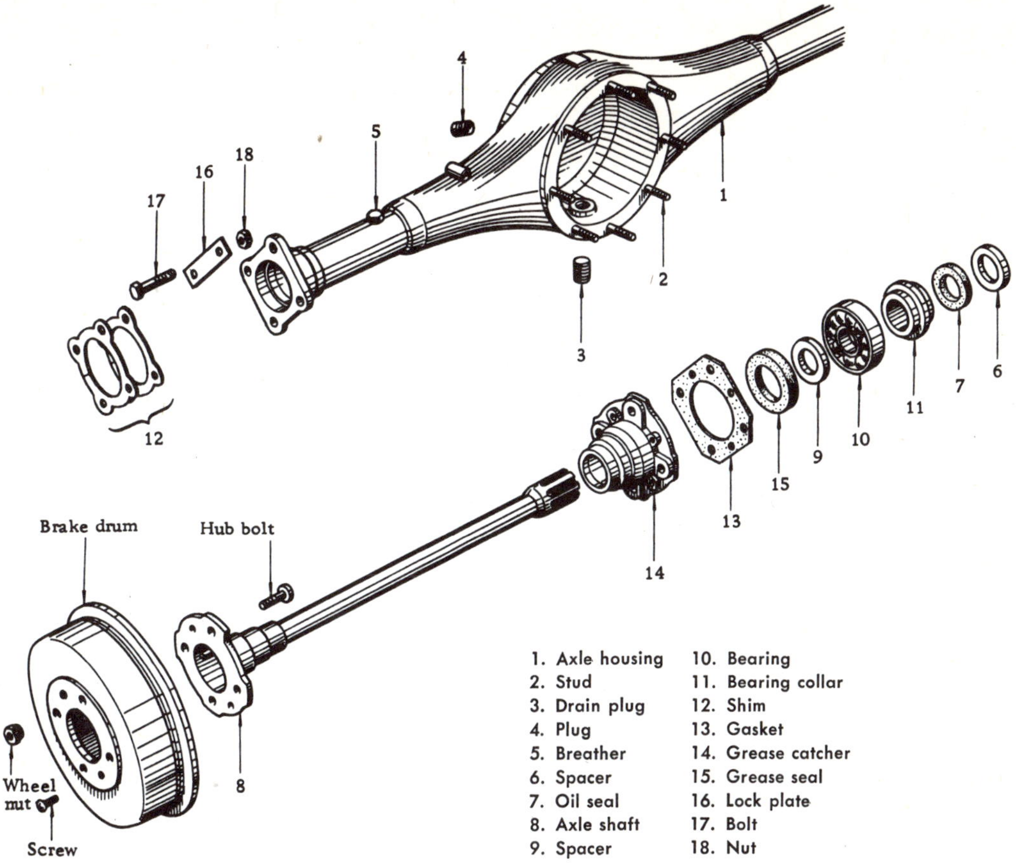

1. Axle housing	10. Bearing
2. Stud	11. Bearing collar
3. Drain plug	12. Shim
4. Plug	13. Gasket
5. Breather	14. Grease catcher
6. Spacer	15. Grease seal
7. Oil seal	16. Lock plate
8. Axle shaft	17. Bolt
9. Spacer	18. Nut

Detail of SPL311 axle shafts

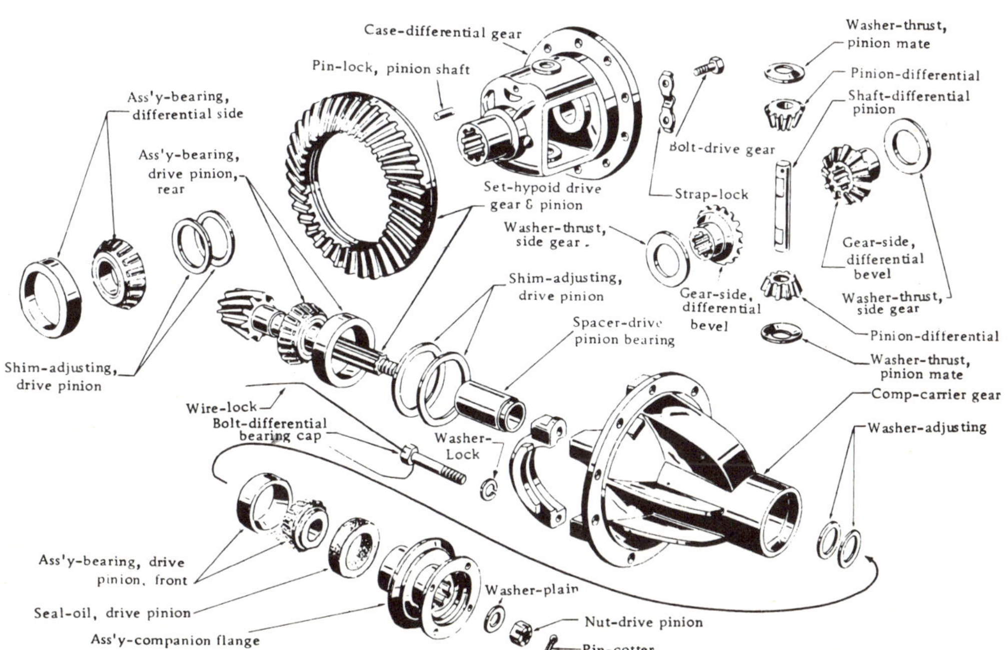

Differential details, WPL510

2. Pull off the side bearings. Do not mix left and right side parts.
3. Flatten the lock tabs and unbolt the ring gear, loosening the bolts diagonally.
4. Drive out pinion shaft lock pin from left to right. Remove pinion shaft and pinions, side gears, and thrust washers. Separate all these parts by original location.
5. Remove drive pinion nut and pull off flange. Tap drive pinion back with a soft hammer and remove with rear bearing inner race, bearing spacer, and adjusting washer.
6. Remove and discard oil seal. Remove front bearing inner race.
7. Pull out front and rear bearing outer races.

Differential Inspection

1. Wash all parts in a safe solvent. Oil bearings immediately.
2. Ring and pinion gears must be replaced only in pairs. If the ring gear is warped more than .002″, replace.
3. Check all parts for wear or distortion. Replace any suspected bearings.

Differential Assembly

1. Assemble pinions, side gears, pinion shaft, and thrust washers in case. Clearance between side gears and thrust washers should be .0020-.0079″. Thrust washers are available in various thicknesses for adjustment.
2. Drive in and peen over the lock pin.
3. Bolt on the ring gear using new lock tabs. Tighten the bolts diagonally. Specified bolt torques are:

Model	*Torque*
L320, L520, WPL510	35-40 ft. lbs.
LB110, KLB110	43-51 ft. lbs.
PL410, PL411, SPL310, SPL311	25-30 ft. lbs.

4. Press the side bearing inner races onto the differential case without shims.
5. The drive pinion height is adjusted with shims behind the rear bearing race. Dealers have special tools for making this measurement. Specified standard pinion heights are:

Model	*Standard Pinion Height*
PL410, PL411, SPL310, SPL311	2.0094″ (51 mm.)
L320, L520, WPL510	2.4034″ (61 mm.)
LB110, KLB110	1.772″ (45 mm.)

Standard pinion height is measured from the axle centerline to the pinion face. The deviation of the drive pinion from standard size is marked on the pinion face with + for larger and − for smaller. All units except the LB110 and KLB110 are marked in thousandths of an inch. The LB110 and KLB110 pinion is marked in hundredths of a millimeter. If no standard pinion height is specified, the adjustment must be made by use of special tools or by comparing the marks on the old and new drive pinion and adjusting the original shim pack to suit.

Pinion face markings, LB110 and KLB110

6. Press in the drive pinion rear bearing outer race and shims. Press in the front bearing outer race. Press the rear bearing inner race onto the drive pinion.
7. Install the drive pinion into the differential carrier without the bearing washer, spacer, and oil seal. The front bearing inner race and the flange should be installed. Tighten the flange nut until the torque required to turn the shaft (bearing preload) is:

Model	*New Bearing*	*Used Bearing*
LB110, KLB110	5.2-6.9 in. lbs.	2.6-3.5 in. lbs.
WPL510	8.7-11.3 in. lbs.	3.5-4.3 in. lbs.
L320, L520, PL410, PL411, SPL310, SPL311	6.1-8.7 in. lbs.	2.4-3.5 in. lbs.

8. Check the drive pinion height again.
9. Remove drive pinion and replace with bearing spacer. Torque flange nut to specified torque.

Model	*Torque*
WPL510	101-130 ft. lbs.
LB110, KLB110	87-123 ft. lbs.
L320, L520, PL410, PL411, SPL310, SPL311	100-120 ft. lbs.

10. Check that pinion bearing preload is as in Step 7. If it is excessive, a new spacer must be installed.

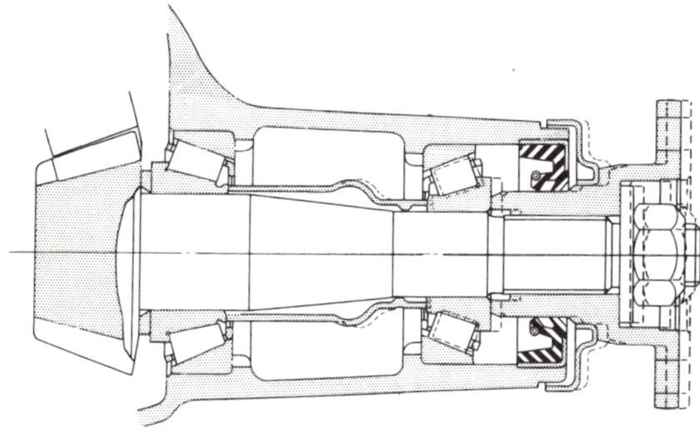

Detail of drive pinion bearing spacer, LB110 and KLB110

11. Remove nut and flange. Press in new oil seal. Pack grease between seal lips. Replace flange and nut, torquing as in Step 9. If cotter pin does not align, file the washer. Do not overtorque.
12. Install differential assembly into carrier, tapping with a soft hammer if necessary. Install side bearing caps in their original locations and torque bolts. Bearing cap bolt torque is 36-43 ft. lbs. for the LB110 and KLB110 and 30-35 ft. lbs. for all others.
13. Side bearing shims are selected by these formulae, for all models except LB110 and KLB110:
    Left side shim thickness=A−C+D+E+.007″
    Right side shim thickness=B−D+F+.006″

Figure	*Location*
A	left bearing housing of gear carrier
B	right bearing housing
C, D	differential case
E	difference from standard size (.7874″) of left bearing
F	difference from standard size of right bearing

All figures are read in thousandths of an inch. If old bearings are being reused, the required shim thickness on each side should be reduced by .001-.003″ to prevent excessive bearing preload.

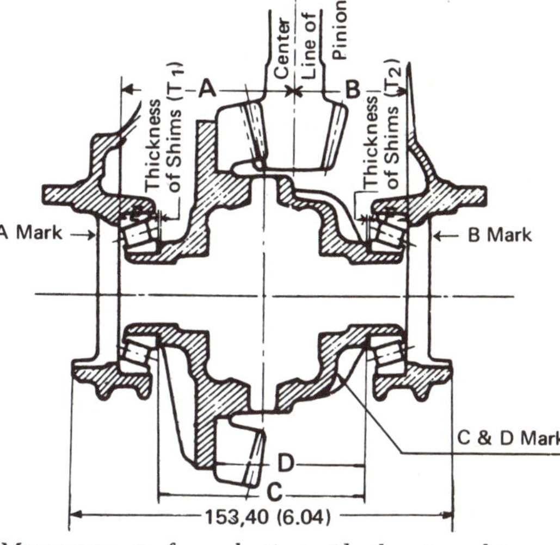

Measurements for selecting side bearing shims, LB110 and KLB110

14. LB110 and KLB110 side bearing shims are selected by these formulae:
    Left side shim thickness=A−C+D+E+.2 mm.
    Right side shim thickness=B−D+F+.2 mm.
    Figures A, B, C, and D are as in Step 13 but are read in hundredths of a millimeter. Figures E and F are the differences of the left and right bearings from standard size (17.5 mm), read in hundredths of a millimeter.
15. Ring and pinion gear backlash should be .0059-.0079″, measured with a dial indicator. If it is excessive, remove some right side shims and place them

on the left. If it is too small, change shims from left to right.

16. Make a tooth contact pattern check with red lead. Adjust the drive pinion height and side bearing shims as required.

Assembly

1. Use a new gasket between the axle housing and differential carrier. Torque the bolts to 14-18 ft. lbs. in a diagonal pattern.
2. Install the grease catcher, bearing spacer, bearing packed with grease, and new bearing collar onto the axle shaft. The seal side of the wheel bearing must face the wheel. Coat the oil seal lips with grease. Press on the bearing collar.
3. Adjust the axle end-play by use of shims between the backing plate and axle housing. Specified end-play is .012-.020″ for the WPL510, and .004″ for the LB110 and KLB110. For the L320 and L520, the first axle shaft to be installed should have an end-play of .033-.043″, and the second .004″.

Shims for adjusting axle shaft end-play

4. Specified bolt torque for the brake backing plate is 20-28 ft. lbs. for the WPL510 and 11-15 ft. lbs. for all other models.
5. Refill with oil. See Capacities and Pressures Chart.

PL510, HLS30

Disassembly

1. Drain oil and remove rear cover.
2. Clamp housing down securely.
3. Check tooth contact pattern with red lead.
4. Check backlash between ring and pinion with a dial indicator. It should be .0039-.0079″.
5. If tooth contact pattern or gear backlash is incorrect, check that runout at the rear of the ring gear does not exceed .0031″.
6. Remove side flange bolts and pull off side flanges with a slide hammer.
7. Unbolt and pull off side retainers. Note original locations of retainers and shims.
8. Remove differential assembly from carrier.
9. Remove bearing outer races from side retainers with an oil seal puller.
10. Hold the drive pinion flange and loosen the nut. Tighten the nut to 123-145 ft. lbs. and check the torque required to turn the drive pinion. It should be 2.6-13 in. lbs. Remove the nut and pull off the flange.
11. Press the drive pinion from the gear carrier with the front and rear bearing inner races, bearing spacers, and adjusting washers. Press out the front pilot bearing.
12. Press the drive pinion from the rear bearing.

NOTE: If the tooth contact pattern and backlash was correct in Steps 3 and 4 and the original ring gear, carrier, drive pinion, rear bearing, and washers are to be reused, it is not necessary to remove the rear bearing.

13. Press the front and rear bearing outer races from the carrier.
14. Pull off the right differential side gear. Spread the lock straps, loosen and remove the ring gear bolts in a diagonal pattern. Remove the ring gear and pull off the left differential side gear. Do not mix right and left side parts.
15. Punch out the pinion shaft lock pin from the ring gear side. Remove the shaft, differential gears, and thrust washers. Note the original location of all parts.
16. To replace the front oil seal, pull off the seal retainer and pull out the seal.

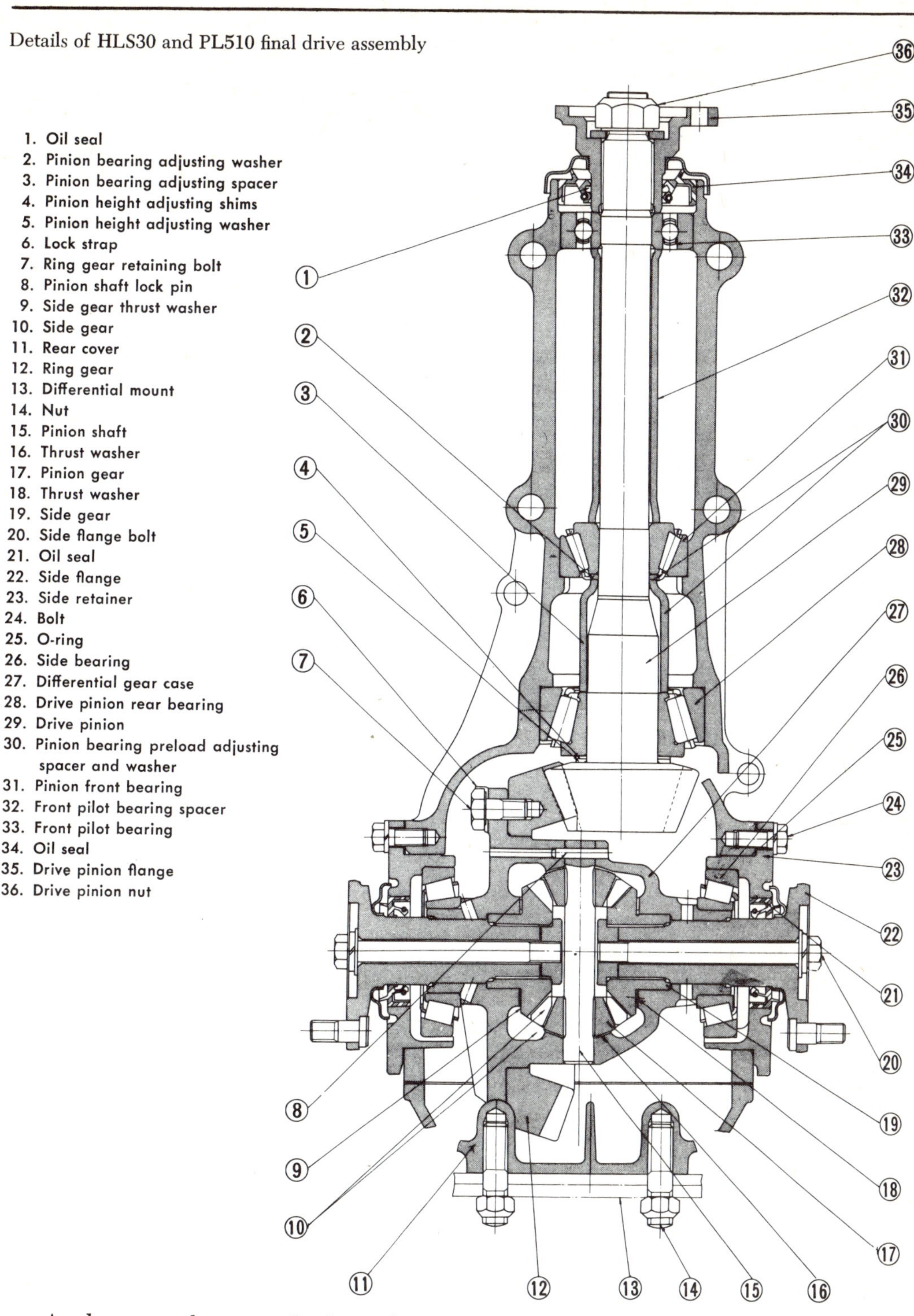

Details of HLS30 and PL510 final drive assembly

Apply grease between the lips of the new oil seal and drive into place. Replace the retainer.

NOTE: The front oil seal can be replaced with the differential mounted on the vehicle, after the driveshaft and flange are removed.

17. To replace the side oil seals, pull out the seal and drive in the new one, applying grease between the seal lips.

NOTE: The side oil seals can be replaced with the differential mounted on the vehicle, after the axle shafts, flanges, and retainers are removed.

Assembly

1. Wash all parts in a safe solvent and oil bearings immediately.
2. Install side and pinion gears into differential case. Replace pinion shaft. Check clearance between side gears and thrust washers. It should be .0039-.0079″ (.1-2 mm). Various thicknesses of thrust washers are available for adjustment.
3. Drive in pinion shaft lock pin. Stake the end of the pin with a punch.
4. Install the ring gear to the differential assembly. Use new lock straps under the bolts. Torque the bolts to 51-58 ft. lbs. in a diagonal pattern, tapping the bolt heads lightly before final torquing.
5. Before pressing on new differential side bearings, check bearing width. Standard width is .787″ (20 mm.).
6. Press front and rear drive pinion bearing outer races into gear carrier.
7. Drive pinion bearing preload turning torque should be 97.2-138.9 in. oz. for new bearings and 41.7-83.3 in. oz. for old bearings, with the pinion flange nut torqued to 123-145 ft. lbs. and without the oil seal. This is normally checked and adjusted with special tools.
8. Normal drive pinion height is 1.909″ (48.5 mm.) from the axle centerline to the pinion face. Special tools are required to make this adjustment. The height is adjusted by a washer and shims between the rear bearing and the drive pinion gear. The deviation of the drive pinion from standard size, in hundredths of a millimeter, is marked on the pinion face with + for larger and — for smaller. If the drive pinion is replaced, compare the old and new marks and adjust the shim pack to suit.

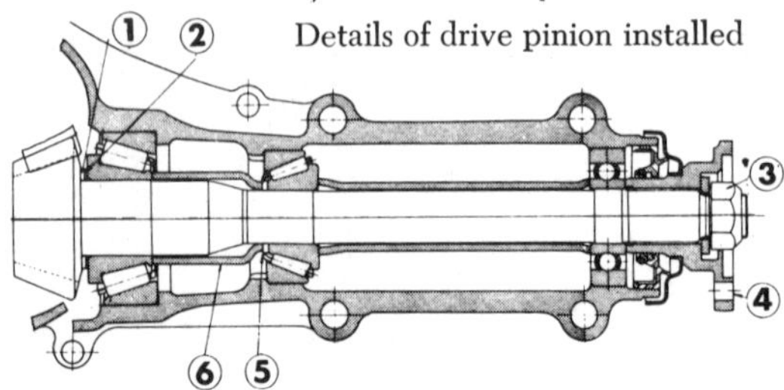

Details of drive pinion installed

1. Pinion bearing adjusting washer
2. Pinion height adjusting shims
3. Pinion nut
4. Pinion flange
5. Pinion bearing adjusting washer
6. Pinion bearing adjusting spacer

9. Install the drive pinion, front pilot bearing, and oil seal. Replace the flange and torque the bolt to 123-145 ft. lbs.
10. Side bearing shims are selected by these formulae:
    Left side shim thickness = A+C+G—D—E+H+.76 mm.
    Right side shim thickness = B+D+G—F—H+.76 mm.

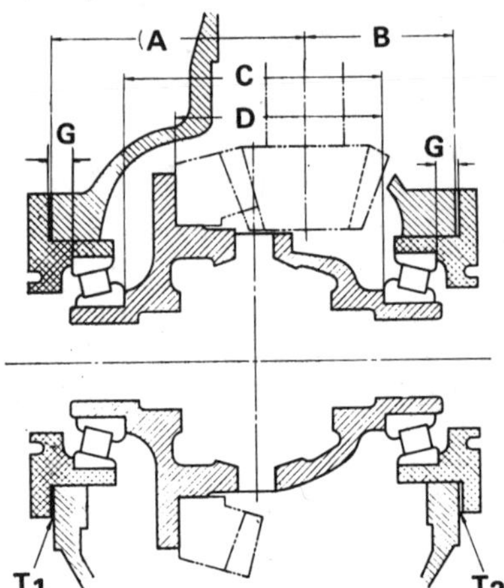

Measurements used in selecting side bearing shims

Figure	*Location*
A,B	on gear carrier
C,D	on differential case
F	difference from standard size (20 mm.) of bearing
G	on side retainers
H	on ring gear

All the figures are read in hundredths of a millimeter. If old side bearings are reused, the required shim thickness on each side should be increased by .001-.003″ (.03-.07 mm.).

11. Install shims selected in Step 10 and O-rings in side retainers. Install retainers. Bolt torque should be 6.5-8.7 ft. lbs.
12. Check ring and pinion gear backlash. It should be .0039-.0079″. If less, move side retainer shims from right to left. If more, move shims from left to right.
13. Check tooth contact pattern with red lead.
14. Replace rear cover and torque bolts to 54-69 ft. lbs. Replace side flanges and torque bolts to 14-19 ft. lbs.
15. Refill differential. See Capacities and Pressures Chart.

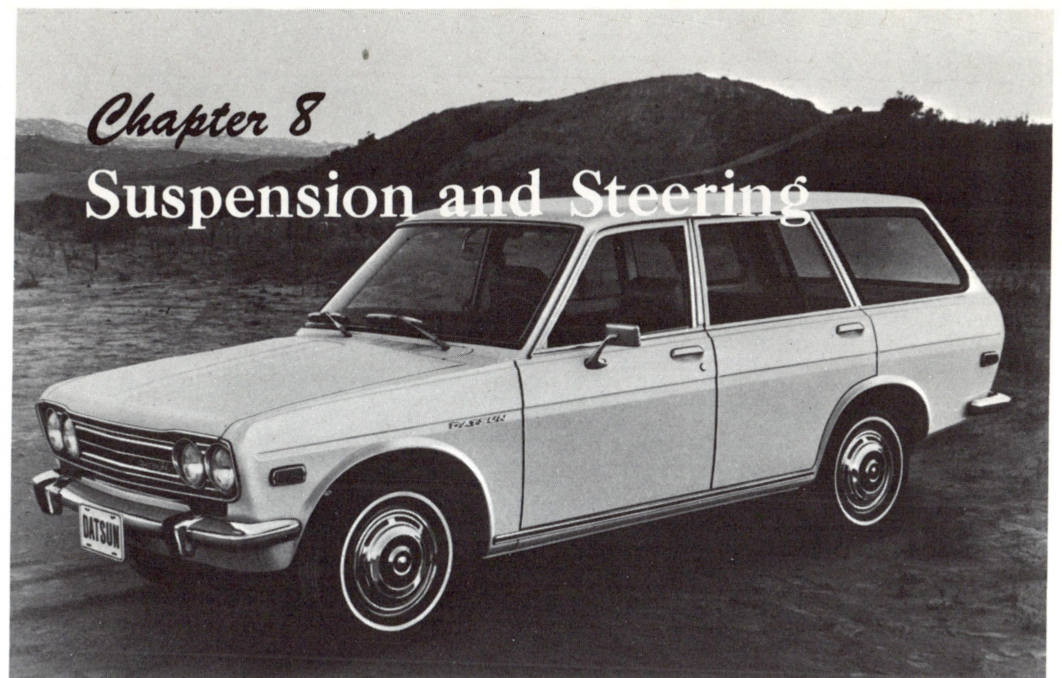

Chapter 8
Suspension and Steering

The L60, Nissan Patrol, is suspended by leaf springs front and rear. The L320, L520, L521, and PL521 pickups have torsion bars in the front and leaf springs in the rear. The PL410, PL411, and RL411 sedans, as well as the SPL310, SPL311, and SRL311 sportscars have front coil and rear leaf springs. The LB110 sedan, KLB110 coupe, and the WPL510 wagon have strut type front suspension with integral coil springs and shock absorbers, and leaf springs in the rear. The PL510 sedan uses struts in the front and coil springs in the rear. The HLS30, 240 Z coupe, has strut type suspension both front and rear. The PL510 and HLS30 have independent rear suspension using axle shafts with U-joints at each end and ball spline joints in the center.

Several types of steering gear are used on Datsun vehicles. These are:

Model	*Type*
L60, L320, L520	Worm and roller
PL410, SPL310, SPL311, SRL311	Cam and lever
PL411, RL411, LB110, KLB110, PL510, WPL510, L521, PL521	Recirculating ball
HLS30	Rack and pinion

PL510, WPL510, SPL311, and SRL311 models starting 1969, and all HLS30, KLB110, and LB110 models, have a steering shaft lock actuated by the ignition lock and a steering column and shaft assembly designed to collapse on impact.

Front Suspension

LEAF SPRING TYPE—L60

The front suspension on this model is quite simple and easily repaired. When replacing the springs, the bolts should be tightened only after the vehicle is resting on its wheels. Spring rear eye bolt torque is 45-50 ft. lbs. The rear eye has a rubber bushing. When tightening the front shackles, which have steel bushings, tighten the nut fully, back off 1/4 turn, and insert the cotter pin. If the pin holes do not align, back the nut off further. The U-bolts holding the axle to the springs should be torqued to 50-60 ft. lbs. The double-acting shock absorbers are not serviceable. An axle rebound stop bolt connects the front axle to the frame. The bottom end of the bolt should protrude from the locknut .47″ and the operating stroke should be 3.34″. The operating stroke can be adjusted but the bolt should always protrude at least .2″. A rubber axle torque arrester bumper is mounted on the left side of the frame. With springs in good condition, there should be 1.81″ clearance between the bumper and the axle.

Wheel Bearing Adjustment

1. Remove front wheels.
2. Pry off drive flange hub cap.
3. Remove snap-ring from axle shaft groove.

4. Unbolt and pull off drive flange.
5. Bend back lockwasher and remove bearing locknut.
6. Using a bearing adjusting wrench, tighten the adjusting nut until the brake drum binds when turned, then back off 1/8 turn.

NOTE: It is very bad practice to use a hammer and chisel on the adjusting nut.

7. Install lockwasher and locknut, bending back lockwasher.
8. 1-3 ft. lbs. torque should be required to turn the hub. If turning torque is excessive, check the condition of the bearing. The brake drum and hub with wheel bearings can be slid off the spindle after removing the adjusting nut.
9. Replace shims, drive flange, lock plates, and nuts. Torque nuts to 25-28 ft. lbs. and bend up lock plates. Replace snap-ring and hub cap.
10. Replace wheels.

Wheel Alignment

The only alignment adjustment possible on the L60 is toe-in. Toe-in is measured between the wheels, in front of and behind the axle, and is adjusted by changing tie rod length. The specified toe-in is .12-.16″.

TORSION BAR TYPE—L320, L520, L521, PL521

This independent front suspension uses torsion bar springs, upper and lower links,

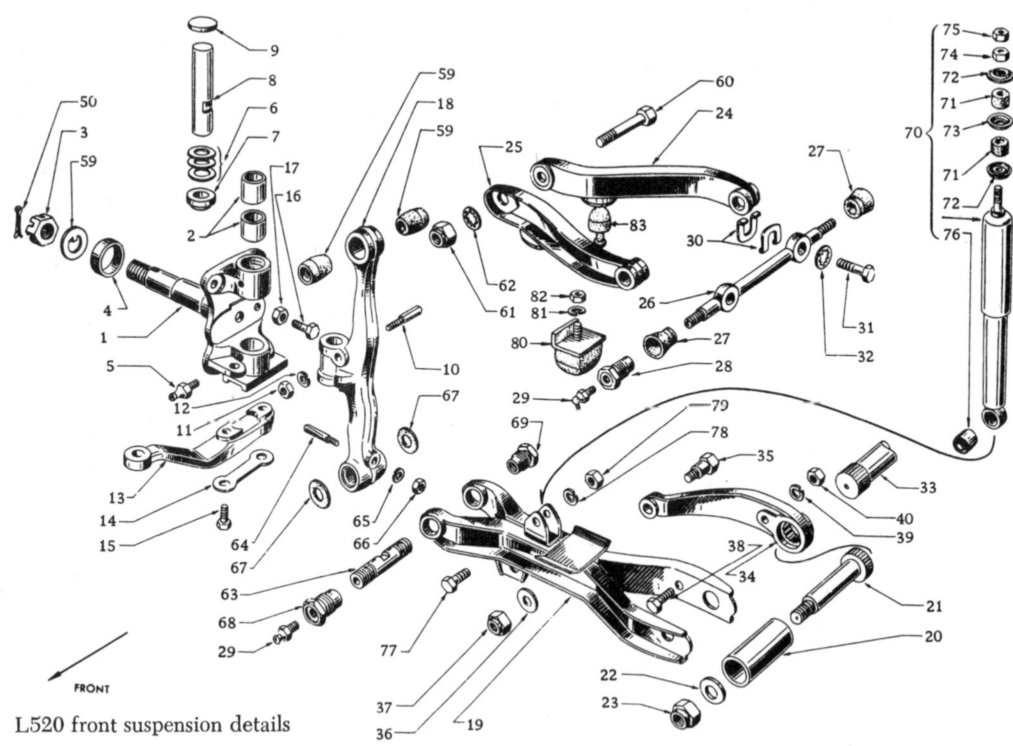

L520 front suspension details

1. Spindle
2. Bushing
3. Spindle nut, used to adjust front wheel bearing
4. Spindle collar
5. Grease nipple
6. Spindle shims
7. Thrust washer
8. Kingpin
9. Plug
10. Lock bolt
11. Nut
12. Lockwasher
13. Steering arm
14. Lockplate
15. Bolt
16. Bolt
17. Nut
18. Spindle support
19. Lower link
20. Lower link bushing
21. Lower link spindle
22. Washer
23. Nut
24. Rear upper link
25. Front upper link
26. Upper link spindle
27. Seal
28. Bushing assembly
29. Grease fitting
30. Camber adjusting shims
31. Spindle upper link bolt
32. Lockwasher
33. Torsion bar
34. Torsion bar front arm
35. Bolt
36. Washer
37. Nut
38. Bolt
39. Lockwasher
40. Nut
41-58. Not used
59. Bushing
60. Fulcrum bolt
61. Nut
62. Lockwasher
63. Fulcrum pin
64. Lock bolt
65. Lockwasher
66. Nut
67. Ring
68. Front bushing assembly
69. Rear bushing assembly
70. Shock absorber assembly
71. Bushing
72. Washer
73. Washer
74. Nut
75. Locknut
76. Bushing
77. Clamp bolt
78. Lockwasher
79. Nut
80. Suspension bound bumper
81. Lockwasher
82. Nut
83. Suspension rebound bumper

tubular shock absorbers, and kingpins. The lower suspension links are located fore and aft by tension rods from the front of the frame. The front end height can be adjusted to compensate for normal spring sagging.

Kingpin and Bushing Replacement

1. Block up the front of the truck.
2. Remove wheels.
3. Unscrew the front wheel brake hose connections.
4. Remove hubcap and spindle nut. Remove the hub and drum with the wheel bearing.
5. Remove the brake backing plate from the spindle.
6. Disconnect the tie rod from each spindle.
7. Take out the kingpin lock bolt and remove the upper spindle plug. Drive the kingpin down to remove the bottom plug. Tap out the kingpins.
8. Remove the spindle with the shims and thrust washer.
9. The old bushings should be driven out of the spindle and the new ones driven in. It is advisable to replace the kingpin also. Ream the new bushings to fit the kingpin. The fit should be such that the kingpin, when oiled, can be turned or pushed in or out readily with thumb pressure. Make sure that the bushing holes for the grease fittings are open.
10. On reassembly, use a new spindle thrust washer. Install spindle shims so that the clearance between the upper end of the kingpin boss on the spindle support knuckle and the spindle is .0032-.0051″ (.08-.13 mm.). Use new kingpin expansion plugs. Use a new front hub grease seal. Adjust the front wheel bearing by torquing it to 30 ft. lbs. and backing off ⅛ turn.
11. Grease suspension and bleed brake system.

Tension Rod Adjustment

There are three adjusting nuts on each tension rod. There is one at the lower suspension link end and two at the frame end. Adjust these nuts until both rubber bushings at the frame end are compressed to .434″ (11 mm.).

Suspension Height Adjustment

1. Jack up the vehicle under the front suspension crossmember to unload the torsion bars.
2. Turn the rear torsion bar anchor bolt right to lower the vehicle and left to raise it.

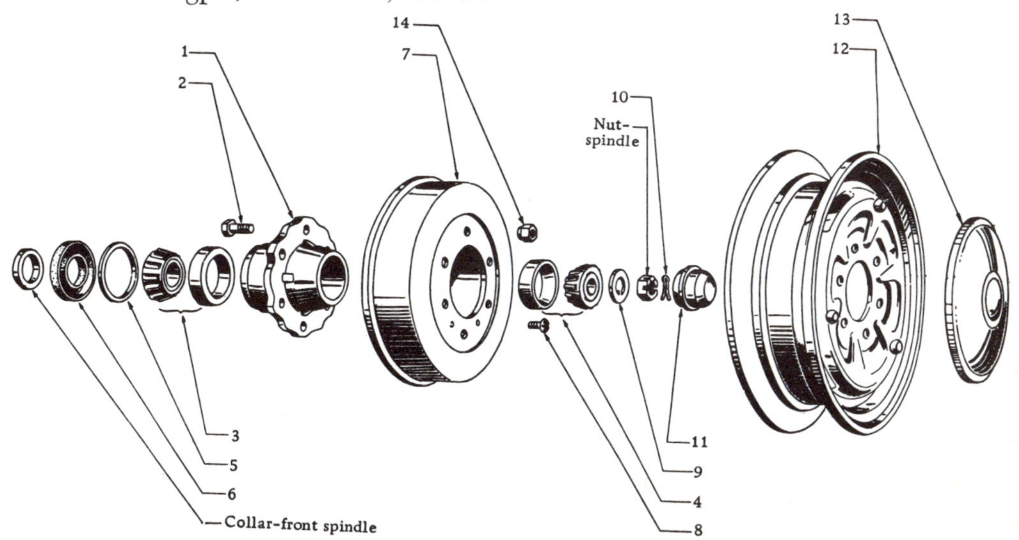

Front hub and drum details, L520

1. Hub
2. Wheel bolt
3. Inner bearing
4. Outer bearing
5. Grease seal spacer
6. Grease seal
7. Brake drum
8. Screw
9. Bearing washer
10. Cotter pin
11. Hubcap
12. Wheel
13. Wheel cover
14. Wheel nut

Tension rod assembly, top, and torsion bar assembly, bottom

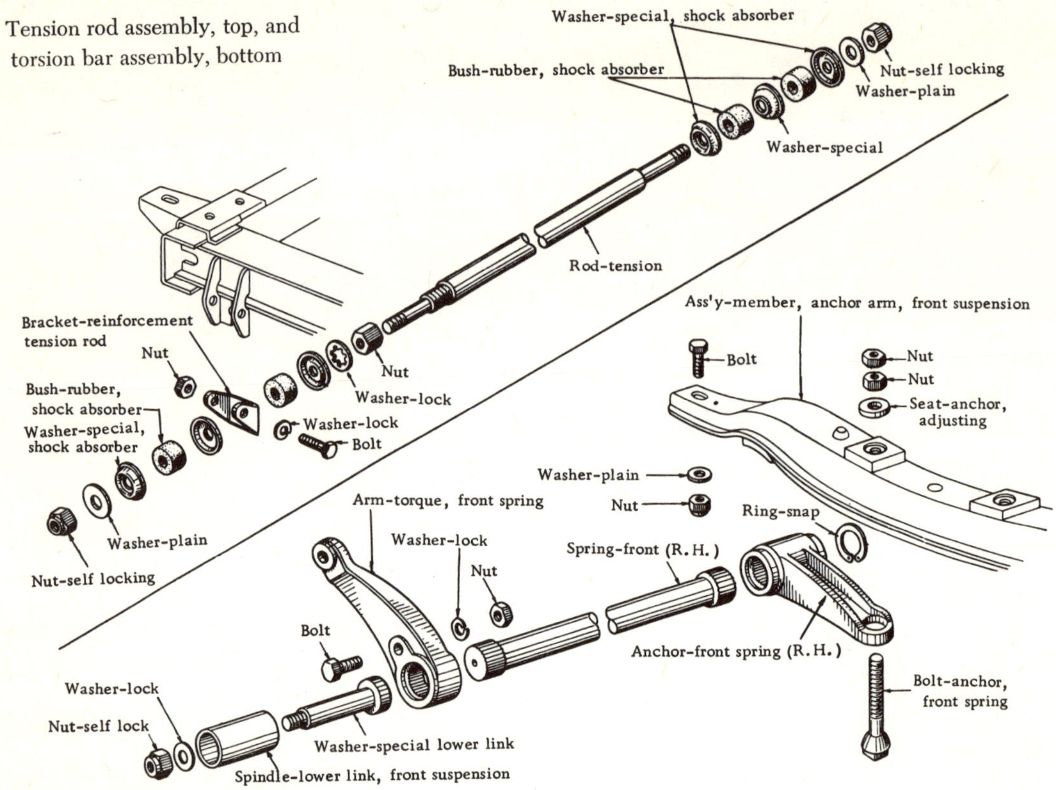

3. Dimension B in the illustration should be 2.93″ (74.5 mm.) on the L320 and 3.07-3.09″ on the L520, with the vehicle empty and resting on its wheels.

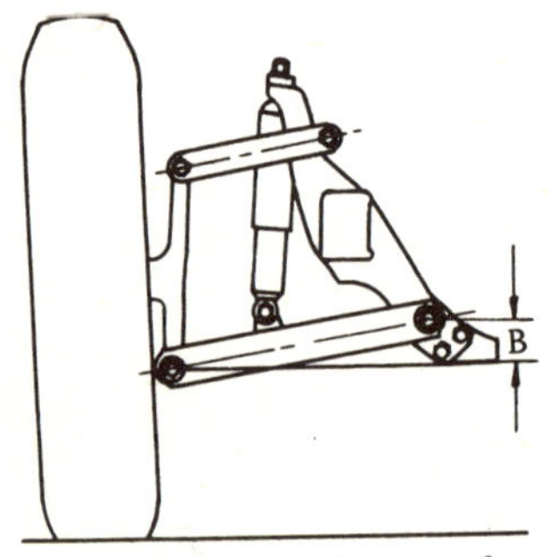

Check measurement B after adjusting front suspension height

Wheel Alignment

Caster and camber are adjusted by shims placed between the upper suspension link spindle and the crossmember. See the Chassis and Wheel Alignment Specifications Chart for alignment specifications.

COIL SPRING TYPE—PL410, PL411, RL411, SPL310, SPL311, SRL311

This independent front suspension uses coil springs between upper and lower wishbones. The shock absorbers are mounted in the center of each spring. The spindles are connected to the wishbones by ball joints. A cross-chassis stabilizer bar is used.

Wheel Bearing Adjustment

1. Jack up car and remove wheel.
2. Remove hubcap and cotter pin.
3. Torque the spindle nut to 33-36 ft. lbs. for the PL410, and 20-30 ft. lbs. for the PL411 and RL411.
4. Turn the hub a few turns in each direction and retorque the nut.
5. Loosen the nut 40-70°. Insert the cotter pin.
6. Turn the hub a few more turns.
7. Check that the hub turns easily. If not, check wheel bearing condition.
8. Replace hubcap and wheel. Lower car.

Spring R&R

1. Raise and support the front of the car.
2. Unbolt top and bottom mounts and remove shock absorber.
3. Install a coil spring compressor.

NOTE: Be extremely cautious when working with chassis coil springs.

Compress the spring.

4. Unbolt the lower link spindle from the

Front suspension details, sedans with coil springs

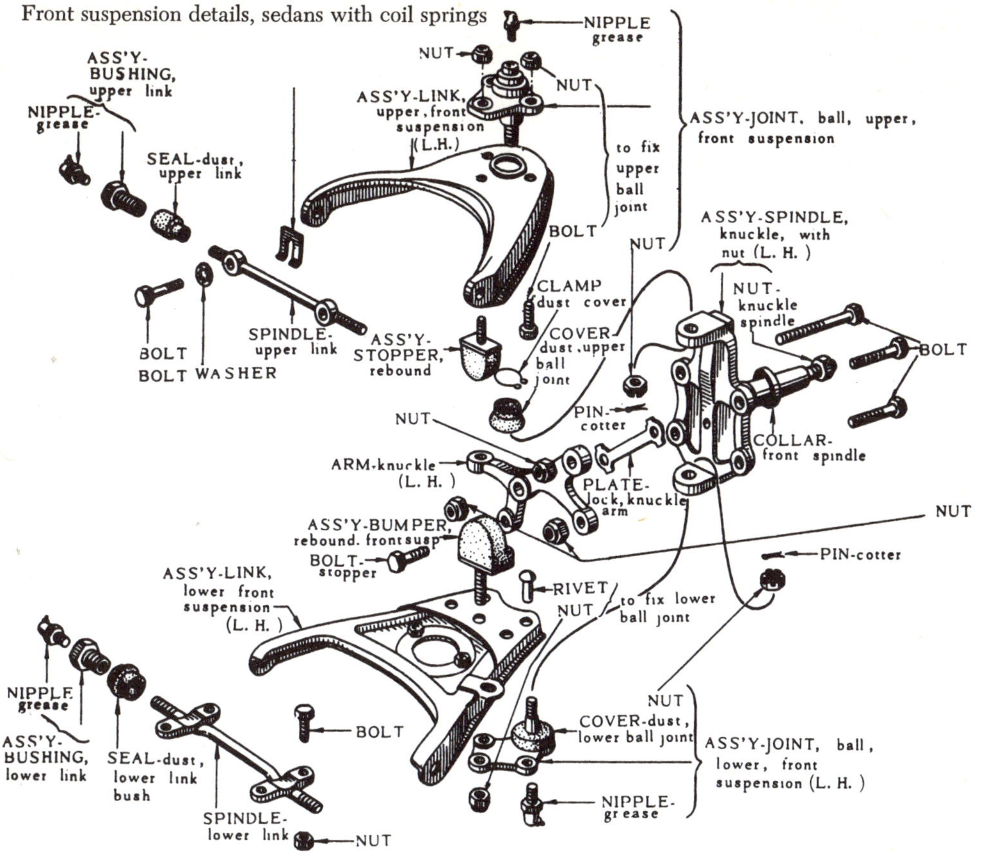

NIPPLE grease
NUT
NUT
ASS'Y-BUSHING, upper link
NIPPLE-grease
ASS'Y-LINK, upper, front suspension (L.H.)
to fix upper ball joint
ASS'Y-JOINT, ball, upper, front suspension
SEAL-dust, upper link
BOLT
NUT
ASS'Y-SPINDLE, knuckle, with nut (L. H.)
NUT-knuckle spindle
CLAMP dust cover
BOLT
COVER-dust, upper ball joint
SPINDLE-upper link
ASS'Y-STOPPER, rebound
BOLT
BOLT WASHER
NUT
PIN-cotter
COLLAR-front spindle
ARM-knuckle (L. H.)
PLATE-lock, knuckle arm
NUT
ASS'Y-BUMPER, rebound, front susp
BOLT-stopper
PIN-cotter
ASS'Y-LINK, lower front suspension (L. H.)
RIVET
NUT
to fix lower ball joint
NIPPLE grease
NUT
ASS'Y-BUSHING, lower link
SEAL-dust, lower link bush
BOLT
COVER-dust, lower ball joint
ASS'Y-JOINT, ball, lower, front suspension (L. H.)
SPINDLE-lower link
NIPPLE-grease
NUT

Front hub details; SPL311, SRL311

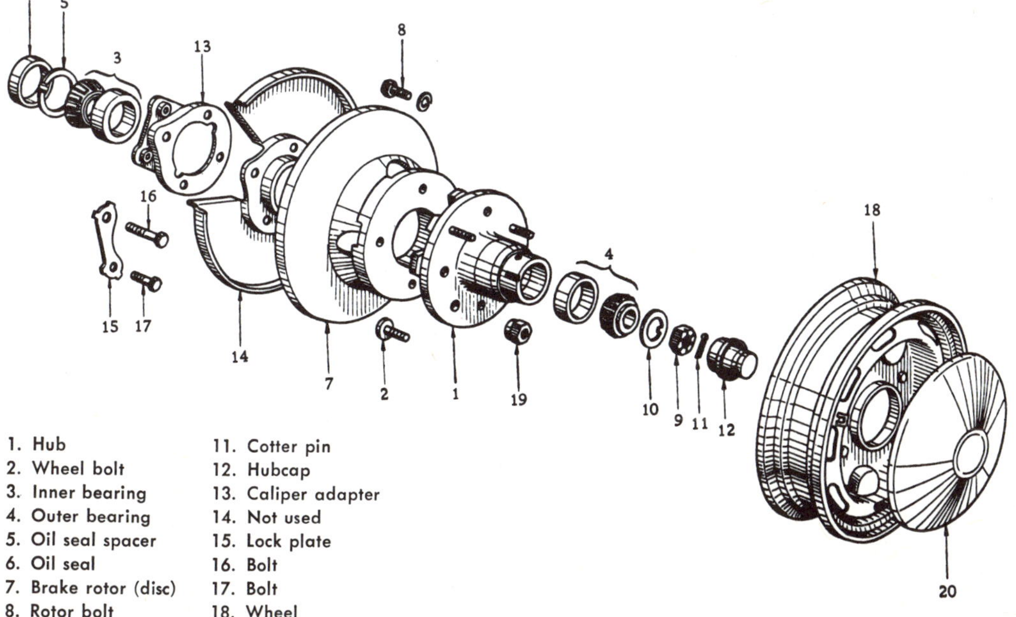

1. Hub
2. Wheel bolt
3. Inner bearing
4. Outer bearing
5. Oil seal spacer
6. Oil seal
7. Brake rotor (disc)
8. Rotor bolt
9. Spindle nut
10. Bearing washer
11. Cotter pin
12. Hubcap
13. Caliper adapter
14. Not used
15. Lock plate
16. Bolt
17. Bolt
18. Wheel
19. Wheel nut
20. Wheel cover

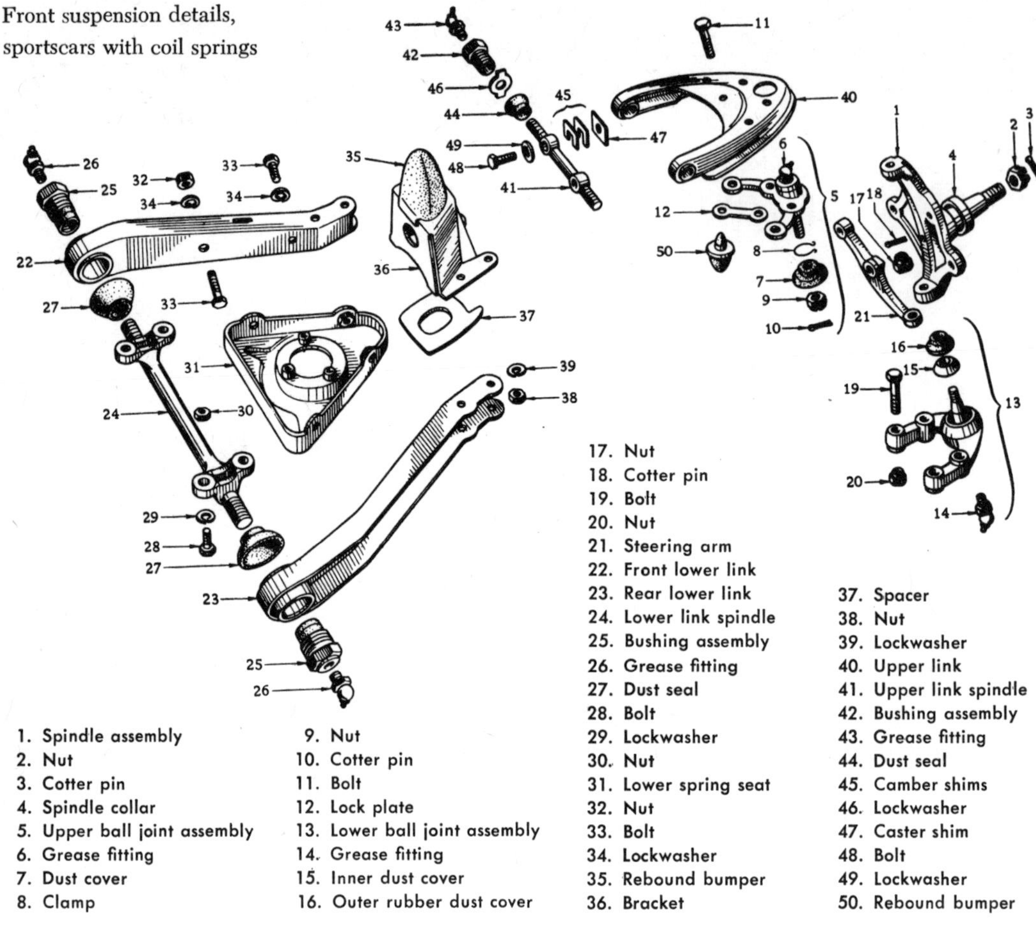

Front suspension details, sportscars with coil springs

1. Spindle assembly
2. Nut
3. Cotter pin
4. Spindle collar
5. Upper ball joint assembly
6. Grease fitting
7. Dust cover
8. Clamp
9. Nut
10. Cotter pin
11. Bolt
12. Lock plate
13. Lower ball joint assembly
14. Grease fitting
15. Inner dust cover
16. Outer rubber dust cover
17. Nut
18. Cotter pin
19. Bolt
20. Nut
21. Steering arm
22. Front lower link
23. Rear lower link
24. Lower link spindle
25. Bushing assembly
26. Grease fitting
27. Dust seal
28. Bolt
29. Lockwasher
30. Nut
31. Lower spring seat
32. Nut
33. Bolt
34. Lockwasher
35. Rebound bumper
36. Bracket
37. Spacer
38. Nut
39. Lockwasher
40. Upper link
41. Upper link spindle
42. Bushing assembly
43. Grease fitting
44. Dust seal
45. Camber shims
46. Lockwasher
47. Caster shim
48. Bolt
49. Lockwasher
50. Rebound bumper

crossmember. An alternate method is to unbolt the lower ball joint. On sportscars, it is also possible to unbolt the lower spring support plate.

5. Slowly and carefully release the coil spring. When the coil is fully extended, remove it.
6. On reinstallation, compress the spring and set it into place. Bolt on the part disconnected in Step 4. Release the coil spring and replace the shock absorber.

Wheel Alignment

Caster and camber are adjusted by shims placed between the crossmember and the spindle of the upper wishbone. See the Chassis and Wheel Alignment Specifications Chart for alignment specifications.

STRUT TYPE—PL510, WPL510, LB110, KLB110, HLS30

This independent front suspension uses McPherson struts. Each strut combines the function of coil spring and shock absorber. The spindle is mounted to the lower part of the strut which has a single ball joint. No upper suspension arm is required in this design. The spindle and lower suspension transverse link are located fore and aft by tension rods to the front part of the chassis on the PL510, WPL510, KLB110, and LB110. Compression rods, which run rearward, are used on the HLS30. A cross-chassis sway bar is used on all models.

Wheel Bearing Adjustment

1. Jack up car and remove wheel.
2. Remove hubcap and cotter pin.
3. Torque the spindle nut to:

Model	*Torque (ft. lbs.)*
HLS30	18-22
PL510, WPL510	22-25
LB110, KLB110	16-17

1. Strut mounting insulator
2. Strut mounting bearing
3. Upper spring seat
4. Bumper rubber
5. Dust cover
6. Pision rod
7. Front spring
8. Strut assembly
9. Hub assembly
10. Spindle
11. Ball joint
12. Transverse link
13. Tension rod
14. Stabilizer
15. Suspension member

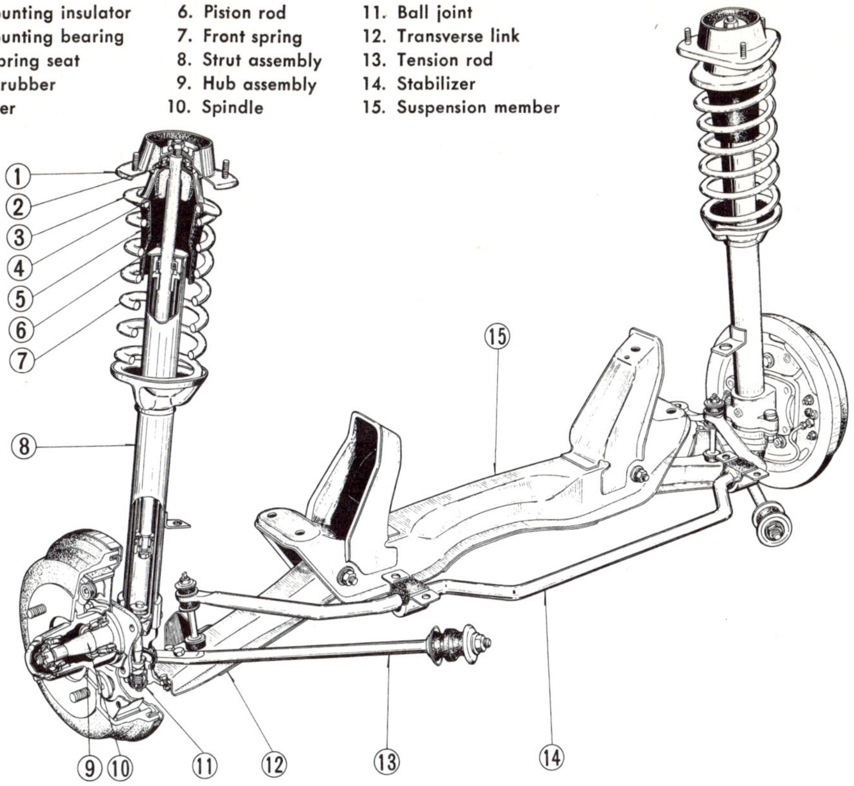

Strut type front suspension, LB110 and KLB110. Other models are quite similar. On HLS30 tension rods are replaced by compression rods which run to the rear.

4. Turn the hub a few turns in each direction and retorque the nut.
5. Loosen the nut 60-75° on the HLS30, 90° on the PL510 and WPL510, and 40-70° on the LB110 and KLB110. Insert the cotter pin.
6. Turn the hub a few more turns.
7. Hub turning torque, with the disc brake pads removed, should be:

Model	*Torque (in. lbs.)*	*Pull at hub bolt (lbs.)*
HLS30	3.5-7.4	1.5-3.3
PL510, WPL510 with new bearing and seal	6.1	
PL510, WPL510 with original bearing and seal	3.5	
LB110, KLB110	15.6-20.0	7.1-8.8

If torque is excessive, check wheel bearing condition. There should be no hub end-play.

8. Replace hubcap, brake pads, and wheel. Lower car.

Hub Assembly Repair

1. Jack up vehicle, remove wheel, and disconnect brake hose.
2. Unbolt and remove brake caliper assembly.
3. Remove hubcap, cotter pin, and spindle nut.
4. Remove wheel hub with bearing washer, bearing, and brake rotor.
5. Remove screws and brake splash shield.
6. Disassemble hub. Use a drift in the two grooves inside the hub to drive out the bearing outer race.
7. Drive or press back in the bearing outer race.
8. Pack the bearings, the hub, and the grease seal lip pocket (use a new seal) with grease. Refer to the illustration.
9. Reassemble, and adjust the wheel bearings. Pack some grease into the hubcap and replace it.

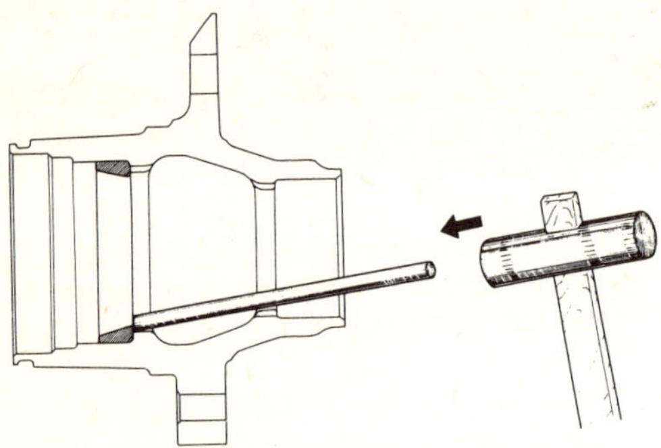

Driving out bearing outer race

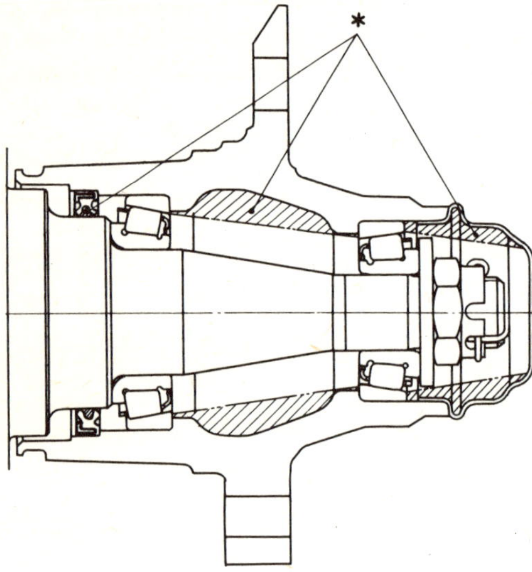

* indicates areas to be filled with grease.

Fastener	Model	Torque (ft. lbs.)
Splash shield screws	All	2-3
Rotor to hub bolts	PL510, WPL510, HLS30	28-38
	LB110, KLB110	20-27
Caliper bolts	HLS30	11-13
	PL510, WPL510	53-72
	LB110, KLB110	33-44

10. Replace caliper, brake hose, and wheel. Lower vehicle.

Strut R&R

1. Jack up car and support safely. Remove wheel.
2. Disconnect and plug brake hose.
3. Disconnect tension rod (compression rod on HLS30) and stabilizer bar from transverse link.
4. Unbolt the steering arm.
5. Place a jack under the bottom of the strut.
6. Open the hood and remove the nuts holding the top of the strut.
7. Lower the jack slowly and cautiously until the strut assembly can be removed.
8. Reverse the procedure to install. The self locking nuts holding the top of the strut must be replaced.

Fastener	Model	Torque (ft. lbs.)
Strut to body nuts	HLS30	18-25
	PL510, WPL510	28-38
	LB110, KLB110	12-15
Steering arm to strut bolts	HLS30	53-72
	PL510, WPL510	43-58
	LB110, KLB110	33-44
Tension or compression rod to transverse link nut	HLS30, PL510, WPL510	36-46
	LB110, KLB110	16-22
Stabilizer to transverse link bolts	HLS30, PL510, WPL510	9-12
	LB110, KLB110	7-9
Stabilizer to frame bracket bolts	HLS30, PL510, WPL510	14-18
	LB110, KLB110	7-9

NOTE: Special tools are required to disassemble the strut. It is recommended that strut repair be left to an authorized repair facility.

Ball Joint R&R

The lower ball joint should be replaced when up and down (axial) play exceeds the standard play of .0118-.0394″ for the LB110 and KLB110 or .0012-.0136″ for the other models. The ball joint should be greased every 30,000 miles. There is a plugged hole in the bottom of the joint for installation of a grease fitting.

1. Raise and support car so wheels hang free. Remove wheel.
2. Unbolt tension rod (compression rod on HLS30) and stabilizer bar from transverse link.
3. Unbolt strut from steering arm.
4. Remove cotter pin and ball joint stud nut. Separate ball joint and steering arm.
5. Unbolt ball joint from transverse link.
6. Reverse procedure to install new ball joint. Grease the joint after installation.

Fastener	Model	Torque (ft. lbs.)
Ball joint to transverse link bolts	HLS30	36-46
	PL510, WPL510	14-18
	LB110, KLB110	16-22
Ball joint stud nut	All	40-55
Tension rod, compression rod, stabilizer bar, and steering arm	All	See Strut R&R.

Wheel Alignment

Caster and camber angles cannot be adjusted except by replacing worn or bent parts. Suspension height is adjusted by replacing the front springs. Various springs are available for adjustment. Toe-in is adjusted by changing the length of the steering side-rods. The length of these rods should always be equal when measured between their ball joint centers. Steering angles are adjusted by means of a stop bolt on each steering arm. On the LB110 and KLB110 make sure that the clearance between the tire and tension rod is at least 1.181″.

Rear Suspension

SPRINGS

Removal and Installation

Nissan Patrol (L60) Leaf Springs

When replacing the springs, the bolts should be tightened only after the vehicle is resting on its wheels. The torque for the front spring eye, which has a rubber bushing, is 45-50 ft. lbs. To tighten the spring rear shackles, which have steel bushings, first tighten the nut fully, back off 1/4 turn, and insert the cotter pin. If the pin holes do not align, back the nut off further. The U-bolts holding the axle to the springs should be torqued to 50-60 ft. lbs. The double-acting shock absorbers are not serviceable. With springs in good condition, there should be .515″ clearance between the main leaf and the rubber bumper on the frame. A cross-chassis sway bar is used on the rear suspension.

LB110, KLB110 Leaf Springs

1. Raise rear axle until wheels hang free. Support the car on stands. Support the rear axle with a jack.
2. Unbolt bottom end of shock absorber.
3. Unbolt axle from spring leaves. Unbolt and remove front spring bracket. Lower the front of the spring to the floor.
4. Unbolt and remove spring rear shackle.
5. Before reinstallation, coat the front bracket pin, bushing, shackle pin, and shackle bushing with a soap solution.
6. Reverse procedure to install. The front pin nut and the shock absorber mounting should be tightened before the vehicle is lowered to the floor.

Fastener	Torque (ft. lbs.)
Axle U-bolts	23-29
Front spring bracket to body	12-15
Shackle pin nuts	12-15
LB110 Sedan shock absorber upper nuts	26-33
KLB110 Coupe shock absorber upper nuts	7-9
LB110 Sedan shock absorber lower nuts	26-33
KLB110 Coupe shock absorber lower nuts	7-9

WPL510 Leaf Springs

1. Raise rear axle until wheels hang free. Support the car on stands. Support the rear axle with a floor jack.
2. Remove the spare tire.
3. Unbolt bottom end of shock absorber.
4. Unbolt axle from spring leaves.
5. Unbolt front spring bracket from body. Lower spring end and bracket to floor.
6. Unbolt and remove rear shackle.
7. Unbolt bracket from spring.
8. Before reinstallation, coat the front bracket pin and bushing, and the shackle pin and bushing with a soap solution.
9. Reverse procedure to install. The front pin nut and the shock absorber mounting should be tightened after the vehicle is lowered to the floor. Make sure that the elongated flange of the rubber bumper is to the rear.

LB110 and KLB110 rear suspension

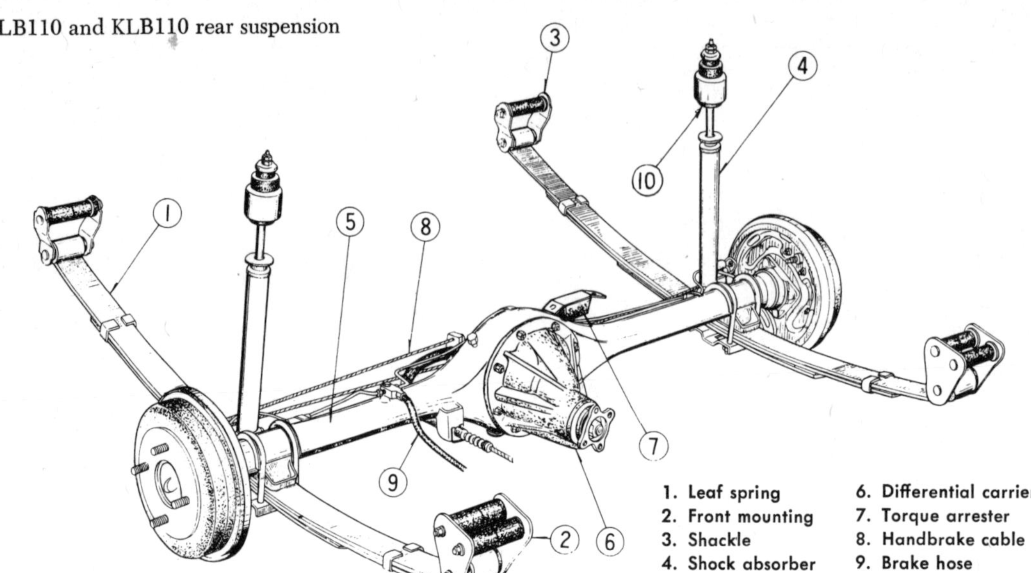

PL510 indépendent rear suspension

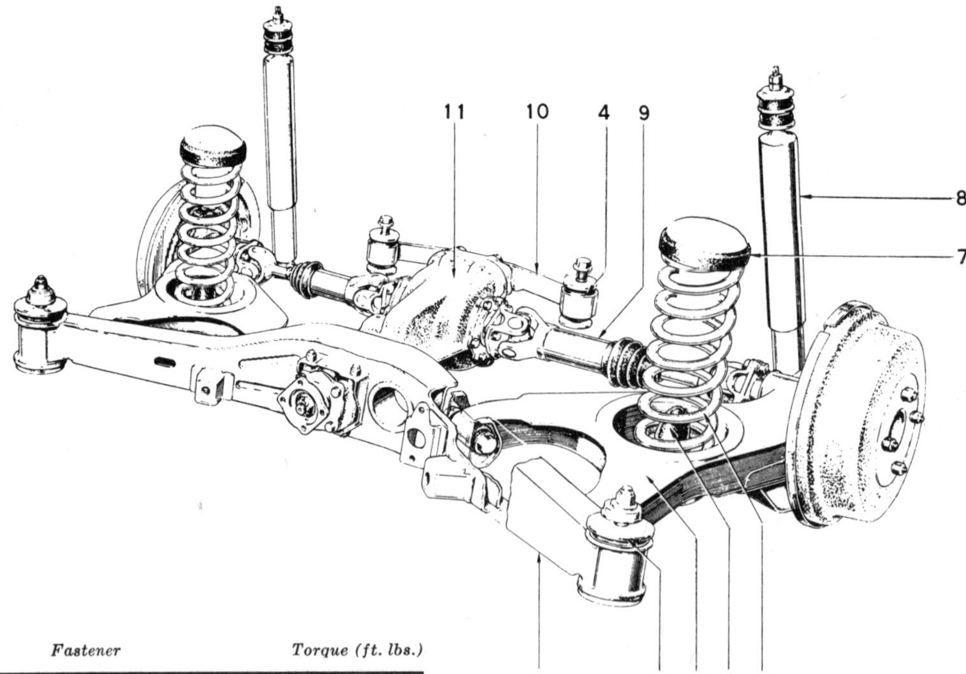

1. Suspension member
2. Suspension arm
3. Member mounting insulator
4. Differential mounting insulator
5. Coil spring
6. Bumper rubber
7. Spring seat
8. Shock absorber
9. Drive shaft
10. Differential mounting member
11. Differential carrier

Fastener	*Torque (ft. lbs.)*
Axle U-bolts	43-47
Shock absorber upper bracket to body	11-18
Shock absorber to upper bracket nuts	12-16
Shock absorber lower nuts	25-33
Spring shackle nuts	33-36
Front pin nuts	33-36
Front bracket to body nuts	13-17

PL510 Coil Springs

1. Raise rear of vehicle and support on stands.
2. Remove wheels.
3. Disconnect handbrake linkage and return spring.
4. Unbolt axle driveshaft flange at wheel end.
5. Unbolt rubber bumper inside bottom of coil spring.
6. Jack up suspension arm and unbolt shock absorber lower mounting.
7. Lower jack slowly and cautiously. Remove coil spring, spring seat, and rubber bumper.
8. Reverse procedure to install, making sure that the flat face of the spring is at the top.

Fastener	*Torque (ft. lbs.)*
Axle driveshaft flange nuts	51-58
Rubber bumper nut	15-19
Shock absorber mounting nuts	17

SHOCK ABSORBERS

Removal and Installation

LB110, KLB110

To remove the rear shock absorbers, simply unbolt the lower and upper ends. The upper nuts are under the rear seat back. The shock absorbers are not serviceable and should be replaced if defective. Mounting bolt torques are given under Spring R & R.

WPL510

When removing the shock absorber, unbolt the upper bracket from the body and remove the shock absorber and bracket as a unit. The shock absorbers are not serviceable and should be replaced if defective. Mounting bolt torques are given under Spring R & R.

PL510

1. Open the trunk and remove the cover panel.
2. Remove the two nuts holding the top of the shock absorber.
3. The shock absorbers can not be repaired. Replace if defective.
4. Reverse procedure to install. See Coil Spring R&R—PL510 for torque figures.

SUSPENSION STRUT

Removal and Installation

HLS30

1. Raise rear of vehicle and support on stands.
2. Remove wheels.
3. Disconnect brake hydraulic line and handbrake cable.
4. Remove nuts from either end of transverse link outer spindle. Remove spindle center locking bolt. Pull out spindle. Separate bottom of strut from transverse link.
5. Unbolt axle driveshaft flange at wheel end.
6. Jack under the lower end of the strut. Remove the strut installation nuts from the tower inside the luggage area. Lower jack and strut gradually.

NOTE: Strut disassembly and repair requires special tools and should be left to an authorized repair facility.

7. Reverse procedure to install. Note that the shorter part of the spindle (measured from the locking bolt notch) should be to the front. Tighten the outer spindle end nuts after the vehicle has been lowered to the floor.

Fastener	*Torque (ft. lbs.)*
Strut installation nut	12-15
Transverse link outer spindle nuts	54-69
Outer spindle locking bolt	7-9
Axle driveshaft flange nuts	36-43

AXLE DRIVESHAFT

Wheel Bearing, Seal, and Axle Driveshaft Service

HLS30, PL510

1. Jack up and support rear of car.
2. Remove wheel and brake drum.
3. Disconnect axle driveshaft from axle shaft at flange.
4. Remove the wheel bearing locknut while holding the axle shaft outer flange from turning.
5. Pull out the axle shaft with a slide hammer. Remove the distance piece and inner flange.
6. Drive the inner wheel bearing and oil

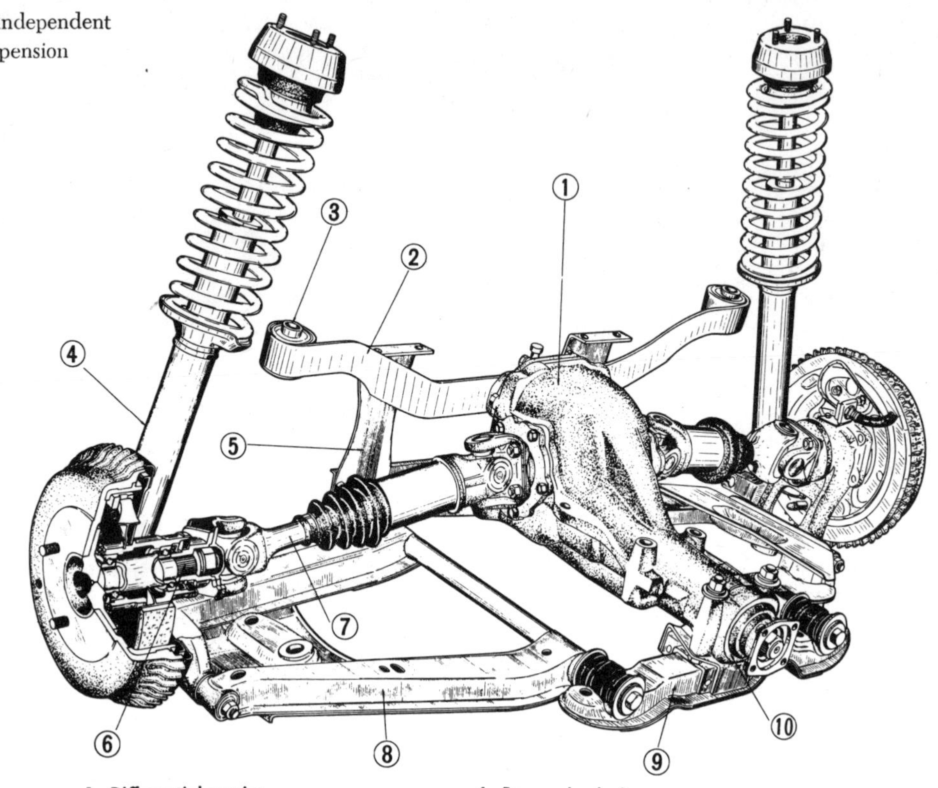

HLS30 independent rear suspension

1. Differential carrier
2. Differential case mount rear member
3. Differential case mount rear insulator
4. Strut assembly
5. Link mount brace
6. Rear axle shaft
7. Drive shaft
8. Transverse link
9. Differential case mount front member
10. Differential case mount front insulator

seal out toward the center of the car.

7. Press or pull the outer wheel bearing from the axle shaft.
8. Pack the wheel bearings with grease. Coat the seal lip also.
9. Reinstall the wheel bearings. Install the outer bearing on the axle shaft so that the side with the seal will be toward the wheel. Always press or drive on the inner bearing race.
10. The distance piece may be reused if it is not collapsed or deformed. The distance piece must always carry the same mark, A, B, or C, as the bearing housing.
11. Fill the area illustrated with grease.
12. Replace the axle shaft and flange. Tighten the bearing locknut to the specified torque.
13. The torque required to start the axle shaft turning should be 390 in. lbs. or less. This is a 28.7 oz. or less pull at the hub bolt. Axle shaft end-play, checked

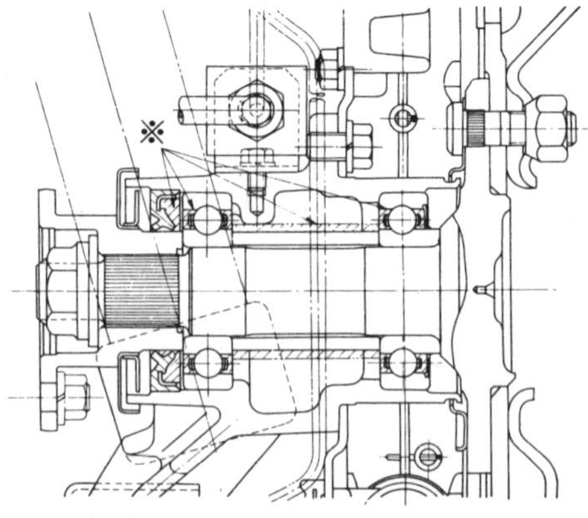

* indicates areas to receive grease

with a dial indicator, should be 0-0057″.

14. If turning torque or axle shaft play is incorrect, disassemble and install a new distance piece.

Fastener	*Model*	*Torque (ft. lbs.)*
Wheel nut	All	58-65
Axle driveshaft flange nuts	PL510	51-58
	HLS30	36-43
Bearing locknut	All	181-239
Axle shaft inner flange nut	All	12-17

Disassembly and Assembly

HLS30, PL510

The axle driveshafts must be removed and disassembled to lubricate the ball splines every 30,000 miles. Handle the driveshaft carefully; it is easily damaged. No repair parts for the driveshafts are available. If a driveshaft is defective in any way, it must be replaced as an assembly.

To disassemble:

1. Remove the U-joint spider from the differential end of the shaft.
2. Remove the snap-ring and sleeve yoke plug.
3. Compress the driveshaft and remove the snap-ring and stopper.
4. Disconnect the boot and separate the driveshaft carefully so as not to lose the balls and spacer.
5. Pack about 10 grams (.35 oz.) of grease into the ball grooves. Also pack about 35 grams (1.23 oz.) of grease into the area illustrated.

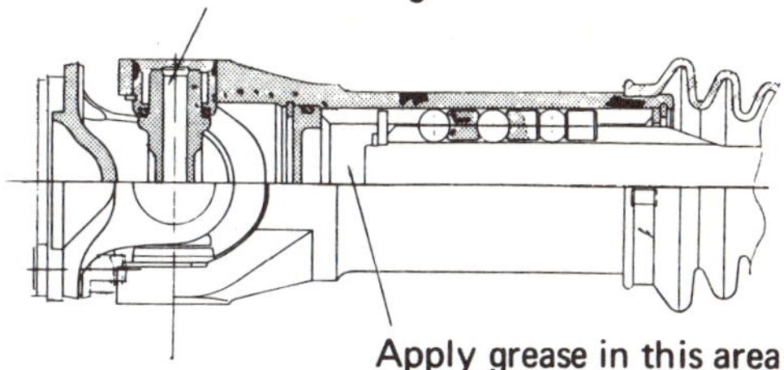

Axle driveshaft cross-section

6. Twisting play between the two shaft halves should not exceed .0039″. Check play with the driveshaft completely compressed.
7. While reassembling, adjust U-joint side play to .0008″ or less by selecting suitable snap-rings. Four different thicknesses are available for adjustment. See Wheel Bearing, Seal, and Axle Shaft Service for driveshaft flange nut torque.

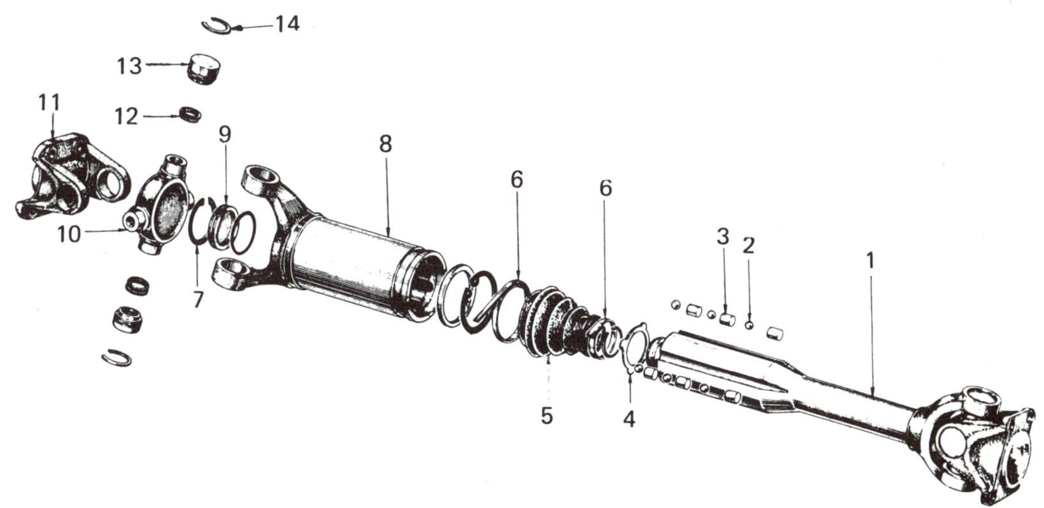

Axle driveshaft for PL510 and HLS30 rear suspension

1. Drive shaft
2. Drive shaft ball
3. Ball spacer
4. Drive shaft stopper
5. Rubber boot
6. Boot band
7. Snap ring
8. Sleeve yoke
9. Sleeve yoke plug
10. Spider journal
11. Flange yoke
12. Oil seal
13. Needle bearing
14. Snap ring

Steering wheel installation, PL410 and PL411

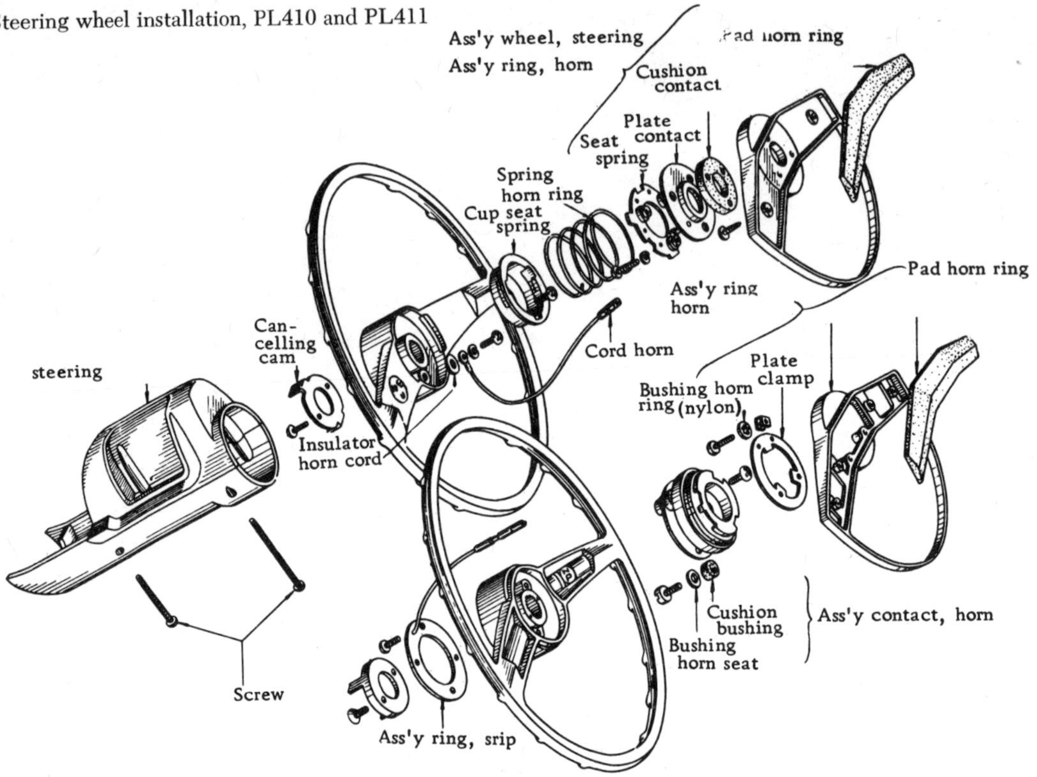

Steering

STEERING WHEEL

Removal and Installation

First remove the horn button or ring. On the L320, L520, and other early models, the horn button assembly is retained by three screws which can be removed from the rear of the wheel. On the PL410, PL411, KLB110 and LB110, the horn ring is retained by two screws which can be removed from the rear of the wheel spokes. On the SPL310, SPL311, and SRL311, the horn button is retained by a wire snap-ring and can be pried loose. To remove the PL510 and WPL510 horn ring, press in and turn to the left. Pull the HLS30 horn button rearward to remove. Next remove the rest of the horn switching mechanism, noting the relative location of the parts. Hold the steering wheel and remove the nut. Using a puller, remove the steering wheel. Do not attempt to pry or hammer off the wheel. This is particularly important in the case of collapsible steering columns. When replacing the wheel, make sure that it is correctly aligned when the wheels are straight ahead. Do not drive or hammer the wheel into place. Tighten the nut while holding the wheel. Specified wheel nut torque is 22-25 ft. lbs. for the LB110 and KLB110 and 29-36 ft. lbs. for the HLS30. Reinstall the horn button or ring.

STEERING GEAR

Removal and Installation

L60, L320, L520, L521, PL521

1. Remove the steering wheel.
2. Unbolt the steering column from the instrument panel. On models with column shift, unbolt the shift linkage from the column.
3. Disconnect the horn wire.
4. Unscrew the drag link end plug and disconnect the steering arm from the drag link on the L60. On the L320 and L520, disconnect the steering rod from the steering arm.
5. Unbolt the steering gear box from the frame.
6. Pull the box, column, and shaft down and out of the vehicle.
7. Reverse the procedure to install.

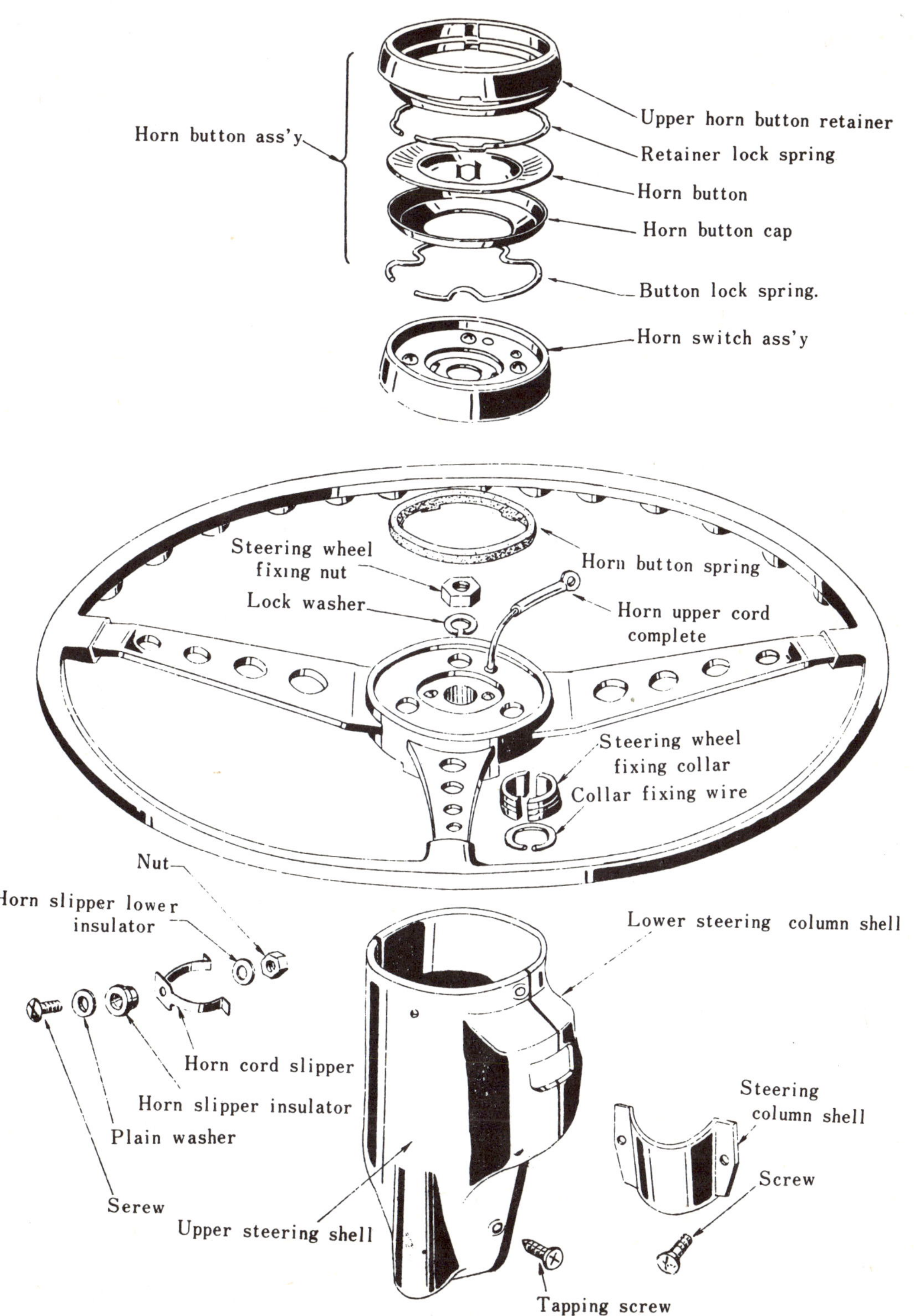

Steering wheel installation; SPL310, SPL311, and SRL311

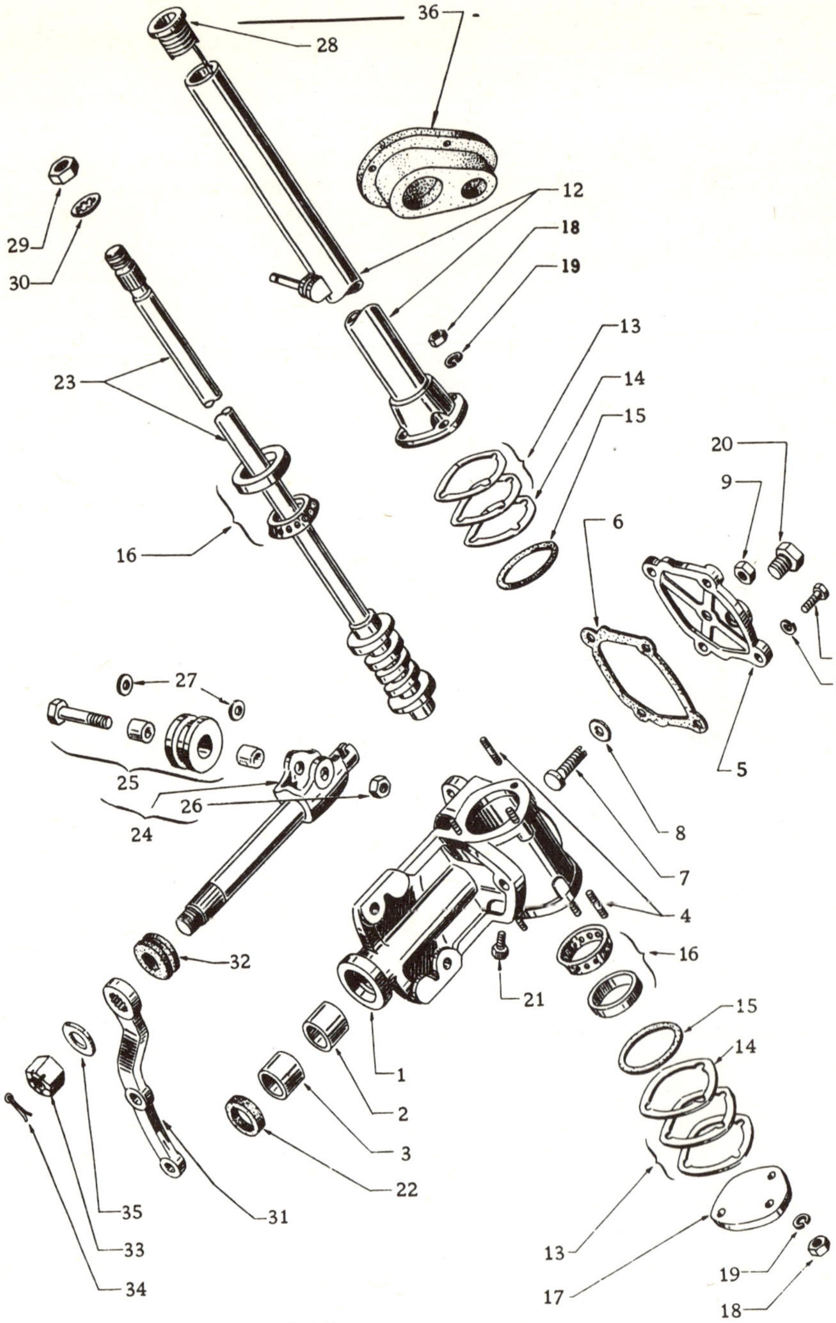

Worm and roller steering gear, L520

1. Steering gear housing
2. Upper bushing
3. Lower bushing
4. Stud
5. Cover
6. Gasket
7. Adjusting screw
8. Adjusting shim
9. Locknut
10. Bolt
11. Lockwasher
12. Steering column
13. Worm bearing shim
14. Shims
15. O-ring
16. Worm bearing
17. Cover
18. Nut
19. Lockwasher
20. Filler plug
21. Drain plug
22. Oil seal
23. Steering shaft
24. Roller shaft
25. Roller and pin
26. Nut
27. Thrust washers
28. Column bushing
29. Wheel nut
30. Lockwasher
31. Steering arm
32. Dust seal
33. Nut
34. Cotter pin
35. Washer
36. Rubber grommet

PL410, PL411

This procedure is the same as that for L60, L320, L520, L521, PL521 above with the substitution of the following step:

4. Remove the stud nut and pull the steering rod ball joint from the steering arm.

SPL310, SPL311, SRL311—Rigid Column SPL31, SRL311, PL510, WPL510—Collapsible Column

1. Remove the steering shaft U-joint clamp bolt.
2. Remove the stud nut and pull the steering rod ball joint from the steering arm.
3. Unbolt steering gear box from frame and remove. If necessary, remove the horn button and pull the steering wheel and shaft up slightly.
4. Reverse procedure to install. Torque U-joint clamp bolt to 22 ft. lbs. If upper and lower shaft sections of collapsible column have been separated, the slit of the universal joint must align with the punch mark on the upper end of the upper steering shaft.

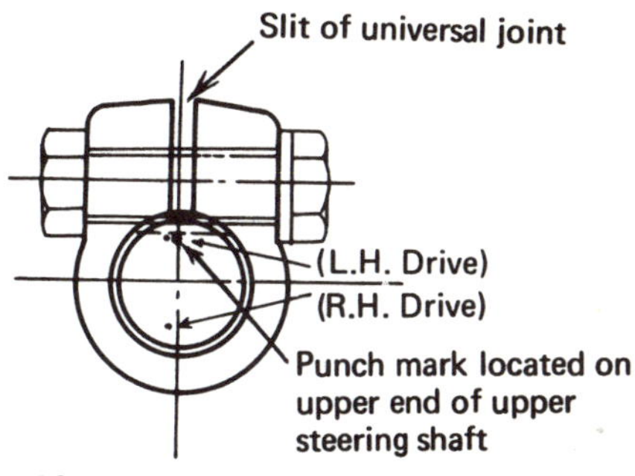

Reassembly details for collapsible column steering shaft

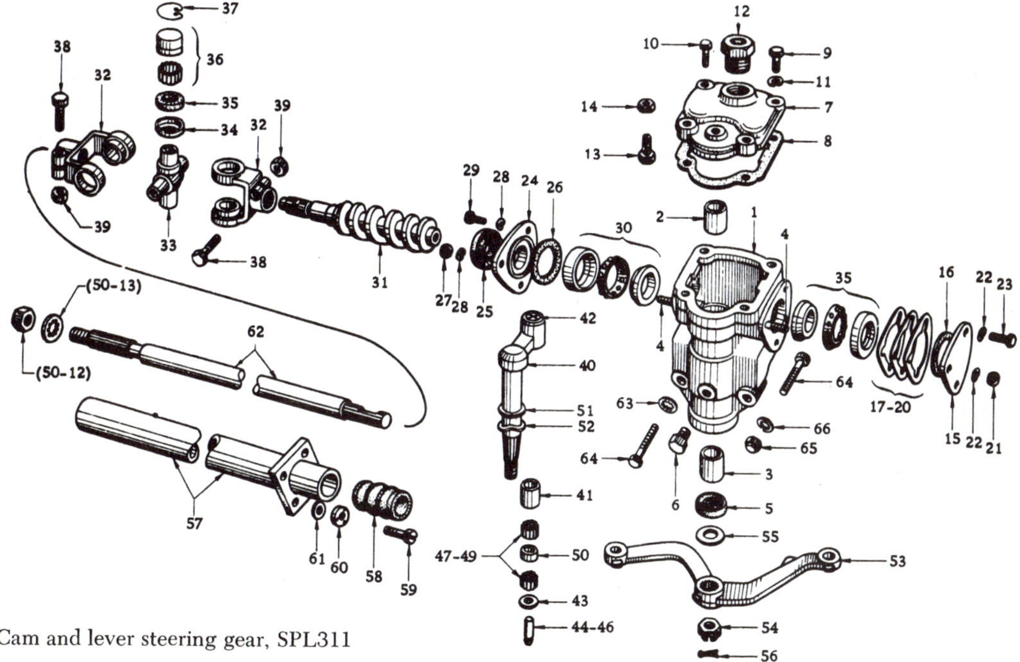

Cam and lever steering gear, SPL311

1. Steering gear housing
2. Bushing
3. Bushing
4. Stud
5. Oil seal
6. Drain plug
7. Cover
8. Gasket
9. Bolt
10. Bolt
11. Lockwasher
12. Filler plug
13. Adjusting screw
14. Locknut
15. Cover
16. O-ring
17-20. Shims
21. Nut
22. Lockwasher
23. Bolt
24. Rear cover
25. Oil seal
26. O-ring
27. Nut
28. Lockwasher
29. Bolt
30. Bearing
31. Worm gear
32. U-joint yoke
33. U-joint spider
34. Oil seal retainer
35. Oil seal
36. Bearing
37. Snap-ring
38. Bolt
39. Nut
40. Rocker shaft (lever)
41. Needle roller race
42. Roller ball plug
43. Needle roller cover
44-46. Roller ball
47-49. Needle rollers
50. Roller spacer
51. Thrust washer
52. Shaft adjusting thrust washer
53. Steering arm
54. Nut
55. Washer
56. Cotter pin
57. Steering column
58. Column bushing
59. Bolt
60. Lockwasher
61. Washer
62. Steering shaft
63. Lockwasher
64. Mounting bolt
65. Nut
66. Lockwasher

PL510, WPL510—Rigid Column LB110, KLB110—Collapsible Column

1. Remove steering wheel.
2. Separate and remove upper steering column shell.
3. Remove turn signal and light switch assembly. Disconnect automatic transmission linkage.
4. Unbolt steering column from instrument panel.
5. Remove steering column hole cover from floorboards.
6. Unbolt steering box from body.
7. Pull assembly out of car toward engine compartment. Be extremely cautious with LB110 and KLB110 collapsible column. Merely dropping or leaning on the assembly could cause enough damage to require replacement.
8. Reverse procedure to install.

Fastener	*Model*	*Torque (ft. lbs.)*
Stud nut	PL510, WPL510	40-55
	LB110, KLB110	22-36
Steering gear box bolts	PL510, WPL510	72
	LB110, KLB110	14-19
Steering column to instrument panel bolts	LB110, KLB110	11-13
Column clamp to column	LB110, KLB110	6-7

HLS30

1. Raise and support front end. Remove front wheels.
2. Loosen clamp bolts at both U-joints. Remove lower joint and shaft assembly from engine compartment.
3. Remove the splash shields.
4. Remove the steering side rod stud nuts and pull the studs from the spindle steering arms.
5. Raise the engine slightly, being careful not to damage the accelerator linkage.
6. Unbolt steering gear housing from suspension crossmember.
7. Remove rack and pinion assembly.
8. Reverse procedure to install. If upper and lower shaft sections of collapsible column have been separated, the slit of the universal joint must align with the punch mark on the upper end of the upper steering shaft.

Fastener	*Torque (ft. lbs.)*
Rubber coupling bolt	11-13
Lower joint bolt	29-36
Side rod stud nut	40-55
Side rod inner socket stopper nut	53-72
Side rod locknut	65

Steering Gear Adjustments

Worm and Roller Adjustment

The backlash adjusting screw is located next to the filler plug on the steering gear box cover.

1. Disconnect the drag link from the steering arm.
2. Loosen the locknut and turn the adjusting screw in clockwise until the mechanism binds.
3. Back off the screw until the unit operates smoothly. Tighten the locknut.
4. Check free play at the end of the steering arm, with the steering gear in the central (straight ahead) position. Free play should be 0-.008″ for the L320 and L520, and 0-.004″ for the L60.
5. Check the force required to turn the steering wheel with a spring scale attached to the wheel rim. It should be .66-1.76 lbs. for the L60, and 1.1-1.5 lbs. for the L320 and L520.
6. Replace the drag link.
7. Maximum permissible play at the steering wheel rim is 1.18″ for the L60, and 1-1.4″ for the other models.

Cam and Lever Adjustment

The adjusting screw is adjacent to the filler plug on the steering gear box cover.

1. Disconnect the steering linkage ball stud from the steering arm.
2. Loosen the locknut and tighten the adjusting screw until there is no steering arm free play in the straight ahead position.
3. Tighten the locknut. Replace the steering linkage.
4. Maximum permissible play at the steering wheel rim is .98-1.38″.

Recirculating Ball Adjustment

The adjusting screw is adjacent to the filler plug on the steering gear box cover.

Recirculating ball steering gear, PL411

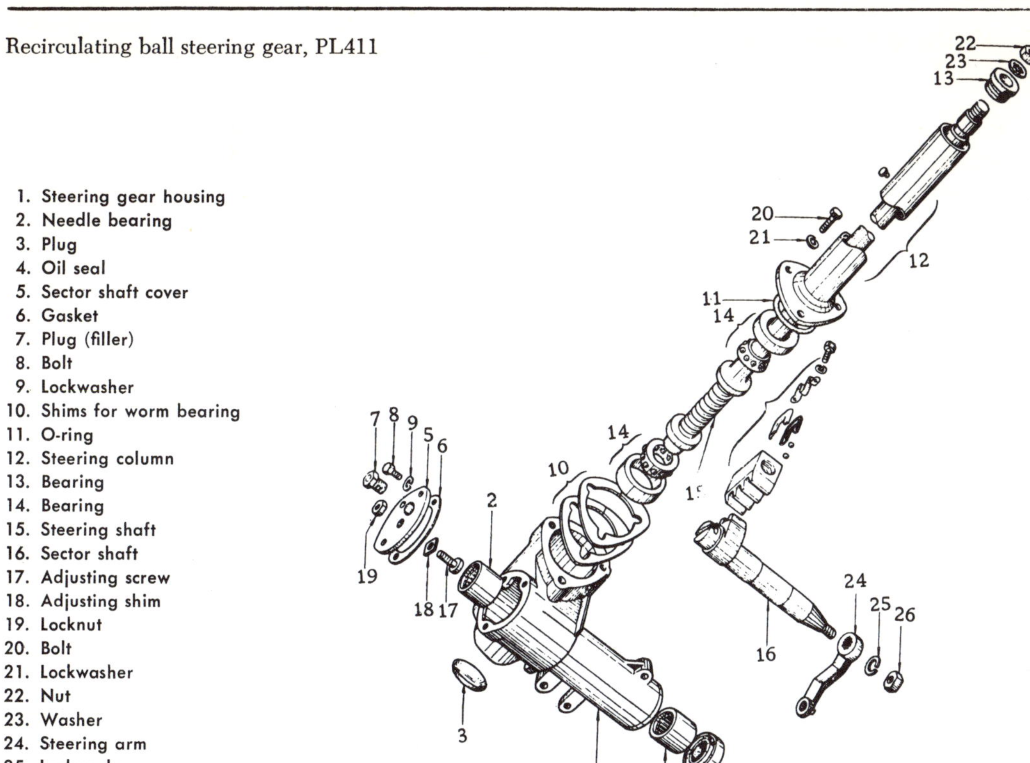

Rack and pinion steering gear, HLS30 (left side shown)

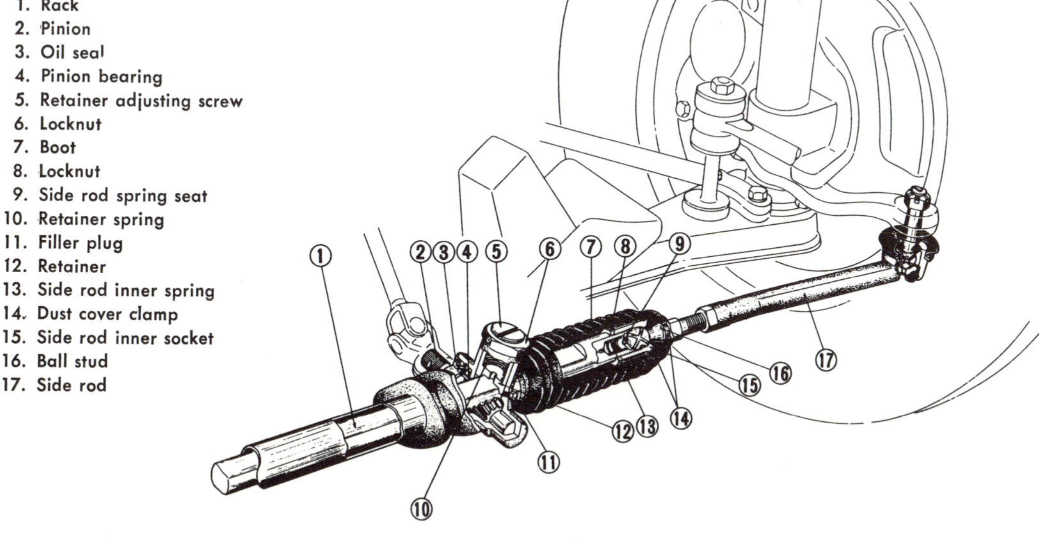

Collapsible shaft and column assembly; SPL311, SRL311, PL510, WPL510

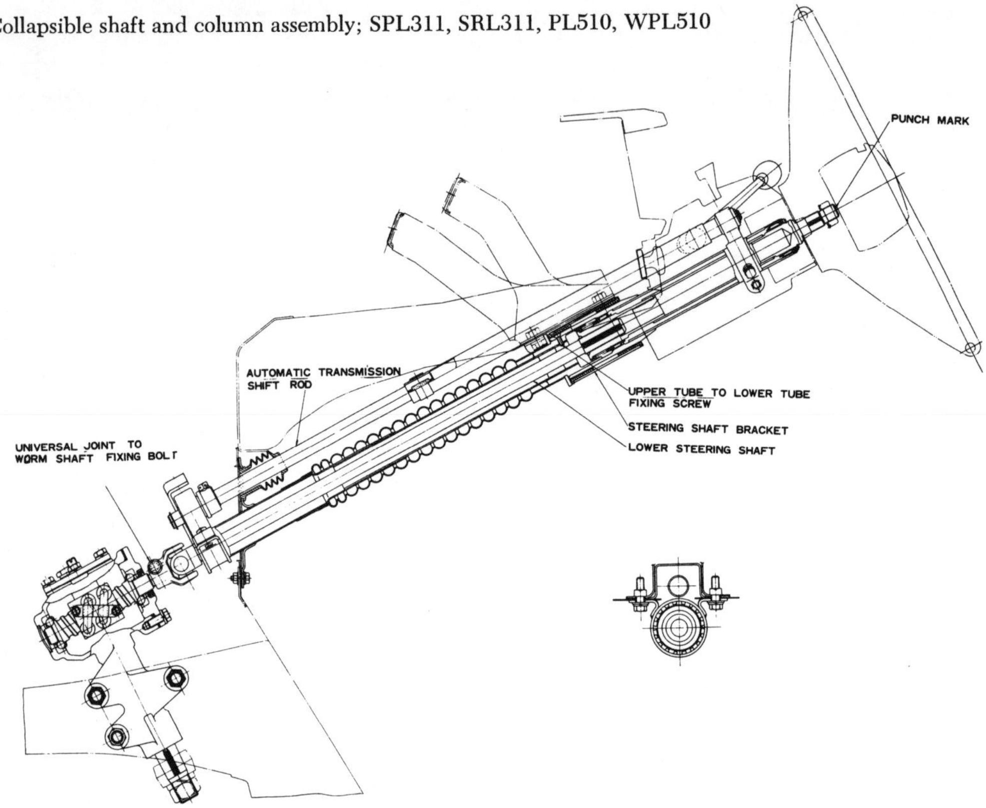

1. Disconnect steering gear arm from steering linkage.
2. Adjust backlash at steering center point so that play at end of steering gear arm is 0-.004″.
3. Tighten adjusting screw 1/8-1/6 turn more and tighten locknut.
4. Reconnect steering linkage. Specified stud nut torque is 22-36 ft. lbs. for the LB110 and KLB110, and 40-55 ft. lbs. for the PL510 and WPL510.
5. Maximum free play at steering wheel rim should be .79-.98″ for the LB110 and KLB110, .98-1.18″ for the PL510 and WPL510, and 1-1.4″ for all other models.

STEERING LOCK

The steering lock/ignition switch/warning buzzer switch assembly is attached to the steering column by special screws whose heads shear off on installation. The screws must be drilled out to remove the assembly. The ignition switch or warning switch can be replaced without removing the assembly. The ignition switch is on the back of the assembly, and the warning switch on the side. The warning buzzer, which sounds when the driver's door is opened with the steering unlocked, is located behind the instrument panel. It is on the left side of the instrument panel on the LB110 and KLB110, and on the steering support on the HLS30.

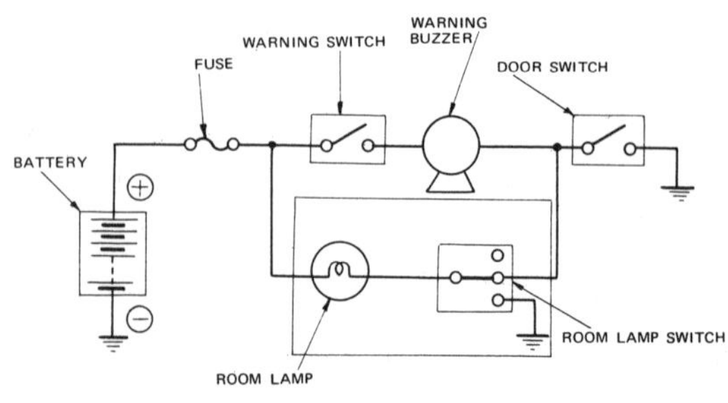

Warning buzzer electrical circuit

Chassis and Wheel Alignment Specifications

Model	Chassis: Wheelbase (in.)	Chassis: Track (in.) Front	Chassis: Track (in.) Rear	Wheel Alignment: Caster (deg.) Range	Wheel Alignment: Caster (deg.) Preferred Setting	Wheel Alignment: Camber (deg.) Range	Wheel Alignment: Camber (deg.) Preferred Setting	Toe-In (in.)	Kingpin Inclination (deg.)	Wheel Pivot Ratio (deg.) Inner Wheel	Wheel Pivot Ratio (deg.) Outer Wheel
L60	86.6	54.6	55.3		1°30′		1°30′	.12-.16	6°45′-7°15′	28	25°32′
WL60	98.4	54.6	55.3		1°30′		1°30′	.12-.16	6°45′-7°15′	28	25°32′
PL410	93.8	47.5	47.0		1°30′		1°30′	.06-.13	6°30′	36	28°36′
SPL310	89.8	47.8	47.1		1°30′		1°26′	.06-.13	6°34′	36	28°36′
PL411	93.7	47.5	47.2		0		1°45′	.06-.13	6°15′	36	28°36′
RL411	93.7	47.5	47.2		0		1°45′	.13	6°15′	36	28°36′
SPL311	89.8	50.2	47.2		1°30′		1°25′	.08-.12	6°35′	36°16′	29°20′
SRL311	89.8	50.2	47.2		1°30′		1°25′	.08-.12	6°35′	36°16′	29°20′
L320	97.2	46.1	46.7		3°30′		1°30′	.08-.12	6	34	29°30′
L520	99.6	49.2	49.9		1°50′	50′-1°50′	1°20′	.08-.12	6	34	29°30′
PL510	95.3	50.4	50.4		1°40′		1	.35-.47	8	38-39	22°30′-33°30′
WPL510	95.3	50.2	49.6		2		1°10′	.12-.24	7°50′	38-39	22°30′-33°30′
L521, PL521	99.6	49.2	49.9		3°50′	50′-1°50′	1°20′	.08-.12	6	34	29°30′
HLS30①	90.7	53.3	53.0	2°25′-3°25′	2°55′	20′-1°20′	50′	08-.20	11°40′-12°40′	32-33	31°24′-32°24′
LB110, KLB110	90.6	48.8	49.0	40′-1°40′	1°10′	35′-1°35′	1°05′	.16-.24	7°55′	42-44	35-37

①—Unloaded

Chapter 9 Brakes

Type

Front disc brakes are used on all current car models, with drum brakes at the rear. All pickups have a drum brake system front and rear. Starting in 1968, all car models are equipped with independent front and rear hydraulic systems with a warning light to indicate loss of pressure in either system. The single circuit master cylinder is retained on pickups. The HLS30 has a vacuum booster system to lessen required pedal pressure. The parking brake, except on the L60, operates the rear brakes through a cable system. On the L60, the handbrake is an external contracting band on the rear output shaft of the transfer case.

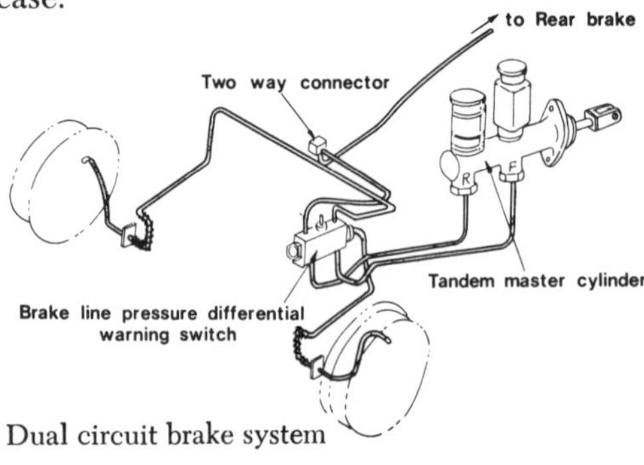

Dual circuit brake system

MASTER CYLINDER

Removal and Installation

Clean the outside of the cylinder thoroughly, particularly around the cap and fluid lines. Disconnect the fluid lines and cap them to exclude dirt. Remove the clevis pin connecting the pushrod to the brake pedal arm inside the vehicle. This pin need not be removed on HLS30 models with the vacuum booster. Unbolt the master cylinder from the firewall and remove. If the pushrod is not adjustable, there will be shims between the cylinder and the firewall. These shims, or the adjustable pushrod, are used to adjust brake pedal free play. After installation, bleed the system and check the pedal free play.

NOTE: Ordinary brake fluid will boil and cause brake failure under the high temperatures developed in disc brake systems. Special fluid for disc brake systems must be used.

Pedal Adjustment

Before adjusting the pedal, make sure that the wheelbrakes are correctly adjusted.

Model	*Pedal free play (in.)*	*Pedal pad free height (in.)*
L60	.25-.75	8.1-8.5
L320, L520	.39-.55	
PL410	.50-1.0	
PL411, RL411	.45	
SPL310	.50-1.0	
SPL311, SRL311	.31-.47	
PL510, WPL510		8.15 manual, 7.76 automatic
LB110, KLB110	.24-.59	5.49-5.65
HLS30		7.99

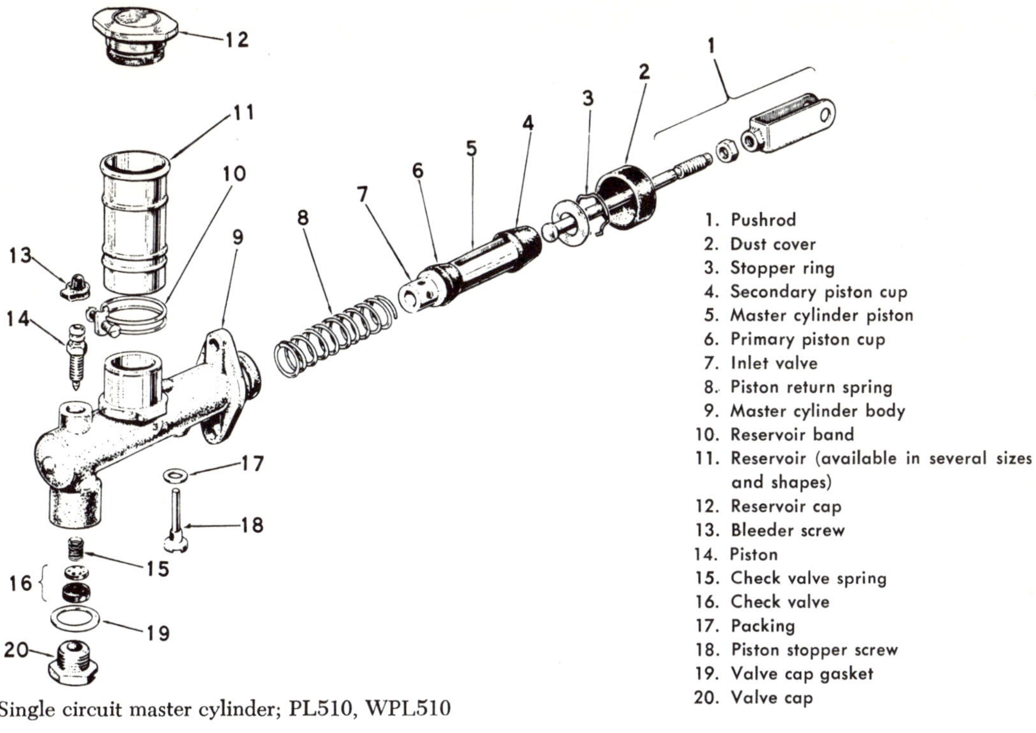

1. Pushrod
2. Dust cover
3. Stopper ring
4. Secondary piston cup
5. Master cylinder piston
6. Primary piston cup
7. Inlet valve
8. Piston return spring
9. Master cylinder body
10. Reservoir band
11. Reservoir (available in several sizes and shapes)
12. Reservoir cap
13. Bleeder screw
14. Piston
15. Check valve spring
16. Check valve
17. Packing
18. Piston stopper screw
19. Valve cap gasket
20. Valve cap

Single circuit master cylinder; PL510, WPL510

Dual circuit master cylinder; PL510, WPL510, SPL311, SRL311

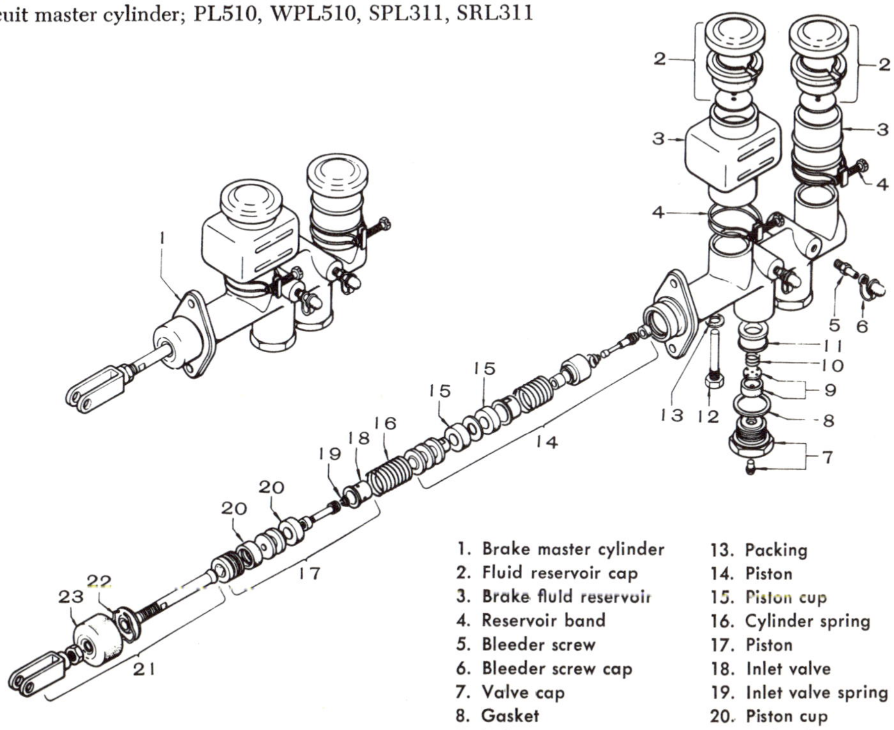

1. Brake master cylinder
2. Fluid reservoir cap
3. Brake fluid reservoir
4. Reservoir band
5. Bleeder screw
6. Bleeder screw cap
7. Valve cap
8. Gasket
9. Valve
10. Valve spring
11. Valve seat
12. Stopper screw
13. Packing
14. Piston
15. Piston cup
16. Cylinder spring
17. Piston
18. Inlet valve
19. Inlet valve spring
20. Piston cup
21. Pushrod
22. Stopper ring
23. Dust cover

PL510, WPL510, LB110, KLB110, HLS30

1. Loosen the stop pad on the brake pedal so that it does not make contact.
2. Adjust the pushrod length to obtain the specified pedal pad height for the PL510 and WPL510, and a pedal height of 8.11″ for the HLS30. On the LB110 and KLB110, adjust the pedal pad height to 5.65″ by changing the number of shims between the master cylinder and the firewall.
3. Tighten the stop pad until the moveable part of the stoplight switch is completely pushed in on the PL510 and WPL510. On the LB110, KLB110, and HLS30, tighten the pedal stop until the specified pedal pad height is obtained. Make sure that the stoplight screw end surface is flush against the bracket.
4. Check that pedal free play is correct and that the stoplight switch functions properly.

All Other Models

Adjust pedal free play to specified figure by means of adjustable pushrod or shims between master cylinder and firewall.

Overhaul

The master cylinder can be disassembled using the illustrations as a guide. Clean all parts in clean brake fluid. Replace cylinder or piston as necessary if clearance between the two exceeds .006″. Lubricate all parts with clean brake fluid on assembly. Master cylinder rebuilding kits, containing all the wearing parts, are available to simplify overhaul.

VACUUM BOOSTER

Test

The vacuum booster is located behind the master cylinder on the firewall. To test the unit:

1. T-connect a vacuum gauge into the vacuum line between the check valve and the booster.
2. Start the engine and run until 19.7″ Hg vacuum is read. Stop the engine.
3. Vacuum should not drop more than .98″ Hg per 15 seconds.
4. Check vacuum line and check valve for leakage before replacing booster unit.

Dual circuit master cylinder, HLS30 with vacuum booster

1. Reservoir cap
2. Brake fluid reservoir
3. Brake fluid reservoir
4. Brake master cylinder
5. Piston assembly
6. Piston cup
7. Cylinder spring
8. Primary piston cup
9. Piston assembly
10. Secondary piston cup
11. Stopper
12. Snap ring
13. Valve spring
14. Check valve assembly
15. Check valve assembly
16. Packing
17. Valve cap screw
18. Stopper bolt
19. Stopper bolt
20. Bleeder

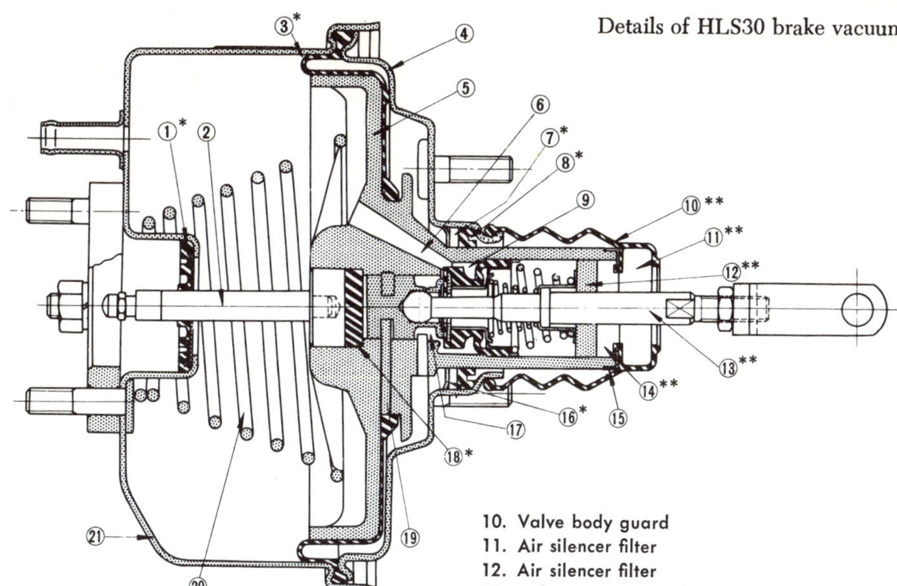

Details of HLS30 brake vacuum booster

1. Plate & seal assembly
2. Push rod
3. Diaphragm
4. Rear shell
5. Power piston (valve body and diaphragm plate)
6. Vacuum route
7. Bearing
8. Seal
9. Vacuum valve
10. Valve body guard
11. Air silencer filter
12. Air silencer filter
13. Valve operating rod assembly
14. Silencer
15. Air silencer retainer
16. Retainer
17. Air valve
18. Reaction disc
19. Stop key
20. Diaphragm return spring
21. Front shell

* Parts in repair Kit A for minor overhaul
** Parts in repair Kit B for major overhaul

Removal and Installation

1. Remove brake pedal clevis pin.
2. Remove master cylinder.
3. Unbolt and remove booster from firewall.
4. Adjust pushrod end height so that it extends .1377-.1575″ above the flange surface. Reverse procedure to install.

Front Disc Brakes

The disc brakes used on the SPL311 and SRL311 are the Dunlop type, manufactured under license in Japan. Lockheed type disc brakes are used on the RL411, PL510, and WPL510. Girling type discs are used on the HLS30, KLB110, and LB110.

Minimum safe disc pad thickness (in.)	*Model*	*Type brakes*
.236	SPL311, SRL311	Dunlop (Sumitomo)
.039	RL411, PL510, WPL510	Lockheed (Akebono)
.063	LB110, KLB110	Girling (Tokiko)
.032	HLS30	Girling (Sumitomo)

Brake Pad Replacement

All four front brake pads must always be replaced as a set. Several grades of pads are available for most models for road use, or racing.

Dunlop Type

1. Jack up car and remove wheel.
2. Remove keeper plate bolt and keeper plate.
3. Pull pads out. A removal tool can easily be made.
4. Thoroughly clean the exposed end of each piston and the caliper assembly. Check rotor (disc) for scoring. If it is badly scored, it must be removed for resurfacing or replacement.
5. Before installing the new pads, the pistons must be pushed back into their cylinders. Be careful not to scratch the pistons or bores.

NOTE: The master cylinder may overflow when the pistons are pushed back. The bleeder screw can be loosened to prevent overflow.

6. Install the new pads. Tighten the bleeder screw if it was loosened.

Dunlop type front disc brake; SPL311, SRL311

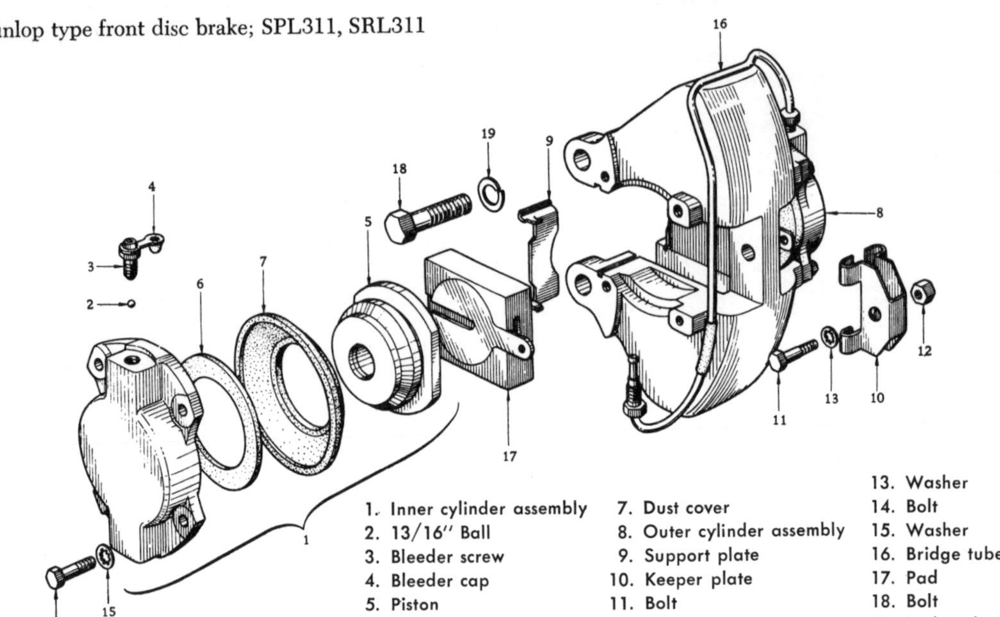

7. Replace the wheels and pump the brake pedal a few times to seat the pads. This must be done before the car is driven.

LOCKHEED TYPE

1. Jack up car and remove wheel.
2. Loosen anti-rattle clip.
3. Loosen bleed screw. Pull caliper plate toward outer end of spindle and push the piston in .118-.157". Be careful not to scratch the pistons or bores.
4. The outer pad can now be pulled out.
5. Pull the caliper plate inward and remove the inner pad.
6. Thoroughly clean the exposed end of each piston and the caliper assembly. Check rotor (disc) for scoring. If it is badly scored, it must be removed for resurfacing or replacement.
7. If the piston has been pushed in far enough, the new pads can be installed.
8. Install the new pads. Tighten the bleeder screw.

GIRLING TYPE

1. Jack up car and remove wheel.
2. Remove clip(s), retaining pins, and anti-squeal clips. Remove coil spring on LB110 and KLB110.
3. Using pliers, pull out pads and anti-squeal shims.
4. Thoroughly clean the exposed end of each piston and the caliper assembly. Check rotor (disc) for scoring. If it is badly scored, it must be removed for resurfacing or replacement.
5. Before installing the new pads, the pistons must be pushed back into their cylinders. Be careful not to scratch the pistons or bores.

NOTE: The master cylinder may overflow when the pistons are pushed back. The bleeder screw can be loosened to prevent overflow.

Be careful not to push the pistons in too far or the seals will be damaged. The pistons need not be pushed in past a position flush with the edge of the cylinder. Install the new pads and tighten the bleeder screw if it was loosened.

6. Install the anti-squeal shims with the arrow marks pointing in the direction of rotor rotation. On LB110, the coil spring should be installed on the retaining pin furthest from the bleed screw.
7. Replace the wheels and pump the brake pedal a few times to seat the pads. This must be done before the car is driven.

Overhaul

LOCKHEED TYPE

1. Jack up and support car. Remove wheel.
2. Disconnect and cap brake hose.
3. Unbolt and remove caliper assembly.

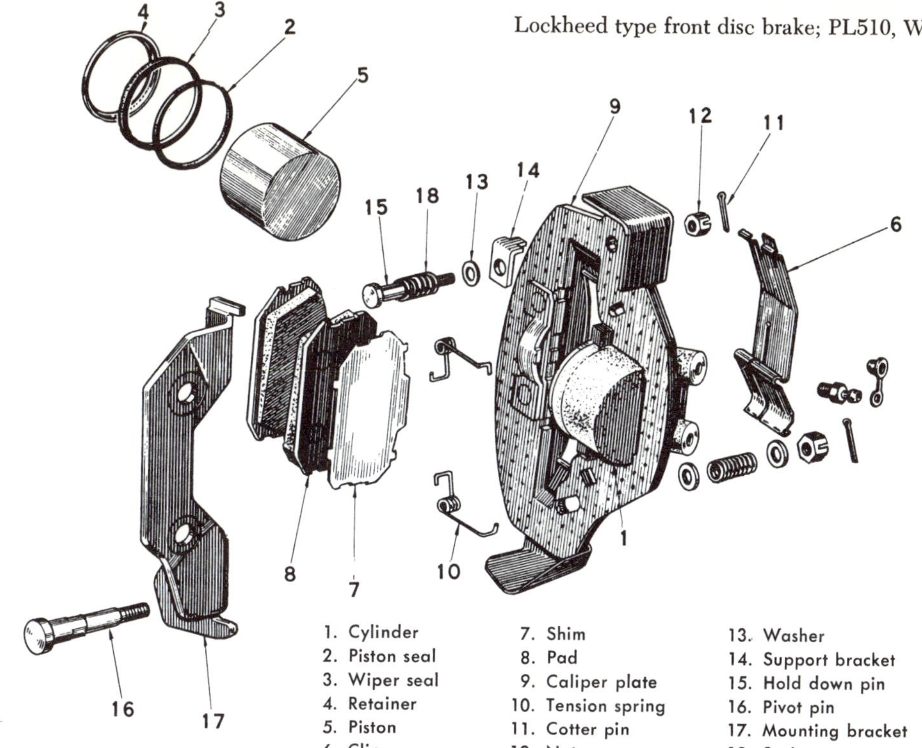

Lockheed type front disc brake; PL510, WPL510

1. Cylinder	7. Shim	13. Washer
2. Piston seal	8. Pad	14. Support bracket
3. Wiper seal	9. Caliper plate	15. Hold down pin
4. Retainer	10. Tension spring	16. Pivot pin
5. Piston	11. Cotter pin	17. Mounting bracket
6. Clip	12. Nut	18. Spring

4. Remove spindle nut and rotor with hub.
5. Unbolt and remove rotor from hub.
6. Remove pads. Remove tension springs and pull out cylinder. Apply air or hydraulic pressure to inlet hole to remove piston from cylinder. Remove retainer and seals. The piston seal also serves to retract the piston and should be replaced at every overhaul.
7. If the rotor is scored, it can be machined. Minimum safe rotor thickness is .331″. Rotor runout must not exceed .0024″.
8. Wash all parts in clean brake fluid. Replace all seals. If cylinder or piston is damaged, replace both.
9. Bolt rotor to hub, torquing bolts to 28-38 ft. lbs. Pack bearings, install hub on spindle, and adjust wheel bearing.
10. Insert new seal in cylinder groove and attach wiper seal. Lubricate cylinder bore with brake fluid. Insert piston cautiously until piston head is almost flush with wiper seal retainer. Relieved part of piston must face pivot pin.
11. Install cylinder into caliper plate and secure with tension springs.
12. Install hold down pin, washer, and nut on support bracket. Install a new cotter pin in the nut.
13. Assemble mounting bracket and caliper plate with pivot pin. Install washer, spring, washer, and nut. Tighten nut completely and lock with a cotter pin.
14. Install caliper assembly to spindle, torquing mounting bolts to 53-65 ft. lbs. Make sure that caliper plate can slide smoothly.
15. Install pads and shims, making sure that they are seated correctly. Seat inner pad first. Make sure anti-rattle clip is positioned correctly.
16. Reconnect brake hose and bleed system.

Girling Type—LB110, KLB110

1. Remove brake pads.
2. Disconnect brake tube.
3. Remove the two bottom strut assembly installation bolts to obtain clearance.
4. Remove caliper assembly mounting bolts.
5. Loosen bleeder screw and press pistons into cylinder.
6. Clamp yoke in a vise and tap yoke head with a hammer to loosen cylinder. Be careful that piston A does not fall out.
7. Remove bias ring from piston A.

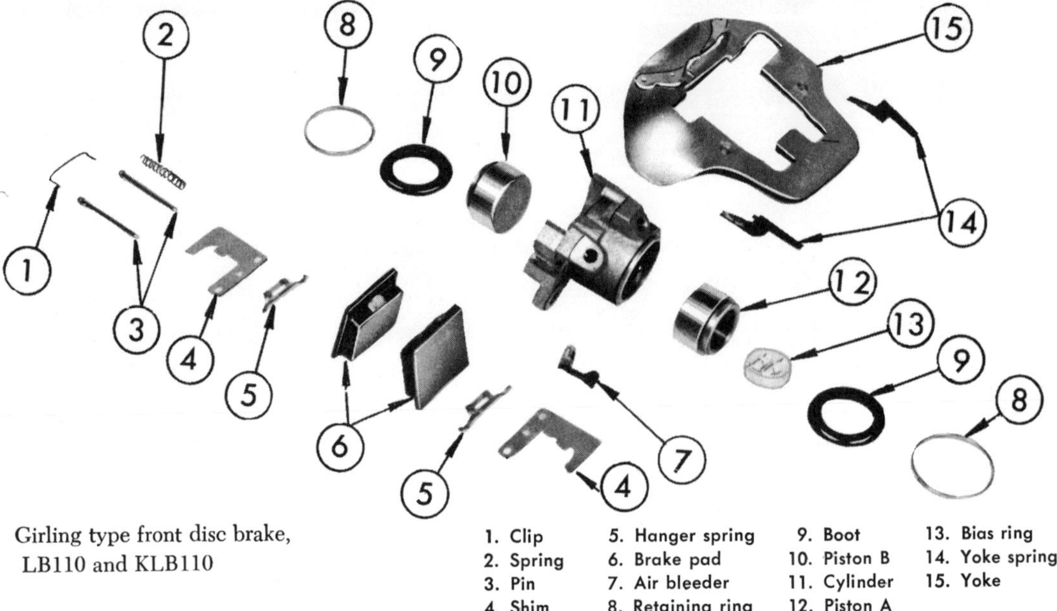

Girling type front disc brake, LB110 and KLB110

1. Clip
2. Spring
3. Pin
4. Shim
5. Hanger spring
6. Brake pad
7. Air bleeder
8. Retaining ring
9. Boot
10. Piston B
11. Cylinder
12. Piston A
13. Bias ring
14. Yoke spring
15. Yoke

Remove retaining rings and boots from both pistons. Depress and remove pistons from cylinder. Remove piston seal from the cylinder carefully with the fingers so as not to mar the cylinder wall.

8. Remove yoke springs from yoke.
9. Wash all parts with clean brake fluid.
10. If piston or cylinder is badly worn or scored, replace both. The piston surface is plated and must not be polished with emery paper. Replace all seals. The rotor can be removed and machined if scored, but final thickness must be at least .331″. Runout must not exceed .0012″.
11. Lubricate cylinder bore with clean brake fluid and install piston seal.
12. Insert bias ring into piston A so that rounded ring portion comes to bottom of piston. Piston A has a small depression inside, while B does not.
13. Lubricate pistons with clean brake fluid and insert into cylinder. Install boot and retaining ring. Yoke groove of bias ring of piston A must align with yoke groove of cylinder.
14. Install yoke springs to yoke so projecting portion faces to disc (rotor).
15. Lubricate sliding portion of cylinder and yoke. Assemble cylinder and yoke by tapping yoke lightly.
16. Replace caliper assembly and pads. Torque mounting bolts to 33-41 ft. lbs. Rotor bolt torque is 20-27 ft. lbs. Strut bolt torque is 33-44 ft. lbs. Bleed the system of air.

Girling Type—HLS30

The caliper halves are not to be separated. If brake fluid leaks from the bridge seal, replace the caliper assembly.

1. Remove pads.
2. Disconnect brake line and caliper mounting bolts.
3. Hold piston in one side and force the other one out with air pressure. Remove the other piston.
4. Remove piston seal from cylinder carefully with the fingers so as not to mar the cylinder wall.
5. Wash all parts with clean brake fluid.
6. If piston or cylinder is badly worn or scored, replace both. The piston surface is plated and must not be polished with emery paper. Replace all seals.
7. With wheel bearing properly adjusted, runout at center of rotor surface should be less then .0059″. The rotor can be resurfaced if scored, but must be at least .413″ thick after resurfacing.
8. Lubricate the piston seal with clean brake fluid and install it.
9. Install dust seals on pistons, lubricate pistons with clean brake fluid, and install pistons into cylinders. Clamp dust seals with retaining rings.
10. Reinstall caliper assembly. Mounting bolt torque is 53-71 ft. lbs. Rotor

Girling type front disc brake, HLS30

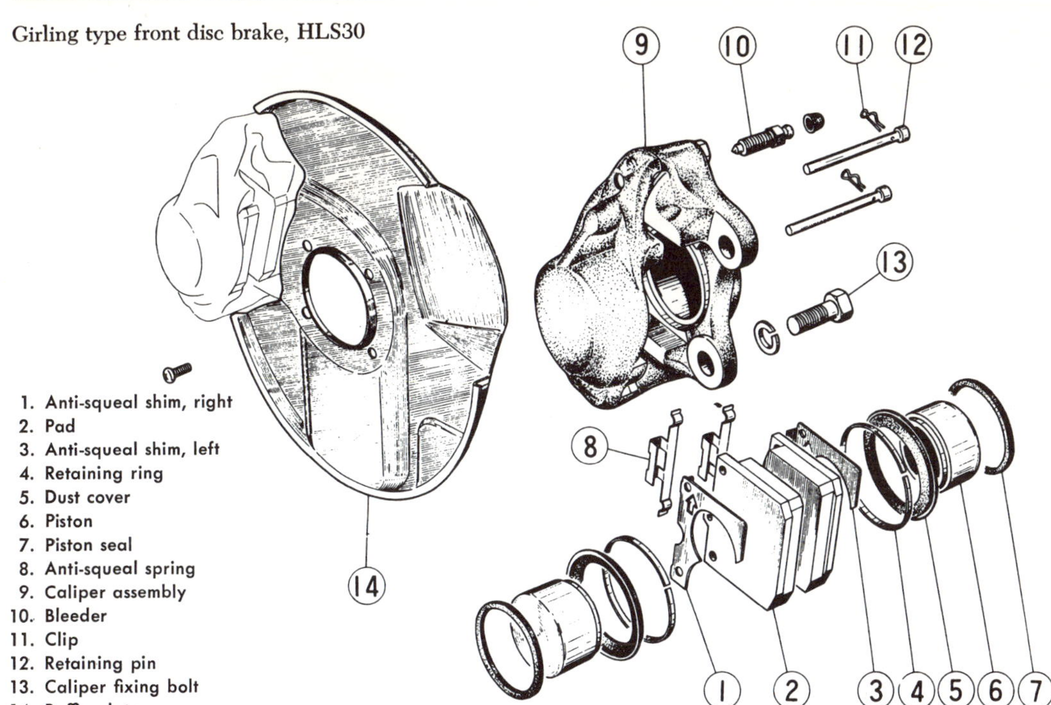

mounting bolt torque is 28-38 ft. lbs.

11. Replace pads and brake line. Bleed system of air.

Adjustment

Disc brakes are self-adjusting for pad wear and require no periodic adjustment. However, the fluid level in the master cylinder will gradually drop as the pads wear. When filling the master cylinder, use only brake fluid specifically designated for disc brakes. Ordinary brake fluid will boil and cause complete loss of braking power at the high operating temperatures attained in disc brakes.

PROPORTIONING VALVE

HLS30

A proportioning valve is installed in the line to the rear brakes on this model to prevent the rear brakes from locking before the front. The valve is operating properly if the front and rear wheels lock simultaneously, or the front wheels lock first. The correct valve is stamped with the part number E4100. Do not use a valve designed for any other vehicle, as the ratio between front and rear pressures will be incorrect. The valve body is marked M on the master cylinder side, and R on the rear brake side. The valve requires no service or adjustment and must be replaced if defective.

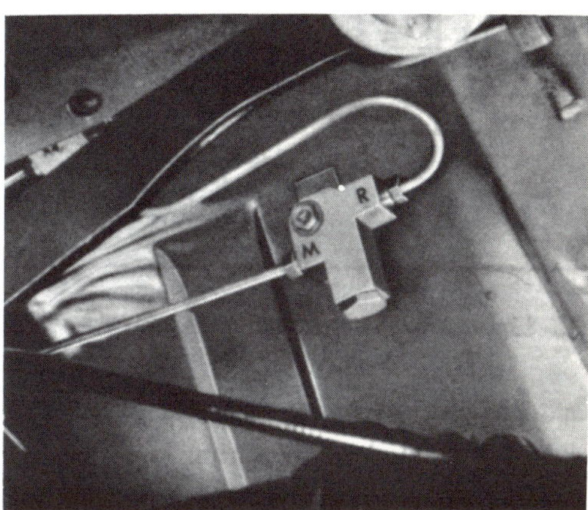

Proportioning valve, HLS30

Drum Brakes

Front drum brakes on all models except the L320 and L520 pickups have two shoes and two hydraulic cylinders at each wheel. These pickups have two shoes and a single hydraulic cylinder at each wheel. The cylinders are bolted to the front brake backing plate. All models have rear drum brakes. Each rear brake assembly has two brake shoes and a single hydraulic cylinder which is free to slide back and forth in a slot in the brake backing plate. On some models the hydraulic cylinder is bolted fast and the adjuster slides.

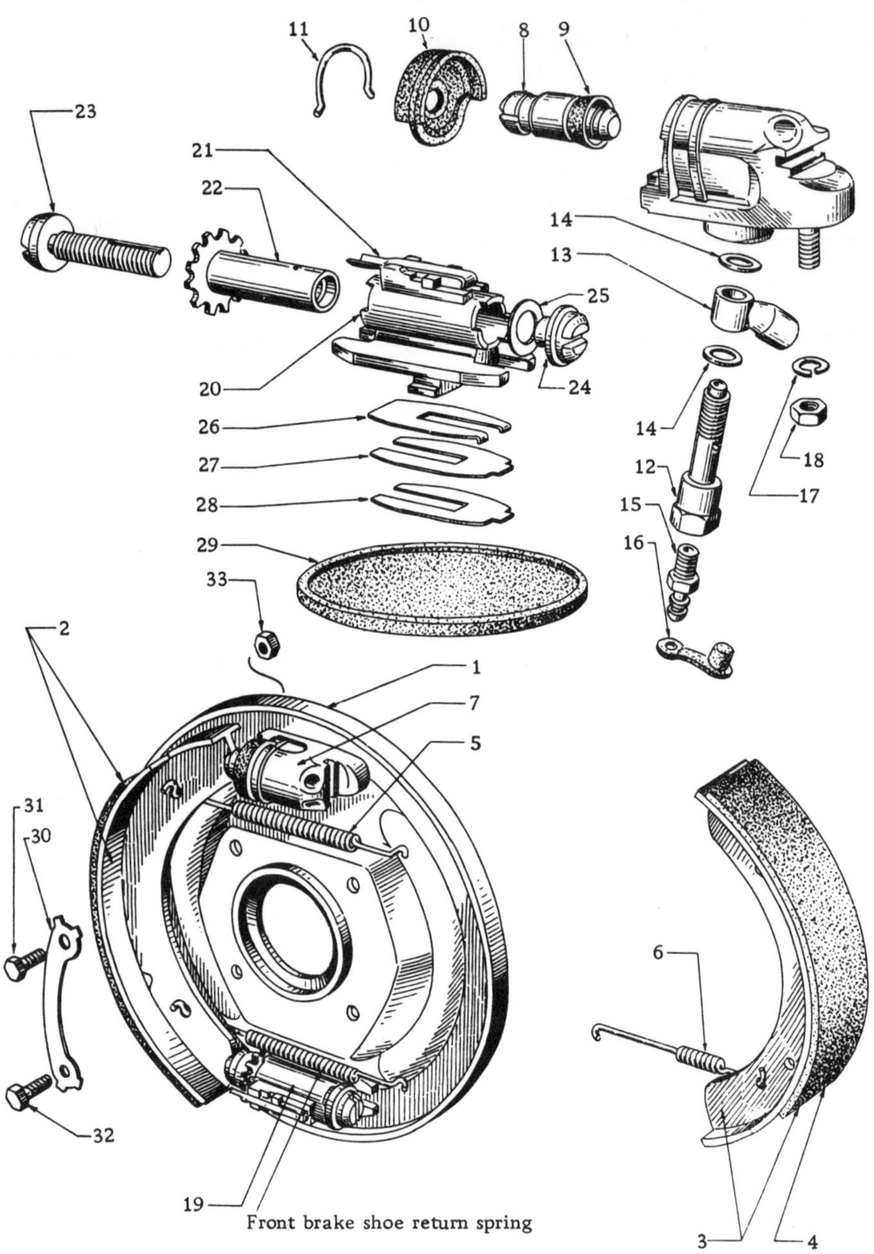

1. Backing plate
2. Forward shoe
3. Rear shoe
4. Lining
5. Rear shoe return spring
6. Rear shoe return spring
7. Wheel cylinder
8. Piston
9. Piston cup
10. Dust shield
11. Dust shield retainer
12. Connector bolt
13. Connector
14. Washer
15. Bleeder screw
16. Bleeder cap
17. Lockwasher
18. Nut
19. Adjuster
20. Adjuster housing
21. Lock spring
22. Adjuster wheel
23. Adjuster screw
24. Adjuster head
25. Adjuster head shim
26. Adjuster retaining spring
27. Retaining spring lock plate
28. Retaining spring adjusting shim
29. Rubber boot
30. Lock plate
31. Bolt
32. Bolt
33. Nut

L520 front brake

Lining Replacement

L60 Front

1. Jack up vehicle. Remove front wheels and brake drums. Loosen brake adjusters if drums are difficult to remove.
2. Lift one shoe first from the wheel cylinder slot at one end, and then from the piston slot at the other. Remove the shoe return springs.
3. Remove the second shoe. Place a heavy rubber band around each cylinder to prevent the piston from coming out.
4. Turn adjusters to fully off position.
5. Clean backing plate and inspect cylinder for leaks. The wheel cylinders are attached to the backing plate by three bolts each.
6. Replace upper shoe first. The short end of the return spring should be attached to the shoe and the long end to the bolt on the backing plate. Replace lower shoe. A very thin film of grease may be applied to the pivot points at the ends of the shoes. Be careful not to get grease on the linings or drums.
7. Replace drums and wheels. Adjust brakes. Bleed the hydraulic system of air if the brake lines were disconnected.

L60 Rear

1. Jack up vehicle, remove wheels and brake drums. Back off adjusters if drums are hard to remove.
2. Remove shoes, one at a time. Place a heavy rubber band around the cylinder to prevent the piston from coming out.
3. Turn adjuster to fully off position.
4. Clean backing plate and inspect for leaks. The wheel cylinder is attached to the backing plate by a spring clip and should be free to slide. A very thin film of grease may be applied behind the wheel cylinder. To remove the adjuster, take off the clip and rubber dust cover and remove the two mounting nuts.
5. Hook the return springs into the new shoes. The springs should be between the shoes and the backing plate. A very thin film of grease may be applied to the pivot points at the ends of the brake shoes. Be careful not to get grease on the linings or drums.
6. Place one shoe in the adjuster and piston slots, and pry the other shoe into position.
7. Replace drums and wheels. Adjust brakes. Bleed the hydraulic system of air if the brake lines were disconnected.

PL510, WPL510 Rear

1. Raise vehicle, remove wheels.
2. Release parking brake. Disconnect cross rod from lever of brake cylinder. Remove brake drum. Place a heavy rubber band around the cylinder to prevent the piston from coming out.
3. Remove return springs and shoes.
4. Clean backing plate and check wheel cylinder for leaks. To remove the wheel cylinder, remove brake line, dust cover, plates, and adjusting shims. Clearance between cylinder and piston should not exceed .0059″.
5. The drums must be machined if scored or out of round more than .002″. The drum inside diameter should not be machined beyond 9.04″. Minimum safe lining thickness is .0591″.
6. Hook the return springs into the new shoes. The springs should be between the shoes and the backing plate. The longer return spring must be adjacent to the wheel cylinder. A very thin film of grease may be applied to the pivot points at the ends of the brake shoes. Grease the shoe locating buttons on the backing plate, also. Be careful not to get grease on the linings or drums.
7. Place one shoe in the adjuster and piston slots, and pry the other shoe into position.
8. Replace drums and wheels. Adjust brakes. Bleed the hydraulic system of air if the brake lines were disconnected.
9. Reconnect the handbrake, making sure that it does not cause the shoes to drag when it is released.

LB110, KLB110 Rear

1. Raise vehicle and remove wheels.
2. Loosen handbrake cable, remove clevis pin from wheel cylinder lever, disconnect handbrake cable, and remove return pull spring.
3. Remove brake drum, shoe retainers, return springs, and brake shoes. Loosen brake adjusters if drums are difficult to remove. Place a heavy rubber band around the cylinder to

L520 rear brake

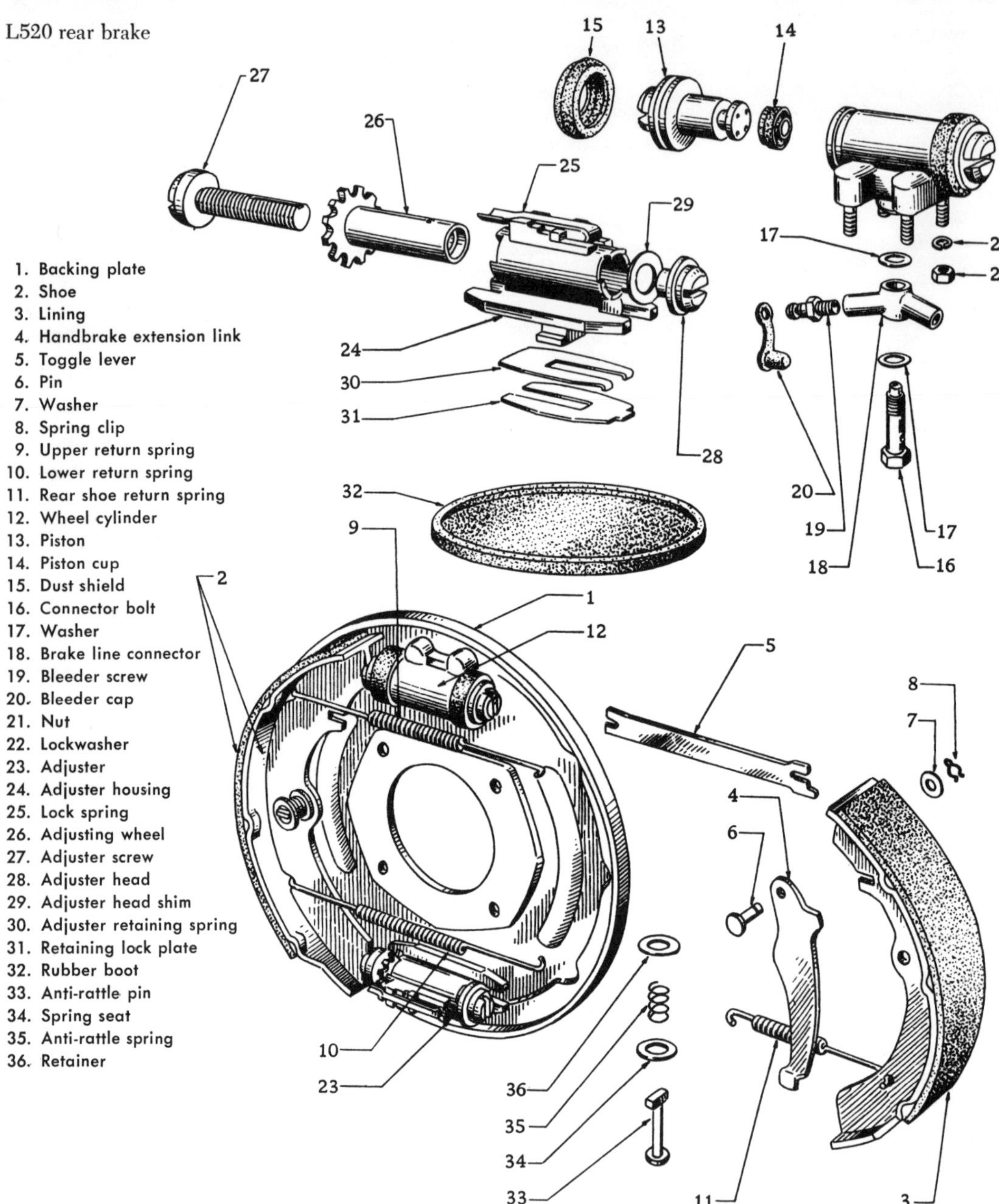

prevent the piston from coming out.

4. Clean backing plate and check wheel cylinder for leaks. To remove the wheel cylinder, remove brake line, dust cover, plates, and adjusting shims. Clearance between cylinder and piston should not exceed .0059″.
5. The drums must be machined if scored or out of round more than .0008″. The drum inside diameter must not be machined beyond 8.04″. Minimum safe lining thickness is .0591″.
6. Follow Steps 6-9 for PL510, WPL510 Rear.

HLS30 Rear

1. Raise and support vehicle. Remove wheel.
2. Remove brake drum. If it is difficult to remove, remove the wheel cylinder lever handbrake clevis pin. Remove the brake drum adjusting hole plug and pry the adjusting lever away from the adjusting wheel with a screwdriver

SPL311, SRL311 rear brake

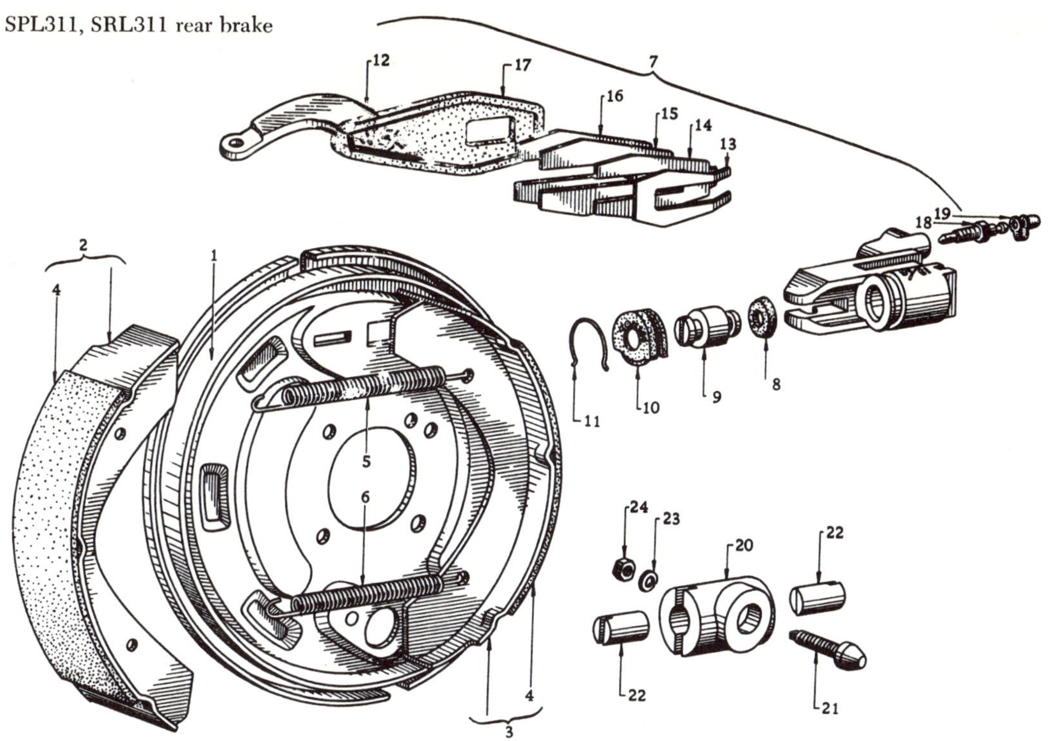

1. Backing plate
2. Forward shoe
3. Rear shoe
4. Brake lining
5. Cylinder side shoe return spring
6. Adjuster side shoe return spring
7. Wheel cylinder assembly
8. Piston cup
9. Cylinder
10. Dust cover
11. Snap-ring
12. Lever
13. Adjusting shim
14. Adjusting shim
15. Plate
16. Plate
17. Dust cover
18. Bleeder screw
19. Bleeder cap
20. Adjuster housing
21. Adjuster wedge
22. Adjuster tappet
23. Lockwasher
24. Nut

inserted through the adjusting hole. Turn the adjusting wheel down with the screwdriver to loosen the brake shoes. Remove the brake drum.

3. Remove the brake shoe retainers and springs. Remove the shoes and return springs. Place a heavy rubber band around the cylinder to prevent the piston from coming out.
4. Clean backing plate and check for wheel cylinder leaks. To remove the wheel cylinder, detach the brake tube and dust cover, drive the lock plate out toward the front, pull the adjusting plate to the rear, and remove the cylinder. Clearance between cylinder and piston should not exceed .006″.
5. The drums should be machined if scored or out of round more than .002″. The drum inside diameter should not be machined beyond 9.04″. Minimum safe lining thickness is .0591″.
6. On reassembly, apply a very light film of grease to all sliding surfaces. Be careful not to get any on the linings or drums. The wheel cylinder must be free to slide. The longer black return spring must be adjacent to the wheel cylinder.

All Other Models

Lining replacement procedures for models not specifically covered above are generally quite similar to the above procedures. Brake drums should not be machined more than .04″ beyond their original inside diameter, and should be machined if scored or out of round more than .002″. Minimum safe lining thickness is .0591″.

Adjustment

There are four basic types of brake adjusting system used.

HLS30 rear brake

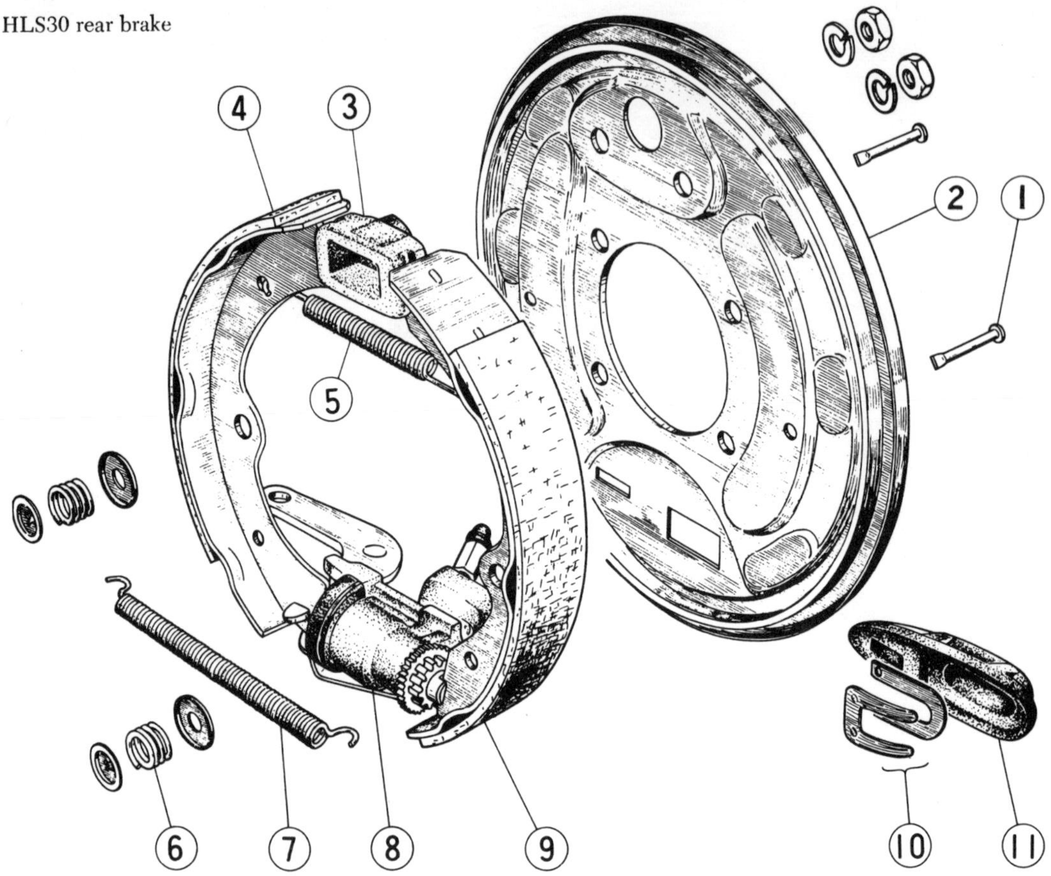

1. Anti-rattle pin
2. Brake backing plate
3. Anchor block
4. After shoe assembly
5. Return spring
6. Anti-rattle spring
7. Return spring
8. Wheel cylinder
9. Fore shoe assembly
10. Retaining shim
11. Dust cover

Loosening HLS30 rear brake adjuster

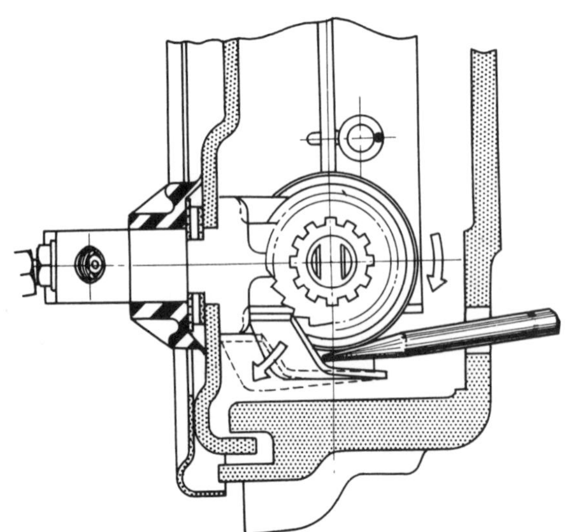

Adjuster type	*Wheel*	*Model*
Bolt	Front	L60, PL410, PL411, SPL310
	Rear	LB110, KLB110
Bolt with click arrangement	Rear	L60, PL410, PL411, RL411, SPL310, SPL311, SRL311, PL510, WPL510
Star wheel	Front, Rear	L320, L520, L521, PL521
Self adjusting	Rear	HLS30

To adjust brakes, raise wheels, disconnect handbrake linkage from rear wheels, apply brakes hard a few times to center drums, and proceed as follows:

Bolt Adjuster

On the front, turn one adjuster bolt on the backing plate until the wheel can no longer be turned, then back off until wheel is free of drag. Repeat the procedure on the other adjuster bolt on the same wheel. On the rear, the adjustment is the same, but one adjuster bolt serves both shoes. The LB110 and KLB110 have two adjusters on each rear wheel.

BOLT ADJUSTER WITH CLICK ARRANGEMENT

This type is used only on rear brakes. The adjuster is located on the backing plate. The adjustment proceeds in clicks or notches. The wheel will often be locked temporarily as the adjuster passes over center for each click. Thus the adjuster is alternately hard and easy to turn. When the wheel is fully locked, back off 1-3 clicks.

STAR WHEEL ADJUSTER

Remove the rubber boot from the backing plate. Insert a screwdriver through the adjusting hole to engage the toothed wheel. Turn the adjuster teeth down until the wheel is locked, then push them up about 12 notches so that the wheel is free of drag.

SELF ADJUSTING

No manual adjustment is required. The self adjusters operate whenever the hand or foot brakes are used.

After Adjustment

After adjusting brakes, reconnect handbrake linkage. Make sure that there is no rear wheel drag with the handbrake released. Loosen the handbrake adjustment if necessary.

Handbrake

HANDBRAKE

Handbrake adjustments are generally not needed, unless the cables have stretched. Before adjusting the handbrake, except on the L60, adjust the rear brakes. There should be no rear wheel drag when the handbrake is released.

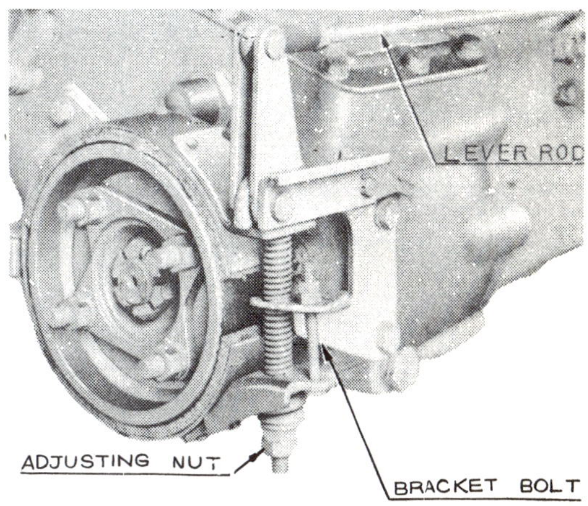

L60 handbrake

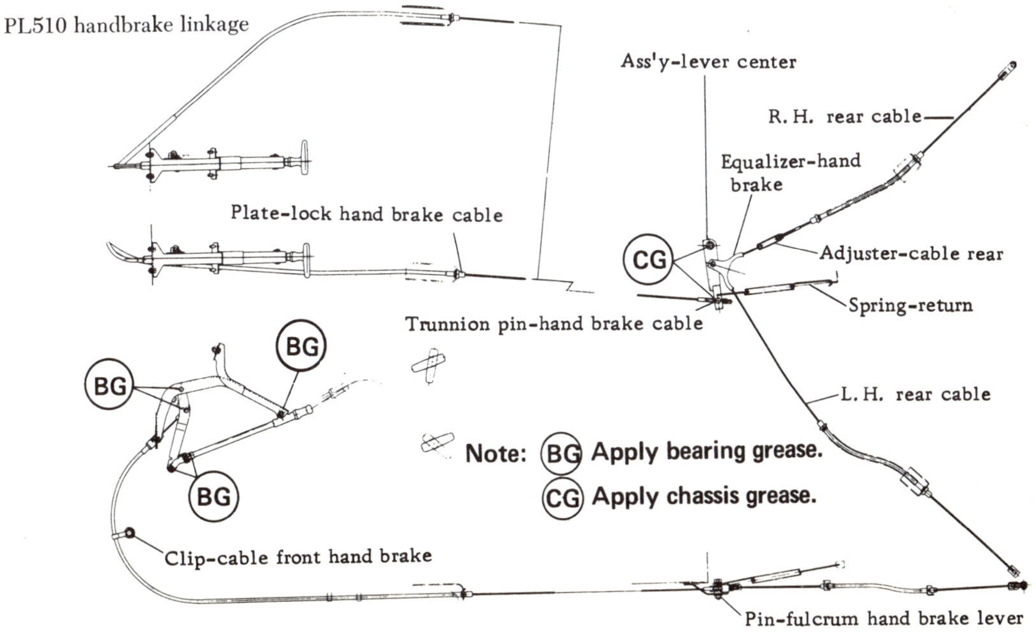

PL510 handbrake linkage

L60

The L60 handbrake is an external contracting band type operating on a drum at the rear of the transfer case. There should be .027-.032″ clearance between the lining and the drum at all points. The upper band is adjusted by an adjusting nut on a large bolt. The lower band is adjusted by a smaller bracket bolt. The length of the rod to the lever can also be adjusted.

All Models Except L60 and HLS30

There is an adjusting nut on the cable under the car, usually at the end of the front cable and near the point at which the two cables from the rear wheels come together (the equalizer). The LB110 and KLB110 have a turnbuckle in the cable. LB110 and KLB110 handbrake lever stroke should be 3.09″ or 6 notches. PL510 handle travel should be 3.35-3.74″. WPL510 handle travel should be 4.33-4.72″.

HLS30

The driveshaft must be removed to gain access to the adjusting nut on the front linkage rod.

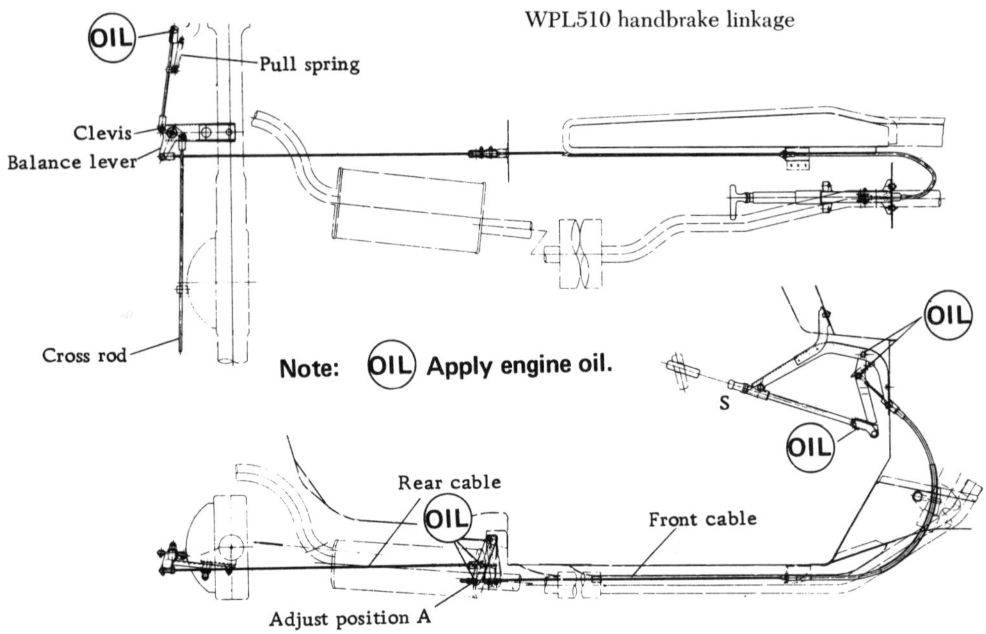

WPL510 handbrake linkage

LB110 and KLB110 handbrake linkage

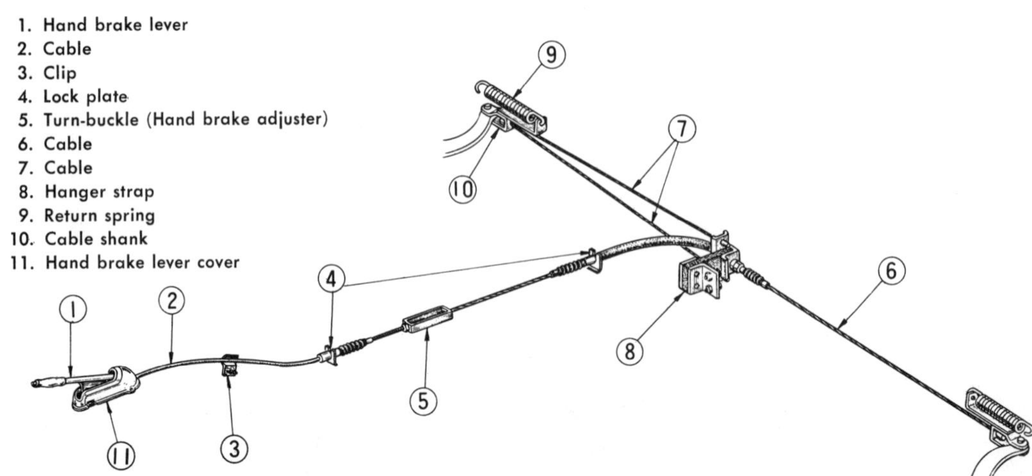

HLS30 handbrake linkage

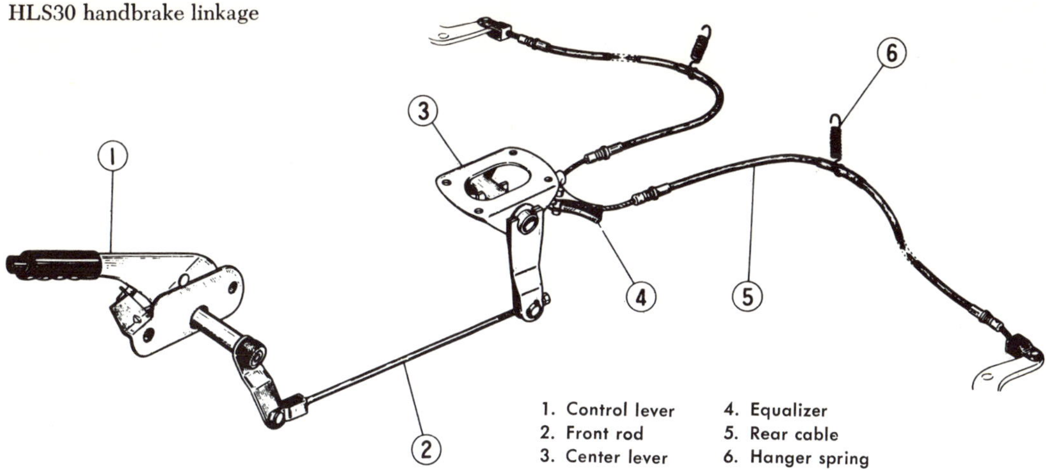

System Bleeding

Bleeding is required whenever air in the hydraulic fluid causes a spongy feeling pedal and sluggish response. This is almost always the case after some part of the hydraulic system has been repaired or replaced.

1. Fill the master cylinder reservoir with the proper fluid. Special fluid is required for disc brakes.
2. The usual procedure is to bleed at the points furthest from the master cylinder first.
3. Fit a rubber hose over the bleeder screw. Submerge the other end of the hose in clean brake fluid in a clear glass container. Loosen the bleeder screw.
4. Slowly pump the brake pedal several times until fluid free of bubbles is discharged. An assistant is required to pump the pedal.
5. On the last pumping stroke, hold the pedal down and tighten the bleeder screw.
6. Bleed the front brakes in the same way as the rear brakes. Note that some front drum brakes have two hydraulic cylinders and two bleeder screws. Both cylinders must be bled.
7. Check that the brake pedal is now firm. If not, repeat the bleeding operation.

Brake Line Pressure Differential Warning Light Switch

A pressure sensitive switch in the engine compartment activates a warning light on the instrument panel when a pressure differential of 185-242 psi exists between the front and rear brake systems on models with dual circuit braking systems. Such a large pressure differential indicates a serious problem, such as a fluid leak, in the system affected. The valve requires no service or adjustment and must be replaced if defective.

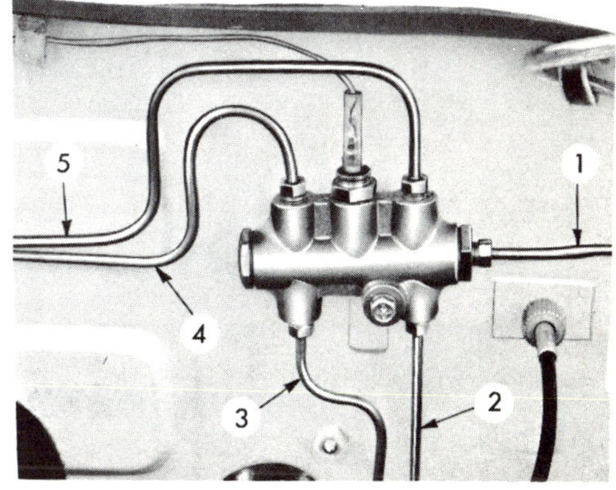

Brake line pressure differential warning light switch

1. To left front brake
2. From master cylinder (Front)
3. From master cylinder (Rear)
4. To rear brakes
5. To right front brake

Brake Specifications

Model	Type		Brake Cylinder Bore (in.)			Brake Drum or Disc Diameter (in.)	
	Front	Rear	Master Cylinder	Wheel Cylinder		Front	Rear
				Front	Rear		
L60	Drum	Drum	1.000	1.000	1.150	11.5	11.5
PL410	Drum	Drum	.875	1.000	.938	N.A.	N.A.
SPL310	Drum	Drum	.875	1.000	.938	N.A.	N.A.
PL411	Drum	Drum	.875	1.000	.938	9.0	9.0
RL411	Disc	Drum	.875	2.000	.938	N.A.	N.A.
SPL311	Disc	Drum	.750	2.125	.813	11.2	9.0
SRL311	Disc	Drum	.750	2.125	.75	11.2	9.0
L320	Drum	Drum	.77	.77	.77	10.0	10.0
L520, L521	Drum	Drum	.750	.750	.750	10.0	10.0
PL510	Disc	Drum	.750	2.000	.813	9.1	9.0
WPL510	Disc	Drum	.750	2.000	.813	9.1	9.0
PL521	Drum	Drum	N.A.	N.A.	N.A.	10.0	10.0
HLS30	Disc	Drum	.875	2.125	.875	10.7	9.0
LB110, KLB110	Disc	Drum	.688	1.894	.688	8.4	8.0

Chapter 10 Body

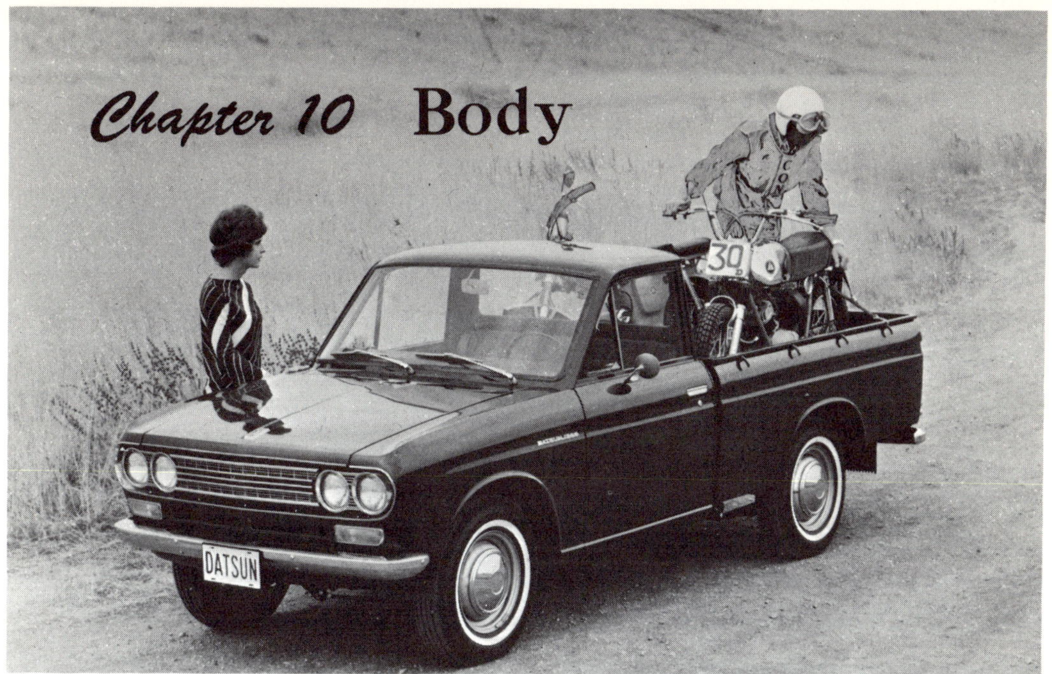

Doors

Removal and Installation

NISSAN PATROL (L60)

1. Remove the door check link from the door.
2. Back off the hinge screws and remove the door.
3. Use a reverse procedure to install, taking care to align the door.
4. Adjustment shims may be placed between the body mounting bracket and frame if necessary.

HLS30

1. The door should be removed with the hinges installed.
2. Disconnect the positive battery cable and the driver's side horn relay on the instrument panel side.
3. Remove the hood lock control installation bracket on the driver's side and the instrument panel side trim.
4. Open the door completely and support with a jack or stand.
5. Remove the door hinge bolts from the body side and remove the door.
6. Install the door using a reverse procedure of the above. Hinge bolt torque is 7–8 ft. lbs.
7. Adjustments can be made at the body side of the hinge.

Door check link

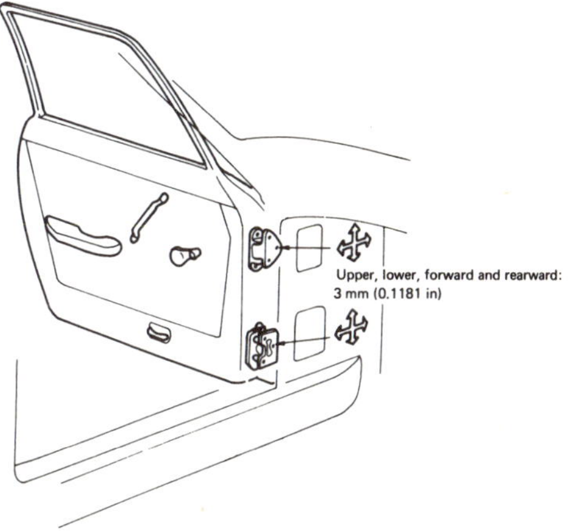

Adjusting door hinges

LB110, KLB110 Front Door

1. Doors should be removed with the hinges attached.
2. Remove the package tray.
3. Remove the hinge access hole cover from the dash side trim.
4. Open the door and support with a jack.

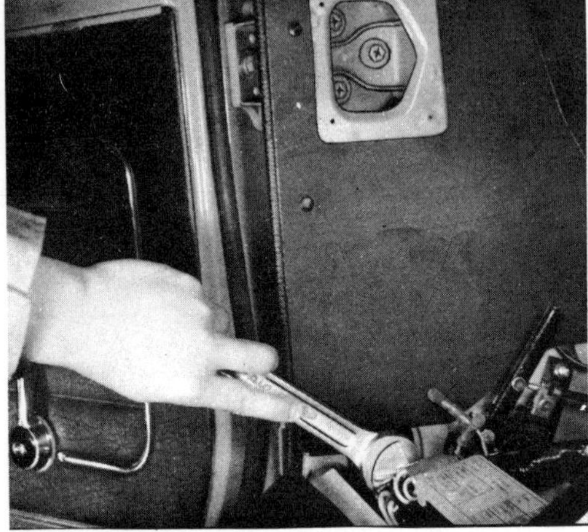

Removing front door hinge bolts

5. Remove the hinge bolts at the body side and remove the door from the body.
6. Reverse the above procedure to install.

Removing rear door hinge bolts

LB110, KLB110 Rear Door

1. Remove the center pillar kick panel and trim. Peel back the body welting on both sides.
2. Follow the same procedure as the front door.
3. Install the door using the reverse of the removal procedure. Torque for both front and rear hinge bolts is 12 ft. lbs.
4. The door striker may be moved to provide additional door adjustment.

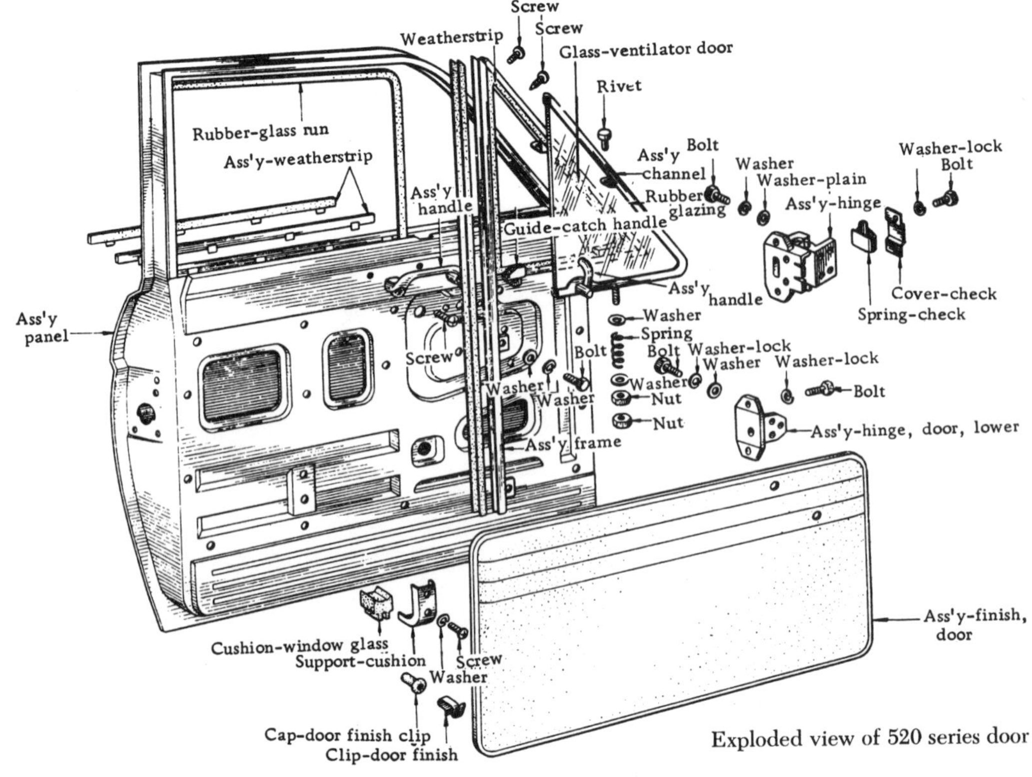

Exploded view of 520 series door

Door Panels

Removal and Installation

L520, L521, PL521 Pickups

1. Remove the inside door handle and the window regulator.
2. Remove the weatherstripping.
3. Unscrew the door clips and remove the panel.
4. Reverse the above procedure to install.

PL411, RL411

1. Remove the inside door handle and window regulator. These are held with a U-shaped clip.
2. Remove the top garnish molding.
3. The door panel is held by spring clips. Carefully pull the panel towards you and release the clips.
4. Reverse the above procedure to install

LB110, KLB110

1. Remove the door handle, lock handle escutcheon, and arm rest.
2. Remove the ash tray outer case and the ash tray.
3. The door panel is held by spring clips. Carefully pull the panel towards you and release the clips.
4. To install, reverse the above procedure.

HLS30

1. Remove the inside handle, escutcheon, and window regulator.
2. Remove the arm rest, grab handle, and door lock knob.
3. Gently pry the panel out with a screwdriver and unhook the door panel clips.
4. Raise the panel and remove it.
5. Reverse the above procedure to install.

Engine Hood Alignment

Nissan Patrol (L60)

Two adjustments are possible to align the hood. The hood lock striker may be moved to correct misalignment and the hood hinges may also be moved to facilitate alignment.

PL411, RL411, L520, L521, PL521

Remove the center bolt of the hood release spring and adjust for correct locking position. Lateral misalignment can be corrected at the hood hinges.

LB110, KLB110, HLS30

The hood lock on these models allows lateral adjustment on the male side lock and longitudinal adjustment on the female side.

PL510, WPL510

Hood alignment adjustment is provided at the hood hinges.

Tailgate Alignment

HLS30

Adjustment is made at the section between the hinge and the body. The tailgate lock and stopper also provide adjustment.

Fuel Tank Removal

PL510

1. Remove the rear seat, seat back, and back trim.
2. Remove the trunk finishing panel from within the trunk.
3. Disconnect the gauge unit lead wire and drain the tank.
4. Remove the filler tube.
5. Remove the retaining bolts and disconnect the rubber lines for fuel outlet and return from the tank.
6. Remove the tank.

WPL510

1. Disconnect fuel lines and gauge wire.
2. Remove the four retaining bolts and remove the tank from underneath the car.

LB110, KLB110

1. Remove the drain plug from the tank bottom and completely drain the tank.
2. Remove the fuel lines.
3. Remove the trunk finishing panel.
4. Remove the four bolts retaining the tank.

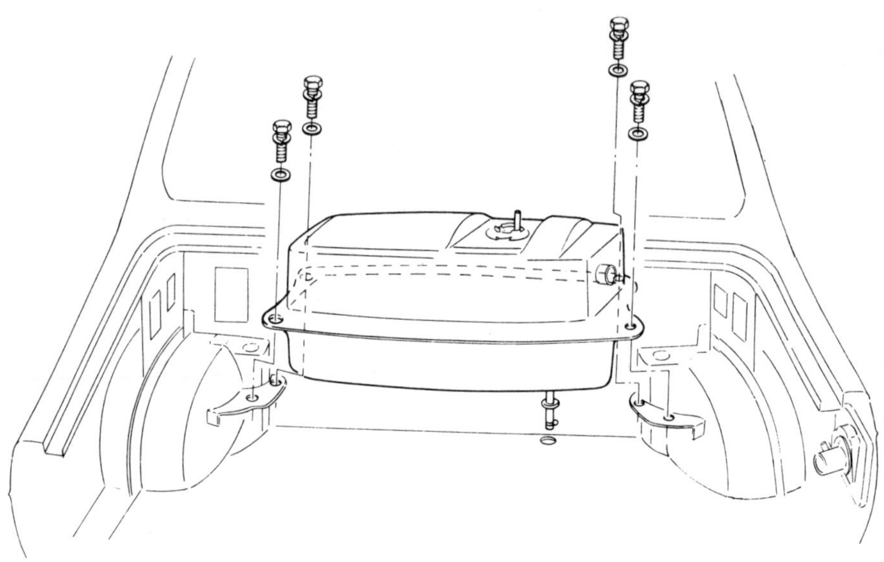

Fuel tank removal LB110

5. Disconnect the hose clamp and gauge wire.
6. Remove the fuel tank.

HLS30

1. Remove the drain plug from the tank bottom, and completely drain the tank.
2. Disconnect the gauge wire, outlet tube, and return hoses from the tank.
3. Remove the two tank securing band nuts and slightly lower the tank.
4. Disconnect the three ventilation tubes and the filler hose from the tank.
5. Remove the fuel tank.
6. Disconnect the breather tube and air tube (used to connect the filler hose to the reservoir), remove the three reservoir bolts, and remove the reservoir.

Appendix

General Conversion Table

Multiply by	*To convert*	*To*	
2.54	Inches	Centimeters	.3937
30.48	Feet	Centimeters	.0328
.914	Yards	Meters	1.094
1.609	Miles	Kilometers	.621
.645	Square inches	Square cm.	.155
.836	Square yards	Square meters	1.196
16.39	Cubic inches	Cubic cm.	.061
28.3	Cubic feet	Liters	.0353
.4536	Pounds	Kilograms	2.2045
4.546	Gallons	Liters	.22
.068	Lbs./sq. in. (psi)	Atmospheres	14.7
.138	Foot pounds	Kg. m.	7.23
1.014	H.P. (DIN)	H.P. (SAE)	.9861
——	To obtain	From	Multiply by

Note: 1 cm. equals 10 mm.; 1 mm. equals .0394″.

Conversion—Common Fractions to Decimals and Millimeters

Inches			Inches			Inches		
Common Fractions	*Decimal Fractions*	*Millimeters (approx.)*	*Common Fractions*	*Decimal Fractions*	*Millimeters (approx.)*	*Common Fractions*	*Decimal Fractions*	*Millimeters (approx.)*
1/128	.008	0.20	11/32	.344	8.73	43/64	.672	17.07
1/64	.016	0.40	23/64	.359	9.13	11/16	.688	17.46
1/32	.031	0.79	3/8	.375	9.53	45/64	.703	17.86
3/64	.047	1.19	25/64	.391	9.92	23/32	.719	18.26
1/16	.063	1.59	13/32	.406	10.32	47/64	.734	18.65
5/64	.078	1.98	27/64	.422	10.72	3/4	.750	19.05
3/32	.094	2.38	7/16	.438	11.11	49/64	.766	19.45
7/64	.109	2.78	29/64	.453	11.51	25/32	.781	19.84
1/8	.125	3.18	15/32	.469	11.91	51/64	.797	20.24
9/64	.141	3.57	31/64	.484	12.30	13/16	.813	20.64
5/32	.156	3.97	1/2	.500	12.70	53/64	.828	21.03
11/64	.172	4.37	33/64	.516	13.10	27/32	.844	21.43
3/16	.188	4.76	17/32	.531	13.49	55/64	.859	21.83
13/64	.203	5.16	35/64	.547	13.89	7/8	.875	22.23
7/32	.219	5.56	9/16	.563	14.29	57/64	.891	22.62
15/64	.234	5.95	37/64	.578	14.68	29/32	.906	23.02
1/4	.250	6.35	19/32	.594	15.08	59/64	.922	23.42
17/64	.266	6.75	39/64	.609	15.48	15/16	.938	23.81
9/32	.281	7.14	5/8	.625	15.88	61/64	.953	24.21
19/64	.297	7.54	41/64	.641	16.27	31/32	.969	24.61
5/16	.313	7.94	21/32	.656	16.67	63/64	.984	25.00
21/64	.328	8.33						

Conversion—Millimeters to Decimal Inches

mm	inches	mm	inches	mm	inches	mm	inches	mm	inches
1	.039 370	31	1.220 470	61	2.401 570	91	3.582 670	210	8.267 700
2	.078 740	32	1.259 840	62	2.440 940	92	3.622 040	220	8.661 400
3	.118 110	33	1.299 210	63	2.480 310	93	3.661 410	230	9.055 100
4	.157 480	34	1.338 580	64	2.519 680	94	3.700 780	240	9.448 800
5	.196 850	35	1.377 949	65	2.559 050	95	3.740 150	250	9.842 500
6	.236 220	36	1.417 319	66	2.598 420	96	3.779 520	260	10.236 200
7	.275 590	37	1.456 689	67	2.637 790	97	3.818 890	270	10.629 900
8	.314 960	38	1.496 050	68	2.677 160	98	3.858 260	280	11.032 600
9	.354 330	39	1.535 430	69	2.716 530	99	3.897 630	290	11.417 300
10	.393 700	40	1.574 800	70	2.755 900	100	3.937 000	300	11.811 000
11	.433 070	41	1.614 170	71	2.795 270	105	4.133 848	310	12.204 700
12	.472 440	42	1.653 540	72	2.834 640	110	4.330 700	320	12.598 400
13	.511 810	43	1.692 910	73	2.874 010	115	4.527 550	330	12.992 100
14	.551 180	44	1.732 280	74	2.913 380	120	4.724 400	340	13.385 800
15	.590 550	45	1.771 650	75	2.952 750	125	4.921 250	350	13.779 500
16	.629 920	46	1.811 020	76	2.992 120	130	5.118 100	360	14.173 200
17	.669 290	47	1.850 390	77	3.031 490	135	5.314 950	370	14.566 900
18	.708 660	48	1.889 760	78	3.070 860	140	5.511 800	380	14.960 600
19	.748 030	49	1.929 130	79	3.110 230	145	5.708 650	390	15.354 300
20	.787 400	50	1.968 500	80	3.149 600	150	5.905 500	400	15.748 000
21	.826 770	51	2.007 870	81	3.188 970	155	6.102 350	500	19.685 000
22	.866 140	52	2.047 240	82	3.228 340	160	6.299 200	600	23.622 000
23	.905 510	53	2.086 610	83	3.267 710	165	6.496 050	700	27.559 000
24	.944 880	54	2.125 980	84	3.307 080	170	6.692 900	800	31.496 000
25	.984 250	55	2.165 350	85	3.346 450	175	6.889 750	900	35.433 000
26	1.023 620	56	2.204 720	86	3.385 820	180	7.086 600	1000	39.370 000
27	1.062 990	57	2.244 090	87	3.425 190	185	7.283 450	2000	78.740 000
28	1.102 360	58	2.283 460	88	3.464 560	190	7.480 300	3000	118.110 000
29	1.141 730	59	2.322 830	89	3.503 903	195	7.677 150	4000	157.480 000
30	1.181 100	60	2.362 200	90	3.543 300	200	7.874 000	5000	196.850 000

To change decimal millimeters to decimal inches, position the decimal point where desired on either side of the millimeter measurement shown and reset the inches decimal by the same number of digits in the same direction. For example, to convert .001 mm into decimal inches, reset the decimal behind the 1 mm (shown on the chart) to .001; change the decimal inch equivalent (.039" shown) to .00039").

Tap Drill Sizes

National Fine or S.A.E.		
Screw & Tap Size	**Threads Per Inch**	**Use Drill Number**
No. 5	44	37
No. 6	40	33
No. 8	36	29
No. 10	32	21
No. 12	28	15
1/4	28	3
5/16	24	1
3/8	24	Q
7/16	20	W
1/2	20	29/64
9/16	18	33/64
5/8	18	37/64
3/4	16	11/16
7/8	14	13/16
1 1/8	12	1 3/64
1 1/4	12	1 11/64
1 1/2	12	1 27/64

National Coarse or U.S.S.		
Screw & Tap Size	**Threads Per Inch**	**Use Drill Number**
No. 5	40	39
No. 6	32	36
No. 8	32	29
No. 10	24	25
No. 12	24	17
1/4	20	8
5/16	18	F
3/8	16	5/16
7/16	14	U
1/2	13	27/64
9/16	12	31/64
5/8	11	17/32
3/4	10	21/32
7/8	9	49/64
1	8	7/8
1 1/8	7	63/64
1 1/4	7	1 7/64
1 1/2	6	1 11/32

Decimal Equivalent Size of the Number Drills

Drill No.	Decimal Equivalent	Drill No.	Decimal Equivalent	Drill No.	Decimal Equivalent
80	.0135	53	.0595	26	.1470
79	.0145	52	.0635	25	.1495
78	.0160	51	.0670	24	.1520
77	.0180	50	.0700	23	.1540
76	.0200	49	.0730	22	.1570
75	.0210	48	.0760	21	.1590
74	.0225	47	.0785	20	.1610
73	.0240	46	.0810	19	.1660
72	.0250	45	.0820	18	.1695
71	.0260	44	.0860	17	.1730
70	.0280	43	.0890	16	.1770
69	.0292	42	.0935	15	.1800
68	.0310	41	.0960	14	.1820
67	.0320	40	.0980	13	.1850
66	.0330	39	.0995	12	.1890
65	.0350	38	.1015	11	.1910
64	.0360	37	.1040	10	.1935
63	.0370	36	.1065	9	.1960
62	.0380	35	.1100	8	.1990
61	.0390	34	.1110	7	.2010
60	.0400	33	.1130	6	.2040
59	.0410	32	.1160	5	.2055
58	.0420	31	.1200	4	.2090
57	.0430	30	.1285	3	.2130
56	.0465	29	.1360	2	.2210
55	.0520	28	.1405	1	.2280
54	.0550	27	.1440		

Decimal Equivalent Size of the Letter Drills

Letter Drill	Decimal Equivalent	Letter Drill	Decimal Equivalent	Letter Drill	Decimal Equivalent
A	.234	J	.277	S	.348
B	.238	K	.281	T	.358
C	.242	L	.290	U	.368
D	.246	M	.295	V	.377
E	.250	N	.302	W	.386
F	.257	O	.316	X	.397
G	.261	P	.323	Y	.404
H	.266	Q	.332	Z	.413
I	.272	R	.339		

ANTI-FREEZE INFORMATION

Freezing and Boiling Points of Solutions According to Percentage of Alcohol or Ethylene Glycol

Freezing Point of Solution	Alcohol Volume %	Alcohol Solution Boils at	Ethylene Glycol Volume %	Ethylene Glycol Solution Boils at
20°F.	12	196°F.	16	216°F.
10°F.	20	189°F.	25	218°F.
0°F.	27	184°F.	33	220°F.
–10°F.	32	181°F.	39	222°F.
–20°F.	38	178°F.	44	224°F.
–30°F.	42	176°F.	48	225°F.

Note: above boiling points are at sea level. For every 1,000 feet of altitude, boiling points are approximately 2°F. lower than those shown. For every pound of pressure exerted by the pressure cap, the boiling points are approximately 3°F. higher than those shown.

To Increase the Freezing Protection of Anti-Freeze Solutions Already Installed

Cooling System Capacity Quarts	Number of Quarts of **ALCOHOL** Anti-Freeze Required to Increase Protection													
	From +20°F. to					From +10°F. to					From 0°F. to			
	0°	−10°	−20°	−30°	−40°	0°	−10°	−20°	−30°	−40°	−10°	−20°	−30°	−40°
10	2	2 3/4	3 1/2	4	4 1/2	1	2	2 2/3	3 1/4	3 3/4	1	1 3/4	2 1/2	3
12	2 1/2	3 1/4	4	4 3/4	5 1/4	1 1/4	2 1/4	3	3 3/4	4 1/2	1 1/4	2	2 3/4	3 1/2
14	3	4	4 3/4	5 1/2	6	1 1/2	2 1/2	3 1/2	4 1/2	5	1 1/4	2 1/2	3 1/4	4
16	3 1/4	4 1/2	5 1/2	6 1/4	7	1 3/4	3	4	5	5 3/4	1 1/2	2 3/4	3 3/4	4 3/4
18	3 3/4	5	6	7	7 3/4	2	3 1/4	4 1/2	5 3/4	6 1/2	1 3/4	3	4 1/4	5 1/4
20	4	5 1/2	6 3/4	7 3/4	8 3/4	2	3 1/4	5	6 1/4	7 1/4	1 3/4	3 1/2	4 3/4	5 3/4
22	4 1/2	6	7 1/2	8 1/2	9 1/2	2 1/4	4	5 1/2	6 3/4	8	2	3 3/4	5 1/4	6 1/2
24	5	6 3/4	8	9 1/4	10 1/2	2 1/2	4 1/2	6	7 1/2	8 3/4	2 1/4	4	5 1/2	7
26	5 1/4	7 1/4	8 3/4	10	11 1/4	2 3/4	4 3/4	6 1/2	8	9 1/2	2 1/2	4 1/2	6	7 1/2
28	5 3/4	7 3/4	9 1/2	11	12	3	5 1/4	7	8 3/4	10 1/4	2 1/2	4 3/4	6 1/2	8
30	6	8 1/4	10	11 3/4	13	3	5 1/2	7 1/2	9 1/4	10 3/4	2 3/4	5	7	8 3/4

Test radiator solution with proper tester. Determine from the table the number of quarts of solution to be drawn off from a full cooling system and replace with concentrated anti-freeze, to give the desired increased protection. For example, to increase protection of a 22-quart cooling system containing Alcohol anti-freeze, from +10°F. to −20°F. will require the replacement of 5 1/2 quarts of solution with concentrated anti-freeze.

Cooling System Capacity Quarts	Number of Quarts of **ETHYLENE GLYCOL** Anti-Freeze Required to Increase Protection													
	From +20°F. to					From +10°F. to					From 0°F. to			
	0°	−10°	−20°	−30°	−40°	0°	−10°	−20°	−30°	−40°	−10°	−20°	−30°	−40°
10	1 3/4	2 1/4	3	3 1/2	3 3/4	3/4	1 1/2	2 1/4	2 3/4	3 1/4	3/4	1 1/2	2	2 1/2
12	2	2 3/4	3 1/2	4	4 1/2	1	1 3/4	2 1/2	3 1/4	3 3/4	1	1 3/4	2 1/2	3 1/4
14	2 1/4	3 1/4	4	4 3/4	5 1/2	1 1/4	2	3	3 3/4	4 1/2	1	2	3	3 1/2
16	2 1/2	3 1/2	4 1/2	5 1/4	6	1 1/4	2 1/2	3 1/2	4 1/4	5 1/4	1 1/4	2 1/4	3 1/4	4
18	3	4	5	6	7	1 1/2	2 3/4	4	5	5 3/4	1 1/2	2 1/2	3 3/4	4 3/4
20	3 1/4	4 1/2	5 3/4	6 3/4	7 1/2	1 3/4	3	4 1/4	5 1/2	6 1/2	1 1/2	2 3/4	4 1/4	5 1/4
22	3 1/2	5	6 1/4	7 1/4	8 1/4	1 3/4	3 1/4	4 3/4	6	7 1/4	1 3/4	3 1/4	4 1/2	5 1/2
24	4	5 1/2	7	8	9	2	3 1/2	5	6 1/2	7 1/2	1 3/4	3 1/2	5	6
26	4 1/4	6	7 1/2	8 3/4	10	2	4	5 1/2	7	8 1/4	2	3 3/4	5 1/2	6 3/4
28	4 1/2	6 1/4	8	9 1/2	10 1/2	2 1/4	4 1/4	6	7 1/2	9	2	4	5 3/4	7 1/4
30	5	6 3/4	8 1/2	10	11 1/2	2 1/2	4 1/2	6 1/2	8	9 1/2	2 1/4	4 1/4	6 1/4	7 3/4

Test radiator solution with proper hydrometer. Determine from the table the number of quarts of solution to be drawn off from a full cooling system and replace with undiluted anti-freeze, to give the desired increased protection. For example, to increase protection of a 22-quart cooling system containing Ethylene Glycol (permanent type) anti-freeze, from +20°F. to −20°F. will require the replacement of 6 1/4 quarts of solution with undiluted anti-freeze.

ANTI-FREEZE CHART

Temperatures Shown in Degrees Fahrenheit
+32 is Freezing

Quarts of **ALCOHOL** Needed for Protection to Temperatures Shown Below

Cooling System Capacity Quarts	1	2	3	4	5	6	7	8	9	10	11	12	13
10	+23°	+11°	− 5°	−27°									
11	+25	+13	0	−18	−40°								
12		+15	+ 3	−12	−31								
13		+17	+ 7	− 7	−23								
14		+19	+ 9	− 3	−17	−34°							
15		+20	+11	+ 1	−12	−27							
16		+21	+13	+ 3	− 8	−21	−36°						
17		+22	+16	+ 6	− 4	−16	−29						
18		+23	+17	+ 8	− 1	−12	−25	−38°					
19		+24	+17	+ 9	+ 2	− 8	−21	−32					
20			+18	+11	+ 4	− 5	−16	−27	−39°				
21			+19	+12	+ 5	− 3	−12	−22	−34				
22			+20	+14	+ 7	0	− 9	−18	−29	−40°			
23			+21	+15	+ 8	+ 2	− 7	−15	−25	−36°			
24			+21	+16	+10	+ 4	− 4	−12	−21	−31			
25			+22	+17	+11	+ 6	− 2	− 9	−18	−27	−37°		
26			+22	+17	+12	+ 7	+ 1	− 7	−14	−23	−32		
27			+23	+18	+13	+ 8	+ 3	− 5	−12	−20	−28	−39°	
28			+23	+19	+14	+ 9	+ 4	− 3	− 9	−17	−25	−34	
29			+24	+19	+15	+10	+ 6	− 1	− 7	−15	−22	−30	−39°
30			+24	+20	+16	+11	+ 7	+ 1	− 5	−12	−19	−27	−35

+ Figures are above Zero, but below Freezing.

− Figures are below Zero. Also below Freezing.

Quarts of **ETHYLENE GLYCOL** Needed for Protection to Temperatures Shown Below

Cooling System Capacity Quarts	1	2	3	4	5	6	7	8	9	10	11	12	13	14
10	+24°	+16°	+ 4°	−12°	−34°	−62°								
11	+25	+18	+ 8	− 6	−23	−47								
12	+26	+19	+10	0	−15	−34	−57°							
13	+27	+21	+13	+ 3	− 9	−25	−45							
14			+15	+ 6	− 5	−18	−34							
15			+16	+ 8	0	−12	−26							
16			+17	+10	+ 2	− 8	−19	−34	−52°					
17			+18	+12	+ 5	− 4	−14	−27	−42					
18			+19	+14	+ 7	0	−10	−21	−34	−50°				
19			+20	+15	+ 9	+ 2	− 7	−16	−28	−42				
20				+16	+10	+ 4	− 3	−12	−22	−34	−48°			
21				+17	+12	+ 6	0	− 9	−17	−28	−41			
22				+18	+13	+ 8	+ 2	− 6	−14	−23	−34	−47°		
23				+19	+14	+ 9	+ 4	− 3	−10	−19	−29	−40		
24				+19	+15	+10	+ 5	0	− 8	−15	−23	−34	−46°	
25				+20	+16	+12	+ 7	+ 1	− 5	−12	−20	−29	−40	−50°
26					+17	+13	+ 8	+ 3	− 3	− 9	−16	−25	−34	−44
27					+18	+14	+ 9	+ 5	− 1	− 7	−13	−21	−29	−39
28					+18	+15	+10	+ 6	+ 1	− 5	−11	−18	−25	−34
29					+19	+16	+12	+ 7	+ 2	− 3	− 8	−15	−22	−29
30					+20	+17	+13	+ 8	+ 4	− 1	− 6	−12	−18	−25

For capacities over 30 quarts divide true capacity by 3. Find quarts Anti-Freeze for the ⅓ and multiply by 3 for quarts to add.

For capacities under 10 quarts multiply true capacity by 3. Find quarts Anti-Freeze for the tripled volume and divide by 3 for quarts to add.

Datsun Distributors

USA MAINLAND

East

Nissan Motor Corporation in USA
400 County Avenue
Secaucus, New Jersey 07094

West

Nissan Motor Corporation in USA
137 East Alondra Boulevard
Gardena, California 90247

HAWAII

Von-Hamm-Young Inc.
711 Kapiolani Boulevard
Honolulu, Hawaii 96813

GUAM

J & G Motor Co., Inc.
P.O. Box 726
Agana, Guam

PUERTO RICO

Motorambar Inc.
G.P.O. Box A0
San Juan, Puerto Rico 00936

SAMOA

B.F. Kneubuhl, Inc.
Pago Pago
American Samoa

CANADA

Nissan Automobile Co., (Canada) Ltd.
480 Audley Boulevard
Annacis Industrial Estate
New Westminster, B.C.
Canada

High Performance and Competition Equipment Sources

The following are sources of high performance/competition equipment, parts, and information.

Bob Sharp Racing
Danbury Road
Box 278
Wilton, Connecticut 06897

BRE
137 Oregon Street,
El Segundo, California 90245

Nissan Motor Corporation in USA
Competition Department
137 E. Alondra Blvd.
Gardena, California 90247